Lecture Notes in Computer

Commenced Publication in 1973
Founding and Former Series Editors:
Gerhard Goos, Juris Hartmanis, and Jan van Leeu

Carlo Blundo   Stelvio Cimato (Eds.)

Security in Communication Networks

4th International Conference, SCN 2004
Amalfi, Italy, September 8-10, 2004
Revised Selected Papers

 Springer

Volume Editors

Carlo Blundo
Stelvio Cimato
Università degli Studi di Salerno, Dipartimento di Informatica ed Applicazioni
84081 Baronissi (SA), Italy
E-mail: {carblu, cimato}@dia.unisa.it

Library of Congress Control Number: 2004117660

CR Subject Classification (1998): E.3, C.2, D.4.6, K.4.1, K.4.4, K.6.5, F.2

ISSN 0302-9743
ISBN 3-540-24301-1 Springer Berlin Heidelberg New York

Springer is a part of Springer Science+Business Media

springeronline.com

© Springer-Verlag Berlin Heidelberg 2005
Printed in Germany

Typesetting: Camera-ready by author, data conversion by Scientific Publishing Services, Chennai, India
Printed on acid-free paper   SPIN: 11375937   06/3142   5 4 3 2 1 0

Preface

The 4th International Conference on Security in Communication Networks 2004 (SCN 2004) was held at the "Diocese Hall" of the Archdiocese of Amalfi-Cava de' Tirreni and the "Armorial Bearings Hall" of the Archbishop Palace in Amalfi, Italy, on September 8–10, 2004. Previous conferences also took place in Amalfi in 1996, 1999 and 2002.

The conference aimed at bringing together researchers in the fields of cryptography and security in communication networks to foster cooperation and the exchange of ideas.

The main topics included all technical aspects of data security, including: anonymity, authentication, block ciphers, complexity-based cryptography, cryptanalysis, digital signatures, distributed cryptography, hash functions, identification, implementations, key distribution, privacy, public key encryption, threshold cryptography, and zero knowledge.

The Program Committee, consisting of 21 members, considered 79 papers and selected 26 for presentation; one of them was withdrawn by the authors. These papers were selected on the basis of originality, quality and relevance to cryptography and security in communication networks.

Due to the high number of submissions, paper selection was a difficult and challenging task, and many good submissions had to be rejected. Each submission was refereed by at least three reviewers and some had four reports or more. We are very grateful to all the program committee members, who devoted much effort and valuable time to read and select the papers. In addition, we gratefully acknowledge the help of colleagues who reviewed submissions in their areas of expertise. They are all listed on page VII and we apologize for any inadvertent omissions.

These preproceedings include the revised versions of the 26 accepted papers and the abstract of the invited talk by Bart Preneel (*ECRYPT: the Cryptographic Research Challenges for the Next Decade*).

Following the example of the previous editions of SCN, we encouraged authors to submit their contributions in electronic format. We handled the submissions with CyberChair (http://www.CyberChair.org) a free Web-based paper submission and reviewing system.

Finally, we would like to thank all the authors who submitted their papers for making this conference possible, the Program Committee members, as well as all the conference participants.

September 2004
C. Blundo
S. Cimato

SCN 2004
September 8–10 2004, Amalfi, Italy

Program Chair

Carlo Blundo   Università di Salerno, Italy

General Chair

Stelvio Cimato   Università di Salerno, Italy

Program Committee

Giuseppe Ateniese	Johns Hopkins University, USA
Carlo Blundo	Università di Salerno, Italy (Chair)
Christian Cachin	IBM Research, Switzerland
Ran Canetti	IBM Research, USA
Xiaotie Deng	City University, Hong Kong, China
Alfredo De Santis	Università di Salerno, Italy
Yvo Desmedt	University College London, UK
Giovanni Di Crescenzo	Telcordia Technology, USA
Rosario Gennaro	IBM Research, USA
Eyal Kushilevitz	Technion, Israel
Tanja Lange	University of Bochum, Germany
Ueli Maurer	ETH Zurich, Switzerland
Eiji Okamoto	Tsukuba University, Japan
Rafail Ostrovsky	UCLA, USA
Giuseppe Persiano	Università di Salerno, Italy
Leonid Reyzin	Boston University, USA
Rei Safavi-Naini	University of Wollongong, Australia
Jacques Stern	ENS, France
Doug Stinson	University of Waterloo, Canada
Gene Tsudik	UCI, USA
Moti Yung	Columbia University, USA

Local Organizing Committee

Paolo D'Arco	Università di Salerno, Italy
Barbara Masucci	Università di Salerno, Italy

Sponsoring Institutions

Dipartimento di Informatica ed Applicazioni, Università di Salerno, Italy
Lanfredi Fund, France

Referees

Michel Abdalla	Pierre-Alain Fouque	Lan Nguyen
Joonsang Baek	Clemente Galdi	Phong Nguyen
Amos Beimel	Louis Granboulan	David Pointcheval
Jan Camenisch	Matthew Green	David Safford
Claude Castelluccia	Daniel Hamburg	Willy Susilo
Dario Catalano	Jason Hinek	Nicolas Tadeusz Courtois
Xi Chen	Seny Kamara	Ivan Visconti
Qi Cheng	Aggelos Kiayias	Duncan Wong
Hung Chim	Hugo Krawczyk	Shouhuai Xu
Stelvio Cimato	TieYan Li	Jianhong Zhang
Paolo D'Arco	Becky Liu	Huafei Zhu
Breno de Medeiros	John Malone-Lee	
Xuhua Ding	Barbara Masucci	

Table of Contents

Authentication and Identification

Zero Knowledge

Public Key Cryptosystems

Distributed Cryptography

Cryptanalysis of Public Key Cryptosystems

ECRYPT: The Cryptographic Research Challenges for the Next Decade

B. Preneel

Katholieke Univ. Leuven, Dept. Electrical Engineering-ESAT,
Kasteelpark Arenberg 10, B-3001 Leuven-Heverlee, Belgium
bart.preneel@esat.kuleuven.ac.be

Abstract. In the past thirty years, cryptology has evolved from a secret art to a modern science. Weaker algorithms and algorithms with
short keys are disappearing, political controls of cryptography have been
reduced, and secure cryptography is becoming more and more a commod-
ity. Moreover, implementations are being becoming more secure as well.
This progress may lead to the belief that the cryptography problem is
"solved." However, this article discusses some of the challenging problems
ahead in the area of cryptographic algorithms and protocols. We also
explain how the ECRYPT Network of Excellence (www.ecrypt.eu.org)
tries to address some of the challenges by bringing together 250 European researchers in the area of cryptology and the related area of
watermarking.

1   Introduction

While cryptology is getting increasingly important in the information society,
it is also becoming less and less visible. Cryptology has been integrated into
smart cards for financial transactions, web browsers, operating systems, mobile
phones and electronic identity cards. This success can be explained by several
factors: first, there is a clear need for cryptographic solutions, second adequate
algorithms and protocols have been developed, and third the decreasing cost of
computation makes it inexpensive to implement symmetric and even asymmetric
cryptology. For outsiders, who have limited understanding of the complexity of
the field, the widespread deployment of cryptology may give the impression
that there a no important problems left in cryptography. We have cryptographic
algorithms and protocols available that can be called as a "black box" by security
engineers to solve some standard problems and the security and performance of
these implementations is improving.

Consequently, one may believe that research efforts in security should be focused exclusively on building trust infrastructures and integrating security into
applications. This (incorrect) impression is strengthened by the (correct) observation that security systems fail usually due to other reasons than cryptographic
flaws (such as incorrect specifications or implementations, bad management,
viruses, social engineering attacks...) [2].

C. Blundo and S. Cimato (Eds.): SCN 2004, LNCS 3352, pp. 1–15, 2005.

A second (but incorrect) conclusion that one may draw from these observations is that research discipline cryptology has ran out of practical problem, and hence researchers now work on purely theoretical problems such as general multi-party computation, exotic protocols and on the question whether or not one-way functions exist. Any cryptographic protocol (encryption, authentication, key establishment, e-payment, e-voting, ...) can be described as a multi-party computation, and generic but highly inefficient solutions to this problem are known since the late 1980s [5, 12, 25]. An interesting challenge is to make these protocols more efficient, either in the general case or for concrete problems (such as group signatures or e-voting) for example by introducing stronger cryptographic assumptions. The most fundamental assumption is the existence of one-way functions: while our intuition seems to suggest that it is very easy to design a function that is "easy" to compute but "hard" to invert, so far the best theoretical result can prove that there exist functions that are twice as hard to invert as to compute [27]; it is clear that such functions would be completely useless to practical cryptography. This is quite remarkable, since one-way functions are a cornerstone of cryptology.

Section 2 presents an overview of the challenges that remain in both practical and theoretical cryptography. Since the area of cryptology is rather broad, the emphasis will be on symmetric cryptology by summarizing the status after recent attacks on block ciphers, stream ciphers and hash functions. We briefly address some research issues in asymmetric cryptology, but due to lack of space we do not provide details on areas such as protocols, secure implementation, watermarking, and perceptual hashing. Next we attempt to explain the problems problems that arise in the standardization of cryptographic algorithms and protocols. Section 3 explains how the ECRYPT project intends to address some of these research challenges. Some concluding remarks are presented in Sect. 4.

2   Research Challenges in Cryptology

2.1   State of the Art

Most of the applications are covered by the block ciphers triple-DES [19] and AES [20]; DES, which was widely used until the late 1990s, is being replaced quickly (NIST has announced in July 2004 that it will withdraw support for the DES algorithm since its strength is no longer sufficient to adequately protect Federal government information). In addition 3rd generation mobile networks (3GPP) use KASUMI [1] and Bluetooth uses SAFER+ [8]. While military environments still use proprietary stream ciphers, RC4 [24] is widely deployed in the commercial world (e.g., SSL/TLS, WEP); GSM uses the stream ciphers A5/1 and A5/2 [7, 42] and Bluetooth uses E0 [8]. The most popular hash functions are MD5 [37], which was broken in August 2004 [43], SHA-1 [23] and in some applications RIPEMD-160 [17] and MDC-2 (see [35]). For MAC algorithms, HMAC and several variants of CBC-MAC are widely used. In the area of public-key cryptology, RSA [38] is clearly the most popular algorithm, both for public key encryption and for digital signatures. For digital signatures, DSA, ECDSA (Elliptic Curve DSA) and variants of these are also successful. For public key encryption, ElGamal and some elliptic curve variants can also be found in applications. For key establishment several variants of authenticated Diffie-Hellman are widely deployed. For entity authentication, there is a limited use of zero-knowledge protocols, o.a. in the pay-TV world and in Novell networks. It is not feasible within the scope of this article to discuss in detail all the cryptographic algorithms and protocols included in standards such as SSL/TLS, IPsec/IKE, SSH, S/MIME, PGP, GSM, 3GPP, WEP, WPA, RSN, Bluetooth, EMV, Global Platform, ...   It is clear that this could be a useful exercise to assess the impact of developments in cryptology.

2.2   Challenges

In this section we discuss the research challenges from a generic perspective. Even if we have currently a large toolbox of cryptographic algorithms and protocols, this may not be adequate for the next years due to several reasons. A first issue is the changing environment and threat models in which cryptology will be deployed: we are evolving towards ambient intelligence, pervasive networking or ubiquitous computing, which have completely new characteristics. A second element is the gradual erosion of the computational difficulty of the mathematical problems on which cryptology is based; this erosion is created in part by developments in computation (progress in electronics and in the future in optical and maybe even quantum computing) and in part by progress in cryptanalytic algorithms. A final element is the requirements of new applications and cryptographic implementations, including the lack of physical security in devices.

In order to structure these new requirements, the areas in which further research is needed can be organized according to three parameters: cost (hardware, memory, power), performance (throughput, latency) and security level. Ideally one would like to achieve a high security level and a high performance at a low cost, but this is not feasible. In practice one has to focus on at least one criterion; depending on the choice, one obtains different solutions. Within this choice, there may still exist trade-offs between the remaining two parameters.

Low Cost and/or Low Power: this can be achieved by giving up high performance or high security; this approach is essential to allow for integration of cryptography in even the tiniest devices (e.g., ambient intelligence). Design goals could be the implementation of a stream cipher that offers a reasonable security level (say 80 bits) with uses less than 1000 gates.

High Performance: this is required for highly efficient solutions for applications such as bus encryption, hard disk encryption, encryption in Terabit networks. If cryptography presents too large an overhead/cost, it will not be deployed, or it will be switched off. In this context, it is important to note that while Moore's 'law' predicts that in 2018, the computational power for the same cost will have increased with a factor of about 100, Gilder's 'law' predicts that the speed of LANs and storage devices will increase with a factor of 10 000. This shows that parallelism will become increasingly important in cryptographic operations, but also demonstrates the need for high performance designs.

High Security: some application areas require cryptographic algorithms and protocols that can offer a higher confidence and assurance level than the state of the art. E.g., for e-voting, we need secure and robust protocols that survive even if a subset of the players are faulty or corrupt and that provide long-term security; for e-health and national security we need cryptographic algorithms which provide guaranteed protection for 50 years or more. As an example, information on our DNA has implications on the DNA of our children and grandchildren, hence this is information that may need to be protected for a very long time.

These requirements guide the approaches taken by the research teams in the ECRYPT project (cf. Sect. 3).

2.3   Symmetric Cryptology

In this section we comment on the challenges in the area of block ciphers, stream ciphers and cryptographic hash functions; we omit MAC algorithms for two reasons: they are mostly derived from other block ciphers and hash functions, and highly efficient constructions based on universal hash functions are known (even if they are not yet widely used).

Block Ciphers. The area of block ciphers has always been very particular in cryptology due to the availability of widely supported standards. The impact of the publication of the Data Encryption Standard (DES) in 1977 by the US NIST [33] (at that time called NBS) on both practice and research is hard to overestimate. DES was obtained after an open competition, in which IBM provided the winning entry; the final design was performed by IBM in cooperation with NSA. After some initial controversy, DES became widely used, first in the financial sector and later on in a broad range of applications.

In the 1990s it became clear that the key length of DES (56 bits) was no longer adequate (see for example Wiener [44]); moreover, the block length of 64 bits will also be too short in the next decade, which means that triple-DES (which is also rather slow) is not an adequate replacement. Therefore NIST launched a call for a successor in 1997. After an open competition with 22 entries, NIST selected the Belgian Rijndael algorithm (designed by J. Daemen and V. Rijmen) as the winner in October 2000. The AES standard FIPS 197 (Federal Information Processing Standard) was published in December 2001 [20]; it is a 128-bit block cipher with a key of 128, 192 and 256 bits. AES is mandatory for sensitive but unclassified data. In 2003, the US government announced that AES can also be used for classified information up to the secret level, while AES with key lengths of 192 and 256 bits can be used for top secret information. In software, AES is more than twice as fast as DES, and thus significantly faster than triple-DES.

In 2004, AES has been included in more than thousand products, and as of August 2004, 171 AES product certifications have been performed by NIST. AES is being adopted very quickly as a standard in other environments (IETF, ISO,

IEEE, 3GPP, ...), with the exception of the financial sector, which is finalizing its slow migration from DES to triple-DES.

While there was a broad consensus on the choice by NIST, there were also some critical comments on the algebraic structure present in the AES. This structure allows for an elegant description and efficient implementations both in hardware and software (8-bit and 32-bit machines), but may also induce weaknesses. For example, it was shown by Courtois and Pieprzyk [11] that the algebraic structure in the AES S-box leads to simple quadratic equations. The authors of [11] claim that it may be possible to solve these equations faster than an exhaustive key search. See also more recent work on algorithms [3,13] to solve quadratic equations. Murphy and Robshaw have shown that the simple overall structure leads to an embedding in larger block cipher BES [31], which has certain weaknesses; however, these weaknesses do not seem to apply to AES. Finally, several authors have shown that the algebraic structure leads to equivalent descriptions of the AES.

In conclusion, more than two years after the announcement of these properties, none of these attacks seems to pose a realistic threat to the security of AES. It is clear that in view of the importance of the AES, more research is needed to increase our understanding of this algorithm. On the other hand, in the past 15 years the cryptographic community has built up some extensive design expertise for block ciphers; even if it would turn out that a less elegant (and less mathematical) design is more desirable, it would not be too difficult to modify the design accordingly.

Stream Ciphers. In contrast to block ciphers, the area of stream cipher has been characterized by many proprietary algorithms and a lack of standards. The first generation of stream ciphers (1920s–1950s) used mechanical and electromechanical designs based on rotors. Subsequently, electronic designs were developed using Linear Feedback Shift Registers (LFSRs); an extensive mathematical theory has been created to analyze these stream ciphers. In the last 15 years a new generation of software-oriented stream ciphers has been proposed, which uses word lengths between 8 and 32 bits and runs efficiently on modern processors.

Designing a secure stream cipher should in principle be easier than designing a block cipher, since a stream cipher has an internal state that cannot be influenced by the opponent (there is no equivalent of a chosen plaintext attack). However, stream cipher designers aim for a significantly better performance than a block cipher in OFB (Output FeedBack) or CTR (CounTeR) mode, which is a natural benchmark. As a consequence, output bits are produced after a few operations, which implies that mixing may be less thorough as desirable. In addition, new attack models are being introduced which exploit the fact that the output stream needs to be restarted or re-synchronized at regular intervals using an Initialization Vector (IV). A chosen IV attack gives an opponent some control over the initialization of the internal state.

The rich algebraic algebraic structure of LFSRs has resulted in a large number of attack strategies: linear attacks, algebraic attacks, correlation attacks, divide and conquer attacks, ...   As a consequence, some researchers are convinced that LFSRs should be eliminated altogether from the design of a stream cipher. As an alternative, one could consider the T-functions proposed by Klimov and Shamir [29]; these functions provide an efficient implementation of a single-cycle non-linear iteration on 2^n bits.

Software-oriented stream ciphers have been analyzed using an ad-hoc approach, that use a broad variety of techniques. The NESSIE project [32], which organized an open competition to develop standard proposals for cryptographic algorithms, concluded that none of the submitted stream ciphers satisfied the security criteria. In most cases, the attacks found were so-called distinguishing attacks with a very high data complexity, which may not represent a realistic threat on applications. However, the NESSIE project asked for a very high security margin, and the submitters initially believed that they could provide this. The motivation was to obtain a sufficient security margin for long-term security. More research is needed to evaluate to which extent we need to reduce the security requirements to obtain the expected performance benefit from stream ciphers.

In order for stream ciphers to be useful in practice, they may also need efficient resynchronization procedures, and an optional mode for authenticated encryption. There is clearly a need for standardized stream ciphers that offer either a very low cost (in terms of gate count or power) or that are highly efficient in software. ECRYPT intends to this

Hash Functions. The area of hash functions has been characterized by a large number of broken schemes in their 25-year history (see [34, 35] for an overview). In practice however, only a limited number of schemes are widely used: MD5 and SHA-1, and to a limited extent RIPEMD-160 and MDC-2.

MD4 was proposed by Rivest in 1990 and broken by Dobbertin in 1996 [16]. MD5 was proposed one year later as a strengthened version of MD4. However, it was discredited by attacks by den Boer and Bosselaers in 1992 [15] and Dobbertin in 1996 [18]; the last attack led RSA Security to withdraw its support for new applications. These attacks showed serious weaknesses of the compression function of MD5, but they did not provide collisions for the complete function. In the mean time, brute force collision attacks on MD5 – which require 2^{64} operations only – are also within reach. In spite of these development, MD5 remained widely used in a broad range of applications until today. In August 2004, four researchers (X. Wang, D. Feng, X. Lai, and H. Yu) announced that they had found collisions for MD5 [43]; their attack requires only 15 minutes on a normal laptop.

The Secure Hash Algorithm, was proposed by NIST [21] in 1993; SHA has a 160-bit hash result. After one year, NIST discovered a certificational weakness in SHA; apparently collisions could be found in less than 2^{80} operations. Consequently a new release of the standard was published. The new algorithm is called SHA-1 [22], which prompted some researchers to rename the original SHA as SHA-0 (this has created some confusion).

After work by Chabaud and Joux in 1998 [10], Biham and Chen in 2004 [6], Joux, Carribault, Jalby and Lemuet presented a collision for SHA in August

2004 [28]; their attack requires 2^{51} compression function computations. Wang et al. [43] claim an improved attack that requires only 2^{40} compression function computations; however, this attack has not yet been implemented.

Biham and Chen have also investigated the extension of their attacks to SHA-1 [6]. The current status is that they can find collisions for 43 (out of 80) rounds of SHA-1; they also show that finding collisions for up to 53 (out of 80) rounds of SHA-1 is faster than a brute force collision attack, which requires 2^{80} steps of the compression function.

The implications of the new cryptanalytic techniques discovered in 2004 on SHA-1 and on RIPEMD-160 are still under study. At this time it is too early to make a reliable assessment, but there does not seem to be an immediate threat to either hash function; however, brute force attacks on these hash functions – requiring 2^{80} compression function evaluations – may become within reach within 10-15 years.

In 2004, Hawkes and Rose [26] have presented some critical observations on the security of SHA-256 (with a 256-bit result). While it is probably too early to draw firm conclusions, it seems now plausible that finding collisions for SHA-256 could take less than 2^{128} evaluations of the compression function, but it may still be out of reach for the next 20 years or more.

For the time being, there is still a lack of understanding of the security of hash function designs. Most practical constructions build on the original ideas of MD4 (32-bit arithmetic and logical operations); we have learned in the last decade that these designs are probably less secure than anticipated. The next generation standards SHA-256 through SHA-512 [23] offers better security levels based on similar principles. However, they are also significantly slower than SHA-1 (about 2-6 times) and it may be that some of the new attack techniques can be extended to these designs.

2.4   Asymmetric Cryptology

The research challenges in asymmetric cryptology are certainly not smaller. The first results in security reductions focused on asymmetric cryptology; in this line of research, one attempts to prove that the security of a cryptographic primitive or protocol can be reduced to an assumption on the difficulty of a mathematical problem (such as extracting modular roots, factoring the product of two large primes or solving the discrete logarithm problem in a specific group). Research concentrates on finding efficient and meaningful reductions, on reducing assumptions used in the proof (such as the 'random oracle model' [4, 9]), on establishing relations between assumptions, and on finding primitives with better and/or more complex security properties. It should also be pointed out that the security of most asymmetric primitives depends on a small set of problems from algebraic number theory; any breakthrough in solving some of these problems could have dramatic consequences. This shows that there is a need for new asymmetric algorithms that depend on new problems.

Cryptology also needs to take into account the ever increasing speed of electronic computers; typically this can be addressed by an adequate upgrade path for key lengths at the cost of a decreased performance and increased key sizes. However, we should also consider the emergence of new computer models such as optical computers and even quantum computers. Shamir, Tromer, and others have shown that optical computers could bring significant progress in factoring large integers [30, 39]. Shor has proved in 1994 [40] that if a large quantum computer could be built, factoring and discrete logarithms in $\mathbb{Z}_p$ would be easy; his results have also been extended to elliptic curve groups. After slow initial progress, in 1992 a 7-bit quantum computer has been demonstrated [41], which managed to factor 15 (note that the technology used in this approach is not scalable). Experts are divided on the question whether sufficiently powerful quantum computers can be built in the next 15-20 years. Nevertheless, this provides an additional motivation to develop asymmetric algorithms that are resistant to quantum computers.

Research on new asymmetric algorithms is progressing slowly; many proposals have a very short lifetime. Candidate systems that are still being studied include algorithms based on the following techniques: large error-correcting codes (e.g., McEliece and variants), multivariate polynomial equations (HFE and variants), lattices (NTRU), number field systems and braid groups. So far it seems very hard to match both the performance and the security of the most popular algorithms.

2.5   Standards

It is well understood that standards are essential for interoperability and economy of scale. Establishing high quality standards is very difficult, particular in areas which are evolving quickly such as information technology. For cryptographic standards, another dimension needs to be added: the standard does not only need to be competitive, it also needs to offer an adequate security level. Several cryptographic standards had to be revised after publication and even deployment because serious security problems were identified. If an adequate security evaluation has been performed, the standard brings some security guarantees as an additional benefit. On the other hand, security standards imply the risks of a single target of attack and of a lack of diversity. There are several standardization bodies in the area of cryptographic algorithms and protocols; the main players include ISO/IEC JTC1/SC27, ISO/TC68, IETF (with limited coordination between the many working groups), NIST, ANSI, IEEE, ETSI, 3GPP, Bluetooth SIG, RSA Labs (PKCS). To quote A.S. Tanenbaum: "The nice thing about standards is there's so many to choose from."

Problems with security standards are not only created by the technical difficulty of developing cryptographic algorithms and protocols as discussed above. Often, there is no time or expertise for an in-depth security analysis. Mechanisms are sometimes selected based on vested interests or 'negotiated', rather than chosen based on merit. In the past there has also be significant political pressure to include on crippled algorithms or protocols. It may also be that commercial considerations result in the introduction in the standard of a weak solution, while at the same time one sells a proprietary high-security solution at a premium price.

Even if a standard is adequate when it is published, progress in research may make it obsolete or insecure. Many standardization bodies do not have efficient maintenance procedures to respond efficiently to such developments. Once a standard has been widely deployed, upgrading it brings significant costs, hence the typical pattern is that upgrades of algorithms and protocols take a very long time; moreover backward compatibility with older insecure solutions may open avenues for attacks. Examples of algorithms that have been widely deployed beyond their useful lifetime include DES and MD5.

3   The ECRYPT Project

ECRYPT is a Network of Excellence funded under the 6th Framework Programme in the thematic area Information Society Technologies (IST); ECRYPT is one of the projects that contribute to the development of a global dependability and security framework. ECRYPT has started on February 1, 2004 and is funded for four years. The total estimated cost of the project is about 8.4 MEURO, of which 5.6 MEURO is funded by the European Commission.

ECRYPT has 32 partners from 14 countries; 7 are large companies, and 2 are small ones; the remaining 23 are universities or research institutions. The ECRYPT partners are: Katholieke Universiteit Leuven (B), Coördinator, École Normale Supérieure, Paris (F), Ruhr-Universität Bochum (D), Royal Holloway, University of London (UK), BRICS, University of Aarhus (DK), University of Salerno (I), Institut National de Recherche en Informatique et en Automatique (F), University of Bristol (UK), Gemplus SA (F), France Telecom R&D (F), IBM Research GmbH (CH), Technical University Eindhoven (NL), Université Catholique de Louvain (B), Universität Duisburg-Essen (D), Technical University of Denmark (DK), University of Bergen (N), Lund University (S), Institute for Applied Information Processing and Communications (A), Institute of Mathematics of the Polish Academy of Sciences (P), Cryptolog International SAS (F), Vodafone Group Services Ltd (UK), Ericsson AB (S), Axalto SA (F), MasterCard Europe sprl (B), Edizone GmbH (D), Fraunhofer Gesellschaft zur Förderung der angewandten Forschung e.V. (D), Otto-von-Guericke University Magdeburg (D), Centre National de la Recherche Scientifique (F), University of Vigo (S), National Inter-University Consortium for Telecommunications (I), University of Geneva (CH), Aristotle University of Thessaloniki (GR).

3.1   Objectives

The main objective of ECRYPT is to ensure a durable integration of European research in both academia and industry and to maintain and strengthen the European excellence in these areas. In order to reach this goal, the ECRYPT partners propose to integrate their research capabilities within five virtual labs focused on the following five core research areas: symmetric key algorithms, public key algorithms, protocols, implementation, and watermarking (cf. Sect. 3.3).

The integration activities include joint workshops, exchange of researchers and students, development of common tools and benchmarks and a website (http://www.ecrypt.eu.org) and forum which will be a focal point for the network and the wider cryptographic community. Each virtual lab organizes one formal *open* workshop per year; in the first project year, there have been open workshops on multi-party protocols, stream ciphers, provable security, and special purpose hardware (for cryptanalysis). In addition there are a number of 'ad hoc' internal research meetings. The ECRYPT website will contain a number of web resources on stream ciphers, AES hardware implementations, side-channel attacks,... A joint infrastructure is being developed which includes tools for the evaluation of cryptographic algorithms, a benchmarking environment for cryptographic hardware and software, infrastructure for side channel analysis measurements and tools, and tools for benchmarking watermarking schemes. It is important to note that ECRYPT has set aside a substantial budget to sponsor research visits and of non-ECRYPT researchers.

Spreading activities include a training program, a substantial contribution towards standardization bodies and an active publication policy. Each year several summer schools will be organized of at least one week, jointly between two virtual labs. The topic for the first schools are elliptic curve cryptology, cryptanalysis (both symmetric and asymmetric), unconditionally secure protocols and multimedia security. ECRYPT intends to improve the interaction between the research community, standardization bodies and the users of cryptology (government, industry, end users). The goal is to make sure that the new developments are integrated into applications and benefit the end-users. ECRYPT will also publish an annual list of recommended algorithms, protocols and parameter sizes for symmetric and asymmetric algorithms (including digital signature suites, encryption algorithms, ...).

3.2   Organization

The highest authority within ECRYPT is the General Assembly, in which each partner has one vote. The General Assembly decides on all strategic matters, including budget allocation. The project is run by the Ecrypt Management Committee (EMC) that meets on a quarterly basis. The EMC consists of the five virtual lab leaders, the chairman of the strategic committee and two additional members in charge of IPR issues and standardization. The EMC is chaired by the project manager, who is in charge of the day to day management; he is supported by the project administrator. The strategic committee consists of highly experienced people from industry and academia; it provides guidance and feedback on the long-term approach taken by the research network. The virtual labs are organized in smaller working groups. A typical working group consists of 5 to 15 people; one or two people are in charge for the directions of the working group. Working groups can be reorganized on a yearly basis depending on the research needs.

3.3   Research Goals of the Virtual Labs

The activities of the ECRYPT Network of Excellence are organized into five virtual laboratories established as follows:

1. Symmetric techniques virtual lab (STVL);
2. Asymmetric techniques virtual lab (AZTEC);
3. Protocols virtual lab (PROVILAB);
4. Secure and efficient implementations virtual lab (VAMPIRE); and
5. Watermarking and perceptual hashing virtual lab (WAVILA).

Each virtual lab intends to promote and facilitate cryptographic research on a pan-European level.

STVL. This virtual lab covers the design and analysis of symmetric cryptosystems. Three particular areas of research have been identified within the scope of the STVL, corresponding to three working groups. The first target for the efforts of the STVL is the development of secure and efficient stream ciphers; a task that will require considerable input from industry and academia alike. A second target for the STVL is a coordinated cryptanalytic assessment of the Advanced Encryption Standard (AES). A third virtual lab of STVL focuses on strategic research; in the next years, one of the items that will be to addressed is the development of lightweight cryptographic primitives as a fundamental building block for ambient intelligence.

AZTEC. The focus of AZTEC is the design and analysis of asymmetric cryptographic techniques. Four main areas of study have been identified. First, it is important to study, compare and propose mechanisms for provable security, to improve and better understand the security of asymmetric schemes. A second target for the AZTEC efforts is to develop alternatives to the RSA scheme, with particular attention to lightweight solutions. In the Internet era, many new applications are emerging for which asymmetric primitives with some specific properties are required; this forms the topic of the third working group. Finally, since it is clear that no unconditionally secure asymmetric cryptography can exist, the fourth area of AZTEC is the study of the hardness of the computational problems that are used as underlying assumptions in asymmetric cryptology.

PROVILAB. This virtual lab is concerned with cryptographic protocols, where two or more agents interact in order to reach some common goal; this can be to establish a secure network connection, to realize a payment transaction securely, or to carry out a secure auction or voting protocol over a network. A large body of theoretical research on protocols already exists, but our basic knowledge is still far from complete. Furthermore, analyzing the security of concrete protocols is notoriously difficult, and several solutions proposed and sometimes even used in practice have later turned out to be insecure. The first objective of PROVILAB is therefore to construct practically useful protocols for a wide range of applications with well understood and provable security. The second is to expand our basic knowledge, for instance in the area of unconditional security, i.e., protocols that remain secure, no matter the resources invested in breaking them. PROVILAB has three working groups, that focus on two-party protocols and secure point-to-point connections, practical multi-party protocols with provable security, and on unconditionally secure protocols.

VAMPIRE. The VAMPIRE lab has a dual role in ECRYPT. On the one hand, it studies new techniques that are related to efficient and secure implementation. On the other hand, VAMPIRE provides a bridge between the research and the user community. In concrete terms, the technical goals of the VAMPIRE lab for the duration of ECRYPT can be summarized as follows: development of novel efficient implementation techniques in hardware and software; development of a solid understanding of existing and new side channel attacks and efficient countermeasures; researching and understanding of cryptanalytical hardware and its impact on cryptographic parameters. There are also non-technical objectives. VAMPIRE intends to stimulate the interesting interplay of secure algorithms and secure implementations; it also hopes to foster cooperation between strong engineering groups and pure crypto groups. Also, it is a major goal to bridge the existing gap between the research community and engineers in industry who need to apply implementation techniques. Another important objective is to assist the researchers in the other (more theoretical) Virtual Labs in understanding the requirements and meeting the needs of applied cryptography. The four working groups of VAMPIRE focus on software implementation, hardware implementation, side-channel attacks, and strategic research.

WAVILA. The watermarking and perceptual hashing virtual lab (WAVILA) intends to broaden the scope of ECRYPT beyond the classical cryptographic techniques into the domain embedded signalling and fuzzy signatures. These two techniques have recently been proposed as important ingredients in digital rights management (DRM) systems, but they have never fully been analyzed with respect to security and usage (protocols), comparable to the standard of cryptography. It is the goal of WAVILA to build tools and techniques for assessing the security aspects of watermarking and perceptual hashing, to design advanced algorithms with a well-defined security level, to design protocols, both stand-alone as well as integrated in cryptographic protocols, and to develop methods and techniques for efficient and secure implementations. The overall and broader goal is to bring watermarking and perceptual hashing to such a level that they can be successfully be integrated into future DRM systems.

4   Conclusion

In this article, we have provided some arguments to support our claim that the cryptographic problem is not solved at all. Both at the practical and at the theoretical level, there are some very interesting problems and challenges that need to be addressed. We are convinced that the coordinated approach towards these research problems that is being developed in the Network of Excellence

ECRYPT will bring significant benefits. By strengthening the cooperation between researchers both in industry and academia and by stimulating interdisciplinary research in the broad area of cryptology and watermarking, substantial progress can be made towards solving the security problems we will face in the next decade.

Acknowledgements and Disclaimer

The author would like to thank all the ECRYPT members and in particular the ECRYPT Management Committee for their contributions towards creating the Network of Excellence. The work described in this paper has been supported in part by the European Commission through the IST Programme under Contract IST-2002-507932 ECRYPT.

The information in this document reflects only the author's views, is provided as is and no guarantee or warranty is given that the information is fit for any particular purpose. The user thereof uses the information at its sole risk and liability.

References

1. 3GPP, http://www.3gpp.org.
2. R.J. Anderson, "Why cryptosystems fail," *Communications ACM*, Vol. 37, No. 11, November 1994, pp. 32–40.
3. G. Ars, J-C. Faugère, M. Sugita, M. Kawazoe, H. Imai, "Comparison between XL and Gröbner Basis Algorithms," *Advances in Cryptology, Asiacrypt 2004, LNCS*, P.J. Lee, Ed., Springer-Verlag, 2004, in print.
4. M. Bellare, P. Rogaway, "Random oracles are practical," *Proc. First Annual Conference on Computer and Communications Security*, ACM, 1993, pp. 62–73.
5. M. Ben-Or, S. Goldwasser, A. Wigderson, "Completeness theorems for noncryptographic fault-tolerant distributed computing," *Proc. of 20th Annual Symposium on the Theory of Computing*, 1988, pp. 1–10.
6. E. Biham, R. Chen, "Near-collisions of SHA-0," *Advances in Cryptology – Crypto'04, LNCS 3152*, M. Franklin, Ed., Springer-Verlag, 2004, pp. 290–305.
7. A. Biryukov, A. Shamir, D. Wagner, "Real time cryptanalysis of A5/1 on a PC," *Fast Software Encryption, LNCS 1978*, B. Schneier, ED., Springer-Verlag, 2001, pp. 1–18.
8. Bluetooth Specification, https://www.bluetooth.org/spec/.
9. R. Canetti, O. Goldreich, S. Halevi, "The random oracle methodology, revisited," *Proc. of 30th Annual Symposium on the Theory of Computing*, 1998, pp. 209–218.
10. F. Chabaud, A. Joux, "Differential collisions: an explanation for SHA-1," *Advances in Cryptology, Proc. Crypto'98, LNCS 1462*, H. Krawczyk, ED., Springer-Verlag, 1998, pp. 56–71.
11. N. Courtois, J. Pieprzyk, "Cryptanalysis of block ciphers with overdefined systems of equations," *Advances in Cryptology, Proc. Asiacrypt'02, LNCS 2501*, Y. Zheng, ED., Springer-Verlag, 2002, pp. 267–287.
12. D. Chaum, C. Crépeau, I. Damgård, "Multi-party unconditionally secure protocols," *Proc. 20th ACM Symposium on Theory of Computing*, 1988, pp. 11–19.

13. C. Diem, "The XL-algorithm and a conjecture from commutative algebra," *Advances in Cryptology, Asiacrypt 2004, LNCS*, P.J. Lee, Ed., Springer-Verlag, 2004, in print.

14. J. Daemen, V. Rijmen, *"The Design of Rijndael. AES – The Advanced Encryption Standard,"* Springer-Verlag, 2001.

15. B. den Boer, A. Bosselaers, "Collisions for the compression function of MD5," *Advances in Cryptology, Proc. Eurocrypt'93, LNCS 765*, T. Helleseth, ED., Springer-Verlag, 1994, pp. 293–304.

16. H. Dobbertin, "Cryptanalysis of MD4," *Journal of Cryptology*, Vol. 11, No. 4, 1998, pp. 253–271. See also *Fast Software Encryption, LNCS 1039*, D. Gollmann, ED., Springer-Verlag, 1996, pp. 53–69.

17. H. Dobbertin, A. Bosselaers, B. Preneel, "RIPEMD-160: a strengthened version of RIPEMD," *Fast Software Encryption, LNCS 1039*, D. Gollmann, ED., Springer-Verlag, 1996, pp. 71–82. See also http://www.esat.kuleuven.ac.be/ ∼ bosselae/ripemd160.

18. H. Dobbertin, "The status of MD5 after a recent attack," *CryptoBytes*, Vol. 2, No. 2, Summer 1996, pp. 1–6.

19. FIPS 46, *"Data Encryption Standard,"* Federal Information Processing Standard, National Bureau of Standards, U.S. Department of Commerce, January 1977 (revised as FIPS 46-1:1988; FIPS 46-2:1993).

20. FIPS 197, *"Advanced Encryption Standard (AES),"* Federal Information Processing Standard, National Institute of Standards and Technologies, U.S. Department of Commerce, December 6, 2001.

21. FIPS 180, *"Secure Hash Standard,"* Federal Information Processing Standard (FIPS), Publication 180, National Institute of Standards and Technology, US Department of Commerce, Washington D.C., May 11, 1993.

22. FIPS 180-1, *"Secure Hash Standard,"* Federal Information Processing Standard (FIPS), Publication 180-1, National Institute of Standards and Technology, US Department of Commerce, Washington D.C., April 17, 1995.

23. FIPS 180-2, *"Secure Hash Standard (SHS),"* Federal Information Processing Standard (FIPS), Publication 180-2, National Institute of Standards and Technology, US Department of Commerce, Washington D.C., August 2002 http://csrc.nist.gov/publications/fips/.

24. S. Fluhrer, I. Mantin, A. Shamir, "Weaknesses in the key scheduling algorithm of RC4," *Selected Areas in Cryptography, SAC 2001, LNCS 2259*, S. Vaudenay, A. Youssef, Eds., Springer-Verlag, 2001, pp. 1–24.

25. S. Goldwasser, S. Micali, A. Wigderson, "How to play any mental game, or: a completeness theorem for protocols with honest majority," *Proc. 19th ACM Symposium on Theory of Computing*, 1987, pp. 221–229.

26. P. Hawkes, G. Rose, "On corrective patterns for the SHA-2 family," *Presented at the Rump Session of Crypto'04*, August 2004.

27. A.P.L. Hiltgen, "Constructions of feebly-one-way families of permutations," *Advances in Cryptology, Proc. Auscrypt '92, LNCS 718*, J. Seberry and Y. Zheng, Eds., Springer-Verlag, 1992, pp. 422-434,

28. A. Joux, P. Carribault, W. Jalby, C. Lemuet, "Collisions in SHA-0," *Presented at the Rump Session of Crypto'04*, August 2004.

29. A. Klimov, A. Shamir, "New cryptographic primitives based on multiword T-functions," *Fast Software Encryption, LNCS 3017*, B. Roy, W. Meier, Eds., Springer-Verlag, 2004, pp. 1–15.

30. A.K. Lenstra, E. Tromer, A. Shamir, W. Kortsmit, B. Dodson, J. Hughes, P.C. Leyland, "Factoring estimates for a 1024-bit RSA modulus," *Advances in Cryptology, Proc. Asiacrypt'03, LNCS 2894*, C.S. Lai, ED., Springer-Verlag, 2003, pp. 55–74.
31. S. Murphy, M.J.B. Robshaw, "Essential algebraic structures within the AES," *Advances in Cryptology, Proc. Crypto'02, LNCS 2442*, M. Yung, ED., Springer-Verlag, 2002, pp. 1–16.
32. NESSIE, http://www.cryptonessie.org.
33. NIST, AES Initiative, http://www.nist.gov/aes.
34. B. Preneel, "Analysis and design of cryptographic hash functions," *Doctoral Dissertation*, Katholieke Universiteit Leuven, 1993.
35. B. Preneel, "Cryptographic primitives for information authentication – state of the art," *State of the Art in Applied Cryptography, LNCS 1528*, B. Preneel, V. Rijmen, Eds., Springer-Verlag, 1998, pp. 50–105.
36. RIPE, *"Integrity Primitives for Secure Information Systems. Final Report of RACE Integrity Primitives Evaluation (RIPE-RACE 1040)," LNCS 1007*, A. Bosselaers, B. Preneel, Eds., Springer-Verlag, 1995.
37. R.L. Rivest, "The MD5 message-digest algorithm," *Request for Comments (RFC) 1321*, Internet Activities Board, Internet Privacy Task Force, April 1992.
38. R.L. Rivest, A. Shamir, L. Adleman, "A method for obtaining digital signatures and public-key cryptosystems," *Communications ACM*, Vol. 21, February 1978, pp. 120–126.
39. A. Shamir, E. Tromer, "Factoring large numbers with the TWIRL device," *Advances in Cryptology, Proc. Crypto'03, LNCS 2729*, D. Boneh, ED., Springer-Verlag, 2003, pp. 1–26.
40. P.W. Shor, "Algorithms for quantum computation: discrete logarithms and factoring," *Proc. 35nd Annual Symposium on Foundations of Computer Science*, S. Goldwasser, Ed., IEEE Computer Society Press, 1994, pp. 124–134.
41. L.M.K. Vandersypen, M. Steffen, G. Breyta, C.S. Yannoni, M.H. Sherwood, I.L. Chuang, "Experimental realization of Shor's quantum factoring algorithm using nuclear magnetic resonance," *Nature*, 414, 2001, pp. 883–887.
42. K. Vedder, "Security aspects of mobile communications," *State of the Art in Applied Cryptography, LNCS 741*, B. Preneel, R. Govaerts, J. Vandewalle, Eds., Springer-Verlag, 1993, pp. 193–210.
43. X. Wang, X. Lai, D. Feng, H. Yu, "Collisions for hash functions MD4, MD5, HAVAL-128 and RIPEMD," *Presented at the Rump Session of Crypto'04*, August 2004.
44. M.J. Wiener, "Efficient DES key search," *Presented at the Rump Session of Crypto'93*. Reprinted in *"Practical Cryptography for Data Internetworks,"* W. Stallings, Ed., IEEE Computer Society, 1996, pp. 31–79.

Relationships Between Diffie-Hellman and "Index Oracles"

Adam Young[1] and Moti Yung[2]

[1] Cigital, Inc.
ayoung@cigital.com
[2] Dept. of Computer Science, Columbia University
moti@cs.columbia.edu

Abstract. The Computational Diffie-Hellman problem and its decisional variant are at the heart of many cryptographic applications. Yet, their exact computational power and their relationship to the Discrete Logarithm problem and the Decision Diffie-Hellman problem (DDH) is not fully understood in all settings. In order to extend the current understanding of the problem we introduce a new decision problem that we call the Jacobi Discrete Logarithm problem. We argue that this is a natural problem and we analyze it in groups in which Decision Diffie-Hellman (DDH) is believed to be intractable. In short, the JDL problem is to return the Jacobi symbol of the exponent x in g^x. We show that JDL is random self-reducible and that it lies in between the Computational Diffie-Hellman (CDH) problem and DDH. Our analysis involves the notion of a powering oracle. Maurer and Wolf showed that a squaring oracle that returns g^{u^2} on input g^u is actually equivalent to a DH oracle. It is weaker in the sense that it can be posed as a specialized DH oracle that need only respond correctly when $u = v$. In this paper we extend the study of the relationships between Diffie-Hellman and oracles for problems which manipulate or give partial information about the index of their input. We do so by presenting a reduction that shows that a powering oracle that responds with $g^{u^a} \mod p$ when given $g^u \mod p$ for an unknown a that is poly-logarithmic in p, is equivalent to DH. Technically, our reduction utilizes the inverse of a particular type of Vandermonde matrix. This inverse matrix has recursively defined entries. Implications for large values of a are also given.

Keywords: Diffie-Hellman (DH), Computational Diffie-Hellman, Decision Diffie-Hellman, Discrete-Log, Public Key Cryptography, Oracles, Black-Box Reductions, JDL, LDL.

1 Introduction

The Diffie-Hellman key exchange [DH76] paved the way for public key cryptography, and is based on the presumed intractability of the Computational Diffie-Hellman problem. A multitude of cryptosystems and protocols depend on the security of DH and its decision version. The ElGamal public key cryptosystem

C. Blundo and S. Cimato (Eds.): SCN 2004, LNCS 3352, pp. 16–32, 2005.

[ElG85] was the first discrete-log based cryptosystem and its semantic security is based on the security of DDH. Also, an efficient cryptosystem which is secure against chosen ciphertext attacks was proven secure under DDH [CS98]. In addition, many key exchange protocols [MvOV99] as well as numerous deployed protocols like IPSEC and SSL designs rely on DH.

The results in this paper are motivated by the following. In typical applications a cyclic group is chosen for which it is believed that solving the Discrete Logarithm (DL) problem is intractable, and then algorithms based on the DH or DDH problems are used within the group. The security therefore rests entirely on the intractability of these problems and so a full understanding of them is mandatory.

One approach to investigate the power of DH is by comparing it to the Discrete Logarithm (or index finding) problem. Much progress has been made in showing the equivalence between the DL problem and the CDH problem [Bo88, Ma94, MW96]. Among other things, these developments show that DH is equivalent to DL whenever Euler's totient function applied to the order of G results in a smooth number. The key idea behind these results is that a DH oracle allows exponents to be multiplied, and thus enables modular exponentiation to be computed in the exponent via a square-and-multiply algorithm. This paves the way for utilizing the Pohlig-Hellman [PH78] algorithm in the exponent.

Other progress has been made by investigating the relationship between the DH oracle and oracles for related problems. It has been shown that the Diffie-Hellman problem is random self-reducible. Hence, it has been shown that given an oracle that solves DH with non-negligible probability, an algorithm exists that solves DH with overwhelming probability. Randomized algorithms which succeed with overwhelming probability will be dubbed "perfect", though clearly they are not strictly perfect since for a randomly chosen input such an oracle fails to give the correct answer with non-zero probability. Thus, the resulting perfect algorithm is called *PerfectDH* (for Perfect-Diffie-Hellman). Another approach to investigating the security of Diffie-Hellman using oracles is to analyze the hardness of computing individual bits of the DH secret vs. computing the entire DH secret. In [BV96] it was shown that an oracle that computes the $O(\sqrt{\log p})$ uppermost (or lower-most) bits of the DH secret can be used to compute all of the bits of the Diffie-Hellman secret. A third oracle result is the work of [MW96, MW98] where the notion of a squaring DH oracle was given. A squaring DH oracle, like a DH oracle, takes as input a value (g^u, g^v) chosen uniformly at random. However, unlike a DH oracle, on a successful call it returns g^{uv} only when $u = v$. The squaring oracle therefore succeeds on far fewer inputs. It was shown that this oracle is random self-reducible and is poly-time equivalent to a DH oracle. The solution is based on the observation that $g^{(u+v)^2}$ divided by g^{u^2} and then divided by g^{v^2} yields g^{2uv}. By taking the square root, the Diffie-Hellman key g^{uv} is obtained.

This paper attempts to extend our understanding of CDH and DDH by presenting a problem that gives partial information about the index. We call it the "Jacobi Discrete Logarithm problem" (which is investigated in groups in which Decision Diffie-Hellman is believed to be intractable). On input g^u the partial information oracle returns the Jacobi character of the index u with non-negligible advantage over guessing. It is shown that this new decision problem resides between CDH and DDH.

In the case that the order of g is a prime q this is the "Legendre Discrete Logarithm problem." Since the Legendre is computed using Euler's criterion, evaluating the Legendre in the exponent amounts to "powering" the exponent (the "power" in this case is $(q-1)/2$). This paper is therefore geared towards the study of *powering oracles*.

We then investigate the notion of powering the exponent using small powers. A reduction is given that shows that an oracle that takes g^u as input and that answers with g^{u^a} with non-negligible probability is equivalent to a DH oracle. Here a is "an unknown constant" such that $1 < a \in \mathbb{Z}$. The novelty here is a reduction that uses a class of matrices with recursively defined entries. We also discuss oacles as above that answer with a large power.

We note that in an independent earlier work, Kiltz extended the notion of a squaring oracle [Ki01] and showed (among other things) that CDH is computationally equivalent to P-DH. Here P-DH is the problem of computing $g^{P(a,b)}$ given g^a and g^b where P is a non-linear polynomial in a and b. This work is related to our powering oracle results, though technically the works take somewhat different paths.

2   Definitions

Denote by $L(a/p)$ the Legendre symbol of a with respect to the prime p. Denote by $J(a/n)$ the Jacobi symbol of a with respect to the odd integer n. The notation $ord_p(g)$ is used to denote the order of element $g \in \mathbb{Z}_p$. When working in $\mathbb{Z}_p$, the notation $log_g(y)$ denotes x such that $y = g^x \bmod p$. The notation $Pr[E]$ is used to denote the probability that event E occurs.

The computational Diffie-Hellman problem will now be reviewed. Let p be prime, let $g \in \mathbb{Z}_p$ be an element having order q, and let G be the group generated by g. The value $\tau = (p, q)$ encodes the group parameters. Finally, let $\mathcal{IG}(\cdot)$ denote an *instance generator*. An instance generator for G is a randomized algorithm that when given an integer n (in unary), runs in polynomial time in n and outputs some random index τ and a generator g of G_τ. Observe that for each n, the instance generator induces a distribution on the set of indices τ. Let $\mathcal{G} = \{G_\tau\}$ be a group family. For one of the reductions a slightly different group parameter will be needed. Let τ' contain the information in τ but also include the "certified" group order, i.e. the factorization of q. The following definition of Computational Diffie-Hellman (CDH) is from [Bon98].

Definition 1. *A CDH algorithm $\mathcal{A}$ for $\mathcal{G}$ is a probabilistic polynomial time (in $|\tau|$) algorithm satisfying, for some fixed $\alpha > 0$ and sufficiently large n:*

$$Pr[\mathcal{A}(\tau, g, g^a, g^b) = g^{ab}] > \frac{1}{n^\alpha}$$

where g is a generator of G_τ. The probability is over the random choice of $<\tau, g>$ according to the distribution induced by $\mathcal{IG}(n)$, the random choice of a, b in the range $[1, |G_\tau|]$ and the random bits used by $\mathcal{A}$. The group family $\mathcal{G}$ satisfies the CDH assumption if there is no CDH algorithm for $\mathcal{G}$.

Let $PerfectDH(\tau, g, g^a, g^b)$ be the same as $\mathcal{A}$ above except that it succeeds with a probability that is overwhelming in α. The Decision Diffie-Hellman problem is as follows.

Definition 2. *A DDH algorithm $\mathcal{A}$ for $\mathcal{G}$ is a probabilistic poly-time algorithm satisfying, for some fixed $\alpha > 0$ and sufficiently large n:*

$$|Pr[\mathcal{A}(\tau, g, g^a, g^b, g^{ab}) = true] - Pr[\mathcal{A}(\tau, g, g^a, g^b, g^c) = true]| > 1/n^\alpha$$

where g is a generator of G_τ. The probability is over the random choice of $<\tau, g>$ according to the distribution induced by $\mathcal{IG}(n)$, the random choice of a, b, c in the range $[1, |G_\tau|]$, and the random bits used by $\mathcal{A}$. The group family $\mathcal{G}$ satisfies the DDH assumption if there is no DDH algorithm for $\mathcal{G}$.

The perfect DDH problem is the same as $\mathcal{A}$ above except that it succeeds with a probablity that is overwhelming in α. It was shown in Proposition 1 of [St96] (see also [NR97]) that DDH and perfect DDH are equivalent in prime order subgroups. An excellent overview of the Decision Diffie-Hellman problem was given in [Bon98]. Elliptic curve groups where DDH is easy and CDH is still believed to be hard were recently shown in [JN01].

3   The Jacobi Discrete Logarithm Problem

In this section a new computational problem is introduced called the Jacobi Discrete Logarithm (JDL) problem. The following is the formal definition of the Jacobi-Discrete-Log (JDL) problem. It is in the same vein as Section 2.

Definition 3. *A JDL algorithm $\mathcal{A}$ for $\mathcal{G}$ is a probabilistic poly-time algorithm satisfying, for some fixed $\alpha > 0$ and sufficiently large n:*

$$Pr[\mathcal{A}(\tau, g, g^a) = J(a/q)] > 1/2 + 1/n^\alpha$$

where g is a generator of G_τ. The probability is over the random choice of $<\tau, g>$ according to the distribution induced by $\mathcal{IG}(n)$, the random choice of a in the range $[1, |G_\tau|]$, and the random bits used by $\mathcal{A}$. The group family $\mathcal{G}$ satisfies the JDL assumption if there is no JDL algorithm for $\mathcal{G}$.

The Perfect Jacobi-Discrete-Log (Perfect-JDL) problem is to do the same as the above, but must succeed with overwhelming probability.

Clearly, when the order q of g is prime, the problem becomes that of computing the Legendre of the exponent (i.e., $L(a/q)$). By Euler's Criterion, $L(a/q) = a^{\frac{q-1}{2}} \mod q$. Taking $a = (q-1)/2$ we see that the investigation of this problem is a natural extension to studying the aforementioned powering oracles.

For the remainder of this section n will be used to denote the order of g. Hence, $n = ord_p(g) = p_1^{t_1} p_2^{t_2} \dots p_m^{t_m}$. The smallest prime is p_1, the next smallest prime is p_2, etc.

4   The JDL Assumption Implies the Perfect-CDH Assumption

The fact that the JDL assumption implies the Perfect-CDH assumption is not hard to see. The reduction algorithm uses an oracle that solves Perfect-CDH to compute Euler's Criterion (the Legendre symbol) in the exponent.

Observe that if we can compute $J(x/p_i)$ for $1 \leq i \leq m$ where $y = g^x \bmod p$, then we can compute $J(x/n)$ in the standard fashion.

$$J(x/n) = \prod_{i=1}^{m} L(x/p_i)^{t_i}$$

Consider the following algorithm which assumes the existence of an oracle *Perfect-CDH* which solves the Perfect Computational Diffie-Hellman problem. Here $y = g^x \bmod p$. The algorithm outputs $g^{x^a} \bmod p$ where $a \geq 0$. Let $a >> b$ denote the bit shift right operation, i.e., the operation of throwing away the b least significant bits of a. For example, $0110 >> 1 = 011$.

EXPSQMUL(τ, q, y, a):
1. let $L = \lceil log_2(a) \rceil$
2. set $SQ[0] = y$
3. for $i = 0$ to $L - 1$ do:
4.   choose $r, r_1, r_2 \in_R \mathbb{Z}_q$
5. $t = $ Perfect-CDH$(\tau, g^r, SQ[i]^{rr_1}, SQ[i]^{rr_2})$
6. $SQ[i + 1] = t^{(rr_1 r_2)^{-1}} \bmod p$
7. let $t = g$ and $s = a$
8. for $i = 0$ to $L - 1$ do:
9.   if $(s \bmod 2)$ equals 1 then
10.   choose $r, r_1, r_2 \in_R \mathbb{Z}_q$
11. $t = $ Perfect-CDH$(\tau, g^r, t^{rr_1}, SQ[i]^{rr_2})$
12. $t = t^{(rr_1 r_2)^{-1}} \bmod p$
13. $s = s >> 1$
14. output t and halt

$\mathcal{A}(\tau, g, y)$:
1. set $\alpha = 1$
2. for $i = 1$ to m do:
3.   if t_i is odd then
4.   compute $w = n/p_i$
5.   compute $g_i = g^w \bmod p$
6.   compute $y' = y^w \bmod p$, and let $y' = g_i^{x'} \bmod p$
7.   compute $b = EXPSQMUL(\tau, p_i, y', (p_i - 1)/2)$
8.   if $b \neq g_i$ then set $\alpha = -\alpha$
9. output α and halt

Step 7 is computed using the Perfect-CDH oracle to compute $x'^{(p_i-1)/2}$ in the exponent in a square-and-multiply fashion.

Theorem 1. *If all calls to Perfect-CDH succeed then* $\mathcal{A}(\tau, g, y) = 1$ *iff* $L(x/n) = 1$.

Proof. Assume that every call to Perfect-CDH succeeds. Clearly $\mathcal{A}$ computes the Jacobi symbol in the standard fashion. Consider the operation of $\mathcal{A}$ when t_i is odd for prime p_i. If it can be shown that $b = g_i$ iff $L(x/p_i) = 1$ then we will be done. Note that $b = g_i \Rightarrow x'^{(p_i-1)/2} \equiv 1 \bmod p_i$ since g_i was raised to w in step 5. But, $x'^{(p_i-1)/2} \equiv 1 \bmod p_i \Rightarrow x^{(p_i-1)/2} \equiv 1 \bmod p_i$, since $x \equiv x' \bmod p_i$. Finally, from Euler's Criterion it follows that $x^{(p_i-1)/2} \equiv 1 \bmod p_i \Rightarrow L(x/p_i) = 1$. To prove the converse, namely that $L(x/p_i) = 1 \Rightarrow b = g_i$, the contrapositive will be proven. In other words, it will be shown that $b \neq g_i \Rightarrow L(x/p_i) = -1$. Clearly, $b \neq g_i$ implies that $x'^{(p_i-1)/2}$ is not congruent to 1 modulo p_i. But the order of $x'^{(p_i-1)/2} \bmod p_i$ is clearly 2 hence, $x'^{(p_i-1)/2} \equiv -1 \bmod p_i$. But, $x'^{(p_i-1)/2} \equiv -1 \bmod p_i \Rightarrow x^{(p_i-1)/2} \equiv -1 \bmod p_i$ since $x = x' \bmod p_i$. From Euler's Criterion it follows that $x^{(p_i-1)/2} \equiv -1 \bmod p_i \Rightarrow L(x/p_i) = -1$. □

Theorem 2. *With probability greater than* $1/2 + 1/n_2^{\alpha_2}$, $\mathcal{A}(\tau, g, y) = J(x/n)$.

Proof. It may be assumed that if one or more calls to Perfect-CDH fails then $\mathcal{A}$ outputs the wrong answer. Clearly, the worst-case is when all prime powers dividing n have a power of unity, since this is the case that requires the most invocations of Perfect-CDH. In this case algorithm $\mathcal{A}$ makes at most $k = \lceil log_2(n) \rceil$ calls to Perfect-CDH. Let γ_1 denote the probability that Perfect-CDH succeeds on a random input. Hence, γ_1 is overwhelming. It follows that $\mathcal{A}$ succeeds with probability at least γ_1^k. It can be shown that this quantity is at least $1/2 + 1/n_2^{\alpha_2}$ for fixed α_2 and sufficiently large n_2. □

5 The Perfect-JDL Assumption Implies the JDL Assumption

It is trivial to prove that the JDL assumption implies the Perfect-JDL assumption. In this section the other direction will be proven. The basic idea is to randomize the problem instance by exponentiating to a random value while taking into account the Jacobi symbol of this random vlaue. Let *JDLAlg* be an oracle solving the JDL problem. Now, consider the following algorithm.

$\mathcal{A}(\tau, g, y)$:
1. if $\sqrt{n} \in \mathbb{Z}$ output "1" and halt
2. for $\ell = 1$ to L do
3.　　choose $r_\ell \in_R \mathbb{Z}_n$
4.　　compute $x_\ell = JDLAlg(\tau, g, y^{r_\ell} \bmod p)$ and store $J(r_\ell/n) * x_\ell$ in list ω
5. output the majority answer in list ω and halt

Denote by property 1 the well known fact that $J(ab/n) = J(a/n)J(b/n)$.

Theorem 3. *With overwhelming probability,* $\mathcal{A}(\tau, g, y) = 1$ *iff* $J(x/n) = 1$.

Proof. If $\sqrt{n} \in \mathbb{Z}$ then the Jacobi symbol of all exponents for g is unity. Hence, step 1 always outputs the correct answer when it halts. It follows from property 1 that $J(log_g(y^{r_\ell})/n) = J(r_\ell/n)J(log_g(y)/n)$. By multiplying both sides by $J(r_\ell/n)$ it follows that $J(log_g(y)/n) = J(r_\ell/n)J(log_g(y^{r_\ell})/n)$ for $\ell = 1, 2, ..., L$. Therefore, $J(r_\ell/n) * x_\ell$ is the Jacobi of $log_g(y)$ with fixed probability s_1 in iteration ℓ where $s_1 \geq 1/2 + 1/n_1^{\alpha_1}$ (ineq. [1]) for some fixed α_1 and sufficiently large n_1. Observe that the loop in steps 2 through 4 constitutes a series of L Bernoulli trials. Theorem 1 (Chernoff Bound - see Appendix B) therefore applies. Let $\mu = s_1 L$ (eq. [2]) and take $L/2 = (1 - \delta)\mu$ (eq. [3]). Here the random variable X is a count of the number of successful trials. It follows that $Pr[X < L/2] < e^{-(s_1 L \delta^2)/2} \leq e^{-((1/2+1/n_1^{\alpha_1})L\delta^2)/2}$. By combining inequality [1] with equalities [2] and [3] it follows that $\delta \geq 2/(n_1^{\alpha_1} + 2)$. From this it can be shown that $Pr[X < L/2] < 2^{-L/(n_1^{2\alpha_1}+2n_1^{\alpha_1})}$. By taking $L = (n_1^{2\alpha_1} + 2n_1^{\alpha_1})n_1$ the theorem is proved. $\square$

An open problem is whether or not CDH and JDL are equivalent and whether or not JDL and DDH are equivalent. The relationship between JDL and the bit hardness of DH is also interesting.

6   The DDH Assumption Implies the Perfect-JDL Assumption

We say that the group DDH *assumption* implies the Perfect-JDL *assumption* since solving DDH is intractable only if solving Perfect-JDL is intractable[1].

Observe that if $2 \mid t_1, t_2, ..., t_m$ then the Jacobi symbol of all elements in $\mathbb{Z}_n$ with respect to n is unity. A straightforward application of PerfectJDL will therefore not always suffice to distinguish DDH triples from random triples. It is not hard to see that as long as one of the t_i is odd, $J(x/n) = 1$ with probability $1/2$ for a randomly chosen x. Now, observe that n must be devoid of small prime factors, otherwise DDH triples can be distinguished based on residuosity (e.g., if $2 \mid n$ then DDH is broken based on testing for quadratic residuosity which can be done in poly-time). Hence, this implication applies to subgroups in which n is odd and free of small prime factors (in many cases the group where DDH is used is a prime order subgroup for a large prime).

Assume that an oracle *PerfectJDL* exists that solves the Perfect-JDL problem. Consider the following algorithm $\mathcal{A}$ which makes calls to PerfectJDL. It will be shown that $\mathcal{A}$ solves the DDH problem. Since PerfectJDL exists iff an algorithm solving JDL exists this proof will show that the DDH assumption implies the JDL assumption. We remark that the reduction can be easily extended to handle an order which is unknown. The problem instances can be transformed into triples that are statistically indistinguishable from DDH triples/random 3-

---

[1] Here we adopt the language of "one assumption implies another assumption," as in [Bon98].

tuples (see [Bon98] for this as well as the randomization technique that we use). Let $X = g^x$, $Y = g^y$, and $Z = g^z$.

$\mathcal{A}(\tau, g, X, Y, Z)$:

1. choose $r, u_1, u_2, v \in_R \mathbb{Z}_n$
2. construct the triplet $(x', y', z') = (X^{rv} g^{ru_1}, Y^r g^{ru_2}, Z^{rv} Y^{ru_1} X^{rvu_2} g^{ru_1 u_2})$
3. compute $s_1 = PerfectJDL(\tau, g^r, x')$, $s_2 = PerfectJDL(\tau, g^r, y')$, and
   $\qquad s_3 = PerfectJDL(\tau, g^r, z')$
4. if $s_3 = s_1 * s_2$ then output true else output false

Theorem 4. *If $\exists$ an algorithm $PerfectJDL$ solving Perfect-JDL then $\mathcal{A}$ breaks DDH.*

The above theorem can be seen from the following. The randomization of the problem instance has the following propertyies. If the input 3-tuple is a DH triple the (x', y', z') is a DH triple. If the input 3-tuple is not a DH triple then (x', y', z') is statisticallly indistinguishable from a random 3-tuple.

With overwhelming probability all three calls to $\mathcal{A}$ will succeed. So, when the input tuple is not a DH triple it will be "caught" with probability close to $1/2$. This detection will arise when $s_3 \neq s_1 * s_2$. When the input tuple is a DH triple then with overwhelming probability $s_3 = s_1 * s_2$.

Since the DDH assumption holds iff the PerfectDDH assumption holds, it follows that any algorithm solving the JDL problem can be used as an oracle to solve PerfectDDH. It has therefore been shown that the JDL problem lies in between CDH and DDH. The potential equivalence of JDL and DDH is left as an open problem.

7   Powering Oracles

In this section we give a reduction that shows that a powering oracle that responds with $g^{u^a} \bmod p$ when given $g^u \bmod p$ for an unknown a that is polylogarithmic in p is equivalent to DH. It is a special case of the prior independent work of [Ki01]. Our approach involves the use of a special type of Vandermonde matrix. The reduction explicitly utilizes the factorized inverse of this type of Vandermonde matrix, an inverse matrix that has recursively defined entries. We also consider the case of unknown a and a that is very large.

Let p be a large prime and let g be an element with order q. For the moment we will consider the case that q is prime. The following is a formal definition of a powering oracle.

Definition 4. *A $PoweringDH_a$ algorithm $\mathcal{A}$ for $\mathcal{G}$ is a probabilistic polynomial time (in $|\tau|$) algorithm satisfying, for some fixed $a > 1, \alpha > 0$, and sufficiently large n:*

$$Pr[\mathcal{A}(\tau, g, g^u) = g^{u^a}] > \frac{1}{n^\alpha}$$

where g is a generator of G_τ and a is poly-logarithmic in p. The probability is over the random choice of $<\tau, g>$ according to the distribution induced by $\mathcal{IG}(n)$, the random choice of u in the range $[1, |G_\tau|]$ and the random bits used by $\mathcal{A}$. The group family $\mathcal{G}$ satisfies the $PoweringDH_a$ assumption if there is no $PoweringDH_a$ algorithm for $\mathcal{G}$.

The oracle $PerfectDH_a$ is the same as $PoweringDH_a$ except that it succeeds with a probability that is overwhelming in α. It was shown by Maurer and Wolf that $PoweringDH_2$ exists iff $PerfectDH_2$ exists. The following are a few simple facts. The problem of computing $s = g^{u^a}$ given (τ, g, g^u) when a is known is random self-reducible. To see this, consider the following algorithm $M(\cdot)$. First, M chooses $r \in_R \mathbb{Z}_q$. M then computes $t = PoweringDH_a(\tau, g, y^r)$. Finally, M outputs $t^{r^{-a}}$ and halts. It is easy to see that a perfect powering oracle for a exists provided a powering oracle for a exists that succeeds with non-negligible probability.

A powering oracle for a can be implemented given a perfect DH oracle. To see this, note that the DH oracle can be used to implement a square and multiply algorithm in the exponent. For example, to implement a powering oracle with $a = 5$, the value

$$PerfectDH(\tau, g, PerfectDH(\tau, g, PerfectDH(\tau, g, y, y),$$
$$PerfectDH(\tau, g, y, y)), y)$$

is computed, where $y = g^u$.

We will now motivate the general solution to the problem of showing that $PoweringDH \Leftrightarrow DH$ by considering powering oracles for $a = 3, 4$. Observe that $(x+1)^3 = x^3 + 3x^2 + 3x + 1$. From this equation it is clear that if we have access to a cubing oracle, we can isolate the $3x^2$ term. Since q is prime, 3 has an inverse mod q. So, x^2 can be isolated. The goal is therefore to utilize the cubing oracle to implement a squaring oracle.

$PerfectDH_2(\tau, g, y)$:
1. compute $t = PerfectDH_3(\tau, g, yg \bmod p)$
2. compute $t = t/(y^3 g) \bmod p$
3. compute $t = t/PerfectDH_3(\tau, g, y) \bmod p$
4. compute $t = t^{3^{-1}} \bmod p$
5. output t and halt

Since given a squaring oracle, we can implement a Diffie-Hellman oracle, the above algorithm proves that given a cubing oracle we can break Diffie-Hellman. Now consider $a = 4$. Again, the goal is to implement a squaring oracle given $PerfectDH_4$. The solution is based on the expansions $(x + 1)^4 = x^4 + 4x^3 + 6x^2 + 4x + 1$ and $(x-1)^4 = x^4 - 4x^3 + 6x^2 - 4x + 1$. Observe that $(x+1)^4 + (x-1)^4 = 2x^4 + 12x^2 + 2$.

$PoweringDH_2(\tau, g, y)$:

1. compute $t = PerfectDH_4(\tau, g, yg \mod p)PerfectDH_4(\tau, g, y/g \mod p) \mod p$
2. compute $t = t/(PerfectDH_4(\tau, g, y))^2 \mod p$
3. compute $t = t/g^2 \mod p$
4. output a twelfth root of t and halt

Given these two reductions it is only natural to ask whether or not there is a general reduction for $a > 2$. This is in fact the case, as will be shown in the sequel.

7.1   Inverse of the Vandermonde Matrix

In order to show that the reduction holds for larger values of a the form of the inverse of a specific class of Vandermonde Matrices will be explored. Recall that the following is an $a + 1$ by $a + 1$ square matrix $D(a + 1)$ called a *Vandermonde Matrix*.

$$\begin{vmatrix} 1 & t_1 & t_1^2 & \cdots & t_1^a \\ 1 & t_2 & t_2^2 & \cdots & t_2^a \\ \vdots & \vdots & \vdots & \ddots & \vdots \\ 1 & t_{a+1} & t_{a+1}^2 & \cdots & t_{a+1}^a \end{vmatrix}$$

It is well known from Linear Algebra that the Determinant of the Vandermonde Matrix is non-zero if all the t_i's are different [Ga59, Me01] and hence that it is non-singular. The inverse therefore exists, is unique, and can be found efficiently via Gauss-Jordan. Given the inverse, the solution to the matrix equation $D(n)\vec{x} = b$ can be easily solved by matrix multiplication since $D(n)^{-1}D(n)\vec{x} = \vec{x} = D(n)^{-1}b$. However, in this paper we will only be concerned with n by n Vandermonde Matrices $M(n)$ whose (i, j) entry is i^{j-1}.

$$[M(n)]_{i,j} = i^{j-1} \tag{1}$$

For example, the value $[M(4)]_{3,2}$ equals 3 and the entire matrix for $M(4)$ is given below.

$$\begin{vmatrix} 1 & 1 & 1 & 1 \\ 1 & 2 & 4 & 8 \\ 1 & 3 & 9 & 27 \\ 1 & 4 & 16 & 64 \end{vmatrix}$$

The reduction algorithm given in the sequel requires the use of the inverse of such matrices. However, rather than having the reduction algorithm perform Gaussian Elimination as a procedural step and rather than relying on the fact that the matrix corresponds to an interpolation operation, we have opted to utilize a recent elegant method. In [BBM02] it was shown how to factor $M(n)^{-1}$ into two matrices in which only the rightmost matrix has recursively defined entries.

$$[M(n)]^{-1} = \frac{1}{(n-1)!} V(n) \qquad\qquad V(n) = T(n)U(n)$$

Here $U(n)$ has recursively defined entries. Thus, the authors give a recurrence describing each entry in $M(n)^{-1}$. Appendix A summarizes this approach. It also shows, by fiat, that all of the entries in $V(n)$ are integers for all n.

7.2   DH-Powering Equivalence When the Order is Prime

The goal in this section is to implement an algorithm that has access to a perfect powering oracle, and that outputs g^{x^2} on input $y = g^x$. It is assumed that q is prime and that a is known where $2 < a \in \mathbb{Z}$. These assumptions will be relaxed in the next section. Using the Binomial Theorem and the inverse of $M(n)$ the general reduction can be given for $a > 2$. Recall that the Binomial Theorem states that for a positive integer n, $(x + b)^n = \sum_{k=0}^{n} \binom{n}{k} x^k b^{n-k}$. The reduction uses $PerfectDH_a(\cdot, \cdot, \cdot)$ as an oracle in an algorithm that computes $PoweringDH_2(\cdot, \cdot, \cdot)$.

The key idea behind the reduction is the following. The powering oracle is used to compute $(x + 1)^a$, $(x + 2)^a$,..., $(x + a)^a$ in the exponent. For instance, $g^{(x+3)^a} = PerfectDH_a(\tau, g, yg^3 \bmod p)$. Using the Binomial Theorem the form of each of these binomial expansions can be found. For each power of x we can define a new variable that is the power of x times the corresponding binomial coefficient. It is then clear that under the new variables, the coefficients that remain form $M(a + 1)$.

$PoweringDH_2(\tau, g, y)$:
1. set $z = g$ and $I = 1$
2. for $j = 1$ to $a + 1$ do:
3. $\qquad V(a + 1)_{a-1,j} = \sum_{k=1}^{a+1} T(a + 1)_{a-1,k} U(a + 1)_{k,j}$
4. $\qquad b_j = PerfectDH_a(\tau, g, yz \bmod p)$
5. $\qquad I = I b_j^{V(a+1)_{a-1,j}} \bmod p$
6. $\qquad z = zg \bmod p$
7. compute $r = a! \frac{a(a-1)}{2} \bmod q$
8. compute $s = r^{-1} \bmod q$ using the Extended Euclidean Algorithm
9. output $I^s \bmod p$ and halt

Theorem 5. *If $a > 2$ and all calls to $PerfectDH_a$ succeed then $PoweringDH_2$ outputs g^{x^2}.*

Proof. The resulting values $V(a+1)_{a-1,j}$ for $j = 1, 2, ..., a+1$ computed in step 3 are equal to the row in $V(a+1)$ which is third from the bottom. The loop over step 5 which computes I effectively multiplies a $1 \times (a+1)$ matrix by an $(a+1) \times 1$ matrix, which yields a single value in the exponent of g in I. The difference is that the elements in $V(a+1)_{a-1,j}$ are in $\mathbb{Z}_q$ and the elements $b_1, b_2, ..., b_{a+1}$ are in $\mathbb{Z}_p$. By performing exponentiation, matrix operations are effectively performed in $\mathbb{Z}_q$. Using the Binomial Theorem and the fact that $[M(n)]^{-1} = \frac{1}{(n-1)!} V(n)$ it can be shown that resulting value in the exponent of g in I is $a!\binom{a}{2}x^2$. Since it was assumed that the order q of g is prime, an inverse s of $r = a!\binom{a}{2} \bmod q$ exists and is unique. Hence, step 8 can be efficiently computed and correctly computes the inverse of r. Since I^s is output it follows that when all calls to $PerfectDH_a$ succeed the resulting output value is g^{x^2}. □

It is straightforward to compose $PoweringDH_2$ with Maurer and Wolf's squaring algorithm to yield the stated DH result. A small numerical example of the above reduction is given in the next subsection to illustrate this algorithm.

7.3 Small Example of the Reduction

It is instructive to analyze an example for $V(n)$. The following is an example of $V(n)$ where $n = 4$. It is straightforward to verify that $(\frac{1}{3!}V(4))M(4) = I$.

$$
V(4) = \begin{vmatrix} 1 & -3 & 2 & -1 \\ 0 & 3 & -6 & 2 \\ 0 & 0 & 3 & -3 \\ 0 & 0 & 0 & 1 \end{vmatrix} \begin{vmatrix} 7 & -2 & 1 & 0 \\ -4 & 7 & -4 & 1 \\ 2 & -5 & 4 & -1 \\ -1 & 3 & -3 & 1 \end{vmatrix} = \begin{vmatrix} 24 & -36 & 24 & -6 \\ -26 & 57 & -42 & 11 \\ 9 & -24 & 21 & -6 \\ -1 & 3 & -3 & 1 \end{vmatrix} \tag{2}
$$

An example will go a long way to illustrate how and why the algorithm works. Suppose we are given a cubing oracle. We would like to show how to use this oracle to implement a squaring DH oracle, and hence an oracle solving computational DH. The loop over step 3 performs the following matrix multiplication.

$$
\begin{vmatrix} 0 & 3 & -6 & 2 \end{vmatrix} \begin{vmatrix} 7 & -2 & 1 & 0 \\ -4 & 7 & -4 & 1 \\ 2 & -5 & 4 & -1 \\ -1 & 3 & -3 & 1 \end{vmatrix} = \begin{vmatrix} -26 & 57 & -42 & 11 \end{vmatrix} \tag{3}
$$

The algorithm then computes I as shown below.

$$
I = g^{3!3x^2} = g^{3!\binom{3}{2}x^2} = b_1^{-26} b_2^{57} b_3^{-42} b_4^{11} \bmod p \tag{4}
$$

This is effectively the following matrix multiplication in the exponent.

$$
\begin{vmatrix} -26 & 57 & -42 & 11 \end{vmatrix} \begin{vmatrix} (x+1)^3 \\ (x+2)^3 \\ (x+3)^3 \\ (x+4)^3 \end{vmatrix} = 18x^2 \tag{5}
$$

7.4   Performance of the Reduction Algorithm

Theorem 6. *If a is poly-logarithmic in p then $PoweringDH_2$ halts in time polynomial in $\log p$ using $a + 1$ oracle calls to $PerfectDH_a$.*

Proof. Computing $V(a+1)_{a-1,j}$ in step 3 requires $a+1$ multiplications. The loop over step 3 therefore constitutes $O(a^2)$ operations. Since $a = \log_2^{O(1)} p$, it follows that this step constitutes a total of $\log_2^{O(1)} p$ operations. The loop over steps 4 through 6 requires $a + 1$ calls to $PerfectDH_a$ requries a polynomial number of operations in $\log p$. Since a is poly-logarithmic in p, computing $a! \bmod q$ in step 7 requires a poly-logarithmic number of multiplications modulo q. From this it is not hard to see that the running time is as claimed.   □

The correct termination of the algorithm is based on the fact that the probability that $PerfectDH_a$ succeeds is $\gamma(\alpha)$ which is overwhelming in some the security parameter α (typically the size of the modulus p) and only fails with negligible probability. Since $PoweringDH_2$ makes $a+1$ calls to the oracle $PerfectDH_a$ it holds that since further $a + 1 \leq p(\alpha)$ where $p(\alpha)$ is a polynomial in α then $PoweringDH_2$ succeeds with non-negligible probability.

7.5   Generalizations

Note that if a is not known, a value for a for which $PerfectDH_a$ succeeds with non-negligible probability can be determined. To see this note that we can invoke the oracle with a randomly chosen index (exponent) x with x known. The values $a = 2, 3, 4, \ldots$ and so on can be tested. It is not hard to see that this process runs in time polynomial in $\log p$. If $a = 2$, then Maurer and Wolf's algorithm for a squaring oracle is performed. Otherwise, our reduction is performed.

Now we will consider the same problem as in the previous section, but generalize it to allow the order of g to be composite. The value q will still be used to denote the order of g, but in this case q may be composite. Provided that $\gcd(w, q)$ is not too large an algorithm can be used to compute $g^{x^2} \bmod p$. Care must be taken now since the existence of unique inverses modulo the composite q is not guaranteed. Recall that the value $g^{a!x_2} = g^{a!\binom{a}{2}x^2} \bmod p$ is readily obtained. By computing the rth root where $r = a!\binom{a}{2} \bmod q$, the answer is found. The work of Scott Lindhurst can be used to analyze the cases in which we can efficiently compute the rth root mod p [SL97]. The following is Proposition 8 from his thesis.

Proposition 1. *Given a cyclic group G and a degree $r = O(\log^2 |G|)$, we can compute r^{th} roots in G deterministically (assuming we are given an rth power residue) using $O(\log^2 |G| \log \log |G|)$ group operations.*

7.6   Equivalence to DH When the Power Is Large

Consider an oracle that on input $g^x \bmod p$ returns $g^{x^{q-a}} \bmod p$ with overwhelming probability. Here $a > 1$ and the order of g is the prime q where q divides $p-1$ evenly. When a is polylogarithmic in p this oracle is equivalent to Diffie-Hellman.

To see this, observe that by applying the oracle twice in succession the value $g^{x^{(q-a)^2}} = g^{x^{q^2-2aq+a^2}}$ is computed with overwhelming probability. Suppose that x generates $\mathbb{Z}_q$. Then since $q^2 - 2aq + a^2$ divided by $q - 1$ results in a remainder of $a^2 - 2a + 1$ it follows that $g^{x^{(q-a)^2}} = g^{x^{(a-1)^2}}$. This yields a powering oracle for a small exponent, which in this case is $(a - 1)^2$, and this has been shown to be equivalent to Diffie-Hellman. Suppose that x does not generate $\mathbb{Z}_q$. To handle this issue it is possible to first randomize x using r to enable $xr \bmod q$ to be a generator of $\mathbb{Z}_q$ with non-negligible probability. This randomization factor can be removed in the final result by computing $(g^{(rx)^{(a-1)^2}})^{r^{-(a-1)^2}}$.

References

[BBM02] C. Bender, D. Brody, B. Meister. Inverse of a Vandermonde Matrix. Preprint 2002 (downloaded from http://theory.ic.ac.uk/~brody/DCB/sa6.pdf).

[Bo88] B. Den Boer. Diffie-Hellman is as strong as discrete log for certain primes. In *Advances in Cryptology—Crypto '88*, LNCS 403, pages 530–539, 1988.

[Bon98] D. Boneh. The Decision Diffie-Hellman Problem. In *Third Algorithmic Number Theory Symposium*, LNCS 1423, pages 48–63, 1998.

[BV96] D. Boneh, R. Venkatesan. Hardness of Computing the Most Significant Bits of Secret Keys in Diffie-Hellman and Related Schemes. In *Advances in Cryptology—Crypto '96*, pages 129–142, 1996.

[CS98] R. Cramer, V. Shoup. A practical public key crypto system provably secure against adaptive chosen ciphertext attack. In *Advances in Cryptology—Crypto '98*, LNCS 1462, 1998.

[DH76] W. Diffie, M. Hellman. New Directions in Cryptography. In *IEEE Transactions on Information Theory*, 22(6), pages 644–654, 1976.

[ElG85] T. ElGamal. A Public-Key Cryptosystem and a Signature Scheme Based on Discrete Logarithms. In *Advances in Cryptology—Crypto '84*, pages 10–18, 1985. Springer-Verlag.

[Ga59] F. R. Gantmacher. The Theory of Matrices vol. 1. AMS Chelsea Publishing, 1959.

[GKP] R. Graham, D. Knuth, O. Patashnik. Concrete Mathematics. Chapter 6 - Special Numbers, Second Edition, Addison-Wesley, 1994.

[JN01] A. Joux, K. Nguyen. Separating Decision Diffie-Hellman from Diffie-Hellman in Cryptographic Groups. Available at http://eprint.iacr.org/2001/003/.

[Ki01] E. Kiltz. A Tool Box of Cryptographic Functions Related to the Diffie-Hellman Function. In *Progress in Cryptology—Indocrypt '01*, pages 339–350, 2001.

[Ma94] U. Maurer. Towards proving the equivalence of breaking the Diffie-Hellman protocol and computing discrete logarithms. In *Advances in Cryptology—Crypto '94*, pages 271–281, 1994. Springer-Verlag.

[Me01] Alfred J. Menezes. Combinatorics and Optimization 331 - Coding Theory. Handout on Vandermonde Matrices. Downloaded by http from www.cacr.math.uwaterloo.ca/~ajmeneze/co331/handouts/vandermonde.ps.

[MW96] U. Maurer, S. Wolf. Diffie-Hellman Oracles. In *Advances in Cryptology—Crypto '96*, pages 268–282, 1996.

[MW98]   U. Maurer, S. Wolf. The Relationship Bewteen Breaking the Diffie-Hellman Protocol and Computing Discrete Logarithms. In *SIAM Journal of Computing*, vol. 28, pages 1689–1721, 1999.

[MvOV99] A. J. Menezes, P. C. van Oorschot, S. A. Vanstone. *Handbook of Applied Cryptography*, CRC Press, 1999.

[NR97]   M. Naor, O. Reingold. Number theoretic constructions of efficient pseudo random functions. In *Proceedings of the 38th Symposium on Foundations of Computer Science—FOCS '97*, pages 458–467.

[PH78]   S. Pohlig, M. Hellman. An improved algorithm for computing logarithms over GF(p) and its cryptographic significance. In *IEEE Trans. on Information Theory*, vol. 24, no. 1, pages 106–110, 1978.

[SL97]   Scott Lindhurst. Computing Roots in Finite Fields and Groups with a Jaunt through sums of Digits. Doctoral Dissertation (advisor - Eric Bach), Chapter 3 - Extensions of Shanks Algorithm, 1997 (downloaded from http://members.aol.com/SokobanMac/scott/papers/papers.html).

[St96]   M. Stadler. Publicly verifiable secret sharing. In *Advances in Cryptology—Eurocrypt '96*, pages 190–199.

A   Inverse of M(n)

We are interested in solving the matrix equation $M(n)\vec{x} = b$ once and for all by obtaining the solution for each element in $M(n)^{-1}$ for all n. Having such a solution is advantageous since it removes the need to do elimination for each n. Fortunately, one such solution which is recursive in nature was pointed out in [BBM02]. We summarize these findings below.

$$[M(n)]^{-1} = \frac{1}{(n-1)!}V(n) \tag{6}$$

The above relationship was shown, and it was noted that all of the entries in $V(n)$ are in $\mathbb{Z}$. However, a clever direct way to build it (which our application may benefit from) will be given explicitly here. The authors give the following factorization of $V(n)$,

$$V(n) = T(n)U(n) \tag{7}$$

where $T(n)$ is upper-triangular. The matrix $U(n)$ is given by the following inhomogeneous recursion relation.

$$[U(n)]_{i,j} = [U(n-1)]_{i-1,j-1} - [U(n-1)]_{i-1,j} + [W(n)]_{i,j} \tag{8}$$

If $i - 1 = 0$ then $[U(n-1)]_{i-1,j-1} = [U(n-1)]_{i-1,j} = 0$. If $j - 1 = 0$ then $[U(n-1)]_{i-1,j-1} = 0$. Finally, if $j = n$ then $[U(n-1)]_{i-1,j} = 0$. The following are the initial values for the recursion relation.

$$U(1) = \begin{vmatrix} 1 \end{vmatrix} \tag{9}$$

$$U(2) = \begin{vmatrix} 1 & 0 \\ -1 & 1 \end{vmatrix} \tag{10}$$

The matrix $W(n)$ is given by the following equations when $n > 2$,

$$[W(n)]_{1,j} = (-1)^j \frac{(n-1)!}{(n-j)!(j-1)!} + \sum_{k=1}^{j} \frac{(-1)^{k+j}(k+1)^{n-1}n!}{(n-j+k)!(j-k)!} \qquad (11)$$

$$[W(n)]_{2,j} = (-1)^j \frac{(n-1)!}{(n-j)!(j-1)!} \qquad (12)$$

$$[W(n)]_{i,j} = 0 \ \ for \ \ i > 2 \qquad (13)$$

The matrices $T(1), T(2), ..., T(5)$ were given along with an explanation of their general form. Below we give the closed form of each entry in $T(n)$. The closed form equation for $[T(n)]_{i,j}$ utilizes Stirling numbers of the first kind. We adopt the notation $\begin{bmatrix} n \\ k \end{bmatrix}$ of [GKP] to represent these numbers.

$$[T(n)]_{i,j} = \begin{cases} 0 & \text{if } i > j \\ (-1)^{n-1} & i=1, j=n \\ (-1)^{j-i}\begin{pmatrix} n-j+i-1 \\ n-j \end{pmatrix}\begin{bmatrix} n-1 \\ n-j+i-1 \end{bmatrix} & \text{otherwise} \end{cases} \qquad (14)$$

Table 1. Stirling numbers of the first kind

n	$\begin{bmatrix} n \\ 0 \end{bmatrix}$	$\begin{bmatrix} n \\ 1 \end{bmatrix}$	$\begin{bmatrix} n \\ 2 \end{bmatrix}$	$\begin{bmatrix} n \\ 3 \end{bmatrix}$	$\begin{bmatrix} n \\ 4 \end{bmatrix}$	$\begin{bmatrix} n \\ 5 \end{bmatrix}$	$\begin{bmatrix} n \\ 6 \end{bmatrix}$
0	1						
1	0	1					
2	0	1	1				
3	0	2	3	1			
4	0	6	11	6	1		
5	0	24	50	35	10	1	
6	0	120	274	225	85	15	1

Theorem 7. *All of the entries in $V(n)$ are integers.*

Proof. From (7) it follows that we need only show that all of the entries in $T(n)$ and all of the entries in $U(n)$ are integers. It is well known that binomial coefficients are contained in $\mathbb{Z}$. It follows that every entry in $T(n)$ is an integer due to (14). It remains to consider $U(n)$. Since $n - j = n - 1 - (j - 1)$ it follows that (12) can be rewritten as,

$$[W(n)]_{2,j} = (-1)^j \binom{n-1}{j-1} \tag{15}$$

Therefore, $[W(n)]_{2,j} \in \mathbb{Z}$. Note that this also shows that the term on the left of (11) is always an integer. Finally, observe that in (11),

$$\frac{(-1)^{k+j}(k+1)^{n-1}n!}{(n-j+k)!(j-k)!} = (-1)^{k+j}(k+1)^{n-1}\binom{n}{j-k} \tag{16}$$

which is clearly always an integer.   □

The solution to $M(n)\vec{x} = b$ is therefore given by $\vec{x} = \frac{1}{(n-1)!}V(n)b$ where $V(n)$ has integer entries.

B   Review of Chernoff Bounds

When n independent trials are conducted such that each trial results in success with fixed probability p, the trials are called *Bernoulli trials*. When the probability of success is p_i in each trial for $1 \le i \le n$ the trails are called *Poisson trials*. The following theorem is due to Chernoff.

Theorem 8. *Let $X_1, X_2, ..., X_n$ be independent Poisson trials such that, for $1 \le i \le n$, $Pr[X_i = 1] = p_i$, where $0 < p_i < 1$. Then, for $X = \sum_{i=1}^{n} X_i$, $\mu = E[X] = \sum_{i=1}^{n} p_i$, and $0 < \delta \le 1$,*

$$Pr[X < (1-\delta)\mu] < e^{-(\mu\delta^2)/2}.$$

On the Security Notions
for Public-Key Encryption Schemes

Duong Hieu Phan and David Pointcheval

École normale supérieure – Dépt d'informatique,
45 rue d'Ulm, 75230 Paris Cedex 05, France
{duong.hieu.phan, david.pointcheval}@ens.fr

Abstract. In this paper, we revisit the security notions for public-key encryption, and namely indistinguishability. We indeed achieve the surprising result that no decryption query before receiving the challenge ciphertext can be replaced by queries (whatever the number is) after having received the challenge, and vice-versa. This remark leads to a stricter and more complex hierarchy for security notions in the public-key setting: the (i, j)-IND level, in which an adversary can ask at most i (j resp.) queries before (after resp.) receiving the challenge. Excepted the trivial implications, all the other relations are strict gaps, with no polynomial reduction (under the assumption that IND-CCA2 secure encryption schemes exist.) Similarly, we define different levels for non-malleability (denoted (i, j)-NM.)

1 Introduction

Relations between security notions for public-key encryption scheme have been deeply studied, namely in the recent papers of Bellare *et al.* [2] and of Bellare and Sahai [4]. These papers are based on the seminal works of Goldwasser and Micali [8] which defined the notions of polynomial security, or indistinguishability denoted IND; Noar and Yung [12] and Rackoff and Simon [15], which introduced stronger scenarios of attacks, and Dolev, Dwork and Naor [5, 6] which proposed a stronger security notion: the non-malleability.

It is now clear that the security notions (indistinguishability and non-malleability) have to be studied under specific attacks: the basic scenario in the public-key setting in the chosen-plaintext attacks (CPA), but more interesting situations are captured by the chosen-ciphertext attacks. Chosen-ciphertext attacks have been split in two families, for historical reasons explained below, the non-adaptive ones (denoted CCA1) and the adaptive ones (denoted CCA2.) In both cases, the adversary has access to a decryption oracle. In the former case, this access is limited until the challenge ciphertext is known, while the latter case allows an unlimited access (with the natural restriction not to ask the challenge ciphertext.)

In this paper, we consider more concrete cases by introducing the (i, j)-IND security level, in which an adversary can ask at most i (j resp.) queries before (after resp.) receiving the challenge ciphertext. The reason for such a more

C. Blundo and S. Cimato (Eds.): SCN 2004, LNCS 3352, pp. 33–46, 2005.
© Springer-Verlag Berlin Heidelberg 2005

precise notation, than just IND-CCA1 thus captured by $(\text{poly}(\cdot), 0)$-IND and IND-CCA2 captured by $(\text{poly}(\cdot), \text{poly}(\cdot))$-IND, is that we can prove that no decryption query before receiving the challenge can be replaced by queries (whatever the number is) after having received the challenge, and vice-versa. Indeed, excepted the trivial implications, all the other relations between the (i, j)-IND security levels are strict gaps, with no polynomial reduction (under the basic assumption that IND-CCA2 secure encryption schemes exist.)

As an application, we introduce a new kind of attack, we call the *post-challenge chosen-ciphertext attack*, denoted CCAO2 (for chosen-ciphertext attacks in the 2nd stage only.) This new scenario completes the above picture with the $(0, \text{poly}(\cdot))$-IND security notion. Furthermore, from a practical point of view, it models very realistic situations since it limits the control the adversary may have on the "a priori" distribution of the plaintexts, but it also encompasses situations where the adversary starts the attack when it becomes aware of the importance of a specific ciphertext (after the latter is generated and sent.)

Even if it seems clear that the CCA1 security model has been introduced because the authors [12] failed at achieving the CCA2 level [15], it is still studied, and considered as a goal to be achieved. However, it seems more realistic to consider scenarios where the adversary has not so much control on the challenge plaintexts: they could just be chosen right after having received the identity and the public-key of the target decryptor. Therefore, the messages m_0 and m_1 should be chosen before having access to any oracle.

1.1   Related Work

In the early 80s, people formally defined the security notions for cryptographic primitives (namely, for signature [10, 11], and for encryption [8] with the notions of polynomial security, or indistinguishability denoted IND.) While these notions did not evolve so much for signatures since adaptive chosen-message attacks were introduced, stronger notions appeared later for encryption, namely after the zero-knowledge concept [9].

Indistinguishability was indeed defined in the basic scenario only, where the adversary has just access to the public information, and can thus encrypt any plaintext of its choice, hence the name of chosen-plaintext attacks (denoted CPA.) Naor and Yung [12] introduced the notion of chosen-ciphertext attacks. However, their solution based on non-interactive zero-knowledge proofs of membership, without the recent non-malleable NIZK or simulation-soundness [16] notions. Therefore, they could not simulate correctly the decryption oracle after the adversary had received the challenge ciphertext. As a consequence, they restricted the chosen-ciphertext attacks to be non-adaptive, in the sense that the decryption queries could not depend on the challenge ciphertext (*a.k.a. lunchtime attacks*, denoted CCA1.) Rackoff and Simon [15] extended this notion, with an unlimited access to the decryption oracle (excepted on the challenge ciphertext), denoted CCA2, and provided a candidate granted the non-interactive zero-knowledge proofs of knowledge.

The above improvements were about the attack model, but then also appeared a relaxed goal for the adversary: the non-malleability [5, 6]. In [2], Bellare *et al.* provided comparisons between all the resulting security notions, but just between the large classes IND/NM combined with CPA, CCA1 or CCA2.

1.2   Contributions

Adaptive chosen-ciphertext attacks (CCA2) are clearly the strongest scenario in the framework of the complexity theory, using perfect oracles and polynomial reductions, or even exact reductions. However, this notion can be considered as a very strong notion. In the real life, which motivated the exact/concrete security [3, 1, 13] (vs. asymptotic or polynomial framework), the adversary may be limited in the number of queries it can ask to the decryption oracle, and then the scheme can be designed to resist such a specified number of queries. Therefore, it's worth considering the exact/concrete security notions. We thus introduce two classes of security notions: (i, j)-IND and (i, j)-NM, or even more precisely (t, i, j)-IND and (t, i, j)-NM secure schemes, which resist (in the indistinguishability sense or non-malleability sense) to adversaries which can make exactly i (j resp.) decryption queries before (after resp.) receiving the challenge within time t.

First, we consider the relations inside each class of security. At a first glance, one could think that a query in the second stage is much more important than a query in the first stage (since then, queries may depend on the challenge ciphertext, and this would justify the consideration of CCA1 and CCA2 only in chosen-ciphertext scenarios.) Surprisingly, we show that no query before receiving the challenge can be replaced by queries (whatever the number is) after having received the challenge, and vice-versa: a query before, helps to correctly choose the messages m_0 and m_1.) This remark leads to a strict and more complex hierarchy for security notions in the public-key setting: excepted the trivial implications, all the other relations are strict gaps, with no polynomial reduction.

As an illustration, we introduce post-challenge chosen-ciphertext attacks (denoted CCAO2.) In this scenario, the adversary has access to the decryption oracle, but after the challenge ciphertext is known only. From the above result, we show that any security notion (IND or NM) under these attacks (CCA1 and CCAO2) are independent. Furthermore, we show that CCA1 + CCAO2 does not necessarily yield CCA2.

2   Security Model

Let us review the main security notions for public-key encryption, but also more theoretical notions, which will be useful for exhibiting gaps, such as the pseudo-random function families.

2.1   Public-Key Encryption

A public-key encryption scheme π is defined by the three following algorithms:

- The *key generation algorithm* $\mathcal{G}$. On input 1^k, where k is the security parameter, the algorithm $\mathcal{G}$ produces a pair (pk, sk) of matching public and private keys.

- The *encryption algorithm* $\mathcal{E}$. Given a message m (in the space of plaintexts $\mathcal{M}$) and a public key pk, $\mathcal{E}_{pk}(m)$ produces a ciphertext c (in the space of ciphertexts $\mathcal{C}$) of m. This algorithm may be probabilistic (involving random coins $r \in \mathcal{R}$) it is then denoted $\mathcal{E}_{pk}(m;r)$.
- The *decryption algorithm* $\mathcal{D}$. Given a ciphertext $c \in \mathcal{C}$ and the secret key sk, $\mathcal{D}_{sk}(c)$ gives back the plaintext $m \in \mathcal{M}$.

2.2   Security Notions

As already noted, the fundamental security notions are the indistinguishability and the non-malleability.

Definition 1 (Indistinguishability). *Let* $\pi = (\mathcal{G}, \mathcal{E}, \mathcal{D})$ *be an encryption scheme. Let us consider a two-stage probabilistic adversary* $\mathcal{A} = (\mathcal{A}_1, \mathcal{A}_2)$ *whose running time is bounded by* t. *We define the advantage of* $\mathcal{A}$ *against the indistinguishability of* π *as follows:*

$$\mathsf{Adv}_\pi^{\mathsf{ind}}(\mathcal{A}) \stackrel{\mathrm{def}}{=} \left| 2 \times \Pr_{b,r} \left[\begin{array}{l} (\mathsf{pk}, \mathsf{sk}) \leftarrow \mathcal{G}(1^k), (m_0, m_1, s) \leftarrow \mathcal{A}_1(\mathsf{pk}), \\ c = \mathcal{E}_{\mathsf{pk}}(m_b, r), b' = \mathcal{A}_2(m_0, m_1, s, c) : b' = b \end{array} \right] - 1 \right|.$$

We insist above on that $\mathcal{A}_1$ *outputs two messages* m_0 *and* m_1 *such that* $|m_0| = |m_1|$. *As usual, we define by* $\mathsf{Adv}_\pi^{\mathsf{ind}}(t)$ *the maximum advantage over all the adversaries* $\mathcal{A}$ *whose running time is bounded by* t. *Then we say that* π *is* (t, ε)-IND *secure if* $\mathsf{Adv}_\pi^{\mathsf{ind}}(t)$ *is less than* ε.

Definition 2 (Non-malleability). *Let* $\pi = (\mathcal{G}, \mathcal{E}, \mathcal{D})$ *be an encryption scheme. Let us consider a two-stage probabilistic adversary* $\mathcal{A} = (\mathcal{A}_1, \mathcal{A}_2)$ *whose running time is bounded by* t. *We define the advantage of* $\mathcal{A}$ *against the non-malleability of* π *by:*

$$\mathsf{Adv}_\pi^{\mathsf{nm}}(\mathcal{A}) \stackrel{\mathrm{def}}{=} \mathsf{Succ}_\pi^{\mathsf{nm}}(\mathcal{A}) - \mathsf{Succ}_\pi^{\mathsf{nm},\$}(\mathcal{A}),$$

where the two successes use the same probability distribution, for a distribution of plaintexts M *and a binary relation* R, *generated by*

$$(\mathsf{pk}, \mathsf{sk}) \leftarrow \mathcal{G}(1^k), (M, s) \leftarrow \mathcal{A}_1(\mathsf{pk});$$
$$m, \tilde{m} \leftarrow M; c \leftarrow \mathcal{E}_{\mathsf{pk}}(m, r); (R, y) \leftarrow \mathcal{A}_2(M, s, c); x \leftarrow \mathcal{D}_{\mathsf{sk}}(y)$$

and

$$\mathsf{Succ}_\pi^{\mathsf{nm}}(\mathcal{A}) \stackrel{\mathrm{def}}{=} \Pr[y \neq c \wedge x \neq \perp \wedge R(x, m)]$$
$$\mathsf{Succ}_\pi^{\mathsf{nm},\$}(\mathcal{A}) \stackrel{\mathrm{def}}{=} \Pr[y \neq c \wedge x \neq \perp \wedge R(x, \tilde{m})].$$

We also define by $\mathsf{Adv}_\pi^{\mathsf{nm}}(t)$ *the maximum advantage over all the adversaries* $\mathcal{A}$ *whose running time is bounded by* t. *Then we say that* π *is* (t, ε)-NM *secure if* $\mathsf{Adv}_\pi^{\mathsf{nm}}(t)$ *is bounded by* ε.

This definition models the above intuition about non-malleability (the adversary cannot output a second ciphertext so that the corresponding plaintexts are meaningfully related.) This is a particular case of the general definition used in [2, 4], and denoted $\mathsf{CNM}^{(k)}$, in which the adversary could output a vector of ciphertexts $(y_1, \ldots, y_k)$ of the plaintexts $(x_1, \ldots, x_k)$ and a relation R so that $R(x_1, \ldots, x_k, m)$ holds more often than $R(x_1, \ldots, x_k, \tilde{m})$. A discussion is provided in Section 3.3.

2.3 Attack Models

For a public-key encryption, the adversary has access, as anybody, to the encryption key. It can thus encrypt any plaintext of its choice. Hence the basic attack is called "Chosen Plaintext Attack", or in short CPA. But the adversary may also have access to more information, and namely some decryptions. This is modeled by an access to the decryption oracle.

Definition 3 (Lunchtime Attacks). *An adversary is called a* non-adaptive chosen-ciphertext adversary, *(or a lunchtime adversary, denoted by* $\mathsf{CCA1}$*-adversary) if it can access the oracle before the challenge ciphertext is known only.*

Definition 4 (Adaptive Attacks). *An adversary is called an* adaptive chosen-ciphertext adversary *(denoted by* $\mathsf{CCA2}$*-adversary) if it can access the oracle whenever it wants, that is before and after the challenge ciphertext is known, with the sole restriction not to use it on the challenge itself.*

These two attack models are the classical ones, but for historical reasons. For more generality, we introduce a more precise definition with a (i, j)-CCA adversary which can ask at most i queries (resp. j queries) before the challenge ciphertext is known (after resp.)

Definition 5 (Chosen-Ciphertext Attack). *An adversary is called an* (i, j) chosen-ciphertext adversary *(denoted by* (i, j)-CCA *adversary) if it can access the oracle, up to* i *times before the challenge ciphertext is known, and up to* j *times after, still with the restriction not to use it on the challenge itself.*
Notation. An encryption scheme $\pi = (\mathcal{G}, \mathcal{E}, \mathcal{D})$ is said to be (t, ε)-XXX-YYY secure if for any YYY-adversary $\mathcal{A}$ against the security XXX within running time t, where XXX can be either IND or NM, and YYY can be either CPA, $\mathsf{CCA1}$, $\mathsf{CCA2}$, or (i, j)-CCA, the advantage of $\mathcal{A}$ is bounded by ε. In the latter case, in short, we say that π is (t, ε, i, j)-IND secure (resp. (t, ε, i, j)-NM secure) if for any (i, j)-CCA adversary $\mathcal{A}$ whose running time is bounded by t, $\mathsf{Adv}_\pi^{\mathsf{ind}}(\mathcal{A}) \leq \varepsilon$ (resp. $\mathsf{Adv}_\pi^{\mathsf{nm}}(\mathcal{A}) \leq \varepsilon$.)

2.4 Trapdoor One-Way Permutations

Some constructions below will need the existence of a trapdoor one-way permutation. Informally, for such a permutation which can be inverted granted the trapdoor, it should be hard to invert without the latter:

Definition 6 (One-Way Permutation). *Let* $f : \{0,1\}^{\ell} \to \{0,1\}^{\ell}$ *be a permutation, and let us consider the adversary* $\mathcal{A}$ *against the one-wayness. We define the success probability of* $\mathcal{A}$ *for inverting* f *by:* $\mathsf{Succ}_f^{\mathsf{ow}}(\mathcal{A}) \overset{\text{def}}{=} \mathrm{Pr}_x[\mathcal{A}(f(x)) = x]$. *As above, we also denote by* $\mathsf{Succ}_f^{\mathsf{ow}}(t)$ *the maximal success over all the adversaries whose running time is bounded by* t. *Therefore, we say that* f *is* (t, ε)-OW *if* $\mathsf{Succ}_f^{\mathsf{ow}}(t)$ *is bounded by* ε.

2.5   Pseudo-Random Functions

The notion of pseudo-random functions [7] requires that any adversary, accessing an oracle $\mathcal{O}_b$, which is either a truly random function F (in case $b = 0$) or a random instance F_K in the family $\mathcal{F} = (F_K)$ (in case $b = 1$), cannot guess the actual bit b. The advantage of such an adversary is defined by:

Definition 7 (Pseudo-Random Functions).

$$\mathsf{Adv}_{\mathcal{F}}^{\mathsf{prf}}(\mathcal{A}) = 2 \times \Pr_{b,F,K}[\mathcal{O}_0 = F, \mathcal{O}_1 = F_K, \mathcal{A}^{\mathcal{O}_b} = b] - 1.$$

We also denote by $\mathsf{Adv}_{\mathcal{F}}^{\mathsf{prf}}(t, n)$ *the maximal advantage over all the adversaries whose running time is bounded by* t, *which makes less than* n *queries to the oracle. Finally, we say that a family* $\mathcal{F}$ *is a* (ε, t, n)-PRF *if* $\mathsf{Adv}_{\mathcal{F}}^{\mathsf{prf}}(t, n)$ *is bounded by* ε.

3   Concrete Security

In this section, we show some non-intuitive gaps in the (i, j)-IND class: a decryption query in the first stage cannot be postponed to the second stage, and reversely. As a consequence, we are interested by a possible comparison of the importance of queries in the first stage and in the second stage. In the following, we formally prove that allowing one more query in the first stage gives a different strength to an adversary than allowing it as many queries as it wants in the second stage. We do the same for an additional query in the second stage, which cannot be compared with even many queries in the first stage.

3.1   Preliminaries

To this aim, we need a new intractability problem, which can hopefully be related to a classical PRF one. Furthermore, we denote below by PRP the analogous notion as PRF, when the functions are permutations. Similarly, we denote by $\mathsf{Adv}_G^{\mathsf{prp}}(\mathcal{A})$ the advantage with which an adversary can distinguish a permutation, randomly drawn from the pseudo-random permutation family, and a truly random permutation. Note that the inverse is not available (*i.e.*, we do not consider the super pseudo-randomness.)

Definition 8. *For any function (or permutation)* G *and any two-stage adversary* $\mathcal{A} = (\mathcal{A}_1, \mathcal{A}_2)$, *we denote by* $\mathsf{Succ}_G^{m,n}(\mathcal{A})$ *the success probability for* $\mathcal{A}_2(v, s)$

to output $G^n(v)$, for a given random value v, and a working tape s transmitted by $\mathcal{A}_1$, when $\mathcal{A}_1$ was limited to m queries to G, and $\mathcal{A}_2$ is limited to $n-1$ queries.

$$\mathsf{Succ}_G^{m,n}(\mathcal{A}) = \Pr[v \xleftarrow{R} \mathcal{M}; s \leftarrow \mathcal{A}_1^G : \mathcal{A}_2^G(v,s) = G^n(v)].$$

As before, we denote by $\mathsf{Succ}_G^{m,n}(t)$ the maximal success probability over all the adversaries whose running time is bounded by t.

Proposition 9. *For any function/permutation G randomly drawn from a pseudo-random function/permutation family $\mathcal{G}$ into a set of cardinality larger than $\{0,1\}^\ell$, we have:*

$$\mathsf{Succ}_G^{m,n}(t) \leq \mathsf{Adv}_{\mathcal{G}}^{\mathsf{prf}}(m + 2n - 1, t) + \frac{mn + 1}{2^\ell}.$$

Proof. We prove that for any adversary $\mathcal{A}$ against the above "one-more evaluation", we can design a PRF-adversary $\mathcal{B}$ such that $\mathsf{Succ}_G^{m,n}(\mathcal{A}) \leq \mathsf{Adv}_{\mathcal{G}}^{\mathsf{prf}}(\mathcal{B})$. Our adversary $\mathcal{B}$ simulates $\mathcal{A}$'s view as follows: whenever $\mathcal{A}$ queries G, $\mathcal{B}$ asks the same query to $\mathcal{O}_b$ and forwards the answer to $\mathcal{A}$ (at most $m + n - 1$ queries.) Eventually, $\mathcal{A}$ outputs x. $\mathcal{B}$ successively queries the oracle $\mathcal{O}_b$ to get $y = \mathcal{O}_b^n(v)$. If $x = y$, $\mathcal{B}$ outputs its guess $b' = 1$, otherwise $\mathcal{B}$ outputs $b' = 0$.

- when $b = 1$, $\mathcal{B}$ actually accesses in fact G and therefore $y = \mathcal{O}_b^n(v) = G^n(v)$, whenever $\mathcal{A}$ outputs the correct value $G^n(v)$. $\mathcal{B}$ always wins the game when $\mathcal{A}$ wins. Since $b' = 1$ means $x = y$:

$$\mathsf{Adv}_{\mathcal{G}}^{\mathsf{prf}}(\mathcal{B} \mid b = 1) = 2\Pr[x = y \mid b = 1] - 1 = 2\mathsf{Succ}_G^{m,n}(\mathcal{A}) - 1.$$

- when $b = 1$, the value $y = \mathcal{O}_b^n(v)$ that $\mathcal{B}$ computes is perfectly random and independent of the view of $\mathcal{A}$ unless $\mathcal{A}_1$ has asked one of the values $\mathcal{O}_b^i(v)$ (for $0 \leq i < n$) to the oracle. We therefore have

$$\mathsf{Adv}_{\mathcal{G}}^{\mathsf{prp}}(\mathcal{B} \mid b = 0) = 2\Pr[x = y \mid b = 0] - 1 \leq 2 \times \left(\frac{mn}{2^\ell} + \frac{1}{2^\ell} \right) - 1.$$

Combining the two cases, with a random bit b, we get the result. □

The following simple proposition will be used several times in the future.

Definition 10. *Let $\pi = (\mathcal{G}, \mathcal{E}, \mathcal{D})$ be a public-key encryption scheme. Let f be a permutation onto $\mathcal{M}$ modeled by the two oracles f and f^{-1}. We define the new encryption scheme $\pi^{(f)} = (\mathcal{G}^{(f)}, \mathcal{E}^{(f)}, \mathcal{D}^{(f)})$ by*

$$\mathcal{M}^{(f)} = \mathcal{M} \qquad \mathcal{R}^{(f)} = \mathcal{R} \qquad \mathcal{C}^{(f)} = \mathcal{C}$$

Algorithm $\mathcal{G}^{(f)}(1^k)$	Algorithm $\mathcal{E}_{\mathsf{pk}^{(f)}}^{(f)}(m,r)$	Algorithm $\mathcal{D}_{\mathsf{sk}^{(f)}}^{(f)}(c)$
$(\mathsf{pk}, \mathsf{sk}) \leftarrow \mathcal{G}(1^k)$	$\mathsf{pk}\|f\|f^{-1} \stackrel{\mathrm{def}}{=} \mathsf{pk}^{(f)}$	$\mathsf{sk} \stackrel{\mathrm{def}}{=} \mathsf{sk}^{(f)}$
$\mathsf{pk}^{(f)} \leftarrow \mathsf{pk}\|f\|f^{-1}$	$return\ \mathcal{E}_{\mathsf{pk}}(f(m), r)$	$return\ f^{-1}(\mathcal{D}_{\mathsf{sk}}(c))$
$\mathsf{sk}^{(f)} \leftarrow \mathsf{sk}$		
$return\ (\mathsf{pk}^{(f)}, \mathsf{sk}^{(f)})$		

Proposition 11. *For any encryption scheme $\pi = (\mathcal{G}, \mathcal{E}, \mathcal{D})$ and for any permutation f (so that f and f^{-1} are efficient), π and $\pi^{(f)}$ have a similar indistinguishability level whatever the kind of attack:*

$$\mathsf{Adv}_{\pi}^{\text{ind-yyy}}(t) \leq \mathsf{Adv}_{\pi^{(f)}}^{\text{ind-yyy}}(t + 2T_f + q_d T_{f^{-1}}) \leq \mathsf{Adv}_{\pi}^{\text{ind-yyy}}(t + (2 + q_d)(T_f + T_{f^{-1}})),$$

where T_f (and $T_{f^{-1}}$ resp.) is an upper-bound of the time required to evaluate f (and f^{-1} resp.)

Proof. We first prove that if $\pi^{(f)}$ is secure then π is secure too. We insist here that both f and f^{-1} are efficiently computable and are included in the *public* key. Let us consider an adversary $\mathcal{A} = (\mathcal{A}_1, \mathcal{A}_2)$ against π, we build an adversary $\mathcal{B} = (\mathcal{B}_1, \mathcal{B}_2)$ against $\pi^{(f)}$: whenever $\mathcal{A}$ makes a decryption query c to the oracle $\mathcal{D}_{\text{sk}}$, $\mathcal{B}$ makes the same query to the decryption oracle $\mathcal{D}_{\text{sk}(f)}^{(f)}$. $\mathcal{B}$ receives the answer m and forwards $f(m)$ to $\mathcal{A}$. When $\mathcal{A}_1$ outputs two candidates m_0 and m_1, $\mathcal{B}_1$ computes $f^{-1}(m_0)$ and $f^{-1}(m_1)$. Finally, when $\mathcal{A}$ outputs its guess b', $\mathcal{B}$ forwards this value. It is clear that the advantage of $\mathcal{B}$ is exactly the advantage of $\mathcal{A}$, while its running time needs extra time for two evaluations of f and q_d evaluations of f^{-1}, where q_d is the number of decryption queries:

$$\mathsf{Adv}_{\pi}^{\text{ind-yyy}}(t) \leq \mathsf{Adv}_{\pi^{(f)}}^{\text{ind-yyy}}(t + 2T_f + q_d T_{f^{-1}}).$$

Since $\pi = \pi^{(f)(f^{-1})}$, and both f and f^{-1} are public and efficient, one easily concludes. $\qquad\square$

3.2   Each Query Is Important

In this section, we show that each query, before receiving the challenge or after having received it, has its own role. This means that no query before receiving the challenge can be replaced by queries (whatever the number is) after having received the challenge, and vice-versa.

Theorem 12. *Under the assumption that* IND-CCA2 *secure encryption schemes exist, for any pair of integers (m, n), there is an encryption scheme that is (m, N)-IND secure and (M, n)-IND secure, but not $(m + 1, n + 1)$-IND secure, whatever M and N are.*

Proof. We first assume that there exists an IND-CCA2 secure encryption scheme $\pi = (\mathcal{G}, \mathcal{E}, \mathcal{D})$, which is thus (i, j)-IND for any pair (i, j). We also need a trapdoor one-way permutation f onto $\mathcal{M}$. The encryption scheme $\pi^{(f)}$ is therefore IND-CCA2 secure, when the trapdoor for computing f^{-1} is included in the public key. We modify $\pi^{(f)}$ into a new encryption scheme $\pi' = (\mathcal{G}', \mathcal{E}', \mathcal{D}')$ which is not $(m + 1, n + 1)$-IND secure anymore, but still both (m, N)-IND secure and (M, n)-IND secure. Note that a main difference comes from the fact that the trapdoor for f^{-1} is now in the private key only. The scheme $\pi' = (\mathcal{G}', \mathcal{E}', \mathcal{D}')$ works as follows:

- We denote by I_M a specific element of $\mathcal{M}$ and we note $p_M = f^{-1}(I_M)$.
- We fix two families, a pseudo-random function family $\mathcal{F} = \{F_K : K \in \{0,1\}^k\}$ and a pseudo-random permutation family $\mathcal{G} = \{G_K : K \in \{0,1\}^k\}$, from the set $\mathcal{C}$ into $\mathcal{C}$. We furthermore assume that the cardinality of $\mathcal{C}$ is larger than 2^ℓ.

  For sake of simplicity, we use the same key sets, domain and range sets for $\mathcal{F}$ and $\mathcal{G}$, but this is not necessary.

Then, the intuition behind the construction is that $m+1$ decryption queries in the first stage will help to determine a specific plaintext μ. It has the specificity that, in the second stage, it will be possible to check after $n + 1$ decryption queries whether a given ciphertext actually encrypts μ or not.

Algorithm $\mathcal{G}'(1^k)$	Algorithm $\mathcal{E}'_{\mathsf{pk}'}(\mu, r)$
$(\mathsf{pk}, \mathsf{sk}) \leftarrow \mathcal{G}(1^k)$	$\mathsf{pk}\|f\|I_M\|m\|n \overset{\text{def}}{=} \mathsf{pk}'$
$I_M \overset{R}{\leftarrow} \mathcal{M}, K_f, K_g \overset{R}{\leftarrow} \{0,1\}^k$	$\varphi \leftarrow f(\mu)$
$\mathsf{pk}' \leftarrow \mathsf{pk}\|f\|I_M\|m\|n$	return $0\|\mathcal{E}_{\mathsf{pk}}(\varphi, r)\|\epsilon$
$\mathsf{sk}' \leftarrow \mathsf{sk}\|f^{-1}\|K_f\|K_g$	
return $(\mathsf{pk}', \mathsf{sk}')$	

Algorithm $\mathcal{D}'_{\mathsf{sk}'}(b\|c\|z)$

$\mathsf{sk}\|f^{-1}\|K_f\|K_g \overset{\text{def}}{=} \mathsf{sk}'$

1. if $(b = 0 \wedge z = \epsilon)$ return $f^{-1}(\mathcal{D}_{\mathsf{sk}}(c))$
2. if $(b = 1 \wedge z = \epsilon)$ return $F_{K_f}(c)$
3. if $(b = 2 \wedge z = \epsilon)$ return $G_{K_g}(c)$
4. if $(b = 1 \wedge z = F_{K_f}^n(c) \wedge \mathcal{D}(c) = G_{K_g}^m(I_M))$ return $f^{-1}(G_{K_g}^m(I_M))$

otherwise, return $\perp$

In the above scheme, $\mu = f^{-1}(G_{K_g}^m(I_M))$ is the crucial plaintext the adversary should send as a challenge, because with a ciphertext $0\|c\|\epsilon$ of this plaintext μ, and the knowledge of $F_{K_f}^n(c)$, one can derive a second ciphertext of μ (and thus break both the non-malleability and the IND-CCA2 security level), using the fourth case in the decryption oracle.

Lemma 13. π' is not $(m + 1, n + 1)$-IND secure.

Proof. The following $(m+1, n+1)$-IND adversary $\mathcal{A} = (\mathcal{A}_1, \mathcal{A}_2)$ can successfully attack π':

- In the first stage, $\mathcal{A}_1$ asks $2\|I_M\|\epsilon$ to $\mathcal{D}'_{\mathsf{sk}'}$ and gets $G_{K_g}(I_M)$. Then for $i = 1$ to $m - 1$, $\mathcal{A}_1$ asks $2\|G_{K_g}^i(I_M)\|\epsilon$ to $\mathcal{D}'_{\mathsf{sk}'}$ and finally gets $G_{K_g}^m(I_M)$, after m decryption queries. It then computes by itself $c = \mathcal{E}_{\mathsf{pk}}(G_{K_g}^m(I_M), r)$ (since pk is part of pk') and asks $0\|c\|\epsilon$ to $\mathcal{D}'_{\mathsf{sk}'}$ to get $m_0 = f^{-1}(G_{K_g}^m(I_M))$. It randomly chooses a second different candidate $m_1 \neq m_0$, and outputs (m_0, m_1), after exactly $m + 1$ decryption queries.

- In the second stage, $\mathcal{A}_2$ receives the challenge ciphertext $y = 0||c^*||\epsilon$, where $c^* = \mathcal{E}(m_b, r)$. $\mathcal{A}_2$ asks $1||c^*||\epsilon$ to $\mathcal{D}'_{\mathsf{sk}'}$ and gets $F_{K_f}(c^*)$. Then, for $i = 1$ to $n - 1$, the adversary asks $1||F^i_{K_f}(c^*)||\epsilon$ and finally gets $F^n_{K_f}(c^*)$ after n decryption queries. As a last query, it asks $1||c^*||F^n_{K_f}(c^*)$ to $\mathcal{D}'_{\mathsf{sk}'}$. If the answer is m_0, the adversary returns 0, otherwise (in which case the answer is $\perp$), the adversary returns 1.

It is easy to see that the value returned by the adversary is always equal to b.   □

Lemma 14. π' is (m, N)-IND secure: for $t' \le t + 2T_f$ and $q_d \le m + N$,

$$\mathsf{Adv}^{(m,N)\text{-ind}}_{\pi'}(t) \le \mathsf{Adv}^{\mathsf{ind\text{-}cca2}}_{\pi}(t' + q_d T_f + 2T_{f-1})$$

$$+2 \times \left(\begin{array}{l} \mathsf{Succ}^{\mathsf{ow}}_f(t') + (m + 2) \times \mathsf{Adv}^{\mathsf{prp}}_{\mathcal{G}}(2m - 1, t') \\ +\mathsf{Adv}^{\mathsf{prp}}_{\mathcal{G}}(q_d, t') + \mathsf{Adv}^{\mathsf{prf}}_{\mathcal{F}}(q_d, t') + (m + 2) \times 2^{-\ell} \end{array} \right).$$

Proof. Since π is IND-CCA2 secure, it is also the case for $\pi^{(f)}$. We then prove that an (m, N)-IND adversary $\mathcal{A}$ against π' can be used by an adversary $\mathcal{B}$ to break the IND-CCA2 security level of $\pi^{(f)}$ with a similar advantage.

Before presenting this adversary, let us claim the following proposition, which proof is straightforward.

Proposition 15. *Providing F_{K_f}, G_{K_g}, f, f^{-1} and the decryption oracle $\mathcal{D}^{(f)}_{\mathsf{sk}^{(f)}}$ of $\pi^{(f)}$, one can perfectly simulate the decryption $\mathcal{D}'_{\mathsf{sk}'}$ of π'.*

Game G_0: In this game, our adversary $\mathcal{B}$ is provided the decryption oracle $\mathcal{D}'_{\mathsf{sk}'}$. It is thus not a $\pi^{(f)}$ adversary yet. Anyway, it can easily simulate the view of the adversary $\mathcal{A}$, granted the oracle access to $\mathcal{D}'_{\mathsf{sk}'}$. When $\mathcal{A}_1$ outputs the candidates (m_0, m_1), $\mathcal{B}_1$ forwards them, as its own output. On the challenge ciphertext c, $\mathcal{B}_2$ runs $\mathcal{A}_2(0||c||\epsilon)$. When $\mathcal{A}_2$ outputs its guess b' for the bit b involved in the challenge, $\mathcal{B}_2$ forwards it as its own guess. We denote by S_0 the event $b' = b$. We clearly have: $\Pr[\mathsf{S}_0] = \Pr[\mathcal{B} = b] = \Pr[\mathcal{A} = b]$.

Game G_1: We modify a little bit $\mathcal{B}_1$, so that it aborts if a bad case occurs. We define $g_m = G^m_{K_g}(I_M)$. When $\mathcal{A}_1$ outputs (m_0, m_1), $\mathcal{B}_1$ computes by itself $f_0 = f(m_0)$ and $f_1 = f(m_1)$. If g_m is one of f_0 or f_1, or appears in a decryption query of the form $1||c||z$ (*i.e.*, $g_m = \mathcal{D}(c)$, see case 4), then $\mathcal{B}$ aborts the game, outputting a random guess, otherwise, it continues as in the previous game. We denote by $\mathsf{EventGM}$ the above bad event that $f_0 = g_m$, $f_1 = g_m$ or g_m appears in a decryption query: $|\Pr[\mathsf{S}_1] - \Pr[\mathsf{S}_0]| \le \Pr[\mathsf{EventGM}]$.

Let us evaluate the probability of this event. To this aim, we consider two situations, since $\mathcal{A}_1$ is allowed to ask at most m decryption queries:

- $\mathcal{A}_1$ asks m queries of the form $2||c||\epsilon$, which are answered by $G_{K_g}(c)$ (see case 3.) Then $\mathcal{B}_1$ does not use any query to f^{-1} to simulate the answers of the decryption queries of $\mathcal{A}_1$. We can thus build an invertor for f: we give every private information to $\mathcal{B}$, except the trapdoor for inverting f. When event

EventGM happens, $\mathcal{B}$ has inverted f on the random element g_m (since I_M is random and G_{K_g} is a public permutation, and thus $G_{K_g}^m$) without making any query to f^{-1}. Indeed, using the private informations, one can compute g_m, and then one can check which one of m_0 or m_1 is the pre-image of g_m by f.

- $\mathcal{A}_1$ asks at most than $m-1$ queries of the form $2\|c\|\epsilon$. Event EventGM means that g_m is one of f_0 or f_1, or appears in a decryption query of the form $1\|c\|z$. This time, we can build an adversary against the PRP property of the family $\mathcal{G}$: we give every private information to $\mathcal{B}$, except K_g, but an oracle access to G_{K_g}. When event EventGM happens, g_m is one of f_0 or f_1, or appears in a decryption query of the form $1\|c\|z$ (note that $g_m = \mathcal{D}(c)$, which can be computed since now $\mathcal{B}$ knows sk.) By randomly outputting f_0, f_1 or $\mathcal{D}(c)$ from one of the m decryption queries of the form $1\|c\|z$, after at most $m-1$ queries to G_{K_g}, with probability of $1/(m+2)$, we get $g_m = G_{K_g}^m(I_M)$, for a random input I_M.

Regrouping these two cases, we have:

$$\Pr[\text{EventGM}] \le \mathsf{Succ}_f^{\mathsf{ow}}(t + 2T_f) + (m+2) \times \mathsf{Succ}_{G_{K_g}}^{0,m}(t + 2T_f)$$

$$\le \mathsf{Succ}_f^{\mathsf{ow}}(t + 2T_f) + (m+2) \times \mathsf{Adv}_{\mathcal{G}}^{\mathsf{prp}}(2m-1, t + 2T_f) + \frac{m+2}{2^\ell}.$$

Game $\mathbf{G_2}$: In this game, we still exclude event EventGM, and thus $\mathcal{B}$ does not need to check g_m, and thus to compute it either. $\mathcal{B}$ is no longer provided with $\mathcal{D}'_{\mathsf{sk}'}$, but $\mathcal{D}_{\mathsf{sk}(f)}^{(f)}$ only. By the Proposition 15, $\mathcal{B}$ can use this decryption oracle $\mathcal{D}_{\mathsf{sk}(f)}^{(f)}$ to perfectly simulate $\mathcal{D}'_{\mathsf{sk}'}$, thanks to the access to F_{K_f}, G_{K_g}, f and f^{-1}. The only situation that $\mathcal{B}$ cannot simulate is when $\mathcal{A}_2$ asks for $1\|c\|z$ because $\mathcal{B}$ cannot ask the decryption oracle on its challenge c. Fortunately, in such a case, $\mathcal{B}$ can safely answer $\perp$ (since we excluded event EventGM): $\Pr[S_2] = \Pr[S_1]$.

Game $\mathbf{G_3}$: In this game, we replace the permutation G_{K_g} by a truly random permutation. Whenever $\mathcal{B}$ needs to use G_{K_g} (for simulating decryptions), it uses G: $|\Pr[S_3] - \Pr[S_2]| \le \mathsf{Adv}_{\mathcal{G}}^{\mathsf{prp}}(q_d, t + 2 \times T_f)$.

Game $\mathbf{G_4}$: We now replace the function F_{K_f} by a truly random function F. Whenever $\mathcal{B}$ needs to use F_{K_f}, it uses F:

$$|\Pr[S_4] - \Pr[S_3]| \le \mathsf{Adv}_{\mathcal{G}}^{\mathsf{prp}}(q_d, t + 2 \times T_f).$$

In this last game, with an access to f and f^{-1}, $\mathcal{B}$ is an actual IND-CCA2 adversary against $\pi^{(f)}$. Since $\mathcal{A}$ is an (m, N)-IND adversary against π', $q_d \le m+N$, hence the result. $\qquad\qquad\square$

Lemma 16. π' is (M, n)-IND secure:

$$\mathsf{Adv}_{\pi'}^{(M,n)\text{-ind}}(t) \le \mathsf{Adv}_{\pi'}^{\mathsf{ind\text{-}cca2}}(t + (M+n)T_f + 2T_{f^{-1}})$$

$$+ n \times \left(\begin{array}{l} 2\mathsf{Adv}_{\mathcal{F}}^{\mathsf{prf}}(M + 2n - 1, t) + (Mn^2 + n + M) \times 2^{-\ell} \\ + \mathsf{Adv}_{\mathcal{F}}^{\mathsf{prf}}(M + n, t) + \mathsf{Adv}_{\mathcal{G}}^{\mathsf{prp}}(M + n, t) \end{array} \right).$$

Proof. As above, we start from an (M,n)-ind adversary $\mathcal{A}$ against π'. We prove that $\mathsf{Adv}^{(M,n)\text{-ind}}_{\pi'}(\mathcal{A})$ is small by exhibiting an IND-CCA2 adversary $\mathcal{B}$ against $\pi^{(f)}$ with a similar advantage.

Game $\mathbf{G_0}$:   In this first game, as above, $\mathcal{B}$ is provided with $\mathcal{D}'_{\mathsf{sk}'}$, and plays exactly the same way:

$$\Pr[\mathsf{S_0}] = \Pr[\mathcal{B} = b] = \Pr[\mathcal{A} = b].$$

Game $\mathbf{G_1}$:   We provide $\mathcal{B}$ with $\mathcal{D}^{(f)}_{\mathsf{sk}(f)}$ instead of $\mathcal{D}'_{\mathsf{sk}'}$, together with oracle access to $F_{\mathcal{K}_f}$, G_{K_g}, but also the trapdoor to compute f^{-1}. By the Proposition 15, $\mathcal{B}$ can use this decryption oracle to perfectly simulate $\mathcal{D}'_{\mathsf{sk}'}$, excepted on a query $1\|c\|z$, where c is the challenge ciphertext for $\mathcal{B}$. Fortunately, in this case, $\mathcal{B}$ can safely output $\perp$. Indeed, it would be a mistake only if $z = F^n_{K_f}(c)$. Note that c is not known to $\mathcal{A}_1$, and thus such a case can appear in the first stage only by chance (less than $M/2^\ell$.) If this happens in the second stage, by randomly outputting a z from a $1\|c\|z$ decryption query, one would break the PRF property of $\mathcal{F}$ with probability of $1/n$, since one would output $F^n_{K_f}(c)$ after only $n-1$ queries (since this critical decryption query is one of the n possible queries of $\mathcal{A}_2$.)

$$|\Pr[\mathsf{S_1}]-\Pr[\mathsf{S_0}]| \leq \frac{M}{2^\ell}+n\cdot\mathsf{Succ}^{M,n}_{F_{K_f}}(t) \leq n\times\mathsf{Adv}^{\mathsf{prf}}_{\mathcal{F}}(M+2n-1,t)+\frac{Mn^2+n+M}{2^\ell}.$$

Game $\mathbf{G_2}$:   In this game, we replace the function F_{K_f} by a truly random function F. Similarly, we replace the permutation G_{K_g} by a truly random permutation G. With the same argument as in the proof of the Lemma 14, in the games $\mathbf{G_3}$ and $\mathbf{G_4}$, we have:

$$|\Pr[\mathsf{S_2}] - \Pr[\mathsf{S_1}]| \leq \mathsf{Adv}^{\mathsf{prf}}_{\mathcal{F}}(q_d,t) + \mathsf{Adv}^{\mathsf{prp}}_{\mathcal{G}}(q_d,t).$$

In this last game, $\mathcal{B}$ is an actual IND-CCA2 adversary against $\pi^{(f)}$, hence the result.   □

From the Lemmas 13, 14 and 16, one completes the proof of the Theorem 12.   □

3.3   Discussion About Non-malleability

We now briefly discuss on the general notion of non-malleability (denoted by $\mathsf{CNM}^{(k)}$) in which the adversary finally outputs a ciphertext vector of size k, instead of a single ciphertext. In [4], Bellare and Sahai introduced the notion of parallel attacks, denoted PA (or more precisely $\mathsf{PA}^{(k)}$ by us), where the adversary can ask a ciphertext vector of size k to the decryption oracle just after the last normal single decryption query (derived in three ways, as usual, with PA0, PA1 and PA2, according to the access of the decryption oracle for single ciphertext queries.) They proved that IND-PAX is equivalent to $CNM^{(k)}$-CCAX, where CCA0 is indeed CPA. Their result can be translated within our formalism under the following theorem, which proof can be found in the full version [14].

Theorem 17. *The two notions (m,n)-IND-PA$^{(k)}$ and (m,n)-CNM$^{(k)}$ are equivalent. In other words, for any encryption scheme $\pi = (\mathcal{G}, \mathcal{E}, \mathcal{D})$:*

$$\frac{1}{2} \times \mathsf{Adv}_\pi^{(m,n)\text{-ind-pa}^{(k)}}(t) \leq \mathsf{Adv}_\pi^{(m,n)\text{-ind-cnm}^{(k)}}(t) \leq \mathsf{Adv}_\pi^{(m,n)\text{-ind-pa}^{(k)}}(t + T_R),$$

where T_R is an upper-bound on the time to evaluate the relation R.

Granted the following identifications,

$$(m,n)\text{-IND-PA}^{(1)} = (m, n+1)\text{-IND} \qquad (m,n)\text{-CNM}^{(1)} = (m,n)\text{-NM},$$

one gets $(m, n+1)$-IND $= (m,n)$-NM.

4   A New Attack Model: CCAO2

Definition 18 (Post-Challenge Attacks). *An adversary is called a post-challenge chosen-ciphertext adversary (denoted by CCAO2-adversary) if it can access the oracle after the challenge ciphertext is known only still with the restriction not to use it on the challenge itself.*

Given this new attack model of post-challenge chosen-ciphertext adversaries, combined with the classical goals, one gets the two security notions: IND-CCAO2 and NM-CCAO2. These notions are independent with the previous ones, excepted the trivial implications. First, it is clear that for any XXX, XXX-CCA2 implies both XXX-CCA1 and XXX-CCAO2. But from the above result, we show that the opposite is not true. In fact, we clearly have the following corollaries:

Corollary 19. IND-CCAO2 *and* IND-CCA1 *are independent notions. In other words, under the assumption that* IND-CCA2 *secure encryption schemes exist, there is a scheme which is* IND-CCA1 *secure but not* IND-CCAO2 *secure and, there is a scheme that is* IND-CCAO2 *secure but not* IND-CCA1 *secure.*

Corollary 20. IND-CCA1 *and* IND-CCAO2 *do not imply, even together,* IND-CCA2. *In other words, under the assumption that* IND-CCA2 *secure encryption schemes exist, there is a scheme which is both* IND-CCA1 *secure and* IND-CCAO2 *secure but not* IND-CCA2 *secure.*

Another Discussion. Since parallel attacks [4] do not give more power to a CCAO2 adversary, we still have equivalence between the two notions of IND and NM under this new kind of attack, as shown in [2] under CCA2.

Acknowledgement. The work described in this paper has been supported in part by the European Commission through the IST Programme under Contract IST-2002-507932 ECRYPT. The information in this document reflects only the authors' views, is provided as is and no guarantee or warranty is given that the information is fit for any particular purpose. The user thereof uses the information at its sole risk and liability.

References

1. M. Bellare, A. Desai, E. Jokipii, and P. Rogaway. A Concrete Security Treatment of Symmetric Encryption: Analysis of the DES Modes of Operation. In *Proc. of the 38th FOCS*. IEEE, New York, 1997.
2. M. Bellare, A. Desai, D. Pointcheval, and P. Rogaway. Relations among Notions of Security for Public-key Encryption Schemes. In *Adv. in Cryptology – Proceedings of Crypto '98*, volume LNCS 1462, pages 26–45, Berlin, 1998. Springer-Verlag.
3. M. Bellare and P. Rogaway. The Exact Security of Digital Signatures – How to Sign with RSA and Rabin. In *Eurocrypt '96*, LNCS 1070, pages 399–416. Springer-Verlag, Berlin, 1996.
4. M. Bellare and A. Sahai. Non-malleable encryption: Equivalence between two notions, and an indistinguishability-based characterization. In *Adv. in Cryptology – Proceedings of Crypto '99*, volume LNCS 1666, pages 519–536, Berlin, 1999. Springer-Verlag.
5. D. Dolev, C. Dwork, and M. Naor. Non-Malleable Cryptography. In *Proc. of the 23rd STOC*. ACM Press, New York, 1991.
6. D. Dolev, C. Dwork, and M. Naor. Non-Malleable Cryptography. *SIAM Journal on Computing*, 30(2):391–437, 2000.
7. O. Goldreich, Goldwasser, and S. Micali. How to construct random functions. *Journal of the ACM*, 33(4):210–217, 1986.
8. S. Goldwasser and S. Micali. Probabilistic Encryption. *Journal of Computer and System Sciences*, 28:270–299, 1984.
9. S. Goldwasser, S. Micali, and C. Rackoff. The Knowledge Complexity of Interactive Proof Systems. In *Proc. of the 17th STOC*, pages 291–304. ACM Press, New York, 1985.
10. S. Goldwasser, S. Micali, and R. Rivest. A "Paradoxical" Solution to the Signature Problem. In *Proc. of the 25th FOCS*, pages 441–448. IEEE, New York, 1984.
11. S. Goldwasser, S. Micali, and R. Rivest. A Digital Signature Scheme Secure Against Adaptative Chosen-Message Attacks. *SIAM Journal of Computing*, 17(2):281–308, April 1988.
12. M. Naor and M. Yung. Public-Key Cryptosystems Provably Secure against Chosen Ciphertext Attacks. In *Proc. of the 22nd STOC*, pages 427–437. ACM Press, New York, 1990.
13. K. Ohta and T. Okamoto. On Concrete Security Treatment of Signatures Derived from Identification. In *Crypto '98*, LNCS 1462, pages 354–369. Springer-Verlag, Berlin, 1998.
14. D. H. Phan and D. Pointcheval. On the Security Notions for Public-Key Encryption Schemes. In *Proc. of SCN '04*. Springer-Verlag, Berlin, 2004. Full version available from http://www.di.ens.fr/users/pointche/.
15. C. Rackoff and D. R. Simon. Non-interactive Zero-knowledge Proof of Knowledge and Chosen Ciphertext Attack. In *Proc. of CRYPTO '91*, volume LNCS 576, pages 433–444, Berlin, 1992. Springer-Verlag.
16. A. Sahai. Non-Malleable Non-Interactive Zero-Knowledge and Chosen-Ciphertext Security. In *Proc. of the 40th FOCS*. IEEE, New York, 1999.

Efficient Unconditional Oblivious Transfer from Almost Any Noisy Channel

Claude Crépeau[1,*], Kirill Morozov[2,**], and Stefan Wolf[3,***]

[1] School of Computer Science, McGill University, Montreal, Canada
Claude.Crepeau@McGill.ca
[2] BRICS[†], FICS [‡], Aarhus University, Denmark
kirill@brics.dk
[3] Département d'Informatique et recherche opérationnelle,
Université de Montréal, Canada
wolf@iro.umontreal.ca

Abstract. *Oblivious transfer (OT)* is a cryptographic primitive of central importance, in particular in two- and multi-party computation. There exist various protocols for different variants of OT, but any such realization from scratch can be broken in principle by at least one of the two involved parties if she has sufficient computing power—and the same even holds when the parties are connected by a quantum channel. We show that, on the other hand, if *noise*—which is inherently present in any physical communication channel—is taken into account, then OT can be realized in an unconditionally secure way for both parties, i.e., even against dishonest players with unlimited computing power. We give the exact condition under which a general noisy channel allows for realizing OT and show that only "trivial" channels, for which OT is obviously impossible to achieve, have to be excluded. Moreover, our realization of OT is efficient: For a security parameter $\alpha > 0$—an upper bound on the probability that the protocol fails in any way—the required number of uses of the noisy channel is of order $O(\log(1/\alpha)^{2+\varepsilon})$ for any $\varepsilon > 0$.

1 Introduction and Motivation

Cryptographic security can either stem from the fact that an adversary's information about the data of interest is zero (or limited), or that these data are difficult to access from her information. The second type of security is based

* Supported by Canada's NSERC and Québec's FQRNT.
** Work carried out while author was with School of Computer Science, McGill University, Montreal, Canada.
*** Supported by Canada's NSERC.
† Basic Research in Computer Science (www.brics.dk), funded by the Danish National Research Foundation.
‡ FICS, Foundations in Cryptography and Security, funded by the Danish Natural Sciences Research Council.

C. Blundo and S. Cimato (Eds.): SCN 2004, LNCS 3352, pp. 47–59, 2005.

on the hardness of certain computational problems and depends on assumptions on the adversary such as her computing power. Unfortunately, there do not exist proven lower bounds on the complexity of solving particular problems that are directly useful in a cryptographic context. The first type of security is called *information-theoretic* security. It can be realized under specific assumptions—such as bounds on an adversary's memory space [17], [12]—, or from no assumptions at all, in which case this type of security is also called *unconditional*. Clearly, this is the most desirable type of security—but it has its price and can generally not be generated from scratch; this is true for encryption, where its price is a secret key of a certain length [20], as well as for so-called *two-* or *multi-party computation*. Examples of two-party tasks that can be shown impossible from scratch in an unconditionally secure way with respect to both parties simultaneously are the computation of the *OR function* or *bit commitment*.

A primitive of particular importance in the context of secure two-party computation is *oblivious transfer (OT)* due to its universality: From information-theoretically secure OT, any two-party computation can be realized in an unconditionally secure way. OT or, more precisely, chosen one-out-of-two bit OT [13], is the following primitive involving a sender A and a receiver B: A sends two bits b_0 and b_1, B inputs a choice bit c and receives b_c, but remains ignorant about b_{1-c}. The sender A, on the other hand, does not learn c. This variant of OT was shown equivalent—given that a small but non-zero failure probability can be accepted—to the original, so-called *Rabin OT* [19] in [6]; Rabin OT in fact corresponds to a binary erasure channel with erasure probability $1/2$.

It is, therefore, a natural question whether OT can as well be realized from other noisy communication channels between the parties. In fact, also in different contexts, such as encryption, noisy channels have proven useful as simple *information-theoretic primitives* [18] allowing for achieving tasks such as (almost) perfectly secret message transmission [10], [24]. In [7], it was shown that any non-trivial *binary-symmetric channel (BSC)* allows for realizing OT in polynomial time, and in [8] a more efficient construction was given and later shown to work as well for *any* non-trivial BSC in [15], [21].

In the present paper, we generalize this result to *arbitrary discrete memoryless channels (DMCs)*—characterized by a conditional probability distribution $P_{Y|X}$. More precisely, we first define *triviality*: Intuitively speaking, a channel $P_{Y|X}$ is trivial if, after removal of all input symbols whose output distribution can be generated by combining other input symbols, the channel is a parallel composition of capacity-zero channels. The main result of our paper then states that any *non-trivial* channel, and only those channels, allow for—efficiently—realizing OT.

Main Result. *Let two players A and B be connected by a non-trivial channel $P_{Y|X}$. Then, for any $\alpha > 0$, there exists a protocol for unconditionally secure OT from A to B with failure probability at most α, where the number of uses of the channel is of order $O(\log(1/\alpha)^{2+\varepsilon})$ for any $\varepsilon > 0$. Trivial channels, on the other hand, do not allow for realizing OT in an unconditional way.*

In [22], the problem of realizing bit commitment from discrete channels was studied. They showed that string commitment with positive rate can be achieved, i.e., the length of the committed string divided by the number of channel uses is bounded from below by a strictly positive constant. They have extended their notion of *commitment capacity* to *OT capacity* [23]. In this context, they independently used the same notion of non-triviality of discrete channels.

The rest of this paper is organized as follows. In Section 2, we briefly review some notions, facts, and constructions from coding theory and information-theoretic cryptography. Section 3 introduces the notion of non-triviality of a discrete memoryless channel. In particular, we prove a property of non-trivial channels that is crucial for the construction of the OT protocol, which is presented in Section 4.

2 Preliminaries

2.1 Coding Theory

We briefly review some basic facts from coding theory. For a more detailed discussion, we refer to, for instance, [16].

A *binary error-correction code* with code-word length or size n, dimension k, and minimal distance d is a subset of cardinality 2^k of $\{0,1\}^n$—the code words—such that for any two elements v, w of this set $d_H(v, w) \geq d$ holds, where d_H denotes the *Hamming distance* between two bit strings. Of particular importance is the special case of *linear codes*, where the subset of code words is in fact a k-dimensional linear subspace of $\{0,1\}^n$. In this case, the code is called a $[n, k, d]$-code and can be represented by a $k \times n$ matrix G, the *generating matrix*, or, alternatively, by the $n \times (n - k)$ *parity-check matrix H*.

In our protocol presented in Section 4, we use a special class of linear codes, so-called *concatenated codes* [14]. Such codes allow for correcting an asymptotically optimal number of errors: For any $\varphi > 0$ there exists $\rho > 1$ such that for all[1] $R < 1 - h(\varphi)$—the latter expression is the capacity of a BSC with bit error probability φ—and sufficiently large N there exists a linear code with length N and dimension at least RN, failing to correct φN uniformly distributed errors only with probability at most $\rho^{(R-1+h(\varphi))N}$.

The idea of concatenated codes is as follows. A straight-forward Las Vegas construction algorithm combines a power-of-two ($N = 2^n$) size $[N, (1 - \alpha)N, \alpha N - 1]$ *Extended Reed-Solomon (outer) code* over the field $\mathbf{F}_{2^n}$ to a rather good (inner) code of size n selected at random among all linear codes $[n, \kappa n, \delta n]$ of appropriate dimension κn. The resulting concatenated code has parameters $[Nn, (1-\alpha)\kappa Nn, \alpha\delta Nn]$ and is able to efficiently correct up to nearly δNn errors on average if they are uniformly distributed (because only very few errors will be uncorrected by the inner code). The error correction procedure uses a brute-force search for the nearest codeword on the inner code and the Berlekamp-Massey

---

[1] Here, $h(x) = -(x \log x + (1 - x) \log(1 - x))$ is the *binary entropy function*. All logarithms are binary.

algorithm for the outer Extended Reed-Solomon code. Both of these algorithms run in polynomial-time with respect to the global code size Nn.

In our protocols, the information transmitted will not be a codeword but only a syndrome $syn(w) = H^T w$—the noisy versions of the information bits are already known to the receiver. From this syndrome, the decoding algorithm allows for recovering w, given its noisy version.

2.2 Privacy Amplification

Privacy amplification is a general technique for distribution uniformizing or—in a cryptographic context—concentrating an adversary's uncertainty. Privacy amplification was first proposed in the context of quantum key agreement for the special case of deterministic side information [2] and later in general [1]. On the other hand, the effect of additional side information, in our case the syndrome the receiver learns, was studied in [5]. Roughly speaking, the number of bits by which the resulting almost secret string will be shorter corresponds to the length of this side information.

For the following, we can restrict ourselves to the special case where one party knows a noisy version—independently bit by bit—of an original string. This case is simpler than the general case since one can deal with typical sequences and almost-uniform distributions.

Let V be a uniformly distributed n-bit string and let W be generated by independently sending each bit over a BSC with error probability φ. Let, furthermore, $syn : \{0,1\}^n \to \{0,1\}^t$ be a linear function and G be a random variable corresponding to the random choice, according to the uniform distribution, of a function from a 2-universal class of functions [9] $\{0,1\}^n \to \{0,1\}^s$ (for instance, G can be a random linear function mapping n bits to s bits). Then we have, except with exponentially (in n) small probability,

$$H(G(V) \,|\, syn(V) = syn(v), W, G) \geq s - 2^{-\Omega(h(\varphi)n-t-s)} \ .$$

3 Trivial Versus Non-trivial Discrete Memoryless Channels

As a first step towards deriving our main result, we prove a property of non-trivial channels. Intuitively, we show the existence of two particular input symbols of such a channel to which the sender can restrict herself in the OT protocol. A crucial point hereby is that, roughly speaking, she can be forced to use only these two symbols—since her failure to do so will be detected by the receiver.

Definition 1. Let $P_{Y|X}$ be a DMC. We call an input symbol $x \in \mathcal{X}$ *redundant* if its output distribution $P_{Y|X=x}$ can be written as a linear combination of the other output distributions as follows:

$$P_{Y|X=x} = \sum_{x' \in \mathcal{X} \setminus \{x\}} \mu_{x'} P_{Y|X=x'}$$

with $\mu_{x'} \in [0,1]$.

Definition 2. We call a channel $P_{Y|X}$ *trivial* if there exist, after removal of all redundant input symbols, partitions of the (remaining) ranges $\mathcal{X}$ of X and $\mathcal{Y}$ of Y, $\mathcal{X} = \mathcal{X}_1 \cup \cdots \cup \mathcal{X}_n$, $\mathcal{Y} = \mathcal{Y}_1 \cup \cdots \cup \mathcal{Y}_n$, and channels $P_{Y_i|X_i}$, where the ranges of X_i and Y_i are $\mathcal{X}_i$ and $\mathcal{Y}_i$, respectively, such that

$$P_{Y|X=x}(y) = \begin{cases} P_{Y_i|X_i=x}(y) & \text{if } x \in \mathcal{X}_i,\ y \in \mathcal{Y}_i \ , \\ 0 & \text{if } x \in \mathcal{X}_i,\ y \in \mathcal{Y}_j,\ i \neq j \end{cases}$$

holds and such that the capacity of the channel $P_{Y_i|X_i}$ is 0 for all i.

The mentioned well-known result that unconditionally secure OT is impossible to realize by noiseless communication immediately carries over to trivial channels. In Section 4 we will show that, on the other hand, any *other* channel *does* allow for realizing OT. Non-triviality is, therefore, a necessary and sufficient condition for a channel to allow for achieving OT in an unconditionally secure way with respect to both parties. We first give an alternative characterization of non-triviality of a channel.

Theorem 1. *Let $P_{Y|X}$ be a non-trivial channel. Then there exist $x_1, x_2 \in \mathcal{X}$ with the following properties.*

1. $P_{Y|X=x_1} \neq P_{Y|X=x_2}$.
2. *There exists $y \in \mathcal{Y}$ such that $P_{Y|X=x_1}(y) > 0$ and $P_{Y|X=x_2}(y) > 0$.*
3. *Let, for $\lambda, \mu_i \in [0,1]$,*

$$\lambda P_{Y|X=x_1} + (1-\lambda)P_{Y|X=x_2} = \sum_i \mu_i P_{Y|X=x_i} \ .$$

Then $\mu_i > 0$ implies that $P_{Y|X=x_i} = \tau P_{Y|X=x_1} + (1-\tau)P_{Y|X=x_2}$ holds for some $\tau \in [0,1]$.

Remark 1. Intuitively speaking, Theorem 1 states that there are two particular input symbols $x_1, x_2 \in \mathcal{X}$ of the channel with the following properties. If a sender is supposed to use only these two symbols as channel inputs (with certain probabilities or frequencies, say p and $1 - p$, respectively), then the receiver can—if the channel is used a large number N of times—detect whenever the sender fails to do so if the latter cheats $\Omega(\sqrt{N})$ times. The only exception is the use of input symbols $x \notin \{x_1, x_2\}$ whose output distribution over $\mathcal{Y}$ is a convex linear combination of the output distributions of x_1 and x_2, i.e., if

$$P_{Y|X=x} = \tau P_{Y|X=x_1} + (1-\tau)P_{Y|X=x_2}$$

holds for some $\tau \in [0,1]$. In our context—where the sender tries to maximize the information he has about the resulting output—, this is, however, not a problem because using x leaves him with less information than if he had used x_1 with probability β and x_2 with probability $1 - \beta$, and then forgot what he sent.

Proof. Because of the non-triviality of the channel, there exist two non-redundant input symbols x_1 and x'_2 and $y \in \mathcal{Y}$ such that $P_{Y|X=x_1} \neq P_{Y|X=x'_2}$, $P_{Y|X=x_1}(y) > 0$, and $P_{Y|X=x'_2}(y) > 0$ hold.

Let us now interpret $P_{Y|X=x}$, for any $x \in \mathcal{X}$, as a point in $\mathbf{R}^{|\mathcal{Y}|-1}$, where the different coordinates correspond to the probabilities $P_{Y|X=x}(y)$ (which sum up to 1). In the following, we will consider the *convex hull* of the set of points

$$\{P_{Y|X=x} \mid x \in \mathcal{X}\} \subseteq \mathbf{R}^{|\mathcal{Y}|-1} . \tag{1}$$

We call $P_{Y|X=x_0}$ a *spanning point* of the convex hull if the convex hull of $\{P_{Y|X=x} \mid x \in \mathcal{X} \setminus \{x_0\}\}$ is strictly smaller than the one of (1).

Since the spanning points of the hull correspond to non-redundant inputs, we can conclude that there exist two spanning points $P_{Y|X=x_1}$ and $P_{Y|X=x'_2}$ of the convex hull such that there exists $y \in \mathcal{Y}$ with $P_{Y|X=x_1}(y) > 0$ and $P_{Y|X=x'_2}(y) > 0$.

Let us now look at the connections between $P_{Y|X=x_1}$ and all other points $P_{Y|X=x}$, $x \in \mathcal{X}$, and let v_x be the unity vector parallel to the vector in $\mathbf{R}^{|\mathcal{Y}|-1}$ connecting $P_{Y|X=x_1}$ and $P_{Y|X=x}$. In a similar way as for points, we define convex linear combinations and the convex hull for these vectors. Let $\{v_x \mid x \in \mathcal{A}\}$, where $\mathcal{A} \subseteq \mathcal{X}$, be the set of spanning vectors.

We will first argue that there exists $x_2 \in \mathcal{A}$ with $P_{Y|X=x_2}(y) > 0$, and secondly, that the representation of any linear combination of x_1 and x_2 as a linear combination of *all points* $P_{Y|X=x}$ is unique—modulo points that are *themselves* linear combinations of x_1 and x_2.

Assume that for all $x \in \mathcal{A}$, we have $P_{Y|X=x}(y) = 0$. Then the same is true also for all distributions in the convex hull of these points. On the other hand, the connection between x_1 and x'_2 has a non-empty intersection with this convex hull by definition of $\mathcal{A}$. Since every distribution in this intersection is a convex linear combination of $P_{Y|X=x_1}$ and $P_{Y|X=x'_2}$—both non-zero in y— there exists a point x_2 in $\mathcal{A}$ with $P_{Y|X=x_2}(y) > 0$.

By construction, x_1 and x_2 have now the following properties. First, they satisfy $P_{Y|X=x_1} > 0$ and $P_{Y|X=x_2} > 0$. Second, any convex linear combination of $P_1 = P_{Y|X=x_1}$ and $P_2 = P_{Y|X=x_2}$ cannot be represented as a convex linear combination involving points $P_{Y|X=x}$ *not* lying on the line connecting P_1 and P_2; this would contradict the fact that P_2 is a spanning point of the connections of P_1 to all other points P; indeed, the line from P_1 to P_2 could in this case be represented as a linear combination of the lines connecting P_1 with the external points occurring in the linear combination. This observation concludes the proof. □

4   A Protocol for Efficient Oblivious Transfer from Any Non-trivial Channel

In this section we describe a protocol for OT based on an arbitrary non-trivial DMC and give, hence, a proof of our main result stated above. Our protocol is an adaptation of the protocol from [8] for the general case (where, at the same time, we reduce the required number of channel uses from *cubic* to, roughly, *quadratic* order in $\log(1/\alpha)$. We develop the protocol in three steps. In Section 4.1, the original channel is used to obtain a binary-symmetric erasure channel with error; in Section 4.2, this is transfered into a weak form of OT vulnerable to active attacks by the sender A; in Section 4.3, finally, we derive the final protocol avoiding these attacks by statistical analysis by the receiver.

4.1   Binary-Symmetric Erasure Channel with Error from Any Non-trivial Channel

From a non-trivial channel $P_{Y|X}$, we first construct a *binary erasure channel with error*. We encode the bits to be transmitted over the DMC as pairs of two fixed distinct input symbols $x_1, x_2 \in \mathcal{X}$ chosen according to Theorem 1: "0" is encoded as $x_1 x_2$ and "1" as $x_2 x_1$. When this is repeated many times, B gets the sent bits with different error rates, depending on the actual output symbols received. We will have B make a decision on 0 or 1 only when he receives certain specific pairs—otherwise, he will decide on erasure Δ. More precisely, B will accept only the pairs which give him the best estimate of what has been sent; we will call these the *most informative pairs*. Note that there might even be output symbols y which allow for deciding *with certainty* whether x_1 or x_2 has sent. Note, however, that the choice of x_1 and x_2 *guarantees* that there exist pairs which are *not* conclusive with certainty. The crucial point is that there are at least two different levels of conclusiveness, and it is the difference between the two that will be used in the protocol. In the following, we will call the pairs providing B with the best *a posteriori* probabilities *good pairs* and denote them by $y_1 y_2$ and $y_2 y_1$, respectively.

Let $\mathcal{Y}'$ be the set of y with $P_{Y|X=x_1}(y) > 0$ or $P_{Y|X=x_2}(y) > 0$. Formally, the *most informative pair* (y_1, y_2) is the pair $(y, \overline{y}) \in \mathcal{Y}' \times \mathcal{Y}'$, $y \neq \overline{y}$, that achieves the following minimum:

$$\varphi = \min_{(y,\overline{y}) \in \mathcal{Y}' \times \mathcal{Y}'} \frac{P_{Y|X=x_1}(\overline{y}) P_{Y|X=x_2}(y)}{P_{Y|X=x_1}(\overline{y}) P_{Y|X=x_2}(y) + P_{Y|X=x_1}(y) P_{Y|X=x_2}(\overline{y})} . \tag{2}$$

Note that (2) is symmetric with respect to x_1 and x_2. The resulting channel is, hence, a binary-symmetric erasure channel (BSEC), i.e., a binary-input channel with some erasure probability and a certain bit-error probability.

Protocol 1. $P_{Y|X} \to \mathrm{BSEC}(r)$

1. A sends $x_1 x_2$ if $r = 0$ and $x_2 x_1$ if $r = 1$.

2. B returns $\begin{cases} 0 & \text{if } y_1 y_2 \text{ is received,} \\ 1 & \text{if } y_2 y_1 \text{ is received,} \\ \Delta & \text{if any other pair is received.} \end{cases}$

4.2   Passively Secure OT

The BSEC obtained above is not a Rabin OT: B might get some information even when deciding on Δ, and there are bit errors. We now describe a protocol, based on the obtained BSEC, for realizing OT under the assumption that A behaves correctly.

In the "weak OT" protocol, A sends $2n$ random bits $r_1, r_2, \ldots, r_{2n}$ to B using BSEC. B should receive roughly $2p_g n$ of them as *good pairs* and $2(1-p_g)n$ "bad" ones, where p_g denotes the probability that B decides on either 0 or 1, but not Δ, in an execution of BSEC given that A is honest, i.e.,

$$p_g = (P_{Y|X=x_1}(y_1)P_{Y|X=x_2}(y_2) + P_{Y|X=x_2}(y_1)P_{Y|X=x_1}(y_2))/2 \ .$$

B then forms two sets I_0 and I_1 of size n if $p_g > 1/2$ and, otherwise, size $n' = (p_g - \gamma)n$, $\gamma > 0$. By the index sets I_0 and I_1, B defines two bit-strings r'_{I_0}, r'_{I_1} such that r'_{I_c} should contain only good pairs.

Let now φ be the bit error probability of the BSEC. The players now establish a code—according to the discussion in Section 2.1—which exactly allows for correcting (except with small probability) all errors of a set consisting only of good pairs. More precisely, the errors are corrected by having A send the syndromes of the two words $syn(r_{I_0})$ and $syn(r_{I_1})$. Using r'_{I_c} and $syn(r_{I_c})$, B can recover r_{I_c} except with small probability. On the other hand, this correction information is *not* sufficient to find out *both* words r_{I_c} and $r_{I_{1-c}}$ as long as the dimension of the code does not exceed $(1 - h(\varphi))n'$.

Finally, a linear privacy amplification function is used to extract one bit per string, such that one of the two bits may be recovered, but not both. This function is the scalar product (we denote it as "$\odot$") with a random n'-bit string m. (Note that *string* OT instead of *bit* OT could be obtained using hashing to a string as the privacy-amplification function.)

Protocol 2. BSEC $\rightarrow \widehat{\text{OT}}(b_0, b_1)(c)$

1. A picks $2n$ random bits r_i, $i = 1, \ldots, 2n$, and sends them to B as BSEC(r_i); B receives r'_i.
2. B picks and sends two disjoint sets I_0, I_1, $|I_0| = |I_1| = n'$, such that $r'_i \neq \Delta$ holds for all $i \in I_c$.
3. A and B agree on a parity-check matrix H of a concatenated code C with parameters $[n', k = (1 - h(\varphi))n', d]$ correcting $\psi\varphi n'$ errors, $\psi > 1$.
4. (a) A computes and sends $s_0 = syn(r_{I_0})$ and $s_1 = syn(r_{I_1})$,
   (b) picks and sends a random n'-bit word m, and
   (c) computes and sends $\hat{b}_0 = b_0 \oplus (m \odot r_{I_0})$ and $\hat{b}_1 = b_1 \oplus (m \odot r_{I_1})$.
5. (a) B recovers r_{I_c} using r'_{I_c}, s_c and the decoding algorithm of C and
   (b) computes and returns $\hat{b}_c \oplus (m \odot r_{I_c})$.

Let us discuss why B is unable to cheat in the weak OT protocol. In fact, the chosen code is such that *complete* error correction is possible only if B collects all the good pairs into one of the two sets. Suppose first that $p_g > 1/2$ holds. Then there exists a constant fraction of bad bits the error rate of which is at least $\varphi' > \varphi$, where φ' is the error rate of the second most informative pairs. Assume for simplicity that the fraction of the second most informative bits is $1 - p_g$, which is the worst case (from A's viewpoint). A dishonest B is not able to put more than $p_g n$ good bits in at least one of the sets I_0 and I_1. The bits of this set do not contain more than $((1 - h(\varphi))p_g + (1 - h(\varphi'))(1 - p_g))n$ bits of Shannon information about the original string with high probability. Therefore, at least $(h(\varphi)p_g + h(\varphi')(1 - p_g))n$ parity-check bits are needed to correct all the errors in each set with high probability; however, $syn(r_{I_0})$, $syn(r_{I_1})$ each contain $(h(\varphi) + \delta)n$ bits only. Thus, at least one of the two words r_{I_0}, r_{I_1} will be undetermined by at least $n(h(\varphi') - h(\varphi))(1 - p_g)$ bits. From the results sketched in Section 2.2, one can conclude that after privacy amplification, B only has an exponentially small amount of information about the corresponding bit. The case of $p_g \leq 1/2$ can be treated in a similar way.

Unfortunately, the weak OT protocol is not secure against cheating by A with the objective of figuring out B's choice bit c. For instance, A can send *incorrect pairs:* $x_1 x_1$ or $x_2 x_2$ instead of $x_1 x_2$ and $x_2 x_1$, hereby increasing the probability that it is received as a bad pair (i.e., $r_i' = \Delta$) by B. Alternatively, A can use any other input symbols but x_1 and x_2 (we call them *forbidden* input symbols) whose support intersects with those of x_1 and x_2. Finally, she can send an incorrect syndrome at Step 4.

In the first and second active attacks, incorrect pairs are more likely to end up in the "bad" set, thus indicating to A which one of I_0 and I_1 is more likely to be the "good" and the "bad" set, respectively, and hence what B's choice is. In the third attack, if A renders only one of the syndromes incorrect, then B will abort or not, depending on which bit he is trying to get.

4.3   The Complete OT Protocol

The main idea is now, as in [8], to avoid cheating by A by repeating the weak OT protocol many times in such a way that A has to cheat in a substantial fraction of all executions of BSEC (namely, in more than the square root of the total number of executions) in order to gain useful information. This, however, can be detected by B when he analyzes his output statistically.

More precisely, Protocol $\widehat{\text{OT}}$ is repeated $\lceil n^{1+\varepsilon} \rceil$ times, $0 < \varepsilon < 1$; thus, we apply BSEC $2\lceil n^{2+\varepsilon} \rceil$ times in total. In order to cheat, A will have to send at least $\lceil n^{1+\varepsilon} \rceil$ wrong pairs (i.e., she forms the pair incorrectly or uses forbidden symbols) in these executions. This will, however, lead to a detectable bias in the output distribution (with probability almost 1). If, on the other hand, A uses *less than* $\lceil n^{1+\varepsilon} \rceil$ incorrect pairs, she finds out nothing about c. Similarly, if A sends wrong syndromes in the protocol for $\widehat{\text{OT}}$ she will, each time, be detected by B with probability $1/2$. If she uses $n^{1+\varepsilon}$ such faulty syndromes it is, hence, only with exponentially small probability that B will not detect her cheating.

Let $n_\varepsilon = \lceil n^{1+\varepsilon} \rceil$, where $\lceil \cdot \rceil$ means rounding up to the next odd integer, and $n_\varepsilon' = n \cdot n_\varepsilon$. The instances are combined by requesting $b_{l,0} \oplus b_{l,1} = b_0 \oplus b_1$ for $1 \leq l \leq n_\varepsilon$. Let

$$b_{0,0} = \bigoplus_{l=1}^{n_\varepsilon} b_{l,0} \quad \text{and} \quad b_{0,1} = \bigoplus_{l=1}^{n_\varepsilon} b_{l,1} \ .$$

Then we get

$$\bigoplus_{l=1}^{n_\varepsilon} b_{l,c_l} = b_{0,z} \quad \text{for} \quad z = \bigoplus_{l=1}^{n_\varepsilon} c_l \ .$$

Thus, in order to find out which of $b_{0,0}$ or $b_{0,1}$ B is trying to receive, A must find out all the c_l.

Let $\psi > 1$. An extra index l is added to each variable of the lth iteration of $\widehat{OT}$. Let us denote by $q_{l,\bar{i}} \in \mathcal{Y}'$ the $\bar{i}$th output symbol $(1 \leq \bar{i} \leq 4n'_\varepsilon)$ and as $r_{l,i} \in \{0,1\}$ the ith output bit $(1 \leq \bar{i} \leq 2n'_\varepsilon)$ received by B in the lth iteration of $\widehat{OT}$. Let

$$\delta = \min_{y \in \mathcal{Y}, \ \bar{x} \in \mathcal{X} \setminus \{x_1, x_2\}} \left| \frac{P_{Y|X=x_1}(y) + P_{Y|X=x_2}(y)}{2} - P_{Y|X=\bar{x}}(y) \right| .$$

Roughly speaking, δ is the closest the sender can get to "the middle point" between the distributions $P_{Y|X=x_1}$ and $P_{Y|X=x_2}$ using forbidden symbols (except the symbols lying on the line between x_1 and x_2, as discussed in Section 3).

Protocol 3. $\widehat{OT} \rightarrow OT$

1. A picks n_ε random bits $b_{1,0}, b_{2,0}, \ldots b_{n_\varepsilon,0}$ and sets $b_{l,1} = b_0 \oplus b_1 \oplus b_{l,0}$ for $1 \leq l \leq n_\varepsilon$.
2. B picks n_ε random bits $c_1, c_2, \ldots, c_{n_\varepsilon}$.
3. **Repeat for** $l = 1, \ldots, n_\varepsilon$
   (a) A runs $\widehat{OT}(b_{l,0}, b_{l,1})(c_l)$ with B who gets b'_l,
   (b) **if** $d_H(r_{l,I_{l,c_l}}, r'_{l,I_{l,c_l}}) > \psi\varphi n'$ **then** B aborts.
4. **if** for some j, $1 \leq j \leq |\mathcal{Y}'| - 1$:

$$\left| \#\{l, \bar{i} | q_{l,\bar{i}} = y_j\} - 2n'_\varepsilon \left(P_{Y|X=x_1}(y_j) + P_{Y|X=x_2}(y_j) \right) \right| > \frac{\delta}{2(|\mathcal{X}|-2)} n_\varepsilon \ ,$$

then B aborts **else if**

$$\#\{l, i \mid r_{l,i} = y_1 y_2 \text{ or } r_{l,i} = y_2 y_1\} < 2p_g n'_\varepsilon - \frac{2p_g - 1}{4} n_\varepsilon \ ,$$

then B aborts **else** B computes and sends $c' = c \oplus \left(\bigoplus_{l=1}^{n_\varepsilon} c_l \right)$.

5. A computes and sends $\hat{b}_0 = b_0 \oplus \left(\bigoplus_{l=1}^{n_\varepsilon} b_{l,c'} \right)$ and $\hat{b}_1 = b_1 \oplus \left(\bigoplus_{l=1}^{n_\varepsilon} b_{l,1-c'} \right)$ to B.

6. B computes and returns $\hat{b}_c \oplus \left(\bigoplus_{l=1}^{n_\varepsilon} b'_l \right)$.

The test in Step 3 of the protocol is to decide whether the syndrome sent by A was valid: If the decoded word has Hamming distance larger than $\psi\varphi n'$ to the received string, then the syndrome was wrong.

We briefly argue that the tests of Step 4 achieve their goals. Let $y \in \mathcal{Y}$ and

$$z_{i,j}^{(y)} = \begin{cases} 0 & \text{if } q_{l,i} \neq y \\ 1 & \text{if } q_{l,i} = y. \end{cases}$$

When A sends only x_1 and x_2, we have for all y that

$$E\left[\sum_{i=1}^{n_\varepsilon}\sum_{j=1}^{4n} z_{i,j}^{(y)}\right] = 4n_\varepsilon' \frac{P_{Y=y|X=x_1} + P_{Y=y|X=x_2}}{2}$$

holds, i.e., B expects to see the "middle distribution" between $P_{Y|X=x_1}$ and $P_{Y|X=x_2}$ for all y. Because of Theorem 1 and the choice of x_1 and x_2, A cannot simulate this "middle point" using the forbidden symbols. Therefore, all she can do is send other symbols in order to get as close as possible to the target distribution, however, she cannot get closer than δ.

For the second test of Step 4 the idea is that the receiver calculates the overall number of accepted symbols $y_1 y_2$ and $y_2 y_1$:

$$w_{i,j} = \begin{cases} 1 & \text{if } r_{l,i} = y_1 y_2 \text{ or } r_{l,i} = y_2 y_1, \\ 0 & \text{otherwise.} \end{cases}$$

Then,

$$E\left[\sum_{i=1}^{n_\varepsilon}\sum_{j=1}^{2n} w_{i,j}\right] = 2p_g n_\varepsilon'$$

holds, where p_g is, as above, the probability to receive a good pair given that $x_1 x_2$ or $x_1 x_2$ was sent. If the actual number of good pairs received is too low, A must have used the incorrect pairs $x_1 x_1$ or $x_2 x_2$; hence, the receiver aborts.

Theorem 2 follows from Bernstein's law of large numbers. Note, hereby, that $n_\varepsilon = \lceil n^{1+\varepsilon} \rceil > \sqrt{n_\varepsilon'} = \sqrt{n \cdot n_\varepsilon}$.

Theorem 2. *There exist constants $\rho_1 < 1$, $\rho_2 < 1$ such that when A does not use the forbidden symbols then*

$$Prob\left[\sum_{i=1}^{n_\varepsilon}\sum_{j=1}^{4n}\left|z_{i,j}^{(y)} - 2n_\varepsilon'\left(P_{Y|X=x_1}(y_j) + P_{Y|X=x_2}(y_j)\right)\right| > \frac{\delta}{2(|\mathcal{X}| - 2)}n_\varepsilon\right] < \rho_1^n$$

holds, whereas, when she cheats n_ε times,

$$Prob\left[\sum_{i=1}^{n_\varepsilon}\sum_{j=1}^{4n}\left|z_{i,j}^{(y)} - 2n_\varepsilon'\left(P_{Y|X=x_1}(y_j) + P_{Y|X=x_2}(y_j)\right)\right| < \frac{\delta}{2(|\mathcal{X}| - 2)}n_\varepsilon\right] < \rho_1^n$$

holds; if A does not use incorrect pairs, then we have

$$Prob\left[\sum_{i=1}^{n_\varepsilon}\sum_{j=1}^{2n} w_{i,j} < 2p_g n_\varepsilon' - \frac{2p_g - 1}{4}n_\varepsilon\right] < \rho_2^n,$$

whereas, when she cheats n_ε times,

$$Prob\left[\sum_{i=1}^{n_\varepsilon}\sum_{j=1}^{2n} w_{i,j} > 2p_g n'_\varepsilon - \frac{2p_g - 1}{4}n_\varepsilon\right] < \rho_2^n.$$

Finally, if A is honest, then the probability that more than $\psi\varphi n'$ transmission errors occur is exponentially small. Thus, an honest A is unlikely to fail the test of Step 3, while a dishonest A who deliberately sends a wrong syndrome will be detected with probability $1/2$ if B picks this syndrome.

This concludes the analysis of the protocol, and, hence, the proof of our main result.

5   Concluding Remarks

All computationally secure cryptography is based on assumptions on a possible adversary, and, hence, threatened by any progress in algorithm design and computer engineering. Functionalities of central importance such as encryption, authentication, or multi-party computation cannot, however, be realized in an unconditionally secure way without any given information-theoretic primitive to start from. In the case of oblivious transfer—as for encryption—, however, this initial primitive can be as simple as *noise*, which is an inherent property of any physical communication channel. More precisely, we have shown that OT can be realized in an unconditionally secure way from almost any discrete memoryless noisy channel. This result should be seen in the context of a number of recent results with the common objective to realize cryptographic functionalities in an unconditional way from simple primitives or weak assumptions.

A non-asymptotic analysis of the presented protocol — the concrete values of failure probability depending on the number of channel uses — is out of scope of this paper. Some non-asymptotic results for the particular case of BSC can be found in [15].

We propose as open problems to realize string OT with non-zero rate in the sense of [22]. A useful result in this context might be a generic reduction of string OT to bit OT based on privacy amplification [4]. Another open problem is to realize OT from more general channels, such as channels *with memory*, or to give a complete characterization with respect to the use of *general unfair channels* [11].

References

1. Bennett, C. H., Brassard, G., Crépeau, C., and Maurer, U. M.: Generalized privacy amplification. In: IEEE Transactions on Information Theory, Vol. 41, Num. 6. IEEE (1995) 1915–1923.
2. Bennett, C. H., Brassard, G., and Robert, J.-M.: Privacy amplification by public discussion. In: SIAM Journal on Computing, vol. 17 (1988) 210–229.

3. Brassard, G., Chaum, D., Crépeau, C.: Minimum disclosure proofs of knowledge. J. of Computer and System Sciences, 37(2). Elsevier (1988) 156–189.
4. Brassard, G., Crépeau, C., and Wolf, S.: Oblivious transfers and privacy amplification. In: *Journal of Cryptology*, vol. 16, no. 4 (2003) 219–237.
5. Cachin, C.: Entropy measures and unconditional security in cryptography. Ph. D. Thesis, ETH Zürich, Hartung-Gorre Verlag, Konstanz, 1997.
6. Crépeau, C.: Equivalence between two flavours of oblivious transfer. In: Advances in Cryptology–CRYPTO '87. Lecture Notes in Computer Science, Vol. 293. Springer-Verlag (1988) 350–354.
7. Crépeau, C., Kilian, J.: Achieving oblivious transfer using weakened security assumptions. In: Proc. 29th Annual Symposium on the Foundations of Computer Science. IEEE (1988) 42–52.
8. Crépeau, C.: Efficient cryptographic primitives based on noisy channels. In: Advances in Cryptology–EUROCRYPT '97. Lecture Notes in Computer Science, Vol. 1233. Springer-Verlag (1997) 306–317.
9. Carter, J.L., Wegman, M.N.: Universal classes of hash functions. J. of Computer and System Sciences, 18. Elsevier (1979) 143–154.
10. Csiszár, I., and Körner, J.: Broadcast channels with confidential messages. In: *IEEE Trans. on Information Theory*, Vol. 24 (1978) 339–348.
11. Damgård, I., Kilian, J., Salvail, L.: On the (im)possibility of basing bit commitment and oblivious transfer on weakened security assumptions. In: Advances in Cryptology–EUROCRYPT '99. LNCS, vol. 1592. Springer-Verlag (1999) 56–73.
12. Dziembowski, S. and Maurer, U. M.: Tight security proofs for the bounded-storage model. In: *Proceedings of STOC 2002* (2002) 341–350.
13. Even, S., Goldreich, O., and Lempel, A.: A randomized protocol for signing contracts. In: Proceedings of CRYPTO '82. Plenum Press (1983) 205–210.
14. Forney, G.D.: Concatenated codes. MIT Press (1966).
15. Korjik, V., Morozov, K.: Generalized oblivious transfer protocols based on noisy channels. In: Proc. Workshop MMM ACNS 2001. LNCS, vol. 2052. Springer-Verlag (2001) 219-229.
16. MacWilliams, F.J., Sloane, N.J.A.: The theory of error-correcting codes. North-Holland (1977).
17. Maurer, U. M., Conditionally-perfect secrecy and a provably-secure randomized cipher. In: *Journal of Cryptology*, Vol. 5, No. 1 (1992) 53–66.
18. Maurer, U. M.: Information-theoretic cryptography. In: *Advances in Cryptology - CRYPTO '99*, LNCS, Vol. 1666. Springer-Verlag. (1999) 47–64.
19. Rabin, M.O.: How to exchange secrets by oblivious transfer. Technical Memo TR-81, Aiken Computation Laboratory, Harvard University (1981).
20. Shannon, C. E.: Communication theory of secrecy systems. In: *Bell System Technical Journal*, Vol. 28 (1949) 656–715.
21. Stebila, D., Wolf, S.: Efficient oblivious transfer from any non-trivial binary-symmetric channel. In: International Symposium on Information Theory (ISIT) (2002) 293.
22. Winter, A., Nascimento, A.C.A., Imai, H.: Commitment capacity of discrete memoryless channels. In: Cryptography and Coding. LNCS, vol. 2898. Springer-Verlag (2003) 35–51.
23. Winter, A., Nascimento, A.C.A.: Oblivious transfer from any genuine noise. Unpublished manuscript (2004).
24. Wyner, A. D.: The wire-tap channel. In: *Bell System Technical Journal*, Vol. 54, No. 8 (1975) 1355–1387.

A Provably Secure Short Transitive Signature Scheme from Bilinear Group Pairs[1]

Siamak Fayyaz Shahandashti[†], Mahmoud Salmasizadeh[‡], and Javad Mohajeri[‡]

[†] School of Electrical Engineering, Sharif University of Technology, Tehran, Iran
siamak@ee.sharif.edu
http://ee.sharif.edu/~siamak

[‡] Electronic Research Center, Sharif University of Technology, Tehran, Iran
{salmasi, mohajer}@sharif.edu

Abstract. We present a realization of the transitive signature scheme based on the algebraic properties of bilinear group pairs. The scheme is proven secure, i.e. transitively unforgeable under adaptive chosen message attack, assuming hardness of the computational co-Diffie-Hellman problem in bilinear group pairs and the security of the underlying standard signature scheme under *known* message attack. Our scheme mostly conforms to previously designed schemes of Micali-Rivest and Bellare-Neven in structure; yet there are two contributions: firstly, we take advantage of bilinear group pairs which were previously used by Boneh, Lynn, and Shacham to build short signature schemes. Secondly, we show that a slight modification in previous definitions of the transitive signature relaxes the security requirement for the underlying standard signature from being secure under chosen message attack to being secure under known message attack; thus shorter and more efficient signatures can be chosen for the underlying standard signature. These two facts eventually yield to short transitive signatures with respect to both node and edge signature size.

1 Introduction

The concept of signature schemes with algebraic properties, later called *homomorphic* [12] or *algebraic* [11] signatures, was first introduced by Rivest in a series of talks [18]. These schemes allow an arbitrary entity to forge signatures on certain messages. Rivest mentioned that algebraic properties must not always be considered as a security threat for cryptosystems. For example, the multiplicative property of RSA function can be advantageous in certain applications. He also presented two design instances of such signature schemes: the *prefix aggregation signature scheme* and the *transitive signature scheme.*

A transitive signature is a scheme for signing vertices and edges of a dynamically growing, transitively closed graph. Transitive closure is the property of including any

---

[1] This research was supported in part by Iran Telecommunication Research Center (ITRC) grant #T/500/3649 through the School of Electrical Engineering, Sharif University of Technology.

C. Blundo and S. Cimato (Eds.): SCN 2004, LNCS 3352, pp.60–76, 2005.

edge if there is a path between two vertices of the two ends of the edge. Depending on the graph, the transitive signature can be directed or undirected. The problem of finding a directed transitive signature is still a challenging open problem. Therefore, the term "transitive signature" is now being used in literature in case of "undirected transitive signature". We will also use this notation through the paper.

A transitive signature has the property that *everyone* can forge a valid signature on the edge *AC* of a graph, knowing the signatures of two edges *AB* and *BC*. This *everyone* does not need to have knowledge of the secret key at all. He/She just knows the public information. Since the graph itself is transitively closed, this property cannot be counted as a deficiency in security. Furthermore, Rivest showed that this property can "provide efficiency for prover and verifier" in comparison with the use of standard signatures [18]. One obvious advantage is that by using a transitive signature, one must sign only $O(n)$ edges of a graph with size n in case of $O(n^2)$ standard signings [15].

To achieve another advantage, a transitive signature must have the property that the *composed* signature on the edge *AC* should be indistinguishable from the signature that could have been produced by the *original* signer on it. This allows the receiver of the signatures to reveal no extra information when presenting the composed signature on the edge *AC* to a third person. A distinguishable composed signature at least bears the information that some other node *B* is between nodes *A* and *C*.

Micali and Rivest introduced the first provably secure (undirected) transitive signature scheme in [15]. Their scheme's security is based on the infeasibility of solving the discrete logarithm problem. Later, Bellare and Neven introduced new schemes whose security proofs were based on the hardness of factoring and on the security of RSA under one-more-inversion [2]. More new schemes based on gap Diffie-Hellman groups also appear in the recent full version of their paper (See [3]).

The security of many recently designed cryptosystems is based on hardness of the computational Diffie-Hellman and co-Diffie-Hellman problems in the so called Gap-Diffie-Hellman (GDH) groups. A GDH group is a group in which decision Diffie-Hellman (DDH) problem is easy, while computational Diffie-Hellman (CDH) problem is hard to solve. Signature schemes with provable security, both in random oracle and in standard model, are designed by Boneh et al. (See [7] and [8].) using bilinear maps in GDH groups. Also many other encryption schemes, signatures (plain, blind, proxy, ring, undeniable, group ...), key agreement protocols (plain, authenticated, group ...), access control, etc. have been constructed based on bilinear maps (See [1] and [14]).

A bilinear map (See [6] for introduction.), also called *pairing*, is a mapping between groups in a way that is "consistent with the group structure of its arguments" [8]. In simple words, it is a mapping that has the linearity property with respect to both its arguments, i.e. there exists three operations $\circ$, $\bullet$, and $*$ such that for every g, h, x, and y we have

$$e(g \circ h, x) = e(g, x) * e(h, x) \text{ and } e(g, x \bullet y) = e(g, x) * e(g, y).$$

This property yields to some useful algebraic properties. Joux and Nguyen showed that an efficiently-computable bilinear map e provides a polynomial time algorithm for solving the decision co-Diffie-Hellman problem [13].

In this paper, we construct a transitive signature from bilinear maps and prove it secure under conventional security assumptions of such maps.

Our Contributions: The main valuable property of our design of the transitive signature scheme is that the signature size on a graph is *shorter* than those of previously designed transitive signatures. Short transitive signatures are useful to shorten the total graph signature size, and this will be vital especially when the size of the graph itself grows too big. It is also apparent that this occurs in many applications where it is needed to transmit a big graph, as graphs themselves are used to simplify understanding large amounts of information.

Our transitive signature is shorter than previous ones in two ways. Firstly, since we use bilinear group pairs to sign edges of a graph in our design as Boneh et al. did to design short signatures, all the discussions on how short the signature could be are still applicable here for edge signatures. For the detailed information, refer to the original paper [7]. Secondly, we propose a slightly modified new definition for transitive signatures, which relaxes the choice of the underlying signature scheme, making it more efficient in sense of signing and verification cost as well as signature length than many conventional signatures. This fact makes the signature on the nodes of the graph shorter and more efficient. We achieve this by showing that the security requirement for the underlying standard signature in our design is just being secure under *known* message attack, rather than adaptive ([3], [15]) or non-adaptive [19] *chosen* message attack for other schemes. Since both edge and node signature size are made shorter than previous schemes, eventually a very short transitive signature on the whole graph is resulted in!

Organization of the Paper: Section 2 is allotted to notations and definitions: In 2.1 we fix the notations we will use through the paper; 2.2 fetches the definitions of the transitive signature schemes and their security. In 2.3 we define the bilinear maps, bilinear group pairs, and their security assumptions. Finally in Section 3 a transitive signature is built using bilinear maps and also proven secure. The concluding remarks, acknowledgements, and references are followed then as usual.

2 Notations and Definitions

A review of notations and definitions used in the paper follows. We will give a mixture of the definitions of transitive signatures presented in [15], [2], and [16], which are all fundamentally the same. Then we will go through bilinear maps and define *bilinear group pairs*, as in [8].

2.1 Notations

All graphs in this paper are undirected. We will use small letters such as i, j, k for the nodes and a concatenation of two small letters (which are the two endpoints of an edge) such as ij, jk for the (undirected) edges of the graph. We will use σ for all signatures on both nodes and edges. The signature on a node i is shown as σ_i and a signature on an edge ij is shown as σ_{ij}. The expression

$$s \xleftarrow{R} S$$

means that a member s is randomly chosen from set S. The italic letter Z represents the set of integer numbers and hence

$$Z_p \text{ and } Z_p^*$$

are used for the additive and multiplicative groups modulo p. We also show the group operation with two operands g and h by $g \cdot h$ or simply by gh (as in multiplicative groups), and by g / h we mean the group operation done with the first operand and inverse of the second one (also, as in multiplicative groups).

2.2 Transitive Signature Schemes

Since, as formerly said, transitive signatures are schemes to authenticate transitively closed graphs. We first review the definition of transitive closure property in graphs.

Transitive Closure of a Graph [15]: Transitive closure of a graph $G = (V, E)$ is the graph $G^* = (V, E^*)$, such that (i,j) is an edge of G^* if and only if there is a path from i to j in G. If $G = G^*$, then we say that the graph G is transitively closed.

Standard Signature Scheme [10]: As a well-known definition, a standard signature scheme is a tuple of three algorithms $SS = (SKeyGen, SSig, Sverify)$ for key generation, signing and verifying. A pair of public and secret keys are generated as $(SPK, SSK) \leftarrow SKeyGen(1^k)$ and the signature is generated as $\sigma \leftarrow SSign(SSK, m)$ for a message m and verified valid as $\texttt{true} \leftarrow SVerify(SPK, m, \sigma)$. The signature is said to be secure against known message attack if no polynomial time adversary can forge a valid signature on a new message, knowing a list of message-signature pairs for some random messages, except with negligible probability in the security parameter k. Here, new message means a message not in the list the adversary is provided with. We denote the probability that adversary F' succeeds in forging a new message-signature pair for the standard signature SS through a known message attack by

$$Adv_{SS,F'}^{uf-kma}(k).$$

We also call the maximum advantage among all adversaries, polynomial time in k, the *insecurity function* of the standard signature SS through a known message attack and denote it by

$$InSec_{SS}^{uf-kma}(k).$$

SS is called secure under known message attack if and only if this function decreases faster than any polynomial in k.

Transitive Signature Scheme ([16] and [2]): An (undirected) transitive signature scheme, which utilizes a standard signature scheme $SS = (SKeyGen, SSign, SVerify)$, is a tuple of six algorithms $TS = (KeyGen, NCert, ESign, VCert, EVerify, Comp)$ such that:

- The algorithm *KeyGen* is the probabilistic *key generation* algorithm. It takes as input 1^k, where k is the security parameter, and calculates a pair (PK, SK) consisting of a *master* public key and a matching secret key. It also calculates a matching key pair (SPK, SSK) for the standard signature using *SKeyGen* algorithm. At last, it outputs the pair $(\,(PK, SK)\,,\,(SPK, SSK)\,)$.
- The *node certification* algorithm *NCert*, can be stateful, randomized, or both. It takes as input the master secret key SK, the standard signature secret key SSK, and a node number n, and produces a node name i and a pair (pk_i, sk_i) consisting of a public key (label) and a matching secret key (label) for node i. It then produces a

signature σ_i using *SSign* algorithm with signing key *SSK* and some message related to i and pk_i. The algorithm finally outputs $(i, (pk_i, sk_i), \sigma_i)$.

- The *edge signing* algorithm *ESign*, which could be stateful, randomized, or both, takes as input the master secret key *SK*, two nodes i and j, and the corresponding secret keys of the nodes sk_i and sk_j, and either computes a value called an *original* signature on edge ij, namely σ_{ij}, or fails.

- The deterministic *certificate verification* algorithm *VCert*, takes as input the standard public key *SPK* and the node certificate (i, pk_i, σ_i), checks the validity of the node certificate using algorithm *SVerify* with verification key *SPK* and returns the validity as a Boolean value.

- The deterministic *edge verification* algorithm *EVerify*, taking the master public key *PK*, two node public keys pk_i and pk_j, and a candidate signature σ_{ij} as input, returns a Boolean value representing the validity of σ_{ij} as a signature of edge ij relative to the public keys.

- The deterministic *composition* algorithm *Comp*, given as input the master public key *PK*, three node public keys pk_i, pk_j and pk_k, and two signatures σ_{ij} and σ_{jk} on nodes ij and jk, either returns a value σ_{ik} as a signature on node ik or fails.

This definition resembles the definitions of [15] and [2] in structure. We also used the ideas of [16]. The paradigm of node certification is used for the public node keys to be brought to others authenticated. By verifying the node certificate to be valid, one can obtain an authenticated message from the original signer saying: "Public key of node i is pk_i." To prove that an edge is in the signed graph, one has to present an *integrated signature* of an edge containing the certificates of its endpoints plus the edge signature and verification of the integrated signature involves verifying both parts. This issue seems to be uncovered in the definition of [16]; therefore we use a mixed definition of [2] and [16], which follows.

It is worth to mention the modification we made in previous definitions. Here, in our definition, we omitted the input i to the node certification algorithm and let the algorithm to choose the node name itself. We later show that by choosing i randomly, the relaxation in the security requirement for *SS* can be achieved. Besides, we know that the algorithm *NCert* is run when the original signer wants to add a new node to the signed graph or wants to recall a certificate. In such a time, there is no difference for the signer what the node name will be. Therefore our modification does not deprive the signer of an important capability, while providing the advantage of short node signatures.

Correctness of Transitive Signature Schemes [2]: As any signature scheme, an original signature is required to be valid with respect to its relative public keys. Furthermore the composition algorithm is required to always produce a valid signature, given as input two valid signatures, either original or composed ones.

Privacy of Transitive Signature Schemes: As stated before, to provide privacy, a valid composed signature must be indistinguishable from a valid original signature on the same edge, which could have been produced by the master signer [15]. This allows using composed signatures as the original ones. In transitive signature schemes whose *ESign* algorithm is deterministic, being indistinguishable reduces to being the same. This means that the composed signature must be equal to the original signature which could have been produced by the master signer.

Security of Transitive Signature Schemes ([15], [2], and [16]): A transitive signature scheme *TS* is called *transitively unforgeable under adaptive chosen message attack* if the advantage in attacking the scheme is negligible for any adversary *F* whose running time is polynomial in the security parameter *k*. The advantage of the best adversary is also known as *insecurity function* and is denoted by

$$InSec_{TS}^{tu-acma}(k).$$

The advantage of *F* in its attack on *TS* is the function defined as

$$Adv_{TS,F}^{tu-acma}(k) = \Pr\left[Exp_{TS,F}^{tu-acma}(k) = 1\right],$$

where the probability is taken over all the random choices made in experiment.

Associated to every transitive signature *TS* = *(KeyGen, NCert, ESign, VCert, Verify, Comp)*, adversary *F*, and security parameter *k* is an experiment, denoted

$$Exp_{TS,F}^{tu-acma}(k),$$

that returns 1 if and only if *F* is successful in its attack on the scheme and 0 otherwise. The experiment begins by running *KeyGen* on input 1^k to get key pair *(PK, SK)*. It then runs *F*, providing this adversary with input *PK* and oracle access to the function *ESign(SK, ·, ·, sk_i, sk_j)*, i.e. it can ask to add any new edge *ij* of its choice to the graph and have the signature σ_{ij} on it. Besides, *F* has a certain kind of limited oracle access to function *NCert(SK, SSK, ·)* such that it cannot have access to the part of algorithm output representing the node secret key, i.e. it can query the oracle on any node number *n* and have only the node name *i*, the public node key pk_i and the node signature σ_i. In other words, the adversary can ask to add any new node to the graph and have the certificate *(i, pk_i, σ_i)* on it. Eventually, *F* will output *i', $pk'_{i'}$, j', $pk'_{j'}$* and values $\sigma'_{i'}$, $\sigma'_{j'}$, and $\sigma'_{i'j'}$. Let *E* be the set of all edges such that *F* made oracle query to *ESign(SK, ·, ·, sk_i, sk_j)*, and let *V* be the set of all nodes which are endpoints of edges in *E*. We say that *F* wins if

$$VCert(i', pk'_{i'}, \sigma'_{i'}) = \text{true},$$
$$VCert(i', pk'_{i'}, \sigma'_{i'}) = \text{true},$$
$$EVerify(PK, pk'_{i'}, pk'_{j'}, \sigma'_{i'j'}) = \text{true},$$

and yet the edge *i'j'* is not in the transitive closure of the graph *G* = *(V, E)*. The experiment returns 1 if *F* wins and 0 otherwise.

2.3 GDH Groups, Bilinear Maps and Bilinear Group Pairs

Let us first review the formal definitions and notations of the well-known Diffie-Hellman problems. Resembling [7], we use the following notations: G_1 and G_2 are two (multiplicative) cyclic groups of prime order *p*, with respective generators of g_1 and g_2. By ψ we mean an isomorphism from G_2 to G_1 with $\psi(g_2) = g_1$. The definitions are simplified versions of those in [7].

Computational co-Diffie-Hellman (co-CDH) on (G_1, G_2): Given g_2, g_2^a in G_2 and *h* in G_1, compute h^a in G_1.

Decision co-Diffie-Hellman (co-DDH) on (G_1, G_2): Given g_2, g_2^a in G_2 and h, h^b in G_1, decide whether $a = b$ or not. When $a = b$ we call (g_2, g_2^a, h, h^b) a (valid) co-Diffie-Hellman *tuple*.

When $G_1 = G_2$ these problems reduce to standard CDH and DDH problems. The advantage of an algorithm A in solving the co-CDH problem on (G_1, G_2) is defined as the probability that A solves the problem correctly given a random instance of the problem specified by a randomly chosen pair for a and h. The probability is taken over the coin tosses of A and the random choices of a and h. We show this probability by

$$Adv_A^{co-CDH}.$$

The maximum advantage among all polynomial time algorithms solving co-CDH problem is also called *insecurity* of co-CDH and is denoted by $InSec^{co-CDH}$. Co-CDH is called hard if and only if its insecurity is negligible.

Co-GDH Group Pair: The group pair (G_1, G_2) is called a Gap co-Diffie-Hellman group pair if it satisfies the following properties:

1. The group operation on both groups and the map ψ can be computed in one time unit.
2. The co-DDH problem on (G_1, G_2) can be solved in one time unit.
3. The co-CDH problem is hard on (G_1, G_2).

In the above definition, if $G_1 = G_2$, then G_1 is said to be a GDH group.

Bilinear Maps: A function $e: G_1 \times G_2 \to G_T$, where $|G_1| = |G_2| = |G_T|$, is bilinear if it satisfies the two properties:

1. For every u in G_1 and every v in G_2, and all integers a and b, $e(u^a, v^b) = e(u,v)^{ab}$.
2. e is non-degenerate, i.e. $e(g_1,g_2) \neq 1$.

Bilinear Group Pair: Two order-p groups (G_1, G_2) are called a bilinear group pair if they satisfy the following properties:

1. The group operation on both groups and the map ψ can be computed in one time unit.
2. A group G_T of order p and a bilinear map $e: G_1 \times G_2 \to G_T$ exist and e is computable in one time unit.
3. The co-CDH is hard on (G_1, G_2).

Joux and Nguyen [13] showed that an efficiently computable bilinear map e provides an algorithm for solving the co-DDH problem as follows:

$$a = b \bmod p \quad \Leftrightarrow \quad e(h, g_2^a) = e(h^b, g_2).$$

As a consequence, if two groups are a bilinear group pair, then they are also a co-GDH group pair. The converse is probably not true [7].

3 A Transitive Signature on Bilinear Group Pairs (BGPTS)

We present a transitive signature scheme, based on the BLS signature ideas, that works in bilinear group pairs. We assume that we have a standard signature scheme *SS* = *(SKeyGen, SSign, SVerify)*, whose message space is the set of all strings made by concatenating a member of the definite set of all node names with a member of the group G_1. We construct the transitive signature scheme, using this standard signature and a bilinear group pair (G_1, G_2). At last, we prove our transitive signature scheme transitively secure under chosen message attack.

Let the bilinear group pair generator G_{BGP} as a randomized polynomial time algorithm that on input 1^k, where k is the security parameter, generates a bilinear group pair (G_1, G_2), where $|G_1| = |G_2| = p(k)$ and the insecurity of the co-CDH problem on (G_1, G_2) is the amount $InSec^{co\text{-}CDH}(k)$. It is obvious that for the group pair to be a bilinear one, this function must decrease faster than any polynomial in k. The formal description of the transitive signature *BGPTS* follows:

- The key generation algorithm *KeyGen*, takes an input 1^k, runs G_{BGP} on this value, and obtains the bilinear group pair (G_1, G_2). It then picks a random member of $Z_{p(k)}$, namely *SK*, and computes $PK \leftarrow g_2{}^{SK}$. The algorithm also runs *SKeyGen* on input 1^k to obtain a key pair *(SPK, SSK)* for the standard signature. At last, the algorithm outputs the group pair (G_1, G_2), the master key pair *(PK, SK)*, and the standard key pair *(SPK, SSK)*.
- The node certifications algorithm *NCert* maintains state *NodeList*, where *NodeList* is a list containing the set of all so-far queried nodes, their secret and public node keys (labels), and their signatures. On input *SK*, *SSK*, and node number n, the algorithm checks if n is on the list. If so, it outputs the corresponding node name, secret node key, and public node key and the corresponding node signature from *NodeList*. Otherwise, it picks a random member of the set of all node names, namely i, and also picks a random member of G_1, namely sk_i. The algorithm then computes $pk_i \leftarrow sk_i{}^{SK}$ and runs *SSign* on inputs *SSK* and the message $i \parallel pk_i$ and obtains σ_i. The algorithm then outputs the node name i and the pair (pk_i, sk_i) as the matching public and secret node keys followed by the node signature σ_i.
- The edge signing algorithm *Esign* takes as input sk_i and sk_j and simply outputs

$$\sigma_{ij} \leftarrow sk_i / sk_j \, .$$

- The certificate verification algorithm *VCert*, on input (i, pk_i, σ_i), runs *SVerify* and outputs $SVerify(SPK, i \parallel pk_i, \sigma_i)$.
- The verification algorithm *EVerify*, takes as input *PK*, pk_i, pk_j, and a candidate signature σ_{ij} and verifies that

$$\left(g_2, PK, \sigma_{ij}, pk_i / pk_j \right)$$

is a (valid) co-Diffie-Hellman tuple. If so, it returns true; if not, returns false.
- The composition algorithm *Comp*, given as input σ_{ij} and σ_{jk}, computes and outputs the value $\sigma_{ik} \leftarrow \sigma_{ij} \cdot \sigma_{jk}$.

Note that, sometimes, it is needed to have σ_{ij}, and sometimes σ_{ji} to compose signatures correctly. Yet since they are inverses of each other and inversion in the multiplicative group G_1 can be made in polynomial time, the transformations $\sigma_{ij} \leftrightarrow \sigma_{ji}$

are both feasible. Therefore, these transformations are omitted from the descriptions of the algorithms.

Eliminating State: As proposed in [2], state *NodeList* can be eliminated through using a pseudorandom function. The master secret key could include a key K to specify an instance F_K from a pseudorandom function family F. Then the signer does not need to save anything. He/She just uses $F_K(i)$ for all the coins needed for the node name and the node keys.

Correctness: It is easy to see that any original signature σ_{ij} produced by the master signer leads to a true output by the verification algorithm. On the other hand, any composed signature of two valid (original or composed) signatures leads to the same output in verification. The proof is up to the reader!

Privacy: The *ESign* algorithm of BGPTS scheme is deterministic. As the composed signature in BGPTS scheme is the same as the signature that could have been produced by the master signer, the privacy property requirement for the signature scheme is met.

Security: As an intuition, it is worth to see that a verifier of a signature σ_{ij} faces a co-DDH problem instance in a bilinear group pair, which is assumed to be easy. On the other side is a forger of the signature. If it wants to forge a signature on an edge, one of whose endpoints is not certified so far, it faces the problem of forging a valid signature for the standard signature scheme, which is infeasible by the assumption of the standard signature's security. Otherwise, it faces the problem of forging a signature on an edge whose endpoints are both certified by the master signer. In this case, it knows three arguments out of four of a tuple, namely g_2, *PK*, and pk_i / pk_j, and it wants to compute σ_{ij} so as the tuple be a valid Diffie-Hellman tuple. This is, obviously, a co-CDH problem instance in a bilinear group pair, which is assumed to be infeasible. The following theorem states that the BGPTS is transitively secure assuming that underlying primitives are flawless. Our method for proving the security of BGPTS is partly similar to Coron's method for proving that of FDH scheme in [9].

Security Theorem: The BGPTS scheme described above is transitively unforgeable under adaptive chosen message attack, assuming that G_{BGP} produces a bilinear group pair and standard signature scheme *SS* is unforgeable under known message attack. More precisely, if the most advantageous adversary asks a maximum of q' queries from the node certification oracle and a maximum of q queries from the edge signing oracle in attacking BGPTS, we have

$$\exp(1) \cdot q \cdot InSec^{co-CDH}(k) + InSec_{SS}^{uf-kma}(k) \geq InSec_{BGPTS}^{tu-acma}(k),$$

where k is the security parameter of the transitive signature input to the key generation algorithm. Furthermore, if we denote the running time of *SSign* and *Esign* algorithms by t_{SSign} and t_{ESign} and that of the best adversaries attacking BGPTS, SS, and co-CDH by t_{BGPTS}, t_{SS}, and t_{co-CDH}, we have

$$t_{BGPTS}(k) \geq \max\{t_{co-CDH}(k) - (q' + q) \cdot O(p^3(k)) - q' \cdot t_{SSign}(k),$$
$$t_{SS}(k) - q' \cdot O(p^3(k)) - q \cdot t_{ESign}(k)\}.$$

Proof Sketch: We will prove the security by reduction as follows. Given any polynomial time forger F for BGPTS asking at most q queries from the edge signing oracle, We will show how to use F to construct two algorithms: An algorithm A to solve the co-CDH problem in (G_1, G_2) and a forger F' breaking the underlying standard signature SS through a known message attack, such that

$$\alpha(q) \cdot Adv_A^{co-CDH}(k) + Adv_{SS,F'}^{uf-kma}(k) = Adv_{BGPTS,F}^{tu-acma}(k),$$

$$\text{where } \alpha(q) = \frac{1}{\left(1 - \dfrac{1}{q+1}\right)^{q+1}} \cdot q.$$

We must show that $\alpha(q)$ is bounded by a polynomial in q, and hence the coefficient $\alpha(q)$ grows polynomially in q, however the advantage of A in solving co-CDH decreases faster than any polynomial in k. This means that controlling k, we can keep the advantage of the adversary attacking BGPTS sufficiently low.

Note that we have

$$\lim_{q \to \infty} \frac{1}{\left(1 - \dfrac{1}{q+1}\right)^{q+1}} = e,$$

therefore $\alpha(q)$ can be bounded linearly in q, i.e. $\alpha(q) = O(q)$.

Since there could be more efficient ways to construct algorithms A and F', the equation

$$\exp(1) \cdot q \cdot InSec^{co-CDH}(k) + InSec_{SS}^{uf-kma}(k) \geq InSec_{BGPTS}^{tu-acma}(k)$$

is proven for large q.

The full description of how the two algorithms A and F' are constructed comes in the full proof of the security theorem in the appendix. We just mention that in the proof, techniques of proving security in [2], [7], and [9] are mixed together.

As in [2], we show that signatures for BGPTS can be forged in only two ways: either there is the forgery that "recycles node certificates from previously issued signatures", or there is the forgery that "includes at least one new node certificate". We will show that the former type of forgery leads us to solve a certain co-CDH problem with a certain probability of success, while a forgery of the latter type can be easily transformed to an attack on SS: the new node certificate is a valid forgery for SS, as it contains a standard node signature that was not produced by the original signer before.

In simulating $NCert$ algorithm, when algorithm A is answering oracle queries made by F, we use the technique of [7]. We simply embed the h argument of our co-CDH instance in some simulated node public keys, while choosing other simulated node public keys randomly. We call the former type of nodes h-node and the latter non-h-node. Then, similar to [7] again, A can answer F's $ESign$ oracle queries only when the edge endpoints are nodes of a type, and succeeds in solving the co-CDH instance it has only when the edge endpoints of the forgey provided by F are nodes of different types.

To get the best success probability in our attack, we use the technique of [9]. We just embed the h argument in simulated node public keys with a certain probability p_0, and choose other simulated node public keys randomly with probability $1 - p_0$. This leads us to maximize A's success probability and hence optimize the security by carefully selecting p_0 with respect to q. The function $\alpha(q)$ is originally an optimized version of a function of two arguments q and p_0 minimized with respect to p_0.

As a time domain analysis, since both t_{SS} and t_{co-CDH} grow faster than any polynomial in k, assuming the standard signature secure and the co-CDH problem hard, the time complexity for the best adversary attacking BGPTS also grows faster than any polynomial in k, for the reason that other subtractive terms in the time complexity equation above are polynomial in k.

We refer the reader to the appendix of this paper for the full description of the proof.

Eliminating Node Certification via Hashing: As stated comprehensively in [2], node certification brings us the disadvantages of "increasing the signature size as well as the computational cost for signing and verifying". Resembling [2], we can eliminate node certificates by specifying the public key of the node i via the output of a hash function by

$$i \| pk_i \leftarrow H(i)$$

and then setting

$$sk_i \leftarrow pk_i^{1/SK}.$$

This provides an "implicit authentication" [2] of node public keys, i.e. there is no need for the original signer to certify nodes anymore. As a consequence, the node certification algorithm collapses to node key generation and the certificate verification algorithm will no more exist. This means that there will be no further need for the standard signature to sign node public keys and verifying them. Fully-described changes in BGPTS are routine and similar to [2] and therefore are omitted here. It is just worth to state that the security of the new scheme relies on the hardness of the co-CDH problem in bilinear group pairs, in the so called *random oracle model (ROM)*. In this model, hash functions are viewed as random functions (See [4] and [5] for further on ROM.).

4   Conclusions

We have constructed a short transitive signature scheme from bilinear maps whose security is proven under reasonable assumptions, such as hardness of the computational Diffie-Hellman problem and existence of secure standard signatures. Shortness of an edge signature is due to the fact of using bilinear group pairs with small representations and that of a node signature is due to the fact of using signatures which are required to be secure only under known message attack. These two, eventually, yield to a very short signature on the whole graph, which is very probable to have a big size in everyday applications. This fact, finally, results in a lower amount of communication traffic load.

Acknowledgement

We firstly thank the anonymous reviewers of the SCN'04 conference for their precious comments. In fact, the idea of eliminating node certification via hashing was a simultaneous idea of a reviewer and the authors. Afterwards, we would like to thank Taraneh Eghlidos for the support and encouragement she gave and Iman Mosavat for helpful discussions, as well. We also thank Mofid Nakhaei, Sara Zaeemdar, and Ebrahim Hedayati for their carefully reading the text and proposing editions.

References

1. P. Barreto. "The Pairing-Based Crypto Lounge" Web Page.
    http://planeta.terra.com.br/informatica/paulobarreto/pblounge.html.
2. M. Bellare and G. Neven. "Transitive Signatures Based on Factoring and RSA". Asiacrypt 2002. LNCS Vol. 2501. Springer-Verlag. 2002.
3. M. Bellare and G. Neven. "Transitive Signatures: New Schemes and Proofs". Cryptology ePrint Archive: Report 2004/215. *http://eprint.iacr.org/2004/215/.* Also at *http://www.cse.ucsd.edu/users/mihir/.* (Full version of [2]).
4. M. Bellare and P. Rogaway. "Random Oracles Are Practical: A Paradigm for Designing Efficient Protocols". The First Annual Conference on Computer and Communications Security. ACM 93. 1993.
    Full Paper: *http://www-cse.ucsd.edu/users/mihir.*
5. M. Bellare and P. Rogaway. "The Exact Security of Digital Signatures – How to Sign with RSA and Rabin". Eurocrypt 96. LNCS Vol. 1070. Springer-Verlag. 1996.
    Full Paper: *http://www-cse.ucsd.edu/users/mihir.*
6. D. Boneh, M. Franklin. "Identity Based Encryption from the Weil Pairing". SIAM Journal of Computing Vol. 32 No. 3 pp. 586-615. Extended Abstract in Crypto 2001.
    Full Paper: *http://crypto.stanford.edu/~dabo/pubs.html.*
7. D. Boneh, B. Lynn, and H. Shacham. "Short Signatures from the Weil Pairing". Asiacrypt 2001. LNCS Vol. 2248. Springer-Verlag. 2001.
    Revised Full Paper: *http://crypto.stanford.edu/~dabo/pubs.html.*
8. D. Boneh, I. Mironov, and V. Shoup. "A Secure Signature Scheme from Bilinear Maps". CT-RSA 2003. LNCS Vol. 2612. Springer-Verlag. 2003.
    Full Paper: *http://crypto.stanford.edu/~dabo/pubs.html.*
9. J. S. Coron. "On the Exact Security of Full Domain Hash". Crypto 2000. LNCS Vol. 1880. Springer-Verlag. 2000.
    http://www.gemplus.com/smart/r_d/publications/pdf/Cor00fdh.pdf.
10. S. Goldwasser, S. Micali, and R. Rivest. "A digital signature scheme secure against adaptive chosen-message attacks". SIAM Journal of Computing Vol. 17 No. 2 April 1988 pp. 281-308.
    http://theory.lcs.mit.edu/~rivest/publications.html.
11. A. Hevia and D. Micciancio. "The Provable Security of Graph-Based One-Time Signatures and Extensions to Algebraic Signature Schemes". Asiacrypt 2002. LNCS Vol. 2501. Springer-Verlag. 2002.
    http://www.cs.ucsd.edu/~ahevia/publications/hm02.pdf.
12. R. Johnson, D. Molnar, D. Song, and D. Wagner. "Homomorphic Signature Schemes". CT-RSA 2002. LNCS Vol. 2271. Springer-Verlag.
    http://citeseer.nj.nec.com/460118.html.
13. A. Joux and K. Nguyen. "Separating Decision Diffie-Hellman from Computational Diffie-Hellman in Cryptographic Groups". Journal of Cryptology Vol. 16 No. 4 pp. 239-247 Sep. 2003. A previous version also available online: "Separating Decision Diffie-Hellman from Diffie-Hellman in Cryptographic Protocols". Cryptology ePrint Archive. Report 2001/003.
    http://eprint.iacr.org/2001/003.

14. H. Lipma0a. "Pairing-based Cryptography" Web Page on Cryptology Pointers.
    http://www.tcs.hut.fi/~helger/crypto/link/public/pairing/.
15. S. Micali and R. Rivest. "Transitive Signature Schemes". CT-RSA 2002. LNCS Vol. 2271.
    Springer-Verlag.
    http://citeseer.nj.nec.com/micali02transitive.html.
16. D. Molnar. "Homomorphic Signature Schemes". BA Thesis, Computer Science Dept.
    Harvard College. Cambridge. Massachusetts. Michael Rabin adv. 2003.
    http://www.cs.berkeley.edu/~dmolnar/papers/papers.html.
17. G. Neven. "Provably secure identity-based identification schemes and transitive
    signatures". Ph.D. thesis. Katholieke Universiteit Leuven, Belgium. May 2004.
    http://www.cs.kuleuven.ac.be/~gregory/papers/phd.html.
18. R. Rivest. "Two New Signature Schemes". Slides from Talk Given at Cambridge
    University. 2000.
    http://www.cl.cam.ac.uk/Research/Security/seminars/2000/rivest-tss.pdf.
19. Z. Sujing. "Transitive Signatures Based on Non-adaptive Standard Signatures".
    Cryptography ePrint Archive. Report 2004/044. *http://eprint.iacr.org.*

Appendix: Proof of Security Theorem

Suppose we are given a feasible forger F for BGPTS. We will show how to use F to construct an algorithm A to solve the co-CDH problem in (G_1, G_2) and a forger F' breaking the underlying standard signature SS through a known message attack, such that

$$\alpha(q) \cdot Adv_A^{co-CDH}(k) + Adv_{SS,F'}^{uf-kma}(k) = Adv_{BGPTS,F}^{tu-acma}(k),$$

where q is the number of $ESign$ queries F makes during its attack on BGPTS and

$$\alpha(q) = \frac{1}{\left(1 - \dfrac{1}{q+1}\right)^{q+1}} \cdot q.$$

Note that for every q we have

$$2q < \alpha(q) \le 4q.$$

Hence, the forger's advantage grows linearly in q, but it descends faster than any polynomial in k. Therefore is proven the security of BGPTS.

Algorithm A performs as follows: given g_2, $u = g_2^a$ in G_2 and h in G_1 as input, it computes h^a in G_1. It maintains state $State$ in which it saves the data it will need later through the algorithm run, such as queries made by F and A's corresponding answers. Using this state A can simply answer repeated queries by repeated answers and just calculate answers to *new* queries. It first generates a fresh key pair *(SPK, SSK)* for SS using the algorithm $SKeyGen$. Then It computes $v = \psi(u)$, which will be used later. Note that since ψ is assumed to be an isomorphism, we have:

$$v = \psi(u) = \psi(g_2^a) = \psi(g_2)^a = g_1^a.$$

Then the algorithm A runs F on input $PK = u \cdot g_2^r = g_2^{a+r}$, where r is chosen randomly from Z_p by algorithm A. Now F will start its $ESign(SK, \cdot, \cdot, sk_i, sk_j)$ and $NCert(SK, SSK, \cdot)$ oracle queries. As A does not know SK it cannot answer the queries by simply running the *ESign* and *NCert* algorithms. Therefore it will simulate these two algorithms as follows.

On an *NCert(SK, SSK, ·)* query for adding a new node n and certifying it, algorithm A first chooses a random node name i from the set of all node names and a random b_i from Z_p. Then it produces a random coin $c_i \in \{0,1\}$, where $c_i = 0$ with probability p_0 and $c_i = 1$ with probability $1 - p_0$. The value p_0 is a fixed probability chosen to get a better reduction (idea from [9]) and will be determined later in this paper. If $c_i = 0$ it sets $pk_i \leftarrow h \cdot g_1^{b_i}$. Otherwise it sets $pk_i \leftarrow g_1^{b_i}$. At last it answers to the query by outputting three values representing the name i, the public key pk_i and the certification signature $\sigma_i = SSign(SSK, i \parallel pk_i)$ of the corresponding node. It also saves the values i, b_i, and c_i for the node n by updating its state *State*. Note that since b_i is random, both $h \cdot g_1^{b_i}$ and $g_1^{b_i}$ are randomly distributed over G_1 and are indistinguishable for the algorithm F from each other and from a real public node key which could have been produced by a real signer. Therefore the simulation is flawless and also F has no idea what c_i could be for a node i.

Before we describe how to simulate answers to *ESign* queries, we introduce a notation we will use in the description. We simply call a node i an "h-node" if $c_i = 0$ and call it a "non-h-node" otherwise. We also assume that when the algorithm F queries its *ESign* oracle on the edge ij it has already queried its *NCert* oracle on nodes named i and j for their certificate. This assumption can be justified since any node name i and the corresponding node keys are chosen independently. Moreover the edge signature is also independent of any single node key. As a result, if at least one of the nodes is not queried before for its certificate, the answer to the *ESign* query will be just a random value independent of other things F knows and will be of no use for it.

On an *ESign(SK, ·, ·, sk_i, sk_j)* query for signing the edge ij of the graph, Algorithm A looks in *State* to recognize one the two possible cases bellow:

1. If i and j are nodes of a type, i.e. both are non-h-nodes or both are h-nodes, then A simply answers the query as $\sigma_{ij} = \left(v \cdot g_1^r\right)^{b_i - b_j}$.

2. If one of i and j is an h-node and the other one is a non-h-node, then A reports failure and terminates.

Note that in the first case we have:

$$\sigma_{ij} = \left(v \cdot g_1^r\right)^{b_i - b_j} = \left(g_1^a \cdot g_1^r\right)^{b_i - b_j} = \left(g_1^{b_i - b_j}\right)^{a+r} \text{ and } pk_i / pk_j = g_1^{b_i - b_j}.$$

Hence the tuple $(g_2, PK = g_2^{a+r}, pk_i / pk_j, \sigma_{ij})$ is a valid co-Diffie-Hellman tuple and σ_{ij} is a valid signature for edge ij. Therefore the simulation works properly.

Finally F will output a forgery including i', $pk'_{i'}$, j', $pk'_{j'}$ and values $\sigma'_{i'}$, $\sigma'_{j'}$, and $\sigma'_{i'j'}$. A will use this output to solve the co-GDH problem, assuming that F manages to win, i.e. manages to forge valid signatures. More precisely, let E is the set of all edges such that F made an *ESign* oracle query on, and let V be the set of all nodes which are endpoints of edges in E. Winning for F means that:

$$\Sigma_1: VCert(i', pk'_{i'}, \sigma'_{i'}) = \texttt{true},$$
$$\Sigma_2: VCert(i', pk'_{i'}, \sigma'_{i'}) = \texttt{true},$$
$$\Sigma_3: EVerify(PK, pk'_{i'}, pk'_{j'}, \sigma'_{i'j'}) = \texttt{true},$$

and yet Σ_4: the edge $i'j'$ is not in the transitive closure of the graph $G = (V, E)$.

We call these statements Σ_1, Σ_2, Σ_3, and Σ_4, respectively. The statement Σ_3 specifically means that $(g_2, PK = g_2^{a+r}, pk'_{i'} / pk'_{j'}, \sigma'_{i'j'})$ is a valid co-Diffie-Hellman tuple, i.e.

$$\sigma'_{i'j'} = \left(pk'_{i'} / pk'_{j'} \right)^{a+r}.$$

Algorithm A now checks that if the node public keys returned by F match those it produced itself or not, i.e. it checks the statements Σ_5 introduced bellow:

$$\Sigma_5: pk'_{i'} = pk_{i'} \text{ and } pk'_{j'} = pk_{j'}.$$

If Σ_5 is not true Algorithm A reports failure and terminates. Otherwise, it checks *State* to find out if i' and j' are nodes of a type. If so, A reports failure and terminates. Otherwise, there are two possibilities:
1. i' is an h-node and j' is a non-h-node. In this case, as we have:

$$\sigma'_{i'j'} = \left(h \cdot g_1^{b_{i'}} / g_1^{b_{j'}} \right)^{a+r}.$$

So A simply computes and outputs h^a as:

$$h^a = \sigma'_{i'j'} / \left(h^r \cdot g_1^{r(b_{i'} - b_{j'})} \cdot v^b \right).$$

2. i' is a non-h-node and j' is an h-node. In this case, as we have:

$$\sigma'_{i'j'} = \left(g_1^{b_{i'}} / h \cdot g_1^{b_{j'}} \right)^{a+r}.$$

So A simply computes and outputs h^a as:

$$h^a = \left(g_1^{r(b_{i'} - b_{j'})} \cdot v^b \right) / \left(h^r \cdot \sigma'_{i'j'} \right).$$

For calculating the success probability of the algorithm A, we observe that it succeeds whenever it does not report failure. First, if F asks q queries from its oracle *ESign*, algorithm A can answer all the q queries with probability $[p_0^2 + (1 - p_0)^2]^q$. This is true for the reason that, in each query, two nodes i and j are both h-nodes with probability p_0^2 and are both non-h-nodes with probability $(1 - p_0)^2$. Secondly, F will succeed in case that the nodes i' and j' are of two different types. The probability that this occurs is $2 p_0 (1 - p_0)$. In these calculations we used the fact that simulation is correct, i.e. h-nodes and non-h-nodes are indistinguishable.

Finally, by defining $\beta(q, p_0) = 2 p_0 (1 - p_0) [p_0^2 + (1 - p_0)^2]^q$, we can calculate the advantage of algorithm A with respect to the advantage of algorithm F as follows:

$$Adv_A^{co-CDH}(k) = \beta(q, p_0) \cdot \Pr\left[\bigwedge_{t=1}^{5} \Sigma_t \right]$$

$$= \beta(q, p_0) \cdot \Pr\left[\Sigma_5 \mid \bigwedge_{t=1}^{4} \Sigma_t \right] \cdot \Pr\left[\bigwedge_{t=1}^{4} \Sigma_t \right]$$

$$= \beta(q, p_0) \cdot \Pr\left[\Sigma_5 \mid \bigwedge_{t=1}^{4} \Sigma_t \right] \cdot Adv_{BGPTS,F}^{tu-acma}(k).$$

Algorithm F' is given SPK as input and a list of random messages and corresponding signatures. It will perform a known message attack on SS using F as a subroutine. Its goal is to eventually output a message-signature pair, where the signature is a valid signature for the message with respect to SPK and yet the message was not on the message-signature list provided for the adversary.

The algorithm F' first runs the algorithm $KeyGen$ of the transitive signature to obtain a pair of keys (PK, SK). It then runs F on input PK and answers the queries of F to the oracles $ESign(SK, \cdot, \cdot, sk_i, sk_j)$ and $NCert(SK, SSK, \cdot)$ as follows:

On an $NCert(SK, SSK, \cdot)$ query n, F' first chooses the n-th entry in the message-signature pair list. It then parses the corresponding message as $i \parallel pk_i$. Afterwards, it computes sk_i as

$$sk_i \leftarrow pk_i^{1/SK}.$$

It also sets the corresponding signature as σ_i. Note that as messages in the message-signature pair list are randomly chosen, both i and pk_i are random and hence is sk_i. Therefore, the simulation works correctly. Moreover, the probability that the node name is repeated in the list is a small *constant* value and we do not take it into account. The reason is that the size of the set of all node names is constant and independent of the security parameter k.

On an $ESign(SK, \cdot, \cdot, sk_i, sk_j)$ query on edge ij, assuming that F has previously queried the two certificates on both nodes, F' looks i and j up in the message-signature pair list and finds the corresponding public and secret node keys. Now, since F' knows SK, sk_i, and sk_j, it simply runs the $ESign$ algorithm of the transitive signature scheme and provides the output σ_{ij} as the answer to the query.

Eventually, F outputs a forgery including i', $pk'_{i'}$, j', $pk'_{j'}$ and values $\sigma'_{i'}$, $\sigma'_{j'}$, and $\sigma'_{i'j'}$. Assuming that F wins, i.e. the statements $\Sigma_1, \Sigma_2, \Sigma_3$, and Σ_4 are all true, F' checks that if the node public keys returned by F match those it produced itself or not, i.e. it checks the statements Σ_5. If Σ_5 is true Algorithm F' reports failure and terminates. Otherwise, at least one of $pk'_{i'}$, $pk'_{j'}$ was not certificated by F' before. In other words, at least one of $i' \parallel pk'_{i'}$ and $j' \parallel pk'_{j'}$ is not a message in the message-signature pair list. Therefore, at least one of the signatures $\sigma'_{i'}$ and $\sigma'_{j'}$ must be a forgery, and is obviously a valid one because Σ_1 and Σ_2 are both true. Hence, all F' has to do is to test whether the string $i' \parallel pk'_{i'}$ is not a message in the list and output $(i' \parallel pk'_{i'}, \sigma'_{i'})$ as a new message-signature pair representing forgery if so, or output $(j' \parallel pk'_{j'}, \sigma'_{j'})$ otherwise.

Algorithm F' succeeds whenever all the statements $\Sigma_1, \Sigma_2, \Sigma_3$, and Σ_4 are true, but Σ_5 is not true. This fact yields to the calculation bellow:

$$Adv_{SS,F'}^{uf-kma}(k) = \Pr\left[\left(\bigwedge_{t=1}^{4}\Sigma_t\right) \wedge \overline{\Sigma_5}\right]$$

$$= \Pr\left[\overline{\Sigma_5} \mid \bigwedge_{t=1}^{4}\Sigma_t\right] \cdot \Pr\left[\bigwedge_{t=1}^{4}\Sigma_t\right]$$

$$= \Pr\left[\overline{\Sigma_5} \mid \bigwedge_{t=1}^{4}\Sigma_t\right] \cdot Adv_{BGPTS,F}^{tu-cma}(k)$$

$$= \left(1 - \Pr\left[\Sigma_5 \mid \bigwedge_{t=1}^{4}\Sigma_t\right]\right) \cdot Adv_{BGPTS,F}^{tu-acma}(k).$$

By eliminating the repeating term in the two calculations we did for the success probability of A and F', we will simply reach the equation:

$$\frac{1}{\beta(q,p_0)} \cdot Adv_A^{co-CDH}(k) + Adv_{SS,F'}^{uf-kma}(k) = Adv_{BGPTS,F}^{tu-acma}(k).$$

To optimize the security, we must maximize the function $\beta(q, p_0)$ by properly selecting p_0 with respect to a given q. Let's rewrite $\beta(q, p_0)$ as:

$$\beta(q,p_0) = 2p_0(1-p_0)\left[p_0^2 + (1-p_0)^2\right]^q$$
$$= 2p_0(1-p_0)\left[1 - 2p_0(1-p_0)\right]^q$$

Defining $p_1 = 2p_0(1-p_0)$ we have

$$\beta(q,p_1) = p_1(1-p_1)^q.$$

The above function is maximized as below:

$$\frac{\partial \beta}{\partial p_1} = 0 \Rightarrow p_1 = \frac{1}{1+q}$$

$$\Rightarrow 2p_0(1-p_0) = \frac{1}{1+q}$$

$$\Rightarrow p_0 = \frac{1}{2} \pm \sqrt{\frac{1}{4}\frac{q-1}{q+1}}.$$

Now $\alpha(q)$ is defined and computed as

$$\alpha(q) = \frac{1}{\max\limits_{p_0}\{\beta(q,p_0)\}} = \frac{1}{\left(1 - \frac{1}{q+1}\right)^{q+1}} \cdot q$$

which is the result we were seeking.

The running time of A equals that of F plus one exponentiation and one $SSig$ algorithm run for every $NCert$ query plus one exponentiation for every $ESign$ query, i.e.

$$t_A(k) = t_F(k) + q' \cdot \left(O\left(p^3(k)\right) + t_{SSign}(k)\right) + q \cdot O\left(p^3(k)\right),$$

for that there are at most q' $NCert$ queries and at most q $ESign$ queries and modular exponentiation time complexity is cubic in group size.

The running time of F' equals that of F plus one exponentiation for every $NCert$ query plus one $ESign$ algorithm run for every $ESign$ query, i.e.

$$t_{F'}(k) = t_F(k) + q' \cdot O\left(p^3(k)\right) + q \cdot t_{ESign}(k),$$

for that there are at most q' $NCert$ queries and at most q $ESign$ queries.

Since there could be more efficient ways to construct algorithms A and F', the claimed equation for the time complexity is proven.

Group Signatures with Separate and Distributed Authorities

Jun Furukawa and Shoko Yonezawa

NEC Corporation
1753, Shimonumabe, Nakahara-Ku, Kawasaki, Kanagawa 211-8666, Japan
j-furukawa@ay.jp.nec.com, s-yonezawa@da.jp.nec.com

Abstract. We propose a new group signature scheme that simultaneously provides the following two properties : (1) the membership authority is able to add a user but not to identify an actual signer, while the tracing authority is able to identify the actual signer but not to add a user, (2) for further decentralization, these two authorities are respectively distributed among multiple entities in a manner efficient enough for practical applications. Previous group signature schemes have only offered one or the other of these two properties. Further, we formalize the security properties

1   Introduction

A group signature scheme, first proposed by Chaum and van Heyst [8] and followed by [7, 6, 1, 2], allows a group member who has registered with the group to sign messages on behalf of a group without revealing his own identity. One notable feature of the group signature scheme is the existence of an authority that can identify this actual signer. In recent group signature schemes, this authority, known as a *group manager*, also had the ability to add a user to a group. Such centralization of power in a single entity, however, was considered undesirable.

To solve this problem, Kilian and Petrank proposed in [11] to separate these roles into a *membership manager*, who would add new members to a group, and a *tracing manager*, who would identify actual signers. Many similar separate-role group signature schemes [6, 1] followed. We believe that it is even more preferable if the capabilities of the membership manager and the tracing manager can be efficiently distributed, respectively. In this sense, the schemes in [6, 1] do not meet our goal, as the secret keys used by the membership manager in these schemes are based on RSA. Namely, in case the RSA-based scheme is used, authorities should collaboratively generate an RSA modulus in a setup process with its prime factors kept secret to all the authorities, which would not be efficiently computable. Moreover, in a process of member addition, it would take large computation for distributed membership managers every time a new user is added. By way of contrast, in the scheme proposed in [2, 12], the secret key for adding a new member is a discrete logarithm of a public key. Therefore the approach of [2, 12] seems promising because distribution could be efficiently executed by using the method proposed in [15]. Unfortunately, the

C. Blundo and S. Cimato (Eds.): SCN 2004, LNCS 3352, pp. 77–90, 2005.

group signature scheme as is presented in [2] does not achieve separation of the membership manager and the tracing manager since, in the scheme in [2], a resulting group signature contains the value which is the output of a deterministic function. Then, those who knows all membership certificates can identify the actual signer of the group signature from the value even if they do not know secret information for tracing. Thus, the scheme in [2] does not achieve separation of authorities. As to [12], the proposed scheme turns out to be insecure [1]. Therefore, none of the scheme suites for separation and distribution of the authorities, and the scheme that achieves separation of the above two authorities and distribution of both capabilities is desired.

In this paper, we give a first group signature scheme that achieves both separation and efficient distribution of the membership manager and the tracing manager. In our scheme, the membership manager uses the Nyberg-Rueppel signature scheme [13] to provide a group member with the ability to create a group signature, and the tracing manager uses the ElGamal cryptosystem to trace the actual signer. Both of these primitives are well-suited to distributed computations, and authority-distribution on our scheme carried out efficiently. Moreover, in our proposed scheme, a signer creates a perfectly hiding commitment of a membership certificate instead of a deterministic function in [2]. This prevents the membership manager from identifying the signer from the signature, thus separation is achieved. The price we pay for simultaneously achieving separation and distribution is the increase in signature length and in computational costs, which is about 4.5 times larger than that of [2].

In this paper, we also formalize the conditions required for security in the group signature scheme in which authorities are both initially separated. The security definitions proposed in Bellare et al. [4] only apply to the case in which all duties of group management are performed by a single manager, and that manager is assumed to be honest. In contrast to this, we formalize our security definition in such a way that (1) neither the tracing manager nor any other entity can add a new member, (2) neither the membership manager nor any other entity can trace an actual signer, and (3) these two managers cannot, even in collusion, create a group signature that would appear to be traceable to an individual group manager. The security of our proposed scheme can be proved in the random oracle and generic model.

2   The Model

In this section, we present a model of our group signature scheme and its security definitions. Note that no previous work has specified security definitions for the case in which a membership manager and a tracing manager act independently of one another.

---

[1] In [12], finding $(r, x, y) \in Z_P \times Z_q^2$ satisfying $ry^r h^x f^y = 1 \bmod P$ is claimed to be difficult, where $P = pq$ and $h^q = y^q = f^q = 1 \bmod P$. However, $r_q := r \bmod q = 1$ holds since $y = h = f = 1 \bmod q$ and finding $r_p \in Z_p^*$ such that $r_p y^{r_q} h^x f^y = 1 \bmod p$ is clearly easy. Hence, from $r \bmod p = r_p$ and $r \bmod q = 1$, we have desired (r, x, y).

2.1   Model of Group Signature Schemes

Our model contains three main entity types: a membership manager (MM), a tracing manager (TM), and group members. The MM is able to add a new member to his group by using a secret key which he generates. More specifically, when a user applies for membership, the MM will conduct a joining procedure together with that user. In completing this procedure, the user will obtain the information which will be required to create a group signature. Such information can only be provided by the MM since the secret key of MM is required to generate it. The MM will subsequently publish these information issued to users. These information would be required for the TM to identify the actual signer of a group signature. The TM is able to identify the actual signer of a given group signature by using a secret generated by himself.

The following is the formalization of our group signature scheme model.

Definition 1. *A group signature scheme $\mathcal{GS}$ consists of the following six algorithms, (KEYGEN-M, KEYGEN-T, JOIN, SIGN, VERIFY, TRACE):*

- *A probabilistic key generation algorithm for the MM, KEYGEN-M(1^k) $\rightarrow$ (mpk, msk), where mpk is the membership public key, msk is the membership secret key, and mpk includes domain parameters.*
- *A probabilistic key generation algorithm for TM, KEYGEN-T(1^k, mpk) $\rightarrow$ (tpk, tsk), where tpk is the tracing public key, and tsk is the tracing secret key.*
- *An interactive member registration protocol for the MM and a user U, JOIN = ⟨JOIN-MM(U, mpk, $\mathcal{L}$, msk), JOIN-U(U, mpk, $\mathcal{L}$)⟩ $\rightarrow$ ($\mathcal{L}$, (cert$_U$, sk$_U$)). The MM outputs a list of all group members $\mathcal{L} = \{⟨U, \text{cert}_U⟩\}_U$. Here, we assume that a tuple $⟨U, \text{cert}_U⟩$ in $\mathcal{L}$ can be confirmed to have been generated by U. The public output of U is a membership certificate cert$_U$, and the secret output of U is a group signing key sk$_U$ corresponding to cert$_U$.*
- *A probabilistic signature generation algorithm for a user U, SIGN(mpk, tpk, cert$_U$, sk$_U$, m) $\rightarrow$ gs, which outputs a group signature gs on a message m.*
- *A deterministic signature verification algorithm for any verifier, VERIFY(mpk, tpk, m, gs) returns either 1 or 0. We say that a group signature gs on m is valid if VERIFY(mpk, tpk, m, gs) = 1.*
- *A deterministic signer tracing algorithm for the TM, TRACE (mpk, tpk, tsk, m, gs, $\mathcal{L}$) $\rightarrow$ (U, proof), where proof assures the validity of the result U. If the algorithm cannot find the actual signer in $\mathcal{L}$, the algorithm outputs $\perp$.*

Let us next define the correctness of a group signature scheme. Informally, a group signature scheme is correct if a group signature generated by a group member is valid and the actual signer is identified by the tracing algorithm.

Definition 2. *(correctness) A group signature scheme $\mathcal{GS}$ = (KEYGEN-M, KEYGEN-T, JOIN, SIGN, VERIFY, TRACE) is correct if, for all (mpk, msk) generated by KEYGEN-M, all (tpk, tsk) generated by KEYGEN-T, all (cert$_U$, sk$_U$) generated by JOIN, all $m \in \{0,1\}^*$, and $\mathcal{L}$, the following properties holds:*

1. $\mathsf{VERIFY}(mpk, tpk, m, \mathsf{SIGN}(mpk, tpk, cert_U, sk_U, m)) = 1$
2. $\mathsf{TRACE}(mpk, tpk, tsk, m, \mathsf{SIGN}(mpk, tpk, cert_U, sk_U, m), \mathcal{L}) = (U, proof)$

2.2   Security Definitions

In this section, we describe the security definitions of a group signature scheme that includes separation of authorities. We define one security notion for each type of entities in the model. With respect to the MM, we require that no one except the MM is able to successfully add a new member to the group. With respect to the TM, we require that no one except the TM is able to successfully identify the actual signer of a signature. With respect to the members, we require that no one except each member is able to successfully create a signature which will be linked to his identity when opened by the TM. These requirements, which is later defined specifically, clarifies the separation of the MM and the TM. We call security properties corresponding the above requirements MM-*invulnerability*, TM-*invulnerability*, *member-invulnerability*, respectively.

MM-**Invulnerability.** MM-invulnerability is the property that no colluding subset of the group members, even colluding with the TM, can create a new signature such that the TM can, in any way, prove that the signer of a signature is not in the member list $\mathcal{L}$. Since a creation of a signature whose signer does not belong to $\mathcal{L}$ implies adding a new member, MM-invulnerability implies that only the MM can play the role of the MM. To define MM-invulnerability, we introduce an adversary $\mathcal{A}$ who attempts to break the group signature scheme in terms of MM-invulnerability. Adversary $\mathcal{A}$ is allowed to collude the TM and all group members. Formally, MM-invulnerability is defined as follows.

Definition 3. *(MM-invulnerability) Let $\mathcal{GS}$ be a group signature scheme, and let $\mathcal{A}$ be an algorithm that has access to an oracle and returns $0/1$. We consider the following experiment:*

Experiment $\mathbf{Exp}_{\mathcal{GS},\mathcal{A}}^{\mathrm{MM}}(k)$
   $(mpk, msk) \leftarrow \mathsf{KEYGEN\text{-}M}(1^k)$
   $(tpk, State) \leftarrow \mathcal{A}(\mathsf{generate}, mpk)$
   $Cont \leftarrow \mathsf{true}$
   While $Cont = \mathsf{true}$ do
      $(\mathcal{L}, (Cont, State)) \leftarrow \langle \mathsf{JOIN\text{-}MM}(U, mpk, tpk, \mathcal{L}, msk), \mathcal{A}(\mathsf{join}, State)\rangle$
   EndWhile
   $(m, gs) \leftarrow \mathcal{A}(\mathsf{forge}, State)$
   If $\mathsf{VERIFY}(mpk, tpk, m, gs) = 0$ then return 0
   If $\mathsf{TRACE}(mpk, tpk, tsk, m, gs, \mathcal{L}) = \bot$ then return 1 EndIf
   Return 0

The MM-invulnerability advantage *is defined as*

$$\mathbf{Adv}_{\mathcal{GS},\mathcal{A}}^{\mathrm{MM}}(k) = \Pr[\mathbf{Exp}_{\mathcal{GS},\mathcal{A}}^{\mathrm{MM}}(k) = 1]$$

A group signature scheme $\mathcal{GS}$ is MM-invulnerable if for all probabilistic, polynomial-time machines $\mathcal{A}$, the advantage $\mathbf{Adv}_{\mathcal{GS},\mathcal{A}}^{\mathrm{MM}}(k)$ is negligible.

TM-**Invulnerability.** *TM*-invulnerability is the property that, given a message and a group signature, no colluding subset of the group members, even colluding with the MM, can identify the signer of the signature unless the TM opens that very signature. TM-invulnerability implies that only the TM can play the role of the TM. To define TM-invulnerability, we introduce an adversary $\mathcal{A}$ who attempts to break a group signature scheme in terms of TM-invulnerability. Adversary $\mathcal{A}$ is allowed to collude the MM and the all group members. $\mathcal{A}$ can also add a new member to the group using the colluding MM. Formally, TM-invulnerability is defined as follows.

Definition 4. *(TM-invulnerability) Let* $\mathcal{GS}$ = (KEYGEN-M, KEYGEN-T, JOIN, SIGN, VERIFY, TRACE)*be a group signature scheme, let* $b \in \{0,1\}$, *and let* $\mathcal{A}$ *be an algorithm that has access an oracle and returns a bit* b'. *We consider the following experiment:*

Experiment $\mathbf{Exp}_{\mathcal{GS},\mathcal{A}}^{\text{TM-}b}(k)$
    $(mpk, State) \leftarrow \mathcal{A}(\text{generate})$
    $(tpk, tsk) \leftarrow \text{KEYGEN-T}(1^k, mpk)$
    If $(tpk, tsk) = \bot$ then return 0 EndIf
    $(State, (cert_0, sk_0), (cert_1, sk_1), m) \leftarrow \mathcal{A}^{\text{TRACE}(mpk,tpk,tsk,\cdot,\cdot,\cdot)}(\text{choose}, State, tpk)$
    $gs \leftarrow \text{SIGN}(mpk, tpk, cert_b, sk_b, m)$
    $b' \leftarrow \mathcal{A}^{\text{TRACE}(mpk,\ tpk,\ tsk,\cdot,\cdot,\cdot)}(\text{guess}, State, gs)$
    If $\mathcal{A}$ did not query its oracle with (m, gs) in the **guess** stage then return b'
    EndIf
    Return 0

The TM-invulnerability advantage *is defined as*

$$\mathbf{Adv}_{\mathcal{GS},\mathcal{A}}^{\text{TM}}(k) = \Pr[\mathbf{Exp}_{\mathcal{GS},\mathcal{A}}^{\text{TM-1}}(k) = 1] - \Pr[\mathbf{Exp}_{\mathcal{GS},\mathcal{A}}^{\text{TM-0}}(k) = 1]$$

A group signature scheme $\mathcal{GS}$ *is* TM-invulnerable *if for all probabilistic, polynomial-time machines* $\mathcal{A}$, *the advantage* $\mathbf{Adv}_{\mathcal{GS},\mathcal{A}}^{\text{TM}}(k)$ *is negligible in* k.

Member-Invulnerability. Member-invulnerability is the property that no colluding subset of the group members, even colluding both the MM and the TM, can create a group signature which is traceable to any non-colluding member. Since to create a group signature of which the member's identity is identified is only allowed for this member, member-invulnerability implies that only each member can play the role of this member. To define member-invulnerability, We introduce an adversary $\mathcal{A}$ who attempts to break the group signature scheme in terms of member-invulnerability. Adversary $\mathcal{A}$ is allowed to collude with the MM, the TM, and any subset of the group members. Formally, member-invulnerability is defined as follows.

Definition 5. *(member-invulnerability) Let* $\mathcal{GS}$ = (KEYGEN-M, KEYGEN-T, JOIN, SIGN, VERIFY, TRACE)*be a group signature scheme, and let* $\mathcal{A}$ *be an algorithm that has access two oracles and returns 0/1. We consider the following experiment:*

Experiment $\mathbf{Exp}_{\mathcal{GS},\mathcal{A}}^{\mathrm{member}}(k)$

    $(mpk, tpk, State) \leftarrow \mathcal{A}(\mathsf{generate})$

    $(State, (sk_U, cert_U)) \leftarrow \langle \mathcal{A}(\mathsf{join}, State), \mathsf{JOIN\text{-}U}(U, mpk, tpk, \mathcal{L})\rangle$

    If $cert_U = \bot$ then return 0 EndIf

    $(m, gs, \mathcal{L}) \leftarrow \mathcal{A}^{\mathsf{SIGN}(mpk, tpk, cert_U, sk_U, \cdot)}(\mathsf{forge}, State)$

    $\mathcal{L} \leftarrow \mathcal{L} \cup \{(U, cert_U)\}$

    If $\mathsf{VERIFY}(mpk, tpk, m, gs) = 0$ then return 0

    If $\mathsf{TRACE}(mpk, tpk, tsk, m, gs, \mathcal{L}) = cert_U$ and m was not queried by $\mathcal{A}$

    to the signing oracle SIGN then return 1

    Else return 0

    EndIf

The member-invulnerability advantage *is defined as*

$$\mathbf{Adv}_{\mathcal{GS},\mathcal{A}}^{\mathrm{member}}(k) = \Pr[\mathbf{Exp}_{\mathcal{GS},\mathcal{A}}^{\mathrm{member}}(k) = 1]$$

A group signature scheme $\mathcal{GS}$ is member-invulnerable *if for all probabilistic, polynomial-time machines $\mathcal{A}$, the advantage $\mathbf{Adv}_{\mathcal{GS},\mathcal{A}}^{\mathrm{member}}(k)$ is negligible.*

Separation of the roles of the managers. From MM-invulnerability and TM-invulnerability, we can see that the TM cannot have the ability to add a new member and that the MM cannot have the ability to identify the signer of a signature. Hence, these definitions imply the complete separation of roles of the TM and the MM. With member-invulnerability, other required notions of security for group signatures are satisfied also. Note that the schemes proposed in [2] do not satisfy the notion of TM-invulnerability.

Relation to the previous definitions. Our definition of TM-invulnerability roughly corresponds to the full-anonymity [4]. If the TM and the MM are unified, the sum of MM-invulnerability and member-invulnerability roughly corresponds to full-traceability [4]. As in the case of [2,10], we are considering the case where the group manager(s) are dishonest and new members are allowed to join the group.

3   Building Blocks

The proposed scheme uses signatures of knowledge [7], a verifiable encryption [17], and the Nyberg-Rueppel signatures [13].

Signature of knowledge. A signature of knowledge is a transformation of corresponding special honest-verifier zero-knowledge interactive proof by using Fiat-Shamir heuristics [9]. A signature of knowledge is denoted by $SPK[\alpha_1, \ldots, \alpha_m : f(\alpha_1, \ldots, \alpha_m) = 0]$, where $\alpha_1, \ldots, \alpha_m$ is secret information for a prover, and $f(\alpha_1, \ldots, \alpha_m) = 0$ is an equation that $\alpha_1, \ldots, \alpha_m$ satisfy. A prover can show a verifier that he knows variables $\alpha_1, \ldots, \alpha_m$ such that $f(\alpha_1, \ldots, \alpha_m) = 0$ holds.

The proposed scheme uses two types of signatures of knowledge as building blocks. One is a *signature of knowledge of representations* denoted by

$$SPK\left[\alpha_1, \ldots, \alpha_u : \left(y_1 = \prod_{j \in \mathcal{J}_1} g_j^{\alpha_{e_{1j}}}\right) \wedge \cdots \wedge \left(y_n = \prod_{j \in \mathcal{J}_n} g_j^{\alpha_{e_{nj}}}\right)\right](m),$$

where the indices $e_{ij} \in \{1, \ldots, u\}$ correspond to the secrets $\alpha_1, \ldots, \alpha_u$ and the elements of $\mathcal{J}_i$ are indices corresponding to the base elements $g_1, \ldots, g_l$. The other is a *signature of knowledge for a range* denoted by

$$SPK[\alpha, \beta : E = g^\alpha h^\beta \wedge \alpha \in [0, b]].$$

The underlying protocol of this signature of knowledge relies on the *interactive proof that a committed value is in an interval* [14]. The scheme proposed in [14] can be constructed only based on the discrete logarithm (DL) problem. In this scheme, a verifier of the signature of knowledge convinces that $\alpha \in [-b, 2b]$, and only when $\alpha \in [0, b]$, the verifier gains no knowledge about α.

There are some more efficient scheme such as [5] in which an RSA modulus is used to make a signature size smaller. It is sufficient to use the scheme in [5] as a proof of the range if authorities are distributed only in the member addition. If distributing authorities require an efficient setup, the DL-based scheme such as [14] is suitable. In this paper, we adopt the scheme for an efficient setup by the distributing authorities.

Verifiable Encryption. A verifiable encryption scheme is an encryption scheme in which a verifier can confirm that a ciphertext C is an encryption of a value such that $c = g^x$. In our scheme, we use a variant of verifiable encryption that uses perfectly hiding commitment $c' = g^x h^y$ instead of $c = g^x$.

Nyberg-Rueppel Signatures. Originally, the Nyberg-Rueppel signature was proposed as a variant of the ElGamal signature scheme with message recovery. In our scheme, we use a variant of the Nyberg-Rueppel signature called a *modified Nyberg-Rueppel signature* in [3] which removes the property of message recovery. The modified Nyberg-Rueppel signature is existentially unforgeable under the chosen message attack (EUF-CMA) in the random oracle and generic model [3].

4   A New Group Signature Scheme

In this section, we give a new group signature scheme that achieves complete separation of the membership manager and the tracing manager. Moreover, the authority of each manager is easily distributed by applying the distributed computation. Our scheme satisfies MM-invulnerability, TM-invulnerability and member-invulnerability defined in Section 2.2 in the random oracle and generic model.

4.1   Basic Idea

At first, the MM generates domain parameters $(p, q, P, g, h, f, G, H, \mathcal{H})$. Then, the MM and the TM generate their public-key/secret-key pairs by executing KEYGEN-M and KEYGEN-T respectively. Their secret keys are discrete logarithm of their public keys. A membership certificate $\langle r_U, \xi_U \rangle$ that the MM issues to a member U is the Nyberg-Rueppel signature on the message I_U given by U during the JOIN protocol. The group signing key σ_U for a member U is a discrete logarithm of I_U with respect to g. In SIGN procedure, a member U first generates an ElGamal ciphertext of a part of its membership certificate r_U with the tracing public key of the TM. Next, the member U generates a signature of knowledge [7], which proves that (1) the knowledge of a membership certificate $\langle r_U, \xi_U \rangle$ and a group signing key σ_U, (2) the knowledge of plaintext r'_U of the ElGamal ciphertext (g', e'), and (3) the fact that the r_U and r'_U are the same. The TM identifies the signer of a group signature by decrypting the membership certificate of the signer r_U from the ElGamal ciphertext (g', e') in the signature.

Roughly, to make the correct signature, a member U needs to prove the knowledge of σ_U, which is possible only by the valid member. This implies member-invulnerability. For an adversary to generate a signature that is not linked to any existing member, the adversary needs to knows a new membership certificate, which means forging of the Nyberg-Rueppel signature. This implies MM-invulnerability. In the SIGN procedure, a user creates an ElGamal ciphertext of r_U and the proof that he correctly computes the ciphertext, which is IND-CCA2 secure assuming random oracle and generic model [16]. Hence, breaking TM-invulnerability which is equivalent to guessing r_U will break IND-CCA2 security of the encryption.

4.2   Construction

We now present the complete construction of the proposed group signature scheme $\mathcal{GS} = $ (KEYGEN-M, KEYGEN-T, JOIN, SIGN, VERIFY, TRACE)as in the following. Let $SPK[\alpha_1, \ldots, \alpha_m : f(\alpha_1, \ldots, \alpha_m) = 0]$ denote a signature of knowledge that proves the knowledge of $\alpha_1, \ldots, \alpha_m$ satisfying $f(\alpha_1, \ldots, \alpha_m) = 0$.

KEYGEN-M. The membership manager MM first randomly chooses sufficiently large primes p, q, P such that $q|p-1$ and $p|P-1$. Let G_q be an order q subgroup of Z_p^*, and let G_p be an order p subgroup of Z_P^*. The MM chooses $g, h, f \in G_q$ and $G, H \in G_p$ such that neither non-trivial $(\alpha_1, \alpha_2, \alpha_3)$ satisfying $g^{\alpha_1} h^{\alpha_2} f^{\alpha_3} = 1 \pmod{p}$ nor non-trivial (β_1, β_2) satisfying $G^{\beta_1} H^{\beta_2} = 1 \pmod{P}$ are not known. The MM initializes a member list $\mathcal{L}$ to $\emptyset$. Let k be a security parameter. Let $\mathcal{H} : \{0,1\}^* \rightarrow \{0,1\}^k$ be a collision-resistant hash function. Then, the MM publishes $PK = (p, q, P, g, h, f, G, H, \mathcal{H})$ as domain parameters.

Next, the MM randomly selects $\upsilon \in_U Z_q$ and computes $y = h^\upsilon \bmod p$. The MM publishes y as a membership public key and stores υ as a membership secret key.

KEYGEN-T. The tracing manager TM randomly selects $\epsilon \in_U Z_q$ and computes $e = g^\epsilon \bmod p$. The TM publishes e as a tracing public key and stores ϵ as a tracing secret key.

JOIN. A user U runs the following protocol with the membership manager MM to join the group.

1. User U randomly chooses $\sigma_U \in_U Z_q$ and computes $I_U = g^{\sigma_U} \bmod p$. U generates the signature of knowledge $spk_U = SPK[\tilde{\sigma}_U : I_U = g^{\tilde{\sigma}_U} \bmod p]$ which assures that U knows a discrete logarithm of I_U to the base g. U also computes the digital signature S_U on the message $I_U \| spk_U$. U sends (I_U, spk_U, S_U) to the membership manager MM.
2. The MM checks the validity of spk_U and S_U. If both are valid, the MM randomly selects $\rho \in_U Z_q$ and computes $r_U := I_U h^\rho \bmod p$ and $\xi_U := \rho - r_U v \bmod q$. The MM sends (r_U, ξ_U) as a membership certificate to U.
3. U checks whether (r_U, ξ_U) sent by the MM satisfies $r_U = y^{r_U} g^{\sigma_U} h^{\xi_U}$ and $r_U \in [0, p-1]$. If it holds, U stores $\langle r_U, \xi_U \rangle$ as his membership certificate, and securely stores σ_U as a group signing key.
4. M adds $\langle I_U, spk_U, r_U, \xi_U, S_U \rangle$ to the member list $\mathcal{L}$.

SIGN. A member U creates a group signature on a message m as follows.

First, a member U chooses a random number $\tau \in_U Z_q$ and computes $(g', e') := (g^\tau, r_U^{-1} e^\tau) \bmod p$, which is an ElGamal encryption of r_U with respect to the tracing public key of the TM. Next, U computes the signature of knowledge:

$$SPK[\tilde{r}_U, \tilde{\xi}_U, \tilde{\sigma}_U, \tilde{\tau} : g' = g^{\tilde{\tau}} \bmod p \ \wedge \ e' = \tilde{r}_U^{-1} e^{\tilde{\tau}} \bmod p \ \wedge$$
$$\tilde{r}_U = y^{\tilde{r}_U} g^{\tilde{\sigma}_U} h^{\tilde{\xi}_U} \bmod p \ \wedge \ \tilde{r}_U \in [0, p-1]](m).$$

This signature of knowledge can be constructed from two components, a perfectly hiding commitments of r_U and a signature of knowledge: The commitments are computed as $h' := y^{r_U} f^\omega \bmod p$ and $J := G^{r_U} H^a \bmod P$, where $\omega \in_U Z_q$ and $a \in_U Z_p$ are chosen uniformly and randomly, and the signature of knowledge is

$$SPK[\tilde{r}_U, \tilde{\xi}_U, \tilde{\sigma}_U, \tilde{\tau}, \tilde{\omega}, \tilde{a} : g' = g^{\tilde{\tau}} \bmod p \ \wedge \ e' = \tilde{r}_U^{-1} e^{\tilde{\tau}} \bmod p \ \wedge$$
$$h' = y^{\tilde{r}_U} f^{\tilde{\omega}} \bmod p \ \wedge \ J = G^{\tilde{r}_U} H^{\tilde{a}} \bmod P \ \wedge \quad (1)$$
$$e'h' = f^{\tilde{\omega}} g^{-\tilde{\sigma}_U} h^{-\tilde{\xi}_U} e^{\tilde{\tau}} \bmod p \ \wedge \ \tilde{r}_U \in [0, p-1]](m).$$

This signature of knowledge can be computed as in the following:

1. For $1 \leq j \leq k$, generate random numbers $\phi_{2j-1} \in_U [0, p-1]$, and sets $\phi_{2j} := \phi_{2j-1} - p$. If $r_U + \phi_{2j-1} \notin [0, p-1]$ and $r_U + \phi_{2j} \in [0, p-1]$, replace ϕ_{2j-1} with ϕ_{2j} to be $r_U + \phi_{2j-1} \in [0, p-1]$. Also, choose $\psi_{2j-1}, \psi_{2j} \in_U Z_q$, $\eta_{2j-1}, \eta_{2j} \in_U Z_p$ randomly. For $1 \leq j \leq k$, compute $V_j := y^{\phi_{2j-1}} f^{\psi_{2j-1}} \| y^{\phi_{2j}} f^{\psi_{2j}} \| G^{\phi_{2j-1}} H^{\eta_{2j-1}} \| G^{\phi_{2j}} H^{\eta_{2j}}$.
2. Choose $t_1, t_2, t_3, t_4, t_5 \in Z_q$ randomly, and compute $T_1 := y^{t_1} f^{t_2} \bmod p$, $T_2 := f^{t_2} g^{-t_3} h^{-t_4} e^{t_5} \bmod p$, and $T_3 := g^{t_5} \bmod p$.

3. For $1 \leq j \leq k$, select $\gamma_j \in_U Z_q$ and $u_j \in_U Z_p$. Set $e_j := e^{\gamma_j} \bmod p$. Then, compute $g_j := g^{\gamma_j} \bmod p$ and $J_j := G^{e_j} H^{u_j} \bmod P$ for $1 \leq j \leq k$.

4. Generate

$$c := \mathcal{H}(g\|h\|f\|G\|H\|y\|e\|V_1\|\cdots\|V_k\|T_1\|T_2\|T_3\|g_1\|\cdots\|g_k\|J_1\|\cdots\|J_k\|m).$$

5. For $1 \leq j \leq k$,
   - If $c[j] = 0$, set $v_{6j-5} := \phi_{2j-1}$, $v_{6j-4} := \phi_{2j}$, $v_{6j-3} := \psi_{2j-1}$, $v_{6j-2} := \psi_{2j}$, $v_{6j-1} := \eta_{2j-1}$, $v_{6j} := \eta_{2j}$, $s_1 := t_1 \bmod q$, $s_2 := t_2 \bmod q$, $s_3 := t_3 \bmod q$, $s_4 := t_4 \bmod q$, $s_5 := t_5 \bmod q$, $w_j := \gamma_j \bmod q$, $z_j := u_j \bmod p$.
   - If $c[j] = 1$, set $v_{6j-5} := r_U + \phi_{2j-1}$, $v_{6j-4} := y^{\phi_{2j}} f^{\psi_{2j}}$, $v_{6j-3} := \omega + \psi_{2j-1}$, $v_{6j-2} := \psi_0 \in_U Z_q$, $v_{6j-1} := a + \eta_{2j-1}$, $v_{6j} := G^{\phi_{2j}} H^{\eta_{2j}}$, $s_1 := t_1 - r_U \bmod q$, $s_2 := t_2 - \omega \bmod q$, $s_3 := t_3 - \sigma_U \bmod q$, $s_4 := t_4 - \xi_U \bmod q$, $s_5 := t_5 - \tau \bmod q$, $w_j := \gamma_j - \tau \bmod q$, $z_j := u_j - ae_j r_U^{-1} \bmod p$

6. The resulting signature of knowledge is $SPK_{gs} = (c, v_1, v_2, v_3, v_4, v_5, v_6, \ldots, v_{6k-5}, v_{6k-4}, v_{6k-3}, v_{6k-2}, v_{6k-1}, v_{6k}, s_1, s_2, s_3, s_4, s_5, w_1, \ldots, w_k, z_1, \ldots, z_k)$.

Finally, U outputs $gs = (g', e', h', J, SPK_{gs})$ as a group signature on m.

VERIFY. A verifier V verifies a group signature gs on a message m by checking the validity of the signature of knowledge involved in gs.

For $gs = (g', e', h', J, c, SPK_{gs})$, V first checks if $v_{6j-5} \in [0, p-1]$ holds at $j \in [1, k]$ such that $c[j] = 1$. If it holds, V checks

$$c = \mathcal{H}(g\|h\|f\|G\|H\|y\|e\|V_1'\|\cdots\|V_k'\|T_1'\|T_2'\|T_3'\|g_1'\|\cdots\|g_k'\|J_1'\|\cdots\|J_k'\|m),$$

where

$$V_j' = \begin{cases} y^{v_{6j-5}} f^{v_{6j-3}} \| y^{v_{6j-4}} f^{v_{6j-2}} \| G^{v_{6j-5}} H^{v_{6j-1}} \| G^{v_{6j-4}} H^{v_{6j}} & c[j] = 0 \\ y^{v_{6j-5}} f^{v_{6j-3}} / h' \| v_{6j-4} \| G^{v_{6j-5}} H^{v_{6j-1}} / J \| v_{6j} & c[j] = 1 \end{cases}$$

$$T_1' = h'^c y^{s_1} f^{s_2}, \quad T_2' = (e'h')^c f^{s_2} g^{-s_3} h^{-s_4} e^{s_5}, \quad T_3' = g'^c g^{s_5}$$

$$g_j' = g'^{c[j]} g^{w_j} \bmod p$$

$$J_j' = \begin{cases} G^{\bar{e}_j'} H^{z_j} \bmod P & c[j] = 0 \\ J^{\bar{e}_j'} H^{z_j} \bmod P & c[j] = 1 \end{cases} \quad (\text{where } \bar{e}_j' := e'^{c[j]} e^{w_j} \bmod p)$$

V accepts gs if and only if the all above equations are satisfied.

TRACE. For an accused group signature gs on m, the tracing manager TM decrypts (g', e') with his tracing secret key by $\bar{r} := g'^{\epsilon}/e' \bmod p$. In addition, the TM computes a signature of knowledge $SPK[\tilde{\epsilon} : g'^{\tilde{\epsilon}} = \bar{r}^{-1} e']$ to prove that he surely used his secret key for decryption.

The TM finds the tuple $\langle I_U, spk_U, r_U, \xi_U, S_U \rangle$ from the member list $\mathcal{L}$ such that $r_U = \bar{r}$ holds. The TM concludes that the member U corresponding to $r_U = \bar{r}$ is the actual signer of gs.

4.3   Distributed Construction

In the group signature scheme shown in the previous subsection, both the membership secret key and the tracing secret key are discrete logarithms of corresponding public keys. Such secret keys can be easily distributed among multiple entities by using the technique proposed by Pedersen in [15].

More specifically, the membership secret key v can be distributed into n elements $v_1, \ldots, v_n$ satisfying $v = v_1 + \cdots + v_n$ for the distributed membership managers $MM_1, \cdots, MM_n$. In the JOIN protocol, each membership manager MM_i computes $r_U = I_U h^t$ and $\xi_i = k_i - r_U v_i$, where t and k_i is a distributedly generated random number satisfying $t = h^{\Sigma k_i}$. The user U obtains a membership certificate (r_U, ξ_U) by computing $\xi_U = \xi_1 + \cdots + \xi_n$.

Similarly, the tracing secret key ϵ can be distributed into $\epsilon_1, \ldots, \epsilon_n$ satisfying $\epsilon = \epsilon_1 + \cdots + \epsilon_n$ for the distributed tracing managers $TM_1, \cdots, TM_n$. In the TRACE algorithm, each tracing manager TM_i computes $g_i' = g'^{\epsilon_i} \bmod p$, and an entire decryption can be executed by computing $\bar{r} = (\prod g_i')/e' \bmod p$.

4.4   Efficiency Analysis

We analyze the efficiency of the proposed scheme. For simplicity, we estimate a basic construction shown in Section 4.2. The signature length is estimated by $|P| + (5k + 3)|p| + (3k + 5)|q|$ bit. If we take $|P| = |p| = 1024$ and $|q| = 160$, the signature length is about 110 KB, which is 4.5 times larger than that of [2]. The computational cost of our scheme is also 4.5 times larger than that of [2]. As mentioned in Section 3, we use an DL-based proof of a range due to the efficient setup by the distributing authorities. If we adopt the proof of a range in [5], the signature size becomes 26.2 KB, which is almost as large as that of [2].

5   Security Considerations

First of all, we prove that the group signature which a signer creates really serves as a signature of knowledge of Equation (1) in the random oracle model. We do prove it by showing that the underlying interactive protocol is honest-verifier zero-knowledge proof of knowledge.

Theorem 1. *The underlying interactive protocol of the proposed group signature scheme is an honest-verifier zero-knowledge proof of knowledge of a membership certificate, corresponding signing key and the random number used for encryption of ElGamal ciphertext, where the common input is a set of domain parameter PK, a membership public key, a tracing public key, and ElGamal ciphertext (g', e').*

Proof. Since the proof of this theorem is straight-forward, we omit the proof.

Next, we prove the entire security of the proposed group signature scheme. We can obtain the following theorem.

Theorem 2. *The proposed group signature scheme $\mathcal{GS}$ is MM-invulnerable in the random oracle and generic model.*

Proof. We show that if there exists an attacker $\mathcal{A}$ that breaks MM- invulnerability of the group signature scheme, then there exists an attacker $\mathcal{A}'$ that breaks the EUF-CMA of the modified Nyberg-Rueppel signature in the random oracle and generic model. The following is the description of $\mathcal{A}'$:

1. Key generation of the target modified Nyberg-Rueppel signature scheme is the same as KEYGEN-M procedure of the proposed group signature scheme.
2. When $\mathcal{A}$ asks a joining oracle to join the group by giving g^{σ_U}, $\mathcal{A}'$ asks its signing oracle to sign on g^{σ_U}. Then $\mathcal{A}'$ sends the answer of the oracle to $\mathcal{A}$, which is the membership certificate.
3. Suppose $\mathcal{A}$ generated a group signature, that is linked, by TRACE procedure, to membership certificate that $\mathcal{A}'$ has never sent to $\mathcal{A}$. Then, $\mathcal{A}$ plays a role of a knowledge extractor, namely, rewinds $\mathcal{A}$ and chooses another random oracle to extract the membership certificate $(\bar{r}_U, \bar{\xi}_U)$ and the signing key $\bar{\sigma}_U$. This is possible from Theorem 1. $(\bar{r}_U, \bar{\xi}_U)$ is a modified Nyberg-Rueppel signature on a message $\bar{\sigma}_U$.

It is shown in [3] that the modified Nyberg-Rueppel signature is EUF-CMA in the random oracle and generic model. Thus, the proposed scheme is TM-invulnerable in the random oracle and generic model. □

Theorem 3. *The proposed group signature scheme $\mathcal{GS}$ is TM-invulnerable in the random oracle and generic model.*

Proof. By construction the group signature generated by SIGN includes an ElGamal encryption of r_U with a random number τ, and the signature of knowledge of τ. This encryption-and-signature pair is regarded as a signed ElGamal encryption [16]. Now we can show that if there exists an attacker $\mathcal{A}$ that breaks TM-invulnerability of the group signature scheme, then there exists an attacker $\mathcal{A}'$ that breaks IND-CCA2 of the above signed ElGamal encryption. The following is the description of $\mathcal{A}'$

1. Key generation of the target cryptosystem is the same as KEYGEN-T procedure of the proposed group signature scheme.
2. When $\mathcal{A}$ asks a tracing oracle to open a signature gs, $\mathcal{A}'$ picks up the signed ElGamal encryption part and throws it to its decryption oracle. Then $\mathcal{A}'$ sends the result to $\mathcal{A}$.
3. When $\mathcal{A}$ chooses a pair of a membership certificate and a signing key, (r_0, ξ_0, σ_0) and (r_1, ξ_1, σ_1), $\mathcal{A}'$ chooses r_0 and r_1 as target plaintexts.
4. When $\mathcal{A}'$ was given a ciphertext as a challenge, $\mathcal{A}'$ generates a group signature that includes this challenge ciphertext by choosing appropriate random oracle. Then $\mathcal{A}'$ gives it to $\mathcal{A}$ as a challenge.
5. When $\mathcal{A}$ gives the answer $b \in \{0, 1\}$, $\mathcal{A}'$ answers b.

It is shown in [16] that the signed ElGamal encryption is IND-CCA2 secure in the random oracle and generic model. Therefore, $\mathcal{GS}$ is TM-invulnerable in the random oracle and generic model. □

Theorem 4. *The proposed group signature scheme $\mathcal{GS}$ is member-invulnerable if the discrete logarithm problem is hard in the random oracle model.*

Proof. It is easy to see from Theorem 1 that each of group signatures includes a signature of knowledge of σ_U.

Now we can show that if there exists an attacker $\mathcal{A}$ that breaks member-invulnerability of the group signature scheme, then there exists an attacker $\mathcal{A}'$ that solves discrete logarithm problem. The following is the description of $\mathcal{A}'$

1. When $\mathcal{A}'$ is given the instance (g, I) as a problem, $\mathcal{A}'$ chooses $h = g^a$ for randomly chosen a.
2. When $\mathcal{A}$ asks a joining oracle to join the group, $\mathcal{A}'$ first generates a simulated signature of knowledge of discrete logarithm of g, I by choosing a random oracle. Next, sends I and this signature of knowledge. Finally, $\mathcal{A}'$ obtains the membership certificate (r_U, ξ_U).
3. When $\mathcal{A}$ asks a signing oracle to sign a message m, $\mathcal{A}'$ generates an ElGamal encryption of r_U and generates a simulated signature of knowledge of a membership certificate, a group signing key, and a random number used for the encryption by choosing a random oracle. Then $\mathcal{A}'$ sends these generated data to $\mathcal{A}$.
4. Suppose $\mathcal{A}$ generated a group signature, that is linked, by TRACE procedure, to a membership certificate r_U. Then, $\mathcal{A}'$ rewinds $\mathcal{A}$ and chooses another random oracle to extract a membership certificate and a signing key. This is possible from Theorem 1. We denote the extracted data $(r_U, \bar{\xi}_U, \bar{\sigma}_U)$.
5. If $\bar{\xi}_U = \xi_U$, then $g^{\bar{\sigma}_U} = I$, which means a success of the attack.
   If $\bar{\xi}_U \neq \xi_U$, then $g^{a(\xi_U - \bar{\xi}_U) + \bar{\sigma}_U} = I$, which also means a successful attack. □

6   Conclusions

We have proposed a new practical group signature scheme with separate and distributed authorities. Our scheme can separate the membership manager and the tracing manager without invading each capability. Moreover, since our scheme is constructed from primitives based on the discrete logarithm problem, our scheme is well suited for distributed authorities. We have also formalized security definitions that describe the complete separation of the capabilities of the two managers and members. We have given the proofs that our scheme is secure under these security definitions.

References

1. G. Ateniese, J. Camenisch, M. Joye and G. Tsudik, "A Practical and Provable Secure Coalition-Resistant Group Signature Scheme," In Advances in Cryptology — CRYPTO 2000, LNCS 1880, pp.255–270, Springer-Verlag, 2000.
2. G. Ateniese and B. de Medeiros, "Efficient Group Signatures without Trapdoors," In Advances in Cryptology — ASIACRYPT 2003, LNCS 2894, pp.246–268, Springer-Verlag, 2003.

3. G. Ateniese and B. de Medeiros, "A Provably Secure Nyberg-Rueppel Signature Variant with Applications," In Cryptology ePrint Archive, Report 2004/093, 2004.
4. M. Bellare, D. Micciancio and B. Warinschi, "Foundations of Group Signatures: Formal Definitions, Simplified Requirements, and a Construction Based on General Assumptions," In Advances in Cryptology — EUROCRYPT 2003, LNCS 2656, pp. 614–629, Springer-Verlag, 2003.
5. F. Boudot, "Efficient Proofs that a Committed Number Lies in an Interval," In Advances in Cryptology — EUROCRYPT 2000, LNCS 1807, pp. 431–444, Springer-Verlag, 2000.
6. J. Camenisch and M. Michels, "A group signature scheme based on an RSA-variant," Technical Report RS-98-27, BRICS, University of Aarhus, November 1998. An earlier version appears in ASIACRYPT '98.
7. J. Camenisch and M. Stadler, "Efficient Group Signature Schemes for Large Groups," In Advances in Cryptology — CRYPTO '97, LNCS 1296, pp. 410–424, Springer-Verlag, 1997.
8. D. Chaum and E. van Heyst, "Group Signatures," In Advances in Cryptology — EUROCRYPT '91, LNCS 547, pp. 257–265, Springer-Verlag, 1991.
9. A. Fiat and A. Shamir, "How to Prove Yourself: Practical Solution to Identification And Signature Problems," In Advances in Cryptology — CRYPTO '86, LNCS 263, pp. 186–194, Springer-Verlag, 1987.
10. A. Kiayias, Y. Tsiounis, and M. Yung, "Traceable Signatures," In Advances in Cryptology — EUROCRYPT 2004, LNCS 3027, pp. 571–589, Springer-Verlag, 2004.
11. J. Kilian and E. Petrank, "Identity Escrow," In Advances in Cryptology — CRYPTO '98, LNCS 1642, pp. 169–185, Springer-Verlag, 1998.
12. A. Miyaji and K. Umeda, "A Fully-Functional Group Signature Scheme over Only Known-Order Group," In ACNS 2004, LNCS 3089, pp. 164–179, Springer-Verlag, 2004.
13. K. Nyberg and R. A. Rueppel, "Message Recovery for Signature Schemes Based on the Discrete Logarithm Problem," In Advances in Cryptology — EUROCRYPT '94, LNCS 950, pp. 182–193, Springer-Verlag, 1994.
14. T. Okamoto, "An Efficient Divisible Electronic Cash Scheme," In Advances in Cryptology — CRYPTO '95, LNCS 963, pp. 438–451, Springer-Verlag, 1995.
15. T. Pedersen, "A Threshold Cryptosystem without a Trusted Party," In Advances in Cryptology — EUROCRYPT '91, LNCS 547, pp. 522–526, Springer-Verlag, 1991.
16. C. P. Schnorr and M. Jakobsson, "Security of Signed ElGamal Encryption," In Advaces in Cryptology — ASIACRYPT 2000, LNCS 1976, pp. 73–89, Springer-Verlag, 2000.
17. M. Stadler, "Publicly Verifiable Secret Sharing," In Advances in Cryptology — EUROCRYPT '96, LNCS 1070, pp. 190–199, Springer-Verlag, 1996.

Threshold Cryptography
in Mobile Ad Hoc Networks[*]

Giovanni Di Crescenzo[1], Gonzalo Arce[2], and Renwei Ge[2]

[1] Telcordia Technologies, Piscataway, NJ, USA
giovanni@research.telcordia.com
[2] University of Delaware, Newark, DE, USA
{arce,ge}@ece.udel.edu

Abstract. The area of Threshold Cryptography investigates the design and analysis of protocols that distribute, in wired networks, cryptographic actions usually performed by a single party into multi-party variants, where the original action is successfully performed only if at least a certain threshold of the participants are available and not corrupted. As of today, several examples of threshold cryptographic protocols (e.g., signatures, public-key cryptosystems, zero-knowledge protocols, etc.) are being investigated in the Cryptography literature.

We note that the impact of the Threshold Cryptography paradigm is of even greater importance to study the security of other types of communication networks, such as Mobile Ad Hoc Networks, where the existence and availability of trusted authorities is severely limited by intrinsic network features, and problems such as avoiding a "single point of failure", or, more generally, "service availability", become crucial.

In this paper we formalize, investigate and present satisfactory solutions for the general problem of Threshold Cryptography in Mobile Ad Hoc Networks. Although we restrict our study to the cryptographic operation of digital signatures schemes, our definitional approaches can be extended to most other cryptographic actions studied in Threshold Cryptography.

1 Introduction

Threshold Cryptography. The area of Threshold Cryptography (starting with [2, 7, 21]) is today receiving a significant amount of attention by the Cryptography literature. In general terms, the threshold cryptography paradigm suggests to divide a cryptographic action, such as the generation and management of a secret key or computation using secret keys, among several parties, in such

[*] Prepared through collaborative participation in the Communications and Networks Consortium sponsored by the U. S. Army Research Laboratory under the Collaborative Technology Alliance Program, Cooperative Agreement DAAD19-01-2-0011. The U. S. Government is authorized to reproduce and distribute reprints for Government purposes notwithstanding any copyright notation thereon.

C. Blundo and S. Cimato (Eds.): SCN 2004, LNCS 3352, pp. 91–104, 2005.

a way to prevent a small number of participants and at the same time allow a larger number of participants to perform the action. A system modified according to the threshold cryptography paradigm enjoys both resiliency with respect to crashes of some of the system components, and tolerance with respect to faulty or malicious behavior of some of the components. For the construction of threshold cryptography schemes, the problem of distributed key generation, that is, generating a shared public key and individual shares as secret keys, is often crucial.

Most popular examples of cryptographic protocols that are being investigated in the literature include digital signatures, public-key cryptosystems, zero-knowledge protocols, etc. An old survey of research on threshold cryptography can be found in [9]. Threshold digital signatures, for instance, satisfy the following properties: at least $t + 1$ parties are able to generate a signature on a given message; at most t parties are not able to generate a signature on a given message, even after having seen several signatures of adaptively chosen messages; finally, any $t < n/2$ parties (where n is the total number of parties) cannot prevent the remaining honest parties to generate a threshold signature. Threshold signatures have been constructed under various hardness assumptions: the hardness of problems related to Discrete Logarithms (see, e.g. [17, 15, 12]); the hardness of inverting the RSA cryptosystem (see, e.g. [7, 8, 13, 5, 16, 14]); the hardness of inverting the RSA cryptosystem with special moduli (see, e.g. [21, 1]); the hardness of solving the Computational Diffie Hellman problem (see, e.g. [2, 4]); the hardness of Factoring (see, e.g. [18]). Several of these papers also study the problem of distributed key generation.

Mobile Ad Hoc Networks. The impact of the threshold cryptography paradigm is of even greater importance when studying the security of other types of communication networks, such as Mobile Ad Hoc Networks (MANETs), that are typically formed by nodes having no pre-established trust or authority relationship. Furthermore, nodes may have significant constraints in all their resources: computation ability, energy, bandwidth and memory. In these networks, even point-to-point connection needs to be carefully modeled because of the limited radio range and mobility of nodes.

Security in MANETs is a large research area (see, e.g., [22]). Most of the research focus on basic issues such as guaranteeing secure routing among any two parties, but also on several other problems that already assume secure routing is in place. Consider, for instance, two basic problems in securing MANETs. The first is avoiding the so-called "single point of failure"; specifically, avoiding that crucial system events are carried out under the responsibility of a single node. The second problem is that of "service availability"; that is, guaranteeing that clients of a certain service are always guaranteed to find enough server resources. For both problems (and others), the threshold cryptography paradigm can provide solutions of fundamental help. We are not aware of a formal treatment of threshold cryptography paradigms for the security of MANETs.

This Paper. We start a comprehensive study of the general Threshold Cryptography problem in MANETs. We specifically restrict our attention to threshold signatures, as these seem to be the most studied as well as among the most relevant primitives needed for practical cryptographic application. We start by presenting a formal definition of Threshold Signatures in MANETs. We note that the intrinsic features of the latter demand stringent constraints on the security requirements for such schemes. We then conclude that (almost) none of the known protocols in the literature realizes the proposed notion. The only exception is represented by a combination of the distributed key generation from [20] and the signature scheme from [4], which, when properly combined, already almost achieve all security and efficiency properties required by our formal definition of threshold signatures in MANETs. We present two solutions and obtain them through some crucial modifications and proper combinations of these two protocols. The first resulting protocol is certainly one of the simplest protocols for Threshold Cryptography in wired networks as well, and is of interest independently from MANETs. The second resulting protocol improves the latency of the first at the cost of increasing communication and computation in correspondence to significant mobile activity from parties. Simulation results on the improved success rate of obtaining valid signatures when using ad hoc groups (rather than fixed ones) are described in [10]. Although we restrict our study to the cryptographic operation of digital signatures schemes, our definitional approaches can be extended to other cryptographic actions such as cryptosystems and zero-knowledge proofs.

We remark that we do not claim to fully secure MANETs, but just to solve a security subproblem and that our solutions provide a component that can be very useful for other tasks. General security solutions for MANETs are quite complex. For instance, our threshold cryptography protocols use an underlying secure routing protocol. Protocols of the latter type typically assume the existence of a public-key infrastructure or pre-shared secret keys. Therefore, if our protocol is used as a subcomponent of a protocol for the secure creation of a distributed certification authority, then one may create a chicken and egg problem. Indeed, our protocols even significantly limit this problem in this particular application as they assume only a limited use of secure routing; specifically, our protocols can be divided into two phases: distributed key generation and signature generation phase; and only the former, which is executed only once at the beginning, requires the secure routing assumption.

2   Definitions

We recall notions and definitions for ordinary and threshold signatures in wired networks and then introduce definitions for threshold signatures in MANETs.

2.1   Threshold Signatures in Wired Networks

Informally, a *digital signature scheme* is a method allowing a party A to append a signature tag to a message such that any other party can verify the tag as a valid signature by A, and another party C cannot produce a tag for a different message that can be verified as a valid signature from A. In (t, n)-*threshold signatures in a wired network*, which we now recall in more detail, we require that up to t servers are not able to generate a signature for a client but at least $t + 1$ are.

Setup and Mechanics. The parties involved in a threshold digital signature scheme are a *dealer*, denoted as D, several *servers*, denoted as $S_1, S_2, \ldots, S_n$, and a *client*, denoted as C. Although in general network connectivity among all parties is allowed, it is specifically required that both the dealer and the client are connected to all servers, and that each pair of servers is also connected. (In some schemes, the dealer's action can be replaced by a protocol run by the servers only.) There are two main phases in a threshold signature scheme: a *key-generation phase* and a *signature phase*. In the former phase all servers and possibly a dealer exchange messages and, at the end of the phase, each server holds some private information (e.g., the share of some secret signing key). In the latter phase, all servers interact with a client, and, at the end of the phase, the client obtains a *message m* and a *signature sig* for m, and can check if *sig* is a valid signature of m.

Security Requirements. Let t, n denote positive integers and k be a security parameter (given in unary). If we denote by Π_{kg} the key generation protocol and by Π_{sgn} the signature protocol, an execution of a threshold signature scheme, denoted as $\Pi \equiv (\Pi_{kg}, \Pi_{sgn})$, consists of one execution of protocol Π_{kg} and polynomially (in k) many executions of protocol Π_{sgn}. A *secure threshold signature scheme* $\Pi \equiv (\Pi_{kg}, \Pi_{sgn})$ has to satisfy the following basic requirements: *correctness* (client C accepts the threshold signature produced by honest parties $S_1, \ldots, S_n$); *unforgeability* (an adversary corrupting at most t servers S_i's, after seeing several (message,signature) pairs for adaptively chosen messages, can produce a signature accepted by client C for a new message only with negligible (in k) probability); *robustness* (any adversary corrupting up to t parties can prevent the remaining parties to generate a valid signature only with negligible (in k) probability). We will not consider in this paper the less basic requirements of *proactive* and *adaptive security*.

Efficiency Requirements. In addition to the above security requirements, great importance in the design of threshold signature schemes has been given to the efficiency requirements of *non-interactive partial signature generation, verification and reconstruction* and *distributed key generation*.

2.2   Threshold Signatures in Mobile Ad-Hoc Networks

In threshold signatures for MANETs we would like any client to be able to make at any time an ad hoc selection of a subset T of servers from which to request a threshold signature, and a threshold parameter. Given this selection, a regular (t, n)-threshold signature should be sent from the servers in T to the client, where $n = |T|$ and t are the size and threshold parameter chosen by the client.

Setup: Parties, Connectivity. Let k be a security parameter (described in unary). We consider a mobile ad hoc network with n parties $P_1, \ldots, P_n$, where each party can act as server by running a *server algorithm S* or as client by running a *client algorithm C*. MANETs put severe constraints on the connectivity among parties and, in general, network connectivity among all parties cannot be guaranteed. Because of the wireless nature of the parties' devices, it is not guaranteed that all parties are in the radio range of a given party; in addition, the shape of a radio range of a given party can differ according to the location, time, device power, and device energy. We will model the connectivity among the parties with a *connectivity graph $\mathcal{G}$*, with the understanding that each node in $\mathcal{G}$ is associated with a different party, and an edge between any two nodes implies connectivity between the two associated parties (for simplicity, we will only consider the case of bidirectional connectivity). In addition, graph $\mathcal{G}$ can vary in time according to *party mobility* or *unavailability*, due to factors such as geographical changes, power disruption or low battery. These events trigger changes in graph $\mathcal{G}$ modeled as *failure* and *creation* of *nodes* and *edges*; therefore the structure of graph $\mathcal{G}$ varies according to such changes (for notational simplicity we omit a time-dependent subscript in the notations related to $\mathcal{G}$ and we assume without loss of generality that n is an upper bound on the number of parties). Each party is assumed to know which nodes are her neighbor, but is not required to have additional knowledge about graph $\mathcal{G}$. In some limited cases, however, we will also make the assumption that a secure routing protocol exists and therefore each party is implicitly aware of identities of all nodes in $\mathcal{G}$. Following the approach in wired networks, we make the simplifying assumption that any two parties connected in $\mathcal{G}$ can communicate through private channels (this is without loss of generality as the two parties can run, for instance, a key agreement protocol before any other protocol).

Threshold Signature Mechanics and Protocols. Consider graph $\mathcal{G} = (V, E)$ denoting the connections between n parties. At any time, a client $C \in V$ may request a signature of some message from the other parties in V. Since C may not be connected to all other parties, an adversary may always choose to corrupt or move some of C's neighbors; as a consequence, C can choose the threshold parameter equal to a number t such that $\tau \le t < n(C)/2$, where τ is the maximum number of parties that C expects to be either corrupted or unavailable, and $n(C)$ is the number of neighbors of C. Therefore, C transfers her signature request to ℓ parties (for simplicity, we will assume wlog that all these ℓ parties are chosen among her $n(C)$ neighbors) by sending the threshold $t < \ell/2$, the message M, and the identities of the parties $i_1, \ldots, i_\ell$. At this point these parties need to run a t-out-of-ℓ threshold signature to sign M. More formally, as for wired networks, we consider two main phases: a *key-generation phase* and a *signature phase*. In the former phase some or all servers run a *key-generation protocol Π_{kg}*. In protocol Π_{kg} each party uses as input some common parameters $Param$ and a different random string; the output of the protocol is a string sk_i for each party P_i, for $i = 1, \ldots, n$. Protocol Π_{sgn} is run by a party acting as a client and a subset T of his choice among his neighbors that will act as servers in this protocol execution. In the rest of the protocol, the client uses as input parameters $Param$, subset T and a message M of his choice, and each server P_i in T uses as inputs parameters $Param$ and string sk_i; the output of the protocol is a pair sig, out for the client, where sig is supposed to be a $(t, |T|)$-threshold signature of m and $out \in \{$ yes, no $\}$ denotes whether sig is a valid signature of m. We stress the ad-hoc selections in protocol Π_{sgn}; that is, at each execution C can arbitrarily choose message M, the subset of servers T, the size ℓ of T, and the threshold t. Finally, we note that the execution of any such protocol takes time at most polynomial in a common security parameter k, described in unary.

Adversarial Model. In threshold signatures for wired networks, the connectivity graph $\mathcal{G} = (V, E)$ is a complete graph; in other words, any two parties are connected. Therefore, if the adversary is assumed to be able to corrupt up to τ parties, then the only requirement necessary to guarantee security is that the number n of parties is at least $2\tau + 1$; that is, $|V(\mathcal{G})| \geq 2\tau + 1$. In MANETs, however, the connectivity graph is arbitrary and might not contain several edges. In addition to the requirement $n \geq 2\tau + 1$, it is necessary that for each execution of a $(t, |T|)$-threshold signature protocol, the number of parties acting as servers is at least $2\tau + 1$. Since the servers are chosen only among neighbors of the client requesting the signature, this condition is rephrased by saying that at any time, a (honest) node starting a signature request has at least $2\tau + 1$ neighbors in $\mathcal{G}$, where we do not necessarily require that τ remains the same during the entire lifetime of the system. We note that in the model a meaningful client's choice of servers can only be among its neighbors. (Assume, instead, that a client C chooses a server S that is 2 hops away; then C cannot trust any message by S as it may be arbitrarily changed or even not forwarded by the intermediate server that is a neighbor of C.)

Basic Requirements. If we denote by Π_{kg} the key generation protocol and by Π_{sgn} the signature protocol, an execution of a threshold signature scheme, denoted as $\Pi \equiv (\Pi_{kg}, \Pi_{sgn})$, consists of one execution of protocol Π_{kg} and polynomially (in k) many executions of protocol Π_{sgn}. A *secure threshold signature scheme* $\Pi \equiv (\Pi_{kg}, \Pi_{sgn})$ *in a mobile ad hoc network* has to satisfy the following requirements:

Correctness. If $P_1, \ldots, P_n$ honestly run all executions of protocols Π_{kg} and Π_{sgn}, then with probability 1 at the end of each execution of protocol Π_{sgn}, the party acting as client in that execution returns $out = $ yes.

Unforgeability. Let A be a probabilistic polynomial time algorithm, called the *adversary*, and consider the following probabilistic experiment. First, A chooses τ indices $i_1, \ldots, i_\tau \in \{1, \ldots, n\}$, and then protocol Π_{kg} is run with A playing as $S_{i_1}, \ldots, S_{i_\tau}$; let $sk_1, \ldots, sk_n$ be its output. Then, the following is repeated until A returns some string out_A and stops: A chooses a node c in $\mathcal{G}$ acting as a client, ℓ new indices $j_1, \ldots, j_\ell \in \{1, \ldots, n\}$ among c's neighbor, a new threshold $t_i < \ell/2$ and a new message m_i. Then the protocol Π_{sgn} is run on input parameters $Param$, message m_i, threshold t_i and the subset of strings $\{sk_i \ : \ i \in T_i\}$, where $T_i = \{j_1, \ldots, j_\ell\}$, and A plays as as each player in $\{P_{i_1}, \ldots, P_{i_\tau}\} \cap \{c, P_{j_1}, \ldots, P_{j_\ell}\}$. This execution of protocol Π_{sgn} returns strings sig_i, out_i. The experiment is *successful* if $out_A = (c'; j'_1, \ldots, j'_\ell; t'; m'; sig')$, where

$\tau \leq t' < \ell/2$, sig' is a valid (t', ℓ)-threshold signature of message m' from parties in subset $T' = \{P_{j_1}, \ldots, P_{j_\ell}\}$, and $(c' \neq c_i) \vee (T' \neq T_i) \vee (t' \neq t_i) \vee (m' \neq m_i)$ for all c_i, T_i, t_i, m_i previously queried by A. We require that for any such A, the above experiment is successful only with probability negligible in the security parameter k.

Robustness. Let A be a probabilistic polynomial time algorithm, called the *adversary*, that chooses τ indices $i_1, \ldots, i_\tau \in \{1, \ldots, n\}$. In the execution of protocol Π_{kg}, A plays as $P_{i_1}, \ldots, P_{i_\tau}$, and in the execution of each protocol Π_{sgn} A plays as $P_{i_1}, \ldots, P_{i_\tau}$, and possibly another party as a client. Then, for any such A, the probability that the correctness requirement does not hold is negligible in the security parameter k.

Additional Security Requirements. Although we will not consider *proactive* and *adaptive security* in MANETs, we note that we can define appropriate notions for both.

Efficiency Requirements. In MANETs we do not rely on a single dealer and therefore the efficiency requirement of *distributed key generation* (as defined for wired networks) is necessary. Potential security problems in the routing of messages through the connectivity graph make the requirements of *non-interactive partial signature generation and verification* and *non-interactive signature reconstruction* (as defined for wired networks) especially desirable. In addition, it is desirable to minimize the *communication latency* of a protocol (which we define as the number of sequential send or forward steps that it takes for the protocol to complete.)

3 Threshold Signatures in Mobile Ad-Hoc Networks

We start by presenting two main tools that we will use in our constructions: a modification of the distributed key generation scheme in [20] and a modification of the signature scheme in [4]. Then we show how to combine them to achieve threshold signature schemes for mobile ad-hoc networks.

3.1 Tools and Subprotocols

Number Theoretic Definitions. Our construction assumes the hardness of the Computational Diffie-Hellman problem on 'so-called' gap-DH groups, based on bilinear maps over elliptic curves. Specifically, consider two groups G_1, G_2 of prime order q and a bilinear map $e : G_1 \times G_1 \to G_2$ between them, that satisfies the following properties:

1. Computable: given $g, h \in G_1$ there is a polynomial time algorithms to compute $e(g, h) \in G_2$.
2. Bilinear: for any integers $x, y \in [1, q]$ we have $e(g^x, g^y) = e(g, g)^{xy}$
3. Non-degenerate: if g is a generator of G_1 then $e(g, g)$ is a generator of G_2.

Here, the size of G_1, G_2 is determined by the security parameter. Such bilinear maps were used in [3] to construct an identity-based public-key cryptosystem and recently to construct other primitives in several other papers. In particular, in [4], the authors construct a very efficient signature scheme, which we describe later, as it will be a component of our scheme. We recall the definition of two well-known computational problems.

Definition 1. CDH Problem: Given a tuple $(< G >, g, g^a, g^b)$, compute g^c, where $c = ab \bmod q$ and $< G >$ denotes the description of group G.

Definition 2. DDH Problem: Given a tuple $(< G >, g, g^a, g^b, g^c)$, decide whether $c = ab \bmod q$. (If so, we say that (g, g^a, g^b, g^c) is a G-DH tuple.)

We define *Gap-DH groups* as groups where the CDH problem is believed to be hard with respect to any probabilistic polynomial algorithm and the DDH problem can be efficiently solved.

A Scheme to Generate a Partial Signature. We describe a scheme that is used by each party while running one execution of a threshold signature subprotocol. This scheme is a slight modification of the signature scheme in [4], that satisfies correctness, unforgeability and robustness (over wired networks) under the assumption that the hash function H is a random oracle and the group G used is a gap-DH group. The modification consists in the fact that, while in the original scheme in [4], the exponentiation of the message is computed over the hash of the message, here we hash the concatenation of the message and various other parameters; specifically, the threshold parameter, the group size and the indices associated with the parties taking part in this execution of a threshold signature protocol. (The modification is crucial in the sense that if only the message were hashed, then an attack violating the unforgeability property would be possible.) We still inherit the very attractive property of the scheme in [4] of having the shortest known signature length (for currently accepted security parameters).

Let G be a gap-DH group of prime order q, and let $H : \{0,1\}^* \to G$ be a full-domain hash function. By $\mathcal{G} = (V, E)$ we denote the connection graph over the n parties; by $T = \{i_1, \ldots, i_\ell\}$, $T \subseteq V$ we denote the subset of parties that is requested by a client C to provide a threshold signature for message M and by $t < \ell/2$ we denote the positive integer denoting the threshold requested by C. We can now define a scheme (S,V) to generate a partial signature, as follows. (Here, S generates a partial signature and V verifies that it was generated correctly.)

- S: on input $r \in Z_q$, message $M \in \{0,1\}^*$, threshold t, integer ℓ, client index c and subset $T = \{i_1, \ldots, i_\ell\}$ of V, do the following: set $m' = M \,|\, t \,|\, \ell \,|\, i_1, \ldots, i_\ell \,|\, c$, $m = H(m')$ and $\sigma = m^r$; return: $sig = \sigma$.
- V: on input $g, v \in G$, message $M \in \{0,1\}^*$, threshold t, integer ℓ, client index c, subset $T = \{i_1, \ldots, i_\ell\}$ of V, and received signature $sig = \sigma$, do the following: compute $m = H(M \,|\, t \,|\, \ell \,|\, i_1, \ldots, i_\ell \,|\, c)$, check that (g, v, m, σ) is a G-DH tuple. If so, return: 1 else return: 0. If no signature sig is received then return: 0.

We note that the last line of V's algorithm deals with the possibility of a signature not reaching the client due to mobility or crashes of any of the two parties. It is not hard to see that even after our modifications, we can still use the proof techniques in [4] to prove the correctness and security properties of this scheme.

A First Distributed Key Generation Protocol. We now present a modified version of the key generation protocol in [20]. Two are the necessary modifications. First, the group G used in the protocol is a gap-DH group, as the private keys returned by the protocol need to be used for the above partial signature generation algorithms S,V. We note that since we are using a multiplicative notation, this will not affect the protocol description. A second modification is necessary as at the end of the protocol in [20] (and similarly in all its applications) a single group key is published. In our scenario, instead, no public key is published as both the threshold parameter and the set of parties that will later generate a threshold signature will be chosen later by a client in an ad hoc manner. Precisely, the protocol in [20] can be divided into three main phases. In the first phase, each party randomly chooses a secret and shares it using the verifiable threshold scheme in [11]. In the second phase, a subset of qualified parties is distributely determined by eliminating all parties that did not perform a correct sharing of their secret, and each party obtains a share by summing the contributions from all parties that have not been eliminated. In the third phase, a joint public key is determined. This latter phase is not necessary in our construction. This is because the first two phases are sufficient to define an implicit public key for any desired subset of parties. We now give a more formal description.

Let G be a gap-DH group of prime order q; we assume that all operations are done over G unless otherwise indicated. Also, we assume that there are n participants and that any two of them are reachable if connected through edges of graph $\mathcal{G} = (V, E)$. (In other words, the routing of messages over $\mathcal{G}$ is reliable. We also assume for simplicity that $\mathcal{G}$ always remains connected.) We define a key distribution protocol $MPed$ as follows (first, we define a protocol where all parties are assumed to be static and then discuss the simple extension to the mobile setting).

- **Input:** threshold t, integer n
- Each party P_i randomly chooses $a_{i0}, \ldots, a_{it} \in Z_q$, defines polynomial $p_i(x) = a_{i0} + a_{i1}x + \cdots + a_{it}x^t$ (where the operations are performed over Z_q), computes $s_{ij} = p_i(j) \bmod q$ for $j = 1, \ldots, n$, and computes $A_{ik} = g^{a_{ik}}$ for $k = 0, \ldots, t$. Each P_i sends A_{ik}, for $k = 0, \ldots, t$, to all parties and s_{ij} secretly to participant P_j.
- Each party P_j verifies the shares received from other parties by checking that, for $i = 1, \ldots, n$, $g^{s_{ij}} = A_{i0}A_{i1}^j A_{i2}^{j^2} \cdots A_{it}^{j^t}$. For any index i for which the check fails, P_j broadcasts a complaint against P_i. If more than t parties complain against P_i, then P_i is disqualified. Otherwise, P_i reveals share s_{ij} for each complaining party P_j. If any of the revealed shares fails the above equation, P_i is disqualified.

- Let $QUAL$ be the set of parties that have not been disqualified.
- Each party P_i returns (as a private output): $(QUAL; \{s_{ij} : j \in QUAL\})$.

The potential mobility of the parties does not significantly affect this protocol. If an edge in $\mathcal{G}$ becomes unavailable, then the secure routing protocol will take care of a different connection between the incident parties (we ruled out the fact that there may be no different connection; but, note that if this is the case, the isolated party or parties have no hope to be part of set $QUAL$ anyway). If a node becomes unavailable, then again this node has no hope to be in $QUAL$ and this fact is advertised to all other parties. If an edge is added, this change to $\mathcal{G}$ is only relevant to how the routing protocol works (whose details we don't deal with). If a node u is added to $\mathcal{G}$, then u runs the steps of a generic party P_i in the above protocol and she is eventually added to $QUAL$ (if she does not cause at least t complaints).

In the single-group version of this protocol, all parties would also return the value $gpk = \Pi_{i \in QUAL} A_{i0}$ as a group public key, which defines the value $gsk = \sum_{i \in QUAL} a_{i0}$ as a shared group secret key. Our protocol defines a public key for each subgroup in $QUAL$ and therefore techniques similar to observations in [15] are essential to prove the unforgeability of our signature scheme. We also note that this subprotocol is constructed assuming the existence of a secure routing protocol as a building block.

A Second Distributed Key Generation Protocol. We will use another modified version of the key generation protocol in [20]. In addition to the two modifications given in the previously described protocol, we add one more modification. Specifically, instead of broadcasting her own information to all other parties, each party will send it only to all parties that are at most some small (i.e., constant) number of hops away. This is sufficient to define an implicit public key for any subset of servers that are later requested to run a threshold signature protocol, as each client will request a signature only from servers that are one hop away from her. The resulting protocol could be seen as a 'bounded' version of the previously described protocol. We now give a more formal description.

Let G be a gap-DH group of prime order q; as before, we assume that there are n participants and that any two of them are reachable through edges of graph $\mathcal{G} = (V, E)$; that is, the routing of messages over $\mathcal{G}$ is reliable, and, for simplicity, $\mathcal{G}$ always remains connected. We denote by $N(i, x)$ the set of nodes in $\mathcal{G}$ that are reachable from party P_i by a path of at most x edges. In this protocol, we also require that each party P_i maintains a connectivity table for $N(i, 2)$. We define a key distribution protocol $BMPed$ (for Bounded MPed) as follows (again, first assuming that the parties are static and then discussing the extension to the general case of mobile parties).

1. **Input:** threshold t, integer n
2. Each party P_i randomly chooses $a_{i0}, \ldots, a_{it} \in Z_q$, defines polynomial $p_i(x) = a_{i0} + a_{i1}x + \cdots + a_{it}x^t$ (where the operations are performed over Z_q), computes $s_{ij} = p_i(j) \bmod q$ for $j = 1, \ldots, n$, and computes $A_{ik} = g^{a_{ik}}$ for $k = 0, \ldots, t$.

Each P_i sends A_{ik}, for $k = 0, \ldots, t$, to all parties in $N(i, 2)$ and s_{ij} secretly to each participant P_j in $N(i, 2)$.

3. Each party P_j verifies the shares received from other parties by checking that, for $i = 1, \ldots, n$, $g^{s_{ij}} = A_{i0} A_{i1}^j A_{i2}^{j^2} \cdots A_{it}^{j^t}$. For any index i for which the check fails, P_j sends a complaint against P_i to all parties in $N(j, 4)$. If any party P_j at ≤ 2 hops away from P_i obtains more than t different complaints against P_i, then P_j broadcasts to all parties evidence to disqualify P_i. Otherwise, P_i reveals share s_{ij} to all parties in $N(i, 6)$ for each complaining party P_j. If any of the revealed shares fails the above equation, evidence that P_i is disqualified is broadcast to all parties.

4. Let $QUAL$ be the set of parties that have not been disqualified.

5. Each party P_i returns (as a private output): $(QUAL; \{s_{ij} \; : \; j \in QUAL \cap N(i, 2)\})$.

The potential mobility of the parties affects $BMPed$ more than the previous protocol $MPed$. This is because we require that each party P_i has to mantain information sent in steps 2 and 3 above from parties in $QUAL \cap N(i, 2)$, and when a party P_j moves, sets $N(i, 2)$ for $i \in N(j, 2)$, may change. Again, we deal with updates by considering additions and deletions of edges or nodes. We do not discuss how the connectivity information is updated as there are many standard non-cryptographic ways to do this, but assume that such a technique is known to the parties. Now, if an edge (i, j) in $\mathcal{G}$ becomes unavailable, then all the connectivity information in $N(a, 2)$, for $a \in N(i, 2) \cup N(j, 2)$ is updated; similarly, if a node i in $\mathcal{G}$ becomes unavailable, then all the connectivity information in $N(a, 2)$, for $a \in N(i, 2)$, is updated.

Now, assume edge (i, j) is added. First of all, the connectivity information in $N(a, 2)$, for $a \in N(i, 1) \cup N(j, 1)$, is updated. Then, each P_b, for $b \in \{i, j\}$ sends A_{bk}, for $k = 0, \ldots, t$, to all new parties in $N(b, 2)$ and s_{ij} secretly to each participant P_j in $N(b, 2)$; and similarly all new parties in $N(b, 2)$ send their $A_{.,k}$ values to P_b. Finally, set $QUAL \cap N(c, 2)$ is updated as in step 2 above for all $c \in N(i, 2) \cap N(j, 2)$.

Now, assume that participant P_i is added. Again, all the connectivity information in $N(a, 2)$, for $a \in N(i, 2)$, is updated. Similarly as before, P_i sends A_{ik}, for $k = 0, \ldots, t$, to each party in $N(i, 2)$ and s_{ij} secretly to each party P_j in $N(i, 2)$; analogously, all parties in $N(i, 2)$ send their $A_{.,k}$ values to P_i. Finally, set $QUAL \cap N(c, 2)$ is updated as in step 2 above for all $c \in N(i, 2)$.

We note that this subprotocol is constructed assuming as a building block the existence of a routing protocol that securely connects each party to any party at a constant number of hops away.

3.2   The Two Threshold Signature Schemes

Recall that graph $\mathcal{G} = (V, E)$ denotes the connections between n parties, and, at any time, client $C \in V$ may request a threshold signature of some message M from her ℓ neighbors $P_{i_1}, \ldots, P_{i_\ell}$, by choosing a threshold parameter t such that $\tau \le t < \ell/2$, and sending t, M, C's index and the indices $i_1, \ldots, i_\ell$ to them. At this point these parties need to run a t-out-of-ℓ threshold signature to sign M. Therefore we solve the problem of designing a threshold signature scheme for MANETs by designing a threshold signature scheme with the following properties: the private keys of the servers are generated in a distributed manner (that is, without help from a central authority or dealer); after the key generation phase, any subset of ℓ parties is able to compute a threshold signature for any arbitrary value t of the threshold such that $t < \ell/2$; the partial signature generation and verification algorithms, as well as the signature reconstruction algorithm require minimal interaction, as they are non-interactive; finally, in our second protocol we even significantly decrease the latency in the key generation protocol.

Given the large amount of threshold signature schemes in the cryptographic literature, we tried to come up with a solution that has as minimal as possible extensions to some known protocols. By inspecting all schemes in the literature, we see that only some schemes satisfy some (and certainly not all) of the mentioned properties. The combination of known schemes that is the closest to our desired solution is obtained by careful modifications of the short signature scheme in [4] and of the distributed key generation scheme in [20]. Specifically, we can obtain a threshold signature scheme for MANETs by properly combining the partial signature scheme and any of the two distributed key generation schemes described in the previous subsection, as follows. We first run several independent copies of the distributed key generation scheme, one for each possible value that the threshold can later assume. Then, upon a request from a client specifying the message to be signed, the threshold and the subset of parties that will generate the threshold signature, we use the described partial signature and verification algorithms on input the various data from the client's request. The input to the partial signing algorithm depends on which parties are requested to participate from the client. The reconstruction of the signature (specifically, the computation of the Lagrange multipliers) depends on which threshold and which set of parties just generated partial signatures for the client. We now give a more formal description of our two protocols.

Our First Protocol. By (S,V) we denote the signing and verification algorithm and by $MPed$ we denote the distributed key generation scheme defined in Section 3.1. We define protocol $MTSig = \Pi = (\Pi_{kg}, \Pi_{sgn})$ as follows. (Subprotocol Π_{kg} is step 1 and subprotocol Π_{sgn} is step 2.)

1. For $t = \tau, \ldots, \lfloor n/2 \rfloor$, parties $P_1, \ldots, P_n$ run an independent execution of protocol $MPed$ on input threshold t and integer n;
   by $A_{t,i,k}$, for $k = 0, \ldots, t$, we denote the values broadcast to all parties from P_i during the execution t of protocol $MPed$
   by $(QUAL^t; \{s_{i,j}^t : j \in QUAL^t\})$ we denote the output of party P_j at the end of execution t of protocol $MPed$
2. For each client C's request $(M; t; \ell; i_1, \ldots, i_\ell; c)$,
   for $j = 1, \ldots, \ell$,
   party P_{i_j} sets $y_{t,j} = \sum_{a=1}^{l} s_{i_j,a}^t$
   party P_{i_j} runs algorithm S on input $(y_{t,j}, M, t, \ell, i_1, \ldots, i_\ell; c)$
   party P_{i_j} sends S's output σ_{i_j} to client C

party C sets $v = A_{t,i_1,0} \cdots A_{t,i_\ell,0}$
party C runs algorithm V on input $(g, v, M, t, \ell, i_1, \ldots, i_\ell, c, \sigma_{i_j})$
party C halts if this execution returns: 0.
    party C computes signature $\sigma = \sigma_{i_1}^{L_{t,1}} \cdots \sigma_{i_\ell}^{L_{t,\ell}}$, where $L_{t,1}, \ldots, L_{t,\ell}$ are the
Lagrange multipliers associated with set $\{P_{i_1}, \ldots, P_{i_\ell}\}$ and threshold t.
party C returns $out = yes$.

We obtain the following

Theorem 1. The protocol $MTSig$ is a threshold signature scheme for mobile ad hoc networks, where: 1) the correctness property holds assuming the existence of a routing protocol that remains secure in the key distribution phase of $MTSig$; 2) the unforgeability and the robustness properties hold with the additional assumptions that H is a random oracle and G is a gap-DH group; 3) the latency of the protocol is $O(d)$, where d is the max diameter of graph $\mathcal{G}$ during the key distribution phase of $MTSig$.

Our Second Protocol. We can define a protocol $BMTSig$ as almost identical to protocol $MTSig$, the only difference being in that $BMTSig$ runs the key distribution protocol $BMPed$ wherever protocol $MTSig$ runs protocol $MPed$. We obtain the following

Theorem 2. The protocol $BMTSig$ is a threshold signature scheme for mobile ad hoc networks, where: 1) the correctness property holds assuming the existence of a routing protocol that remains secure in the key distribution phase of $BMTSig$; 2) the unforgeability and the robustness properties hold with the additional assumptions that H is a random oracle and G is a gap-DH group; 3) the latency of the protocol is $O(1)$.

Remarks. Both proofs cannot be included for lack of space. We note that in both protocols the choice of t from party C should, in practice, depend on the expected number of parties corrupted by the adversary, on the number of expected failures during the execution of the protocol, and on the number of neighbors of C.

Acknowledgement. We thank David Carman for useful discussions.

References

1. J. Algesheimer, J. Camenisch, and V. Shoup, *Efficient Computation Modulo a Shared Secret with Application to the Generation of Shared Safe-Prime Products*, in Proc. of CRYPTO 2002.

2. A. Boldyreva, *Efficient Threshold Signatures, Multisignature and Blind Signature Schemes based on the Gap-Diffie-Hellman-group Signature Scheme*, in Proc. of Public-Key Cryptography 2003.
3. D. Boneh and M. Franklin, *Efficient Generation of Shared RSA Keys*, in Proc. of CRYPTO 97.
4. D. Boneh, B. Lynn, and H. Shacham, *Short Signatures from the Weil Pairing*, in Proc. of Asiacrypt 2001.
5. A. De Santis, Y. Desmedt, Y. Frankel, and M. Yung, *How to Share a Function Securely*, in Proc. of STOC 1994.
6. Y. Desmedt, G. Di Crescenzo and M. Burmester, *Multiplicative Non-Abelian Sharing Schemes and their Application to Threshold Cryptography*, in Proc. of Asiacrypt 94.
7. Y. Desmedt and Y. Frankel, *Threshold Cryptosystems*, in Proc. of CRYPTO 89.
8. Y. Desmedt and Y. Frankel, *Shared Authentication of Authenticators and Signatures*, in Proc. of CRYPTO 91.
9. Y. Desmedt, *Threshold Cryptography*, in European Transaction of Telecommunications, vol. 5, n, 4, 1994.
10. G. Di Crescenzo, R. Ge and G. Arce, *Secure Service Provision for Reliable Service Pooling in MANET*, in Proc. of 24th Army Science Conference 2004, to appear.
11. P. Feldman, *A Practical Scheme for Non-Interactive Verifiable Secret Sharing*, in Proc. of FOCS 87.
12. A. Fouque and J. Stern, *One Round Threshold Discrete-Log Key Generation without Private Channels*, in Proc. of Public Key Cryptography 2001.
13. A. Fouque and J. Stern, *Fully Distributed Threshold RSA under Standard Assumptions*, in Proc. of Asiacrypt 2001.
14. Y. Frankel, P. MacKenzie, and M. Yung, *Robust Efficient Distributed RSA Key Generation*, in Proc. of STOC 98.
15. R. Gennaro, S. Jarecki, H. Krawczyk and T. Rabin, *Revisiting the Distributed Key Generation for Discrete Log Based Cryptosystems*, in Proc. of RSA security conference 03.
16. R. Gennaro, S. Jarecki, H. Krawczyk and T. Rabin, *Robust and Efficient Sharing of RSA Functions*, in Proc. of CRYPTO 96.
17. R. Gennaro, S. Jarecki, H. Krawczyk and T. Rabin, *Robust Threshold DSS*, in Proc. of Eurocrypt 96.
18. J. Katz and M. Yung, *Threshold Cryptosystems based on Factoring*, in Proc. of Asiacrypt 2002.
19. T. Pedersen, *Non-Interactive and Information-Theoretic Secure Verifiable Secret Sharing*, in Proc. of CRYPTO 91.
20. T. Pedersen, *A threshold Cryptosystem without a Trusted Party*, in Proc. of Eurocrypt 91.
21. V. Shoup, *Practical Threshold Signatures*, in Proc. of Eurocrypt 2000.
22. L. Zhou and Z. J. Haas. *Securing Ad Hoc Networks*, in IEEE Network Magazine, vol. 13, no.6, 1999.

Designated Verifier Signatures: Anonymity and Efficient Construction from *Any* Bilinear Map

Fabien Laguillaumie[1,2] and Damien Vergnaud[2]

[1] France Telecom Research and Development,
42, rue des Coutures, B.P. 6243, 14066 Caen Cedex 4, France
[2] Laboratoire de Mathématiques Nicolas Oresme,
Université de Caen, Campus II, B.P. 5186,
14032 Caen Cedex, France
{laguillaumie, vergnaud}@math.unicaen.fr

Abstract. The concept of *Designated Verifier Signatures (DVS)* was introduced by Jakobsson, Sako and Impagliazzo at Eurocrypt'96. These signatures are intended to a specific verifier, who is the only one able to check their validity. In this context, we formalize the notion of *privacy of signer's identity* which captures the *strong designated verifier property* investigated in their paper. We propose a variant of the pairing-based DVS scheme introduced at Asiacrypt'03 by Steinfeld, Bull, Wang and Pieprzyk. Contrary to their proposal, our new scheme can be used with any admissible bilinear map, especially with the low cost pairings and achieves the new anonymity property (in the random oracle model). Moreover, the unforgeability is *tightly* related to the Gap-Bilinear Diffie-Hellman assumption, in the random oracle model and the signature length is around 75 % smaller than the original proposal.

Keywords: Designated verifier signatures, Privacy of signer's identity, Bilinear Diffie-Hellman problems, Exact security, Tight reduction

1 Introduction

Recently, Steinfeld, Bull, Wang and Pieprzyk [17] proposed a designated verifier signature scheme based on pairings. In this article, we propose three techniques which significantly improve this protocol. First of all, a novel use of a hash function in a context of digital signatures permits to rehabilitate the low cost pairing, namely the discrete exponentiation, which has been turned down because it suffers from some unavoidable drawbacks as a bilinear map. The efficiency is increased by a factor of 3.5 to 16, and the signature length is around 75 % smaller than the original proposal. Secondly, we formally define a notion of anonymity of signers, and, randomizing the signatures makes our scheme achieve this property. As a side effect, its unforgeability is *tightly* related to the Gap Bilinear Diffie-Hellman assumption. Finally, the proofs of security rely on a new use of a Decisional Bilinear Diffie-Hellman oracle in the simulation of a random oracle.

C. Blundo and S. Cimato (Eds.): SCN 2004, LNCS 3352, pp. 105–119, 2005.

Related Work. The *self-authenticating* property of digital signatures can be suitable for some applications such as dissemination of official announcements, but it is sometimes undesirable in personally or commercially sensitive applications. Therefore it may be preferable to put some restrictions on this property to prevent potential misuses of signatures. To address this concern, several techniques that allow users to generate a signature with anonymity have been developed over the years. The concept of **D**esignated **V**erifier **S**ignatures (DVS) was introduced by Jakobsson, Sako and Impagliazzo at Eurocrypt'96 [10] and independently by Chaum in the patent [7], under the name of *private signatures*. They are intended to a specific and unique designated verifier, who is the only one able to check their validity. This verifier cannot convince another party that the signature is actually valid, essentially because he can also perform this signature by himself. This means, in particular, that DVS do not provide the main property of ordinary digital signatures, namely non-repudiation. As explained in [10], in some cases, it may be desirable that DVS provide an even stronger notion of privacy: given a DVS and two potential signing public keys, it is computationally infeasible for an eavesdropper to determine under which of the two corresponding secret keys the signature was performed. Following [10], we call *strong designated verifier signatures*, the DVS schemes that achieve this property.

In [14], Rivest, Shamir and Tauman introduced the ring signatures (see also [6]). By setting the size of the ring to two members, these signatures provide DVS. Many ring signatures have been proposed but they do not achieve the strong designated verifier property. Recently, in [15], Saeednia, Kremer and Markowitch proposed very efficient DVS with signatures *à la* Schnorr. They proved the existential unforgeability of their scheme under a no-message attack and argued that their scheme performs the strong designated verifier property (this property is defined in terms of simultability). But lacking a good security model, they could not prove that their scheme achieves these security notions under adaptive chosen-message attack. In [19], Susilo, Zhang and Mu proposed an identity-based strong DVS which is a pairing-based variant of [15] and whose security is investigated in the same model. In [17], Steinfeld, Bull, Wang and Pieprzyk proposed a formalization of *Universal DVS* (UDVS). These are ordinary digital signatures with the additional functionality that any holder of a signature is able to convert it into a DVS specified to any designated verifier of his choice. Moreover they showed that bilinear maps allow an elegant construction of a UDVS scheme (DVSBM). A similar construction has been proposed independently by the authors in [11]. At PKC'04 [18], Steinfeld, Wang and Pieprzyk proposed a slightly stronger security model, which allows the attacker, while mounting a chosen-message attack, to query the verification of any couple message/signature of its choice. In their article they give three new DVS constructions based on Schnorr and RSA signatures.

Our Contributions. In this paper, we formalize the notion of *privacy of signer's identity* which captures the strong designated verifier property. For public-key encryption, Bellare, Boldyreva, Desai and Pointcheval defined, in [1], an additional security requirement which includes the notion that an attacker cannot determine under which key an encryption was performed: it is the idea of *key-privacy*. Our formalization follows this notion. Steinfeld *et al.* proposed at Asiacrypt'03 [17] an interesting and promising scheme based on pairing, which however suffers from a lack of efficiency (compared to [15]'s scheme for instance). Moreover their scheme is not secure with low cost pairings.

We revise it such that, at equal security guarantees, we obtain the most efficient UDVS scheme, and instantiated with the discrete exponentiation we obtain the most efficient DVS protocol in practice (*cf.* Section 4.2), but loose the universal property. The first modification which consists in a novel use of hash function in the asymmetric signature setting makes it possible to shorten the signatures and allows the scheme to be used with any admissible bilinear map. Short signatures are useful for low-bandwidth devices and environments where a person is asked to manually type in the signature. By using this technique, for a security level of 2^{80} bit operations, the signature length is 271 bits and does not depend on the size of the ground field. The second trick consists in making the signature generation not deterministic. With this randomization we can draw a scheme which achieves privacy of signer's identity under an adaptive chosen-message attack in the random oracle model [3]. As in [8], it also makes the unforgeability of the modified scheme *tightly* related to the underlying problem, in the random oracle model. We introduce a new use of a Decisional Bilinear Diffie-Hellman oracle in the security proofs to maintain a random oracle list. We obtain a very tight link between the security of the scheme and the Gap Bilinear Diffie-Hellman assumption, with a quadratic time reduction.

In the rest of the paper, we recall the definition of DVS, then we formalize the new anonymity requirement for DVS. In section 4, we present our new scheme with a precise security treatment. In appendix, we discuss the security of some other schemes.

2   Definition and Security Assumptions for Designated Verifier Signatures

In this section, we state the definition of DVS schemes induced by Steinfeld *et al.*'s formalization.

Definition 1 (Designated Verifier Signature Scheme). *Given an integer k, a (weak) designated verifier signature scheme DVS with security parameter k is defined by the following:*

- *a common parameter generation algorithm DVS.Setup: it is a probabilistic algorithm which takes k as input. The outputs are the public parameters;*
- *a signer key generation algorithm DVS.SKeyGen: it is a probabilistic algorithm which takes the public parameters as input and outputs a pair of signing keys* $(\mathbf{pk_A}, \mathbf{sk_A})$;
- *a verifier key generation algorithm DVS.VKeyGen: it is a probabilistic algorithm which takes the public parameters as inputs, and outputs a pair of verifying keys* $(\mathbf{pk_B}, \mathbf{sk_B})$;

- a designated verifier signing algorithm *DVS.Sign: it takes a message m, a signing secret key* sk_A, *a verifying public key* pk_B *and the public parameters as inputs . The output* σ *is a B-designated verifier signature of m. This algorithm can be either probabilistic or deterministic;*
- a designated verifying algorithm *DVS.Verify: it is a deterministic algorithm which takes a bit string* σ, *a message m, a signing public key* pk_A, *a verifying secret key* sk_B *and the public parameters as inputs, and tests whether* σ *is a valid B-designated verifier signature of m with respect to the keys* (pk_A, sk_A, pk_B, sk_B).

Moreover, a designated verifier signature scheme must satisfy the following properties (formally defined in [18] and discussed below):

1. **correctness**: *a properly formed B-designated verifier signature must be accepted by the verifying algorithm;*
2. **unforgeability**: *given a pair of signing keys* (pk_A, sk_A) *and a pair of verifying keys* (pk_B, sk_B), *it is computationally infeasible, without the knowledge of the secret key* sk_A *or* sk_B, *to produce a valid B-designated verifier signature;*
3. **source hiding**: *given a message m and a B-designated verifier signature* σ *of this message, it is (unconditionally) infeasible to determine who from the original signer or the designated verifier performed this signature, even if one knows all secrets;*

For digital signatures, the widely accepted notion of security was defined by Goldwasser, Micali and Rivest in [9] as *existential forgery against adaptive chosen-message attack* (EF-CMA). For a DVS scheme, the security model proposed in [17] and [18] (under the designation ST-DV-UF) is similar, with the notable difference that, while mounting a chosen-message attack, we allow the attacker to query a verifying oracle on any couple message/signature of its choice. As usual, in the adversary answer, there is the natural restriction that the returned message/signature has not been obtained from the signing oracle (for more details, we refer the reader to [17] and [18]). In order to be consistent with the classical security model for usual signatures, also for DVS we denote this security point by EF-CMA.

In their formalization of UDVS [17] [18], Steinfeld *et al.* defined the *Non-Transferability Privacy* property to prevent a designated-verifier from using a DVS to produce evidence which convinces a third-party that this DVS was actually computed by the signer. However, their notion is computational, and we believe that the identity of the signer should be unconditionally protected (*i.e.* DVS should provide information theoretical anonymity), as in ring signatures (where this security requirement is called *source hiding*).

Finally, even with this unconditional ambiguity, anyone can check that there are only two potential signers for a DVS. If signatures are captured on the line before reaching the verifier, an eavesdropper will be convinced that the designated verifier did not produce the signature. Therefore, in [10], Jakobsson *et al.* suggested a stronger notion of anonymity:

Definition 2 (Strong Designated Verifier Signature Scheme). *Given an integer k, a strong designated verifier signature scheme DVS with security param- eter k is a designated verifier signature scheme with security parameter k, which satisfies the following additional property (formally defined in the next section):*

4. *privacy of signer's identity: given a message m and a B-designated verifier sig- nature σ of this message, it is computationally infeasible, without the knowl- edge of the secret key of B or the one of the signer, to determine which pair of signing keys was used to generate σ.*

3   Anonymity of DVS

3.1   Formal Definition

In this section, we define formally the *privacy of signer's identity* under a chosen message attack (PSI-CMA). We consider a PSI-CMA-adversary $\mathcal{A}$ in the random oracle model, which runs in two stages: in the `find` stage, it takes two signing public keys $\mathbf{pk_{A_0}}$ and $\mathbf{pk_{A_1}}$ and a verifying public key $\mathbf{pk_B}$, and outputs a message $m^\star$ together with some state information $\mathcal{I}^\star$. In the `guess` stage, it gets a challenge B-designated verifier signature $\sigma^\star$ formed by signing the message $m^\star$ at random under one of the two keys and the information $\mathcal{I}^\star$, and must say which key was chosen. The adversary has access to the random oracle(s) $\mathcal{H}$, to the signing oracles $\Sigma_{A_0,B}$, $\Sigma_{A_1,B}$ and to the verifying oracle Υ_B, and is allowed to invoke them on any message with the restriction of not querying $(m^\star, \sigma^\star)$ from the verifying oracle in the second stage.

Definition 3 (Privacy of Signer's Identity). *Let k be an integer and DVS a designated verifier signature scheme with security parameter k. We consider the following random experiment, for $r \in \{0, 1\}$:*

Experiment $\mathbf{Exp}_{DVS,\mathcal{A}}^{psi\text{-}cma-r}(k)$

params $\xleftarrow{R}$ DVS.Setup(k)

$(\mathbf{pk_{A_0}}, \mathbf{sk_{A_0}}) \xleftarrow{R}$ DVS.SKeyGen(params)

$(\mathbf{pk_{A_1}}, \mathbf{sk_{A_1}}) \xleftarrow{R}$ DVS.SKeyGen(params)

$(\mathbf{pk_B}, \mathbf{sk_B}) \xleftarrow{R}$ DVS.VKeyGen(params)

$(m^\star, \mathcal{I}^\star) \leftarrow \mathcal{A}^{\Sigma_{A_0,B}, \Sigma_{A_1,B}, \Upsilon_B, \mathcal{H}}(\textbf{find}, \mathbf{pk_B}, \mathbf{pk_{A_0}}, \mathbf{pk_{A_1}})$

$\sigma^\star \leftarrow$ DVS.Sign(params, $m^\star$, $\mathbf{sk_{A_r}}$, $\mathbf{pk_B}$)

$d \leftarrow \mathcal{A}^{\Sigma_{A_0,B}, \Sigma_{A_1,B}, \Upsilon_B, \mathcal{H}}(\textbf{guess}, m^\star, \mathcal{I}^\star, \sigma^\star, \mathbf{pk_B}, \mathbf{pk_{A_0}}, \mathbf{pk_{A_1}})$

Return d

We define the advantage *of the adversary $\mathcal{A}$, via*

$$\mathbf{Adv}_{DVS,\mathcal{A}}^{psi\text{-}cma}(k) = \left| Pr\left[\mathbf{Exp}_{DVS,\mathcal{A}}^{psi\text{-}cma-1}(k) = 1 \right] - Pr\left[\mathbf{Exp}_{DVS,\mathcal{A}}^{psi\text{-}cma-0}(k) = 1 \right] \right|.$$

Let $t \in \mathbb{N}$ and $\varepsilon \in [0, 1]$. The scheme DVS is said to be (k, t, ε)-PSI-CMA se- cure, if the function $\mathbf{Adv}_{DVS,\mathcal{A}}^{psi\text{-}cma}(k)$ is smaller than ε for any PSI-CMA-adversary $\mathcal{A}$ running in time complexity less than t.

3.2   Semantically Secure Encryption Implies Anonymity

In [10], Jakobsson *et al.* suggested that "in order to make protocols strong designated verifier, transcripts can be probabilistically encrypted using the public key
of the intended verifier". This is not sufficient in general (for instance a plaintext
El Gamal encryption does not protect the anonymity of the signers). However,
in this paragraph, we prove that using an additional IND-CCA2 public-key encryption layer is actually sufficient to make any DVS scheme strong.

Basically, being able to distinguish two potential signing keys in the signature
scheme will give an advantage to distinguish two potential encrypted messages.

Let k be an integer, let DVS be a (weak)-designated verifier signature scheme
with security parameter k and let Π be any IND-CCA2 encryption scheme. We
define a designated verifier signature DVS^{Π} as follows: the generation of a DVS^{Π}
signature of a message m is done by encrypting a DVS signature σ of m under
the designated verifier public key. Its verification is performed by first decrypting
the signature, then verifying it with the DVS.Verify algorithm.

Proposition 1. *Let k be an integer, let DVS be a (weak)-designated verifier signature scheme with security parameter k, and let Π be an IND-CCA2 encryption
scheme with security parameter k. Then DVS^{Π} is a strong designated verifier
signature scheme. More precisely, for any PSI-CMA adversary $\mathcal{A}$ with security
parameter k which takes advantage $\mathbf{Adv}^{psi-cma}_{DVS^{\Pi},\mathcal{A}}$ against DVS^{Π} within time t, making $q_{\mathcal{H}}$, q_{Σ} and q_{Υ} queries to the random oracle(s), the signing oracle and the
verifying oracle respectively, there exists an IND-CCA2 adversary $\mathcal{A}'$ against Π,
making $q_{\mathcal{H}}$ queries to the random oracle(s), and q_{Υ} queries to the decrypting
oracle, within time t, which has the same advantage as $\mathcal{A}$.*

Proof (sketch). A general study of the security notions and attacks for encryption
schemes was conducted in [2]. We refer the reader to this paper for the definition
of IND-CCA2 encryption.

We construct the algorithm $\mathcal{A}'$ as follows:

– $\mathcal{A}'$ is fed with a public key $\mathbf{Epk_B}$ for Π and chooses two pairs of signing
  keys $(\mathbf{sk_{A_0}}, \mathbf{pk_{A_0}})$ $(\mathbf{sk_{A_1}}, \mathbf{pk_{A_1}})$ and a pair of verifying keys $(\mathbf{sk_B}, \mathbf{pk_B})$.
– $\mathcal{A}$ is fed with $\mathbf{Epk_B}$, $\mathbf{pk_B}$, $\mathbf{pk_{A_0}}$ and $\mathbf{pk_{A_1}}$.
– In both stages, for any signing query from $\mathcal{A}$, $\mathcal{A}'$ answers using the secret
  key of either A_0 or A_1. For any verifying query from $\mathcal{A}$, $\mathcal{A}'$ answers using
  the secret key $\mathbf{Dpk_B}$ of B and the decryption oracle.
– Eventually, in the find stage, $\mathcal{A}$ outputs a message $m \in \{0,1\}^*$.
– $\mathcal{A}'$ computes two pre-signatures σ_0 and σ_1 using the DVS.Sign algorithm
  of the message m, and queries these signatures to the IND-CCA2 challenger
  which answers with an encryption of σ_b where $b \in_R \{0,1\}$.
– $\mathcal{A}'$ gives this challenge to $\mathcal{A}$ as the answer to the PSI-CMA challenge. The
  only verification query that $\mathcal{A}'$ cannot answer is the one $\mathcal{A}$ is not allowed to
  ask.
– Finally $\mathcal{A}$ outputs a bit b' in the guess stage.

By definition of $\mathcal{A}$, $b' = b$ with probability $\mathbf{Adv}^{\text{psi-cma}}_{\text{DVS}^{\Pi},\mathcal{A}}$ and $\mathcal{A}'$ distinguishes the two messages σ_0 and σ_1 encrypted by Π with the same advantage $\mathbf{Adv}^{\text{ind-cca}}_{\Pi,\mathcal{A}'} = \mathbf{Adv}^{\text{psi-cma}}_{\text{DVS}^{\Pi},\mathcal{A}}$. This concludes the proof.

4   The New Scheme : DVSBMH

4.1   Bilinear Maps and Underlying Problems

In this section, we recall some definitions concerning bilinear maps.

Definition 4 (Admissible Bilinear Map [4]). *Let* $(\mathbb{G}_0, +)$, $(\mathbb{G}_1, +)$ *and* $(\mathbb{H}, \times)$ *be three groups of the same prime order* q *and let* P_0 *and* P_1 *be two generators of* $\mathbb{G}_0$ *and* $\mathbb{G}_1$ *(respectively). An* admissible bilinear map *is a map* $e : \mathbb{G}_0 \times \mathbb{G}_1 \longrightarrow \mathbb{H}$ *satisfying the following properties:*

- *bilinear:* $e(aQ, bR) = e(Q, R)^{ab}$ *for all* $(Q, R) \in \mathbb{G}_0 \times \mathbb{G}_1$ *and all* $(a, b) \in \mathbb{Z}^2$;
- *non-degenerate:* $e(P_0, P_1) \neq 1$;
- *computable: there exists an efficient algorithm to compute* e.

Definition 5 (Prime-Order-BDH-Parameter-Generator [4]). *A prime-order-BDH-parameter-generator is a probabilistic algorithm that takes a security parameter* k *as input and outputs a 7-tuple* $(q, P_0, \mathbb{G}_0, P_1, \mathbb{G}_1, \mathbb{H}, e)$ *satisfying the following conditions:* q *is a prime with* $2^k < q < 2^{k+1}$, *the groups* $\mathbb{G}_0, \mathbb{G}_1$ *and* $\mathbb{H}$ *are of order* q, P_0 *and* P_1 *generates* $\mathbb{G}_0$ *and* $\mathbb{G}_1$ *(respectively), and* $e : \mathbb{G}_0 \times \mathbb{G}_1 \longrightarrow \mathbb{H}$ *is an admissible bilinear map. A prime-order-BDH-parameter-generator* $\mathcal{G}en$ *is said to be* symmetric *if* $P_0 = P_1$ *and* $\mathbb{G}_0 = \mathbb{G}_1$ *for any 7-tuple* $(q, P_0, \mathbb{G}_0, P_1, \mathbb{G}_1, \mathbb{H}, e)$ *output by* $\mathcal{G}en$.

Let $(\mathbb{G}_0, +)$, $(\mathbb{G}_1, +)$ and $(\mathbb{H}, \times)$ be three groups of the same large prime order q, P_0 and P_1 be two generators of $\mathbb{G}_0$ and $\mathbb{G}_1$ (respectively), and let $e : \mathbb{G}_0 \times \mathbb{G}_1 \longrightarrow \mathbb{H}$ be an admissible bilinear map. For most of the applications of pairings in cryptography, it is necessary to know an efficient way to compute an isomorphism $\varphi : \mathbb{G}_0 \simeq \mathbb{G}_1$. Contrary to Weil or Tate pairings, this is not true for the discrete exponentiation $e : \langle P_0 \rangle \times (\mathbb{Z}/q\mathbb{Z}, +) \longrightarrow \langle P_0 \rangle, (P, x) \longmapsto xP$ where the map $\langle P_0 \rangle \longrightarrow \mathbb{Z}/q\mathbb{Z}$ is the discrete logarithm.

At PKC'01, Okamoto and Pointcheval proposed a new class of computational problems, called gap problems [13]. Essentially, a gap problem is a dual to inverting and decisional problems. More precisely, this problem is to solve an inverting problem with the help of an oracle for a decisional problem. Following this idea, we state the following problems (where $\mathbb{G}_0$ and $\mathbb{G}_1$ have not a symmetric role):

Computational Bilinear Diffie-Hellman (CBDH): let a, b and c be three integers. Given aP_0, bP_0, cP_1, compute $e(P_0, P_1)^{abc}$.

Decisional Bilinear Diffie-Hellman (DBDH): let a, b, c and d be four integers. Given aP_0, bP_0, cP_1 and $e(P_0, P_1)^d$, decide whether $d = abc \mod q$.

Gap-Bilinear Diffie-Hellman (GBDH): let a, b and c be three integers. Given aP_0, bP_0, cP_1, compute $e(P_0, P_1)^{abc}$ with the help of a DBDH Oracle.

Definition 6 (CBDH and GBDH Assumption). *Let $\mathcal{G}en$ be a prime-order-BDH-parameter-generator. Let D be an adversary that takes as input a 7-tuple $(q, P_0, \mathbb{G}_0, P_1, \mathbb{G}_1, \mathbb{H}, e)$ generated by $\mathcal{G}en$ and $(X, Y, Z) \in \mathbb{G}_0^2 \times \mathbb{G}_1$. He returns an element of $h \in \mathbb{H}$. We consider the following random experiments, where k is a security parameter and $\mathcal{O}_{DBDH}$ is a DBDH oracle:*

Experiment $\mathbf{Exp}^{\mathsf{cbdh}}_{\mathcal{G}en, D}(k)$	Experiment $\mathbf{Exp}^{\mathsf{gbdh}}_{\mathcal{G}en, D}(k)$
$(q, P_0, \mathbb{G}_0, P_1, \mathbb{G}_1, \mathbb{H}, e) \xleftarrow{R} \mathcal{G}en(k)$	$(q, P_0, \mathbb{G}_0, P_1, \mathbb{G}_1, \mathbb{H}, e) \xleftarrow{R} \mathcal{G}en(k)$
$\mathbf{setup} \leftarrow (q, P_0, \mathbb{G}_0, P_1, \mathbb{G}_1, \mathbb{H}, e)$	$\mathbf{setup} \leftarrow (q, P_0, \mathbb{G}_0, P_1, \mathbb{G}_1, \mathbb{H}, e)$
$x \xleftarrow{R} [\![1, q-1]\!],\ X \leftarrow xP_0$	$x \xleftarrow{R} [\![1, q-1]\!],\ X \leftarrow xP_0$
$y \xleftarrow{R} [\![1, q-1]\!],\ Y \leftarrow yP_0$	$y \xleftarrow{R} [\![1, q-1]\!],\ Y \leftarrow yP_0$
$z \xleftarrow{R} [\![1, q-1]\!],\ Z \leftarrow zP_1$	$z \xleftarrow{R} [\![1, q-1]\!],\ Z \leftarrow zP_1$
$h \leftarrow D(\mathbf{setup}, X, Y, Z)$	$h \leftarrow D^{\mathcal{O}_{DBDH}}(\mathbf{setup}, X, Y, Z)$
Return 1 if $h = e(P_0, P_1)^{xyz}$,	Return 1 if $h = e(P_0, P_1)^{xyz}$,
0 otherwise	0 otherwise

We define the success of D in solving the CBDH and the GBDH problems via

$$\mathbf{Succ}^{\mathsf{cbdh}}_{\mathcal{G}en, D}(k) = \Pr[\mathbf{Exp}^{\mathsf{cbdh}}_{\mathcal{G}en, D}(k) = 1] \text{ and } \mathbf{Succ}^{\mathsf{gbdh}}_{\mathcal{G}en, D}(k) = \Pr[\mathbf{Exp}^{\mathsf{gbdh}}_{\mathcal{G}en, D}(k) = 1]$$

Let t be an integer and ε a real in $[0, 1]$. $\mathcal{G}en$ is said to be (k, t, ε)-CBDH-secure (resp. (k, t, ε)-GBDH-secure) if no adversary D running in time t has success $\mathbf{Succ}^{\mathsf{cbdh}}_{\mathcal{G}en, D}(k) \geq \varepsilon$ (resp. $\mathbf{Succ}^{\mathsf{gbdh}}_{\mathcal{G}en, D}(k) \geq \varepsilon$).

Notations : we denote by $T_{\mathrm{Exp-G}}$ the time complexity for evaluating exponentiation in a group $\mathbb{G}$ and $T_{\mathcal{O}}$ the time complexity of the oracle $\mathcal{O}$.

4.2   Description of the New Scheme DVSBMH

The scheme DVSBM, proposed at Asiacrypt'03 by Steinfeld *et al.* [17] is a pairing-based DVS. The signature generation is deterministic, therefore this scheme can certainly not achieve the PSI-CMA security point. The authors required that the isomorphism between $\mathbb{G}_0$ and $\mathbb{G}_1$ is known and efficiently computable. In fact, DVSBM is trivially *not* secure if we use the discrete exponentiation.

We introduce a variant of DVSBM which is more efficient, achieves the property of privacy of signer's identity and whose security is proven even if we use the discrete exponentiation. For industrial purposes, where efficiency prevails over exact security, the choice of the parameters is oriented by the underlying algorithmic problems without consideration of the reduction cost in the security proof (we call it *industrial security*). Considering the best algorithms to solve GBDH in both settings, the scheme with the discrete exponentiation will be prefered in practice, whereas the scheme with the Weil or Tate pairing has a tighter security reduction.

In DVSBM, the verification of signatures consists only in checking an equality between two quantities which can be computed independently by the signer and the verifier, it is actually sufficient to check the equality of some hash values of these quantities. This first remark, which seems to have been overlooked in [17], makes it possible to shorten the signature considerably and to use the discrete exponentiation to instantiate the protocol.

Our second trick aims at randomizing the signature. We prove that this is sufficient to obtain the anonymity of signers. Moreover, the security of the signature is *tightly* related to the GBDH and this random salt ensures the anonymity of signers. Using these tricks, we define DVSBMH.

Description of DVSBMH

Setup Let k be a security parameter. Let $\mathcal{G}en$ be a prime-order-BDH-parameter-generator, f_1, f_2, $f_r : \mathbb{N} \to \mathbb{N}$ be three functions. We denote $k_1 = f_1(k)$, $k_2 = f_2(k)$ and $n_r = f_r(k)$. Let $(q, P_0, \mathbb{G}_0, P_1, \mathbb{G}_1, \mathbb{H}, e)$ be a 7-tuple generated by $\mathcal{G}en(k_1)$. Let $[\{0,1\}^* \times \{0,1\}^{n_r} \longrightarrow \mathbb{G}_1]$ be a hash function family, and h be a random member of this family. Let $[\mathbb{H} \longrightarrow \{0,1\}^{k_2}]$ be a hash function family, and g be a random member of this family.

SKeyGen $a \in [\![1, q-1]\!]$ is the secret key, $P_A = aP_0$ is the public one
VKeyGen $b \in [\![1, q-1]\!]$ is the secret key, $P_B = bP_0$ is the public one

Sign Given a message m, the secret key a of the signer, the public key P_B of the designated verifier, compute $H = h(m, r)$ for some random string r of length n_r and $s = g(e(P_B, aH))$ and the signature is $\sigma = (r, s)$.

Verify Given a pair $(m, (s, r))$, the signer's public key P_A, and the verifier's secret key b, the algorithm accepts the signature if and only if $s = g(e(P_A, bh(m, r)))$.

In practice, for a security requirement of 2^{80} operations (*i.e.* $k = 80$), we use the values $k_1 = k_2 = 160$ and $n_r = 111$ which are derived from the security proofs (*cf.* [12]). The correctness and source hiding properties of DVSBMH are straightforward. In general, the new scheme does not satisfy the universal property from [17] any more, because the security of BLS signatures [5] relies on the existence of an efficiently computable isomorphism from $\mathbb{G}_0$ to $\mathbb{G}_1$.

4.3   Security of DVSBMH When $\mathbb{G}_0 = \mathbb{G}_1$

Here we formally investigate the security of the version of DVSBMH for which we know an algorithm to compute the isomorphism between $\mathbb{G}_0$ and $\mathbb{G}_1$ in the random oracle model (*i.e.* we replace the hash functions h and g by random oracles $\mathcal{H}$ and $\mathcal{G}$). For simplicity, we assume $\mathbb{G}_0 = \mathbb{G}_1 = \mathbb{G}$. In practice such a setting can be obtained with, for instance, the Weil or Tate pairing. In this case our new scheme can be extended to a UDVS scheme related to the randomized BLS signatures [5, 8]. This is an important consideration because we prove that the unforgeability is *tightly* related to the GBDH problem, therefore this scheme offers the best exact security of all DVS protocols. Moreover, it achieves the privacy of signer's identity under the CBDH assumption (with the random salt but without the g hash function, the anonymity would have been related to DBDH, an easier problem). These results are described in the following theorems.

Theorem 1 (Unforgeability of DVSBMH). *Let $\mathcal{G}en$ be a symmetric prime-order-BDH-parameter-generator, let f_1, f_2, $f_r : \mathbb{N} \rightarrow \mathbb{N}$ be three functions and let DVSBMH be the associated DVS scheme. For any EF-CMA-adversary $\mathcal{A}$, in the random oracle model, against DVSBMH, with security parameter k which has success $\varepsilon = \mathbf{Succ}_{DVSBMH,\mathcal{A}}^{ef-cma}(k)$, running time t, and makes $q_{\mathcal{H}}$ and $q_{\mathcal{G}}$ queries to the random oracles, q_{Σ} queries to the signing oracles and q_{Υ} queries to the verifying oracle, there exists an adversary D for GBDH which has advantage $\varepsilon' = \mathbf{Succ}_{\mathcal{G}en,D}^{gbdh}(k)$ running in time $t' \in \mathbb{N}$ such that*

$$\begin{cases} \varepsilon' \geq \varepsilon - \dfrac{(q_{\mathcal{H}} + q_{\Sigma})q_{\Sigma}}{2^{n_r}} - (1 + q_{\Upsilon})\left(\dfrac{q_{\mathcal{G}}}{2^{k_1}} + \dfrac{1}{2^{k_2}}\right) \\ t' \leq t + (q_{\mathcal{H}} + q_{\Sigma})\left(T_{Exp-\mathbb{G}} + O(1)\right) + q_{\Sigma}\left(T_{Exp-\mathbb{H}} + O(1)\right) \\ \qquad + (q_{\Upsilon} + 1)\left(T_{DBDH} + O(1)\right) \end{cases}$$

where $k_1 = f_1(k)$, $k_2 = f_2(k)$ and $n_r = f_r(k)$.

Proof. The proof is a straightforward modification of the proof of [17] using the additional technique in [8]. Due to the lack of space, we have not written it down.

Theorem 2 (Anonymity of DVSBMH). *Let $\mathcal{G}en$ be a symmetric prime-order-BDH-parameter-generator, let f_1, f_2, $f_r : \mathbb{N} \rightarrow \mathbb{N}$ be three functions and let DVSBMH be the associated DVS scheme. For any PSI-CMA-adversary $\mathcal{A}$, in the random oracle model, against DVSBMH, with security parameter k which has advantage $\varepsilon = \mathbf{Adv}_{DVSBMH,\mathcal{A}}^{psi-cma}(k)$, running time t, and makes $q_{\mathcal{H}}$ and $q_{\mathcal{G}}$ queries to the random oracles, q_{Σ} queries to the signing oracles and q_{Υ} queries to the verifying oracle, there exists an adversary D for CBDH which has advantage $\varepsilon' = \mathbf{Succ}_{\mathcal{G}en,D}^{cbdh}(k)$ running in time $t' \in \mathbb{N}$ such that*

$$\begin{cases} \varepsilon' \geq \dfrac{\varepsilon}{2q_{\mathcal{G}}} - \dfrac{(q_{\mathcal{H}} + q_{\Sigma} + 1)(q_{\Sigma} + 1)}{2^{n_r}q_{\mathcal{G}}} - \dfrac{q_{\Upsilon}}{2^{k_2}q_{\mathcal{G}}} - \dfrac{q_{\mathcal{G}}q_{\Upsilon}}{2^{k_1}q_{\mathcal{G}}} \\ t' \leq t + (q_{\mathcal{H}} + q_{\Sigma})(T_{Exp-\mathbb{G}} + O(1)) + (q_{\Sigma} + q_{\Upsilon})(T_{Exp-\mathbb{H}} + O(1)) \end{cases}$$

where $k_1 = f_1(k)$, $k_2 = f_2(k)$ and $n_r = f_r(k)$.

Proof. Due to lack of space, the proof will be given in the full version of the paper [12].

4.4   Security of the General Scheme

It is not necessary, thanks to our construction, to know explicitly an isomorphism between $\mathbb{G}_0$ and $\mathbb{G}_1$ to achieve a secure scheme. In this general case, we have a leak in terms of exact security compared to the previous case. In fact, we obtain a very tight link between the success probability of the adversary and the success in solving the GBDH problem but the reduction is quadratic time. When we use the discrete exponentiation as the underlying pairing (and so without the isomorphism), we get the best *industrial security*. We provide here the proof of the unforgeability, with the use of a decisional oracle to maintain the random oracle lists. The proof of the anonymity follows the same lines.

Theorem 3 (Unforgeability of DVSBMH). *Let $\mathcal{G}en$ be a prime-order-BDH-parameter-generator, let f_1, f_2, $f_r : \mathbb{N} \to \mathbb{N}$ be three functions and let DVSBMH be the associated DVS scheme. For any EF-CMA-adversary $\mathcal{A}$, in the random oracle model, against DVSBMH, with security parameter k which has success $\varepsilon = \mathbf{Succ}^{ef-cma}_{DVSBMH,\mathcal{A}}$, running time t, and makes $q_{\mathcal{H}}$ and $q_{\mathcal{G}}$ queries to the random oracles, q_{Σ} queries to the signing oracles and q_{Υ} queries to the verifying oracle, there exists an adversary D for GBDH which has success $\varepsilon' = \mathbf{Succ}^{gbdh}_{\mathcal{G}en,D}(k)$ running in time $t' \in \mathbb{N}$ such that*

$$
\begin{cases}
\varepsilon' \geq \varepsilon - \dfrac{q_{\Sigma}(q_{\mathcal{H}} + q_{\Sigma} + 1)}{2^{n_r}} - \dfrac{(q_{\mathcal{G}} + q_{\Sigma} + 1)(q_{\Sigma} + q_{\Upsilon} + 1)}{2^{k_1}} - \dfrac{(q_{\Upsilon} + 1)(q_{\Sigma} + 1)}{2^{k_2}} \\
t' \leq t + (q_{\mathcal{H}} + 2q_{\Sigma} + 1)\left(T_{Exp-\mathbb{G}_1} + O(1)\right) \\
\qquad + (q_{\mathcal{G}} + q_{\Sigma} + 1)(q_{\mathcal{G}} + q_{\Sigma} + q_{\Upsilon})\left(T_{DDH} + O(1)\right),
\end{cases}
$$

where $k_1 = f_1(k)$, $k_2 = f_2(k)$ and $n_r = f_r(k)$.

Proof. The method of our proof is inspired by Shoup [16]: we define a sequence of games of modified attacks starting from the actual adversary. Let k be a security parameter, let $(q, P_0, \mathbb{G}_0, P_1, \mathbb{G}_1, \mathbb{H}, e)$ be a 7-tuple generated by $\mathcal{G}en(k_1)$ and (R_1, R_2, R_3) be a random instance of the GBDH problem.

Game$_0$ We consider an EF-CMA-adversary $\mathcal{A}$ with success $\varepsilon = \mathbf{Succ}^{ef-cma}_{DVSBMH,\mathcal{A}}(k)$, within time t. The key generation algorithms are run and produce two pairs of keys $(\mathbf{sk_A}, \mathbf{pk_A})$ and $(\mathbf{sk_B}, \mathbf{pk_B})$. The adversary $\mathcal{A}$ is fed with $\mathbf{pk_A}$ and $\mathbf{pk_B}$ and, querying the random oracles $\mathcal{H}$ and $\mathcal{G}$, the signing oracle $\Sigma_{A,B}$ and the verifying oracle $\Upsilon_{A,B}$, it outputs a $(m^\star, (r^\star, s^\star))$ pair.

We denote by $q_{\mathcal{H}}$, $q_{\mathcal{G}}$, q_{Σ} and q_{Υ} the numbers of queries from the random oracles $\mathcal{H}$ and $\mathcal{G}$, from the signing oracle $\Sigma_{A,B}$ and from the verifying oracle $\Upsilon_{A,B}$. The only requirement is that the output signature $(r^\star, s^\star)$ has not been obtained from the signing oracle. When the adversary outputs its forgery, it can be checked whether it is actually valid or not. In any Game$_j$, we denote by Forge$_j$ the event DVSBMH.Verify$(m^\star, (r^\star, s^\star), \mathbf{sk_B}, \mathbf{pk_A}) = 1$.

By definition, we have $\Pr[\mathsf{Forge_0}] = \mathbf{Succ}^{ef-cma}_{DVSBMH,\mathcal{A}}(k)$.

Game$_1$ We modify the simulation by replacing $\mathbf{pk_A}$ by R_1 and $\mathbf{pk_B}$ by R_2. The distribution of $(\mathbf{pk_A}, \mathbf{pk_B})$ is unchanged since (R_1, R_2, R_3) is a random instance of the GBDH problem. Therefore we have $\Pr[\mathsf{Forge_1}] = \Pr[\mathsf{Forge_0}]$.

Game$_2$ In this game, we simulate the random oracle $\mathcal{H}$. For any fresh query $(m, r) \in \{0,1\}^\star \times \{0,1\}^{n_r}$ to the oracle $\mathcal{H}$, we pick $u \in [\![1, q-1]\!]$ at random and compute $Q = uR_3$. We store (m, r, u, Q) in the H-List and return Q as the answer to the oracle call. In the random oracle model, this game is clearly identical to the previous one. Hence, $\Pr[\mathsf{Forge_2}] = \Pr[\mathsf{Forge_1}]$.

Game₃ We simulate the random oracle $\mathcal{G}$ by maintaining an appropriate G-List. For any query $\tilde{s} \in \mathbb{H}$,
  - we check whether the G-List contains a triple $(\tilde{s}, \perp, s)$. If it does, we output s as the answer to the oracle call,
  - else, we browse the G-List and check for all triples $(\perp, u, s)$ whether $(\mathbf{pk_A}, \mathbf{pk_B}, uP_1, \tilde{s})$ is a valid Bilinear Diffie-Hellman quadruple. If it does, we give s as the answer,
  - otherwise we pick at random $s \in \{0,1\}^{k_2}$, record $(\tilde{s}, \perp, s)$ in the G-List, and output s as the answer to the oracle call.

  We have $\Pr[\mathsf{Forge_3}] = \Pr[\mathsf{Forge_2}]$.

Game₄ We now simulate the signing oracle: for any m, whose signature is queried, we pick at random three elements $r \in \{0,1\}^{n_r}$, $s \in \{0,1\}^{k_2}$, $u \in [\![1, q-1]\!]$, and compute $Q = uP_1$.
  - If the H-List includes a quadruple $(m, r, ?, ?)$ we abort the simulation, else we store (m, r, u, Q) in the H-List,
  - we browse the G-List and check for all triples $(\tilde{s}, \perp, ?)$ (resp. $(\perp, v, ?)$) whether $(\mathbf{pk_A}, \mathbf{pk_B}, uP_1, \tilde{s})$ is a valid Bilinear Diffie-Hellman quadruple (resp. wether $u = v$). If it does, we abort the simulation,
  - otherwise, we record $(\perp, u, s)$ in the G-List, and output (r, s).

  Since there are at most $q_{\mathcal{H}} + q_{\Sigma} + 1$ messages queried to the random oracle $\mathcal{H}$ and $q_{\mathcal{G}} + q_{\Sigma} + 1$ messages queried to the random oracle $\mathcal{G}$, the new simulation aborts with probability at most $(q_{\mathcal{H}} + q_{\Sigma} + 1) \cdot 2^{-n_r} + (q_{\mathcal{G}} + q_{\Sigma} + 1) \cdot 2^{-k_1}$. Otherwise, this new oracle perfectly simulates the signature. Summing up for all signing queries, we obtain

$$|\Pr[\mathsf{Forge_4}] - \Pr[\mathsf{Forge_3}]| \leq \left(\frac{(q_{\mathcal{H}} + q_{\Sigma} + 1)}{2^{n_r}} + \frac{(q_{\mathcal{G}} + q_{\Sigma} + 1)}{2^{k_1}} \right) q_{\Sigma}$$

Game₅ In this game, we make the verifying oracle reject all couples message/signature $(m, (r, s))$ such that s has not been obtained from $\mathcal{G}$. As in **Game₅** of the previous proof, we get $|\Pr[\mathsf{Forge_5}] - \Pr[\mathsf{Forge_4}]| \leq (q_{\Upsilon} + 1)2^{-k_2}$.

Game₆ In this game, we finally simulate the verifying oracle. For any couple message/signature $(m, (r, s))$, whose verification is queried, we check whether the H-List includes a quadruple $(m, r, ?, ?)$. If it does not, we reject the signature. Therefore the H-List includes a quadruple (m, r, u, Q), and we browse the G-List: if it includes a triple $(\tilde{s}, \perp, s)$, we accept the signature if and only if $(\mathbf{pk_A}, \mathbf{pk_B}, Q, \tilde{s})$ is a valid Bilinear Diffie-Hellman quadruple; else the G-List includes a triple $(\perp, v, s)$ and we accept the signature if and only if $u = v$. As in **Game₆** of the previous proof, we get

$$|\Pr[\mathsf{Forge_6}] - \Pr[\mathsf{Forge_5}]| \leq \frac{(q_{\mathcal{G}} + q_{\Sigma} + 1)(q_{\Upsilon} + 1)}{2^{k_1}} + \frac{q_{\Sigma}(q_{\Upsilon} + 1)}{2^{k_2}}.$$

When the game **Game₆** terminates, outputting a valid message/signature $(m^\star, (r^\star, s^\star))$ pair, by definition of existential forgery, the H-List includes a quadruple $(m^\star, r^\star, u^\star, Q^\star)$ with $Q^\star = u^\star R_3$.

By the simulation $(\mathbf{pk_A}, \mathbf{pk_B}, Q^\star, \tilde{s}^\star)$ is a valid Bilinear Diffie-Hellman quadruple, and therefore $z = (\tilde{s}^\star)^{(u^\star)^{-1}}$ gives the solution to the GBDH problem instance (R_1, R_2, R_3), and we obtained the claimed bounds.

Theorem 4 (Anonymity of DVSBMH). *Let $\mathcal{G}en$ be a prime-order-BDH-parameter-generator, let f_1, f_2, $f_r : \mathbb{N} \to \mathbb{N}$ be three functions and let DVSBMH be the associated DVS scheme. For any PSI-CMA-adversary $\mathcal{A}$, in the random oracle model, against DVSBMH, with security parameter k which has advantage $\varepsilon = \mathbf{Adv}_{DVSBMH,\mathcal{A}}^{psi-cma}(k)$, running time t, and makes $q_{\mathcal{H}}$ and $q_{\mathcal{G}}$ queries to the random oracles, q_Σ queries to the signing oracles and q_Υ queries to the verifying oracle, there exists an adversary D for GBDH which has success $\varepsilon' = \mathbf{Succ}_{\mathcal{G}en,D}^{gbdh}(k)$ running in time $t' \in \mathbb{N}$ such that*

$$\begin{cases} \varepsilon' \geq \dfrac{\varepsilon}{2} - \dfrac{q_\Sigma(q_{\mathcal{H}}+q_\Sigma+1)}{2^{n_r}} - \dfrac{(q_{\mathcal{G}}+q_\Sigma+1)}{2^{k_1}}(q_\Sigma + q_\Upsilon + 1) - \dfrac{(q_\Upsilon+1)(q_\Sigma+1)}{2^{k_2}} \\ t' \leq t + (q_{\mathcal{H}} + 2q_\Sigma + 1)\left(T_{Exp-\mathbb{G}_1} + O(1)\right) \\ \qquad + (q_{\mathcal{G}} + q_\Sigma + 1)(q_{\mathcal{G}} + q_\Sigma + q_\Upsilon)\left(T_{DDH} + O(1)\right), \end{cases}$$

where $k_1 = f_1(k)$, $k_2 = f_2(k)$ and $n_r = f_r(k)$.

5 Conclusion

We designed an efficient construction for strong DVS based on *any* bilinear map (which is a variant of DVSBM from [17]), and clarified the property of anonymity of the signers. Unlike Steinfeld *et al.*, our construction can be instantiated with the discrete exponentiation. In this case, the unforgeability and the privacy of signer's identity are related to the Gap Diffie-Hellman problem, since the discrete logarithm in $\mathbb{G}_1$ is easy. This new scheme offers the best performance in terms of computational cost and signature length. The DVSBMH scheme built on the discrete exponentiation is closely bound to a Diffie-Hellman session key exchange. The general relationship between session key exchange and DVS seems to be an interesting topic for further research.

Ackowledgements. We express our gratitude to Jacques Traoré, Pascal Paillier and Éric Reyssat for their helpful comments. Many thanks to Pierre and Laura for correcting some misprints and our broken english.

References

1. M. Bellare, A. Boldyreva, A. Desai, D. Pointcheval: Key-Privacy in Public-Key Encryption. Proc. of Asiacrypt'01, Springer LNCS Vol. 2248, 566-582 (2001)
2. M. Bellare, A. Desai, D. Pointcheval and P. Rogaway: Relations among Notions of Security for Public-Key Encryption Schemes. Proc of Crypto'98, Springer LNCS Vol. 1462, 162-177 (1998)
3. M. Bellare, P. Rogaway: Random Oracles are Practical: a Paradigm for Designing Efficient Protocols. Proc. of 1st ACM Conference on Computer and Communications Security, 62-73 (1993)
4. D. Boneh, M. Franklin: Identity-based Encryption from the Weil Pairing. SIAM J. Computing, 32(3), 586-615 (2003)
5. D. Boneh, B. Lynn, H. Shacham: Short Signatures from the Weil Pairing. Proc of Asiacrypt'01, Springer LNCS Vol. 2248, 514-532 (2001)

6. J. Camenisch: Efficient and Generalized Group Signatures. Proc of Eurocrypt'97, Springer LNCS Vol. 1233, 465–479 (1997)
7. D. Chaum: Private Signature and Proof Systems. United States Patent 5,493,614 (1996)
8. E.-J. Goh, S. Jarecki: A Signature Scheme as Secure as the Diffie-Hellman Problem. Proc of Eurocrypt'03, Springer LNCS Vol. 2656, 401–415 (2003)
9. S. Goldwasser, S. Micali, R. L. Rivest: A digital signature scheme secure against adaptive chosen-message attacks. SIAM J. of Computing, 17 (2) 281–308 (1988)
10. M. Jakobsson, K. Sako, R. Impagliazzo: Designated Verifier Proofs and their Applications. Proc. of Eurocrypt'96, Springer LNCS Vol. 1070, 142–154 (1996)
11. F. Laguillaumie, D. Vergnaud: Efficient and Provably Secure Designated Verifier Signature Schemes from Bilinear Maps. Crypto'03 rump session. Rapport de Recherche LMNO, 2003-25, 16 pages (2003)
12. F. Laguillaumie, D. Vergnaud: Designated Verifier Signatures: Anonymity and Efficient Construction from *any* Bilinear Map. Full version, IACR e-print.
13. T. Okamoto, D. Pointcheval: The Gap-Problems: a New Class of Problems for the Security of Cryptographic Schemes. Proc. of PKC'01 Springer LNCS Vol. 1992, 104–118 (2001)
14. R. L. Rivest, A. Shamir, Y. Tauman: How to Leak a Secret. Proc. of Asiacrypt'01, Springer LNCS Vol. 2248, 552–565 (2001)
15. S. Saeednia, S. Kremer, O. Markowitch: An Efficient Strong Designated Verifier Signature Scheme. Proc. of ICISC 2003, Springer LNCS Vol. 2836, 40–54 (2003)
16. V. Shoup: OAEP reconsidered. J. Cryptology, Vol. 15 (4), 223–249 (2002)
17. R. Steinfeld, L. Bull, H. Wang, J. Pieprzyk: Universal Designated Verifier Signatures. Proc. of Asiacrypt'03, Springer LNCS Vol. 2894, 523–542 (2003)
18. R. Steinfeld, H. Wang, J. Pieprzyk: Efficient Extension of Standard Schnorr/RSA signatures into Universal Designated-Verifier Signatures. Proc. of PKC'04, Springer LNCS Vol. 2947, 86–100 (2004)
19. W. Susilo, F. Zhang, Y. Mu: Identity-based Strong Designated Verifier Signatures Schemes. Proc. of ACISP'04, Springer LNCS Vol. 3108, 313–324 (2004)

A   Review of Other Schemes

A.1   Privacy of Signer's Identity of SchDVS$_1$, SchDVS$_2$ and RSADVS

In [18], Steinfeld *et al.* proposed three Universal DVS schemes SchUDVS$_1$, SchUDVS$_2$ and RSAUDVS. We refer the reader to [18], for the description of these schemes. The DVS schemes induced by SchUDVS$_2$ and RSAUDVS do not satisfy the PSI-CMA security property. Indeed, the designated verifier secret key is not involved in the verifying algorithm. However it is easy to see that SchDVS$_1$, the DVS scheme induced by SchUDVS$_1$, fulfills this property assuming the difficulty of the Decision Diffie-Hellman (DDH) problem:

Theorem 5 (Anonymity of SchDVS$_1$). *Let $\mathcal{A}$ be a PSI-CMA-adversary, in the random oracle model, against the SchDVS$_1$ scheme, with security parameter k. Assume that $\mathcal{A}$ has advantage $\varepsilon = \mathbf{Adv}^{\mathrm{psi-cma}}_{SchDVS_1, \mathcal{A}}(k)$, running time t, and makes $q_{\mathcal{H}}$, q_{Σ}, q_{Υ} queries to the hash function $\mathcal{H}$, to the signing oracles and* *to the verifying oracle (respectively). Then there exist $\varepsilon' \in [0,1]$ and $t' \in \mathbb{N}$ verifying*

$$
\begin{cases}
\varepsilon' \geq \dfrac{\varepsilon}{2} - \dfrac{q_\Upsilon + q_\mathcal{H} q_\Sigma + 1}{2^k} \\
t' \leq t + (q_\Sigma + q_\Upsilon)(3T_{Exp-\mathbb{G}} + O(1))
\end{cases}
$$

such that the DDH problem can be solved with probability ε', within time t'.

Proof. Due to lack of space, the proof will be given in the full version of the paper [12].

A.2 Security of Saeednia, Kremer and Markowitch's Scheme (SKM)

The unforgeability of the DVS scheme in [15] is only considered under a no-message attack which is not acceptable in terms of security requirements. By using the technique introduced in the proof of Theorem 3, we can prove the unforgeability of SKM's scheme against a chosen message attack:

Theorem 6 (Unforgeability of SKM Signatures). *Let $\mathcal{A}$ be an EF-CMA-adversary against SKM's scheme with security parameter k, in the random oracle model, which produces an existential forgery with probability $\varepsilon = \mathbf{Succ}_{SKM,\mathcal{A}}^{ef-cma}(k)$, within time t, making $q_\mathcal{H}$, q_Σ and q_Υ queries to the hash oracle, to the signing oracle and to the verifying oracle. Then there exist $\varepsilon' \in [0,1]$ and $t' \in \mathbb{N}$ verifying*

$$
\begin{cases}
\varepsilon' \geq \varepsilon - \dfrac{(q_\mathcal{H} + q_\Sigma)q_\Sigma + q_\Upsilon}{2^k}, \\
t' \leq t + (q_\Sigma + q_\Upsilon)\left(2T_{Exp-\mathbb{G}} + O(1)\right) + (q_\mathcal{H} + q_\Sigma)(q_\mathcal{H} + q_\Sigma + q_\Upsilon)\left(T_{DDH} + O(1)\right),
\end{cases}
$$

such that the Gap Diffie-Hellman (GDH) problem can be solved with probability ε', within time t'.

Theorem 7 (Anonymity of SKM Signatures). *Let $\mathcal{A}$ be a PSI-CMA-adversary, in the random oracle model, against SKM's scheme, with security parameter k. Assume that $\mathcal{A}$ has advantage $\varepsilon = \mathbf{Adv}_{SKM,\mathcal{A}}^{psi-cma}(k)$, running time t, and makes $q_\mathcal{H}$, q_Σ, q_Υ queries to the hash function $\mathcal{H}$, to the signing oracles and to the verifying oracle. Then there exist $\varepsilon' \in [0,1]$ and $t' \in \mathbb{N}$ verifying*

$$
\begin{cases}
\varepsilon' \geq \dfrac{\varepsilon}{2} - \dfrac{(q_\mathcal{H} + q_\Sigma)q_\Sigma + q_\Upsilon}{2^k} \\
t' \leq t + (q_\Sigma + q_\Upsilon)\left(2T_{Exp-\mathbb{G}} + O(1)\right) + (q_\mathcal{H} + q_\Sigma)(q_\mathcal{H} + q_\Sigma + q_\Upsilon)\left(T_{DDH} + O(1)\right)
\end{cases}
$$

such that GDH can be solved with probability ε', within time t'.

Proofs. They are straightfoward adaptations of the proof of Theorem 3. Due to lack of space, they will be omitted.

Group Signatures: Better Efficiency and New Theoretical Aspects

Jan Camenisch[1] and Jens Groth[2,3]

[1] IBM Research, Zurich Research Lab
jca@zurich.ibm.com
[2] Cryptomathic
[3] BRICS*, Dept. of computer Science, University of Aarhus
jg@brics.dk

Abstract. A group signature scheme allows members of a group to anonymously sign messages. To counter misuse, the anonymity can be revoked by the so-called group manager.

This paper contributes two results to the area of group signatures. First, we improve the state-of-the-art scheme by Ateniese et al. by an order of magnitude. Our new scheme satisfies the recent security definition by Bellare et al. Second, and of a more theoretical nature, we study the Bellare et al. definitions and show that their notion of full-anonymity may require stronger assumptions than what is needed to achieve a relaxed but reasonable notion of anonymity.

1   Introduction

Group signatures, introduced by Chaum and van Heyst [11], allow a member to anonymously sign on behalf of the group. More precisely, distinguishing whether or not two group-signatures originated by the same or by different group members is infeasible to everyone but the group manager. A number of group signature schemes are proposed in the literature [11, 10, 9, 1, 3, 6, 4, 2, 5, 8]. Many of them also allow members to join and leave the group at arbitrary times [3, 6, 21].

Group signatures have many applications in the space of privacy protection. The most prominent one is probably in trusted computing, where a computing device is required to authenticate as proper (i.e., secure) device, i.e., that it has obtained *attestation* by some third party. To protect privacy of the device's user, this authentication should not allow identification of the device. In fact, the protocol standardized by the Trusted Computing Group to achieve this [20] basically uses the Ateniese et al. group signature scheme [1] but without its anonymity revocation feature.

In this paper, we present a new practical group signature scheme that is related to the Ateniese et al. scheme [1]. We prove that it satisfies a strong security definition very similar to [4]. Security is proved in the random oracle model under the strong RSA assumption and a DDH assumption.

* Basic Research in Computer Science (www.brics.dk), funded by the Danish National Research Foundation.

Our scheme is considerably faster than the state of the art scheme in [1]. Moreover, in our scheme the protocol to join the group only takes two rounds. The prospective member sends a join request to the group manager. The group manager sends a certificate back to the member.

The scheme supports dynamically joining new members to the group without changing the public key. Furthermore, it is possible to revoke a secret key such that it can no longer be used to sign messages. Revocation of a membership does require the public key to be modified. However, the modification is of constant size and allows group members in good standing to update their secret keys easily. To accomplish this goal we use methods similar to those of [6] and [21]. Their schemes are not as efficient as our scheme.

We present a modification of our scheme that with only a small loss of efficiency also allows us to make a full revocation, i.e., reveal all signatures signed with a revoked key. This scheme does not satisfy the [4] definition of security though. The problem is that given a private signature key it *is* possible to determine which signatures belong to the member in question.

As a separate theoretical contribution we show that the existence of one-way functions and NIZK arguments can be used to construct a group signature scheme. Again, we obtain a scheme that does not satisfy the [4] definition because a member's secret key does make it possible to identify signatures made by this member. We propose how to define security of group signature schemes when compromise of members' secret keys does matter.

We prove that the [4] definition implies IND-CCA2 secure public key bit-encryption. The existence of one-way functions and NIZK arguments does to our knowledge not entail the existence of public key encryption. Therefore, it seems that to satisfy [4] one must use stronger security assumptions than what is needed for just making a group signature scheme.

State of the Art. The current state of the art group signature scheme is due to Ateniese et al. [1]. While being reasonably efficient, this scheme does not support certificate revocation. An extension by Ateniese, Song and Tsudik [3] implements the full revocation mentioned before, i.e., all bad signatures by the revoked member are revealed. Unfortunately, this scheme is rather inefficient. Camenisch and Lysyanskaya [6] and Tsudik and Xu [21] propose schemes with dynamic revocation. This means that after a certificate has been revoked the member cannot any longer make signatures. Both schemes are less efficient than [1]. [21] is more efficient than [6], but relies on a trusted third party to generate some of the data, and need to update the key both when members join and leave the group. [6] can easily be modified to only updating the verification key when memberships are revoked.

All the schemes mentioned here include in their assumptions the strong RSA assumption and the random oracle model. Ateniese and de Medeiros [2] suggest a scheme that does not rely on knowledge of the factorization of the modulus, but this scheme is much less efficient than [1]. [4] suggest a scheme based on any trapdoor permutation and without the random oracle model. This scheme is only a proof of concept; it is very inefficient.

Concurrent with our work, Boneh, Boyen, and Shacham [5] as well as Camenisch and Lysyanskaya [8] presented groups signatures schemes based on bilinear maps. While these schemes are more efficient, they are based on new and alternative number theoretic assumptions.

2   Definitions

A group signature scheme involves three types of parties: members, non-members and a group manager. It further consists of five algorithms KeyGen, Join, Sign, Verify, Open, and Revoke. The key generation algorithm produces $(vk, gmsk) \leftarrow$ KeyGen() as output, where vk is a public verification key and $gmsk$ is the group managers secret key. If the group of members is fixed, we may assume that the algorithm also outputs a vector $\boldsymbol{sk}$ of secret keys to be used by the members. If, however, the group of members is dynamic, KeyGen does not output secret keys for the members. Instead the Join protocol can be used to let non-members join the group. As a result of this protocol, a new member obtains a secret key sk_i, while the group manager obtains some information Y_i related to the new member that he includes into his secret key $gmsk$. To sign a message m the member runs $\sigma \leftarrow$ Sign(sk_i, m). To verify a signature σ on message m one computes Verify(vk, m, σ). Furthermore, given a signature σ on m, the group manager can identify the originating member by computing Open$(gmsk, m, \sigma)$, which outputs the identity of the member who created the signature. Finally, using the Revoke algorithm $(vk, gmsk) \leftarrow$ Revoke$(gmsk, Y_i)$, the group manager can exclude the member relating to Y_i from the group.

Bellare, Micciancio, and Warinschi [4] propose two properties, full-traceability and full-anonymity, that capture the security requirements of group signatures. These definition assume that the key generation is run by a trusted party and do not consider members joining or leaving the group after the key generation [4].

Full-Traceability. The short description of full-traceability is that without a member's secret key it must be infeasible to create a valid signature that frames this member. This must hold even if the group manager's secret key and an arbitrary number of the members' secret keys are exposed.

Formally, we say that the group signature scheme has full-traceability if the expectation of the following experiment is negligible.

$\mathbf{Exp}_A^{\text{f}-\text{trace}}(k)$:

$(vk, gmsk, \boldsymbol{sk}) \leftarrow$ KeyGen(k)
$(m, \sigma) \leftarrow \mathcal{A}^{\text{Sign}(sk.,\cdot),\text{Corrupt}(\cdot)}(vk, gmsk)$
If Verify$(vk, m, \sigma) = 1$, $i = $ Open$(gmsk, m, \sigma) \in [k]$, i was not queried Corrupt$(\cdot)$ and (i, m) was not queried to Sign$(sk., \cdot)$ then return 1
If Verify$(vk, m, \sigma) = 1$ and $i = $ Open$(gmsk, m, \sigma) \notin [k]$ then return 1
Else return 0

Here Corrupt$(\cdot)$ is an oracle that on query $i \in [k]$ returns sk_i.

[4] argue that full-traceability implies what is meant by the more informal notions of unforgeability, no-framing, traceability, and coalition resistance as defined, e.g., in [1].

Full-Anonymity. We want to avoid that signatures can be linked to group members or other signatures. For this purpose, we define full-anonymity as the notion that an adversary cannot distinguish signatures from two different members. This must hold even when we give the secret keys to the adversary. In other words, even if a member's key is exposed, then it is still not possible for the adversary to see whether this member signed some messages in the past, neither is it possible to see if any future messages are signed by this member.

$\mathbf{Exp}_{\mathcal{A}}^{\text{f-anon}}(b, k)$:

    $(vk, gmsk, \boldsymbol{sk}) \leftarrow \text{KeyGen}(k)$

    $(i_0, i_1, m) \leftarrow \mathcal{A}^{\text{Open}(gmsk, \cdot, \cdot)}(vk, \boldsymbol{sk}); \sigma \leftarrow \text{Sign}(sk_{i_b}, m)$

    $d \leftarrow \mathcal{A}^{\text{Open}(gmsk, \cdot, \cdot)}(\sigma)$

    If $\mathcal{A}$ did not query m, σ return d, else return 0

We say the group signature scheme has full-anonymity if $\Pr[\mathbf{Exp}_{\mathcal{A}}^{\text{f-anon}}(1, k) = 1]$ - $\Pr[\mathbf{Exp}_{\mathcal{A}}^{\text{f-anon}}(0, k) = 1]$ is negligible.

[4] argue that full-anonymity entails what is meant by the more informal notions of anonymity and unlinkability.

Anonymity. The [4] model is strict in its anonymity requirements. It demands that even if a member's secret key is exposed it must still be impossible to tell which signatures are made by the member in question. This is a good definition of security in a threat model where parties may be corrupted adaptively but can erase data. The schemes in [1] and [6] have this strong anonymity property as does our new scheme with Join and Revoke.

In other threat models, this may be aiming too high. Consider for instance a static adversary, then the key is exposed before any messages are signed or it is never exposed. Or consider an adaptive adversary where parties cannot erase data, in this case full-anonymity does not buy us more security. We therefore define a weaker type of anonymity that is satisfied if both the group manager's secret key and the member's secret key are not exposed. We note that for instance the scheme in [11, 2, 21] satisfy only this weaker property. One positive effect of not requiring full-anonymity is that potentially it makes it possible for the member to claim a signature she made, i.e., prove that she signed a particular signature, without having to store specific data such as randomness, etc., used to generate the signature. This latter property is called claiming in [16].

$\mathbf{Exp}_{\mathcal{A}}^{\text{anon}}(b, k)$:

    $(vk, gmsk, \boldsymbol{sk}) \leftarrow \text{KeyGen}(k)$

    $(i_0, i_1, m) \leftarrow \mathcal{A}^{\text{Open}(gmsk, \cdot, \cdot), \text{Sign}(sk., \cdot), \text{Corrupt}(\cdot)}(vk); \sigma \leftarrow \text{Sign}(sk_{i_b}, m)$

    $d \leftarrow \mathcal{A}^{\text{Open}(gmsk, \cdot, \cdot), \text{Sign}(sk., \cdot)}(\sigma)^1$

    If $\mathcal{A}$ did not query m, σ to Open and did not query i_0, i_1 to Corrupt$(\cdot)$ then return d, else return 0

---

[1] We do not allow $\mathcal{A}$ to corrupt member's in the second phase. This is simply because we WLOG may assume that it corrupts all other members than i_0 and i_1 before getting the challenge signature.

We say the group signature scheme is anonymous if $\Pr[\mathbf{Exp}_{\mathcal{A}}^{\mathrm{anon}}(1, k) = 1]$ - $\Pr[\mathbf{Exp}_{\mathcal{A}}^{\mathrm{anon}}(0, k) = 1]$ is negligible.

As Bellare et al. [4], we can argue that anonymity implies the informal notions of anonymity and unlinkability mentioned in the introduction.

3   Preliminaries

Protocols to Prove Knowledge of and Relations Among Discrete Logarithms. In our scheme we will use various protocols to prove knowledge of and relations among discrete logarithms. To describe these protocols, we use notation introduced by Camenisch and Stadler [10] for various proofs of knowledge of discrete logarithms and proofs of the validity of statements about discrete logarithms. For instance, $PK\{(\alpha, \beta, \gamma) : y = g^{\alpha}h^{\beta} \wedge \tilde{y} = \tilde{g}^{\alpha}\tilde{h}^{\gamma} \wedge (u \leq \alpha \leq v)\}$ denotes a *"zero-knowledge* P*roof of* K*nowledge of integers* α*,* β*, and* γ *such that* $y = g^{\alpha}h^{\beta}$ *and* $\tilde{y} = \tilde{g}^{\alpha}\tilde{h}^{\gamma}$ *holds, where* $u \leq \alpha \leq v$*,"* where $y, g, h, \tilde{y}, \tilde{g}$, and $\tilde{h}$ are elements of some groups $G = \langle g \rangle = \langle h \rangle$ and $\tilde{G} = \langle \tilde{g} \rangle = \langle \tilde{h} \rangle$. The convention is that Greek letters denote the quantities the knowledge of which is being proved, while all other parameters are known to the verifier. Using this notation, a proof protocol can be described by just pointing out its aim while hiding all details.

In the random oracle model, such protocols can be turned into signature schemes using the Fiat-Shamir heuristic [12, 19]. We use the notation $SPK\{(\alpha) : y = g^{\alpha}\}(m)$ to denote a signature obtained in this way.

The Camenisch-Lysyanskaya Signature Scheme. The group signature scheme is based on the Camenisch-Lysyanskaya (CL) signature scheme [7, 18]. Unlike most signature schemes, this one is particularly suited for our purposes as it allows for efficient protocols to prove knowledge of a signature and to retrieve signatures on secret messages efficiently using discrete logarithm based proofs of knowledge [7, 18]. We recall the signature scheme here.

Key generation. On input 1^k, choose an RSA modulus $n = pq$, $p = 2p' + 1$, $q = 2q' + 1$ as a product of safe primes. Choose, uniformly at random, $g_1, \ldots, g_L, h, a \in QR_n$. Output the public key $(n, g_1, \ldots, g_L, h, a)$ and the secret key p. Let ℓ_n be the length of n.

Message space. Let ℓ_m be a parameter. The message space is the set $\{(m_1, \ldots, m_L) : m_i \in \pm\{0, 1\}^{\ell_m}\}$.

Signing algorithm. On input $m_1, \ldots, m_L$, choose a random prime number e of length $\ell_e > \ell_m + 2$, and a random number r of length $\ell_r = \ell_n + \ell_m + \ell_s$, where ℓ_s is a security parameter. Compute the value y such that $y^e \equiv ag_1^{m_1} \ldots g_L^{m_L} h^r$ (mod n). The signature on the message $(m_1, \ldots, m_L)$ consists of (e, y, r).

Verification algorithm. To verify that the tuple (e, y, r) is a signature on message $(m_1, \ldots, m_L)$, check that $y^e \equiv ag_1^{m_1} \ldots g_L^{m_L} h^r$ (mod n), and check that $2^{\ell_e} > e > 2^{\ell_e - 1}$.

Theorem 1 ([7]). *The signature scheme is secure against adaptive chosen message attacks [14] under the strong RSA assumption.*

Remarks. The original scheme considered messages in the interval $[0, 2^{\ell_m} - 1]$. Here, however, we allow messages from $[-2^{\ell_m}+1, 2^{\ell_m}-1]$. The only consequence of this is that we need to require that $\ell_e > \ell_m + 2$ holds instead of $\ell_e > \ell_m + 1$.

Further note that a signature can be randomized: It is clear that if $y^e = ag^m h^r \bmod n$, then we also have $(yh)^e = ag^m h^{r+e} \bmod n$. Thus the signature scheme is not strong but it is secure against chosen message attack.

The CL-signature scheme makes it possible to sign a committed message. One party computes the commitment $g^m h^{r'} \bmod n$, where $r' \in_R \mathbb{Z}_n$ such that m is statistically hidden. This party also proves knowledge of m, r'. The signer now picks e as a random $\ell_e = \ell_2$-bit prime, and picks $r'' \in \mathbb{Z}_{E_i}$. He then computes y so $y^e = ag^m h^{r'+r''}$ and returns (y, e, r''). Now the party has a signature on m without the signer having any knowledge about which message was signed.

We note that careful analysis of the signature scheme's security proof shows that in fact the requirement of Camenisch and Lysyanskaya that $\ell_r = \ell_n + \ell_m + \ell_s$ holds can be relaxed to $\ell_r = \ell_e$, by picking $r \in_R \mathbb{Z}_e$. However, if the goal is to sign a commitment message that shall be kept secret from the signer, one requires a larger r, for instance $r \in_R \mathbb{Z}_n$.

4   The Basic Group Signature Scheme

The Ideas Underlying Our Group Signature Scheme. We base our group signature scheme on two groups. One group is QR_n, where n is an RSA modulus chosen as a safe-prime product. The other group is of order Q in $\mathbb{Z}_P^*$, where $Q|P-1$.

Each member receives a CL-signature (y_i, e_i, r_i) on a message x_i. As part of a group signature they will prove knowledge of such a CL-signature. Since outsiders cannot forge CL-signatures this ensures that the signer is member of the group. As the group manager must be able to open signatures and identify the signer we include in the group signature also an encryption of $Y_i = G^{x_i} \bmod P$. The signer proves knowledge of x_i and that it is the same x_i that she knows a CL-signature on. The group manager knowing the secret key can decrypt and identify the signer. Because the group manager does not know x_i we avoid members being framed by malicious group managers. The group manager simply cannot compute the discrete logarithm x_i, and therefore not make a group signature pointing to the member.

In Figure 1 we present the actual protocol. Following the model of [4], it assumes that the key generation algorithm is run by a trusted third party. We later extend this scheme to include dynamic join and revocation such that this third party is not required.

The parameters of our schemes are as follows. We use ℓ_s as a bit-length such that for any integer a when we pick r as a $|a| + \ell_s$-bit random number then $a + r$ and r are statistically indistinguishable. ℓ_c is the length of the output of the hash-function. ℓ_e is a number large enough that we can assign all members different numbers and make the E_i's prime.

It must be the case that $\ell_c + \ell_e + \ell_s + 1 < \ell_Q$ and $\ell_Q + \ell_c + \ell_s + 1 < \ell_E < \ell_n/2$.

A suggestion for parameters is $\ell_n = 2049$, $\ell_P = 1600$, $\ell_E = 404$, $\ell_Q = 282$, $\ell_c = 160$, $\ell_e = \ell_s = 60$. This choice should ensure that factoring an ℓ_n bit number is about as hard as computing discrete logarithms in a subgroups of size 2^{ℓ_Q} modulo an ℓ_P-bit prime [17].

Theorem 2. *The basic group signature scheme has full-traceability and full-anonymity.*

The proof of Theorem 2 can be found in the full paper.

5   Join and Revoke

Flexible Join. It may be impractical to set up the signature scheme with all members in advance. Often groups are dynamic and we may have members joining after the public keys have been generated. The recent schemes [1, 6, 21] support members joining at arbitrary points in time. The schemes [6, 21] require that the public key be updated when a new member joins. However, they can easily be modified to the more attractive solution where the public key does not need to be updated when a member joins.

Our scheme supports members joining throughout the protocol. The idea is that the member generates $Y_i = G^{x_i} \bmod P$ herself, so only she knows the discrete logarithm x_i. Jointly the group manager and the member generate $a g^{x_i} h^{r_i} \bmod n$, where r_i is so large that x_i is statistically hidden. Then she gives it to the group manager who generates (y_i, e_i) and give them to the member. Here we use that the CL-signature scheme is secure against adaptive chosen message attack such that members cannot forge signatures and thereby falsely join themselves.

Revocation. On occasions, it may be necessary to revoke a member's secret key. Since signatures are anonymous, the standard approach of using certificate revocation lists cannot be used. Following [6] we suggest using roots of some element w to implement revocation. A signature contains an argument of knowledge of a pair (w_i, E_i) such that $w = w_i^{E_i} \bmod n$. If we want to revoke a membership we update the public key to contain $w \leftarrow w_i$. Now this member may no longer prove knowledge of a root of w and thus she cannot sign messages any more.[2]

When changing the public key we need to communicate to the remaining members how they should update their secret keys. In our scheme, we do this by publishing e_i corresponding to the revoked member. Members in good standing may use this to obtain a root of the new w through a simple computation. This means that the change in the public key is of constant size, and old members may update their secret keys by downloading only a constant amount of public information.

The protocol is described in Figure 2.

---

[2] A member with a revoked key can still sign messages under the old verification key and claim that they were signed when this key was valid. Whether such an attack makes sense depends on the application of the group signature scheme and is beyond the scope of the paper. One obvious solution is of course to add a time-stamp.

Basic Group Signature Scheme

KeyGen(k): Choose an ℓ_n-bit RSA modulus $n = pq$ as a product of two safe primes $p = 2p' + 1, q = 2q' + 1$. Select at random $a, g, h \in QR_n$. Select at random ℓ_Q-bit and ℓ_P-bit primes Q, P such that $Q | P - 1$. Let F be an element of order Q in $\mathbb{Z}_P^*$. Choose at random $X_G, X_H \in \mathbb{Z}_Q$ and set $G = F^{X_G} \bmod P, H = F^{X_H} \bmod P$.
Select at random $x_1, \ldots, x_k \in Z_Q$ and select also at random $r_1, \ldots, r_k \in \mathbb{Z}_n$. Choose different random ℓ_e-bit numbers $e_1, \ldots, e_k$ such that $E_1 = 2^{\ell_E} + e_1, \ldots, E_k = 2^{\ell_E} + e_k$ are primes. Compute $y_1, \ldots, y_k$ such that $y_1^{E_1} = ag^{x_1}h^{r_1} \bmod n, \ldots, y_k^{E_k} = ag^{x_k}h^{r_k} \bmod n$.
Public key: $vk = (n, a, g, h, Q, P, F, G, H)$.
Group managers private key:
$gmsk = (vk, X_G, Y_1 = G^{x_1} \bmod P, \ldots, Y_k = G^{x_k} \bmod P)$.
Member i's private key: $sk_i = (vk, x_i, y_i, e_i, r_i)$.

Sign(sk_i, m): Select at random $r \in \{0, 1\}^{\ell_n/2}$ and $R \in \mathbb{Z}_Q$. Set $u = h^r y_i \bmod n$, $U_1 = F^R \bmod P$, $U_2 = G^{R+x_i} = G^R Y_i \bmod P$, and $U_3 = H^{R+e_i} \bmod P$.[a]
Compute the (sub-)signature

$$SPK\{(\xi, \rho, \varepsilon, \tau) : a = u^{2^{\ell_E}+\varepsilon} g^{-\xi} h^\rho \bmod n \ \wedge \ U_1 = F^\tau \bmod P \ \wedge$$
$$U_2 = G^{\tau+\xi} \bmod P \ \wedge \ U_3 = H^{\tau+\varepsilon} \bmod P \ \wedge$$
$$\varepsilon \in \{-2^{\ell_e+\ell_c+\ell_s}, +2^{\ell_e+\ell_c+\ell_s}\} \ \wedge \ \xi \in \{-2^{\ell_Q+\ell_c+\ell_s}, 2^{\ell_Q+\ell_c+\ell_s}\}\}(m) \ ,$$

i.e., choose $r_x \in \{0, 1\}^{\ell_Q+\ell_c+\ell_s}$, $r_r \in \{0, 1\}^{\ell_n/2+\ell_c+\ell_s}$, $r_e \in \{0, 1\}^{\ell_e+\ell_c+\ell_s}$, and $R_R \in \mathbb{Z}_Q$ and compute

$$v = u^{r_e} g^{-r_x} h^{r_r} \bmod n, \qquad\qquad V_1 = F^{R_R} \bmod P,$$
$$V_2 = G^{R_R+r_x} \bmod P, \qquad\qquad V_3 = H^{R_R+r_e} \bmod P \ .$$

Compute a challenge $c = \text{hash}(vk, u, v, U_1, U_2, U_3, V_1, V_2, V_3, m)$ and set $z_x = r_x + cx_i, z_r = r_r + c(-r_i - rE_i), z_e = r_r + ce_i$, and $Z_R = R_R + cR \bmod Q$.
Signature: $\sigma = (c, u, U_1, U_2, U_3, z_x, z_r, z_e, Z_R)$.

Verify(vk, m, σ): Check that $z_e \in \{0, 1\}^{\ell_e+\ell_c+\ell_s}$ and $z_x \in \{0, 1\}^{\ell_Q+\ell_c+\ell_s}$. Compute

$$v = a^{-c} g^{-z_x} h^{z_r} u^{c2^{\ell_E}+z_e} \bmod n, \qquad V_1 = U_1^{-c} F^{Z_R} \bmod P,$$
$$V_2 = U_2^{-c} G^{Z_R+z_x} \bmod P, \qquad V_3 = U_3^{-c} H^{Z_R+z_e} \bmod P$$

and verify that $c = \text{hash}(vk, u, v, U_1, U_2, U_3, V_1, V_2, V_3, m)$

Open$(gmsk, m, \sigma)$: Verify that the signature is valid.
Using X_G decrypt $(U_1^{\frac{P-1}{Q}} \bmod P, U_2^{\frac{P-1}{Q}} \bmod P)$ to get $G^{\frac{P-1}{Q} x_i} \bmod P$ and return i.

---

[a] Without knowledge of the factorization of n, $h^r \bmod n$ for $r \in_R \{0, 1\}^{\ell_n/2}$ is indistinguishable from a random element in QR_n [13]. Therefore, u does not reveal y_i to outsiders.

Fig. 1. The Basic Group Signature Scheme

Join and Revoke

KeyGen(): Run KeyGen(0) of the basic scheme. Choose also at random
$w \in QR_n$ and include it in vk. Prove that $g \in \langle h \rangle$ by running $PK\{(\alpha) : g = h^\alpha\}$
using binary challenges. Set $gmsk = (vk, p, q, X_G)$ where $n = pq$.

Join: The member selects at random $x_i \leftarrow \mathbb{Z}_Q$ and computes $Y_i = G^{x_i} \bmod P$.
She also forms a commitment to x_i, $g^{x_i} h^{r'_i} \bmod n$ with $r_i \in_R \mathbb{Z}_n$ and proves
knowledge of x_i, r'_i fitting the above. She sends $Y_i, g^{x_i} h^{r'_i} \bmod n$ and the proof
to the group manager.

The group manager selects $e_i \in \{0,1\}^{\ell_e}$ such that $E_i = 2^{\ell_E} + e_i$ is prime. He
computes $w_i = w^{E_i^{-1}} \bmod n$. He selects at random $r''_i \in \mathbb{Z}_e$ and sets
$y_i = (ag^{x_i} h^{r'_i + r''_i})^{E_i^{-1}} \bmod n$. He sends w_i, y_i, E_i, r''_i back to the new member.
Her secret key is $sk_i = (vk, w_i, x_i, r_i = r'_i + r''_i, y_i, e_i)$.

Sign(vk, sk_i, m): Select at random $r \in \{0,1\}^{\ell_n/2}$ and $R \in \mathbb{Z}_Q$. Set
$u = h^r y_i w_i \bmod n$, $U_1 = F^R \bmod P$, $U_2 = G^{R+x_i} \bmod P$, and
$U_3 = H^{R+e_i} \bmod P$. Compute the (sub-)signature

$$SPK\{(\xi, \rho, \varepsilon, \tau) : aw = u^{2^{\ell_E}+\varepsilon} g^{-\xi} h^\rho \bmod n \ \wedge \ U_1 = F^\tau \bmod P \ \wedge$$

$$U_2 = G^{\tau+\xi} \bmod P \ \wedge \ U_3 = H^{\tau+\varepsilon} \bmod P \ \wedge$$

$$\varepsilon \in \{-2^{\ell_e+\ell_c+\ell_s}, +2^{\ell_e+\ell_c+\ell_s}\} \ \wedge \ \xi \in \{-2^{\ell_Q+\ell_c+\ell_s}, 2^{\ell_Q+\ell_c+\ell_s}\}\}(m) \ ,$$

i.e., choose $r_x \in \{0,1\}^{\ell_Q+\ell_c+\ell_s}$, $r_r \in \{0,1\}^{\ell_n/2+\ell_c+\ell_s}$, $r_e \in \{0,1\}^{\ell_e+\ell_c+\ell_s}$, and
$R_R \in \mathbb{Z}_Q$ and compute

$$v = u^{r_e} g^{-r_x} h^{r_r} \bmod n, \qquad\qquad V_1 = F^{R_R} \bmod P,$$

$$V_2 = G^{R_R+r_x} \bmod P, \qquad\qquad V_3 = H^{R_R+r_e} \bmod P.$$

Compute a challenge $c = \text{hash}(vk, u, v, U_1, U_2, U_3, V_1, V_2, V_3, m)$ and
$z_x = r_x + cx_i$, $z_r = r_r + c(-r_i - rE_i)$, $z_e = r_e + ce_i$, $Z_R = R_R + cR \bmod Q$.
Signature: $\sigma = (c, u, U_1, U_2, U_3, z_x, z_r, z_e, Z_R)$.

Verify(vk, m, σ): Check that $z_e \in \{0,1\}^{\ell_e+\ell_c+\ell_s}$ and $z_x \in \{0,1\}^{\ell_Q+\ell_c+\ell_s}$. Compute

$$v = (aw)^{-c} g^{-z_x} h^{z_r} u^{c2^{\ell_E}+z_e} \bmod n, \qquad V_1 = U_1^{-c} F^{Z_R} \bmod P,$$

$$V_2 = U_2^{-c} G^{Z_R+z_x} \bmod P, \qquad V_3 = U_3^{-c} H^{Z_R+z_e} \bmod P$$

and verify that $c = \text{hash}(vk, u, v, U_1, U_2, U_3, V_1, V_2, V_3, m)$

OpenProof($gmsk, i, m, \sigma$): This is the same as in the basic scheme.

Revoke($gmsk, i$): Publish E_i. Replace in vk the element w with w_i.
Any member in good standing may update her secret key sk_j as follows. She
selects α, β such that $\alpha E_i + \beta E_j = 1$. Then she computes the new
$w_j \leftarrow w_i^{\beta E_i} w_j^{\alpha E_j} \bmod n$.

Fig. 2. Protocol for Dynamic Join and Revoke

Performance. We now discuss the performance of our group signature with
join and revoke and compare it to the ACJT scheme [1] and it's extension to

revocation by Camenisch and Lysyanskaya [7]. To compute a group-signature, one needs to do six exponentiations modulo P with exponents from $\mathbb{Z}_Q$, one exponentiation modulo n with an exponent of length $\ell_n/2$, and one multi-base exponentiation with one exponent of length $\ell_n/2 + \ell_c + \ell_s$ and two of length at most $\ell_Q + \ell_s + \ell_c$. In a good implementation, the computation of the multi-base exponentiation takes about 10 percent more time than a single exponentiation with an exponent of length $\ell_n/2 + \ell_c + \ell_s$.

The verification of a signature requires three two-base exponentiations modulo P and one multi-base exponentiation modulo n. As one of the exponents of the two-base exponentiations modulo P is rather small (ℓ_c bits), these three take roughly the same time as three ordinary exponentiations modulo P. Concerning the multi-base exponentiation modulo n, the same statements as for the multi-base exponentiation modulo n in the signature generation holds.

Let us compare this with the [1] group signature scheme. In order to achieve the same security as in our scheme, the modulus n used there needs to be about 3200 bits. The reason is that in their scheme, the group manager is given a value $B_i = a^{x_i} a_0 \bmod n$ by a member, where x_i is the member's secret. As the group manager knows the factorization of n, he has an advantage when trying to compute discrete logarithms modulo n and hence to compute x_i.

Now, the computation of a signature in the ACJT scheme takes four exponentiations modulo n with exponents about the size of n^2 and three multi-base exponentiations with exponents the size of about n^3. Assuming that all the exponentiations in the ACJT and our scheme were carried out with the same modulus (which is quite a bit in favor of the ACJT scheme), our scheme is about 20 times more efficient.) Moreover, our scheme also provides revocation which the ACJT scheme does not. The extension of the ACJT to revocation proposed by Camenisch and Lysyanskaya requires about four multi-base base exponentiation with a 2048-bit modulus and exponents, in which case our scheme is more than 26 times more efficient.

Finally we note that the ACJT scheme requires that the member are assured that the modulus n is a safe prime product while in our scheme it is sufficient that they are convinced that $g \in \langle h \rangle$. The latter can be achieved *much* more efficiently than the former.

Separating the Membership Management and the Anonymity Revocation Capability. There may be cases where we want to separate the process of granting (and revoking) membership and the process of revoking anonymity of signatures. A simple modification to our scheme allows for this.

The idea is that n is generated by the membership manager who can produce the needed CL signatures that we use in our scheme. On the other hand we let the anonymity revocation manager generate G, H. The membership manager then registers $G^{x_i} \bmod P$ and $H^{e_i} \bmod P$ with the anonymity revocation managers.

Now, if the member that wants to sign a message picks r and r_r large enough (for instance from $\{0,1\}^{\ell_n + \ell_s}$), then in the group QR_n everything is statistically hidden. Furthermore in $\mathbb{Z}_P^*$ everything is encrypted. Therefore, the membership manager can no longer see who signs a particular message. However, the membership manager needs to prove that $y_i, g, w_i \in \langle h \rangle$, otherwise the side-classes might leak information. We refer to the full paper for the details of this,

6   Full Revocation

Revocation Revisited. The current method of revocation does not allow us to revoke signatures valid under an old key. It would be highly impractical to demand that all members re-sign messages when the public key is updated. Instead, we would prefer a solution parallel to that of certificate revocation lists that allow us to publish information that marks signatures signed by the now distrusted member. Nevertheless, of course we still want to preserve the privacy of all other members so we cannot simply reveal the group manager's secret key.

We propose an addition that solves this problem. The idea is to pick a random element $s_i \in \mathbb{Z}_Q$ when the member joins. The member can now form $F^R \bmod P$ and $F^{Rs_i} \bmod P$ and include them in a group signature. According to the DDH assumption this will just look like two random elements. However, if the group manager releases s_i, then all signatures suddenly become clearly marked as belonging to said member.

We do need to force the member to use s_i, otherwise the member could create group signatures that could not be full-revoked. Therefore, we include a random element $f \in QR_n$ in the public key and give the member a CL-signature on the form (y_i, E_i, r_i), where $y_i^{E_i} = af^{s_i}g^{x_i}h^{r_i} \bmod n$. The member will form U_4, V_4 as $U_4 = F^{Rs_i} \bmod P$ and $V_4 = F^{d_s} \bmod P$, when making the signature and argues correctness of this together with an argument that s_i is included in the CL-signature that she knows.

The protocol is described in Figure 3.

Security. A member's secret key contains s_i. Therefore, if the secret key is exposed it is easy to link the member with the signatures she has made. We can therefore not hope to have full anonymity but must settle for anonymity.

In theory, it is possible to construct a signature scheme that supports full revocation and full-anonymity. One idea could be that the group manager selects elements A_i, B_i with $B_i = A_i^{X_i} \bmod P$ and signs these elements. Then the member must produce in addition to the standard signature a pair $(A_i^R \bmod P, B_i^{RX_i} \bmod P)$ and prove in zero-knowledge that it has been properly formed. Once the group manager wants to make a full revocation he publishes X_i. However, the member's secret key does not include X_i so exposure of this key does not reveal which messages she has signed. This method is not very efficient though. It is an open problem to come up with an efficient group signature scheme that has full-anonymity and supports full revocation.

On the flip side we note that it may be seen as a positive thing that the member's signing key reveals which messages she signed. In [16]'s notion of traceable signatures it is a requirement that the member should be able to claim his signature. When the member's secret key links him to her signatures then this

---

Group Signature with Full Revocation

KeyGen(): As in the basic scheme except we now also include a random element f from QR_n in the public key, as well as $w \in_R QR_n$.

Join: The Join protocol remains the same except now the member chooses a random element $s_i \in \mathbb{Z}_Q$ and gets $y_i = (af^{s_i}g^{x_i}h^{r'_i+r''_i})^{E_i^{-1}} \bmod n$, while the group manager learns s_i.

Sign(vk, sk_i, m): Choose randomizers as in the Join and Revoke scheme and set $u = h^r y_i w_i \bmod n$, $U_1 = F^R \bmod P$, $U_2 = G^{R+x_i} \bmod P$, $U_3 = H^{R+e_i} \bmod P$, and $U_4 = U_1^{s_i} \bmod P$.

Compute the (sub-)signature

$$SPK\{(\psi, \xi, \rho, \varepsilon, \tau) : aw = u^{2^{\ell_E}+\varepsilon}f^{-\psi}g^{-\xi}h^{\rho} \bmod n \ \wedge \ U_1 = F^{\tau} \bmod P \ \wedge$$
$$U_2 = G^{\tau+\xi} \bmod P \ \wedge \ U_3 = H^{\tau+\varepsilon} \bmod P \ \wedge \ U_4 = U_1^{\psi} \bmod P \ \wedge$$
$$\varepsilon \in \{-2^{\ell_e+\ell_c+\ell_s}, +2^{\ell_e+\ell_c+\ell_s}\} \ \wedge \ \psi, \xi \in \{-2^{\ell_Q+\ell_c+\ell_s}, 2^{\ell_Q+\ell_c+\ell_s}\}\}(m) \ ,$$

i.e., choose $r_s \in \{0,1\}^{\ell_Q+\ell_c+\ell_s}$, $r_x \in \{0,1\}^{\ell_Q+\ell_c+\ell_s}$, $r_r \in \{0,1\}^{\ell_n/2+\ell_c+\ell_s}$, $r_e \in \{0,1\}^{\ell_e+\ell_c+\ell_s}$, and $R_R \in \mathbb{Z}_Q$ and compute

$$v = u^{r_e}f^{-r_s}g^{-r_x}h^{r_r} \bmod n, \qquad V_1 = F^{R_R} \bmod P,$$
$$V_2 = G^{R_R+r_x} \bmod P, \qquad V_3 = H^{R_R+r_e} \bmod P, \qquad V_4 = U_1^{r_s} \bmod P,$$

Compute a challenge $c = \text{hash}(vk, u, v, U_1, U_2, U_3, V_1, V_2, V_3, m)$ and $z_s = r_s + cs_i$, $z_x = r_x + cx_i$, $z_r = r_r + c(-r_i - rE_i)$, $z_e = r_e + ce_i$, $Z_R = R_R + cR \bmod Q$.

Signature: $\sigma = (c, u, U_1, U_2, U_3, U_4, z_s, z_r, z_x, z_e, Z_R)$.

Verify(vk, m, σ): Check that $z_e \in \{0,1\}^{\ell_e+\ell_c+\ell_s}$ and $z_s, z_x \in \{0,1\}^{\ell_Q+\ell_c+\ell_s}$.

Compute

$$v = (aw)^{-c}f^{-z_s}g^{-z_x}h^{z_r}u^{c2^{\ell_E}+z_e} \bmod n, V_1 = U_1^{-c}F^{Z_R} \bmod P,$$
$$V_2 = U_2^{-c}G^{Z_R+z_x} \bmod P, V_3 = U_3^{-c}H^{Z_R+z_e} \bmod P, V_4 = U_4^{-c}U_1^{z_s} \bmod P$$

and verify that $c = \text{hash}(vk, u, v, U_1, U_2, U_3, U_4, V_1, V_2, V_3, V_4, m)$

Open($gmsk, m, \sigma$): The opening protocol remains the same.

Revoke($gmsk, i$): The revocation protocol remains the same.

FullRevoke($gmsk, i$): Look up s_i and publish it on the certificate revocation list. Execute Revoke($gmsk, i$).

Since s_i is now public anybody may check in old signatures whether $U_4^{\frac{P-1}{Q}} = U_1^{\frac{P-1}{Q}s_i} \bmod P$ and therefore whether the signatures have been formed by the fully revoked member.

Fig. 3. Group Signature with Full Revocation

can be done easily without her having to store old randomness used in specific signatures that she might later want to claim.

7   Separating Full-Anonymity and Anonymity

Full-Anonymity Implies IND-CCA2 Public Key Bit-Encryption. To appreciate the strength of the [4] definition of security of a group signature scheme, we note that full-anonymity implies CCA2 secure public key bit-encryption.

Theorem 3. *If a group signature scheme satisfying full-anonymity exists, then an* IND-CCA2 *public key cryptosystem for encrypting bits exists.*

We refer to the full paper for the proof.

[2] speculate whether it is possible to construct a group signature scheme based only on one-way functions. Following [15] we believe it is not possible to construct public key encryption from one-way functions, and therefore not possible to construct a group signature scheme from one-way functions that satisfies the security definition of [4].

Group Signature from One-Way Function and NIZK Argument. From the full paper we get the following theorem.

Theorem 4. *If one-way functions and non-interactive zero-knowledge arguments exist for some suitable language, then group signature schemes with full-traceability and anonymity exist.*

We do not know of any construction of public key encryption from one-way functions and non-interactive zero-knowledge arguments. Theorems 3 and 4 therefore indicate that a group signature scheme having full-anonymity may require stronger assumptions than what is needed to obtain anonymity.

The scheme in the full paper can easily be extended to a traceable signature scheme [16]. Theorems 3 and 4 can then be seen as indications that group signatures require stronger assumptions than traceable signature schemes.

Acknowledgement

Part of the first author's work reported in this paper is supported by the European Commission through the IST Programme under Contract IST-2002-507932 ECRYPT and by the IST Project PRIME. The PRIME projects receives research funding from the European Community's Sixth Framework Programme and the Swiss Federal Office for Education and Science. The information in this document reflects only the author's views, is provided as is and no guarantee or warranty is given that the information is fit for any particular purpose. The user thereof uses the information at its sole risk and liability.

References

1. G. Ateniese, J. Camenisch, M. Joye, and G. Tsudik. A practical and provably secure group signature scheme. In *CRYPTO 2000*, LNCS, vol. 1880, pp. 255–270.

2. G. Ateniese and B. de Medeiros. Efficient group signatures without trapdoors. In *ASIACRYPT '03*, LNCS, vol. 2894, pp. 246–268, 2003.
3. G. Ateniese, D. X. Song, and G. Tsudik. Quasi-efficient revocation in group signatures. In *Financial Cryptography '02*, pp. 183–197, 2002.
4. M. Bellare, D. Micciancio, and B. Warinschi. Foundations of group signatures: Formal definitions, simplified requirements, and a construction based on general assumptions. In *EUROCRYPT '03*, LNCS vol. 2656, pp. 614–629.
5. D. Boneh, X. Boyen, and H. Shacham. Short group signatures using strong diffie hellman. In *CRYPTO 2004*, LNCS. Springer Verlag, 2004.
6. J. Camenisch and A. Lysyanskaya. Dynamic accumulators and application to efficient revocation of anonymous credentials. In *CRYPTO '02*, LNCS, vol. 2442.
7. J. Camenisch and A. Lysyanskaya. A signature scheme with efficient protocols. In *SCN '02*, LNCS, vol. 2576, pp. 268–289, 2002.
8. J. Camenisch and A. Lysyanskaya. Signature schemes and anonymous credentials from bilinear maps. In *CRYPTO 2004*, LNCS. Springer Verlag, 2004.
9. J. Camenisch and M. Michels. A group signature scheme with improved efficiency. In *ASIACRYPT '98*, vol. 1514 of *LNCS*, pp. 160–174, 1998.
10. J. Camenisch and M. Stadler. Efficient group signature schemes for large groups. In *CRYPTO '97, LNCS, vol. 1294*, pp. 410–424, 1997.
11. D. Chaum and E. van Heyst. Group signatures. In *EUROCRYPT '91, LNCS, vol. 547*, pp. 257–265, 1991.
12. A. Fiat and A. Shamir. How to prove yourself: Practical solutions to identification and signature problems. In *CRYPTO '86, LNCS, vol. 263*, pp. 186–194, 1986.
13. O. Goldreich and V. Rosen. On the security of modular exponentiation with application to the construction of pseudorandom generators. *Journal of Cryptology*, 16(2):71–93, 2003.
14. S. Goldwasser, S. Micali, and R. Rivest. A digital signature scheme secure against adaptive chosen-message attacks. *SIAM J. on Comp.*, 17(2):281–308, Apr. 1988.
15. R. Impagliazzo and S. Rudich. Limits on the provable consequences of one-way permutations. In *proceedings of STOC '89*, pp. 44–61, 1989.
16. A. Kiayias, Y. Tsiounis, and M. Yung. Traceable signatures. Cryptology ePrint Archive, Report 2004/007, 2004. http://eprint.iacr.org/.
17. A. K. Lenstra and E. K. Verheul. Selecting cryptographic key sizes. *Journal of Cryptology*, 14(4):255–293, 2001.
18. A. Lysyanskaya. Unique signatures and verifiable random functions from the DH-DDH separation. In *CRYPTO 2002*, LNCS, pp. 597–612, 2002.
19. D. Pointcheval and J. Stern. Security proofs for signature schemes. In *EURO-CRYPT '96*, vol. 1070 of *LNCS*, pp. 387–398. Springer Verlag, 1996.
20. Trusted Computing Group. TCG TPM specification 1.2. Available at www.trustedcomputinggroup.org, 2003.
21. G. Tsudik and S. Xu. Accumulating composites and improved group signing. In *proceedings of ASIACRYPT '03, LNCS series, volume 2894*, pp. 269–286, 2003.

Efficient Blind Signatures Without Random Oracles

Jan Camenisch[†], Maciej Koprowski[‡,∗], and Bodgan Warinschi[♯]

[†] IBM Research, Zurich Research Laboratory,
CH–8803 Rüschlikon
jca@zurich.ibm.com
[‡] Intel Technology Poland,
PL–80-298 Gdansk
maciejx.koprowski@intel.com
[♯]Computer Science Dept.,
UC Santa Cruz, Santa Cruz, CA 95064, USA
bogdan@soe.ucsc.edu

Abstract. The only known blind signature scheme that is secure in the standard model [19] is based on general results about multi-party computation, and thus it is extremely inefficient. The main result of this paper is the first provably secure blind signature scheme which is also efficient. We develop our construction as follows. In the first step, which is a significant result on its own, we devise and prove the security of a new variant for the Cramer-Shoup-Fischlin signature scheme. We are able to show that for generating signatures, instead of using randomly chosen *prime* exponents one can securely use randomly chosen *odd integer* exponents which significantly simplifies the signature generating process. We obtain our blind signing function as a secure and efficient two-party computation that cleverly exploits its algebraic properties and those of the Paillier encryption scheme. The security of the resulting signing protocol relies on the Strong RSA assumption and the hardness of decisional composite residuosity; we stress that it does not rely on the existence of random oracles.

1   Introduction

Provable Security: Standard Versus the Random Oracle Model. Provable security is the defining paradigm of modern cryptography. Here, complex cryptographic constructs are designed starting from simpler ones, and the security of the former is *proved* exhibiting a reduction to the security of the latter. Although security proved this way is not unconditional, the guarantees that are obtained in this framework (known as the "standard model") typically rely only on a few widely studied and accepted assumptions.

[∗] Work done at IBM Zurich Research Laboratory and BRICS, University of Aarhus, Denmark.

C. Blundo and S. Cimato (Eds.): SCN 2004, LNCS 3352, pp. 134–148, 2005.

The *random oracle* [2] model is a popular alternative to the above paradigm. Here, protocols are designed and proved secure under the additional assumption that publicly available functions that are chosen truly at random exist,[1] and concrete implementations are obtained by replacing the random oracles with cryptographic hash functions (such as SHA-1).

Although existence of random oracles enables very efficient cryptographic solutions for a large number of problems (digital encryption and signing, identification protocols etc.), in general, security proofs in this model are not sound with respect to the standard model: there exist constructions of various cryptographic schemes [5, 22, 17, 1] provably secure in the random oracle model, but for which no instantiation of the random oracle yields a secure scheme in the standard model. As a consequence, a central line of research in modern cryptography is designing efficient schemes provably secure in the standard model. We address this issue in the context of blind signature schemes.

Blind Signatures. Since their introduction [6], blind signature schemes have been used in numerous applications, most prominently in anonymous voting schemes and anonymous e-cash.

Informally, blind signature schemes allow a user to obtain signatures from an authority on any document, in such a way that the authority learns nothing about the message that is being signed. A bit more formal, a signer S with public key pk and secret secret key sk, interacts with user U having as private input m. At the end of the interaction, the user obtains a signature σ on m. Two seemingly contradictory properties must be satisfied. The first property, termed *blindness*, requires that after interacting with various users, the signer S is not able to link a valid message-signature pair (m, σ) obtained by some user, with the protocol session during which σ was created. The second security property, termed *unforgeability*, requires that it be impossible for any malicious user that engages in k runs of the protocol with the signer, to obtain strictly more than k valid message-signature pairs. These security notions were formalized in [19] building on previous work [24, 26].

In contrast with the random oracle model where several very efficient schemes are already known [24, 25], in the standard model only one such scheme has been designed [19]. The construction is based on general results regarding two-party computation and is thus extremely inefficient. In fact the authors themselves present their construction as an existence result.

Our Results. Our main result is the design of an efficient blind signature scheme, provably secure in the standard model. The idea of the construction is similar to the one of [19]: consider the signing function $\mathsf{Sig}(\cdot, \cdot)$ of a signature scheme provably secure in the standard model, with input arguments a secret signing key sk and a message m. The output of the function is a signature σ on m which can later be verified using the public key pk associated to sk. We obtain a secure blind

---

[1] These random oracles can only be accessed in a black-box way, by providing an input and obtaining the corresponding output.

signature protocol by providing a secure two-party computation of this signing function in which the signer provides as input its secret key sk and the user provides the message m to be signed. In our implementation only the user learns the outcome of the computation, i.e., learns a signature $\sigma = \mathsf{Sig}(sk, m)$, and the signer learns nothing. Security of the resulting protocol is implied by standard properties of secure two-party computation: because S learns nothing about the message that it signed the protocol satisfies the blindness condition. Since after each interaction the user only learns a signature on a message of his choice, and nothing else, our blind signature scheme is also unforgeable.[2]

We start with a more efficient and *provably secure* variant of the Cramer-Shoup signature scheme proposed by Fischlin [15]. Still, due to efficiency reasons, we do not implement this scheme directly; one of its essential ingredients is the use of a randomly chosen prime exponent each time a signature is created. In order to avoid this step, which seems to be a difficult and time consuming task, we further modify the Cramer-Shoup-Fischlin scheme by replacing the randomly chosen *prime* exponents with randomly chosen *odd integers*. An interesting result on its own, we show that the resulting scheme(mCSF) remains secure. We note that the same modification can be applied to the original Cramer-Shoup signature scheme, leading to a scheme which does not involve prime number generation. Next, we show how to implement the signing algorithm of the mCSF signature scheme as a secure two-party computation as discussed above. Efficiency is achieved by exploiting in a crucial way the algebraic properties of the mCSF signature scheme and those of Paillier's encryption scheme.

We prove the security of our scheme in a slightly weaker sense than the one captured by the the model of [19]. There, the setting that is considered involves an adversary interacting with the the honest party via multiple, possibly interleaved executions of the protocol. In contrast, we prove security of our scheme in a setting the signer executes the protocol sequentially only. The reason for this is that our proof of unforgeability requires rewinding of the user which, in the case of interleaved sessions, typically leads to an exponential blow-up of the reduction. This is similar to what Dwork et al. observed for rewinding w.r.t. to proving zero-knowledge for arbitrary proof systems [13]. We note that in fact, similar restrictions need to be applied to the scheme of Juels et al. [19], a point which until today has been overlooked. We postpone for the full version of the paper a discussion on the techniques that could potentially be used to achieve security of the protocol in such a concurrent setting.

The rest of the paper is organized as follows. In §2 we present some background on ingredients that go into our construction. §3 contains formal definitions of security for blind signatures. We then introduce and prove secure the mCSF signature scheme, §4. Finally we present a two party protocol computing the signing function of this scheme and prove that the resulting blind signature scheme is indeed secure.

---

[2] A secure two-party computation is also used by Mackenzie and Reiter in [21] for generating DSA signatures. The problem they address is different and it does not seem possible to extend their solution to achieve blind signing.

2   Preliminaries

Statistically Hiding Commitment Schemes. A building block, fundamental for our scheme, is a *statistically hiding commitment scheme* with an efficient statistical zero-knowledge proof of knowledge of the committed value. Consider a domain X. A commitment scheme to elements in X is given by a family $\{\mathsf{Comit}\}_{n \in \mathbf{N}}$, where $\mathsf{Comit}_n : X \times \{0,1\}^{r(n)} \to \{0,1\}^{l(n)}$; here $r(n)$ represents the number of random coins used to commit, and $l(n)$ is the bit-length of such a commitment. The security requirement that we need is that the scheme is statistically hiding, i.e., for any $x_0, x_1 \in X$, the distribution ensembles $\{\mathsf{Comit}(x_0, U(r(n))\}_n$ and $\{\mathsf{Comit}(x_1, U(r(n))\}_n$ are statistically indistinguishable, where $U(r(n))$ denotes the random variable of choosing an integer uniformly from $\{0,1\}^{r(n)}$. We are using essentially the scheme of [16, 10]: if G is a group of unknown order (for example $\mathbb{Z}_n$ with $\mathfrak{n}$ an RSA modulus with unknown factorization,) and $\mathfrak{g}$ and $\mathfrak{h}$ are random group elements then $\mathsf{Comit}(x)$ is defined by $\mathfrak{g}^x \mathfrak{h}^r$, where r is randomly chosen from a big enough domain.

Paillier Encryption. Our protocol also makes use of the Paillier encryption scheme. Following [23], the algorithms defining the scheme, i.e., $(\mathcal{K}, \mathcal{E}, \mathcal{D})$ are as follows. For a security parameter k, the key generation $\mathcal{K}$ algorithm picks two primes p and q of of bit-length k, sets n to be the product of the two primes and $\mathsf{h} := \mathsf{n} + 1$. The public key is (h, n), and the secret key is $\mathsf{d} = \mathsf{lcm}(\mathsf{p} - 1, \mathsf{q} - 1)$. A message $m \in [0, n-1]$ is encrypted by choosing $\mathsf{u} \in_R \mathbb{Z}_{\mathsf{n}^2}$ and computing the ciphertext $\mathsf{c} := \mathsf{h}^m \mathsf{u}^\mathsf{n} \bmod \mathsf{n}^2$. Given the secret key d, the clear-text $\hat{m}$ can be obtain from the cipher-text c as $\hat{m} := \tilde{m}\mathsf{d}^{-1} \bmod \mathsf{n}$ with $\tilde{m} := (\frac{(\mathsf{c}^\mathsf{d} \bmod \mathsf{n}^2) - 1}{\mathsf{n}})$.

We will use the homomorphic properties of the Paillier encryption: if c_1 and c_2 are the encryptions of m_1 and m_2 respectively, then c_1^r is the encryption of $m_1 r$ and $\mathsf{c}_1 \mathsf{c}_2$ is the encryption of $m_1 + m_2 \bmod \mathsf{n}$.

Efficient Proof Protocols. A Σ-protocol [8] is a protocol between a prover and a verifier, running on some common input y. Additionally, the prover has some additional input x. Such protocols are three move protocols: in the first move the prover sends the verifier a "commitment" message t, in the second move the verifier sends the prover a random "challenge" message c, and in the third move the prover sends the verifier a "response" message s.

Such a protocol is *special honest verifier zero knowledge* if there exists a simulator that, on input (y, c), outputs (t, s) such that the distribution of the triple (t, c, s) is is indistinguishable from that of an actual conversation, conditioned on the event that the verifier's challenge is c. This property implies (ordinary) honest verifier zero knowledge, and also allows the protocol to be *easily and efficiently* transformed into one satisfying much stronger notions of zero knowledge (e.g., using techniques in [9]).

Such a protocol is said to satisfy the *special soundness condition with respect to a property P* if it is computationally infeasible to find two valid conversations (t, c, s) and (t, c', s'), with $c \neq c'$, unless the input y satisfies P. Via standard rewinding arguments, this notion of soundness implies the more general notion of computational soundness.

We use notation introduced by Camenisch and Stadler [4] for the various zero-knowledge proofs of knowledge of discrete logarithms and proofs of the validity of statements about discrete logarithms. For instance,

$$PK\{(\alpha, \beta, \gamma) : y = g^\alpha h^\beta \ \wedge \ \mathfrak{y} = \pm \mathfrak{g}^\alpha \mathfrak{h}^\gamma \ \wedge \ (u \le \alpha \le v)\}$$

denotes a *"zero-knowledge Proof of Knowledge of integers α, β, and γ such that $y = g^\alpha h^\beta$, $\mathfrak{y} = \pm \mathfrak{g}^\alpha \mathfrak{h}^\beta$, and $u \le \alpha \le v$ holds,"* where $y, g, h, \mathfrak{y}, \mathfrak{g}$, and $\mathfrak{h}$ are elements of some groups $G = \langle g \rangle = \langle h \rangle$ and $\mathfrak{G} = \langle \mathfrak{g} \rangle = \langle \mathfrak{h} \rangle$. The convention is that the elements listed in the round brackets denote quantities the knowledge of which is being proved (and are in general not known to the verifier), while all other parameters are known to the verifier. To make this distinction easier, we use Greek letters to denote the quantities the knowledge of which is proved, and non-Greek letters for all quantities.

Smoothness of Integers. Our proofs use several number theoretical facts related to the smoothness of randomly chosen integers. We will denote

$$\Psi(x, y) = \# \{0 < n \le x : n_1 \le y\}, \quad \Psi(x, y, z) = \# \{0 < n \le x : n_1 \le y, n_2 \le z\}.$$

where n_1 and n_2 are the first and the second biggest prime factors of n. Various bounds on these quantities are known from the existing literature (see for example [12, 11, 20, 18]) and these bounds are further used to derive concrete bounds on the probability that certain randomly chosen integers are (semi-)smooth.

3   Formal Model for Blind Signatures

In this section we recall the formal definition and the standard security notion for blind signature schemes introduced in [19].

Syntax. A blind signature scheme $\mathcal{BS} = (\mathsf{Kg}, \mathsf{Signer}, \mathsf{User}, \mathsf{Vf})$ is given by:

- the probabilistic key generation algorithm Kg takes as input security parameters params and outputs a pair (pk, sk) of public-secret keys; we write $(pk, sk) \in_R \mathsf{Kg}(\mathsf{params})$ for the process of running the key generation algorithm with fresh coins;
- Signer and User are two interactive probabilistic Turing machines that run in polynomial time. Each machine has a read-only input tape, a write-only output tape, a read/write work tape, and a read-only random tape. The machines communicate using a read-only and a write-only tape. Both machines have a common input that consists of a public key pk produced by the key generation algorithm. As private inputs, the Signer machine has the secret key sk corresponding to pk, and the User machine has a message m to be signed. The two parties interact, and, at the end of the interaction the expected local output is as follows. The Signer outputs one of the two messages

completed, not-completed, and the User outputs either *fail* or a signature σ on m.

We write $\sigma \in_R [\mathsf{User}(pk, m), \mathsf{Signer}(pk, sk)]$ for the process of producing signature σ on message m.

- the deterministic Vf verification algorithm takes as input the public key pk, a message m and a candidate signature σ and outputs $0/1$, i.e., it either rejects or accepts.

It is required that for all (pk, sk) that have non-zero probability of being output by Kg, and all messages m, if $\sigma \in_R [\mathsf{Signer}(sk), \mathsf{User}(m)]$ then $\mathsf{Vf}(pk, (m, \sigma)) = 1$. The essential security properties for blind signatures, defined in [19] are unforgeability and blindness:

Unforgeability and Strong Unforgeability. Unforgeability is defined via an experiment parameterized by a security parameter k. The experiment involves an adversarial user user $\mathcal{U}$ and is as follows: First a public/secret key pair for the signer is generated by running the key generation algorithm $(pk, sk) \in_R \mathsf{Kg}(k)$. Then, $\mathcal{U}$ engages in polynomially many runs of the protocol with the signer, interleaved at its own choosing. Finally $\mathcal{U}$ outputs a list of message-signature pairs $((m_1, \sigma_1), (m_2, \sigma_2), ..., (m_l, \sigma_l))$ with $m_i \neq m_j$. Let s be the number of runs successfully completed by the signer. We define the advantage of $\mathcal{U}$ by

$$\mathbf{Adv}_{\mathcal{BS}, \mathcal{U}}^{\text{unforg}}(k) = \Pr\left[(\forall 1 \leq i \leq l, \mathsf{Vf}(pk, (m_i, \sigma_i)) = 1) \wedge (s < l)\right]$$

and say that blind signature scheme $\mathcal{BS}$ is unforgeable if $\mathbf{Adv}_{\mathcal{BS}, \mathcal{U}}^{\text{unforg}}(\cdot)$ is negligible for any adversary $\mathcal{U}$. If $(m_i, \sigma_i) \neq (m_j, \sigma_j)$ instead of $m_i \neq m_j$ holds for message-signature pairs output by the adversary, the blind signature scheme is said to be *strongly* unforgeable[3].

Blindness. We define blindness via an experiment involving an adversarial signer $\mathcal{S}$. The experiment is parameterized by a bit b and security parameter k. It starts out by generating public/secret keys (pk, sk) by running the key generation algorithm on the security parameter. Then, the adversary outputs a pair of messages (m_0, m_1) lexicographically ordered. In the next stage of the experiment $\mathcal{S}$ engages in two (possibly correlated and interleaved) runs with two honest users, with inputs m_b and $m_{\bar{b}}$, respectively. If both users obtain valid signatures, on their respective message, $\mathcal{S}$ is also given these two signatures; otherwise there is no extra input to $\mathcal{S}$; in either case, $\mathcal{S}$ is required to output a bit d. We define the advantage of $\mathcal{S}$ by:

$$\mathbf{Adv}_{\mathcal{BS}, \mathcal{S}}^{\text{blind}}(k) = 2 \cdot \Pr[b = d] - 1$$

and say that $\mathcal{BS}$ satisfies the blindness property, if for all polynomial time adversaries $\mathcal{S}$, the function $\mathbf{Adv}_{\mathcal{BS}, \mathcal{S}}^{\text{blind}}(\cdot)$ is negligible (in the security parameter) for any polynomial time adversary $\mathcal{S}$.

---

[3] This distinction which is analogous to the case of standard signature schemes, was not explicitly made in [19]. We note that for the main application of blind signatures, i.e., electronic cash, unforgeability (rather than strong unforgeability) suffices.

4   A Modification of the Cramer-Shoup-Fischlin Signature Scheme

In this section we introduce the mCSF signature scheme. Recall that the original scheme [15] is parameterized by two security parameters k (the length of the RSA moduli) and l (the length of the hash function outputs), with $l < k$, and is strongly unforgeable under chosen message attack, assuming that the strong RSA assumption holds.

Before we provide our modified scheme, we discuss our motivation for the modifications. If we wanted to use the plain Cramer-Shoup-Fischlin signature scheme as a basis for our blind signatures scheme, we would have to implement the generation of a random prime exponent as a two party protocol. This would be quite costly and thus not result in an efficient blind signature scheme. However, jointly generating a random integer can be done very efficiently, using a suitable commitment scheme. From our analysis on smooth numbers, it turns out that one can indeed replace the random *prime* exponents by random sufficiently large integers. That is, if one considers a random interval I of size $2^{l'}$ of integers of size at least 2^{ul}, one finds that the probability that *all* integer in the interval have a prime factor that is bigger than $2^{l'}$ is overwhelming for suitably large u (and suitable l'). In fact, these prime factors will be unique: Assume the contrary, i.e., let $e_0 = pk_0$ and $e_1 = pk_1$, with p being a common factor larger than $2^{l'}$. Now $e_0 - e_1 = p(k_0 - k_1)$. As $p > 2^{l'}$, it follows that not both e_0 and e_1 can lie in I and hence any (prime) factor $p > 2^{l'}$ of an element in I is unique.

Considering the security proof of the Cramer-Shoup-Fischlin scheme, one finds that it requires the exponents to have a unique prime factor that is bigger than the outputs of the hash function. So, if we set l' to be bigger than the output length l of the hash function used, we can indeed replace the random primes by random integers from the interval I. However, it turns out that this required to choose rather large integers. Fortunately, we can do better: A closer inspection of the signature scheme's security proof shows that it is sufficient that (1) every integer in the interval has a unique prime factor larger than $2^{l'}$ and (2) that the integers the signer uses to sign have either a prime factor larger than 2^l or two prime factors larger than $2^{l'}$ with $2l' > l$. This facts allow us to choose much smaller integers. We will give a detailed concrete treatment of the security of the resulting scheme in the full version of this paper.

We are now ready to describe our modification of the Cramer-Shoup-Fischlin signature scheme. Apart from using random integer exponents instead of prime ones, we operate two further modifications. The reason for both of them is purely technical. The first one takes care of the problem of when doing proofs of knowledge modulo an RSA modulus that is safe-prime product. That is, we introduce an extra squaring in the verification equations which will allow us later in the blind signature generation protocol to square the "blinded message" to cast it into the group of squares modulo n. The second one is splitting the signing algorithm in two stages: To sign message m, the algorithm first outputs some random data and then, in the second stage, outputs the remaining part of the signature on m, deterministically determined by the message and the output of the first stage. This modification will allow us to reduce the security of our blind signature scheme to the security of the mCSF scheme.

The mCSF Signature Scheme. The scheme uses parameters k, l, l', and u where $l/2 \leq l' < l$ and u is a real number. The parameters l', and u are as above. The parameter k denotes here the bit-length of the prime factor of the RSA modulus, l is the bit-length of the output of a public, collision resistant hash function $\mathcal{H}() : \{0,1\}^* \rightarrow \{0,1\}^l$. Also, let t be the maximal number of messages to be signed.

The parameters l' and u strictly depend on l and can be chosen such that the discussed above smoothness probabilities are sufficiently small. Also, we note that for practical purposes it is possible to choose u based on concrete bounds. We will show how to derive these bounds in the full version of our paper.

The algorithms defining the mCSF signature scheme are the following:

- The key generation algorithm KGen generates two random safe primes $p = 2p' + 1$ and $q = 2q' + 1$ of bit-length k and sets $N := pq$. It also draws at random $x, h_1, h_2 \in QR_N$ and a random integer $f_0 \in_R]0, 2^{lu-l'}[$ and sets $f := 2^{l'} f_0 + 1$. Then, it chooses a public collision-resistant hash function $\mathcal{H}()$. The public key is $(N, h_1, h_2, x, \mathcal{H}(), f, l')$, and the corresponding secret key is $\phi = (p - 1)(q - 1) = 4p'q'$.

- Signing a message m is done as follows. Pick a random l-bit string a and a random odd number e from the interval $[f, f + 2^{l'}[$ and output it. This completes the first stage of the signing process. Then, on a further request (not necessarily executed immediately afterwards) compute y such that $y^e = (xh_1^a h_2^{(a+\mathcal{H}(m) \bmod 2^l)})^2$. The signature on m is $\sigma = (e, a, y)$.

- A signature (e, a, y) on message m is valid if e is odd and the following two relations are valid

$$f \leq e < f + 2^{l'} \quad \text{and} \quad y^e = (xh_1^a h_2^{(a+\mathcal{H}(m) \bmod 2^l)})^2 . \tag{1}$$

Security Analysis. The security of the mCSF signature scheme is captured by the following theorem:

Theorem 41. *Let $\mathcal{H}()$ be a collision-resistant hash function, let $l > l' \geq l/2$ and u be such that $\Psi\left(2^{lu}, 2^{l'}\right) 2^{-lu+l'}$ and $\Psi\left(2^{lu}, 2^l, 2^{l'}\right) 2^{-lu+4l'/5}$ are negligible. Then mCSF is strongly unforgeable under adaptive chosen message attack provided that the strong RSA assumption holds.*

Moreover, the signature scheme is secure under the more general attack, where the adversary is allowed to query for pairs (e, a) and then, at some later point, ask for signatures on a hash of a message w.r.t. some of these pairs (but only once per pair).

We postpone the proof for the full version of this paper.

Notice that if we are interested in signing only short messages, we do not need to assume a collision resistant hash functions.

Two issues are raised in comparing the original scheme to our modified version. On the one hand, our scheme has a more efficient signing algorithm: the prevailing cost for signing in the original scheme is to find the prime exponent e. In our scheme the signer just needs to choose a random number which, for the computation of y, the signer can further reduce it modulo $\phi(n)$. On the other hand, our verification protocol is less efficient, as the verifier has to perform a computation with an exponent e that is much larger in our case (and the verifier cannot reduce it modulo $\phi(n)$).

5   Our Blind Signature Protocol

In this section we give the construction of our blind signature scheme. As we have anticipated, its signing protocol is a two-party computation of the signing function of the mCSF signature scheme, while the verification algorithms is the same. The two parties, henceforth a user U and a signer S, provide as private inputs to the signing protocol a message m and a secret key ϕ, respectively, and jointly compute an mCSF signature $\sigma = (a, e, y)$ on m. The properties of the joint computation are such that S learns absolutely no information (in a strong, information-theoretic sense), and the user U learns the signature σ, but no information on ϕ (in a computational sense.)

We start by discussing the main ideas behind our construction. Recall that given the public key $(N, h_1, h_2, x, \mathcal{H}(), f, l')$, the signer, which has the corresponding secret key ϕ, and the user, having some private input m, need to compute values (e, a, y) such that $y^e \equiv (xh_1^a h_2^{(a+\mathcal{H}(m) \bmod 2^l)})^2 \pmod{N}$. This is done as follows.

First the parties jointly generate a random e and a in such a way that only U learns their values. For this, U first commits to random shares for e and a (via a statistically hiding commitment scheme), and sends these commitments to the signer. The signer replies with his own shares, allowing U to compute the resulting e and a as sum of the corresponding shares. At this point, U computes the value $xh_1^a h_2^{(a+\mathcal{H}(m) \bmod 2^l)}$ by himself, blinds it using a mechanism similar to the one in Chaum's RSA-based blind signature scheme [7], and sends the resulting value to the signer.

The signer and the user together compute the value $\hat{e} = e\bar{e} + r\phi$, which is statistically independent from e and thus reveals no information about e to the signer. At this point the signer can compute an $e\bar{e}$-th root modulo N of the blinded message which he then returns to the user. Finally, the user eliminates the blinding factor and obtains (e, a, y), a signature on m. A key element of our protocol are *efficient* zero-knowledge proofs that all messages of the user follow the protocol as outlined above. We note that the signer does not need to prove that it behaves according to the protocol: the signer can only cheat in the computation of the last message it sends which will result in an invalid signature therefore the user will note cheating here. We now proceed with the detailed description of our scheme.

Key Generation. The key generation algorithm Kg takes as input four security parameters k, k', l, l' (k, l, l' are as in Theorem 41 and $k' \approx 100$ is a parameter that controls the statistical blindness of e) and is as follows:

Algorithm $\mathsf{Kg}(k, k', l, l')$:

1. Select keys for the Paillier encryption scheme, i.e., pick two primes $\mathsf{p}, \mathsf{q} > 2^{(lu+2k+k'+1)/2}$; set $\mathsf{n} := \mathsf{pq}$, $\mathsf{h} := (1 + \mathsf{n})$, $\mathsf{d} := \mathrm{lcm}(\mathsf{p} - 1, \mathsf{q} - 1)$
2. Choose $u > 1$ as described in §4.
3. Select keys for the mCSF signature scheme, i.e., pick two safe prime p and q of bit-length k, set $N := pq$, and $\phi := (p - 1)(q - 1)$.
4. Pick $\mathcal{H}()$ at random from a collision resistant hash function family with an output size of l bits;
5. Select a random f_0 from the interval $]0, 2^{lu-l'}[$; set $f := 2^{l'} f_0 + 1$;
6. Select random $x, h_1, h_2, h_3 \in_R QR_N$.
7. Select $\mathsf{v} \in_R \mathbb{Z}_\mathsf{n}^*$ and set $\mathsf{c} := \mathsf{h}^\phi \mathsf{v}^\mathsf{n} \bmod \mathsf{n}^2$.
8. Select auxiliary keys for the proof-protocols, i.e., pick two safe prime $\mathfrak{p}, \mathfrak{q}$ of bit-length k, set $\mathfrak{n} := \mathfrak{pq}$. Select two generators $\mathfrak{g}$ and $\mathfrak{h}$ of $QR_\mathfrak{n}$.
9. Set the public key of S to $(N, h_1, h_2, h_3, x, f, \mathfrak{n}, \mathfrak{h}, \mathfrak{g}, \mathsf{n}, \mathsf{c}, \mathsf{h}, k, k', l, l', u)$, set the secret key of S to (ϕ, d).

We imagine that this key generation algorithm is either run by a trusted third party which then hands over the secret key to the signer or, alternatively, the signer runs the key generation by itself, and then proves to a trusted party that it had followed the protocol. Specifically, it needs to prove that 1) the moduli N and $\mathfrak{n}$ are indeed products of safe-primes, 2) that $h_1, h_2 \in \langle h_3 \rangle$ and $\mathfrak{g} \in \langle \mathfrak{h} \rangle$, and 3) that c is a Paillier encryption of $\phi(N)$. Proving these statements can be done via standard protocols: Showing that N and $\mathfrak{n}$ are products of two safe prime can be done as in Camenisch and Michels [3]. In order to prove that $h_1, h_2 \in \langle h_3 \rangle$, it is sufficient to show that the h_i's are squares [14] and to check that $\gcd(h_3 \pm 1, N) = 1$. Similarly, one can show that $\mathfrak{g} \in \langle \mathfrak{h} \rangle$. Finally, the statement that c is an encryption of ϕ can be proved, given an auxiliary modulus $\hat{\mathfrak{n}}$ that is the product of two safe primes of bit-size k and two generators $\hat{\mathfrak{g}}$ and $\hat{\mathfrak{h}}$ of $QR_{\hat{\mathfrak{n}}}$ such that the signer does not knows the factorization of $\hat{\mathfrak{n}}$ or an integer $\hat{u}$ such that $\hat{\mathfrak{h}} = \hat{\mathfrak{g}}^{\hat{u}}$. (Such parameters could be generated either by a trusted third party, or by the party verifying the proof). Because this proof is less known, we give its details in the sequel: The signer chooses $v_1, v_2 \in_R [1, \lfloor \frac{\hat{\mathfrak{n}}}{4} \rfloor]$, computes $\Phi := \hat{\mathfrak{g}}^\phi \hat{\mathfrak{h}}^{v_1}$ and $P := \hat{\mathfrak{g}}^{p-1} \hat{\mathfrak{h}}^{v_2}$, sends Φ and P to the verifier and runs the protocol

$$Proof\ 0 = PK\{(\alpha, \beta, \gamma, \delta, \xi_1, \ldots, \xi_4) : \Phi = \pm\hat{\mathfrak{g}}^\alpha \hat{\mathfrak{h}}^{\xi_1} \wedge P = \pm\hat{\mathfrak{g}}^\beta \hat{\mathfrak{h}}^{\xi_2} \wedge$$

$$\Phi = \pm P^\gamma \hat{\mathfrak{h}}^{\xi_3} \wedge \frac{\hat{\mathfrak{g}}^N}{\hat{\mathfrak{g}}P} = \pm(\hat{\mathfrak{g}}P)^\gamma \hat{\mathfrak{h}}^{\xi_4} \wedge \mathsf{c} = \mathsf{h}^\alpha \delta^\mathsf{n} \pmod{\mathsf{n}^2} \wedge 1 \leq \beta \leq N - 2\}$$

with the verifier. (See Theorem 51 for an analysis of this protocol.) The signer could prove these statements just once to the certification authority (or to

$U(m, \text{params})$	$S((\phi, \mathsf{d}), \text{params})$

$e_U \in_R \{0,1\}^{l'-1}$ $e_S \in_R \{0,1\}^{l'-1}$

$a_U \in_R \{0,1\}^l,$ $a_S \in_R \{0,1\}^l$

$\bar{e}' \in_R \{0,1\}^{2k+k'-1}, r \in_R \{0,1\}^{lu+k'}$

$u_0, u_1, u_2 \in_R [1, \lfloor \frac{n}{4} \rfloor]$

$E_U := \mathfrak{g}^{e_U} \mathfrak{h}^{u_0}, A_U := \mathfrak{g}^{a_U} \mathfrak{h}^{u_1}$

$M := \mathfrak{g}^{\mathcal{H}(m)} \mathfrak{h}^{u_2}$

$$\xrightarrow{\quad A_U, E_U, M, \text{Proof 1} \quad}$$

$$\xleftarrow{\quad e_S, a_S \quad}$$

$e := 2\big((e_U + e_S) \bmod 2^{l'-1}\big) + f$

$\bar{e} := 2\bar{e}' + 1$

$u_3, u_4, u_5, u_9 \in_R [1, \lfloor \frac{n}{4} \rfloor]$

$E := \mathfrak{g}^e \mathfrak{h}^{u_3}, R := \mathfrak{g}^r \mathfrak{h}^{u_9}$

$\bar{E} := \mathfrak{g}^{\bar{e}} \mathfrak{h}^{u_4}, \tilde{E} := \mathfrak{g}^{e\bar{e}} \mathfrak{h}^{u_5}$

$\mathsf{u} \in_R \mathbb{Z}_n^*$

$\bar{\mathsf{c}} := \mathsf{c}^r \mathsf{h}^{e\bar{e}} \mathsf{u}^n \bmod n^2$

$$\xrightarrow{\quad \bar{\mathsf{c}}, E, R, \bar{E}, \tilde{E}, \text{Proof 2} \quad}$$

$b \in_R [1, \lfloor \frac{N}{4} \rfloor]$

$a := a_U + a_S \bmod 2^l$

$\tilde{m} := \big(h_3^{be} x h_1^a h_2^{(a+\mathcal{H}(m) \bmod 2^l)}\big)^{\bar{e}}$

$u_6, u_7, u_8 \in_R [1, \lfloor \frac{n}{4} \rfloor]$

$A := \mathfrak{g}^a \mathfrak{h}^{u_6}, B := \mathfrak{g}^b \mathfrak{h}^{u_7}$

$\tilde{A} := \mathfrak{g}^{(a+\mathcal{H}(m) \bmod 2^l)} \mathfrak{h}^{u_8}$

$$\xrightarrow{\quad \tilde{m}, A, B, \tilde{A}, \text{Proof 3} \quad}$$

$\hat{e} := \big(\big(\tfrac{(\bar{\mathsf{c}}^d \bmod n^2) - 1}{n}\big) \mathsf{d}^{-1} \bmod n\big) \bmod \phi$

$\tilde{y} := \tilde{m}^{2/\hat{e}} \pmod{N}$

$$\xleftarrow{\quad \tilde{y} \quad}$$

$y := \tilde{y} h_3^{-2b} \pmod{N}$

$y^e \stackrel{?}{=} \big(x h_1^a h_2^{(a+\mathcal{H}(m) \bmod 2^l)}\big)^2$

Output (e, a, y)

Fig. 1. A two-party protocol for producing mCSF signatures. The signer does not learn any information about the signed message. Here, the common parameters params are $((N, h_1, h_2, h_3, x, f, \mathfrak{n}, \mathfrak{h}, \mathfrak{g}, \mathsf{n}, \mathsf{c}, \mathsf{h}, k, k', l, l', u))$

some other representative trusted by the users in this respect) or to each user individually.

Blind Signing Protocol. We give the details of the blind signature protocol in Figure 1. The protocol is as follows:

The user U sends to the signer S commitments E_U, A_U, and M to random values e_U and a_U and to $\mathcal{H}(m)$, respectively, and proves to the signer that she knows how to open these commitments by running the interactive protocol

$$Proof\ 1 = PK\{(\alpha, \beta, \gamma, \delta, \varepsilon, \varrho) : \ E_U = \pm \mathfrak{g}^\alpha \mathfrak{h}^\beta \ \wedge \ M = \pm \mathfrak{g}^\gamma \mathfrak{h}^\delta \ \wedge \ A_U = \pm \mathfrak{g}^\varepsilon \mathfrak{h}^\varrho\}$$

with the signer. If the proof succeeds, the signer S responds with random values a_S and e_S with which U to computes e and a. Thus both parties are assured that a and e are chosen randomly but S does not learn anything more about a and e.

Next, the two parties compute (an encryption $\bar{c}$ of) $\hat{e} = e\bar{e} + r\phi(N)$ from the encryption c of $\phi(N)$: U picks random blinding factors $\bar{e}$ and r, computes $\bar{c} := c^r h^{e\bar{e}} u^n \bmod n^2$, and sends $\bar{c}$ to S. By means of the auxiliary commitments E, $\bar{E}$, and $\tilde{E}$ and the Σ-protocol

$$Proof\ 2 = PK\{(\alpha, \beta, \gamma, \delta, \varepsilon, \xi_1, \ldots, \xi_8) : \ \frac{E}{\mathfrak{g}^f} = \pm(\mathfrak{g}^2)^\alpha \mathfrak{h}^{\xi_1} \ \wedge$$

$$\frac{E}{E_U^2 \mathfrak{g}^{(2e_s+f)}} = \pm(\mathfrak{g}^{2^{l'}})^{\xi_2} \mathfrak{h}^{\xi_3} \ \wedge \ \bar{E}/\mathfrak{g} = \pm(\mathfrak{g}^2)^\beta \mathfrak{h}^{\xi_4} \ \wedge \ \tilde{E} = \pm \mathfrak{g}^\gamma \mathfrak{h}^{\xi_6} \ \wedge$$

$$\tilde{E}/E = \pm(E^2)^\beta \mathfrak{h}^{\xi_5} \ \wedge \ R = \pm \mathfrak{g}^\delta \mathfrak{h}^{\xi_8} \ \wedge \ \bar{c} = c^\delta h^\gamma \xi_7^n \pmod{n^2} \ \wedge$$

$$\alpha \in \{0,1\}^{l'-1} \ \wedge \ \beta \in \{0,1\}^{2k+k'-1} \ \wedge \ \delta \in \{0,1\}^{lu+k'}\}$$

U convinces S that $\bar{c}$ was correctly computed, that r and $\bar{e}$ have the required length, that e was computed as $2(e_U + e_S \bmod 2^{l'-1}) + f$, and that $\bar{e}$ is odd (cf. Theorem 51). It is not hard to show that $e\bar{e} + r\phi(N)$ is statistically independent of e.

Next, U computes the "blinded message" $\tilde{m} = (h_3^{be} x h_1^a h_2^{(a+\mathcal{H}(m) \bmod 2^l)})^{\bar{e}}$, where b is the randomly chosen blinding factor, and sends $\tilde{m}$ to S. Using the auxiliary commitments A, B, and M and the Σ-protocol

$$Proof\ 3 = PK\{(\alpha, \beta, \gamma, \delta, \varepsilon, \mu, \varphi, \rho, \omega, \nu, \kappa, \xi_1, \ldots, \xi_{11}) : \ \ A = \pm \mathfrak{g}^\alpha \mathfrak{h}^{\xi_1} \ \wedge$$

$$B = \pm \mathfrak{g}^\beta \mathfrak{h}^{\xi_2} \ \wedge \ \tilde{A} = \pm \mathfrak{g}^\gamma \mathfrak{h}^{\xi_3} \ \wedge \ \tilde{E} = \pm \mathfrak{g}^\delta \mathfrak{h}^{\xi_4} \ \wedge \ \bar{E} = \pm \mathfrak{g}^\varepsilon \mathfrak{h}^{\xi_5} \ \wedge$$

$$M = \pm \mathfrak{g}^\mu \mathfrak{h}^{\xi_6} \ \wedge \ \tilde{m} = \pm h_3^\varphi x^\varepsilon h_1^\sigma h_2^\rho \ \wedge \ 1 = \pm A^\varepsilon (\frac{1}{\mathfrak{g}})^\sigma (\frac{1}{\mathfrak{h}})^{\xi_7} \ \wedge$$

$$1 = \pm B^\delta (\frac{1}{\mathfrak{g}})^\varphi (\frac{1}{\mathfrak{h}})^{\xi_8} \ \wedge \ 1 = \pm \tilde{A}^\varepsilon (\frac{1}{\mathfrak{g}})^\rho (\frac{1}{\mathfrak{h}})^{\xi_9} \ \wedge \ A_U = \pm \mathfrak{g}^\omega \mathfrak{h}^{\xi_{12}} \ \wedge$$

$$\frac{A}{A_U \mathfrak{g}^{a_S}} = \pm(\mathfrak{g}^{2^l})^\nu \mathfrak{h}^{\xi_{10}} \ \wedge \ \frac{\tilde{A}}{MA} = \pm(\mathfrak{g}^{2^l})^\kappa \mathfrak{h}^{\xi_{11}} \ \wedge \ \alpha, \mu, \gamma \in \{0,1\}^l\}$$

she convinces S that $\tilde{m}$ is correctly formed, that a is computed as $a_U + a_S \bmod 2^l$, and that $\mathcal{H}(m) \in \{0,1\}^l$ (cf. Theorem 54).

Next, the signer decrypts $\bar{c}$ to obtain $\hat{e}(\equiv e\bar{e}+r\phi(N) \pmod{\phi(N)})$, calculates $\tilde{y} := \tilde{m}^{2/\hat{e}}$, and sends $\tilde{y}$ to U. It is immediate that

$$\tilde{y} = (h_3^{be}xh_1^ah_2^{(a+\mathcal{H}(m) \bmod 2^l)})^{2\bar{e}/(e\bar{e}+r\phi(N))} = h_3^{2b}(xh_1^ah_2^{(a+\mathcal{H}(m) \bmod 2^l)})^{2/e}).$$

Finally, U removes the blinding factor by computing $y := \tilde{y}h_3^{-2b}$ and thereby obtains the signature (e, a, y) on m.

5.1   Security of the Scheme for Sequential Sessions

Proving security of our protocol requires analyzing the Σ-subprotocols. Their security is captured by Theorems 51, 52, 53, and 54 whose proofs are postponed for the full version of this paper.

Theorem 51. *Under the strong RSA assumption and provided that N is a product of two primes, Proof 0 constitutes a statistical zero-knowledge argument that* c *is an encryption of $\phi(N)$.*

Theorem 52. *Under the strong RSA assumption Proof 1 constitutes a statistical zero-knowledge proof of knowledge of the integers committed to by E_U, A_U, and M. Also, the proof is witness indistinguishable w.r.t. the integers committed to by E_U, A_U, and M.*

The proof of this theorem follows from the explanations in §2 and the fact the commitments E_U, A_U, and M are statistically hiding.

Theorem 53. *Under the strong RSA assumption and provided that* c *encrypts a value μ such that $0 \le \mu \le 2^{2k}$, Proof 2 constitutes a statistical zero-knowledge argument that*

1. $\bar{c}$ *is an encryption of the integer $e\bar{e}+r\mu$, where r is an integer in $\{0,1\}^{l_U+k'}$.*
2. $e = 2((e_U+e_S) \bmod 2^{l'-1})+f$ *and $\bar{e}$ is odd, where e is the integer committed by E, $\bar{e}$ is the one committed by $\bar{E}$, and e_U is the integer committed by E_U.*

Moreover, the protocol is witness indistinguishable w.r.t. all $\bar{e}$, e, and r such that $e\bar{e}+r\mu$ equals the value encrypted in $\bar{c}$.

Theorem 54. *Under the strong RSA assumption Proof 3 constitutes a statistical zero-knowledge argument that*

$$\tilde{m} = \pm h_3^{b\bar{e}}(xh_1^ah_2^{(a+\dot{m} \bmod 2^l)})^{\bar{e}} \ , \quad a = a_U + a_S \bmod 2^l \ , \quad \text{and} \quad \tilde{e} = e\bar{e} \quad (2)$$

holds, where a is the integer committed to by A, a_U is the integer committed to by A_U, e the integer committed to by E, $\bar{e}$ the integer committed to by $\bar{E}$, $\tilde{e}$ the integer committed to by $\tilde{E}$, and $\dot{m}$ the integer committed to by M. Also, the protocol is witness indistinguishable w.r.t. all a, a_U, b, e, $\bar{e}$, $\tilde{e}$, and $\dot{m}$ such that the Equations (2) hold.

Our main results is the following theorem.

Theorem 55. *Under the strong RSA and the decisional n-residuosity assumptions the blind signature scheme depicted in Figure 5 is blind and strongly unforgeable under an adaptive chosen message attack, if executed sequentially polynomially many times.*

References

1. M. Bellare, A. Boldyreva, and A. Palacio. An un-instantiable random-oracle-model scheme for a hybrid-encryption problem. In *EUROCRYPT 2004*, LNCS, 2004.
2. M. Bellare and P. Rogaway. Random oracles are practical: A paradigm for designing efficient protocols. In *ACM CCS* , pp. 62–73, 1993.
3. J. Camenisch and M. Michels. Proving in zero-knowledge that a number n is the product of two safe primes. In *EUROCRYPT '99*, vol. 1592 of *LNCS*.
4. J. Camenisch and M. Stadler. Efficient group signature schemes for large groups. In *CRYPTO '97*, vol. 1296 of *LNCS*. Springer Verlag, 1997.
5. R. Canetti, O. Goldreich, and S. Halevi. The random oracle methodology, revisited. In *Proceedings of the 13th Annual ACM STOC*, pp. 209–218, 1998.
6. D. Chaum. Blind signatures for untraceable payments. In *Advances in Cryptology — Proceedings of CRYPTO '82*, pp. 199–203. Plenum Press, 1983.
7. D. Chaum. Blind signature systems. In *Advances in Cryptology — CRYPTO '83*, p. 153. Plenum Press, 1984.
8. R. Cramer. *Modular Design of Secure yet Practical Cryptographic Protocol*. PhD thesis, University of Amsterdam, 1997.
9. I. Damgård. Efficient concurrent zero-knowledge in the auxiliary string model. In *EUROCRYPT 2000*, vol. 1807 of *LNCS*. Springer Verlag, 2000.
10. I. Damgård and E. Fujisaki. A statistically-hiding integer commitment scheme based on groups with hidden order. In *ASIACRYPT 2002*, vol. 2501 of *LNCS*.
11. N. de Bruijn. On the number of positive integers $\leq x$ and free of prime factors $> y$. *Nederl. Akad. Wetensch. Proceedings*, 53:813–821, 1950.
12. K. Dickman. On the frequency of numbers containing prime factors of a certain relative magnitude. *Arkiv för Matematik, Astronomi och Fysik*, 22A(10), 1930.
13. C. Dwork, M. Naor, and A. Sahai. Concurrent zero-knowledge. In *Proceedings of the 30th Annual STOC*, pp. 409–418, Dallas, TX, USA, May 1998. ACM Press.
14. A. Fiat and A. Shamir. How to prove yourself: Practical solution to identification and signature problems. In *CRYPTO '86*, vol. 263 of *LNCS*. Springer Verlag, 1987.
15. M. Fischlin. The Cramer-Shoup Strong-RSA signature scheme revisited. In *PKC 2003*, vol. 2567 of *LNCS*, pp. 116–129. Springer-Verlag, 2003.
16. E. Fujiski and T. Okamoto. Statistical zero-knowledge protocols to prove modular polynomial relations. In *CRYPTO '97*, vol. 1294 of *LNCS*, pp. 16–30, 1997.
17. S. Goldwasser and Y. Tauman. On the (in)security of the Fiat-Shamir transform. In *Proceedings of Foundations of Computer Science*, 2003.
18. A. Hildebrand. On the number of positive integers $\leq x$ and free of prime factors $> y$. *Journal of Number Theory*, 22:289–307, 1986.
19. A. Juels, M. Luby, and R. Ostrovsky. Security of blind digital signatures. In *Proceedings of Crypto'97*, vol. 1294 of *LNCS*, pp. 150–164. Springer-Verlag, 1997.
20. D. E. Knuth and L. T. Pardo. Analysis of a simple factorization algorithm. *Theoretical Computer Science*, 3(3):321–348, Dec. 1976.
21. P. MacKenzie and M. K. Reiter. Two-party generation of DSA signatures. *International Journal of Information Security*, 2(3), 2004.

22. J. B. Nielsen. Separating random oracle proofs from complexity theoretic proofs: The non-committing encryption case. In *CRYPT0 2002*, vol. 2442 of *LNCS*.
23. P. Paillier. Public-key cryptosystem based on composite degree residuosity classes. In *Proceedings of EUROCRYPT'99*, vol. 1592 of *LNCS*, pp. 223–238, 1999.
24. D. Pointcheval and J. Stern. Provably secure blind signature schemes. In *Advances in Cryptology – ASIACRYPT '96*. LNCS, Springer-Verlag, 1996.
25. D. Pointcheval and J. Stern. New blind signatures equivalent to factorization. In *ACM CCS*, pp. 92–99. ACM Press, 1997.
26. D. Pointcheval and J. Stern. Security arguments for digital signatures and blind signatures. *Journal of Cryptology*, 13(3):361–396, 2000.

Minimalist Cryptography for Low-Cost RFID Tags
(Extended Abstract)

Ari Juels

RSA Laboratories,
Bedford, MA 01730, USA
ajuels@rsasecurity.com

Abstract. A radio-frequency identification (RFID) tag is a small, inexpensive microchip that emits an identifier in response to a query from a nearby reader. The price of these tags promises to drop to the range of $0.05 per unit in the next several years, offering a viable and powerful replacement for barcodes.

The challenge in providing security for low-cost RFID tags is that they are computationally weak devices, unable to perform even basic symmetric-key cryptographic operations. Security researchers often therefore assume that good privacy protection in RFID tags is unattainable. In this paper, we explore a notion of *minimalist cryptography* suitable for RFID tags. We consider the type of security obtainable in RFID devices with a small amount of rewritable memory, but very limited computing capability. Our aim is to show that standard cryptography is not necessary as a starting point for improving security of very weak RFID devices. Our contribution is twofold:

1. We propose a new security model for authentication and privacy in RFID tags. This model takes into account the natural computational limitations and the likely attack scenarios for RFID tags in real-world settings. It represents a useful divergence from standard cryptographic security modeling, and thus a new basis for practical formalization of minimal security requirements for low-cost RFID-tag security.
2. We describe a protocol that provably achieves the properties of authentication and privacy in RFID tags in our proposed model, and in a good practical sense. It involves no computationally intensive cryptographic operations, and relatively little storage.

Keywords: authentication, privacy, pseudonyms, RFID tags.

1 Introduction

A passive *radio-frequency identification* (RFID) tag is a microchip capable of transmitting a static identifier or serial number for a short distance. It is typically activated by a query from a nearby reader, which also transmits power for the operation of the tag. Several varieties of RFID tag are already familiar in

C. Blundo and S. Cimato (Eds.): SCN 2004, LNCS 3352, pp. 149–164, 2005.

daily life. Examples include the small plaques mounted on car windshields for the purpose of automated toll payment and the proximity cards used to control physical access to buildings. More expensive RFID tags can execute advanced cryptographic and other functions, but we concern ourselves in this paper with the inexpensive variety geared to serve as a next-generation successor to barcodes.

The cost of rudimentary RFID tags promises to drop to roughly $0.05/unit in the next several years [23], while tags as small as 0.4mm × 0.4mm, and thin enough to be embedded in paper are already commercially available [27]. Such improvements in cost and size augur a rapid proliferation of RFID tags into many areas of use. Indeed, Wal-Mart has issued a directive to its top one-hundred suppliers requiring deployment of RFID at the pallet level [5], while The Gillette Company has recently placed an order for half a billion tags for use in supply-chain and retail environments [6]. A goal of researchers in RFID tag development is to see them serve ubiquitously as a replacement for barcodes. This change promises more flexible and intelligent handling of consumer goods and devices. Here are just a few enticing possibilities: Microwave ovens that can read the tags on packages and cook food without explicit instructions, refrigerators that can recognize expired and depleted foodstuffs, and closets that can inventory their contents (and perform a Web search for custom fashion advice). Towards this end, for example, researchers have recently designed RFID-based systems to monitor medication compliance in the elderly [8].

The impending ubiquity of RFID tags, however, also poses a potentially widespread threat to consumer privacy [17]. If RFID tags are easily readable, then tagged items will be subject to indiscriminate physical tracking, as will their owners and bearers. Researchers have recognized this problem for some time [13, 24], and have yet to propose a truly satisfactory remedy. The issue has also seen recent attention in the popular press, whose negative coverage has vexed a number of potential RFID users, such as the clothing retailer Benetton [4, 25]. Corporate privacy is similarly problematic, as RFID tags can facilitate corporate espionage by revealing information about the operation of supply chains.

Auto-ID Labs and EPC Global (together formerly known as the Auto-ID Center) have been leading institutions in the development and standardization of RFID tags. Their initial RFID-chip designs are geared toward general corporate and consumer use. To permit inexpensive manufacture, they carry only the most basic functionality, emitting a static, 96-to-256-bit identifier on receiving a reader query [23]. Auto-ID Center chip designs seek to enforce privacy by permitting an RFID tag to be "killed," i.e., rendered permanently inoperable on receiving a short, specially designated key [24]. Other design proposals propose a pair of complementary "sleep" and "wake" commands that allow a chip to be rendered inoperable on a temporary basis. Thus, for example, a supermarket might deploy RFID tags to facilitate tracking of shipments and monitoring of shelf stocks. To protect the privacy of customers, checkout clerks might "kill" the tags of purchased goods. Alternatively, to permit tag use in the home, a consumer might furnish a secret "sleep" key at the time of checkout. This key could be used to put tags to sleep when the consumer leaves the supermarket, and to reawaken them for later use.

There are many environments, however, in which simple measures like use of "kill" or "sleep" commands are unworkable or undesirable for privacy enforcement. Consumers may wish RFID tags in their possession to remain active, or may simply find it inconvenient to manage their wake/sleep patterns. Businesses may have concerns about unauthorized monitoring of tags before they are "killed." We enumerate a few examples here of important uses and privacy concerns for which "kill" or "sleep" commands are unsatisfactory:

- **Access Delegation**: A consumer may wish certain tags in her possession to be permanently active so as to enable reading by other parties. For example, a consumer might wish to use RFID tags for effortless physical access control,[1] for theft-protection of belongings, for wireless cash and fidelity cards, and so forth. New and clever consumer applications are already beginning to emerge. For example, a Prada store in New York City tracks the RFID tags of items held by customers in order to display related accessories on nearby screens [2]. Function creep promises to result in many more uses unimagined or unimaginable today.
- **Consumer Use**: As mentioned above, RFID readers may eventually be inexpensive enough and RFID tags prevalent enough to make a range of smart appliances practical in the home. In the shorter term, there are other consumer benefits, like the ability of consumers to return RFID-tags items to shops without the need for a receipt.
- **Industrial Espionage**: Industrial espionage is a likely concern prior to the "killing" of tags. This is true, for example, in a retail environment, where a competitor capable of reading tags in shops or warehouses may gather business intelligence regarding the turnover rate of stocks, the shopping patterns of customers, and so forth.
- **Banknote Tracking**: If tags are embedded in banknotes, then they must be permanently accessible to law enforcement agencies. One straightforward approach to enforcing privacy would be to distribute banknotes in a "sleep" state, and to assign a "waking" key to law enforcement. This is problematic in that to awaken banknote tags, a law enforcement reader must transmit the key, rendering it easily vulnerable to capture. Keys cannot be assigned on a fixed per-banknote basis, because in that case a banknote would have to emit a unique identifier in order to enable law enforcement to determine the correct key for that banknote. Thus a given awakening key would potentially have to be associated with a wide batch of banknotes, in which case one would expect privacy to be swiftly and broadly compromised.

RFID tags that promiscuously emit static serial numbers pose another serious problem, namely that of authentication. Such tags may be easily cloned by an

---

[1] Smartcards with RF-enabled chips are in fact in use for this purpose today, but generally only function in very close proximity to readers.

attacker that has read access: The attacker need merely read the RFID tags of passersby to harvest their identifiers for later re-use. This is highly problematic for a number of the current and projected uses of RFID tags, most notably physical access to buildings via passive RFID tokens, and inventory tracking (especially with an eye to protection against counterfeiting). Privacy protection and the problem of authentication are thus intimately related, a fact highlighted by our investigations in this paper.

Projections on the likely resources in several years of RFID tags with cost in the vicinity of $0.05 include several hundred bits of memory and several thousand logical gates [22], of which a considerable fraction will be required for basic tag functions. Such RFID tags may be expected to perform some basic computational operations, but not conventional cryptographic ones. At best, they may include security functions involving static keys, such as keyed reads and keyed writes, i.e., essentially just PIN-controlled data accesses.

Remark: One might take the view that Moore's law will ensure greater processing power on tags in the coming years, and thus that cryptographic functionality will eventually be available in five-cent tags. There is a competing phenomenon, though: Users of low-end RFID tags are more concerned to see prices drop and RFID tags become more widespread than to see functionality increase. This means that cryptography in basic tags may be some time in coming.

1.1   Our Work: Minimalist Cryptography

Our goal in this paper is to elaborate for RFID tags a notion of *minimalist cryptography*. We first seek to characterize common adversarial capabilities in the special security environment that RFID tags present. As a complementary endeavor, we investigate security designs and key management involving severely restricted computing resources. Our main goal is to show that standard cryptographic functionality is not needed to achieve stronger security in RFID tags.

To begin with, we present a security model for an adversary that we consider representative of real-world attack scenarios for RFID. This is an important new contribution of our work. As we show, despite the limited capabilities of RFID tags, RFID systems offer the security architect a special advantage. Like normal users, adversaries in an RFID-system are physically constrained: They must have physical proximity to RFID tags in order to read (and therefore attack) them. Such adversaries are necessarily weaker than in a traditional cryptographic setting. They also have more complex restrictions on their palette of attacks. The model we propose aims to capture these distinct adversarial characteristics. This model may not be perfect, but it aims to undercut some of the standard cryptographic assumptions that may not be appropriate for real-world deployments.

A fortunate feature of our security model is the fact that it is possible to design protocols without reliance on traditional cryptographic primitives. This turns out to be essential in the setting we consider. As explained above, low-cost RFID tags in particular are incapable of performing the most basic cryptographic operations – even those involving symmetric-key primitives. Such RFID tags cannot in fact withstand strong adversarial attacks of the kind usually considered in cryptographic security models, where an adversary has general "oracle" access, i.e., a largely unrestricted ability to interact with devices.

We show how privacy and authentication may be considerably improved in low-cost RFID tags with only a small enhancement of their capabilities. We propose a scheme that may be implemented in RFID tags with just several hundred bits of memory and read/write enablement, that is, in tags roughly comparable to the $0.05-per-unit tags anticipated in the near future. We refer to our basic scheme as *pseudonym throttling*.

Pseudonym throttling is conceptually simple approach to RFID-tag authentication in which an RFID tag stores a short list of random identifiers or pseudonyms (known by authorized verifiers to be equivalent). Each time the tag is queried, it emits the next pseudonym in the list, cycling to the beginning when the list is exhausted. Combined with this feature is the physical imposition of a low query-response rate in the tag. By using hardware-based delays, tags may be made to emit identifiers at a relatively low prescribed rate. (Indeed, delay-based throttling has already seen practical demonstration: Alien Technologies incorporates a throttling mechanism into its current generation of inexpensive RFID tags to prevent guessing of "kill" codes, i.e., the PINs used to disable tags in retail environments [21].)

Alternatively, in higher-end RFID tags that permit user involvement, a user might need to press a button to initiate reading of the tag: This would constitute a different form of throttling. Given the presence of a throttling mechanism, an attacker can only track an RFID tag with a high likelihood of success if she has access to it for a long, continuous period of time, or at many different times. In the latter case, the ability of the attacker to link pseudonyms is still limited, as the tag continually changes appearance.

Pseudonym throttling is simple and practical, but has a shortcoming: The small storage capacity of RFID tags permits only a small list of pseudonyms, and hence only limited privacy protection. Our full protocol allows pseudonyms in an RFID tag to be refreshed by authorized verifiers. In consequence, an additional feature required of our scheme is authentication between tags and verifiers. This is a useful contribution of our work, and interrelated with our exploration of privacy. Given its range of security features, our full pseudonym-throttling protocol necessarily involves multiple flows, and is thus more complex than mere identifier emission. Adhering to the design principle of minimalist cryptography, our protocol involves operations no more computationally intensive than rudimentary memory management, string comparisons, and a basic XOR. To achieve privacy, we propose a special scheme involving composition of one-time pads across protocol sessions.

We emphasize that writeable memory of the type needed for our full-blown protocol may or may not ultimately be more expensive than the logic required to perform standard cryptographic operations. Our main goal here is to demonstrate how a different allocation of resources – namely a shift in favor of memory rather than computation – can subserve important security goals in a new way. This is particularly true as resource costs change on a regular basis. Given emerging breakthroughs in non-organic storage media, re-writeable memory may ultimately prove inexpensive [16].

There is also some practical offshoot of our work with more immediate potential. We describe reduced-functionality variants of our basic pseudonym scheme that require virtually no supplementation of existing tag resources. These simple variants help offer security against the real-world threat of passive eavesdropping. Although the effective read distance of RFID tags is fairly short, the readers themselves broadcast tag identifiers for long distances – indeed, up to as much as a kilometer. Our techniques help address this problem.

1.2   Related Work on RFID

Researchers have from the outset recognized the possibility of privacy threats from physical tracking in the deployment of RFID tags [24]. A number of recent papers have proposed ways of addressing the problem. Juels and Pappu [13] consider a purported plan by the European Central Bank to embed RFID tags in Euro banknotes [1]. They propose a privacy-protecting scheme in which RFID tags carry ciphertexts on the serial numbers of banknotes. These ciphertexts are subject to re-encryption by computational devices in shops, thereby rendering multiple appearances of a given RFID tag unlinkable. The Juels/Pappu scheme, however, assumes a single verifying entity – namely a law-enforcement organization – and is not obviously extensible to the multi-verifier systems likely in commercial and consumer environments. A scheme of Golle, Jakobsson, Juels, and Syverson [11] builds on this idea with a primitive known as universal encryption, essentially a special extension of the El Gamal cryptosystem [9] in which re-encryption is possible without knowledge of public keys. It has the practical drawback, though, of requiring an infrastructure of agents capable of performing public-key-based re-encryption for privacy protection of RFID tags.

Weis, Sarma, Rivest, and Engels [28] also propose a collection of privacy-enforcement ideas for RFID tags in general environments. One scheme involves the use of a hash function to protect the key used for read-access to the tag. Another includes use of a pseudo-random number generator to protect tag identities. As they note, it is unclear how and when adequate pseudo-random number generators can be deployed on inexpensive RFID tags.

Juels, Rivest, and Szydlo [14] describe a privacy-protection tool they call a "blocker" tag. This is an RFID tag that can obstruct reading of tag identifiers within a certain numerical range by simulating the presence of RFID tags bearing *all* identifiers in that range. This is accomplished through non-standard interaction with the anti-collision protocols employed in tag-reading prtoocols [15, 23]. So as not to serve as a purely disruptive mechanism, the blocker may be accompanied by a form of privacy "zoning," in which only the reading of a certain subset of identifiers is disrupted. This permits tags to be transparently readable by businesses and yet shielded from scrutiny when they reach the hands of consumers. In follow-up work, Juels and Brainard [12] describe the notion of "soft blocking," an approach to blocking that provides weaker security guarantees, but simpler tags and more flexible policy, e.g., the possibility of an "opt-in" regime for consumers.

While a practical and attractive proposal for businesses and consumers alike, the "blocker" tag and its variants have limited applicability. For example, this approach does not address the problem of industrial espionage: In most portions of the supply chain, it is impractical to block tags, because they must be readable for industrial use. In contrast, the privacy protection of our proposal functions under general conditions, and requires no special action on the part of the user. Our proposal has a slightly different aim than the blocker, however: It permits reading of a tag by an authorized verifier, while the blocker prohibits reading categorically within the limits of its policy.

In recent work, Molnar and Wagner [19] explore the issue of RFID privacy in detail in the special and imminently important context of libraries. Their work includes several proposals, including concealment of transmissions on the (more easily tapped) reader-to-tag channel, and also pseudonym-based privacy techniques akin to variants of our proposal here.

Fishkin, Roy, and Jiang have performed intriguing preliminary experiments on a physical mechanism for RFID privacy in which a tag monitors the signal-to-noise ratio of reader queries to approximate the physical proximity of the reader [7]. In their work, physical proximity can serve as a metric for trust.

A rather different, complementary perspective on privacy for RFID tags is that of Garfinkel [10], who elaborates a policy for consumer privacy-protection in the form of a proposed "RFID Bill of Rights." Proposed there are: The right of the consumer to know what items possess RFID tags and the right to have tags removed or deactivated upon purchase of these items, the right of the consumer to access of the data associated with an RFID tag, the right to access of services without mandatory use of RFID tags, and finally the right to know to when, where, and why the data in RFID tags is used.

The problem of security modeling for RFID-tag systems may be viewed as similar in flavor to that for ad-hoc wireless networks. This is true both in terms of the restricted power of participating devices and in terms of the rapid changes in their physical and therefore logical relationships. There is little formal work on security modeling particular to the special characteristics of ad-hoc networks, although it is an emerging area of interest. Of particular note is the "resurrecting duckling" idea of Stajano and Anderson [26], who consider secure authentication between devices in ad-hoc networks. As we do here, they examine the way that physical proximity may be treated as an element in security modeling.

1.3   Organization

In section 2, we outline our security model for privacy and authentication in RFID tags. We describe our scheme for RFID-tag privacy in section 3. In section 4, we discuss practical deployment issues and introduce some reduced-functionality variants of our scheme with potential for short-term, real-world application. We conclude in section 5 with some discussion of future research directions. Space limitations require the omission of formal modelling details and security proofs, as well as PRNG-based extensions from this extended abstract. These essential details may be found in a full version of the paper, available at www.ari-juels.com.

2   A Security Model for RFID Tags

Given the very basic functionality of RFID tags, it is natural to consider an adversary in an RFID-tag system whose capabilities are quite limited. In most cryptographic security definitions, as for IND-CCA security on public-key encryption schemes [3], an adversary is presumed to be able to experiment extensively with elements of the system in the course of mounting an attack. In particular, the adversary is regarded as capable of submitting a large number of "oracle" queries, that is, exploratory inputs to the cryptographic operations composing the system. (In asymptotic analyses, the number of such oracle queries is polynomially bounded in the security parameters for the system; in concrete analyses, the bound on queries aims to reflect the limits of current computing ability, and may be on the order of, say, 2^{80} for local computation. Smaller bounds, e.g., 2^{30} may be imposed for practical modeling where interaction with, e.g., an actual signing or decrypting party is involved.)

In modeling an RFID system, it is natural to treat both tags and tag-verifiers as oracles. Given the limited computing ability of tags, however, a practical system cannot feasibly withstand an adversary that can submit a large number of arbitrarily ordered queries to all oracles in the system. Moreover, a high degree of adversarial power would not accurately reflect the physical characteristics of an RFID-tag system. Both readers and tags operate only at short range, and tags may in many cases be highly mobile. Thus, the collection of "oracles" available to an adversary at a given time is likely to be small in practice.

We seek to model the limitations on adversarial power in an RFID-tag system by the following key assumption: *An adversary may only interact with a given tag on a limited basis before that tag is able in turn to interact in a protected manner with a valid verifier.* We refer to this protected interaction as a *refresh*. In particular, a refresh is a privacy and integrity-protected session between a verifier and tag in which the verifier may update keying data in the tag. A refresh models the use of a tag with a legitimate reader outside the range of the adversary. In our security model, we impose two restrictions on adversarial interaction with tags between refreshes:

Limited Successive Tag Queries: We assume that an adversary may interact with targeted RFID tags only a relatively small number of times in rapid succession prior to a refresh. This restriction would follow naturally from use of the throttling mechanism that we propose. Suppose, for example, that an RFID tag only permits reading once every several seconds. Given that an RFID-tag typically has a read range of at most a few meters, a rogue reader would have difficulty in harvesting more than, say, one or two pseudonyms from most passersby; tags might easily store half-a-dozen or so pseudonyms, however.[2] An attacker bringing a reader into a monitored environment like a shop or warehouse might similarly face difficulties in attempting prolonged intelligence gathering.

We rely on this assumption to enforce privacy protection in our scheme.

Limited Interleaving: We assume a restriction on the ability of an adversary to mount man-in-the-middle attacks between tags and legitimate readers. This assumption reflects the following adversarial constraints in real-world scenarios:

- *Stationary attacker:* A sophisticated adversary has the potential to mount a full-blown man-in-the-middle attack. Such an adversary might, for example, maintain a physical presence in proximity to a legitimate reader and alter, eavesdrop on, or inject messages to and from tags. There are two complementary impediments to such an attacker, one innate to many RFID-tag environments, another part of our proposal in this paper:

    1. Mobility of tags: In many cases, it is operationally inconvenient for an adversary to interact for an extended period of time with tags in the vicinity of legitimate readers. For example, if a reader were stationed so as to regulate physical access to a building or to permit automated checkout at a supermarket, then the mobility of users (and consequently of tags) would help ensure only a limited number of protocol flows for attack by the adversary.

    2. Throttling: Part of our proposal in this paper, throttling helps restrict the number of successive adversarial queries. It may be thought of as a defensive measure exercised by stationary or lightly mobile tags against a persistent attacker. (In a sense, throttling boosts or simulates the natural security properties of mobile tags.) Moreover, in the face of a passive attack, a reader can help implement its own throttling policy by, e.g., refusing to initiate sessions with a particular tag in rapid succession.[3]

- *Mobile attacker:* An attacker might scan RFID tags and then use harvested information to interact with readers. Such an attacker, however, has only a limited ability to perform a man-in-the-middle attack, since this requires shuttling back and forth between tags and legitimate readers. (Indeed, our proposed scheme achieves secure authentication against an attacker of this kind irrespective of the amount of interleaving.)

---

[2] Other throttling schemes are possible of course. For example, a tag might permit the reading of two pseudonyms a few seconds apart (in case of an initial read failure), but restrict access to others for a number of minutes. This would render attack even more difficult. Care is required to minimize the risk of denial-of-service attacks. We do not explore the issue of delay scheduling in detail here.

[3] A more sophisticated adversary might make use of two communicating devices: One simulating a valid tag near a reader, and another simulating a reader near a valid tag. This type of adversary can straightforwardly perform a full man-in-the-middle attack on any type of RF system that does not involve explicit user participation. Even a system employing sophisticated cryptography cannot defend against such an attack.

We rely on the assumption of limited interleaving to help enforce both privacy and authentication properties in our proposed protocol.

We reiterate that our assumptions *do not characterize the strongest possible type of adversary.* One can easily envisage a sophisticated adversary violating these assumptions to a greater or lesser degree – particularly if targeting a single or small number of RFID tags or individuals. Our goal in this paper is to achieve good, practical security by defending against a broad, real-world class of attacks. Viewed another way, we try to minimize security vulnerabilities in this constrained environment, but do not expect to eliminate them.

Due to space limitations, we are forced to relegate formal security definitions and proofs for our proposed protocol to the full version of this paper.

Remark: Our model does not explicitly capture one important feature of RFID systems. While tags may be feasibly read at only a short distance, it is possible to eavesdrop on readers from a considerably larger distance, as they are powered broadcast devices. Thus, a passive attacker can in principle harvest reader-to-tag data more easily than tag-to-reader data. Our model does characterize this situation if it is assumed that an adversary eavesdrops only intermittently – or, more realistically, that tags are read by different readers at different times, and therefore not always near readers monitored by the adversary. More importantly, in the protocol we propose here, an eavesdropper on reader-to-tag transmissions does not receive tag identifiers. Therefore, such an eavesdropper has no way of determining which data correspond to which tags.

3   Our Proposed Scheme

As explained above, our proposed protocol relies upon rotation by a tag through multiple pseudonyms, which we denote by $\alpha_1, \alpha_2, \ldots, \alpha_k$. These pseudonyms, however, do not themselves serve as the sole means of authentication for tags. If a tag authenticated itself to a verifier merely by releasing a key α_i, then an adversary could clone a tag very simply as follows. The adversary would query the target tag, obtaining α_i; the adversary would then separately interact with the verifier, using the key α_i to simulate a valid tag. Indeed, this is precisely the type of cloning attack to which standard RFID tags with static identifiers are vulnerable, e.g., current EPC designs [23]. Any single-flow protocol is necessarily vulnerable to such an attack.

To prevent this type of attack in our protocol, a tag only authenticates to a verifier after the verifier has itself authenticated to the tag. The verifier authenticates to a tag by releasing a key β_i; this key β_i is unique to a given pseudonym α_i. Once the verifier has authenticated to the tag, the tag authenticates itself to the verifier by releasing an authentication key γ_i. Like β_i, this authentication key γ_i is unique to an identifier α_i. Briefly stated, we propose a kind of challenge-response protocol, but one that is carefully interwoven with pseudonym rotation.

In order to maintain the integrity of a tag over an extended period of time and in the face of multiple probing attacks by an adversary, we take the approach in our protocol of having the verifier update the $\{\alpha_i\}$, $\{\beta_i\}$, and $\{\gamma_i\}$ values in an RFID tag after successful mutual authentication between tag and verifier. This introduces a new problem, however: An adversary can eavesdrop on or tamper with the secrets used in this update process. Our strategy for addressing this problem is to update values using one-time pads that have been transmitted across multiple authentication protocols. Thus an adversary that only eavesdrops periodically is unlikely to learn the updated $\{\alpha_i\}$, $\{\beta_i\}$, and $\{\gamma_i\}$ values.

Updating tag values in this way provides integrity protection as an important side-benefit. An adversary without knowledge of the one-time pads used during a update cannot, for instance, mount a swapping attack by substituting keys from one compromised tag into another tag.

3.1   One-Time Pads in Our Scheme

The one-time pad is, of course, a simple, classical form of encryption. (See, e.g., [18] for discussion.) We briefly recall the underlying idea. If two parties share a secret one-time pad δ, namely a random bitstring of length l, then one party may transmit an l-bit message M secretly to the other via the ciphertext $M \oplus \delta$, where $\oplus$ denotes the XOR operation. It is well known that this form of encryption provides information-theoretic secrecy.

In our scheme, the verifier transmits one-time padding data that the tag uses to update its shared $\{\alpha_i\}$, $\{\beta_i\}$, and $\{\gamma_i\}$ values. Provided that an eavesdropper does not obtain the padding data, she achieves no knowledge of the updated tag values. Although this procedure does not explicitly involve encryption by means of one-time pads, it is equivalent to encryption. We may think of the pads as keys used to "encrypt" and thereby update the $\{\alpha_i\}$, $\{\beta_i\}$, and $\{\gamma_i\}$ values.

Additionally, we introduce a special twist into our use of the one-time pad. Our scheme involves composition of one-time pads across multiple verifier-tag sessions. This has the effect of retaining secrecy in the face of partial adversarial eavesdropping (or tampering). Suppose, for instance, that pads from two different verifier-tag sessions are XORed with a given tag value κ in order to update it. Then even if the adversary intecepts the pad used in one session, it may be seen that she will learn no information about the updated value of κ.

Application of a one-time pad requires only the lightweight computational process of XORing. Like encryption based on the one-time pad, updating tag values via one-time padding also provides information-theoretic security. While this latter property renders security proofs for our system somewhat simpler, it is not a motivation for our choice. Indeed, one-time padding results in less communications efficiency than that achievable with standard cryptographic encryption tools like block or stream ciphers. The problem, as we have already explained, is that standard cryptographic primitives require more computational power than is available in a low-cost RFID tag. This is the real motivation behind our use of one-time pads.

As explained above, we employ a strategy of updating tag values using pads from multiple authentication sessions. Let κ be some value stored in a tag, i.e., $\kappa \in \{\alpha_i\} \bigcup \{\beta_i\} \bigcup \{\gamma_i\}$. Let m parameterize the resistance of the protocol to adversarial eavesdropping. For every value κ, we maintain in the tag a vector $\Delta_\kappa = \{\delta_\kappa^{(1)}, \delta_\kappa^{(2)}, \ldots, \delta_\kappa^{(m)}\}$ of one-time pads. The pad $\delta_\kappa^{(1)}$, which we refer to as the *live* pad, is used to update the tag value κ. In particular, to update κ, the tag computes $\kappa \leftarrow \kappa \oplus \delta_\kappa^{(1)}$.

Prior to update of κ, the pads in Δ_κ are updated with new padding material received from the verifier. Let $\tilde{\Delta}_\kappa = \{\tilde{\delta}_\kappa^{(1)}, \tilde{\delta}_\kappa^{(2)}, \ldots, \tilde{\delta}_\kappa^{(m)}\}$ be a vector of newly generated one-time pads received from the verifier in our protocol. The vector Δ_κ is updated as follows. The live pad $\delta_\kappa^{(1)}$ is discarded – as it has already been used to update κ. The indices of all other pads in Δ are then shifted downward, i.e., in increasing index order, we set $\delta_\kappa^{(i)} = \delta_\kappa^{(i+1)}$ for $1 \le i \le n-1$. We set $\delta_\kappa^{(m)} = 0^l$, i.e., we fill the last, missing element in the vector with a '0' bitstring. (Alternatively, it is possible to rotate the discarded, previously live pad to the last position in the vector.[4]) Finally, we "overlay" the newly received vector $\tilde{\Delta}_\kappa$ on the existing vector Δ_κ, by performing an element-wise XOR. That is, we let $\delta_\kappa^{(i)} = \delta_\kappa^{(i)} \oplus \tilde{\delta}_\kappa^{(i)}$.

As a result of these manipulations, the vector Δ_κ consists of a set of m one-time pads with decreasing levels of backward secrecy. After the completion of a session, the live pad $\delta_\kappa^{(1)}$, for instance, consists of the XOR of independent pads from the previous m successfully completed sessions. At the other end of the spectrum, the value $\delta_\kappa^{(m)}$ is constituted of only a single pad, namely the one just transmitted in the most recent session. This is why we update κ using the strongest pad in Δ_κ, namely the live one, and then strengthen and "promote" the other pads in Δ_κ by overlaying a vector of newly transmitted ones.

This approach provides information-theoretic security guarantees. In particular, an adversary that has knowledge of only $m-1$ of the last m pad-transmissions from the verifier has no knowledge at all about $\delta_\kappa^{(1)}$. Thus, when the live pad is employed to update κ, such an adversary learns no information whatever about the new value of κ.

The drawback to this approach is that the transmission cost to maintain pads is lm bits per session. In other words, the communications costs in our protocol are linear in the length of individual tag values *and* in the number of consecutive authentication sessions relative to which we wish to achieve security against the adversary. Given that there are $3k$ tag values, this translates into a total cost of $3klm$. This cost is less than ideal, but still permits a range of practical parameterizations, as we discuss below in section 4.

We use the notation $\mathsf{update}(\Delta_\kappa, \tilde{\Delta}_\kappa)$ to denote the function that updates Δ_κ and "overlays" it with $\tilde{\Delta}_\kappa$. We let $\mathsf{pad}(\kappa, \Delta_\kappa)$ denote the update of κ using the live pad $\delta_\kappa^{(1)}$ – again, the one with the strongest backward security. For brevity of notation, we let ABC denote the set of values $\{\alpha_i\} \bigcup \{\beta_i\} \bigcup \{\gamma_i\}$. We let Δ_{ABC} denote padding vectors for all values κ in the set ABC.

---

[4] This option is probably easier to implement. It also has the (slight) advantage of not causing a newly initialized tag to discard one of its original, secret values.

3.2   The Protocol

As above, let k be a parameter denoting the number of pseudonyms stored in a given tag and let m denote the number of authentication sessions over which one-time pads are constructed; in other words, the higher the value of m, the stronger the eavesdropping-resistance of the system. For visual clarity in our protocol figure, we omit variable ranges and tag subscripts on variables for keys. The variables i and j, however, always span the ranges $\{1, 2, \ldots, k\}$ and $\{1, 2, \ldots, m\}$ respectively. We use $\in_R$ here and elsewhere to denote uniform random selection. In case of a message-delivery failure, we assume the input of a special symbol $\perp$ (leading to protocol termination). We assume initialization of all entities by a trusted party, who generates a key set ABC for every tag and distributes this to both the tag and the verifier. All counters are initialized at 0. Details of our protocol are provided in Figure 1.

Again, we present formal modelling and proofs only in the full version of this paper.

Tag   **Verifier**

$d \leftarrow (c \bmod k) + 1$
$c \leftarrow c + 1$
$\alpha' \leftarrow \alpha_d$ $\xrightarrow{\alpha'}$ if $\alpha' = \alpha_i$ for some T_x then
                                                                              $tag \leftarrow x$
                                                                              $\beta' \leftarrow \beta_i$
                                                                              $\gamma \leftarrow \gamma_i$
                                                                              mark α_i as invalid for T_x
                                                                        else
                                                                              output("reject") and abort

                                                              $\xleftarrow{\beta'}$

if $\beta' \neq \beta_d$ then
        output("reject") and abort
$\gamma' \leftarrow \gamma_d$ $\xrightarrow{\gamma'}$

                                                                        if $\gamma' \neq \gamma$ or $\gamma' = \perp$ then
                                                                              output("reject") and abort
                                                                        $\tilde{\Delta}_{ABC} \in_R \{\{0,1\}^l\}^{3km}$

                                                              $\xleftarrow{\tilde{\Delta}_{ABC}}$

                                                                        output(tag, "accept")
$\{\mathsf{update}(\Delta_\kappa, \tilde{\Delta}_\kappa)\}_{\kappa \in ABC}$ $\{\mathsf{update}(\Delta_\kappa, \tilde{\Delta}_\kappa)\}_{\kappa \in ABC}$
$\{\kappa \leftarrow \mathsf{pad}(\kappa, \Delta_\kappa)\}_{\kappa \in ABC}$ $\{\kappa \leftarrow \mathsf{pad}(\kappa, \Delta_\kappa)\}_{\kappa \in ABC}$

Fig. 1. Full RFID-tag authentication protocol

Remarks: We assume no collisions among tag identifiers here – a property that can be enforced during tag initialization and updates with only a very slight skew from a uniform random distribution over identifiers.

4   Some Practical Variants

The full-blown scheme we have proposed is practical for very low-cost tags only with the use of small security parameters. There are several ways, however, to reduce its functionality while still retaining important properties.

To begin with, in real-world deployments, the moderate security afforded by relatively short keys $\{\beta_i\}$ and perhaps also short $\{\gamma_i\}$ keys would be acceptable in many cases. For example, if β_i and γ_i keys are a mere twenty bits each, then an adversary would have roughly a one-in-a-million chance of defeating the authentication protocol in a single try. Tag pseudonyms, i.e., the $\{\alpha_i\}$ keys, must be considerably longer to permit unique identification of tags and to avoid pseudonym collisions. We believe that 100-bit α values would suffice for this purpose in most environments. (It should be noted, however, that if a pseudonym collision occurs in the naming of a new tag, then different pseudonyms may be selected by the verifier. Such a naming strategy would probably permit a reduction in the lengths of α_i tags to around 80 bits.) In any event, large values of m or k are unlikely to be practical. Indeed, $m = 0$ (no updates via refresh) or 1 and $k = 4$ or 5 might be a reasonable choice for a real-world system.

A range of truncated versions of the protocol itself is also interesting. One example is a scheme that excludes the fourth flow from our protocol. In other words, the *ABC* values in the tag may remain the same throughout its lifetime. A much reduced variant might involve only the first flow in our protocol. This would mean that a tag merely cycles through a static set of pseudonyms, preferably with the benefit of throttling. This approach offers better privacy assurances than a system using static identifiers, but does not protect against cloning. (Such a degenerate case of our protocol also does not meet our security definitions unless the process of tag refresh in our model is replaced with elimination of a tag from the system.) Simple approaches like this might be especially attractive as a low-cost way of realizing privacy protection for RFID-enabled banknotes, weaker in some respects but involving much less overhead than the scheme proposed in [13]. Another, similarly useful truncation is one in which multiple identifiers $\{\alpha_i\}$ are stored in a tag, but only a single key β and single key γ for common use with all identifiers.

These and kindred approaches have the advantage of backward compatibility with existing RFID systems employing just a static identifier or challenge-response. In other words, a reader does not have to have awareness of the fact than an identifier is in fact a pseudonym: Only the verifying application on the back-end needs to. Such systems would merely have to include some application-level support for linkage of pseudonyms, but would not necessarily require any software or firmware adjustments at the level of the reader.

Another interesting, restricted case is that involving just one identifier, but with the challenge-response and pseudonym replacement protocols intact. This limited variant would be useful for cases in which consumers are borrowing RFID-tagged books from libraries or renting RFID-tagged videos. Use of a single pseudonym like this would not prevent physical tracking. But authenticated rotation of the pseudonym *would* help prevent the bigger problem of passersby being scanned to determine what books or videos they are carrying via "hotlisting." Given plans by the San Francisco public library to implant RFID tags in books, and the resistance of civil libertarians in reaction to the USA Patriot Act [20], solutions like ours and those proposed recently by Molnar and Wagner [19] seem very attractive.

5   Conclusion: Further Research

RFID security modeling is a line of research that deserves further attention. We feel that the model proposed here captures a range of the special characteristics of RFID-tag environments in an effective way. It is especially important as a way of showing how to reduce reliance on standard cryptographic security modelling in situations where it might not be entirely appropriate. We hope that our model will benefit from refinement as real-world experience with RFID-tag systems evolves, and as it becomes possible to draw on analogous experience and results from the field of ad-hoc networking.

Acknowledgements

Thanks to Markus Jakobsson, Burt Kaliski, Ravi Pappu, and Sanjay Sarma for their suggestions and comments on this work. Thanks also to Peter Trei for providing useful references.

References

1. Security technology: Where's the smart money? *The Economist*, pages 69–70. 9 February 2002.
2. Prada's smart tags too clever? *Wired News*, 27 October 2002.
3. M. Bellare, A. Desai, D. Pointcheval, and P. Rogaway. Relations among notions of security for public-key encryption schemes. In H. Krawczyk, editor, *CRYPTO '98*, pages 26–45. Springer-Verlag, 1998. LNCS no. 1462.
4. Benetton undecided on use of 'smart tags'. *Associated Press*, 8 April 2003.
5. J. Collins. The cost of Wal-Mart's RFID edict. *RFID Journal*, 10 Sept. 2003.
6. D.M. Ewatt and M. Hayes. Gillette razors get new edge: RFID tags. *Information Week*, 13 January 2003. Referenced at http://www.informationweek.com/story/IWK20030110S0028.
7. K.P. Fishkin, S. Roy, and B. Jiang. Some methods for privacy in rfid communication. In *1st European Workshop on Security in Ad-Hoc and Sensor Networks*. Springer-Verlag, 2004. To appear.

8. K.P. Fishkin, M. Wang, and G. Borriello. A ubiquitous system for medication monitoring. In *Second International Conference on Pervasive Computing*. Springer-Verlag, 2004. To appear.

9. T. El Gamal. A public key cryptosystem and a signature scheme based on discrete logarithms. *IEEE Transactions on Information Theory*, 31:469–472, 1985.

10. S. Garfinkel. An RFID Bill of Rights. *Technology Review*, page 35, October 2002.

11. P. Golle, M. Jakobsson, A. Juels, and P. Syverson. Universal re-encryption for mixnets. Springer-Verlag, 2004. To appear.

12. A. Juels and J. Brainard. Soft blocking: Flexible blocker tags on the cheap. In *WPES 04*. ACM Press, 2004. To appear.

13. A. Juels and R. Pappu. Squealing Euros: Privacy protection in RFID-enabled banknotes. In R. Wright, editor, *Financial Cryptography '03*, pages 103–121. Springer-Verlag, 2003. LNCS no. 2742.

14. A. Juels, R.L. Rivest, and M. Szydlo. The blocker tag: Selective blocking of RFID tags for consumer privacy. In V. Atluri, editor, *ACM CCS 03*, pages 103–111. ACM Press, 2003.

15. Auto-ID Labs. 13.56 MHz ISM band class 1 radio frequency identification tag interference specification: Candidate recommendation, version 1.0.0. Technical Report MIT-AUTOID-WH-002, Auto-ID Labs, 2003. Referenced at http://www.autoidlabs.org.

16. L. Ma, Q. Xu, and Y. Yang. Organic non-volatile memory by controlling the dynamic copper-ion concentration within the organic layer. *Nature*, 2003. submitted.

17. D. McCullagh. RFID tags: Big Brother in small packages. *CNet*, 13 January 2003. Referenced at http://news.com.com/2010-1069-980325.html.

18. A.J. Menezes, P.C. van Oorschot, and S.A. Vanstone. *Handbook of Applied Cryptography*. CRC Press, 1996.

19. D. Molnar and D. Wagner. Privacy and security in library RFID : Issues, practices, and architectures. In *ACM CCS 04*. ACM Press, 2004. To appear.

20. Associated Press. Libraries eye RFID to track books: Privacy issues raised as San Francisco plans chips' use. 3 Oct. 2003.

21. RFID, privacy, and corporate data. *RFID Journal*, 2 June 2003. Feature article. Referenced at www.rfidjournal.com on subscription basis.

22. S. E. Sarma, S. A. Weis, and D.W. Engels. Radio-frequency-identification security risks and challenges. *CryptoBytes*, 6(1), 2003.

23. S.E. Sarma. Towards the five-cent tag. Technical Report MIT-AUTOID-WH-006, Auto-ID Labs, 2001. Referenced at http://www.autoidlabs.org/.

24. S.E. Sarma, S.A. Weis, and D.W. Engels. RFID systems and security and privacy implications. In B. Kaliski, editor, *CHES '02*, pages 454–469. Springer-Verlag, 2002. LNCS no. 2523.

25. R. Shim. Benetton to track clothing with ID chips. *CNET*, 11 March 2003. Referenced at http://news.com.com/2100-1019-992131.html.

26. F. Stajano and R. Anderson. The resurrecting duckling: Security issues for ad-hoc wireless networks. In *7th International Workshop on Security Protocols*, pages 172–194. Springer-Verlag, 1999. LNCS no. 1796.

27. K. Takaragi, M. Usami, R. Imura, R. Itsuki, and T. Satoh. An ultra small individual recognition security chip. *IEEE Micro*, 21(6):43–49, 2001.

28. S. A. Weis, S. Sarma, R. Rivest, and D. Engels. Security and privacy aspects of low-cost radio frequency identification systems. In *First International Conference on Security in Pervasive Computing*, 2003.

On the Key Exposure Problem in Chameleon Hashes

Giuseppe Ateniese[1] and Breno de Medeiros[2]

[1] Information Security Institute and
Department of Computer Science,
The Johns Hopkins University
ateniese@cs.jhu.edu
[2] Department of Computer Science,
Florida State University
breno@cs.fsu.edu

Abstract. Chameleon signatures were introduced by Krawczyk and Rabin, being non-interactive signature schemes that provide non-transferability. However, that first construction employs a chameleon hash that suffers from a key exposure problem: The non-transferability property requires willingness of the recipient in consequentially exposing a secret key, and therefore invalidating all signatures issued to the same recipient's public key. To address this key-revocation issue, and its attending problems of key redistribution, storage of state information, and greater need for interaction, an identity-based scheme was proposed in [1], while a fully key-exposure free construction, based on the elliptic curves with pairings, appeared later in [7].

Herein we provide several constructions of exposure-free chameleon hash functions based on different cryptographic assumptions, such as the RSA and the discrete logarithm assumptions. One of the schemes is a novel construction that relies on a single trapdoor and therefore may potentially be realized over a large set of cryptographic groups (where the discrete logarithm is hard).

Keywords: Digital signatures, undeniable signatures, collision-resistant hashing, trapdoor commitments, chameleon signatures, chameleon hashing.

1 Introduction

A chameleon hash function is a trapdoor collision-resistant hash function: Without knowledge of the trapdoor information, a chameleon hash function has the same characteristics of any cryptographic hash function, such as pre-image and collision-resistance; however, collisions and second pre-images can be easily computed once the trapdoor is known.

An interesting application of chameleon hashing is to obtain non-transferable signature algorithms known as chameleon signatures.

C. Blundo and S. Cimato (Eds.): SCN 2004, LNCS 3352, pp. 165–179, 2005.
© Springer-Verlag Berlin Heidelberg 2005

1.1   Chameleon Signatures

Chameleon signatures, introduced in [12], are signature schemes based on the hash-and-sign paradigm. To authenticate a message m, a signer computes its digest value h using a chameleon hash function, and then signs h using an arbitrary signing algorithm of the signer's choice.

In applications, users include the description of a particular chameleon hash as part of their public keys, attesting their knowledge of the corresponding trapdoors. In this scenario, a signer who wished to provide a recipient with a nontransferable signature could hash the message to be signed with the chameleon hash function of the recipient, signing the resulting digest value. While the recipient is able to verify the signature as correct, a third party would only be able to ascertain that *some* message was signed (by the signer to the recipient). The third party would be aware that the signing value could have been re-used by the recipient to authenticate any message of choice, since the signature is a function of the hash value h alone and not of the original message, and because the recipient can easily find collisions for the hash value h. Therefore, a third party would not be willing to accept a proposed message content from the recipient in the absence of further evidence.

To determine the original message content one depends on a secondary signer affirmation or, if the signer is uncooperative, on the dispute settlement method described next.

Settlement of Disputes. In case of disputes, it is easy to ascertain whether or not a proposed message content is indeed the original one committed by the signer. A judge would summon both signer and recipient. If the signer can produce a different message that is authenticated by the same signing value of the proposed message, the contested signature is considered invalid. Remember that such a collision proves that the recipient has put forth a forged signature at some point in time, as nobody apart from the recipient has more than a negligible probability of successfully finding a second message that produces the same signing value.

The dispute-settling procedure described above shows that chameleon signatures provide non-repudiation, as well as non-transferability. Unlike undeniable signatures (introduced in [6]), which similarly provide both of these features, chameleon signatures require no interaction between the signer and recipient for the purpose of issuing a signature. This great improvement in communication complexity comes at a mild disadvantage that, as mentioned above, chameleon signatures leak the information that a user signed something for a specific recipient, a characteristic not shared with undeniable signatures.

Applications of Chameleon Signatures. The non-transferability property is convenient in many scenarios in which the signer has a legitimate interest in controlling subsequent disclosures of the signed information. One application suggested in [1] is private auctions. In this context, the signer is an auction bidder, and does not wish to have its signed bid value published before the auction closing time and/or unless it wins the bidding. If the bid is leaked by the auctioneer, a second bidder (who does not trust the auctioneer) cannot ascertain the validity of the claimed bid without first contacting the original bidder. Another application that has been widely proposed for both undeniable and chameleon signatures is secure software distribution, resistant to bootlegging. Here a software vendor would distribute multiple binaries implementing the same functionality, making it difficult to recognize between bona-fide versions and potentially virotic ones. To protect legitimate users, the software vendor issues recipient-specific signatures on a particular binary. If later the user were to post the signed binary in a file-sharing network, others downloading the software would do so at their own risk – the presence of the non-transferable signature would not confer authenticity onto the posted binary.

1.2   The Key Exposure Problem

The first construction of a chameleon signature [12] employed for hash function the Chaum-Pedersen trapdoor commitment. More precisely, a potential recipient chooses and publishes a regular discrete logarithm-based public key $y = g^x$, where g is the generator of a cyclic group G and x is the secret key. Later, a user who wishes to sign message m can compute the chameleon hash value $h = y^m g^r$, where r is an auxiliary integer chosen uniformly at random by the signer. Here it is understood that m is a short binary message that has value smaller than the order of the group G when interpreted as the binary expansion of a non-negative integer. However, to extend the scheme to arbitrary length messages, it is sufficient to first hash the long message using a regular, cryptographic hash function.

Notice that if the recipient forges the signature, and two pairs (m, r) and (m', r') become known to the signer (during a dispute), the signer can recover the secret key x of the recipient from $h = g^m y^r = g^{m'} y^{r'}$, giving $x = \frac{m'-m}{r-r'}$.

This is a highly undesirable outcome from the recipient's viewpoint, as it invalidates all signatures ever issued to the associated public key y. A third-party is therefore more likely to believe claims made by the recipient about presenting an original (non-forged) signature, knowing that such forgery would negatively affect the recipient. In fact, the deterrent effect of key exposure on forgeries threatens the claims of non-transferability provided by the scheme. Therefore, to support non-transferability in any practical sense, we believe chameleon signatures schemes should *necessarily* rely on key-exposure free chameleon hash function, described next.

Previous Work on Key Exposure Freeness. The problem of key exposure was partly addressed in [1], where it is shown how to build identity-based chameleon hash functions. The advantage of using the identity-based primitives is that applications could direct the use of transaction-specific chameleon hashes: The public key associated to a transaction-specific hash function is computed by the signer from specially formatted strings that describe the transaction, and which include the signer and recipient information as well as some nonce or time-stamp. In that paper, these strings were called *customized identities*. Later, if the recipient wishes to forge the signature, it suffices for him to communicate with the trusted authority (of the identity-based scheme) to recover the trapdoor information associated with the transaction-specific public key. It is understood that the trusted authority will only provide the trapdoor information to the recipient designated in the formatted string. Notice that the trapdoor recovery is an optional step, the trapdoor information being necessary only when the recipient wishes to deviate from the basic protocol by finding hash collisions and re-using signing tokens. This extra interaction adds less communication complexity than key revocation and key update in a classical public key infrastructure, but may still be too burdensome in certain applications, and therefore offering only a partial answer to the key exposure problem.

In [7], Chen et al. provide a specific construction of a key-exposure free chameleon hash function, working in the setting of Gap groups with bilinear pairings. While that certainly constitutes the first full construction of a key-exposure free chameleon hash, it does not settle the question of whether constructions exist that are either based on other cryptographic assumptions, or of more efficient schemes, for instance of comparable performance to the original chameleon hash function in [12].

Our Contribution. In this paper we show that key-exposure-free solutions exist whose security depends on non-pairing-based assumptions, such as the security of the RSA signature scheme. In fact, we show that the construction of [1] already enjoys the key-exposure-freeness property when used in a PKI setting instead of as the proposed identity-based application.

In all of the constructions, the public key is divided into two components, one permanent and the other ephemeral. Except for the scheme in section §4, all require a double-trapdoor context, and the components of the public key is made to correspond to each of the trapdoors. Non-transferability is supported through eventual compromise of the ephemeral component of the public key only. We also show that this technique can be applied broadly whenever a double-trapdoor is available.

More surprisingly, we have a novel construction of a key-exposure free chameleon hash function that does *not* rely on a double-trapdoor mechanism (section §4). To the best of our knowledge this is a novel result, of independent interest.

Organization of the Paper. In the following section, we provide the precise definition of key-exposure free chameleon hashes, and present several requirements that such hashes should satisfy for efficient application to a chameleon signature scheme. We follow that with a section that shows how chameleon hashes satisfying different subsets of these security requirements correspond to trapdoor commitment schemes satisfying different properties. Sections §4 and §5 present constructions of key-exposure free chameleon hashes based on single, and double trapdoors, respectively, and are followed by a few concluding remarks.

2   Definition and Requirements

A key-exposure free chameleon hash function is defined by a set of efficient algorithms:

Key Generation. accepts as input a security parameter κ in unary form, and outputs a pair $(\mathcal{SK}, \mathcal{PK})$. It is a probabilistic algorithm, denoted as:

$$\textbf{KeyGen}: \ 1^{\kappa} \longrightarrow (\mathcal{SK}, \mathcal{PK})$$

Hash. accepts as input a public key $\mathcal{PK}$, a *label* $\mathcal{L}$, a message m and an auxiliary random parameter r and outputs a bitstring h of fixed length τ.

$$\textbf{Hash}: \ (\mathcal{PK}, \mathcal{L}, m, r) \longrightarrow C \in \{0,1\}^{\tau}$$

Universal Forge. accepts as input the secret key $\mathcal{SK}$ associate to public key $\mathcal{PK}$, a label $\mathcal{L}$, a message m, and auxiliary parameter r, and computes a second message m' and random parameter r' such that $\textbf{Hash}(\mathcal{PK}, \mathcal{L}, m, r) = C = \textbf{Hash}(\mathcal{PK}, \mathcal{L}, m', r')$.

$$\textbf{UForge}(\mathcal{SK}, \mathcal{L}, m, r) \longrightarrow (m', r'), \text{ such that}$$

$$\textbf{Hash}(\mathcal{PK}, \mathcal{L}, m, r) = C = \textbf{Hash}(\mathcal{PK}, \mathcal{L}, m', r')$$

Instance Forge. accepts as input a tuple $(\mathcal{PK}, \mathcal{L}, m, r, m', r')$ of a public key, a label, and two pairs of a message and auxiliary random parameter, where $C = \textbf{Hash}(\mathcal{PK}, \mathcal{L}, m, r) = \textbf{Hash}(\mathcal{PK}, \mathcal{L}, m', r')$, and computes another collision pair (m'', r'') that also satisfies $C = \textbf{Hash}(\mathcal{PK}, \mathcal{L}, m'', r'')$.

$$\textbf{IForge}(\mathcal{PK}, \mathcal{L}, m, r, m', r') \longrightarrow (m'', r''), \text{ such that}$$

$$\textbf{Hash}(\mathcal{PK}, \mathcal{L}, m, r) = C = \textbf{Hash}(\mathcal{PK}, \mathcal{L}, m', r') = \textbf{Hash}(\mathcal{PK}, \mathcal{L}, m'', r'')$$

The security requirements of a chameleon hash include:[1]

Collision-Resistance: There is no efficient algorithm that given only $\mathcal{PK}$, $\mathcal{L}$, m and r, (but not the secret key $\mathcal{SK}$) can find a second pair m', r' such that $C = \textbf{Hash}(\mathcal{PK}, \mathcal{L}, m, r) = \textbf{Hash}(\mathcal{PK}, \mathcal{L}, m', r')$ with more than negligible probability over the choices of $\mathcal{PK}$, $\mathcal{L}$, m and r.

Semantic Security: The chameleon hash value C does not reveal anything about the possible message m that was hashed. In formal terms, let $H[X]$ denote the entropy of a random variable X, and $H[X|Y]$ the entropy of the variable X given the value of a random function Y of X. Semantic security is the statement that the conditional entropy $H[m|C]$ of the message given its chameleon hash value C equals the total entropy $H[m]$ of the message space.

---

[1] We adopt information-theoretic formulations of semantic security and message hiding properties because these lead to simpler proofs. Moreover, information-theoretic security (with respect to semantic security and message hiding) is indeed achieved by all constructions of chameleon hashing schemes currently in the literature as well the ones proposed in this paper.

Message hiding: Assume the recipient has computed a collision using the universal forgery algorithm, i.e., a second pair (m', r') s.t. $\textbf{Hash}(\mathcal{PK}, \mathcal{L}, m, r) = C = \textbf{Hash}(\mathcal{PK}, \mathcal{L}, m', r')$, where (m, r) was the original value signed. Then the signer, upon seeing the claimed values (m', r'), can successfully contest this invalid claim by releasing a third pair (m'', r''), without having to reveal the original signed message. Moreover, the entropy of the original value (m, r) is unchanged by the revelation of the pairs (m', r'), (m'', r''), and any further collisions: $H[(m, r)|C, (m', r'), (m'', r'')] = H[(m, r)|C]$.

Key Exposure Freeness: If a recipient with public key $\mathcal{PK}$ has never computed a collision under label $\mathcal{L}$, then given $C = \textbf{Hash}(\mathcal{PK}, \mathcal{L}, m, r)$ there is no efficient algorithm that can find a collision (a second pair m', r' mapping to the same digest C). This must remain true even if the adversary has oracle access to $\textbf{UForge}(\mathcal{SK}, \cdot, \cdot, \cdot)$ and is allowed polynomially many queries on triples $(\mathcal{L}_i, m_i, r_i)$ of his choice, except that $\mathcal{L}_i$ is not allowed to equal the challenge label $\mathcal{L}$.

Remark: Notice that when a chameleon hash with key-exposure freeness is employed within a chameleon signature then any label $\mathcal{L}$ must be explicitly committed to the signature along with the identity of the recipient and a description of the hashes (see [12]).

3   Previous Work on Trapdoor Commitments

Trapdoor commitment schemes were introduced as early as 1988, with the work of Brassard et al. [4]. Trapdoor commitment schemes are closely related to chameleon hashes. Yet the two notions are not truly equivalent. The reason is that chameleon hashes, intended for use in combination with signature schemes, require extra properties that are not enjoyed by every trapdoor commitment scheme. Indeed, in reviewing the literature in trapdoor commitments, we have identified at least four categories of commitments, which have all different degrees of suitability for use as a chameleon hashing scheme. The first category, what we called "stateful" trapdoor commitment schemes, cannot be used at all as chameleon hashes.

Stateful Trapdoor Commitments: These refer to trapdoor commitments which have the property that the knowledge of the trapdoor by itself is not sufficient to enable the computation of alternate de-commitments. In fact, it is necessary that the committing party know the trapdoor, execute a variant commitment algorithm that produces the commitment plus some auxiliary information, and save that auxiliary information (state) for later use in the alternate de-commitment algorithm. One example of such constructions are simulation-sound trapdoor commitments, see [13].

Such trapdoor commitment schemes cannot be used as chameleon hashes. In the chameleon hashing setting it is required that the recipient be able to find collisions (alternate de-commitments) from the digest value and the trapdoor information alone. *All chameleon hashes must be stateless trapdoor commitment schemes.*

Key Exposing Commitments: The chameleon hashing algorithm of Krawczyk and Rabin suffered from the key exposure problem, which limits its application in the chameleon hashing setting. It corresponds to the well-known Pedersen commitment scheme [17]. Another example of a trapdoor commitment that suffer from the key exposure problem is given by several constructions in Marc Fischlin's thesis [10], including one based on factoring, originally introduced in [8] (without reference to trapdoors). Another construction is provided by Shamir and Kalai [20] in relation to *online/offline* signatures (notion introduced by Even, Goldreich, and Micali [9]). In short, a signature on a chameleon hash is computed *offline* and then a signature on a new message is derived by computing a collision of the hash (*online* phase). Although very efficient, their original chameleon hash scheme, based on factoring, also suffers from the key exposure problem. This implies, in particular, that the online phase of their mechanism can actually be performed only once.

Non-Perfect-Hiding Commitments: These schemes are key exposure free, but they do not allow the execution of the instance forge algorithm **IForge**. In other words, they do not permit adjudication without the original valid signature being disclosed at some stage. These schemes might be interesting in a variety of application scenarios for which key exposure is not acceptable due to high cost of key-redistribution, but where the privacy of the message signed is no longer important at the time the matter comes for adjudication. In the following section we describe one original scheme of this type.

Message-Hiding and Key-Exposure-Free Commitments: This lead to the most flexible and suitable application as chameleon hashes. The first claim of construction of such a scheme is included in [7], where a pairings-based algorithm is given. However, the property is actually present (though not recognized as such) in the scheme in [1], based on a well-known RSA commitment scheme, first described in [15]. Therefore the use of pairings is not needed to obtain key-exposure-free schemes. In the following we explain how the RSA commitment scheme can be used to provide both guarantees, and we also present two new constructions. The first is based on a trapdoor commitment scheme [5] based on the Paillier's cryptosystem [16]. The second requires pairings, and is based on the trapdoor scheme described in [11]. Its security is dependent on the so-called Strong Diffie-Hellman assumption.

The crucial feature enjoyed by the commitment schemes in this category is that they are all double-trapdoor. One of the trapdoors is the secret key (used in the algorithm **UForge** to find collisions) and the other is some trapdoor function of the label used in the **IForge**.

4   Key Exposure Freeness Without Message Hiding

In this section we describe a trapdoor commitment scheme that can be seen as a chameleon hash providing key exposure freeness but no perfect message hiding. Unlike other schemes, it has the unique and appealing feature of relying on a single trapdoor.

The scheme is related to a twin Nyberg-Rueppel signature, introduced in [14]. The key generation is similar to that of other discrete logarithm-based schemes. Notice that while we describe the scheme in the finite field setting, the scheme may potentially be instantiated in other groups where the DL is hard.

Key Generation: The scheme specifies a *safe* prime p of bitlength κ. This means that $p = 2q + 1$, where q is also prime, and a generator g of the subgroup of quadratic residues $\mathbf{Q}_p$ of $\mathbf{Z}_p^*$, i.e, g has order q. The recipient chooses as secret key x at random in $[1, q - 1]$, and his public key is computed as $(g, y = g^x)$. Let $\mathcal{H}$ be a collision-resistant hash function, mapping arbitrary-length bitstrings to strings of fixed length τ: $\mathcal{H} : \{0, 1\}^* \to \{0, 1\}^\tau$.

The Hash Scheme: To commit to a message m, it is sufficient to choose random values $(r, s) \in \mathbf{Z}_q \times \mathbf{Z}_q$, and compute:

$$e = \mathcal{H}(m, r); \text{ and } \mathbf{Hash}(m, r, s) = r - (y^e g^s \bmod p) \bmod q.$$

Collision Finding: Let C denote the output of the chameleon hash on input the triple (m, r, s). A collision (m', r', s') can be found by computing (m', r', s') such that:

$$e' = \mathcal{H}(m', r'); \text{ and } C = r' - (y^{e'} g^{s'} \bmod p) \bmod q.$$

First, the recipient chooses a random message m', a random value $k' \in [1, q-1]$, and computes $r' = C + (g^{k'} \bmod p) \bmod q$, $e' = \mathcal{H}(m', r')$, and $s' = k' - e'x \bmod q$. Notice that indeed:

$$r' - (y^{e'} g^{s'} \bmod p) \bmod q = C + (g^{k'} \bmod p) - (g^{xe'} g^{s'} \bmod p) \bmod q) = C.$$

Key Exposure Freeness and Collision-Resistance: The security of the scheme depends on whether twice signing a message (without redundancy), using the above variant of Nyberg-Rueppel, is secure. This was proven in appendix A to [14], where the concept of twinning signature schemes is considered. The only difference from the scheme above is that we have substituted $e = \mathcal{H}(m, r)$ for r in the exponent of y. The only modification to the proof, which is formally the same, is that the probability of collisions is changed from finding collisions in the whole ring $\mathbf{Z}_q$ to finding them over the image of $\mathcal{H}(\cdot)$. Therefore, provided that this hash is collision-resistant, the conclusion of security is unchanged. Notice that we do not need to model the function $\mathcal{H}(\cdot)$ as a random oracle. Instead, the proof of security for the twin Nyberg-Rueppel works in the generic model of computation.

Semantic Security: Notice that when the committing party computes the value C, it can choose s completely independently of m and r. Since g is an element of order q, the term g^s uniformly covers the whole subgroup of quadratic residues, independently of the value $ry^{\mathcal{H}(m,r)}$. The result follows. More formally, from the commitment equation, for each random r and message m, there is a one-to-one correspondence between the commitment C and the value s. This implies that the conditional probability $\mu(m, r|C)$ equals $\mu(m, r|s)$. But the latter value is simply $\mu(m, r)$ since s is chosen independently of m and r.

Now, consider the definition of conditional entropy:

$$H[m, r|C] = -\sum_{m,r \in \{0,1\}^\tau \times \mathbf{Z}_q} \sum_{C \in \mathbf{Z}_q} \mu(m, r, C) \log(\mu(m, r|C)).$$

The internal summation becomes $\sum_{C \in \mathbf{Z}_q} \mu(m, r, C) \log(\mu(m, r))$, which equals $\mu(m, r) \log(\mu(m, r))$. Therefore,

$$H[m, r|C] = -\sum_{m,r \in \{0,1\}^\tau \times \mathbf{Z}_q} \mu(m, r) \log(\mu(m, r)) = H[m, r].$$

Notice that the proof is automatic once shown that the probability of the message conditioned on the commitment value is really equal to the unconditioned probability. In the remaining schemes we describe here, our proofs of semantic security will be shortened to only show the equality between conditioned and unconditioned probabilities.

Remark: We have defined the above scheme using the short version of the Nyberg-Rueppel signature, for convenience of reference to the twin signatures work [14]. It is also possible to define a trapdoor commitment scheme using the long form, as:

$$e = \mathcal{H}(m, r); \text{ and } \mathbf{Hash}(m, r, s) = ry^e g^s \bmod p.$$

5   Key Exposure Freeness with Message Hiding

In this section we provide some examples of chameleon hash with key exposure freeness. Any stateless trapdoor commitment with two trapdoors may be adequate, but the schemes below are based on common assumptions and well-known constructions.

We stress that these candidate functions are not new but are rather well-known and have been proposed as trapdoor commitments by others. We are showing that, unlike other trapdoor commitment schemes, they can be easily adapted and transformed in chameleon hashes that provide simultaneously key exposure freeness and message hiding.

5.1   Scheme Based on RSA and Factoring

The scheme below is based on a well-known trapdoor commitment and has two
trapdoors, the factors of an RSA modulus and roots of elements in the RSA
ring. This fact has been exploited in [1] to build an identity-based chameleon
hash and was independently noticed by Gennaro in [11], where the basic scheme
is also extended to allow for several trapdoors and applied to the construction
of concurrently non-malleable proofs of knowledge.

Key Generation: Let τ and κ be security parameters. As before, let $\mathcal{H}$ be a
collision-resistant hash function mapping strings of arbitrary length to strings
of fixed length τ. Let $n = pq$ with the two prime numbers p and q in the set
$\{2^{\kappa-1}, \ldots, 2^{\kappa} - 1\}$. A random prime integer e is computed s.t. $e > 2^{\tau}$, and such
that it is relatively prime to the order $\phi(n) = (p-1)(q-1)$ of the multiplicative
residues modulo n. The secret key d is computed such that $ed \equiv 1 \bmod \phi(n)$.

The recipient's public key is (n, e) and his secret key is (p, q, d).

The Hash Scheme: Let S be the string uniquely identifying the recipient and
let $\mathcal{L}$ be a label. Let $\mathcal{C} : \{0,1\}^* \to \{0, \cdots, 2^{2\kappa-1}\}$ be a secure hash-and-encode
scheme, mapping arbitrary bit-strings to integers less than n. In general, such
schemes are probabilistic, requiring an auxiliary random string. For instance,
the EMSA-PKCS encoding, defined in [19], requires a random (or pseudo-random) salt at least 64 bits long, while the EMSA-PSS encoding, defined in [2, 18],
can take an auxiliary random string of bit-length equal to τ, the output length
of the cryptographic hash function $\mathcal{H}$. Our notation will not make the random
parameter explicit, as the nature of the encoding (i.e., deterministic or non-
deterministic) is immaterial to the following discussion as long as the encoding
scheme is uniquely invertible, i.e., the output of the encode function can be
decoded to recover the hash value.

Given $J = \mathcal{C}(\mathcal{L})$ in $\mathbf{Z}_n$, the secret trapdoor is extracted as $B = J^d \bmod n$,
i.e., a secure RSA signature on $\mathcal{L}$.

The **Hash**$(\cdot)$ algorithm is:

$$\mathbf{Hash}(\mathcal{L}, m, r) = J^{\mathcal{H}(m)} r^e \bmod n, \text{ where } J = \mathcal{C}(\mathcal{L})$$

Collision Finding: To compute a collision (m', r'), the recipient would chose
a random message m' and consider the following equation:

$$J^{\mathcal{H}(m)} r^e = J^{\mathcal{H}(m')} r'^e,$$

and solve it for r' modulo n, that is:

$$r' = r B^{\mathcal{H}(m)-\mathcal{H}(m')} \bmod n.$$

Collision-Resistance and Key Exposure Freeness: Exposing a collision
allows anybody to extract the secret key B associated to the value $J = \mathcal{C}(L)$.
Indeed,

$$J^{\mathcal{H}(m)}r^e = J^{\mathcal{H}(m')}r'^e \Longrightarrow r'/r = B^{\mathcal{H}(m)-\mathcal{H}(m')}.$$

Clearly, the absolute value of $\Delta = \mathcal{H}(m) - \mathcal{H}(m')$ is smaller than 2^τ and given that e is a prime integer larger than 2^τ, it follows that $\gcd(\Delta, v) = 1$. Using the extended Euclidean algorithm for the GCD, one computes α and β such that $\alpha\Delta + \beta v = 1$. B can now be extracted:

$$B = (r'/r)^\alpha J^\beta.$$

As B is a secure RSA signature on $\mathcal{L}$, and computing collisions is equivalent to breaking this signature scheme, we conclude that finding collisions is hard without knowledge of the trapdoor. Finally, notice that since revealing collisions is equivalent to computing signatures, the scheme is safe from key exposure as the EMSA-PSS RSA signature scheme is resistant against active attacks.

Semantic Security: For each message m, the value $C = \mathbf{Hash}(\mathcal{L}, m, r)$ is uniquely determined by the value r, and vice-versa. Therefore, the conditional probability $\mu(m|C)$ equals that of $\mu(m|r)$, which equals $\mu(m)$, as m and r are independent variables. The semantic security follows – see the example in the previous section for details.

Message Hiding: Let C be the commitment value. It is sufficient to show that, once a collision is revealed, a person who does not know the trapdoor can compute a de-commitment to C under any message m'' of her choice. From the above proof of the collision-resistance property we see that the revelation of a collision $(m, r), (m', r')$ discloses the trapdoor information $B = \mathcal{C}(\mathcal{L})^d$. In order to find another collision, it is sufficient to choose m'' and set $r'' = rB^{\mathcal{H}(m)-\mathcal{H}(m')}$.

Remark: This RSA-based scheme is a multi-trapdoor scheme in the sense of Gennaro [11], as the second trapdoor is multiply instantiated – in other words, there is one trapdoor per label. Instead of relying on the Strong RSA assumption as the scheme described in [11], the version described above relies on the security of the EMSA-PSS RSA signature.

5.2   Scheme Based on RSA[n,n] and Factoring

In [16], Paillier proved that, for each $h \in \mathbf{Z}_{n^2}^*$ of order a non-zero multiple of n, the function $\mathcal{F}_h$ that maps elements in $(\mathbf{Z}_n, \mathbf{Z}_n^*)$ to elements in $\mathbf{Z}_{n^2}^*$, defined as:

$$\mathcal{F}_h : (a, b) \longrightarrow h^a b^n \bmod n^2,$$

is a trapdoor permutation.

In [5], a trapdoor commitment scheme was introduced that is based on the Paillier trapdoor permutation. The authors of [5] suggest to use their trapdoor commitment to build a chameleon signature. However, if used directly as they described (i.e., a standard signature over a trapdoor commitment), the problem of key exposure would arise. We simply observe that their trapdoor commitment has actually two trapdoors and can be easily extended to support labels as described below.

Key Generation: Let $n = pq$ with p and q large primes. Let $\mathcal{H}(\cdot)$ be a cryptographic hash function that maps elements of arbitrary length to element of a subset of $\mathbf{Z}_{n^2}^*$. The public key of the scheme is n, while the private key is (p, q).

The Hash Scheme: Given a message $m \in \mathbf{Z}_n$, and a label $\mathcal{L}$, compute $h = \mathcal{H}(\mathcal{L})$. Next, generate randomly the pair $(r_1, r_2) \in (\mathbf{Z}_n, \mathbf{Z}_n^*)$, and compute ([5]):

$$C = \mathbf{Hash}(\mathcal{L}, m, r_1, r_2) = (1 + mn)h^{r_1}r_2^n \bmod n^2.$$

To extend the scheme to commit arbitrary length messages, it is sufficient to employ a cryptographic hash function with codomain in $\mathbf{Z}_n$.

Collision-Finding and Collision-Resistance: Let C be a commitment with respect to label $\mathcal{L}$, where $h = \mathcal{H}(\mathcal{L})$. From here to compute a collision under a second message m', the recipient finds $C' = C(1 - m'n) \bmod n^2$ and computes its inverse under the trapdoor permutation $\mathcal{F}_h$:

$$\mathcal{F}_h^{-1}(C') = (a, b), \text{ with } a \in \mathbf{Z}_n \text{ and } b \in \mathbf{Z}_n^*.$$

The new de-commitment is $(m', r_1' = a, r_2' = b)$. Without knowledge of the trapdoor, computing this collision is equivalent to breaking the RSA[n, n] assumption, as shown in [5].

Key Exposure Freeness: Suppose a party can compute a collision under label $\mathcal{L}$, i.e., values $(m, r_1, r_2, m', r_1', r_2')$ such that

$$(1 + mn)h^{r_1}r_2^n = (1 + m'n)h^{r_1'}(r_2')^n,$$

where $h = \mathcal{H}(\mathcal{L})$. It follows that (see full argument in [5]) the one can recover values a and b such that

$$\mathcal{H}(\mathcal{L}) = h = (1 + an)b^n, \tag{1}$$

i.e., the party can compute the Paillier signature (a, b) on the "message" $\mathcal{L}$. This is not feasible, since the Paillier signature is resistant against existential forgeries under active attacks in the random oracle model, by reduction to the RSA[n,n] assumption.

Semantic Security: The semantic security of this commitment scheme has been shown in [5].

Message Hiding: Assuming a collision (m', r_1', r_2') has been revealed to the committing party, she has learned a Paillier signature (a, b) on the value $\mathcal{L}$. To obtain a collision, she computes the value $\delta = a^{-1} \bmod n$, chooses an arbitrary message m'', and computes $r_1'' = r_1' + \delta(m' - m'')$ (as an integer) and $r_2'' = r_2' + \delta(m'' - m') \bmod n$. One may readily verify that (m'', r_1'', r_2'') commits to the same value as (m', r_1', r_2').

Remark: Note that when computing the collision, the new value r_1' may fall outside the interval $[1, n-1]$. This is not a problem, as there is no requirement that collisions look like plausible initial commitments. In a chameleon hashing scheme the goal is just to prove that the trapdoor-owner has revealed a collision. If it is required that derived collisions look like plausible commitments, the scheme can be "fixed" by redefining the interval where r_1 is chosen to be much larger than $[1, n-1]$.

5.3   Scheme Based on SDH and DL

Gennaro in [11] proposes a new trapdoor commitment scheme based on the Strong Diffie-Hellman (SDH) assumption introduced by Boneh and Boyen [3]. Informally, the ℓ-SDH assumption says that if G is a cyclic gap-DDH group of prime order q and g is a generator of such a group, then an attacker that sees $G, g, g^x, \ldots, g^{x^\ell}$, for an $x \in \mathbf{Z}_q$, should not be able to compute h and e such that $h^{x+e} = g$.

We show here that such a trapdoor commitment scheme can support labels and that collisions cannot be used to compute the master trapdoor.

Key Generation: Let $G = \langle g \rangle$ be a gap-DDH group of order q and let $x \in \mathbf{Z}_q$. The public key of the recipient is $h = g^x$. Let $\mathcal{H}(\cdot)$ be a cryptographic hash function that maps elements of arbitrary length to elements of $\mathbf{Z}_q$.

The Hash Scheme: Let $e = \mathcal{H}(\mathcal{L})$, where $\mathcal{L}$ is the label. Given a message m, select a random $r \in \mathbf{Z}_q$ and compute ([11]):

$$\mathbf{Hash}(\mathcal{L}, m, r) = g^{\mathcal{H}(m)}(g^e h)^r.$$

Let F denote the output of the chameleon hash divided by $g^{\mathcal{H}(m)}$. To verify that the hash was computed correctly, one can check whether (g^r, hg^e, F) is a Diffie-Hellman triple. Remember that Gap groups have efficient algorithms to decide the Diffie-Hellman problem.

Collision Finding, Collision-Resistance, and Key Exposure Freeness: Following [11], given a pair (m, g^r), it is efficient to find a collision $(m', g^{r'})$ if x is known by setting:

$$g^{r'} = g^r g^{[(\mathcal{H}(m) - \mathcal{H}(m'))/(x+e)]}. \tag{2}$$

Conversely, exposing a collision (m, g^r) and $(m', g^{r'})$ allows anybody to efficiently compute $g^{1/(x+e)}$ (which, in general, is a hard computational problem under the SDH assumption). To obtain key exposure freeness, one needs the result that even if several values $f_i = g^{1/(x+e_i)}$ are known, it is difficult computing other values f_j under different e_j – i.e., under different labels $\mathcal{L}_j$. As remarked in [11], this result has been proved in [3], where the values f_i are shown to be "weak signatures." Moreover, since the knowledge of x permits computing such values efficiently, it is clear that deriving x from collisions is infeasible.

Semantic Security and Message Hiding: From the discussion above, it is clear that with the trapdoor information, exactly one collision can be computed under each message m', proving the semantic security of the scheme. It remains to be shown that collisions, and the consequent exposure of the value $f_e = g^{1/(x+e)}$, permit finding other collisions under the same label. It is sufficient to observe that the collision-finding equation (2) does not require knowledge of x, but only of the value f_e.

6   Conclusions and Open Problems

In this paper we outline a formal security model for chameleon hash functions, including precise specifications of the message-hiding and key-exposure freeness properties. We conclude that single-trapdoor commitment schemes are not sufficient for the construction of chameleon hashes – instead a double-trapdoor mechanism is required. Here an interesting question poses itself: The double-trapdoor mechanism can either be used to construct an identity-based chameleon hash scheme (in the sense of [1]) or a key-exposure free one, but not both. Are there *efficient* schemes that are simultaneously identity-based and key-exposure free, perhaps based on a construction with multiple (more than two) consecutive trapdoors?

Our results include three constructions of schemes satisfying the full security model, two based on RSA, as well as a construction based on pairings. This significantly augments the family of chameleon hashes satisfying both key-exposure freeness and message hiding, of which only one example was previously known ([7]), based on pairings. We have also provided an example of trapdoor commitment that provides key-exposure freeness, but not message hiding – and that relies on a single trapdoor, the first such construction to our knowledge.

Acknowledgments. We are grateful to Rosario Gennaro and David Molnar for their insightful comments. This work was partly funded by a NSF grant.

References

1. Ateniese, G., de Medeiros, B.: Identity-based chameleon hash and applications. In Financial Cryptography 2004. LNCS 3110, Springer-Verlag (2004) 164–180. Available online at http://eprint.iacr.org/2003/167/.
2. Bellare, M., Rogaway, P.: PSS: Provably secure encoding method for digital signature. IEEE P1363a: Provably secure signatures. http://grouper.ieee.org/groups/1363/p1363a/pssigs.html (1998)
3. Boneh, D. and Boyen, X.: Short Signatures Without Random Oracles, Proc. of Advances in Cryptology – EUROCRYPT '04, Volume 3027 of LNCS Springer-Verlag (2004) 56–73
4. Brassard, G., Chaum, D., and Crepeau, C.: Minimum disclosure proofs of knowledge. Journal of Computer an Systems Sciences, vol. 37 no. 2, (1988) 156-189.
5. Catalano, D., Gennaro, R., Howgrave-Graham, N., Nguyen, P.Q.: Paillier's Cryptosystem Revisited. ACM CCS 2001.

6. Chaum, D., Antwerpen, H.: Undeniable signatures. In: Advances in Cryptology – CRYPTO'89. Volume 435 of LNCS., Springer-Verlag (1991) 212–216
7. Chen, X., Zhang, F., and Kim, K.: Chameleon hashing without key exposure. To appear in the proceedings of the 7th Information Security Conference (ISC '04), Palo Alto, California. Available online at http://eprint.iacr.org/2004/038/.
8. Damgård, I.: Practical and provable secure release of a secret and exchange of signature. In: Journal of Cryptology, Volume 8. Springer-Verlag (1995) 201–222
9. Even S., Goldreich O., Micali S.: On-line/off-line Digital Signatures. In: Advances in Cryptology – CRYPTO '89. LNCS of Springer-Verlag, 263–277. August 1990.
10. Fischlin, M.: Trapdoor commitment schemes and their applications. Ph.D. thesis, 2001.
11. Gennaro, R.: Multi-trapdoor commitments and their applications to proofs of knowledge secure under concurrent man-in-the-middle attacks. In: Advances in Cryptology – CRYPTO '04. LNCS of Springer-Verlag. August 2004.
12. Krawczyk, H., Rabin, T.: Chameleon signatures. In: Proceedings of NDSS 2000. (2000) 143–154
13. MacKenzie, P. and Yang, K.: On Simulation-Sound Trapdoor Commitments. In: Proc. of Advances in Cryptology – EUROCRYPT '04. Volume 3027 of LNCS, Springer-Verlag (2004) 382–400
14. Naccache, D., Pointcheval, D., and Stern, J.: Twin signatures: an alternative to the hash-and-sign paradigm. In: Proc. of the 8th ACM Conference on Computer and Communication Security (ACM CCS), ACM Press (2001) 20–27
15. Okamoto, T.: Provably secure and practical identification schemes and corresponding signature schemes. In: Proc. of Advances in Cryptology – CRYPTO '92. Volume 740 of LNCS, Springer-Verlag (1992) 31–53
16. Paillier, P.: Public key cryptosystems based on composite degree residuosity classes. In: Proc. of Advances in Cryptology – EUROCRYPT '99. Volume 1592 of LNCS, Springer-Verlag (1999) 223–238
17. Pedersen, T. Non-interactive and information-theoretic secure verifiable secret sharing. In: Proc. of Advances in Cryptology – CRYPTO '91. Volume 576 of LNCS, Springer-Verlag (1991) 129–149
18. RSA Labs: RSA Crypt. Std: EMSAPSS – PKCS#1 v2.1., pp. 26–28, 32–37 (2002)
19. RSA Labs: RSA Crypt. Std: EMSAPKCS1-v1_5 - PKCS#1 v2.1. pp. 29–33, 37–38 (2002)
20. Shamir A, Kalai, Y.: Improved Online/Offline Signature Schemes. In: Proc. of Advances in Cryptology – CRYPTO'01, Volume 2139 of LNCS. Springer-Verlag (2001) 355–367.

Identity-Based Zero-Knowledge

Jonathan Katz[1,*], Rafail Ostrovsky[2,**], and Michael O. Rabin[3]

[1] Dept. of Computer Science, University of Maryland
jkatz@cs.umd.edu
[2] Dept. of Computer Science, UCLA
rafail@cs.ucla.edu
[3] Dept. of Computer Science, Harvard University
rabin@deas.harvard.edu

Abstract. We introduce and define the notion of *identity-based zero-knowledge*, concentrating on the non-interactive setting. In this setting, our notion allows any prover to widely disseminate a proof of a statement while protecting the prover from plagiarism in the following sense: although proofs are *transferable* (i.e., publicly verifiable), they are also *bound* to the identity of the prover in a way which is recognizable to any verifier. Furthermore, an adversary is unable to change this identity (i.e., to claim the proof as his own, or to otherwise change the authorship), unless he could have proved the statement on his own.

While we view the primary contribution of this work as a formal definition of the above notion, we also explore the relation of this notion to that of *non-malleable (non-interactive) zero-knowledge*. On the one hand, we show that these two notions are incomparable: that is, there are proof systems which are non-malleable but not identity-based, and vice versa. On the other hand, we show that a proof system of either type essentially implies a proof system of the other type.

1 Introduction

One of the motivations behind the introduction of the fundamental notion of zero-knowledge (ZK) proof systems by Goldwasser, Micali, and Rackoff [9] was to allow a prover to convince a verifier about the validity of a theorem without enabling the verifier to later convince someone else [2]. When viewing ZK proofs in this way, one sees that a primary concern of such proofs is to prevent plagiarism; in other words, the prover wishes to prevent the verifier from learning some valuable information from the proof and later claiming the proof as his own (without properly referencing the original prover).

We remark that the above concerns are handled, to some extent, by ZK proofs in the *interactive* setting. Here, we have a prover P and a (possibly malicious) verifier V who will (at some *later* point) try to convince a second verifier V'. Since the transcript of the interaction between P and V can be simulated, by definition

---

* Work done while this author was at Columbia University.
** Supported in part by a gift from Teradata and Intel equipment grant

of zero-knowledge, a copy of the proof transcript will not be convincing to V'. Additionally, if V and V' interact *after* completion of the interaction between P and V, the zero-knowledge property implies that V gains no advantage in trying to convince V'.

Of course, the concern remains that V might interact with V' *while* interacting with P (i.e., act as man-in-the-middle). A related concern, in the public-key setting, was considered by Jakobsson, Sako, and Impagliazzo [10] (see also the related work by Cramer and Damgård [5]) who introduce proofs meant to convince only a single, designated verifier. Note that such a notion, if extended to the non-interactive setting, would fundamentally *limit* the widespread dissemination of proofs; on the other hand, frequently one would like to *disseminate* proofs as widely as possible (e.g., to announce results to the scientific community).

Indeed, *non-interactive* ZK (NIZK) proof systems introduced by Blum, Feldman, and Micali [3] paradoxically allow (in the presence of a common-random string available to all parties) the widespread dissemination of zero-knowledge proofs. However, although NIZK proofs "hide" the witness to the truth of the theorem, NIZK proofs do not seem to offer any guarantees against plagiarism. That is, if P gives a non-interactive proof π to V, this proof is still convincing when V transfers it to V'. Note that, here, V's interaction with V' does not need to be simultaneous with his interaction with P, since π can be copied and stored until needed. Indeed, one *advantage* of NIZK proofs is that they are *transferable* and can be passed from verifier to verifier yet still remain a convincing proof of the theorem claimed. However, NIZK proofs are not *bound* in any way to the original discoverer of the proof. That is, once a prover gives a convincing NIZK proof to the first verifier, the verifier can claim that proof as his own!

Ideally, one would like to retain the ability to disseminate proofs as widely as possible while maintaining clear (and unalterable) information about who actually created the proof. To protect the original prover P, some mechanism needs to be developed which ensures that (1) if the proof is passed from verifier to verifier it remains a convincing proof; yet (2) if the proof is simply copied, V' will recognize that P was the one who actually composed the proof. Furthermore, (3) any adversary V' should be unable to modify the proof to make it appear as though he (V') actually composed the proof.

Toward this end, we formally define the notion of *identity-based* proof systems which satisfy the security requirements implied by the discussion above. We also show a simple and provably-secure construction of an identity-based scheme achieving the stated requirements, starting from any non-malleable zero-knowledge scheme [7]. In our construction, we do not rely on public-key infrastructure.

1.1   Related Work

The notion informally outlined above is related to the notion of non-malleability as introduced by Dolev, Dwork, and Naor [7]. Yet, these two notions are technically very different and non-malleability does not automatically imply security in the sense esdescribed above. Specifically, we note that although Dolev, et al.

discuss a way to simplify the construction of non-malleable cryptosystems when identities are present, they *do not* formally define the idea of "binding" or "linking" an identity with a proof. One can also see that a non-malleable NIZK proof system does *not* achieve the security desired in our setting; in particular, the definition of non-malleability does not protect against copying (something we are explicitly concerned with here), and known non-malleable NIZK proof systems [7, 16, 6] do not consider the notion of having the prover's identity associated with the proof. Furthermore, an identity-based proof system (as defined below) is not necessarily non-malleable.

We show, however, an underlying connection between (non-interactive) non-malleable and identity-based proof systems: our construction of an identity-based proof system uses any non-malleable proof system as a building block, and we show how any identity-based system can be used to construct a non-malleable scheme without much additional complexity.

Since the original version of this manuscript was written, an improved construction of (interactive) non-malleable zero-knowledge has been proposed [1]. See also the work of [11, 15] which, *inter alia*, construct identity-based zero-knowledge proofs for identities of *logarithmic* length which are fixed *a priori* (note, however, that neither of these works formally define the notion of identity-based zero knowledge). Also related to this work is recent work of Pass [14] which is concerned with the transferability of NIZK proofs, but is not explicitly concerned with associating proofs with identities. We remark also that NIZK proof systems in the universally composable (UC) framework [4] incorporate identities to some extent (as a consequence of the definition of the UC framework), but not quite the way we do so here. For one thing, in the UC framework there is no notion of "transferability" of NIZK proofs (indeed, such proofs inherently *cannot* be transfered in the UC framework), and there is no direct requirement that identities be "extractable" from proofs. Nevertheless, known constructions of NIZK proofs in the UC framework do achieve our definition.

The complementary notion of identity-based *interactive* proof systems is also of interest. Although the notion seems not to have been considered explicitly in the early work on non-malleability [7] (and no formal definition of such a notion has previously appeared), the techniques given there may be adapted to yield identity-based proof systems in the interactive setting. Our results below, showing that identity-based proof systems can be used to construct non-malleable proof systems, extend to the interactive setting as well. In particular, the methods of Theorem 2 show that the existence of an r-round identity-based (interactive) proof system implies the existence of an r-round non-malleable proof system, indicating that the complexity of identity-based systems is not any lower than non-malleable ones.

2   Definitions

We begin with the standard definition of (adaptive) NIZK proof systems, with one additional feature: The prover algorithm $\mathcal{P}$ takes as one of its inputs a string id representing an identity. The verification algorithm $\mathcal{V}$, on input a proof π, outputs both a bit denoting acceptance/rejection of the proof as well as a string id indicating which party it believes was the one who generated the proof. The intention is that the identity information id is embedded in π by the prover (in some way) such that it can be extracted efficiently by the verifier $\mathcal{V}$. The following definition deals simply with the correctness of this process; however, this embedding of the id will be crucial when we define security for an identity-based scheme further below.

Definition 1. $\Pi = (p, q, \mathcal{P}, \mathcal{V}, \mathcal{S} = (\mathcal{S}_1, \mathcal{S}_2))$ *is an* NIZK *proof system with extractable identity for language L with witness relation R if p, q are polynomial (with $q(k) = \omega(\log k)$) and $\mathcal{P}, \mathcal{V}$, and $\mathcal{S}$ are* PPT *algorithms such that:*

1. **(Completeness):** *For all $x \in L$, all w such that $(x, w) \in R$, all $\sigma \in \{0,1\}^{p(|x|)}$, and all $id \in \{0,1\}^{q(|x|)}$, we have $\mathcal{V}(x, \mathcal{P}(x, w, id, \sigma), \sigma)_1 = \text{true}$ (where $\mathcal{V}(\cdot, \cdot, \cdot)_1$ represents the first component of $\mathcal{V}$'s output).*
2. **(Extractable Identities):** *For all $x \in L$, all w such that $(x, w) \in R$, all $\sigma \in \{0,1\}^{p(|x|)}$, and all $id \in \{0,1\}^{q(|x|)}$, we have $\mathcal{V}(x, \mathcal{P}(x, w, id, \sigma), \sigma)_2 = id$.*
3. **(Soundness):** *For all unbounded algorithms $\mathcal{P}'$, if $\sigma \in \{0,1\}^{p(|x|)}$ is chosen randomly, the probability that $\mathcal{P}'(\sigma)$ outputs (x, π) such that $\mathcal{V}(x, \pi, \sigma)_1 = \text{true}$ and $x \notin L$ is negligible.*
4. **(Zero-Knowledge):** *For all $x \in L$, all w such that $(x, w) \in R$, and all $id \in \{0,1\}^{q(|x|)}$, the following distributions are computationally indistinguishable (where $k \stackrel{\text{def}}{=} p(|x|)$):*

$$\left\{ \sigma \leftarrow \{0,1\}^k ; \pi \leftarrow \mathcal{P}(x, w, id, \sigma) : (\sigma, \pi) \right\}$$

$$\left\{ (\sigma, s) \leftarrow \mathcal{S}_1(1^k) ; \pi \leftarrow \mathcal{S}_2(x, id, s) : (\sigma, \pi) \right\}.$$

We remark that our results extend to a stronger (robust) notion of Non-Interactive Zero-knoweldge, considered in [6], where σ is identical in the real interaction and in the simulation[1].

We further remark that the above definition says nothing about a prover who chooses to use some arbitrary identity (i.e., as opposed to their own identity) when constructing a proof. Indeed, this cannot be prevented without the additional assumption of some infrastructure who "binds" physical entities to identities.

Following [8, 6], we extend the above definition to allow for simulation of any polynomial number of proofs:

Definition 2. $\Pi = (p, q, \mathcal{P}, \mathcal{V}, \mathcal{S})$ *is an* unbounded NIZK *proof system with extractable identity for language L with witness relation R if Π is an* NIZK *proof system with extractable identity and for all* PPT *A, we have that:*

---

[1] That is, the two experiemnts are as follows: First, generate $(\sigma, s) \leftarrow \mathcal{S}_1(1^k)$, where we require the distribution on σ to be uniform, and them we require that the following two distributions are indistinguishable:$\{\pi \leftarrow \mathcal{P}(x, w, id, \sigma) : (\sigma, \pi)\}$ and $\{\pi \leftarrow \mathcal{S}_2(x, id, s) : (\sigma, \pi)\}$.

$$\left| \Pr[\mathsf{Expt}_{A,\Pi}(k) = 1] - \Pr[\mathsf{Expt}^{\mathcal{S}}_{A,\Pi}(k) = 1] \right|$$

is negligible; where:

$\mathsf{Expt}_{A,\Pi}(k)$:	$\mathsf{Expt}^{\mathcal{S}}_{A,\Pi}(k)$:
$\sigma \leftarrow \{0,1\}^k$	$(\sigma, s) \leftarrow \mathcal{S}_1(1^k)$
return $A^{\mathcal{P}(\cdot,\cdot,\cdot,\sigma)}(\sigma)$	return $A^{\mathcal{S}'(\cdot,\cdot,\cdot,s)}(\sigma)$

and $\mathcal{S}'(x, w, \mathsf{id}, s) \stackrel{\text{def}}{=} \mathcal{S}_2(x, \mathsf{id}, s)$ *(we assume, above, that if* x, w, id *is a query of A, then* $(x, w) \in R$*; note that this can be verified easily).*

We now turn to the definition of security (as sketched in the Introduction) for this setting. Informally, we want to ensure that an adversary cannot take a proof π given by a prover $\mathcal{P}(x, w, id, \sigma)$ and convert it to a proof π' (for the same theorem) such that $\mathcal{V}(x, \pi', \sigma)_1 = \mathsf{true}$, yet $\mathcal{V}(x, \pi', \sigma)_2 \neq id$. In fact, our definition is even stronger as it rules out the possibility of an adversary claiming *any* proof with respect to a "new" identity unless (informally) the adversary could have proved such a statement on its own. More specifically, anything the adversary can prove with respect to a *new* identifier after seeing any (polynomial) number of proofs $\pi_1, \ldots, \pi_\ell$ given by provers with (possibly) multiple identities (adaptively chosen by the adversary), could have been proved by the adversary without seeing these proofs.[2] Our definition is based on that of [6], who present definitions in the context of non-malleable NIZK. However, we stress (as pointed out previously) that non-malleable and identity-based proof systems are incomparable, in the sense that a proof system satisfying one need not satisfy the other. We make this explicit in Lemmas 1 and 2, below.

Definition 3. *Let* $\Pi = (p, q, \mathcal{P}, \mathcal{V}, \mathcal{S})$ *be an unbounded NIZK proof system with extractable identity for language L with witness relation R_L. We say that Π is an* identity-based *NIZK proof system for L if there exists an extractor* Ext *such that, for all* PPT *adversaries A and all poly-time relations R, the following is negligible:*

$$\left| \Pr[\mathsf{ExptID}^{\mathcal{S}}_{A,R,\Pi}(k)] - \Pr[\mathsf{ExptID}'_{A,R,\Pi}(k)] \right|,$$

where:

$\mathsf{ExptID}^{\mathcal{S}}_{A,R,\Pi}(k)$:	$\mathsf{ExptID}'_{A,R,\Pi}(k)$:
$(\sigma, s) \leftarrow \mathcal{S}_1(1^k)$	$(x, w, \mathsf{aux}) \leftarrow \mathsf{Ext}^A(1^k)$
$(x, \pi, \mathsf{aux}) \leftarrow A^{\mathcal{S}_2(\cdot,\cdot,s)}(\sigma)$	return true *iff*
Let I be the list of identities queried by A	$(x, w) \in R_L$ and
return true *iff*	$R(x, \mathsf{aux}) = 1$
$\quad \mathcal{V}(x, \pi, \sigma)_1 = \mathsf{true}$ and	
$\quad \mathcal{V}(x, \pi, \sigma)_2 \notin I$ and	
$\quad R(x, \mathsf{aux}) = 1$	

(we assume, above, that if x, id is a query of A, then $x \in L$).

---

[2] When we say that x "could have been proved by the adversary", we mean that an actual witness w for x can be extracted from the adversary (see Definition 3).

We remark that the above definition actually corresponds to an NIZK proof *of knowledge* (in the sense that Ext "extracts" a witness from A). It is possible to relax the definition (and our constructions) for the case of NIZK *proofs* but we omit the details here.

The next two lemmas indicate that identity-based schemes and non-malleable schemes are incomparable. For self-containment, we include in Appendix A a definition of non-malleable NIZK proof systems (adapted from [6]).

Lemma 1. *Assuming the existence of trapdoor permutations and*[3] *dense cryptosystems, there exists a proof system Π which is a non-malleable NIZK proof system yet is not an identity-based NIZK proof system.*

Proof (sketch). Consider, for example, the non-malleable schemes given in [6]. In these schemes, there is no notion of prover identities at all, and thus no connection whatsoever between a proof and the identity of the prover.

Lemma 2. *Assuming the existence of trapdoor permutations and dense cryptosystems, there exists a proof system Π which is an identity-based NIZK proof system yet is not a non-malleable NIZK proof system.*

Proof (sketch). An identity-based NIZK proof system only prevents an adversary from modifying an existing proof to yield a proof which is not associated with any of the legitimate provers, yet it may be possible for an adversary to modify an existing proof to yield a proof of a different statement (but in the name of the original prover). In particular, consider the construction Π of an identity-based proof system given in Section 3. Define proof system Π' in which a prover appends an extra bit to the end of every proof which is ignored by the verifier. Since flipping the final bit of a valid proof yields a new valid proof, clearly the scheme is not non-malleable. Yet it is not difficult to show that Π' remains an identity-based proof system

3   An Identity-Based Proof System

We construct an identity-based NIZK proof system Π starting from any non-malleable NIZK proof system $\widetilde{\Pi} = (\tilde{p}, \widetilde{\mathcal{P}}, \widetilde{\mathcal{V}}, \widetilde{\mathcal{S}})$ for languages in $\mathcal{NP}$. We make the additional assumption that $\widetilde{\Pi}$ has *uniquely applicable proofs* (see [16]). This means that, for all $x, x'\pi, \sigma$ with $x \neq x'$, if $\widetilde{\mathcal{V}}(x, \pi, \sigma) = \text{true}$ then we must have $\widetilde{\mathcal{V}}(x', \pi, \sigma) = \text{false}$. Known techniques for constructing non-malleable NIZK proof systems [16, 6] give proof systems which have uniquely applicable proofs.

---

[3] The assumption of dense cryptosystems is needed only for the definitions as currently presented. By relaxing the definitions to consider *proofs* rather than *proofs of knowledge* (see the remark following Def. 3) we can, following [6–Footnote 6], base our results on the assumption of trapdoor permutations alone.

The intuition behind our construction[4] of proof system Π for language $L \in \mathcal{NP}$ is as follows: an identity-based proof of the theorem $x \in L$ using identity id will consist of a proof (under $\widetilde{\Pi}$) of the theorem that *either* $x \in L$ *or* (a portion of) the common random string specifies a commitment to id. A formal description follows:

- **Common Random String.** Let $k \overset{\text{def}}{=} |x|$. Define $p(k) \overset{\text{def}}{=} \tilde{p}(6k^2 + 2k) + 6k^2$. The random string $\sigma \in \{0,1\}^{p(k)}$ is parsed as $\sigma_1 \circ \sigma_2$, with $|\sigma_1| = 6k^2$. String σ_1 is parsed as $r_1, c_1, \ldots, r_k, c_k$ where $|r_i| = |c_i| = 3k$, for all i. Pair (r_i, c_i) will be viewed as a bit commitment as follows [12]: let $G : \{0,1\}^k \rightarrow \{0,1\}^{3k}$ be a pseudorandom generator. If $c_i = G(y)$ for some y, then (r_i, c_i) represents a 0. If $c_i \oplus r_i = G(y)$ for some y, then (r_i, c_i) represents a 1. Note that with all but negligible probability over random choice of r_i, c_i, the pair will not represent a valid commitment to any value.

- **Prover Strategy.** Any $q(k) = poly(k)$ is possible; for simplicity, we set $q(k) \overset{\text{def}}{=} k$. Define language $\widetilde{L} \in \mathcal{NP}$ as consisting of tuples (x, id), with $|x| = k$ and $|\sigma_1| = 6k^2$, such that at least one of the following is true:

  1. $x \in L$
  2. σ_1 is a commitment (see above) to the k-bit string id.

  (Note that $\widetilde{L}$ depends on a fixed value of σ_1. Thus, technically, we should write $\widetilde{L}_{\sigma_1}$; however, we suppress σ_1 in the notation.) Algorithm $\mathcal{P}(x, w, id, \sigma)$, where $id \in \{0,1\}^k$, is defined as follows: First, σ is parsed as $\sigma_1 \circ \sigma_2$. $\mathcal{P}$ sets $\tilde{x} := (x, id)$ and runs $\widetilde{\mathcal{P}}(\tilde{x}, w, \sigma_2)$, where $\widetilde{\mathcal{P}}$ is the proof system for language $\widetilde{L}$. Let $\tilde{\pi}$ be the output of $\widetilde{\mathcal{P}}$. The output of $\mathcal{P}$ is then $\pi := (id, \tilde{\pi})$.

- **Verifier Strategy.** $\mathcal{V}(x, (id, \tilde{\pi}), \sigma)$ runs as follows: First, σ is parsed as $\sigma_1 \circ \sigma_2$. The verifier sets $\tilde{x} := (x, id)$ and outputs $(\widetilde{\mathcal{V}}(\tilde{x}, \tilde{\pi}, \sigma_2), id)$.

- **Simulation.** We define $(\mathcal{S}_1, \mathcal{S}_2)$ as follows: $\mathcal{S}_1(1^k)$ chooses $\sigma_1 \in \{0,1\}^{6k^2}$ at random and then runs $\widetilde{\mathcal{S}}_1(1^k)$ to generate (σ_2, s). The output of $\mathcal{S}_1$ is (σ, s), where $\sigma = \sigma_1 \circ \sigma_2$. Algorithm $\mathcal{S}_2(x, id, s)$ sets $\tilde{x} := (x, id)$, and runs $\widetilde{\mathcal{S}}_2(\tilde{x}, s)$ to obtain output $\tilde{\pi}$. Finally, $\mathcal{S}_2$ sets $\pi := (id, \tilde{\pi})$ and outputs π.

The security offered by this construction is described by the following theorem:

Theorem 1. *If $\widetilde{\Pi}$ is a non-malleable NIZK proof system (with uniquely applicable proofs) for $\widetilde{L}$, then Π is an identity-based NIZK proof system for L.*

Using [6], we immediately obtain the following corollary:

Corollary 1. *Assuming the existence of trapdoor permutations and dense cryptosystems, there exists an identity-based NIZK proof system for any $L \in NP$.*

We now prove the theorem.

---

[4] In fact, a simpler construction is possible. Informally, to prove $x \in L$ we first construct the language $L' \overset{\text{def}}{=} \{(id, x) \mid x \in L\}$ and then give a non-malleable proof that $(id, x) \in L'$. We omit the details and a proof of security for this construction.

Proof. One-way functions are sufficient for the construction given above; furthermore, the fact that $\widetilde{\Pi}$ is an NIZK proof system for languages outside $\mathcal{BPP}$ implies that one-way functions exist (assuming $\mathcal{NP} \neq \mathcal{BPP}$) [13]. We first show that Π is an NIZK proof system with extractable identity (cf. Definition 1). Completeness and identity extraction are trivial. Soundness of Π follows from the soundness of $\widetilde{\Pi}$ and the observation that, with all but negligible probability over randomly chosen $\sigma = \sigma_1 \circ \sigma_2$, the string σ_1 cannot be interpreted as a commitment to *any* string *id*. Zero-knowledge will follow from the stronger property proved below.

To show that Π is unbounded, consider an arbitrary PPT adversary A (cf. Definition 2). Define $\widetilde{A}$ as follows: on input σ_2, adversary $\widetilde{A}$ generates $\sigma_1 \in \{0,1\}^{6k^2}$ at random and runs $A(\sigma_1 \circ \sigma_2)$. When A submits query (x, w, id), algorithm $\widetilde{A}$ sets $\tilde{x} := (x, id)$ and submits query $(\tilde{x}, w)$ to its oracle. Upon receiving $\tilde{\pi}$ in response, $\widetilde{A}$ returns to A the value $(id, \tilde{\pi})$. Finally, $\widetilde{A}$'s final output is whatever A outputs. Note that:

$$\Pr[\mathsf{Expt}_{A,\Pi}(k) = 1] = \Pr[\mathsf{Expt}_{\widetilde{A},\widetilde{\Pi}}(k) = 1]$$

and

$$\Pr[\mathsf{Expt}^{\mathcal{S}}_{A,\Pi}(k) = 1] = \Pr[\mathsf{Expt}^{\widetilde{\mathcal{S}}}_{\widetilde{A},\widetilde{\Pi}}(k) = 1].$$

Thus, if $\widetilde{\Pi}$ is an unbounded NIZK proof system (cf. Definition 5), Π is an unbounded, identifiable NIZK proof system.

We now prove that Π is an identity-based NIZK proof system. Let A be a PPT adversary, and let R be a poly-time relation. Define $\widetilde{A}$ as follows: on input σ_2, adversary $\widetilde{A}$ generates $\sigma_1 \in \{0,1\}^{6k^2}$ at random and runs $A(\sigma)$, where $\sigma = \sigma_1 \circ \sigma_2$. When A submits query x, id to its oracle for $\mathcal{S}_2$, algorithm $\widetilde{A}$ sets $\tilde{x} := (x, id)$ and submits query $\tilde{x}$ to its oracle for $\widetilde{\mathcal{S}}_2$. Upon receiving $\tilde{\pi}$ in response, $\widetilde{A}$ returns to A the response $(id, \tilde{\pi})$. When A outputs $(x_f, \pi_f = (id_f, \tilde{\pi}_f), \mathsf{aux})$, algorithm $\widetilde{A}$ checks whether id_f appears in the list of identities queried by A. If it does not, $\widetilde{A}$ outputs $(\tilde{x}_f = (x_f, id_f), \tilde{\pi}_f, \mathsf{aux})$; otherwise, $\widetilde{A}$ outputs $\bot$.

Furthermore, define relation $\widetilde{R}$ as follows: $\widetilde{R}(\tilde{x} = (x, id), \mathsf{aux}) = 1$ if and only if $R(x, \mathsf{aux}) = 1$.

We claim that:

$$\Pr[\mathsf{ExptID}^{\mathcal{S}}_{A,R,\Pi}(k)] = \Pr[\mathsf{ExptNM}^{\widetilde{\mathcal{S}}}_{\widetilde{A},\widetilde{R},\widetilde{\Pi}}(k)]. \tag{1}$$

To see this, first note that the simulation (in ExptNM) provided by $\widetilde{A}$ for A is perfect. Thus, the distribution on the values $(x_f, \pi_f = (id_f, \tilde{\pi}_f), \mathsf{aux}, \sigma)$ in the two experiments is identical. Furthermore, note that (as above, we let $\tilde{x}_f \overset{\text{def}}{=} (x_f, id_f)$):

$$
\begin{array}{ccc}
\mathcal{V}(x_f, \pi_f, \sigma)_1 = \mathsf{true} & \widetilde{\mathcal{V}}(\tilde{x}_f, \tilde{\pi}_f, \sigma_1) = \mathsf{true} \\
\mathcal{V}(x_f, \pi_f, \sigma)_2 \notin I & \Longleftrightarrow & \tilde{\pi}_f \notin Q \\
R(x_f, \mathsf{aux}) = 1 & \widetilde{R}(\tilde{x}_f, \mathsf{aux}) = 1
\end{array} \quad ,
$$

where I is the list of identities queried by A and Q is the list of proofs which $\widetilde{A}$ received from oracle $\widetilde{S}_2$ (here, we use the property that $\widetilde{\Pi}$ has uniquely applicable proofs). This completes the proof of the claim.

Let $\widetilde{\mathsf{Ext}}$ be the extractor for proof system $\widetilde{\Pi}$ guaranteed by Definition 6. We now specify extractor Ext. Algorithm $\mathsf{Ext}^A(1^k)$ first chooses $\sigma_1 \in \{0,1\}^{6k^2}$ at random and fixes it for the remainder of its execution; note that this defines $\widetilde{L}$. Next, Ext runs $\widetilde{\mathsf{Ext}}(1^k)$, responding to the oracle calls of $\widetilde{\mathsf{Ext}}$ as follows: when $\widetilde{\mathsf{Ext}}$ submits σ_2 to its oracle for $\widetilde{A}$, Ext submits $\sigma_1 \circ \sigma_2$ to its oracle for A. When A queries x, id, algorithm Ext responds by first setting $\tilde{x} := (x, id)$ and sending query $\tilde{x}$ to $\widetilde{\mathsf{Ext}}$. When $\widetilde{\mathsf{Ext}}$ responds with $\tilde{\pi}$, algorithm Ext responds to A with $\pi = (id, \tilde{\pi})$. Ultimately, when A generates its final output $(x_a, \pi_a = (id_a, \tilde{\pi}_a), \mathsf{aux}_a)$, algorithm Ext gives $(\tilde{x}_a = (x_a, id_a), \tilde{\pi}_a, \mathsf{aux}_a)$ to $\widetilde{\mathsf{Ext}}$. When $\widetilde{\mathsf{Ext}}$ outputs $(\tilde{x}_f = (x_f, id_f), \tilde{w}, \mathsf{aux}_f)$, algorithm Ext outputs $(x_f, \tilde{w}, \mathsf{aux}_f)$.

Note that, in the simulation above, Ext perfectly simulates oracle $\widetilde{A}$ for $\widetilde{\mathsf{Ext}}$ (where $\widetilde{A}$ is defined as before). Furthermore, note that if $\tilde{w}$ is a witness to $\tilde{x}_f \in \widetilde{L}$ then, with all but negligible probability, $\tilde{w}$ is also a witness to $x_f \in L$. This is so because, with all but negligible probability, string σ_1 is not a well-defined commitment to *any* string id. Therefore, the following is negligible:

$$\left| \Pr[\mathsf{ExptID}'_{A,R,\Pi}(k)] - \Pr[\mathsf{ExptNM}'_{\widetilde{A},\widetilde{R},\widetilde{\Pi}}(k)] \right|. \tag{2}$$

Equations (1) and (2) complete the proof that Π is identity-based.

4   From Identity-Based Schemes to Non-malleability

In this section, we further study the relation between identity-based NIZK proof systems and non-malleable NIZK proof systems. Section 3 shows how to construct an identity-based proof system based on any non-malleable proof system. Yet, since the definition of identity-based proof systems seems weaker than the definition of non-malleable proof systems, one may wonder whether more efficient constructions of identity-based proof systems are possible. Our results indicate that, in some sense, this is not possible. More formally, we show that any identity-based NIZK proof system can be converted to a non-malleable NIZK proof system with minimal additional overhead. Below, we consider the non-interactive case; however, our results extend to the interactive setting as well. In particular, one can show (using a construction much like the one given below) that any identity-based, interactive ZK proof system can be converted to a non-malleable, interactive ZK proof system without any increase in round-complexity.

We begin with an identity-based NIZK proof system $\widetilde{\Pi} = (\tilde{p}, \tilde{q}, \widetilde{P}, \widetilde{V}, \widetilde{S})$ in which $q(k) = \omega(\log k)$. We make the additional assumption that $\widetilde{\Pi}$ has uniquely-applicable proofs [16] (the construction given in Section 3 satisfies this assumption). In non-malleable proof system Π which we construct, a proof that $x \in L$ will consist of the following: (1) a verification key VK for a one-time signature scheme, (2) a proof $\tilde{\pi}$, in proof system $\widetilde{\Pi}$ and using $id = \mathsf{VK}$, that $x \in L$, and (3) a signature τ on $\tilde{\pi}$, using the secret key SK which corresponds to VK. A complete description of the protocol follows:

- **Common Random String.** Let $|x| = k$ and define $p(k) \stackrel{\text{def}}{=} \tilde{p}(k)$. Thus, the random string σ used by Π to prove statements of length k will have the same length as that used by $\widetilde{\Pi}$.
- **Prover Strategy.** We use a one-time signature scheme secure against existential forgery: algorithm $\mathsf{KeyGen}(1^k)$ generates signing/verification keys $(\mathsf{SK}, \mathsf{VK})$. We assume for simplicity that VK output by $\mathsf{KeyGen}(1^k)$ has length $\tilde{q}(k)$ (recall the definition requires $\tilde{q}(k) = \omega(\log k)$). Algorithm $\mathcal{P}(x, w, \sigma)$ first runs $\mathsf{KeyGen}(1^k)$ to generate $(\mathsf{SK}, \mathsf{VK})$. Then, $\mathcal{P}$ runs $\widetilde{\mathcal{P}}(x, w, \mathsf{VK}, \sigma)$ to give proof $\tilde{\pi}$. Finally, $\mathcal{P}$ signs $\tilde{\pi}$ (using SK) to obtain signature τ. The output is $\pi = (\mathsf{VK}, \tilde{\pi}, \tau)$.
- **Verifier Strategy.** $\mathcal{V}(x, (\mathsf{VK}, \tilde{\pi}, \tau), \sigma)$ runs as follows: if τ is not a valid signature of $\tilde{\pi}$ under VK or $\widetilde{\mathcal{V}}(x, \tilde{\pi}, \sigma)_2 \neq \mathsf{VK}$, output false. Otherwise, output $\widetilde{\mathcal{V}}(x, \tilde{\pi}, \sigma)_1$.
- **Simulation.** $\mathcal{S}_1(1^k)$ simply outputs the result σ, s of running $\widetilde{\mathcal{S}}_1(1^k)$. To simulate a proof, $\mathcal{S}_2(x, s)$ runs $\mathsf{KeyGen}(1^k)$ to obtain $(\mathsf{SK}, \mathsf{VK})$, and then runs $\widetilde{\mathcal{S}}_2(x, \mathsf{VK}, s)$ to obtain $\tilde{\pi}$. Finally, $\mathcal{S}_2$ signs $\tilde{\pi}$ using SK, giving signature τ. The output is $\pi = (\mathsf{VK}, \tilde{\pi}, \tau)$.

The security of this construction is given by the following theorem:

Theorem 2. *If $\widetilde{\Pi}$ is an identity-based NIZK proof system (with $q(k) = \omega(\log k)$ and uniquely applicable proofs) for L, then Π is a non-malleable NIZK proof system for L.*

Proof. One-way functions are sufficient for the construction above; furthermore, the fact that $\widetilde{\Pi}$ is an NIZK proof system for languages outside $\mathcal{BPP}$ implies that one-way functions exist (assuming $\mathcal{NP} \neq \mathcal{BPP}$) [13]. Completeness, soundness, and (unbounded) zero-knowledge of Π follow from the fact that $\widetilde{\Pi}$ satisfies Definitions 1 and 2. Therefore, we focus on proving that Π satisfies Definition 6.

Let A be a PPT adversary and R be a poly-time relation (cf. Definition 6). Define $\widetilde{A}$ as follows: on input σ, adversary $\widetilde{A}$ simply runs $A(\sigma)$. When A submits query x to its oracle for $\mathcal{S}_2$, algorithm $\widetilde{A}$ runs algorithm $\mathsf{KeyGen}(1^k)$ to obtain $(\mathsf{SK}, \mathsf{VK})$, and submits query x, VK to its oracle for $\widetilde{\mathcal{S}}_2$. Upon receiving $\tilde{\pi}$ in response, $\widetilde{A}$ generates signature τ for $\tilde{\pi}$ using SK, and returns to A the proof $\pi = (\mathsf{VK}, \tilde{\pi}, \tau)$. When A outputs $(x_f, \pi_f = (\mathsf{VK}_f, \tilde{\pi}_f, \tau_f), \mathsf{aux})$, algorithm $\widetilde{A}$ checks that π_f is a valid proof for x and that π_f was not one of the proofs which $\widetilde{A}$ gave to A. If both conditions are satisfied, $\widetilde{A}$ outputs $(x_f, \tilde{\pi}_f, \widetilde{\mathsf{aux}} = (\mathsf{aux}, \mathsf{VK}_f, \tau_f))$; otherwise $\widetilde{A}$ outputs $\perp$.

We claim that the following is negligible:

$$\left| \Pr[\mathsf{ExptNM}^{\mathcal{S}}_{A,R,\Pi}(k)] - \Pr[\mathsf{ExptID}^{\widetilde{\mathcal{S}}}_{\widetilde{A},R,\widetilde{\Pi}}(k)] \right|. \tag{3}$$

To see this, note that the simulation provided by $\widetilde{A}$ for A is perfect. Thus, the distribution on $(x_f, \pi_f, \mathsf{aux})$ in the two experiments is identical. Assuming π_f is a valid proof for x_f and that π_f was not one of the proofs given to A, there are two possibilities: either VK_f is equal to one of the verification keys which $\widetilde{A}$ already used or not. The probability of the first possibility is negligible, by the security of the one-time signature scheme. On the other hand, when the second possibility occurs, we have:

$$\begin{array}{ll} \mathcal{V}(x_f, \pi_f, \sigma) = \mathsf{true} \\ \pi_f \notin Q \end{array} \Longleftrightarrow \begin{array}{ll} \widetilde{\mathcal{V}}(x_f, \tilde{\pi}_f, \sigma)_1 = \mathsf{true} \\ \widetilde{\mathcal{V}}(x_f, \tilde{\pi}_f, \sigma)_2 \notin I \end{array},$$

where Q is the list of proofs received by A and I is the list of verification keys used by $\widetilde{A}$. This completes the proof of the claim.

Let $\widetilde{\mathsf{Ext}}$ be the extractor for proof system $\widetilde{\Pi}$ guaranteed by Definition 3. Define $\mathsf{Ext}(1^k)$ which runs $\widetilde{\mathsf{Ext}}(1^k)$, responding to the oracle calls of $\widetilde{\mathsf{Ext}}$ as follows: when $\widetilde{\mathsf{Ext}}$ submits σ to its oracle for $\widetilde{A}$, this query is forwarded by Ext to its oracle for A. When A queries x, algorithm Ext runs KeyGen to obtain keys $(\mathsf{SK}, \mathsf{VK})$ and submits query x, VK to $\widetilde{\mathsf{Ext}}$. When $\widetilde{\mathsf{Ext}}$ responds with $\tilde{\pi}$, algorithm Ext generates signature τ on $\tilde{\pi}$ using SK, and returns $\pi = (\mathsf{VK}, \tilde{\pi}, \tau)$ to A. When A generates its final output $(x_a, \pi_a = (\mathsf{VK}_a, \tilde{\pi}_a, \tau_a), \mathsf{aux}_a)$, algorithm Ext gives $(x_a, \tilde{\pi}_a, \mathsf{aux}_a)$ to $\widetilde{\mathsf{Ext}}$. Finally, when $\widetilde{\mathsf{Ext}}$ outputs $(x_f, w_f, \mathsf{aux}_f)$, algorithm Ext outputs the same. It is clear that:

$$\Pr[\mathsf{ExptNM}'_{A,R,\Pi}(k)] = \Pr[\mathsf{ExptID}'_{\widetilde{A},R,\widetilde{\Pi}}(k)]. \tag{4}$$

Equations (3) and (4) complete the proof that Π is non-malleable.

Acknowledgments

We thank the referees for their helpful comments.

References

1. B. Barak. Constant-Round Coin-Tossing with a Man in the Middle or Realizing the Shared Random String Model. FOCS 2002.
2. M. Blum. How to Prove a Theorem so No One Else Can Claim It. *Proceedings of the International Congress of Mathematicians*, 1986.
3. M. Blum, P. Feldman, and S. Micali. Non-Interactive Zero-Knowledge and Its Applications. STOC '88.
4. R. Canetti. Universally Composable Security: A New Paradigm for Cryptographic Protocols. FOCS 2001.
5. R. Cramer and I. Damgård. Fast and Secure Immunization Against Adaptive Man-in-the-Middle Impersonation. Eurocrypt '97.
6. A. De Santis, G. Di Crescenzo, R. Ostrovsky, G. Persiano, and A. Sahai. Robust Non-Interactive Zero Knowledge. Crypto 2001.

7. D. Dolev, C. Dwork, and M. Naor. Non-Malleable Cryptography. *SIAM J. Computing* 30(2): 391–437 (2000).
8. U. Feige, D. Lapidot, and A. Shamir. Multiple Non-Interactive Zero Knowledge Proofs Under General Assumptions. SIAM J. Comp. 29(1): 1–28 (1999).
9. S. Goldwasser, S. Micali, and C. Rackoff. The Knowledge Complexity of Interactive Proof Systems. SIAM J. Comp. 18(1): 186–208 (1989).
10. M. Jakobsson, K. Sako, and R. Impagliazzo. Designated-Verifier Proofs and their Applications. Eurocrypt '96.
11. J. Katz, R. Ostrovsky, and A. Smith. Round Efficiency of Multi-Party Computation with a Dishonest Majority. Eurocrypt 2003.
12. M. Naor. Bit Commitment Using Pseudorandomness. J. Crypto. 4(2): 151–158 (1991).
13. R. Ostrovsky and A. Wigderson. One-Way Functions are Essential for Non-Trivial Zero-Knowledge. 2nd Israeli Symp. on Theory of Computing and Systems, 1993.
14. R. Pass. On Deniability in the Common Reference String and Random Oracle Models. Crypto 2003.
15. R. Pass. Bounded-Concurrent Multi-Party Computation with a Dishonest Majority. STOC 2004.
16. A. Sahai. Non-Malleable Non-Interactive Zero Knowledge and Adaptive Chosen-Ciphertext Security. FOCS '99.

A   Definitions for Non-malleable NIZK

For completeness, we include relevant definitions from [6].

Definition 4. ([6–Def. 1]) $\Pi = (p, \mathcal{P}, \mathcal{V}, \mathcal{S} = (\mathcal{S}_1, \mathcal{S}_2))$ *is a single-theorem NIZK proof system for a language L with witness relation R if p is polynomial and $\mathcal{P}, \mathcal{V}$, and $\mathcal{S}$ are* PPT *algorithms such that:*

1. **(Completeness):** *For all $x \in L$ and all w such that $(x, w) \in R$, for all $\sigma \in \{0,1\}^{p(|x|)}$, we have $\mathcal{V}(x, \mathcal{P}(x, w, \sigma), \sigma) = \mathsf{true}$.*

2. **(Soundness):** *For all unbounded algorithms $\mathcal{P}'$, if $\sigma \in \{0,1\}^{p(|x|)}$ is chosen randomly, the probability that $\mathcal{P}'(\sigma)$ outputs (x, π) such that $\mathcal{V}(x, \pi, \sigma) = \mathsf{true}$ and $x \notin L$ is negligible.*

3. **(Zero-knowledge):** *For all $x \in L$ and all w such that $R(x, w) = \mathsf{true}$, the following distributions are computationally indistinguishable (where $k \overset{\text{def}}{=} p(|x|)$):*

$$\{\sigma \leftarrow \{0,1\}^k; \pi \leftarrow \mathcal{P}(x, w, \sigma) : (\sigma, \pi)\}$$

and

$$\{(\sigma, s) \leftarrow \mathcal{S}_1(1^k); \pi \leftarrow \mathcal{S}_2(x, s) : (\sigma, \pi)\}.$$

Definition 5. ([6–Def. 2]) $\Pi = (p, \mathcal{P}, \mathcal{V}, \mathcal{S})$ *is an* unbounded *NIZK proof system for language L if Π is a single-theorem NIZK proof system for L and for all* PPT *algorithms A, we have that $|\Pr[\mathsf{Expt}_{A,\Pi}(k) = 1] - \Pr[\mathsf{Expt}^{\mathcal{S}}_{A,\Pi}(k) = 1]|$ is negligible; where:*

$\mathsf{Expt}_{A,\Pi}(k):$	$\mathsf{Expt}^{\mathcal{S}}_{A,\Pi}(k):$
$\quad \sigma \leftarrow \{0,1\}^k$	$\quad (\sigma, s) \leftarrow \mathcal{S}_1(1^k)$
$\quad \text{return } A^{\mathcal{P}(\cdot,\cdot,\sigma)}(\sigma)$	$\quad \text{return } A^{\mathcal{S}'(\cdot,\cdot,s)}(\sigma)$

where $\mathcal{S}'(x, w, s) \stackrel{\text{def}}{=} \mathcal{S}_2(x, s)$ (we assume, above, that if x, w is a query of A, then $(x, w) \in R$).

Definition 6. ([6–Def. 5]) *Let* $\Pi = (p, \mathcal{P}, \mathcal{V}, \mathcal{S})$ *be an unbounded NIZK proof system for language* L *with witness relation* R_L. *We say that* Π *is a non-malleable NIZK proof system for* L *if there exists an extractor* Ext *such that, for all* PPT *adversaries* A *and all poly-time relations* R, *the difference*

$$|\Pr[\mathsf{ExptNM}^{\mathcal{S}}_{A,R,\Pi}(k)] - \Pr[\mathsf{ExptNM}'_{A,R,\Pi}(k)]|$$

is negligible, where:

$\mathsf{ExptNM}^{\mathcal{S}}_{A,R,\Pi}(k):$	$\mathsf{ExptNM}'_{A,R,\Pi}(k):$
$\quad (\sigma, s) \leftarrow \mathcal{S}_1(1^k)$	$\quad (x, w, \mathsf{aux}) \leftarrow \mathsf{Ext}^A(1^k)$
$\quad (x, \pi, \mathsf{aux}) \leftarrow A^{S_2(\cdot, s)}(\sigma)$	$\quad \text{return true } \textit{iff}$
$\quad \textit{Let } Q \textit{ be the list of proofs returned by } \mathcal{S}_2$	$\quad\quad (x, w) \in R_L \text{ and}$
$\quad \text{return true } \textit{iff}$	$\quad\quad R(x, \mathsf{aux}) = 1$
$\quad\quad \mathcal{V}(x, \pi, \sigma) = \text{true and}$	
$\quad\quad \pi \notin Q \text{ and}$	
$\quad\quad R(x, \mathsf{aux}) = 1$	

(we assume, above, that if x is a query of A then $x \in L$).

A Robust Multisignature Scheme with Applications to Acknowledgement Aggregation

Claude Castelluccia[1,2], Stanisław Jarecki[1], Jihye Kim[1], and Gene Tsudik[1]

[1] University of California, Irvine
Computer Science Department, Irvine, CA 92697-3425
{stasio,jihyek,gts}@ics.uci.edu
[2] INRIA Rhône-Alpes, 655 Avenue de l'Europe, 38334 Saint Ismier CEDEX, France
claude.castelluccia@inrialpes.fr

Abstract. A multicast communication source often needs to securely verify which multicast group members have received a message, but verification of individually signed acknowledgments from each member would impose a significant computation and communication cost. As pointed out by Nicolosi and Mazieres [NM04], such cost is minimized if the intermediate nodes along the multicast distribution tree aggregate the individual signatures generated by the multicast receivers into a single *multisignature*.

While the solution of [NM04], based on a multisignature scheme of Boldyreva [Bol03], relied on so-called "Gap Diffie-Hellman" groups, we propose a solution using a multisignature scheme which is secure under just the discrete logarithm assumption. However, unlike the previously known discrete-log based multisignature scheme of Micali et al. [MOR01a], our multisignature scheme is robust, which allows for an efficient multisignature generation even in the presence of (possibly malicious) node and communication failures.

1 Introduction

Multicast (or one-to-many) communication is widespread in a variety of settings. Popular examples include IP Multicast, p2p content sharing, digital cable TV transmission, mobile ad hoc networks and application-layer replication protocols. Multicast security has been the subject of much attention in the research literature. Most of the relevant work has been in the context of key management, multicast/broadcast encryption and efficient content authentication. One of the related issues that has not been sufficiently considered is the problem of secure (authenticated) acknowledgments. After sending out a multicast message, the source is often interested in establishing which group members have received the message.

In this paper we propose several new techniques for efficient authentication of acknowledgments generated in response to a multicast message. We are interested in schemes which are efficient, scalable, robust with respect to failures and malicious participants, and provably secure under long-standing cryptographic assumptions like the hardness of computing discrete logarithms.

C. Blundo and S. Cimato (Eds.): SCN 2004, LNCS 3352, pp. 193–207, 2005.

Importance of Multicast Acknowledgment Aggregation. We assume that the packets are sent from the source to the members along a delivery tree. This tree is rooted at the source and the members are represented as leaves and, possibly, also as intermediate nodes. The delivery tree is no necessarily binary, i.e., a node can have more than two children. This model is general enough to cover the standard client-server and peer-to-peer multicast flavors. In the former, the group members are the leaves, whereas, in the latter, intermediate nodes can also be group members. However, for the sake of simplicity in the presentation, we will assume that the group members are leaves of a binary multicast tree rooted at the source.

After multicasting a message M to the group, the source needs to make sure that all members have received it. One simple solution is to ask each member to send an authenticated acknowledgment back to the source. However, this solution is not scalable as it results in the acknowledgment implosion problem, i.e. the individual acknowledgments take up too much bandwidth, which in many application will be a scarce resource. While the computational cost of verifying the individual acknowledgments can be sped up by various batch signature verification techniques, such techniques do not address the need to save the communication resources as well.

Prior Art: Acknowledgment Aggregation Using Multisignatures Based on GDH Groups. Nicolosi and Mazieres [NM04] recently proposed to reduce the computation and the communication costs associated with acknowledgment verification by aggregating the acknowledgments using a multisignaturescheme of Boldyreva [Bol03]. A multisignature scheme is a generalization of the standard notion of a signature to messages signed by *groups* of users. It was formally defined only recently by Micali et al. in [MOR01a],[1] a long time after the (less formal) introduction of this concept by Itakura and Nakamura [IN83], and after several such schemes were proposed and a few were shown to have serious security vulnerabilities. In a multisignature scheme s is called a multisignature on message M issued by a group of players G if (s, M) passes certain verification equation involving the set of all public keys in group G. If the multisignature scheme is secure, this happens only (except for negligible probability) if *all* players in group G indeed signed M.[2]

It is easy to illustrate multisignatures using the multisignature scheme of Boldyreva [Bol03], which is a generalization of a regular signature scheme proposed by Boneh et al. [BLS01]. Assuming that an element g is a generator of such a group, in a BLS signature the user's private key is x, the public key is a group element $y = g^x$, the signature on a (hashed) message M is $s = M^x$, and signature verification consists of checking that (g, y, M, s) is a Diffie-Hellman tuple. Boldyreva's multisignature scheme generalizes the BLS signatures by defining

---

[1] A full version of this paper is available as [MOR01b].

[2] Thus multisignatures, referred to as "accountable subgroup multisignatures" by Micali et al., are a special case of so-called "aggregate signatures" [BGLS03] which enable aggregation of signatures by multiple signers on possibly *different* messages.

string s as a multisignature on M issued by a *group* of players G if (g, y, M, s) is a DDH tuple for $y = \prod_{i \in G} y_i$. Note that if each s_i is a BLS signature issued by player i on M, then $s = \prod_{i \in G} s_i$ is a multisignature on M issued by players in G. Both schemes are secure in the Random Oracle Model under the so-called "Gap Diffie-Hellman" (GDH) group assumption, which requires that even if it is easy to *decide* whether a tuple of four group elements (g, y, z, w) is a Diffie-Hellman tuple, i.e. whether $DL_g(y) = DL_z(w)$, still *computing* a DH function $F_x(z) = (z)^x$ on a random group element z is intractable without the knowledge of x. GDH is assumed to hold for certain elliptic curve groups with Weil pairings, where decisional Diffie-Hellman can be efficiently computed via the pairing, but where computational Diffie-Hellman still appears to be hard [Jou02, Gag02].

Since the aggregation of BLS signatures into a multisignature does not require participation of the signers, this multisignature scheme enables robust aggregation of acknowledgments by the intermediate nodes on the multicast delivery tree: Each intermediate node can verify, given the (combined) public keys of the nodes below him, whether the (aggregated) acknowledgments he receives are correct, and then aggregate them further for the node above. Together with an aggregation of the valid multisignatures he receives, each node also passes up identities of members involved in this multisignature. In this way the source receives the final multisignature and the identities of members whose signatures are aggregated in it. Note that the scheme uses constant bandwidth on every link, and that the cost of the multisignature verification is the same as the verification of a standard BLS signature. Furthermore, this solution implicitly provides *traceability* by allowing the source to eventually identify the malicious participants who send bogus acknowledgments.

Our Contribution: A Robust DL-Based Multisignature and Acknowledgment Aggregation. While efficient and robust, the above scheme is based on relatively new cryptographic assumption of GDH. In this paper we show that a robust multisignature scheme, and thus a robust acknowledgment aggregation, can be done securely based (in ROM) on a more standard cryptographic assumption of hardness of discrete logarithm. Our solution is an improvement on the DL-based multisignature scheme proposed by Micali et al. [MOR01a]. Just as the multisignature of [MOR01a], our scheme is a variant of the Schnorr's signature scheme [Sch89], provably secure (in ROM) under the discrete logarithm assumption. However, by tying together the individual players' commitments in Schnorr signatures with Merkle tree hashes [Mer89], our multisignature scheme has a novel property of *robustness*, because it enables the group of signers to efficiently generate a multisignature even in the presence of (some number of) communication failures between the participating players and/or malicious behavior on the part of (some of) the players. By contrast, the multisignature scheme of [MOR01a] would have to be restarted from scratch in the case of a single communication or node fault during a multisignature generation protocol.

Our robust multisignature scheme is provably secure only for a limited number of faults t. Specifically, if q is the size of the multiplicative group this discrete-log scheme is instantiated with and n is the maximum number of players allowed to participate in the multisignature generation protocol, then our scheme is secure as long as quantity $S_{t,n}/q$ is negligible, where $S_{t,n}$ is a sum of consecutive combinations, $S_{t,n} = \binom{n}{0} + \binom{n}{1} + \ldots + \binom{n}{t}$. Although we do not see any attack on our scheme for larger values of n and t, our proof of security does not extend beyond these limitations, and an existence of a discrete-log multisignature scheme which is robust (without having to re-start the generation protocol) against any number of faults remains an open problem. However, we note that our scheme works for parameters like $(q, n, t) = (2^{1024}, 2^{10}, 100)$, which should be useful in practice. Furthermore, note that the if the number of faults t crosses the above limit the multisignature protocol fails and needs to be restarted for the remaining players, hence the above bounds really limit only the robustness property, and not security.

The robustness property we introduce to Schnorr-based multisignatures comes either at no extra communication cost, or at a modest communication cost increase, depending on the communication medium connecting the players. In the case when the players communicate in a ring as in [MOR01b], the total communication cost grows from $O(n)$ group elements to $O(n \log n)$. If the players communicate via a reliable broadcast medium, as in [MOR01a], then the communication costs do not change. Finally, if the players communicate via a multicast tree, as is the case in our application of multisignatures to multicast acknowledgement aggregation, the total communication cost is $O(n + t(\log n)^2)$ group elements, where t is the number of faults. This is the communication setting in which we will describe our multisignature scheme, but the scheme is applicable to the other settings as well.

When we apply our multisignatures to multicast acknowledgement aggregation, the comparison of the resulting scheme to that of Nicolosi and Mazieres [NM04] is as follows. Assuming that the source shares symmetric keys with the receivers, if no *malicious* node faults occur then our scheme can run in an "optimistic" mode which provides an all-or-nothing verification of aggregated acknowledgments and matches the communication cost of the scheme of Nicolosi and Mazieres, i.e. it takes one round of communication and total bandwidth of $O(n)$ group elements, where n is the size of the multicast group. Moreover, our scheme has a smaller *computational* overhead because we avoid the pairing operations used in the GDH-based scheme of [NM04]. In the case of malicious node faults, our robustness mechanisms kick in and the scheme takes three communication rounds, and the total bandwidth grows to $O(n + t(\log n)^2)$ bandwidth where t is the number of faults, whereas the scheme of [NM04] takes only one round and the total bandwidth remains $O(n)$. Our scheme is therefore most applicable when the number of malicious faults and link failures is moderate, which we believe is the case for many applications.

Limitations of Current Multisignature Schemes. We point out that the multisignature scheme we propose continues to suffer from the problem identified by Micali et al., a problem which is shared by both the scheme of Micali et al. and by the scheme of Boldyreva. Namely, none of these schemes, including ours, is known to be secure without special requirements on the generation of the participants' public keys. Micali et al. list a number of such possible requirements on the key-generation process (see esp. [MOR01b]), which apply equally to the scheme of Micali et al., Boldyreva, and ours, but we will mention here only two.

The first requirement under which all three schemes are provably secure is the assumption that *all* certificate authorities who certify the participants' public keys are first of all honest, and second, that they verify a zero-knowledge proof of knowledge of the private key when certifying some user's private key. As pointed out in [MOR01a], this requirement makes delegation problematic, disallows self-delegation completely, and is probably sensible only when all certificates are signed by very few completely trusted entities. The second possible requirement is that all participants generate and certify their public keys in a special distributed protocol. While this requirement avoids trusted third parties completely, it is applicable only to small groups, and is unsuitable for general public key infrastructure.

Moreover, unlike in the scheme of Boldyreva but like in the scheme of Micali et al., we will require that the players involved in the multisignature generation protocol take as input the set G of players (potentially) participating in this protocol.

However, while these limitations remain a serious problem for general applications of multisignatures, they do not influence the application of multisignatures to multicast acknowledgement aggregation. In this application we can assume not only that all participants' keys are certified by a single trusted certification authority, but we can in fact simply give everyone's private key to this authority. Therefore in the subsequent sections we choose to present our multisignature scheme assuming a single trusted certification authority. Similarly, in the multicast acknowledgement aggregation application it can be safely assumed that the intended set of recipients G who would participate in the multisignature generation can be known to each of the participants.

Paper Organization: In the next section we describe the proposed multisignature scheme. In section 3 we describe its optimized variant suited to multicast acknowledgement aggregation. Finally, in section 4 we sketch the security proof for our scheme.

2   A Robust Discrete-Log Based Multisignature Scheme

2.1   Computational Setting and Initialization

We propose a multisignature scheme based on an extension of the Schnorr signature scheme [Sch89]. We assume common parameters (p, q, g) where p, q are large primes and g is an element of order q in $\mathbb{Z}_p^*$. As in the Schnorr signature scheme we assume a hash function $h : \{0,1\}^* \rightarrow \mathbb{Z}_q$, which we will model as a random oracle. All equations involving multiplication or exponentiation are meant modulo p.

As mentioned in the introduction, we will assume a single trusted Certification Authority who signs all participants' public keys. We will describe our multisignature scheme using the application to acknowledgment aggregation as a context. Namely, we assume that the group of players who are potential participants in the multisignature generation are multicast group members, and that they are logically organized in a binary tree, with the group members represented as the leaves of the delivery tree, the intermediary tree nodes occupied by the multicast delivery network, and the multicast source S at the root. We note, however, that the scheme is generally applicable, in which case the tree data structure needs to be computed by the participating players, and both the intermediary nodes and the "source" node will be just special functions played by the players to whom the data structure assigns these roles.

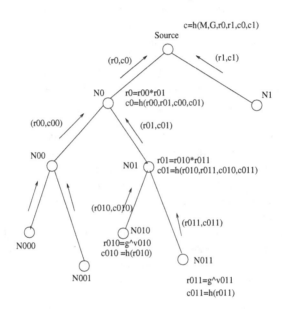

Fig. 1. Computation of the Merkle Tree

We denote the left and right children of S as N_0 and N_1. More generally, the left and right children of N_i are defined as N_{i0} and N_{i1} (see Figure 1 for example). Each member N_i randomly selects its secret key $x_i \in [0, q-1]$ and sets its public key $y_i = g^{x_i}$. As discussed in the introduction, under the assumption of a single trusted CA, the proof of security requires that during the registration of the public key y_i a player must pass a zero knowledge proof of possession of the discrete logarithm $x_i = DL_g(y_i)$.[3] When our scheme is used for efficient acknowledgment aggregation, the trusted source can either check each player's ZK proof, or, to support the "optimistic" mode of the protocol operation, the source simply picks N_i's secret x_i himself and shares it with the player.

---

[3] If no trusted CA's can be assumed, to assuage the problem of concurrent composition of such proofs, our multisignature scheme would have to generate all public keys simultaneously, in a distributed protocol proposed by [MOR01a].

We assume that each node N_i knows the public keys of all members (tree leaves) in the subtree rooted at N_i. Each node can also aggregate the keys of all the members in his subtree. The aggregated public key y_i is computed as $y_i = y_{i0} * y_{i1}$, where y_{i0}, y_{i1} are (possibly aggregated) public keys of N_i's children.

2.2   Overview of the Scheme

In the original Schnorr signature the signature on message M under key $y = g^x$ is generated by taking one-time "commitment" $r = g^v$ for random $v \in [0, q-1]$, computing the challenge $c = h(m, r)$, and issuing a response $z = v + cx \bmod q$. The signature is then a pair (r, z) s.t. $g^z = ry^c \bmod p$ and $c = h(m, r)$. Micali et al., aggregate such signatures, i.e. pairs (r_i, z_i) produced by members of some group G, by running a 3-stage protocol: In the first phase everyone *broadcasts* its $r_i = g^{v_i}$, all players combine $r = \prod_{i \in G} r_i$, compute $c = h(m, r)$, each player broadcasts $z_i = v_i + cx_i$ and (c, z) where $z = \sum_{i \in G} z_i$ is a Schnorr multisignature for group G, with $y = \prod_{i \in G} y_i$ as a verification key.[4]

However, this solution is not robust in the face of node and link failures during the computation of the multisignature. For example, if any node first sends a commitment r_i but fails to send a valid response z_i, the multisignature has to be recomputed from scratch. To alleviate this problem, instead of hashing a simple product of all r_i's as above, we compute the challenge c via a Merkle Tree-like [Mer89] aggregation of the r_i values.[5] Because a Merkle Tree is a commitment to all the r_i's, the resulting challenge c is meaningful for all subsets of r_i's that were used to create it. Therefore the challenge can be used for a multisignature involving those and only those players that respond to it with proper z_i's. We note that the Merkle tree we construct is not exactly standard because we fold into it the intermediary values r_i, which allows for a more efficient handling of network or malicious faults occurring in the protocol. The exact computation of the Merkle Tree is illustrated in Figure 1.

2.3   The Multisignature Generation Protocol

Our multisignature generation protocol has 3 stages. Each player always stores all the information passing through it. As in the scheme of Micali et al. [MOR01a], for the sake of provable security we forbid the players to participate in more than one instance of this protocol at a time. Moreover, as in the scheme of Micali et al., we also require that each participant is informed about the (potential, in our case) set of participants G willing to sign the same message M.

---

[4] In the fuller version [MOR01b] of their work the authors show that the same scheme works also without broadcast, for example if the players communicate in a ring-like fashion. However, that version of the protocol is similarly not robust.

[5] We note that Micali et al. use a Merkle Tree in the key generation protocol, but they use it to enable provable security in the absence of a trusted CA, while we use it in the multisignature generation protocol instead, to enable its robustness.

Stage 1: Each member N_i that receives M randomly selects $v_i \in [0, q-1]$ and sends to its parent the commitment $r_i = g^{v_i}$ and the *partial* challenge $c_i = h(r_i)$. A node N_j that receives two commitments and partial challenges $\{r_{j0}, c_{j0}\}$ and $\{r_{j1}, c_{j1}\}$ from its two children, N_{j0} and N_{j1}, stores these values, generates its own commitment and partial challenge $r_j = r_{j0} * r_{j1}$ and $c_j = h(r_{j0}, r_{j1}, c_{j0}, c_{j1})$. It then forwards $\{r_j, c_j\}$ to its parent, as illustrated in Figure 1. Each N_i also passes up the identities of nodes in N_i's subtree which participated in the protocol. If some node N_j on the tree does not send correct values to its parent, the parent assigns $r_j = 1$ and $c_j = 0$.

Stage 2: When the source receives the two tuples $\{r_0, c_0\}$ and $\{r_1, c_1\}$ from its two children N_0 and N_1, it computes $r = r_0 * r_1$ and the challenge $c = h(M, G, r_0, r_1, c_0, c_1)$. It then sends (c, r_1, c_1) to N_0 and (c, r_0, c_0) to N_1. N_0 then sends $(c, r_1, c_1, r_{01}, c_{01})$ to N_{00} and $(c, r_1, c_1, r_{00}, c_{00})$ to N_{01} and so on. Figure 2 shows an example of how the challenge c is propagated from the source to the members.

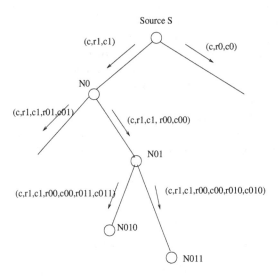

Fig. 2. Transmission of the challenge value c

As a result of this process, each member N_j receives the challenge c and the values $copath_j = \{(r_i, c_i)\}$ on its *co-path* to the root c of the Merkle tree. Every N_j can then reconstruct values $path_j = \{(r_i, c_i)\}$ that lie on its *path* to the root, and verify that c is correct. We denote this operation as checking if $c = h_{MHT}(M, G, r_j, copath_j)$. For example, N_{011} receives values c and $copath_{011} = \{(r_{010}, c_{010}), (r_{00}, c_{00}), (r_1, c_1)\}$. The verification if $c = h_{MHT}(M, G, r_{011}, copath_{011})$ consists of recomputing $r_{01} = r_{010} * r_{011}$ and $c_{01} = h(r_{010}, r_{011}, c_{010}, c_{011})$, $r_0 = r_{00} * r_{01}$ and $c_0 = h(r_{00}, r_{01}, c_{00}, c_{01})$, and checking if $c = h(M, G, r_0, r_1, c_0, c_1)$.

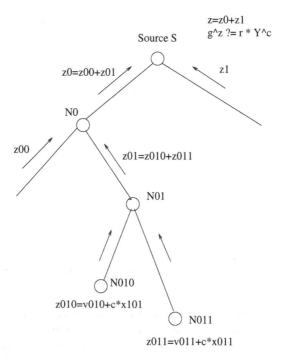

Fig. 3. Default propogation of the responses z_i

Stage 3: If the challenge c verifies, each signer N_i sends back its response $z_i = v_i + c * x_i \mod q$. An intermediary node N_j that receives values z_{j0} and z_{j1} from its two children verifies each of them by checking that $g^{z_{j0}} = r_{j0} * (y_{j0})^c$ and $g^{z_{j1}} = r_{j1} * (y_{j1})^c$. If the equations verify, N_j forwards to its parent the aggregated value $z_j = z_{j0} + z_{j1} \mod q$, and so on until the aggregated $z = z_0 + z_1$ value reaches the source, as illustrated in Figure 3.

If one of the signatures is incorrect (let's say z_{j1}), N_j sets z_j to z_{j0} instead of $z_{j0} + z_{j1}$, and sends $(z_j, r_{j0}, r_{j1}, c_{j0}, c_{j1})$ to its parent. The parent, let's say N_k such that $j = k1$, can perform two checks: (1) N_k can check if $g^{z_j} = r_j/r_{j1} * (y_j/y_{j1})^c$; and (2) N_k can check if $h(r_{j0}, r_{j1}, c_{j0}, c_{j1})$ is equal to c_j given to N_k by N_j in stage 1 of the protocol.

In general, each intermediary node N_j passes up a set $\mathcal{M}_j$ of pairs $(r_i, copath_i)$ where each r_i is a (possibly accumulated) value corresponding to players which have not delivered a valid z_i response, either due to communication failure or a malicious fault. Each node N_k upon receiving these messages first performs the following tests for both its branches $b = 0$ and $b = 1$:

1. N_k sets $r'_{kb} = r_{kb}/(\prod_{i \in \mathcal{M}_{kb}} r_i)$ and $y'_{kb} = y_{kb}/(\prod_{i \in \mathcal{M}_{kb}} y_i)$ and checks if $g^{z_{kb}} = r'_{kb} * (y'_{kb})^c$.
2. N_k checks if $c = h_{MHT}(M, G, r_i, copath_i)$ for each $i \in \mathcal{M}_{kb}$.

If everything verifies, N_k passes up $z_k = z_{k0} + z_{k1}$ and $\mathcal{M}_k = \mathcal{M}_{k0} \cup \mathcal{M}_{k1}$. In case of a failure in branch b, N_k passes up only the correct values, i.e. $z_k = z_{k\bar{b}}$,

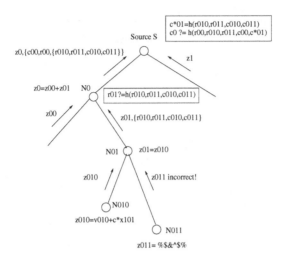

Fig. 4. Propagation of responses z_i in case of faults

and passes up the set of the missing values as $\mathcal{M}_k = \mathcal{M}_{k\bar{b}} \cup \{(r_{kb}, copath_{kb})\}$. If both branches fail, N_k passes up just $\mathcal{M}_k = \{(r_k, copath_k)\}$.

Figure 4 illustrated this step when one of the member's signature is incorrect. In this example, N_{01} detects that the signature generated by N_{011} is incorrect because $g^{z_{011}} \neq r_{011} * y_{011}^c$. N_{01} then sets z_{01} to z_{010} and forwards the message $\{z_{01}, r_{010}, r_{011}, c_{010}, c_{011}\}$ to its parent N_0. N_0 then computes $c_{01}^* = h(r_{010}, r_{011}c_{010}, c_{011})$. If c_{01}^* is equal to the value committed by N_{01} in the first stage of the protocol, then N_0 can verify if the signature z_{01} is correct by checking whether $g^{z_{01}} = r_{01}/r_{011} * (y_{01}/y_{011})^c$.

2.4   Multisignature Verification

We call σ a multisignature on message M issued by the group $G \setminus \mathcal{M}$ if

$$\sigma = [z, (r_0, r_1, c_0, c_1), \mathcal{M}, \{(r_i, copath_i)\}_{i \in \mathcal{M}}]$$

such that:

$$g^z = \left(\frac{r}{\prod_{i \in \mathcal{M}} r_i}\right) * \left(\prod_{i \in G \setminus \mathcal{M}} y_i\right)^c$$

where

$$c = h(M, G, r_0, r_1, c_0, c_1)$$
$$r = r_0 * r_1$$

and moreover:

1. $c = h_{MHT}(M, G, r_i, copath_i)$ for each $i \in \mathcal{M}$, and all the co-paths contain values (r_0, r_1, c_0, c_1) in the appropriate places
2. $|G| \leq n_{max}$, and the number of *individual participants* (implicitly) specified by the missing set $\mathcal{M}$ is smaller or equal to t_{max}

Importantly, the criterion in point 2 above limits the number of the missing *individual participants* represented by the $\mathcal{M}$ set, and not the *size* of that set, i.e. the number of (possibly aggregated) r_i values supplied in $\{(r_i, copath_i)\}_{i \in \mathcal{M}}$.

The values n_{max}, t_{max} are set so quantity $S_{t_{max}, n_{max}}/q$ is negligible, e.g. less than 2^{-80}, where $S_{t,n} = \binom{n}{0} + \binom{n}{1} + \ldots + \binom{n}{t}$.

3   A "MultiMAC" Variant of the Multisignature Scheme

If acknowledgment non-repudiation is not required, the multicast source can have a copy of each participant's private key, in which case our aggregation scheme can be called "multiMAC" rather than a multisignature. Moreover, while the basic scheme described above requires three stages of communication, its MultiMAC variant can run in an "optimistic" fashion, which requires only one communication stage if none of the intermediary nodes acts maliciously. Since this is very likely to be the common case of operation, the communication cost of the resulting solution matches the cost of the scheme of Nicolosi and Mazieres.

In this variant, each member has a unique secret key x_i shared with the source. We assume that each such key is agreed upon or distributed at the time when the member joins the source's multicast group. Knowing all such keys, the source can add them all up and obtain the aggregated key for any group G of players, $x_G = \sum_{i \in G} x_i$. When a member N_i receives a message M from the source, it replies by sending the acknowledgment $ack_i = m^{x_i}$, where $m = h(M)$, to its parent N_k, which, in turn, multiplies the acknowledgments of its children and sends the resulting aggregated message $ack_i = ack_{i0} * ack_{i1}$ to its parent. The parent also passes up the identities of players that participated in the acknowledgment in his subtree. If most members usually do participate, the parent can instead attach a vector identifying all subtree members who do not participate. When the source computes the final aggregated acknowledgment $ack = ack_0 * ack_1$ and combines the sets of participating members sets into one set G, it can verify if all these members indeed acknowledge receipt of M by checking whether $ack = h(M)^{x_G}$.

Note that this "optimized" protocol by itself is secure but not robust against malicious faults. It is, however, robust against non-malicious communication faults. Note also that to save memory, the source could pick all the members' keys as $x_k = h(s, k)$ where s is the source's short secret. In this way the source would not have to store all the secrets keys since it can easily retrieve each of them.

The optimization allows the source to verify the aggregated acknowledgment in one stage. However, this solution is not robust since, if the aggregated acknowledgment is invalid, the source is unable to identify the malicious member(s). We therefore propose to combine the two schemes by piggybacking the commitment of the basic scheme with the authenticators of the second scheme. As a result, the source can verify – in one stage – the aggregated acknowledgment. If this acknowledgment is incorrect, *Stage 2* and *Stage 3* of the basic scheme can be executed to trace the malicious nodes and robustly compute the desired multisignature.

4   Security Analysis of the New Multisignature Scheme

We briefly recall the definition of security for a multisignature scheme given by Micali et al. [MOR01a]. The adversary A can corrupt any group member at any time, and he conducts a *chosen message and subgroup* attack, i.e. he specifies the message M and the subgroup of players G which participate in the multisignature generation protocol, and then gets to participate in the multisignature generation protocol involving group G and message M.

Definition 1. ([MOR01a]) *We say that a multisignature scheme is secure if every efficient adversary A which stages a chosen message and subgroup attack against the multisignature scheme has at best negligible chance of outputting triple (M, G, σ) s.t. (1) σ is a valid multisignature on M issued by the group G, and (2) there exists an uncorrupted player N_{i*} in G who has never been asked by A to participate in a multisignature protocol on M.*

The multisignature scheme resulting from the addition of the optimistic "multiMAC" protocol as explained in section 3, is similar enough to the basic scheme of section 2 that its security proof follows very simply from the security proof for the basic multisignature scheme, given below.

Theorem 1. *The multisignature scheme described in Section 2 is secure in the Random Oracle Model under the Discrete Logarithm assumption.*

Proof. The proof goes by exhibiting a simulator S which, with sizable probability, converts a successful attack algorithm A against our new multisignature scheme into an algorithm that computes discrete logarithms. The simulation of this scheme is very similar to the simulation of the Schnorr signature scheme, although it is less efficient, and hence the exact security of our scheme is not optimal. However, a similar degradation, although for a different reason, is suffered by the exact security of the multisignature scheme of [MOR01a]. The simulator's goal is to compute, on input a random y in $\mathbb{Z}_p^*$ a discrete logarithm $x = DL_g(y)$. Without loss of generality we can assume that the adversary forges a multisignature issued by players $G = \{1, \ldots, n\}$, all of whose members are corrupted except of player N_n, on some message M which N_n is never ask to sign. (This assumption does not hold if the adversary is adaptive, but the same proof holds there too, except that the simulator has to guess the identity of an uncorrupted player against whom the forgery claim is made.) The simulator assigns $y_n = y$ as the public key of N_n, while it picks the private keys x_i of *all the other players* at random.

Since S knows the private data of all uncorrupted players except for N_n, the only thing that the simulator needs to simulate are N_n's responses. This is done similarly as in the Pointcheval and Stern's proof [PS96] of security of Schnorr signatures, except that as in the security proof [MOR01b] of the Schnorr-based multisignature scheme of Micali et al., the simulator will need to rewind the adversary in this simulation. Namely, when N_n is asked to participate in the multisignature generation on message M, S picks c and z_n at random in $\mathbb{Z}_q$, outputs value $r_n = g^{z_n} y_n^{-c}$, and then embeds c in the answer to *one* of the A's queries (M, r_0, r_1, c_0, c_1) to the h oracle. If this is not the c that comes down to N_n in the second stage of the protocol together with some co-path $copath_n$ such that $c = h_{MHT}(M, G, r_n, copath_n)$, then S cannot proceed and the simulation has to wind back to right after N_n outputs his commitment r_n. (Note that the Merkle Tree hashing does not help us here in any obvious way because the adversary can still try any number of values $r_1, \ldots, r_{n-1}$ he likes, form them together with r_n into many different Merkle Tree hash constructions, and pick any of the resulting c values.) If q_h is the maximal number of hash queries made by A, this trial and error procedure will eventually succeed in expected number of at most q_h repeats,[6] which will slow the Schnorr-like simulation of this signature process by only a polynomial factor. (We crucially use here the assumption that the players do not participate in two multisignature protocol instances at the same time.) When S is finally lucky and the right c comes down to N_n, the simulator outputs its prepared answer z_n.

Thus the simulation proceeds slowly but surely, and A eventually creates a valid multisignature involving N_n with non-negligible probability. Similarly as in the "forking lemma" proof of [PS96], we can argue that with high enough probability it is the case that if A uses some values $(M, G, (r_0, r_1, c_0, c_1))$ in this forgery, then A has a high enough probability of forging a message using the same tuple of values, where the probability is taken over all the remaining randomness used by the simulator in answering A's oracle queries, *including* the randomness c used in answering the very query $c = h(M, G, r_0, r_1, c_0, c_1)$. Thus, following the "forking lemma" technique, the simulator re-runs the adversary A from the point of this query on, each time using fresh randomness and thus answering this query with a fresh random value c. In any successful round of such rewinding, the simulator gets a forgery which consists of:

1. set $\mathcal{M}$ such that the number of individual participants implicitly specified by this set is no more than t_{max}
   (For simplicity, we will use $\mathcal{M}$ here to describe this set of participants; Note that then $\mathcal{M} \subseteq G$ and $n \notin \mathcal{M}$.)
2. a set of pairs $\{(r_i, copath_i)\}_{i \in \mathcal{M}}$ s.t. for every $i \in \mathcal{M}$ we have $c = h_{MHT}(M, G, r_i, copath_i)$, and all the co-paths $copath_i$ contain values that match value (r_0, r_1, c_0, c_1) above
3. value z s.t. $g^z = r/r_{\mathcal{M}} * (y_n \bar{y}/y_{\mathcal{M}})^c$, where $r = r_0 * r_1$, $r_{\mathcal{M}} = \prod_{i \in \mathcal{M}} r_i$, $\bar{y} = \prod_{i \in G \setminus \{n\}} y_i$, and $y_{\mathcal{M}} = \prod_{i \in \mathcal{M}} y_i$

---

[6] Thanks to the Merkle Tree hashing, this bound can be improved to q_h/n.

Note that if there are n members in G then there can be at most n values r_i which the adversary can "open" in item (2) above, unless A finds a collision in the hash function, but that can happen only with negligible probability in ROM.

Let's denote $v = DL(r)$ where $r = r_0 * r_1$, $v_i = DL(r_i)$ for $i = 1, .., n$, $x_n = DL(y_n)$, and $\bar{x} = \sum_{i \in G \setminus \{n\}} x_i$. Then the condition in item (3) translates into a linear equation on $n + 2$ unknowns $v, v_1, \ldots, v_n, x_n$:

$$z = v - \sum_{i \in \mathcal{M}} v_i + c(x_n + \bar{x} - \sum_{i \in \mathcal{M}} x_i) \bmod q \qquad (1)$$

For every successful round of such re-run of A, the simulator gets another equation of type (1). Once the simulator gets $n + 2$ of such equations then with an overwhelming probability it can can solve for x_n (and thus answer its DLP challenge). This is because for every choice of membership in the set $\mathcal{M}$, there is at most one c which can make the new equation linearly dependent on the previous ones. Thus the number of c's which can possibly make the new equation dependent on the previous ones is at most $S_{t,n}$. Since c is chosen at random, if $S_{t,n} \ll q$ and n is polynomial in the security parameter then the probability that any of the $n + 2$ equations is linearly dependent on the previous ones is negligible.

The necessity of rewinding A creates a polynomial factor blow-up in the running time of the simulation. However, it is not substantially worse then the blow-up encountered in the security argument for the regular Schnorr signature scheme, because the expected number of simulation rewindings that leads to a single successful forgery is the same as in Schnorr signatures, and since we need $n + 2$ successes, our simulation running time will only grow by the additional factor of $n + 2$.

References

[BGLS03]   D. Boneh, C. Gentry, B. Lynn, and H. Shacham. Aggregate and verifiable encrypted signatures from bilinear maps. In *Advances in Cryptology - Eurocrypt 2003*, 2003.

[BLS01]   Dan Boneh, Ben Lynn, and Hovav Shacham. Short Signatures from the Weil Pairing. In Colin Boyd, editor, *ASIACRYPT'01*, pages 514–532, 2001.

[Bol03]   A. Boldyreva. Efficient threshold signatures, multisignatures and blind signatures based on the gap-diffie-hellman-group signature scheme. In *Public Key Cryptography 2003*, 2003.

[Gag02]   Martin Gagne. Applications of bilinear maps in cryptography. Master's thesis, University of Waterloo, 2002.

[IN83]   K. Itakura and K. Nakamura. A public-key cryptosystem suitable for digital multisignatures. In *NEC Research and Development (71):1-8*, October 1983.

[Jou02]   A. Joux. The weil and tate pairings as building blocks for public key cryptosystems. In *Proceedings of the 5th International Symposium on Algorithmic Number Theory*, 2002.

[Mer89]   Ralph C. Merkle. A certified digital signature. In *Advances in Cryptology - CRYPTO 1989*, 1989.

[MOR01a]   S. Micali, K. Ohta, and L. Reyzin. Accountable-subgroup multisignatures. In *ACM Conference on Computer and Communications Security*, October 2001.

[MOR01b]   S. Micali, K. Ohta, and L. Reyzin. Accountable-subgroup multisignatures. available from *www.cs.bu.edu/~reyzin/research.html*, 2001.

[NM04]   A. Nicolosi and D. Mazieres. Secure acknowledgement of multicast messages in open peer-to-peer networks. In *3rd International Workshop on Peer-to-Peer Systems (IPTPS '04)*, San Diego, CA, February 2004.

[PS96]   D. Pointcheval and J. Stern. Security proofs for signature schemes. In *Advances in Cryptology - Eurocrypt 1996*, pages 387 – 398, 1996.

[Sch89]   C. Schnorr. Efficient identification and signatures for smart cards. In *Advances in Cryptology - CRYPTO 1989*, Santa Barbara, CA, August 1989.

Efficient Key Encapsulation to Multiple Parties

N.P. Smart

Dept. Computer Science, University of Bristol,
Merchant Venturer's Building, Woodland Road,
Bristol, BS8 1UB, United Kingdom
nigel@cs.bris.ac.uk

Abstract. We present the notion of an mKEM, which is a Key Encapsulation Mechanism (KEM) which takes multiple public keys as input. This has applications where one wishes to encrypt a single large document to a set of multiple recipients, as when one sends an encrypted email to more than one person. We present a security definition and show that the naive approach to implementing an mKEM is secure under this definition. We then go on to present a more efficient construction of an mKEM, which is secure in the random oracle model.

1 Introduction

Public key cryptography has been traditionally concerned with two parties communicating. In the traditional scenario one party, Alice, wishes to communicate securely with one other party, Bob. Alice obtains Bob's authentic public key and then encrypts the data she wishes to send to Bob. Bob, knowing the associated private key, is able to decrypt the ciphertext to obtain Alice's message. Since public key algorithms are very slow, if Alice wishes to send a large amount of data she first encrypts a per message symmetric "session key" to Bob using Bob's public key algorithm and then encrypts the actual data using a fast symmetric cipher keyed by the session key. Such a combination of public key and symmetric techniques is called a hybrid encryption algorithm.

This hybrid technique has been strengthened in recent years with the use of the KEM-DEM philosophy, see [4] and [5]. In this approach to hybrid encryption one defines a symmetric data encapsulation mechanism (DEM) which takes a key K and a message M and computes

$$C \leftarrow DEM_K(M).$$

Given knowledge of K one can also recover M via

$$M \leftarrow DEM_K^{-1}(C).$$

To transport the key K to the recipient of the ciphertext the sender uses a key encapsulation mechanism (KEM). This is an algorithm which takes as input a public key pk and outputs a session key K plus an encapsulation E of this session key under the public key,

$$(K, E) \leftarrow KEM(\text{pk}).$$

C. Blundo and S. Cimato (Eds.): SCN 2004, LNCS 3352, pp. 208–219, 2005.

Notice, that the session key is not used as input to the KEM. The recipient recovers the key K using his private key sk via the decapsulation mechanism

$$K \leftarrow KEM^{-1}(E, \mathsf{sk}).$$

The full ciphertext of the message M is then given by

$$E \| C.$$

The use of the KEM-DEM philosophy allows the different components of a hybrid encryption scheme to be designed in isolation, leading to a simpler analysis and hopefully more efficient schemes.

However, as soon as one moves away from the traditional two-party setting problems occur. Suppose Alice now wishes to send a large file to two parties (say Bob and Charlie), for example she may wish to encrypt an email to Bob and Charlie, or encrypt a file on her system such that either Bob or Charlie can decrypt it. ¿From one's own experience one notices that very few emails are sent to a single recipient, hence such a one-to-many model is clearly of importance.

A number of possible solutions exist to this problem. All of which have disadvantages. In the first naive solution one simply encrypts the data twice, once for Bob and once for Charlie, using their respective public key schemes. This is clearly wasteful especially if the data to be encrypted is large. A more efficient solution would be to encrypt the data once with a symmetric encryption key K and then encrypt this key under Bob and Charlie's public keys, i.e. the ciphertext would look like

$$\mathcal{E}_{\mathrm{pk}_B}(K) \| \mathcal{E}_{\mathrm{pk}_C}(K) \| \mathcal{E}_K(M).$$

Whilst this is probably sufficient for two users, this can become very expensive for a large number of users.

In addition it is unclear what security definition one is using for such a scheme. The work of Bellare, Boldyreva and Micali [2] looks at the security of encryption schemes in the presence of many users but did not consider the fact that a "ciphertext" could correspond to different users. In their definition the above hybrid encryption to two parties would be considered as two encryptions, whereas we wish to treat it as a single encryption.

The use of the KEM-DEM philosophy in such a situation is also not applicable. After all the KEM produces the session key, hence application of a KEM for two users would result in two different session keys. What is required is a KEM like construction which takes as input n public keys and outputs a session key and an encapsulation of that session key under each of the input public keys. We would like such a multiple KEM (or mKEM) which is more efficient than the above concatenation of public key encryptions of a session key.

In this paper we propose such mKEMs and propose a security definition for them. We show that the above naive concatenation method is secure, in the standard model, under this definition, although inefficient. We then present a public key mKEM based on the Diffie–Hellman problem which is more efficient than repeated encryption of a session key using an analogous traditional public key system, yet is still secure in the random oracle model under the proposed security definition.

2   Notation

We let $v \leftarrow u$ for variables v and u to denote assignment. For a set S we let $v \leftarrow S$ denote the variable v being assigned the set S and $v \xleftarrow{R} S$ to denote v being assigned an element of the set S chosen uniformly at random.

If A is a, possibly probabilistic, algorithm then $v \leftarrow A$ denotes v being assigned the output of algorithm A with the probability distribution induced by A's input and internal random choices. If we wish to make explicit precisely what value r is used as the randomness in a probabilistic algorithm $A(x)$ with input x we write $A(x; r)$.

A function f is said to be negligible if for all polynomials p there exists a constant N_p such that $f(x) \leq \frac{1}{p(x)}$ for all $x \geq N_p$.

3   Security of a KEM

A KEM (key encapsulation mechanism) is a public key scheme which allows a sender to generate an encryption of a random session key, and allows the holder of the correct private key to recover the session key from the ciphertext. We let $\mathbb{D}$ denote a set of domain parameters which could consist of only the security parameter k written in unary 1^k, or could consist of a public group and generator as in ElGamal systems.

More formally we define a KEM [4] is a triple of algorithms:

- $\mathcal{G}_{KEM}(\mathbb{D})$ which is a probabilistic key generation algorithm. On input of $\mathbb{D}$ this algorithm outputs a public/private key pair $(\mathbf{pk}, \mathbf{sk})$.
- $\mathcal{E}_{KEM}(\mathbf{pk})$ which is a probabilistic encapsulation algorithm. On input of a public key $\mathbf{pk}$ this algorithm outputs an encapsulated key-pair (K, C), where $K \in \mathbb{K}$ is the session key and C is an encapsulation of the key K under the public key $\mathbf{pk}$. In other words C is a ciphertext of the message K. We assume that the space $\mathbb{K}$ of all keys output by $\mathcal{E}$ are of some fixed length.
- $\mathcal{D}_{KEM}(C, \mathbf{sk})$ which is a decapsulation algorithm. This takes as input an encapsulation C and a private key $\mathbf{sk}$ and outputs a key K or a special symbol $\perp$ representing the case where C is an invalid encapsulation with respect to the private key $\mathbf{sk}$.

For such a scheme to be useful we require that it is complete in the following sense,

$$\Pr\left((\mathbf{pk}, \mathbf{sk}) \leftarrow \mathcal{G}_{KEM}(\mathbb{D}), (K, C) \leftarrow \mathcal{E}_{KEM}(\mathbf{pk}) : K = \mathcal{D}_{KEM}(C, \mathbf{sk})\right) = 1.$$

Security of a KEM is defined in the following way. We assume an adversary $\mathcal{A}$ which runs in two stages. In the first stage it is allowed to produce encapsulations and (depending on the precise security definition we require) it may be allowed access to a decapsulation oracle on encapsulations of its choosing. At the end of this stage it returns some state information.

In the second stage it is provided with a challenge encapsulation C^*, its state information from the first stage plus two keys K_0 and K_1. The adversaries goal in the second stage is to decide which key K_b is encapsulated by C. In this second stage it may also have access to an decapsulation oracle, but if it does it is not allowed to request the decapsulation of the challenge C^*.

Consider the following game played with such an adversary:

$(\mathsf{pk}, \mathsf{sk}) \leftarrow \mathcal{G}_{KEM}(\mathbb{D}).$
$s \leftarrow \mathcal{A}^1(\mathsf{pk}).$
$b \xleftarrow{R} \{0, 1\}.$
$(K_b, C^*) \leftarrow \mathcal{E}_{KEM}(\mathsf{pk}).$
$K_{1-b} \xleftarrow{R} \mathbb{K}.$
$b' \leftarrow \mathcal{A}^2(C^*, \{K_0, K_1\}, s).$
Output whether $b = b'$.

The adversary is said to win the game if $b = b'$. The advantage of an adversary is defined to be

$$\mathrm{Adv}_{\mathcal{A}} = |\Pr(b = b') - 1/2|.$$

If the maximum advantage over all possible adversaries $\mathcal{A}$ is a negligible function of the security parameter k then we say that the KEM is IND-xxx secure, where xxx denotes what access $\mathcal{A}$ is allowed to a decapsulation oracle. If $\mathcal{A}$ is not allowed any access to such an oracle then we say the scheme is IND-CPA secure, if it is only allowed access during stage one then we say the scheme is IND-CCA1 secure and if it is allowed access in both stages (subject to the earlier restriction on requesting the decapsulation of C^*) then we say the scheme is IND-CCA2 secure.

A KEM needs to be used with a DEM (data encapsulation mechanism) to provide a hybrid encryption algorithm. A DEM is a symmetric encryption algorithm which takes a symmetric key k and a message (resp. ciphertext) and provides the corresponding ciphertext (resp. message). Security definitions can be provided for such DEMs, which are independent of the security definition of the associated KEM. In [4] Cramer and Shoup show that a combined KEM-DEM encryption scheme is secure in the standard IND-CCA2 sense (for a public key encryption scheme) if the DEM is secure and the KEM is secure in the IND-CCA2 sense above. Hence, the goal is to define KEM's which are IND-CCA2 secure.

4   Review of Dent's Construction

In this section we recap on some prior work on classical KEM's, in particular a construction of a secure KEM given a public key encryption algorithm which is secure in the sense of OW-CPA [3].

We first turn our attention to probabilistic public key encryption schemes. We formally define these as a triple of algorithms:

- $\mathcal{G}(\mathbb{D})$ which is a probabilistic key generation algorithm. On input of $\mathbb{D}$, the domain parameters, this algorithm outputs a public/private key pair (pk, sk).
- $\mathcal{E}(m, \text{pk})$ which is a probabilistic public key encryption algorithm. On input of a public key pk and a message $m \in \mathcal{M}$ this algorithm output a ciphertext c, it makes use of a random value drawn from a space $\mathcal{R}$.
- $\mathcal{D}(c, \text{sk})$ which is a decryption algorithm. This takes as input a ciphertext c and a private key sk and outputs the associated message m or a special symbol $\perp$ representing the case where c is an invalid ciphertext with respect to the private key sk.

For such a scheme to be useful we require that it is sound in the following sense,

$$\Pr\left((\text{pk}, \text{sk}) \leftarrow \mathcal{G}(\mathbb{D}), m \xleftarrow{R} \mathcal{M}, c \leftarrow \mathcal{E}(m, \text{pk}) : m = \mathcal{D}(c, \text{sk})\right) = 1.$$

We also require that the scheme is truly probabilistic in that the proportion of values of r, used as input into $\mathcal{E}(m, \text{pk}; r)$, that encrypt a given message to a given ciphertext is negligible as a function of the security parameter.

We shall require the security notion of OW-CPA for public key schemes, which we recap on now. We assume an adversary $\mathcal{A}$ which takes a challenge ciphertext c^* and a public key and is asked to produce the associated plaintext. The scheme said to be OW-CPA secure if no adversary exists which wins the following game with probability greater than a negligible function of the security parameter k.

$(\text{pk}, \text{sk}) \leftarrow \mathcal{G}(\mathbb{D})$.
$m \xleftarrow{R} \mathcal{M}$.
$c^* \leftarrow \mathcal{E}(m, \text{pk})$.
$m' \leftarrow \mathcal{A}(\text{pk}, c^*)$.
Output whether $m = m'$.

The adversary is not given access to any decryption oracles, but is clearly allowed to encrypt arbitrary messages of its choice since it has access to pk.

Dent [3] proposes a KEM, derived from a OW-CPA probabilistic public key algorithm $(\mathcal{G}, \mathcal{E}, \mathcal{D})$, a hash function H with codomain $\mathcal{R}$ (the space of randomness used by algorithm $\mathcal{E}$) and a key derivation function KDF with domain $\mathcal{M}$. Dent's scheme is described as follows:

$\mathcal{G}_{KEM}(\mathbb{D})$: $\mathcal{G}_{KEM} = \mathcal{G}$.

$\mathcal{E}_{KEM}(\text{pk})$:
    $m \xleftarrow{R} \mathcal{M}$.
    $r \leftarrow H(m)$.
    $C \leftarrow \mathcal{E}(m, \text{pk}; r)$.
    $K \leftarrow KDF(m)$.
    Output (K, C).

$\mathcal{D}_{KEM}(C, \text{sk})$:
    $m \leftarrow \mathcal{D}(C, \text{sk})$.
    If $m = \perp$ then output $\perp$ and halt.
    $r \leftarrow H(m)$.
    Check that $C = \mathcal{E}(m, \text{pk}; r)$,
        if not output $\perp$ and halt.
    $K \leftarrow KDF(m)$.
    Output K.

One then has the following result, when one models the functions H and KDF as random oracles,

Theorem 1 (Dent [3]). *If $(\mathcal{G}, \mathcal{E}, \mathcal{D})$ is a OW-CPA probabilistic public key encryption algorithm then in the random oracle model the KEM*

$$(\mathcal{G}_{KEM}, \mathcal{E}_{KEM}, \mathcal{D}_{KEM})$$

derived from $(\mathcal{G}, \mathcal{E}, \mathcal{D})$ is secure in the sense of IND-CCA2.

5   mKEMs

We now extend the notion of KEM to deal with the case where one wants to encrypt a large amount of data to multiple people, say n people. In such a situation it makes sense to apply the DEM once and so one requires a mechanism which creates the symmetric key for the DEM and an encapsulation which encapsulates the key to many parties at once. We call such a system an mKEM for "multiple KEM".

Note, a trivial solution would be to generate a session key K for the DEM and then encrypt this to the various intended receivers by encrypting using an IND-CCA2 public key encryption algorithm. This would produce n distinct ciphertexts $c_1, \ldots, c_n$, each encrypting K for n different users. We would then define the key encapsulation as

$$C = c_1 \| c_2 \| \cdots \| c_n.$$

Our goal however is to do this in a more efficient manner, where one measures efficiency either in terms of computing resources or in terms of length of the resulting encapsulation C.

Note, in the above trivial system one would need to specify which ciphertext component c_i corresponded to which user u_i. Hence, the ciphertext should actually contain some information specifying which ciphertext corresponds to which user, i.e. we need to have something like

$$C = u_1 \| c_1 \| u_2 \| c_2 \cdots \| u_n \| c_n.$$

In our future discussion we shall drop this explicit reference to which users which component corresponds to. Instead we shall pass the list of recipients to the decryption function as an optional additional parameter.

Just as for a KEM, we define an mKEM formally as a triple of algorithms, $(\mathcal{G}_{mKEM}, \mathcal{E}_{mKEM}, \mathcal{D}_{mKEM})$, by adapting the earlier definition, we have

- $\mathcal{G}_{mKEM}(\mathbb{D})$ which is a probabilistic key generation algorithm. On input of $\mathbb{D}$, the domain parameters, this algorithm outputs a public/private key pair (pk, sk).
- $\mathcal{E}_{mKEM}(\mathcal{P})$ which is a probabilistic encapsulation algorithm. On input of a set of public key $\mathcal{P} = \{pk_1, \ldots, pk_n\}$ this algorithm outputs an encapsulated key-pair (K, C), where $K \in \mathbb{K}$ is the session key and C is an encapsulation of the key K under the public keys $\{pk_1, \ldots, pk_n\}$.

– $\mathcal{D}_{mKEM}(C, sk, \mathcal{P})$ which is a decapsulation algorithm. This takes as input an encapsulation C and a private key sk, plus optionally the set of all recipients $\mathcal{P}$, and outputs a key K or a special symbol $\perp$ representing the case where C is an invalid encapsulation with respect to the private key sk.

Completeness is now defined as follows.

$$\Pr\left(\begin{array}{l} (\mathrm{pk}_i, \mathrm{sk}_i) \leftarrow \mathcal{G}_{mKEM}(\mathbb{D}) \forall i \in \{1, \ldots, n\} \\ (K, C) \leftarrow \mathcal{E}_{mKEM}(\{\mathrm{pk}_1, \ldots, \mathrm{pk}_n\}), \\ j \stackrel{R}{\leftarrow} \{1, \ldots, n\} \end{array} : K = \mathcal{D}_{mKEM}(C, \mathrm{sk}_j)\right) = 1.$$

Security of an mKEM is defined in a similar manner to a KEM via the following game.

$(\mathrm{pk}_i, \mathrm{sk}_i) \leftarrow \mathcal{G}_{mKEM}(\mathbb{D}) \forall i \in \{1, \ldots, n\}$.
$\mathcal{P}' \leftarrow \{\mathrm{pk}_1, \ldots, \mathrm{pk}_n\}$
$\{s, \mathcal{P}\} \leftarrow \mathcal{A}^1(\mathcal{P}')$, where $\mathcal{P} \subseteq \mathcal{P}'$ and $m = \#\mathcal{P} \leq n$.
$b \stackrel{R}{\leftarrow} \{0, 1\}$.
$(K_b, C^*) \leftarrow \mathcal{E}_{mKEM}(\mathcal{P})$.
$K_{1-b} \stackrel{R}{\leftarrow} \mathbb{K}$.
$b' \leftarrow \mathcal{A}^2(C^*, \{K_0, K_1\}, s)$.
Output whether $b = b'$.

Notice in stage one the adversary picks a set $\mathcal{P}$ of public keys on which it wants to be challenged. Unlike the case of security models for multisignatures we do not allow the adversary to generate their own keys to be challenged on, after all if we allowed the adversary to generate its own public keys to be challenged on it could simply remember the corresponding private keys and decapsulate honestly.

One needs to be careful about the oracle access to the decapsulation oracle. To see why consider our earlier trivial mKEM with two parties, the challenge is given by

$$C^* = c_1 \| c_2.$$

However, using a traditional CCA2 definition of security an adversary could produce the encapsulation

$$C = c_1$$

and ask the decapsulation oracle to return the associated private key. Since $C \neq C^*$ this is a valid oracle query, which would result in the adversary breaking the system. However, we feel such an oracle query is too lenient for our purposes. We therefore restrict decapsulation oracle queries in the second stage to be only allowed if the resulting key is different from the key encapsulated by C^*. Such a restricted oracle access is used in other works to deal with the public key encryption algorithms which suffer from benign malleability, see for example [5].

We say an mKEM is (m, n)-IND-CCA2 secure, for an integers n and m with $m \leq n$, if the advantage of the adversary winning the above game is negligible as a function of the security parameter. We assume the adversary is allowed access to decapsulation oracle queries in both stages, subject to the above restriction on C^*.

6 Constructions of mKEMs

We start this section by giving a generic construction which mirrors the naive construction of the introduction. Then we go on to provide a more efficient construction based on the ElGamal encryption function.

6.1 A Generic Construction

We let $(\mathcal{G}, \mathcal{E}, \mathcal{D})$ denote a public key encryption algorithm which is IND-CCA2 secure, and let KDF denote a key derivation function with domain $\mathcal{M}$.

We define a KEM from $(\mathcal{G}, \mathcal{E}, \mathcal{D})$ as follows, where $\mathcal{M}$ is the message space of $\mathcal{E}$ and $\mathcal{R}$ is the space of randomness used by $\mathcal{E}$,

$\mathcal{G}_{mKEM}(\mathbb{D})$:
   $(\mathbf{sk}, \mathbf{pk}) \leftarrow \mathcal{G}(\mathbb{D})$.
   Output $(\mathbf{pk}, \mathbf{sk})$.

$\mathcal{E}_{mKEM}(\{\mathbf{pk}_1, \ldots, \mathbf{pk}_n\})$:
   $m \xleftarrow{R} \mathcal{M}$.
   $r_i \xleftarrow{R} \mathcal{R}$ for all i.
   $c_i \leftarrow \mathcal{E}(m, \mathbf{pk}_i; r_i)$ for all i.
   $K \leftarrow KDF(m)$.
   $C \leftarrow (c_1, \ldots, c_n)$.
   Output (K, C).

$\mathcal{D}_{mKEM}(C, \mathbf{sk}_i)$:
   Parse C as $(c_1, \ldots, c_n)$.
   $m \leftarrow \mathcal{D}(c_i, \mathbf{sk}_i)$.
   If $m = \perp$ then output $\perp$ and halt.
   $K \leftarrow KDF(m)$.
   Output K.

Theorem 2. *If $(\mathcal{G}, \mathcal{E}, \mathcal{D})$ is IND-CCA2 secure as a public key encryption scheme and n grows as a polynomial function of the security parameter then the mKEM $(\mathcal{G}_{mKEM}, \mathcal{E}_{mKEM}, \mathcal{D}_{mKEM})$ is (m, n)-IND-CCA2 for all $m \leq n$.*

Proof. Since $(\mathcal{G}, \mathcal{E}, \mathcal{D})$ is IND-CCA2 secure as a public key encryption algorithm it is secure in the multi-user setting described in [2].

We recap on the security definition from [2]. The adversary is given n public keys $\mathbf{pk}_1, \ldots, \mathbf{pk}_n$ and is given access to a left-right oracle $\mathcal{O}_{LR}$ which on input of $\{\{m_0, m_1\}, \mathbf{pk}_i\}$ will output the encryption of m_b under $\mathbf{pk}_i$ for some fixed hidden bit b. The adversary is given access to a decryption oracle $\mathcal{O}_D$ for all the public keys $\mathbf{pk}_i$, subject to the constraint it is not allowed to ask for the decryption of the result of a call to the left-right oracle $\mathcal{O}_{LR}$.

We assume an adversary $\mathcal{A}$ against the mKEM $(\mathcal{G}_{mKEM}, \mathcal{E}_{mKEM}, \mathcal{D}_{mKEM})$ and show how one can use this to produce an adversary $\mathcal{B}$ against $(\mathcal{G}, \mathcal{E}, \mathcal{D})$ in the above multi-user setting. Thus we will derive a contradiction.

Algorithm $\mathcal{B}$ takes as input the n public keys $\mathcal{P}' = \{\mathbf{pk}_1, \ldots, \mathbf{pk}_n\}$. These are then passed into algorithm $\mathcal{A}^1$. We answer the decapsulation oracle queries of $\mathcal{A}^1$ using the decryption provided to $\mathcal{B}$ in an obvious way, i.e. on input of $C = (c_1, \ldots, c_n)$ with respect to some public key $\mathbf{pk}_i$ we execute

$m \leftarrow \mathcal{O}_D(c_i, \mathbf{pk}_i)$.
If $m = \perp$ then output $\perp$ and halt.

$K \leftarrow KDF(m)$.
Output K.

Algorithm $\mathcal{A}^1$ eventually will terminate and will return a list of public keys

$$\mathcal{P} = \{\mathrm{pk}_{i_1}, \ldots, \mathrm{pk}_{i_m}\} \subseteq \mathcal{P}',$$

and a state s.

Algorithm $\mathcal{B}$ then computes two random messages $m_0, m_1 \in \mathcal{M}$ and computes $K_0 = KDF(m_0)$ and $K_1 = KDF(m_1)$. Then using the left-right oracles it computes

$$C^* = (c_{i_1}, \ldots, c_{i_m})$$

where

$$c_{i_j} = \mathcal{O}_{LR}(\{m_0, m_1\}, \mathrm{pk}_{i_j}).$$

One then executes $\mathcal{A}^2(C^*, \{K_0, K_1\}, s)$. The decapsulation oracle queries of $\mathcal{A}^2$ are answered as above on noting that any oracle query allowed in the game being played by $\mathcal{A}^2$ will be able to be answered by the oracle provided to $\mathcal{B}$.

Finally $\mathcal{A}^2$ will respond with its guess b' as to the hidden bit b, we let this bit b' be the output of $\mathcal{B}$. If $\mathcal{A}^2$ answers correctly then algorithm $\mathcal{B}$ will also answer correctly.

We note that the KDF function used need have very weak properties in the above construction. Namely, it maps a uniform distribution on its input space into a uniform distribution on its output space. There is no requirement on it being one-way or anything else. This should be constrasted with the construction in the next section where we require that the KDF is modelled as a random oracle.

6.2   An Efficient ElGamal Based mKEM

We now present an efficient mKEM based on the ElGamal encryption algorithm for a group G of prime order $q \approx 2^k$ with generator g. We let $\mathbb{D} = \{q, g, G\}$ denote the domain parameters of the scheme, ElGamal is then given by the triple of algorithms:

$\mathcal{G}(\mathbb{D})$:
$\quad \mathrm{sk} \xleftarrow{R} \mathbb{F}_q^*$.
$\quad \mathrm{pk} \leftarrow g^{\mathrm{sk}}$.
$\quad$ Output $(\mathrm{pk}, \mathrm{sk})$.

$\mathcal{E}(m, \mathrm{pk}; r)$:
$\quad c_1 \leftarrow g^r$.
$\quad c_2 \leftarrow m \cdot \mathrm{pk}^r$.
$\quad$ Output (c_1, c_2).

$\mathcal{D}((c_1, c_2), \mathrm{sk})$:
$\quad m = c_2 / c_1^{\mathrm{sk}}$.
$\quad$ Output m.

This is OW-CPA secure assuming the Diffie–Hellman problem for the group G is hard. Hence, the KEM derived from ElGamal by Dent's construction, is IND-CCA2 secure.

We now derive an mKEM from ElGamal by letting the key generation function be as in standard ElGamal. We then define encapsulation and decapsulation via

$\mathcal{E}_{mKEM}(\{pk_1, \ldots, pk_n\})$:
$\qquad m \xleftarrow{R} G.$
$\qquad r \leftarrow H(m).$
$\qquad c_0 \leftarrow g^r.$
$\qquad c_i \leftarrow m \cdot pk_i^r$ for $i = 1, \ldots, n.$
$\qquad K \leftarrow KDF(m).$
$\qquad C \leftarrow (c_0, c_1, \ldots, c_n).$
$\qquad$ Output $(K, C).$

$\mathcal{D}_{mKEM}(C, sk_i)$:
$\qquad$ Parse C as $(c_0, c_1, \ldots, c_n).$
$\qquad m \leftarrow c_i / c_0^{sk_i}.$
$\qquad r \leftarrow H(m).$
$\qquad$ If $c_0 \neq g^r$ the output $\perp$ and halt.
$\qquad K \leftarrow KDF(m).$
$\qquad$ Output $K.$

Theorem 3. *If n grows as a polynomial function of the security parameter k and the Diffie–Hellman problem in G is hard then, in the random oracle model the above mKEM is secure, for n users, in the sense of (m,n)-IND-CCA2 for mKEMs for all $m \leq n$.*

Proof. We let $(\mathcal{G}_{KEM}, \mathcal{E}_{KEM}, \mathcal{D}_{KEM})$ denote the ordinary KEM derived from the ElGamal system via Dent's transform for OW-CPA probabilistic public key algorithms. It is known, by Theorem 1, that in the random oracle model the scheme $(\mathcal{G}_{KEM}, \mathcal{E}_{KEM}, \mathcal{D}_{KEM})$ is secure in the IND-CCA2 sense assuming the Diffie–Hellman problem is hard.

We let $(\mathcal{G}_{mKEM}, \mathcal{E}_{mKEM}, \mathcal{D}_{mKEM})$ denote our mKEM. We shall assume we have an IND-CCA2 adversary $\mathcal{A}$ against this scheme in the random oracle model which works against n public keys. We shall show how to use $\mathcal{A}$ to create an adversary $\mathcal{B}$ against $(\mathcal{G}_{KEM}, \mathcal{E}_{KEM}, \mathcal{D}_{KEM})$. Since such an adversary is assumed, in the random oracle model, not to exist we can then conclude that $\mathcal{A}$ could not exist either.

We first describe algorithm $\mathcal{B}^1(pk)$. Let $pk_1 = pk$ denote the public key input into algorithm $\mathcal{B}^1$. We first generate some extra public keys via, $k_i \xleftarrow{R} \mathbb{F}_q^*$ and $pk_i = pk \cdot g^{k_i}$, for $i = 2, 3, \ldots, n$. We now pass the set $\mathcal{P}' = \{pk_1, \ldots, pk_n\}$ into $\mathcal{A}^1$. We then obtain a subset $\mathcal{P} \subseteq \mathcal{P}'$ and a state s'. We shall discuss how to answer all decapsulation oracle queries of $\mathcal{A}^1$ later. We let s denote the state

$$s = \{(k_2, pk_2), \ldots, (k_n, pk_n), \mathcal{P}, s'\}$$

and return s as the output of $\mathcal{B}^1(pk)$.

Algorithm $\mathcal{B}^2$ takes as input two keys K_0 and K_1, the state information s and an encapsulation C^* of one of the keys $K_b \in \{K_0, K_1\}$ from the algorithm $\mathcal{E}_{KEM}$ with respect to the public key pk. We first need to create a valid encapsulation C_m^* of the key K_b with respect to the algorithm $\mathcal{E}_{mKEM}$ and the set of keys $\mathcal{P} = \{pk_{i_1}, \ldots, pk_{i_m}\}$. We have

$$C^* = (\mathfrak{c}_0^*, \mathfrak{c}_1^*) = (g^{\mathfrak{r}}, \mathfrak{m} \cdot pk^{\mathfrak{r}}),$$

with $K_b = KDF(\mathfrak{m})$ and $\mathfrak{r} = H(\mathfrak{m})$, whereas

$$C_m^* = (c_0^*, c_1^*, \ldots, c_m^*) = (g^{\mathfrak{r}}, \mathfrak{m} \cdot pk_{i_1}^{\mathfrak{r}}, \ldots, \mathfrak{m} \cdot pk_{i_m}^{\mathfrak{r}}).$$

Hence, we set $c_0^* = \mathfrak{c}_0^*$ and for $j = 1, \ldots, m$

$$
\begin{aligned}
c_j^* &= \mathfrak{c}_1^* \cdot \mathfrak{c}_0^{*k_{ij}} \\
&= \mathfrak{m} \cdot \mathrm{pk}^r \cdot g^{rk_{ij}} = \mathfrak{m} \cdot \left(\mathrm{pk} \cdot g^{k_{ij}} \right)^r \\
&= \mathfrak{m} \cdot \mathrm{pk}_{ij}^r,
\end{aligned}
$$

where we let $k_1 = 0$.

Having constructed C_m^* we can now pass $C_m^*, \{K_0, K_1\}$ and s' to algorithm $\mathcal{A}^2$. If $\mathcal{A}$ is a successful adversary against the mKEM then we will obtain with non-negligible probability a bit b' such that $K_b = K_{b'}$. Hence, by returning this bit b' as our output from the algorithm $\mathcal{B}^2$ we obtain an algorithm $\mathcal{B}$ which with non-negligible probability will break the security of the $(\mathcal{G}_{KEM}, \mathcal{E}_{KEM}, \mathcal{D}_{KEM})$ in the IND-CCA2 sense.

All that remains is to show how to answer the decapsulation oracle queries of algorithm $\mathcal{A}$. Recall we have a decapsulation oracle $\mathcal{O}_{KEM}$ for the scheme $(\mathcal{G}_{KEM}, \mathcal{E}_{KEM}, \mathcal{D}_{KEM})$ which will respond with respect to the key pk on all requests C except one is not allow to query it with $C = C^*$. The decapsulation queries of $\mathcal{A}$ must be answered correctly unless the query C_m corresponds to the key K_b.

Suppose we are given the, possibly invalid, encapsulation

$$
C_m = (c_0, c_1, \ldots, c_m) = (g^r, \mathfrak{m} \cdot \mathrm{pk}_{i_1}^{r_1}, \ldots, \mathfrak{m} \cdot \mathrm{pk}_{i_m}^{r_m})
$$

and we are asked to decapsulate it with respect to the public key pk_{ij}. This should result in the key $K = KDF(\mathfrak{m})$ if and only if $r = H(\mathfrak{m})$ and $r_j = r$.

We first form the encapsulation $(\mathfrak{c}_0, \mathfrak{c}_1)$ with respect to the scheme KEM, via setting $\mathfrak{c}_0 = c_0$ and

$$
\begin{aligned}
\mathfrak{c}_1 &= c_{ij} \cdot c_0^{-k_{ij}} \\
&= \mathfrak{m} \cdot \mathrm{pk}_{ij}^{r_j} \cdot g^{-rk_{ij}} \\
&= \mathfrak{m} \cdot \mathrm{pk}^{r_j} \cdot g^{(r_j - r)k_{ij}} \\
&= \mathfrak{m} \cdot \mathrm{pk}^r \text{ if } r_j = r.
\end{aligned}
$$

Note since we are not allowed to query $\mathcal{A}$'s decapsulation oracle with any encapsulation which corresponds to K_b we must have $m \neq \mathfrak{m}$.

The oracle $\mathcal{O}$ will not respond if $\mathfrak{c}_0 = \mathfrak{c}_0^*$ and $\mathfrak{c}_1 = \mathfrak{c}_1^*$. Such a situation would mean that $\mathcal{O}$ returns K_b, i.e. the encapsulation C_m is an encapsulation of K_b with respect to pk_{ij}, and such a query is invalid under the security model for mKEMs.

We can, therefore, assume that either $\mathfrak{c}_0 \neq \mathfrak{c}_0^*$ or $\mathfrak{c}_1 \neq \mathfrak{c}_1^*$. In either case the oracle $\mathcal{O}$ will compute

$$
m' = m \cdot \mathrm{pk}^{r_j} \cdot g^{(r_j - r)k_{ij}} \cdot \mathfrak{c}_0^{-\mathrm{sk}} = m \cdot \left(\mathrm{pk} g^{k_{ij}} \right)^{r_j - r}.
$$

For the oracle $\mathcal{O}$ to return $K = KDF(m')$ we must have $r = H(m')$. In which case $(\mathfrak{c}_0, \mathfrak{c}_1)$ is a (possibly badly formed) ciphertext for the KEM which nevertheless passes the validity check and C_m is a (possibly badly formed) ciphertext for the mKEM which also passes the validity check of the mKEM. Hence, $\mathcal{A}$s oracle should return K, unless $K = K_b$ in which case we have found a collision in KDF since

$$KDF(\mathfrak{m}) = KDF(m').$$

Such a collision will only occur with negligible probability since KDF is modelled as a random oracle.

7   Efficiency Comparison

We first compare our ElGamal based mKEM for n users against naive concatenation of n ElGamal ciphertexts together. We let $EG(n)$ denote a IND-CCA2 version of ElGamal (such as EC-IES/DH-IES [1]) applied n-times to encrypt a session key. We let $EG_{KEM}(n)$ denote the ElGamal based mKEM described in Section 6.2 applied to n public keys. We compare the number of group exponentiations performed in the following table:

	$EG_{KEM}(n)$	$EG(n)$
Encapsulation	$n + 1$	$2n + 2$
Decapsulation	2	1

Hence we see that our method is more efficient than simply concatenating n-ElGamal ciphertexts together. In addition our method only requires the transmission of $n + 1$ group elements as opposed to $2n$ group elements for the naive method.

References

1. M. Abdalla, M. Bellare and P. Rogaway. DHAES : An encryption scheme based on the Diffie–Hellman problem. Preprint, 1999.
2. M. Bellare, A. Boldyreva and S. Micali. Public-key encryption in the multi-user setting : Security proofs and improvements. In *Advances in Cryptology – EuroCrypt 2000*, Springer-Verlag LNCS 1807, 259–274, 2000.
3. A.W. Dent. A designer's guide to KEMs. To appear *Coding and Cryptography*, Springer-Verlag LNCS 2898, 133–151, 2003.
4. R. Cramer and V. Shoup. Design and analysis of practical public-key encryption schemes secure against adaptive chosen-ciphertext attack. Preprint, 2002.
5. V. Shoup. A proposal for the ISO standard for public-key encryption (version 2.0). Preprint, 2001.

Improved Signcryption from q-Diffie-Hellman Problems

Benoît Libert[1,2,*] and Jean-Jacques Quisquater [1]

[1]UCL Crypto Group Place du Levant,
3. B-1348 Louvain-La-Neuve. Belgium
{libert, jjq}@dice.ucl.ac.be
[2] Laboratoire d'Informatique de l'École Polytechnique (LIX)
F-91128 Palaiseau CEDEX, France

Abstract. This paper proposes a new public key authenticated encryption (signcryption) scheme based on the hardness of q-Diffie-Hellman problems in Gap Diffie-Hellman groups. This new scheme is quite efficient: the signcryption operation has almost the same cost as an El Gamal encryption while the reverse operation only requires one pairing evaluation and three exponentiations. The scheme's chosen-ciphertext security is shown to be related to the hardness of the q-Diffie-Hellman Inversion $(q-\text{DHI})$ problem in the random oracle model while its unforgeability is proved under the q-Strong Diffie-Hellman assumption (q-SDH). It also provides detachable signatures that are unlinkable to the original anonymous ciphertext. We also show that most of the sender's workload can be computed offline. Our construction is based on a signature scheme independently studied by Boneh-Boyen and Zhang et al. in 2004.

Keywords: signcryption, bilinear maps, provable security.

1 Introduction

Public key encryption and digital signatures are primitives that aim at achieving very different purposes. The former has to yield communication privacy while the latter is used for authentication and non-repudiation of sensitive data. However, in many cryptographic applications, such as secure e-mail or secure channel establishment protocols, these requirements need to be simultaneously fulfilled. To achieve them in the asymmetric setting, the concept of public key authenticated encryption, or 'signcryption', was introduced by Zheng in 1997 ([30]). This kind of primitive aims to efficiently perform encryption and signature in a single logical step in order to obtain confidentiality, integrity, authentication and non-repudiation. We recall that the basic encrypt-then-sign composition is generally insecure (except for some particular constructions such as [1] or [15] or if, as in [2], we consider a relaxed security notion for this kind of composition)

---

* This author was supported by the DGTRE's First Europe Project.

against chosen-ciphertext attacks as well as the encrypt-and-sign approach. The drawback of most of the latter solutions is to expand the final ciphertext size and increase the sender and receiver's computing time. Zheng's original discrete logarithm based signcryption proposal ([30]) was only proven secure in 2002 ([3]) by Baek et al. who described a formal security model in a multi-user setting. In [27], Steinfeld and Zheng proposed another scheme for which the unforgeability of ciphertexts relies on the intractability of the integer factoring problem but they provided no proof of chosen-ciphertext security.

The previously cited schemes have the shortcoming not to offer easy non-repudiation of ciphertexts: a recipient cannot convince a third party that a plaintext actually emanates from its sender. A method was proposed in ([4]) to overcome this limitation but it was shown ([26]) to leak information on the plaintext as other schemes described in [19] and [28]. This weakness can easily be fixed by slightly modifying the schemes but no strong guarantee of unforgeability can be obtained since only loose reductions from computational problems to a ciphertext forger currently exist. Formal security notions were considered in [1] where general composition methods for asymmetric encryption and digital signatures together are analyzed but these security models do not consider that, in a multi-user setting, an adversary can be an insider as stressed in [2]: a chosen-ciphertext attacker can learn some user's private key and threaten the confidentiality of messages previously signcrypted by that user.

Another CCA2-secure discrete logarithm based signcryption scheme was described in [26] but no proof of unforgeability was given for it. An RSA-based scheme was described by Malone-Lee and Mao ([20]) who provided proofs for unforgeability under chosen-message attacks and chosen-ciphertext security but they only considered the security in a two-user setting rather than the more realistic multi-user setting. Furthermore, the security of that scheme is only loosely related to the RSA assumption. However, none of the aforementioned schemes is provably secure against insider attacks: in some of them, an attacker learning some user's private key can recover all the messages previously sent by that user.

An et al. ([2]) presented an approach consisting in performing signature and encryption in parallel: a plaintext is first transformed into a commitment/de-commitment pair (c, d) in such a way that c reveals no information about m while the pair (c, d) allows recovering m. The signer can then jointly sign c and encrypt d in parallel using appropriate encryption and signature schemes. The de-signcryption operation is also achieved by the recipient in a parallel fashion: the signature on c is verified while the decryption reveals d and the pair (c, d) is finally used to recover the plaintext. This approach was further investigated by Pieprzyk and Pointcheval ([25]) who proposed to use a commitment scheme based on a $(2, 2)$-Shamir secret sharing of an appropriately salted plaintext: the first resulting share s_1, which does not individually reveal any information on m, is used as a commitment and is signed while the second share s_2 is encrypted as a de-commitment. That method also provides a construction allowing to integrate any one-way encryption system (such as the basic RSA) with a weakly secure signature (a non-universally forgeable signatures) into a CCA2-secure and existentially unforgeable scheme.

Dodis et al. ([11]) recently proposed other possibly parallel signcryption techniques, one of which which can be viewed as a generalization of existing probabilistic paddings such as OAEP, OAEP+ or PSS-R. They showed that their constructions allow optimal exact security as well as compatibility with PKCS standards and has other interesting properties. In fact, the latter schemes might be the most practical ones among all solutions based on trapdoor functions.

In a discrete logarithm context, Libert and Quisquater recently proposed a solution based on bilinear maps and the properties of Gap Diffie-Hellman groups. This scheme was shown to satisfy strong security notions (namely, notions of chosen-ciphertext security and 'ciphertext strong unforgeability' even against insider attacks that were introduced in [2] where the multi-user setting was considered for the first time) and to provide anonymous ciphertexts (i.e. a ciphertext contains no information identifying its originator nor its recipient) as well as a notion called 'invisibility' (that informally captures the fact that an actual ciphertext for a given recipient's public key and a chosen sender's private key is indistinguishable from a random element of the ciphertext space). Unfortunately, the latter Diffie-Hellman based scheme, that was obtained from Boneh et al.'s short signature ([9]) in a randomized version, only spares one elliptic curve scalar multiplication on the receiver's side as well as a 160-bit bandwidth overhead in the ciphertext size when compared to a sequential composition of the BLS signature with a CCA2-secure El Gamal encryption.

The present paper aims at proposing a more efficient Diffie-Hellman based signcryption solution that satisfies the same strong security requirements: the scheme that is described here has essentially the same cost as a mere El Gamal encryption on the sender'side while only one pairing evaluation and three exponentiation are required for the simultaneous decryption/verification tasks. This is a real efficiency improvement: the signcryption operation is roughly 33% faster while the de-signcryption algorithm is almost twice more efficient than in Libert and Quisquater's original scheme. The price to pay for such improvements is that our scheme's security relies on stronger assumption than the one depicted in [18]: the chosen-ciphertext security is proved under the q-Diffie-Hellman Inversion assumption already considered in [6], [7] and [29] while the scheme's strong unforgeability relies on the q-Strong Diffie-Hellman assumption introduced by Boneh and Boyen ([6]).

Before starting with describing our scheme, we have to recall the properties of the bilinear maps that are needed to achieve our purposes. We then discuss about formal security models for signcrytpion and we then give a description of our scheme before discussing about its efficiency and we finally give security proofs in the random oracle model.

2 Preliminaries

2.1 Bilinear Maps

Let k be a security parameter and p be a k-bit prime number. Let us consider groups $\mathbb{G}_1$ and $\mathbb{G}_2$ of the same prime order p. For our purposes, we need a bilinear map $e : \mathbb{G}_1 \times \mathbb{G}_1 \to \mathbb{G}_2$ satisfying the following properties:

1. Bilinearity: $\forall\ u, v \in \mathbb{G}_1,\ \forall\ a, b \in \mathbb{Z}_p^*$, we have $e(u^a, v^b) = e(u, v)^{ab}$
2. Non-degeneracy: $\forall\ u \in \mathbb{G}_1,\ e(u, v) = 1$ for all $v \in \mathbb{G}_1$ iff $u = 1_{\mathbb{G}_1}$
3. Computability: $\forall\ u, v \in \mathbb{G}_1,\ e(u, v)$ can be efficiently computed

Such admissible bilinear maps can be instantiated by modifications ([8]) of the Weil or the Tate pairing over elliptic curves or abelian varieties. We now first recall some problems that provided underlying assumptions for many previously proposed pairing based cryptosystems and we also recall what are the q-Diffie-Hellman and q-Strong Diffie-Hellman problems.

Definition 1. *Given groups $\mathbb{G}_1$ and $\mathbb{G}_2$ of prime order p, a bilinear map $e : \mathbb{G}_1 \times \mathbb{G}_1 \to \mathbb{G}_2$ and a generator g of $\mathbb{G}_1$,*

- *The **Computational Diffie-Hellman problem** (CDH) in $\mathbb{G}_1$ is, given (g, g^a, g^b) for unknown $a, b \in \mathbb{Z}_p^*$, to compute $g^{ab} \in \mathbb{G}_1$.*
- *The **Decision Diffie-Hellman problem** (DDH) is, to decide whether $ab \equiv c \pmod{p}$ given (g, g^a, g^a, g^c) for unknown $a, b, c \in \mathbb{Z}_p^*$. Tuples of the form (g, g^a, g^a, g^{ab}) are called "Diffie-Hellman tuples". In our notations, we will sometimes write $g^c = DH_g(g^a, g^b)$.*
- *The **Gap Diffie-Hellman problem** (GDH) is to solve an instance (g, g^a, g^b) of the CDH problem with the help of a DDH oracle deciding whether given tuples $(g, g^{a'}, g^{b'}, g^{c'})$ satisfy $c' \equiv a'b' \pmod{p}$ or not.*
- *The q-**Diffie-Hellman Inversion problem** (q-DHI) consists of, given a tuple $(g, g^x, g^{(x^2)}, \ldots, g^{(x^q)}) \in \mathbb{G}_1^{q+1}$, computing $g^{1/x} \in \mathbb{G}_1$.*
- *The q-**Strong Diffie-Hellman problem** (q-SDH) consists of, given a tuple $(g, g^x, g^{(x^2)}, \ldots, g^{(x^q)})$, coming up with a pair $(c, g^{1/(x+c)}) \in \mathbb{Z}_p \times \mathbb{G}_1$.*

As shown in [16], the DDH problem is easy in any group where bilinear mappings of the above form can be efficiently computed. These groups are called Gap Diffie-Hellman groups according to the terminology of [24].

The q-Diffie-Hellman inversion problem was introduced in [21]. It was also used in [29] where it was shown to be equivalent to the $(q + 1)$-exponent problem (namely, finding $g^{(x^{q+1})}$ given $(g, g^x, g^{(x^2)}, \ldots, g^{(x^q)})$). The relaxed q-Strong Diffie Hellman assumption (i.e. the hardness of the q-Strong Diffie-Hellman problem) was introduced in [6] where it was used to prove the security of a new signature scheme in the standard model.

3   Security Notions for Signcryption Schemes

We recall the two usual security notions: the security against chosen ciphertext attacks and the unforgeability against chosen-message attacks. In the former, we consider a multi-user security model as already done in [2],[3],[11],[25] and [10] to let the adversary obtain ciphertexts created with the attacked private key under arbitrary public keys. We also consider the "inside attackers" that are allowed to choose the private key under which the challenge is signcrypted: for confidentiality purposes, we require the owner of a private key to be unable to find any information on a ciphertext created with that key without knowing which random coins were used to produce that ciphertext. This further allows us to show that an attacker stealing a private key does not threaten the confidentiality of messages previously signcrypted using that private key.

Definition 2. *We say that a signcryption scheme is **secure against chosen ciphertext attacks** (we call this security notion IND-SC-CCA) if no probabilistic polynomial time (PPT) adversary has a non-negligible advantage in the following game:*

1. *The challenger CH generates a private/public key pair (sk_U, pk_U). sk_U is kept secret while pk_U is given to the adversary $\mathcal{A}$.*
2. *$\mathcal{A}$ performs a first series of queries of the following kinds:*
   - *Signcryption queries: $\mathcal{A}$ produces a message $m \in \mathcal{M}$ and an arbitrary public key pk_R (which may differ from pk_U) and requires the result $Signcrypt(m, sk_U, pk_R)$ of the signcryption oracle.*
   - *De-signcryption queries: $\mathcal{A}$ produces a ciphertext σ and requires the result of $De\text{-}signcryt(\sigma, sk_U)$ which consists of a signed plaintext together with a sender's public key if the obtained signed plaintext is valid for the recovered sender's public key and the $\perp$ symbol otherwise (indicating that the ciphertext was not properly formed).*

   These queries can be asked adaptively: each query may depend on the answers to previous ones.
3. *$\mathcal{A}$ produces two equal length-plaintexts $m_0, m_1 \in \mathcal{M}$ and an arbitrary private key sk_S. CH flips a coin $b \xleftarrow{R} \{0, 1\}$ to compute a signcryption $\sigma = Signcrypt(m_b, sk_S, pk_U)$ of m_b with the sender's private key sk_S under the attacked public key pk_U. σ is sent to $\mathcal{A}$ as a challenge.*
4. *$\mathcal{A}$ performs new queries as in step 2. It may not ask the de-signcryption of the challenge σ with the private key sk_U of the attacked receiver.*
5. *At the end of the game, $\mathcal{A}$ outputs a bit b' and wins if $b' = b$.*

$\mathcal{A}$'s advantage is defined to be $Adv^{ind\text{-}cca}(\mathcal{A}) := 2 \times Pr[b' = b] - 1$.

A lot of provably unforgeable signcryption schemes ([2],[3],[11],[15],[25], etc.) provide non-repudiation with respect to the whole ciphertext. As noticed in [10], in many contexts, it is sufficient to only consider the non-repudiation with respect to the signature embedded in the ciphertext. Even though we still doubt on whether non-repudiation with respect to entire ciphertexts is a relevant or useful security notion, for applications that would be requiring it, we will show to turn our scheme into a ciphertext-existentially unforgeable one at the cost of increasing the size of the detachable signatures by a factor of 3 (but without any other loss of efficiency). The notion of unforgeability w.r.t. embedded signature, that was introduced for the first time in [10], is recalled below.

Definition 3. *We say that a signcryption scheme is said to be **existentially signature-unforgeable** against chosen-message attacks (ESUF-SC-CMA) if no PPT adversary has a non-negligible advantage against a challenger CH in the following game:*

1. *CH generates a key pair (sk_U, pk_U) and pk_U is given to the forger $\mathcal{F}$.*
2. *$\mathcal{F}$ adaptively performs queries to the same oracles as in definition 2.*
3. *$\mathcal{F}$ eventually produces a ciphertext σ and a key pair (sk_R, pk_R) and wins if the result of De-signcrypt(σ, sk_R) is a triple (m, s, pk_U) such that the pair (m, s) is valid for the public key pk_U and no query to the signcryption oracle involving the message m and some receiver's public key pk'_R resulted in a ciphertext σ' for which the output of De-signcrypt(σ', sk'_R) is (m, s, pk_U).*

As stressed by [10], considering non-repudiation only w.r.t. signatures is useful for schemes providing detachable signatures that should be *unlinkable* to the ciphertext they were conveyed in: anyone seeing a valid message-signature pair can use his/her private key to encrypt it into a valid signcryption under his/her public key. A notion complementary to the latter was called *ciphertext authentication* and means that a receiver is always convinced that a ciphertext was (jointly) signed and encrypted by the same person. We refer to [10] for a formal definition of this notion that is omitted here and that our scheme can be shown to satisfy.

4   The Scheme

The protocol makes use of a semantically secure[1] symmetric cryptosystem and relies on a signature scheme independently proposed by Zhang et al. ([29]) and Boneh and Boyen ([6]). In the latter papers, this scheme was shown to efficiently produce 160 bits long signatures without requiring the use of a special hash function mapping messages to be signed onto an elliptic curve subgroup (unlike the original BLS short signature proposed in [9]). In [6], it was also shown that this scheme has a tight security reduction w.r.t. the q-strong Diffie-Hellman problem in the random oracle model (Zhang et al. gave in [29] a reduction w.r.t. the $(q + 1)$-exponent problem but their reduction is loose as mentioned in [6]).

The protocol depicted on figure 1 makes use of such a (masked) signature as an El Gamal like ephemeral key as well as a checksum showing that a message was properly encrypted in chosen-ciphertext security concerns: the sender first

---

[1] Actually, an adversary against such a symmetric cipher is required to be unable to decide which one of two messages of its choice matches a challenge ciphertext without having access to encryption or decryption oracles. This is a very weak requirement.

computes an exponent $r = \gamma/(h_1(b_m||m) + x_S) \in \mathbb{Z}_p^*$ where γ is randomly chosen from $\mathbb{Z}_p^*$, $m \in \{0,1\}^*$ is the message to signcrypt and b_m is a message-dependent bit computed as a pseudo-random function of m and the private key x_s according to Katz and Wang's proof technique ([17]) (that aims at achieving tight security reductions without random salts). This exponent r is then used to compute an ephemeral Diffie-Hellman key g^r as in the El Gamal cryptosystem ([12]) and to scramble the secret γ using a hash value of Y_R^r, where Y_R is the recipient's public key, while a digest of γ is used to encrypt the message m together with the sender's public key.

The use of a masked signature as a "one-time" Diffie-Hellman key allows to spare one exponentiation (actually an elliptic curve scalar multiplication) w.r.t. a sequential signature/encryption composition.

When computing the second component of the ciphertext, the recipient's public key and the first component (which is an embedded signature as well as a Diffie-Hellman ephemeral key) are hashed together with the "one-time" Diffie-Hellman key Y_R^r in order for the security proof to work.

In order to convince a third party that a recovered message m emanates from the sender S, the receiver reveals σ, the message m and the associated bit b_m and the third party can run the regular signature verficication algorithm as done in step 3 of the de-signcryption algorithm. The scheme then provides detachable signatures that cannot be linked to their original ciphertext: the signature is masked by a randomly chosen factor γ and anyone observing a valid message-signature pair can use his/her private key to built a signcryption of that message-signature pair under his/her public key. The scheme thus provides *ciphertext unlinkability* in the sense of Boyen ([10]) in a very simple manner.

As Boyen's identity based scheme, the present one is obviously not existentially ciphertext-unforgeable in the sense of [18] (because of its inherent ciphertext unlinkability property) but we believe that it is actually useless to consider ciphertext non-repudiation (that appears as being antagonist to the useful notion of ciphertext unlinkability and thus might even be undesirable) rather the mere signature non-repudiation: an adversary should not be rewarded for achieving the trivial task of using a valid signature and a randomly chosen x_R' as a recipient's private key to output a claimed forged ciphertext under the public key $Y_R' = g^{x_R'}$.

Efficiency Discussions. As mentioned above, the scheme is quite efficient since, beside a modular inversion and a symmetric encryption, the sender only computes two exponentiations. The receiver's workload is dominated by one pairing computation (as $e(g,g)$ can be computed once-and-for-all and cached in memory) and three exponentiation. From both the sender and the receiver's side the protocol is much more efficient than Libert and Quisquater's scheme ([18]).

Interestingly, unlike what appears at first glance, the two exponentiations that are the bulk of the sender's workload can be computed offline (i.e. before the message to be sent is known). Indeed, in an offline phase, the sender can already pick a random $r \xleftarrow{R} \mathbb{Z}_p^*$, compute $c_1 = g^r$ and $\omega = Y_R^r$, store them in memory and then, once the message m is known, compute $\gamma = r(h_1(b_m||m) + x_S) \bmod p$, $c_2 = \gamma \oplus h_2(c_1, Y_R, \omega) \in \{0,1\}^k$ and $c_3 = \mathcal{E}_{h_3(\gamma)}(m||Y_S)$. In this case, care must

Common-Keygen: given security parameters k, λ, this algorithm outputs a prime number p such that $2^{k-1} < p < 2^k$, the description of two groups $\mathbb{G}_1$ and $\mathbb{G}_2$ such that $|\mathbb{G}_1| = |\mathbb{G}_2| = p$ and the bitlength ℓ of $\mathbb{G}_1$'s elements is polynomial in k, a generator $g \in \mathbb{G}_1$, a bilinear map $e : \mathbb{G}_1 \times \mathbb{G}_1 \to \mathbb{G}_2$, and hash functions $h_1 : \{0,1\}^* \to \mathbb{Z}_p$, $h_2 : \mathbb{G}_1^3 \to \{0,1\}^k$ and $h_3 : \{0,1\}^k \to \{0,1\}^\lambda$ as well as an pseudo-random function $h' : \{0,1\}^* \to \{0,1\}$. The algorithm also chooses a semantically secure symmetric encryption scheme $(\mathcal{E}, \mathcal{D})$ of keylength λ. The common key is then

$$I = \{p, \mathbb{G}_1, \mathbb{G}_2, g, e, h_1, h_3, h_3, h', n, \mathcal{E}, \mathcal{D}, \lambda\}$$

where n denotes the size of plaintexts.

Keygen: each user picks $x_u \xleftarrow{R} \mathbb{Z}_p^*$ and computes $Y_u = g^{x_u} \in \mathbb{G}_1$ obtains a public/private key pair $(pk_u, sk_u) = (Y_u, x_u)$.

Signcrypt: given a message $m \in \{0,1\}^n$, the recipient's public key Y_R and her private key x_S, the sender does the following:

1. pick $\gamma \xleftarrow{R} \mathbb{Z}_p^*$ and compute $r = \frac{\gamma}{h_1(b_m||m) + x_S} \bmod p$ where $b_m = h'(x_S, m) \in \{0,1\}$ is a message-dependent bit.

2. Compute $c_1 = g^r \in \mathbb{G}_1$, $c_2 = \gamma \oplus h_2(c_1, Y_R, Y_R^r) \in \{0,1\}^k$ and then $c_3 = \mathcal{E}_\kappa(m||Y_S) \in \{0,1\}^{n+\ell}$ where $\kappa = h_3(\gamma) \in \{0,1\}^\lambda$

The ciphertext is

$$C = \langle b_m, c_1, c_2, c_3 \rangle = \langle b_m, g^r, \gamma \oplus h_2(g^r, Y_R, Y_R^r), \mathcal{E}_{h_3(\gamma)}(m||Y_S) \rangle$$

De-signcrypt: given a ciphertext $C = \langle b, c_1, c_2, c_3 \rangle \in \{0,1\} \times \mathbb{G}_1 \times \{0,1\}^{n+k+\ell}$, the recipient runs the following process:

1. compute $\gamma = c_2 \oplus h_2(c_1, Y_R, c_1^{x_R}) \in \{0,1\}^k$. Return $\perp$ if $\gamma \notin \mathbb{Z}_p^*$.

2. Compute $(m||Y_S) = \mathcal{D}_\kappa(c_3) \in \{0,1\}^{n+\ell}$ with $\kappa = h_3(\gamma) \in \{0,1\}^\lambda$.

3. Compute $\sigma = c_1^{\gamma^{-1}}$ and accept the message if and only if

$$e(\sigma, Y_S g^{h_1(b||m)}) = e(g,g). \tag{1}$$

Fig. 1. The q-DH signcryption scheme

be taken not to re-use the same r to sign and encrypt distinct messages because this would expose the private key but this is not a problem since all signatures obtained through the Fiat-Shamir heuristic ([13]) have this feature.

As an observation of independent interest, we note that a similar technique can increase the online efficiency of Boneh and Boyen's short signature ([6]) that is proven secure in the standard model. Indeed recall that, in this scheme, each user has a key pair $PK = (X = g^x, Y = g^y)$, $SK = (x, y)$ and a signature on a message $m \in \mathbb{Z}_p^*$, given by a pair $(r, \sigma) = (r, g^{1/(m+x+yr)}) \in \mathbb{Z}_p^* \times \mathbb{G}_1$, can be verified by checking that $e(\sigma, XY^r g^m) = e(g,g)$. In an offline phase, the signer can pick a random $\mu \xleftarrow{R} \mathbb{Z}_p^*$, compute $\sigma = g^\mu \in \mathbb{G}_1$, store it in memory together with μ and, once the message is known, compute $r = y^{-1}(\mu^{-1} - m - x) \bmod p$. The cost of the online phase can thus be reduced to a simple modular operation (since y^{-1} can be computed once and for all at the key setup while μ^{-1} is also pre-computed in the offline stage) and the overall cost of a signature generation remains unchanged.

Again, care must be taken not to re-use the same μ to sign distinct messages because this would reveal the signer's private key (although it does not prevent the signer to use the same random r to sign distinct messages in the usual signing procedure). For both schemes, in the absence of reliable pseudo-random generators, we may choose random powers as digests of the message and the signer's public/private key pair according to a technique suggested in [23].

Short Detachable Signatures. The version of the scheme depicted in figure 1 is only instantiable with modified Weil or Tate pairings obtained from distortion maps (and thus requires the use of supersingular curves). As a result, if we use the same curves as in [8], the scheme cannot allow detachable signatures shorter than 512 bits[2].

If shorter signatures are needed (by using ordinary curves such as those described in [22] as suggested in [9]), it is possible to modify the scheme so that it can be instantiated with pairings $e : \mathbb{G}_1 \times \mathbb{G}_2 \rightarrow \mathbb{G}_T$ over distinct cyclic subgroups among which only $\mathbb{G}_1$'s elements have short representations. In this case, public keys are elements of $\mathbb{G}_2$ and the first part of the ciphertext must be computed as $c_1 = g_2^r$, where g_2 is a generator of $\mathbb{G}_2$, in such a way that, upon decryption, the receiver can detach a short signature by computing $\sigma = \psi(c_1)^{\gamma^{-1}} \in \mathbb{G}_1$ (the description of a group isomorphism $\psi : \mathbb{G}_2 \rightarrow \mathbb{G}_1$ must then be a part of the common public parameters and is not only needed in the security proof). The price to pay consists of more expensive exponentiations since operations in $\mathbb{G}_2$ are usually less efficient than in $\mathbb{G}_1$.

The security proofs presented in the next section are easily adaptable to provide a validation on the security of the aforementioned modification of the scheme.

5   Security Proofs for q-DH Signcryption

The present section gives proofs in the random oracle model of chosen-ciphertext security and of existential signature unforgeability.

Theorem 1. *In the random oracle model, if an adversary $\mathcal{A}$ has a non-negligible advantage ϵ in breaking the IND-SC-CCA security of the scheme when runnning in a time τ, asking q_{h_i} queries to random oracles h_i (for $i = 1, 2, 3$), q_{sc} signcryption queries and q_{dsc} de-signcryption queries, then there exists a PPT algorithm $\mathcal{B}$ to solve the q-Diffie-Hellman Inversion problem for $q = q_{sc} + 1$ with an advantage*

---

[2] We recall that supersingular curves in characteristic 3 are not recommended for applications requiring short signatures as explained in [9]

$$\epsilon' > \epsilon - q_{dsc}\left(\frac{q_{h_3}}{2^k} + \frac{1}{2^\lambda} + \frac{1}{2^k}\right) - \frac{q_{h_3}}{2^\lambda}$$

when running in a time $\tau' < \tau + O(q^2\tau_e) + 2q_{h_2}\tau_p$ where τ_e is the cost of an exponentiation in $\mathbb{G}_1$ and τ_p denotes the time for a bilinear map evaluation.

Proof. We show how $\mathcal{B}$ can use $\mathcal{A}$ as a subroutine to solve a random given instance $(g, g^x, g^{(x^2)}, \ldots, g^{(x^q)})$ of the $(q+1)$-exponent problem problem. We can assume w.l.o.g. that $q_{sc} = q-1$ since, otherwise, $\mathcal{B}$ can issue dummy signcryption queries for itself. In a preparation phase, $\mathcal{B}$ uses its input to compute a generator $h \in \mathbb{G}_1$ and a public key $X = h^x$ such that it knows $q-1$ pairs $(w_i, h^{1/(w_i+x)})$ for $w_i \xleftarrow{R} \mathbb{Z}_p^*$ as in the proof technique of [6]. To do so, $\mathcal{B}$ picks $w_1, \ldots, w_{q-1} \xleftarrow{R} \mathbb{Z}_p^*$, expands the polynomial $f(z) = \prod_{i=0}^{q-1}(z + w_i) = \sum_{i=0}^{q-1} c_i z^i$. A generator $h \in \mathbb{G}_1$ and the public key X are then obtained as

$$h = \prod_{i=0}^{q-1}(g^{x^i})^{c_i} = g^{f(x)} \quad \text{and} \quad X = \prod_{i=1}^{q}(g^{x^i})^{c_{i-1}} = g^{xf(x)} = h^x$$

(as in the proof of lemma 1 in [6]). As in [6], the pairs $(w_i, h^{1/(w_i+x)})$ are obtained by expanding $f_i(z) = f(z)/(z + w_i) = \sum_{i=0}^{q-2} d_i z^i$ and computing

$$h_i = \prod_{j=0}^{q-2}(g^{x^j})^{d_j} = g^{f_i(x)} = g^{f(x)/(z+w_i)} = h^{1/(z+w_i)}$$

for $i = 1, \ldots, q-1$.

The adversary $\mathcal{A}$ is then initialized with the generator h and on the public key X. It starts probing the oracles it is given access to. These oracles are simulated by $\mathcal{B}$ as explained below. The queries to the h_2 oracle need to be simulated using two lists L_2, L_2' that are initially empty.

- h' queries on an input $(\alpha_i, m_i) \in \mathbb{Z}_p^* \times \{0,1\}^*$: $\mathcal{B}$ first checks if $X = h^{\alpha_i}$. In this case, we are done and $\mathcal{B}$ can easily compute $g^{1/x}$. Otherwise, it responds with a random bit $b_{m_i} \xleftarrow{R} \{0,1\}$.
- h_1 queries: these queries are indexed by a counter t that is initially set to 1. When a pair $(d, m) \in \{0,1\} \times \{0,1\}^*$ is submitted in a h_1 query for the first time, $\mathcal{B}$ checks whether d equals the bit b_m (which is set at the first time the message m is submitted in a $h_1(.)$ query). If $d = b_m$, $\mathcal{B}$ returns w_t and increments t (in such a way that $\mathcal{B}$ is able to create a valid signature on m). Otherwise, $\mathcal{B}$ returns a random $c \xleftarrow{R} \mathbb{Z}_p^*$ and updates L_1.
- h_2 queries on triples $(y_{1,i}, y_{2,i}, y_{3,i}) \in \mathbb{G}_1^3$: $\mathcal{B}$ checks if $(h, y_{1,i}, y_{2,i}, y_{3,i})$ is a valid Diffie-Hellman tuple by two pairing evaluations. If it is, $\mathcal{B}$ checks if L_2' contains an entry of the form $(y_{1,i}, y_{2,i}, ., \tau_i)$ for some $\tau_i \in \{0,1\}^k$. In this case, τ_i is returned and an entry $(y_{1,i}, y_{2,i}, y_{3,i}, \tau_i, 1)$ is added in L_2. If no entry of the form $(y_{1,i}, y_{2,i}, ., \tau_i)$ is found in L_2', $\mathcal{B}$ returns a string $\tau_i \xleftarrow{R} \{0,1\}^k$ and inserts $(y_{1,i}, y_{2,i}, y_{3,i}, \tau_i, 1)$ in L_2. If $(h, y_{1,i}, y_{2,i}, y_{3,i})$ is not a DH tuple, the entry $(y_{1,i}, y_{2,i}, y_{3,i}, \tau_i, 0)$ is added in L_2. At most $2q_{h_2}$ pairings must be computed overall.

- h_3 queries: are answered by picking a random element from $\{0,1\}^\lambda$.
- Signcryption queries on a plaintext m, for an arbitrary receiver's key Y: we assume that m was previously submitted in a h_1 and that the message-dependent bit b_m was previously defined. Since $h_1(b_m, m)$ was (or will be) defined to be w_j for some $j \in \{1, \dots, t\}$, $\mathcal{B}$ knows that the previously computed $h_j = h^{1/(w_j+x)}$ appears as a valid signature on m from $\mathcal{A}$'s view. So, it computes $c_1 = h_j^\gamma \in \mathbb{G}_1$ for a $\gamma \xleftarrow{R} \mathbb{Z}_p^*$, obtains $\kappa = h_3(\gamma) \in \{0,1\}^\lambda$ through h_3-simulation and computes $c_3 = \mathcal{E}_\kappa(m||X) \in \{0,1\}^{n+\ell}$. It then checks if L_2 contains an entry $(c_1, Y, y_3, \tau, 1)$ (indicating that $y_3 = DH_h(c_1, Y)$). If this entry exists, $\mathcal{B}$ returns $C = \langle b_m, c_1, c_2, c_3 \rangle$ with $c_2 = \gamma \oplus \tau \in \{0,1\}^k$. Otherwise it returns $C = \langle b_m, c_1, c_2, c_3 \rangle$ for a random $c_2 \xleftarrow{R} \{0,1\}^k$ and inserts $(c_1, Y, ., \gamma \oplus c_2)$ in the special list L_2'.
- De-signcryption queries: when $\mathcal{A}$ submits a ciphertext $C = \langle b, c_1, c_2, c_3 \rangle$, $\mathcal{B}$ checks whether L_2 contains the unique entry $(c_1, X, Y, \tau, 1)$ for some $Y \in \mathbb{G}_1$ and $\tau \in \{0,1\}^k$ (indicating that $Y = DH_h(c_1, X)$). If it does not, C is declared as being ill-formed. Otherwise, $\mathcal{B}$ obtains $\gamma = c_2 \oplus \tau \in \{0,1\}^k$, $\kappa = h_3(\gamma)$ (C is rejected if h_3 was not queried on γ) and finally $(m||X_S) = \mathcal{D}_\kappa(c_3) \in \{0,1\}^{n+\ell}$ (C is also rejected if X_S is not a $\mathbb{G}_1$ element). Finally, $\mathcal{B}$ extracts $\sigma = c_1^{\gamma^{-1}}$ and returns the plaintext $m \in \{0,1\}^n$ and the associated signature c_1 together with the sender's public key X_S if the verfication equation (1) holds.

After the find stage, $\mathcal{A}$ outputs messages m_0, m_1 and a sender's private key $x_S \in \mathbb{Z}_p^*$. At this moment, $\mathcal{B}$ chooses a random $a \xleftarrow{R} \mathbb{Z}_p^*$ and computes $c_1^* = h^{x+a} \in \mathbb{G}_1$ as $c_1^* = Xh^a$. It also expands the polynomial $f'(z) = f(z)(z+a) = \sum_{j=0}^q f_i z^i \in \mathbb{Z}_p[x]$ and returns the challenge $C^* = \langle c_1^*, c_2^*, c_3^* \rangle$, where $c_2^* \xleftarrow{R} \{0,1\}^k$ and $c_3^* = \mathcal{E}_\kappa(m_b||g^{x_S}) \in \{0,1\}^{n+\ell}$ for a random bit $b \xleftarrow{R} \{0,1\}$ and a random string $\kappa \xleftarrow{R} \{0,1\}^\lambda$. Clearly, if $(\mathcal{E}, \mathcal{D})$ is semantically secure and κ does not hit the output of a h_3 query (the probability for this to occur is at most $q_{h_3}/2^\lambda$), $\mathcal{A}$'s view is independent from the bit b unless the hash value $h_2(c_1^*, X, DH_h(c_1^*, X))$ is asked during the simulation. Such an event, that we call AskH$_2$, is easily detected by the h_2 simulator and is very likely to happen[3]: one can easily show that in a real attack, $\Pr[\text{AskH}_2]$ is at least ϵ if $\mathcal{A}$'s advantage in definition 2 is ϵ. Furthermore, as long as $\mathcal{A}$ is provided with a consistent view, $\Pr[\text{AskH}_2]$ is the same in the simulation as in the real world.

Queries made by $\mathcal{A}$ in the second stage are handled as above and, as already argued, the h_2 simulator must detect the AskH$_2$ event with high probability. At this moment, $\mathcal{B}$ obtains $Z = DH_h(c_1^*, X) = h^{(x+a)x} = g^{f(x)(x+a)x}$. Since we have $f(z)(z+a)z = zf'(z) = \sum_{j=0}^q f_j z^{j+1}$ and, since $Z = \prod_{j=0}^q (g^{x^{j+1}})^{f_j}$, $\mathcal{B}$ can compute

---

[3] In fact, the challenge C^* can be computed after the preparation phase (i.e. before $\mathcal{A}$ enters in the find stage) without any modification of the probability space. The event AskH$_2$ is then detected even if it occurs in the find stage.

$$g^{(x^{q+1})} = [Z \prod_{j=0}^{q-1} (g^{x^{j+1}})^{-f_j}]^{1/f_q} \in \mathbb{G}_1$$

which is the solution to the $(q+1)$-exponent problem. At that moment, we are done since the latter is known to be equivalent to the q-Diffie-Hellman Inversion problem (as explained in [21] and [7]).

From a computational point of view, $\mathcal{B}$'s running time is dominated by $q + 2$ multi-exponentiations with q elements that reach an overall cost of $O(q^2)$ exponentiations. Computing $f(z)$ also involves a cost in $O(q^2)$ while computing each $f_i(z)$ also implies $O(q)$ modular multiplications just like the computation of the product $f(z)(z+a)$. When handling h_2 queries, $\mathcal{B}$ also has to compute $2q_{h_2}$ pairings.

The bound on $\mathcal{B}$'s advantage derives from the fact that it only provides $\mathcal{A}$ with an incoherent view when a rejected ciphertext subsequently appears as valid (because of 'bad' values taken by oracles for inputs on which they were not defined at the moment of the query). The probability of such an event is less than $q_{dsc}(q_{h_3}/2^k + 1/2^\lambda + 1/2^k)$. □

Theorem 2. *In the random oracle model, if an ESUF-SC-CMA adversary $\mathcal{F}$ has a non-negligible advantage ϵ in the game of definition 3 when running in a time τ, making q_{h_i} queries to oracles h_i ($i = 1,2,3$), q_{dsc} de-signcryption queries and q_{sc} signcryption queries, then there exists an algorithm $\mathcal{B}$ that solves the q-strong Diffie-Hellman problem with a probability*

$$\epsilon' > \frac{1}{2}\left(\epsilon - q_{dsc}\left(\frac{q_{h_3}}{2^k} + \frac{1}{2^\lambda} + \frac{1}{2^k}\right)\right) - \frac{1}{2^k} - \frac{1}{2^\lambda}$$

within a time $\tau' < \tau + O(q^2\tau_e) + 2q_{h_2}\tau_p$ where τ_e is the cost of an exponentiation in $\mathbb{G}_1$ and τ_p denotes the time for a bilinear map evaluation.

Proof. We build a simulator $\mathcal{B}$ that behaves almost exactly as in the previous proof. The generator $h \in \mathbb{G}_1$, that is given to the forger $\mathcal{F}$ as a part of the output of the common key generation algorithm, is generated as in the proof of theorem 1 so that the simulator $\mathcal{B}$ knows $q-1$ pairs $(w_i, h^{1/(1+x)})$ (where $x \in \mathbb{Z}_p^*$ is the unknown element that implicitly defines its input $g, g^x, g^{(x^2)}, \ldots, g^{(x^q)}$). By doing so, $\mathcal{B}$ is always able to answer signcryption queries that are handled, as all other oracle queries, exactly as in the proof of theorem 1.

Eventually, the forger $\mathcal{F}$ halts and outputs a forged signature embedded into a signcrypted message $C^* = (b^*, c_1^*, c_2^*, c_3^*)$ and an arbitrary recipient's key pair $(x_R^*, Y_R^* = g^{x_R^*})$ that allows $\mathcal{B}$ recovering the fake message-signature pair $(m^*, \sigma^* = h^{1/(\tilde{h}_1(b^*||m^*)+x)})$ embedded into C^*. With a probability $1/2$, b^* differs from the message-dependent bit b_{m^*} (that indicates how a message the message m^* should be signed with the private key corresponding to X in the underlying signature scheme and that is independent from $\mathcal{F}$'s view) and $\mathcal{B}$ can extract a solution to the q-Strong Diffie-Hellman problem as follows: if $\mathcal{F}$ is successful, $\mathcal{B}$ recovers a valid message-signature pair for the sender's public key X by computing $\gamma^* = c_2 \oplus h_2(c_1^*, Y_R^*, c_1^{*x_R^*})$, $(m^*||X) = \mathcal{D}_{h_3\gamma^*}(c_3^*)$ and

$\sigma^* = c_1^{*\gamma^{*-1}}$. A q-Strong Diffie-Hellman pair $\langle h_1^*, g^* \rangle$ can then be extracted by expanding $f(z)/(z + h_1^*)$ into

$$\frac{\gamma_{-1}}{z + h_1^*} + \sum_{i=0}^{q-2} \gamma_i z^i,$$

where $h_1^* = h_1(b^*, m^*) \in \mathbb{Z}_p$, and computing $g^* = [\sigma^* \prod_{i=0}^{q-2} (g^{(x^i)})^{-\gamma_i}]^{1/\gamma_{-1}}$.

A lower bound on the simulator's probability to obtain it is thus one half of the advantage of the simulator of the previous proof decreased by the (negligible) probability for $\mathcal{F}$ to produced a valid encryption of the fake signature without asking the appropriate h_2 and h_3 values during the simulation (in that case, $\mathcal{B}$ is unable extract a q-Strong Diffie-Hellman pair).   □

The ciphertext authentication property can be proven in the same way as its signature unforgeability and the proof, as well as the proof of ciphertext anonymity, is also omitted here because of space limitation.

For applications that would require the ciphertext unforgeability, adapting the scheme is straightforward: the first part of the ciphertext must be $c_1 = g^{1/(h_1(m||\gamma||Y_R)+x_S)}$ where $\gamma \in \mathbb{Z}_p^*$ is encrypted in the component c_2 and Y_R is the receiver's public key. As a consequence, γ and Y_R become a part of the detached signature and the sender of a message is not only committed to the plaintext's content but he/she is also responsible for having sent it to the owner of the key Y_R. Moreover, the ciphertext unlinkability property is also lost.

6   Conclusion

We presented an efficient signcryption scheme based on discrete logarithm related assumptions and we proved its security in the random oracle model. The scheme was shown to have a great online efficiency (similarly to the basic El Gamal cryptosystem but unlike a Fujisaki-Okamoto/El Gamal encryption scheme).

As an observation of independent interest, we extended our method to achieve this online efficiency to the Boneh-Boyen short signature ([6]).

References

1. J.-H. An, *Authenticated Encryption in the Public-Key Setting: Security Notions and Analyses*, eprint available at http://eprint.iacr.org/2001/079/, 2001.
2. J.-H. An, Y. Dodis, T. Rabin, *On the security of joint signature and encryption*, Advances in Cryptology - Eurocrypt'02, LNCS 2332, pp. 83–107, Springer, 2002.
3. J. Baek, R. Steinfeld, Y. Zheng, *Formal Proofs for the Security of Signcryption*, PKC'02, LNCS 2274, pp. 80–98, Springer, 2002.
4. F. Bao, R.-H. Deng, *A signcryption scheme with signature directly verifiable by public key*, PKC'98, LNCS 1988, pp. 55–59, 1998.

5. M. Bellare, P. Rogaway, *Random oracles are practical: A paradigm for designing efficient protocols*, 1st ACM Conference on Computer and Communications Security, pp. 62-73, 1993.
6. D. Boneh, X. Boyen, *Short Signatures Without Random Oracles*, Advances in Cryptology - Eurocrypt'04, LNCS 3027, Springer, pp. 56–73, 2004.
7. D. Boneh, X. Boyen, *Efficient Selective-ID Secure Identity Based Encryption Without Random Oracles*, Advances in Cryptology - Eurocrypt'04, LNCS 3027, Springer,pp. 223–238, 2004.
8. D. Boneh, M. Franklin, *Identity Based Encryption From the Weil Pairing*, Advances in Cryptology - Crypto'01, LNCS 2139, pp. 213–229, Springer, 2001.
9. D. Boneh, B. Lynn, H. Shacham, *Short signatures from the Weil pairing*, Advances in Cryptology - Asiacrypt'01, LNCS 2248, pp. 514–532, Springer, 2001.
10. X. Boyen, *Multipurpose identity-based signcryption: A swiss army knife for identity-based cryptography*, Advances in Cryptology (CRYPTO '03), LNCS 2729, pp. 382–398, Springer, 2003.
11. Y. Dodis, M.-J. Freedman, S. Jarecki, S. Walfish, *Versatile Padding Schemes for Joint Signature and Encryption*, to appear at ACM Conference on Computer and Communication Security (CCS), October 2004.
12. T. El Gamal, *A Public Key Cryptosystem and Signature Scheme Based on Discrete Logarithms*, IEEE Trans. on Information Theory, vol. 31, 1985.
13. A. Fiat, A. Shamir, *How to Prove Yourself: Practical Solutions to Identification and Signature Problems* , Advances in Cryptology - Crypto'86, LNCS 0263, Springer, pp. 186-194, 1986.
14. E. Fujisaki, T. Okamoto, *Secure integration of asymmetric and symmetric encryption schemes*, Advances in Cryptology - Crypto'99, LNCS 1666, pp. 537–554, Springer, 1999.
15. I.-R. Jeong, H.-Y. Jeong, H.-S. Rhee, D.-H. Lee, I.-L. Jong, *Provably secure encrypt-then-sign composition in hybrid signcryption*, ICISC'02, LNCS 2587, 2002.
16. A. Joux, K. Nguyen. *Separating Decision Diffie-Hellman from Diffie-Hellman in cryptographic groups*, available at http://eprint.iacr.org/2001/003/, 2001.
17. J. Katz, N. Wang, *Efficiency improvements for signature schemes with tight security reductions*, 10th ACM Conference on Computer and Communications Security, pp. 155–164, 2003.
18. B. Libert, J.-J. Quisquater, *Efficient Signcryption with Key Privacy from Gap Diffie-Hellman Groups*, PKC'04, LNCS 2947, pp. 187-200, Springer, 2004.
19. J. Malone-Lee, *Signcryption with non-repudiation*, Technical report available at http://www.cs.bris.ac.uk/Tools/Reports/Ps/2002-malonelee.pdf, 2002.
20. J. Malone-Lee, W. Mao, *Two birds one stone: Signcryption using RSA*, Topics in Cryptology - CT-RSA 2003, LNCS 2612, pp. 211-225, Springer, 2003.
21. S. Mitsunari, R. Sakai, M. Kasahara, *A new traitor tracing*, IEICE Trans. Vol. E85-A, No.2, pp. 481-484, 2002.
22. A. Miyaji, M. Nakabayashi, S. Tanako, *New Explicit Conditions of Elliptic Curve Traces for FR-Reduction*. IEICE Trans. Fundamentals, E84-A(5):1234-43, 2001.
23. D. M'Raïhi, D. Naccache, D. Pointcheval, S. Vaudenay, *Computational Alternatives to Random Number Generators*, Selected Areas in Cryptography'98 (SAC'98), LNCS 1566, pp. 72-80, Springer, 1998.
24. T. Okamoto, D. Pointcheval, *The Gap-Problems: A New Class of Problems for the Security of Cryptographic Schemes*, PKC'01, LNCS 1992, Springer, 2001.
25. J. Pieprzyk, D. Pointcheval, *Parallel Authentication and Public-Key Encryption*, ACISP'03, LNCS 2727, pp. 383–401, Springer, 2003.

26. J.-B. Shin, K. Lee, K. Shim, *New DSA-verifiable signcryption schemes*, ICISC'02, LNCS 2587, pp. 35–47, Springer, 2002.
27. R. Steinfeld, Y. Zheng, *A signcryption scheme based on integer factorization*, ISW'00, LNCS 1975, pp. 308–322, Springer, 2000.
28. D.-H. Yum, P.-J. Lee, *New signcryption schemes based on KCDSA*, ICISC'01, LNCS 2288, pp. 305–317, Springer, 2001.
29. F. Zhang, R. Safavi-Naini, W. Susilo, *An Efficient Signature Scheme from Bilinear Pairings and Its Applications*, PKC'04, LNCS 2947, pp. 277–290, 2004.
30. Y. Zheng, *Digital signcryption or how to achieve cost (signature & encryption) << cost(signature) + cost(encryption)*, Advances in Cryptology - Crypto'97, LNCS 1294, pp. 165–179, 1997.

Colored Visual Cryptography Without Color Darkening

S. Cimato, R. De Prisco*, and A. De Santis

Università di Salerno,
Dipartimento di Informatica ed Applicazioni,
84081 Baronissi (SA), Italy
{cimato, robdep, ads}@dia.unisa.it

Abstract. Visual cryptography schemes allow the encoding of a secret image into shares, in the form of transparencies, which are distributed to the participants. The shares are such that only qualified subsets of participants can visually recover the secret image by superimposing the transparencies.

In this paper we study colored visual cryptography schemes. Most of previous work on colored visual cryptography allows the superposition of pixels having the same color assuming that the resulting pixel still has the same color. This is not what happens in reality since when superimposing two pixels of the same color one gets a darker version of that color, which effectively is a different color. Superimposing many pixels of the same color might result in a so dark version of the color that the resulting pixel might be not distinguishable from a black pixel.

Thus we propose a model where the reconstruction has to guarantee that the reconstructed secret pixel has the same color of the original one and not a darker version of it. We give a construction of c-color (k, n)-threshold visual cryptography schemes. Since we have to guarantee the reconstruction of the exact original color, in many cases our schemes have a bigger pixel expansion than previous ones. However, for the case of $k = n$, we get a smaller pixel expansion when compared with schemes that to do not guarantee the exact reconstruction of the original color. We also prove that, in the model introduced in this paper, our schemes for $k = n$ have optimal pixel expansion.

1 Introduction

A visual cryptography scheme (VCS for short) for a set $\mathcal{P}$ of n participants is a method to encode a secret image into n shadow images in the form of transparencies, called shares, where each participant in $\mathcal{P}$ receives one share. Certain subsets of participants, called qualified sets, can "visually" recover the secret

---

* This author is also a member of the Akamai Faculty Group, Akamai Technologies, 8 Cambridge Center, Cambridge, MA 02142, USA.

C. Blundo and S. Cimato (Eds.): SCN 2004, LNCS 3352, pp. 235–248, 2005.

image, but other subsets of participants, called forbidden sets, have no information on the secret image. A "visual" recovery for a set $X \subseteq \mathcal{P}$ consists of superimposing the shares (transparencies) given to the participants in X. The participants in a qualified set X will be able to see the secret image without any knowledge of cryptography and without performing any cryptographic computation. Forbidden sets of participants will have no information on the secret image.

This cryptographic paradigm was introduced by Naor and Shamir [12]. They analyzed the case of (k, n)-threshold VCS in which a black and white (b&w for short) secret image is visible if and only if any k transparencies are stacked together. It should be noted that "white" is actually the transparent color.

In order to implement a visual cryptography scheme, each pixel of the secret image is subdivided into a certain number m of subpixels. Hence, there is a loss of resolution proportional to m. The *pixel expansion* m is the most important measure of the goodness of a scheme. Obviously, schemes with a smaller pixel expansion are better. Optimal schemes are those that have the minimum pixel expansion. Another important measure for the goodness of a scheme is the contrast, which is a measure of the quality of the reconstructed image; roughly speaking, the contrast tells us how much the reconstructed image differs from the original one.

Most of the work done focused on b&w VCS, where the secret image to be shared is composed of b&w pixels. There is a quite large body of literature on b&w visual cryptography (see for example [2, 3, 4, 6, 8, 9, 12]). Naor and Shamir in their seminal paper [12] provide a construction of b&w (k, k)-threshold schemes with perfect reconstruction of black pixels whose pixel expansion is 2^{k-1}. We will use such schemes as building blocks in order to construct our colored VCS.

In this paper we are concerned with colored visual cryptography, where the secret image is made up with a certain number c of colors. The b&w visual cryptography paradigm is based on the fact that superimposing pixels the resulting color is black if anyone of the superimposed pixels is black and white if all the superimposed pixels are white. To be more precise each pixel can be seen as a filter that stops some of the original light. The original light is perceived by the human eye as white. A black pixel blocks all the light so that the result is black (no light left), while a white (transparent) pixel does not stop any light leaving unchanged the original color. When we deal with colors something similar happens. The difference is that while black and white are the extreme cases (all or no light blocked), other colors partially block some light. As we discuss more formally in Section 2, this means that when superimposing pixels which are not white, the resulting color becomes darker. The only color that does not alter the original light is white. For this reason we call white the *identity* color. For the opposite reason we call black the *annihilator* color.

Taking into account the real law of color superposition into colored schemes seems to be quite a challenge and, as far as we know, only a few papers do actually use it [11, 1, 10]. The problem is that superimposing two colors one gets a third color that might not even be in the original palette of colors. The papers that use a model where different colors can be superimposed solve the above cited problem by considering only restricted sets of colors which enjoy the nice property of being closed with respect to the superposition operation. For example the set of colors consisting of white, black, red, green and blue and the set of colors consisting of white, black, red, green, blue, cyan, yellow and magenta are closed with respect to the color superposition.

Many other papers use a model where the annihilator color is used to cover up the result of a color superposition that would give a color that is not in the original palette of colors. This can be done either by requiring the special property that superimposing pixels with different colors one gets black [13], or by ensuring that we have at least one black pixel in the superposition (e.g. [14,7]). The artificial property used in [13] can be simulated by subdividing each pixel into c subpixels. However this simulation not only implies a bigger pixel expansion but also a diminishment of the contrast because when a pixel is reconstructed with the right color, its size is actually $1/c$ of the normal pixel size.

Previous Work. The papers [13,5,14,7] use a model that is very close to our own. The difference is that those paper allow pixels of the same color to be superimposed (assuming that the resulting color is still the same one).

Verheul and Van Tilborg [13] provided c-color (k,n)-threshold schemes; the pixel expansion is not given as a closed formula. In [5] constructions of c-color $(2,n)$-threshold and (n,n)-threshold schemes are provided and they both improve on [13].

The schemes of [13,5] require the special property that superimposing two pixels of different colors one gets black, which can be implemented paying a loss of resultion of a factor equal to c. In [14,7] such a special property is not required because the schemes provided in those papers never superimpose pixels with different colors; hence the extra factor of c in the pixel expansion is avoided.

Yang and Laih [14] provide new constructions for c-color (k,n)-threshold schemes which use as building blocks schemes for the b&w model. The schemes improve on the pixel expansion of those of [13,5].

In [7] a tight lower bound on the pixel expansion of c-color (n,n)-threshold schemes has been provided. Such a lower bound is:

$$m \geq \begin{cases} c \cdot 2^{n-1} - 1, \text{if } n \text{ is even} \\ c \cdot 2^{n-1} - c + 1, \text{if } n \text{ is odd} \end{cases} \tag{1}$$

It turns out that the (n,n)-threshold schemes of [14] are optimal since they match the above lower bound. In [7] a construction of (contrast-optimal) c-color (k,n)-threshold scheme is also given and the resulting pixel expansion improves in some cases the one of [14].

In [7] a construction of c-color $(2,n)$-threshold scheme is provided. The pixel expansion of such a construction improves on the other c-color $(2,n)$-threshold schemes. Unfortunately, a closed formula for the pixel expansion is not given.

The above cited papers are the ones that use a model which is the one closest to the model considered in this paper. Other work on colored visual cryptography is provided in [11,1,10].

This paper. All the papers discussed above use the black color to cover up undesired colors in the reconstructed image; however the model of [13, 14, 5, 7] requires that the superposition of pixels of the same color results in that same color. This property is not real, because the result is a darker version of the original color.

In this paper we consider a model where when superimposing pixels we can only superimpose black pixels, white pixels and at most 1 pixel of a given color. Thus we consider the identity and annihilator color as special colors. Clearly using this constraint the reconstruction of a color is perfect, in the sense that it gives the exact original color and not a darker version of it.

Using the above model we build c-color (k, n)-threshold schemes whose pixel expansion is $m = c\binom{n}{k}2^{k-2}$.

Clearly our schemes are not comparable with the previous ones, since the model used is different. Our model requires an extra property so it is not surprising that our pixel expansion is, in general, worst than the corresponding schemes in the previous models. What it is surprising, however, is that for the case of $k = n$, our c-color (n, n)-threshold schemes achieve a better pixel expansion. However, it should be noted that we use also the white color as a special color.

Finally, we also provide a proof of optimality, with respect to the pixel expansion, of the c-color (n, n)-threshold scheme.

This paper is organized as follows. Section 2 contains some observation about the real properties of color superposition which justify the model used in this paper. In Section 3 we provide a formal definition of the model. Then, in Section 4, we provide the construction of c-color (k, n)-threshold schemes. In Section 5 we provide a proof of optimality, with respect to the pixel expansion, of the c-color (n, n)-threshold scheme. Finally Section 6 contains some concluding remarks and directions for future work.

2   Light and Colors

Roughly speaking, light is a flux of photons, with each photon having a particular energy (frequency). The energy of a photon corresponds to the color we see when that photon hits our eyes. The intensity of the light depends on the number of photons. A white light is a flux of photons of all possible visible frequencies (all colors).

A filter (or the surface of an object) of a particular color C absorbs all of the frequencies except the ones that "make up" color C, so that, when looking at the light through the filter (or reflected by the surface of the object), we see color C.

Combining the fundamental colors, which are red, green and blue, and varying their intensity, it is possible to obtain any other color. So, for our purposes, a color C can be represented by a triple (x, y, z), where x, y and z denote the amount of red, green and blue, respectively, that color C consists of. Each component of the triple can be considered as a a filter absorbing red, green and blue photons, respectively; the amount of light left is described by an integer in the range $[0, L]$. With this setting, we can produce $(L+1)^3$ different colors, which, for L sufficiently large, are enough to approximate all colors that the human eye is able to distinguish. Typically, for computers, we have $L = 255$; for simplicity we will use $L = 100$.

The color $(0, 0, 0)$, which we will denote with $\bullet$, is the black color: indeed all filters are 0 meaning that there is no light left. The color $(100, 100, 100)$, which we will denote with $\circ$ is white (transparent) because no light is absorbed by the filters. The colors red, green and blue are represented, respectively, by $(100, 0, 0), (0, 100, 0)$ and $(0, 0, 100)$; we will refer to these colors also as R, G and B, respectively. The colors yellow, magenta and cyan are represented, respectively, by $(100, 100, 0), (100, 0, 100)$ and $(0, 100, 100)$; we will refer to these colors also as Y, M and C, respectively. The color $(50, 0, 0)$ is also a red, because that is the only component present, but it is darker since some red light is absorbed. The higher is the value of the component the lighter is the color. If all components are equal, i.e. (x, x, x), then the resulting color is a gray whose intensity depends on x: the smaller is x, the darker is the gray.

Let $C_1 = (x_1, y_1, z_1)$ and $C_2 = (x_2, y_2, z_2)$ be two colors and assume that two pixels of color C_1 and of color C_2 are printed on two different transparencies. Superimposing the transparencies, one on the top of the other, the resulting color can be expressed (approximately) as:

$$\text{add}(C_1, C_2) = \left(\text{int} \left(\frac{x_1 x_2}{L} \right), \text{int} \left(\frac{y_1 y_2}{L} \right), \text{int} \left(\frac{z_1 z_2}{L} \right) \right), \qquad (2)$$

where the int function approximates its argument to the nearest integer. Operator add defines the "color superposition". The add operation can naturally be extended to any number of colors. The add operation is commutative and thus the order in which we superpose the colors is irrelevant. Color $\circ$ is the "identity" color, in the sense that for any color C we have that $\text{add}(C, \circ) = C$, while color $\bullet$ is the "annihilator" color, in the sense that for any color C we have that $\text{add}(C, \bullet) = \bullet$. As expected, it results that $\text{add}(\text{Y}, \text{M}) = \text{R}$, $\text{add}(\text{R}, \text{G}) = \text{Y}$, $\text{add}(\text{Y}, \text{M}, \text{C}) = \bullet$. Other examples of the result of color superposition are the following: $\text{add}((80, 80, 80), (80, 80, 80)) = (64, 64, 64)$, $\text{add}((63, 40, 65), (50, 92, 31)) = (31, 37, 20)$.

Hence superimposing two pixels of the same color one gets a different color. For example consider color $(90, 0, 0)$, which is an almost full intensity red. If we superimpose two pixels with such a color we get a pixel of color $(81, 0, 0)$. If we superimpose 5 pixels all with color $(90, 0, 0)$ the resulting pixel has color $(59, 0, 0)$. The difference between $(90, 0, 0)$ and $(59, 0, 0)$ is quite evident to the human eye. Clearly the more pixels we superimpose the darker the result will be and thus the recognition of the color might become problematic. Figure 1 illustrates this situation: on the left it is shown a pixel with color $(78, 78, 78)$, a light gray, then the result of superimposing pixels with that color is shown. On the far right of the figure it is shown the result of superimposing 16 such pixels; the resulting pixel is hardly distinguishable from black.

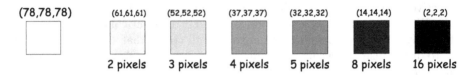

Fig. 1. Example of darkening in color superposition. The original color is a light gray $(78, 78, 78)$

This problem is even more evident if the original color is not very intense as the resulting superposition gets close to black very quickly. For example superimposing 5 pixels of color $(50, 0, 0)$, which is an half-red, one gets $(3, 0, 0)$ which is hardly distinguishable from black by the human eye.

Hence in this paper we focus on a model that avoids superimposing pixels with the same color.

3   The Model

A secret image, consisting of colored pixels, has to be shared among a set $\mathcal{P} = \{1, \ldots, n\}$ of *participants*. A trusted party, which is called the *dealer* and is not a participant, knows the secret image. The dealer has to distribute *shares* to the n participants in the form of printed transparencies. The subsets of $\mathcal{P}$ consisting of at least k participants are called *qualified sets*. Participants in a qualified subset have to be able to "visually" recover the secret image, by stacking together their shares (transparencies) and holding the stacked set of transparencies to the light. All other subsets, that is, those which have less than k participants, are called *forbidden sets*. Participants in a forbidden set must be not able to get any information on the secret image from their shares, neither by stacking together the transparencies nor by any other computation. Schemes where the forbidden and qualified sets are defined as above are called (k, n)-threshold schemes. Sometimes more general access structures are used, however in this paper we are concerned only with (k, n)-threshold schemes.

From now on we concentrate on how to deal with just one pixel of the image. In order to share the whole image it is enough to repeat the sharing process for each pixel of the image.

Each secret pixel is divided into m subpixels. This implies a loss of resolution: the pixels of the reconstructed image will be m times bigger compared to the ones of the original image. A *share* is a "version" of the secret pixel consisting of a particular assignment of colors to the m subpixels.

Each pixel, either in the original image or in the shares, has one of c colors which we denote by $\{1, 2, \ldots, c\}$. We augment the set of colors with the "annihilator" color black, which we denote with the symbol •, and with the "identity" (transparent) color white, which we denote with the symbol ∘.

We remark that we still have only c colors in the original image; the added black and white colors are needed to cover up the noise introduced in the reconstructed image in order to not reveal information to forbidden sets of participants.

Superimposing two pixels one gets a pixel of a color which depends on the color of the superimposed pixels. The add operator, defined in Equation (2), gives the superposition color.

The add operator is easily extended to (column) vectors of colors for which it returns the result of superimposing all the pixels of the vector. We also extend it to matrices: given a matrix M the $\mathrm{add}(M)$ is the (row) vector with elements in $\{\bullet, \circ, 1, 2, ..., c\}$ obtained by letting the ith entry be the add of the ith column of M. We also use a generalized Hamming weight $w_i(\Psi)$ for a vector of colors Ψ, which gives the number of colors in Ψ that are equal to color i. Notice that $w_\bullet(\Psi)$ returns the number of components equal to the special $\bullet$ color (and similarly for $\circ$).

Given a matrix M and a set X of natural numbers, which represent participants, we denote by $M|X$ the matrix consisting of only the rows of M corresponding to the integers in X, if they exists in M. For example, assuming that M has at least 6 rows, if $X = \{2, 3, 6\}$, then $M|X$ is the submatrix of M consisting of the second, the third and the sixth row of M.

Next we provide the definition of a colored visual cryptography scheme.

Definition 1. *Consider a set of c colors $\{1, 2, \ldots, c\}$ and let h and ℓ be integers such that $0 \leq \ell < h \leq m$. A c-color (k, n)-threshold visual cryptography scheme for a set of n participants, consists of c collections (multisets) of $n \times m$ matrices $\mathcal{C}^0, ..., \mathcal{C}^{c-1}$, whose elements are in the set $\{\circ, \bullet, 1, 2, \ldots, c\}$, satisfying:*

1. *Given a qualified set X, $|X| = k$, for any $M \in \mathcal{C}^i$, it holds that $w_i(\mathrm{add}(M|X)) \geq h$ and $w_j(\mathrm{add}(M|X)) \leq \ell$ for any $j \neq i$.*
2. *Given a forbidden set X, $|X| < k$, the c collections of $|X| \times m$ matrices, $\mathcal{D}^i$, $i = 0, 1, ..., c - 1$, consisting of $M|X$ for each $M \in \mathcal{C}^i$, are equal.*
3. *For any column Ψ in any base matrix we have that $w_\bullet(\Psi) + w_\circ(\Psi) = n - 1$.*

To share a secret pixel of color i, the dealer randomly chooses one of the matrices in $\mathcal{C}^i$ and distributes row j to participant j. Thus, the chosen matrix defines the m subpixels in each of the n transparencies.

Since matrices in $\mathcal{C}^i$ are used to share pixels of color i we say that i is the *primary* color for $\mathcal{C}^i$, while any other color $j \neq i$ is a *secondary* color for $\mathcal{C}^i$.

Property 1 of Definition 1 is called the *contrast property* because it guarantees that the secret image will be visible for a qualified set of participants. Property 2 is called the *security property* because it guarantees that a forbidden set of participants has no information on the secret image. Property 3 guarantees that the reconstruction of the secret pixel gives the exact same color as the original secret pixel.

Notice that the contrast property guarantees the reconstruction only for qualified sets X whose cardinality is exactly k and not for qualified sets of cardinality greater than k. This is without loss of generality since a qualified set of participants consisting of more than k members can anyway reconstruct the image by simply using only k shares and leaving out the remaining ones.

Finally we remark that, although the definition of a VCS is almost identical to that given in [13] and used also in other papers, the definition differs in that it allows also the use of the identity color ∘, beside the annihilator color •, and more fundamentally it differs because of the underlying rule the regulates the result of color superposition. In particular while in previous models it is assumed that superimposing pixels with the same color one gets that color, in our model the superposition of pixels with the same color gives a darker version of the original color. As we have discussed in Section 2, this is what happens in reality.

Base matrices. Given a matrix B we denote by $\mathcal{C}(B)$ the set of matrices obtained by permuting in all possible ways the columns of B. In most schemes, the c collections $\mathcal{C}^i$ are obtained by fixing c matrices B^i and letting $\mathcal{C}^i = \mathcal{C}(B^i)$. The matrices B^i are called the "base matrices". Base matrices constitute an efficient representation of the scheme. Indeed, the dealer has to store only the base matrices and in order to randomly choose a matrix from $\mathcal{C}(B^i)$ he has to randomly choose a permutation of the columns of the base matrix B^i.

Notice that the security property for a base matrices scheme is equivalent to: Given a forbidden set X, the matrices $B^i|X$, for $i = 0, 1, \ldots, c-1$ are the same up to a permutation of the columns.

4   Construction of c-Color (k, n)-Threshold Schemes

The construction uses as a building block a b&w $(k-1, k-1)$-threshold scheme with perfect reconstruction of black pixels. A scheme with perfect reconstruction of black pixels is a scheme where a black secret pixel is reconstructed with all subpixels black. We remark that for the case of $k = 2$ one would need a $(1, 1)$-threshold b&w scheme which, for obvious reasons, is not a scheme. For the scope of the next construction, we let $S_1^\bullet = [\bullet]$ and $S_1^\circ = [\circ]$ be the base matrices of a $(1, 1)$-threshold scheme.

Construction 1 *Fix k and n, $2 \le k \le n$. Let S_{k-1}° and $S_{k-1}^\bullet$ be the basis matrices of a $(k-1, k-1)$-threshold scheme with perfect reconstruction of black pixels and let m' be the pixel expansion of such a scheme. Denote the rows of S_{k-1}° and $S_{k-1}^\bullet$ with w_i and b_i, respectively:*

$$S_{k-1}^\circ = \begin{bmatrix} w_1 \\ w_2 \\ \ldots \\ \ldots \\ w_{k-1} \end{bmatrix}, \qquad S_{k-1}^\bullet = \begin{bmatrix} b_1 \\ b_2 \\ \ldots \\ \ldots \\ b_{k-1} \end{bmatrix}.$$

Let $F_{k,n}(i, S_{k-1}^\phi)$, where $i \in \{1, 2, ..., c\}$ and $\phi \in \{\circ, \bullet\}$ be the $n \times \binom{n}{k}m'$ matrix constructed by $\binom{n}{k}$ submatrices, called "blocks", with dimension $n \times m'$ each consisting of the following rows: $n - k$ ("black") rows of m' elements $\bullet$; each block differs from the others in the choice of the $n - k$ "black" rows; The *remaining k rows are filled with one row of elements equal to i followed in order by the $k - 1$ rows of S_{k-1}^{ϕ}.*

Base matrix for color i, for $i \in \{1, 2, ..., c\}$, is given by:

$$B^i = F_{k,n}(1, S_{k-1}^{\bullet}) + ... + F_{k,n}(i - 1, S_{k-1}^{\bullet}) + F_{k,n}(i, S_{k-1}^{\circ}) + F_{k,n}(i + 1, S_{k-1}^{\bullet}) + ... + F_{k,n}(c, S_{k-1}^{\bullet}).$$

☐

Some examples will clarify the above construction. Let us start with the case $k = n$ for which the construction becomes very simple: The matrix $F_{n,n}(i, S_{k-1}^{\circ})$ is simply given by the first row consisting of all i's and the remaining rows are given by S_{k-1}°, and similarly for $F_{n,n}(j, S_{k-1}^{\bullet})$.

For example consider $k = n = 4$ and S_{k-1}° and $S_{k-1}^{\bullet}$ given by the Naor and Shamir $(4, 4)$-threshold scheme [12], that is

$$S_{k-1}^{\circ} = \begin{bmatrix} \circ \circ \circ \bullet \circ \bullet \bullet \bullet \\ \circ \circ \bullet \circ \bullet \circ \bullet \bullet \\ \circ \bullet \circ \circ \bullet \bullet \circ \bullet \\ \circ \bullet \bullet \bullet \circ \circ \circ \bullet \end{bmatrix} \qquad S_{k-1}^{\bullet} = \begin{bmatrix} \circ \circ \circ \bullet \circ \bullet \bullet \bullet \\ \circ \circ \bullet \circ \bullet \circ \bullet \bullet \\ \circ \bullet \circ \circ \bullet \bullet \circ \bullet \\ \bullet \circ \circ \circ \bullet \bullet \bullet \circ \end{bmatrix}$$

The following are the base matrices of a 3-color $(5,5)$-threshold scheme (the vertical bars identify the F matrices) obtained with Construction 1.

$$B^1 = \begin{bmatrix} 1\,1\,1\,1\,1\,1\,1\,1 & 2\,2\,2\,2\,2\,2\,2\,2 & 3\,3\,3\,3\,3\,3\,3\,3 \\ \circ \circ \circ \bullet \circ \bullet \bullet \bullet & \circ \circ \circ \bullet \circ \bullet \bullet \bullet & \circ \circ \circ \bullet \circ \bullet \bullet \bullet \\ \circ \circ \bullet \circ \bullet \circ \bullet \bullet & \circ \circ \bullet \circ \bullet \circ \bullet \bullet & \circ \circ \bullet \circ \bullet \circ \bullet \bullet \\ \circ \bullet \circ \circ \bullet \bullet \circ \bullet & \circ \bullet \circ \circ \bullet \bullet \circ \bullet & \circ \bullet \circ \circ \bullet \bullet \circ \bullet \\ \circ \bullet \bullet \bullet \circ \circ \circ \bullet & \bullet \circ \circ \circ \bullet \bullet \bullet \circ & \bullet \circ \circ \circ \bullet \bullet \bullet \circ \end{bmatrix}$$

$$B^2 = \begin{bmatrix} 2\,2\,2\,2\,2\,2\,2\,2 & 1\,1\,1\,1\,1\,1\,1\,1 & 3\,3\,3\,3\,3\,3\,3\,3 \\ \circ \circ \circ \bullet \circ \bullet \bullet \bullet & \circ \circ \circ \bullet \circ \bullet \bullet \bullet & \circ \circ \circ \bullet \circ \bullet \bullet \bullet \\ \circ \circ \bullet \circ \bullet \circ \bullet \bullet & \circ \circ \bullet \circ \bullet \circ \bullet \bullet & \circ \circ \bullet \circ \bullet \circ \bullet \bullet \\ \circ \bullet \circ \circ \bullet \bullet \circ \bullet & \circ \bullet \circ \circ \bullet \bullet \circ \bullet & \circ \bullet \circ \circ \bullet \bullet \circ \bullet \\ \circ \bullet \bullet \bullet \circ \circ \circ \bullet & \bullet \circ \circ \circ \bullet \bullet \bullet \circ & \bullet \circ \circ \circ \bullet \bullet \bullet \circ \end{bmatrix}$$

$$B^3 = \begin{bmatrix} 3\,3\,3\,3\,3\,3\,3\,3 & 1\,1\,1\,1\,1\,1\,1\,1 & 2\,2\,2\,2\,2\,2\,2\,2 \\ \circ \circ \circ \bullet \circ \bullet \bullet \bullet & \circ \circ \circ \bullet \circ \bullet \bullet \bullet & \circ \circ \circ \bullet \circ \bullet \bullet \bullet \\ \circ \circ \bullet \circ \bullet \circ \bullet \bullet & \circ \circ \bullet \circ \bullet \circ \bullet \bullet & \circ \circ \bullet \circ \bullet \circ \bullet \bullet \\ \circ \bullet \circ \circ \bullet \bullet \circ \bullet & \circ \bullet \circ \circ \bullet \bullet \circ \bullet & \circ \bullet \circ \circ \bullet \bullet \circ \bullet \\ \circ \bullet \bullet \bullet \circ \circ \circ \bullet & \bullet \circ \circ \circ \bullet \bullet \bullet \circ & \bullet \circ \circ \circ \bullet \bullet \bullet \circ \end{bmatrix}$$

The case of $k = n$ is particularly easy to understand because we only have 1 block and we don't have to add any "black" row. So let us now consider another example. Let $k = 3$ and $n = 4$ and once again consider the matrices S°_{k-1} and $S^{\bullet}_{k-1}$ given by the Naor and Shamir $(2, 2)$-threshold scheme [12], that is

$$
S^{\circ}_2 = \begin{bmatrix} \circ & \bullet \\ \circ & \bullet \end{bmatrix}, \qquad S^{\bullet}_2 = \begin{bmatrix} \circ & \bullet \\ \bullet & \circ \end{bmatrix}.
$$

In this case the F matrices will have $\binom{n}{k} = 4$ blocks, since we have to place 1 black row in each of 4 possible positions. Hence we have:

$$
F_{3,4}(i, S^{\circ}_2) = \begin{bmatrix}
i & i & i & i & i & i & \bullet & \bullet \\
\circ & \bullet & \circ & \bullet & \bullet & \bullet & i & i \\
\circ & \bullet & \bullet & \bullet & \circ & \bullet & \circ & \bullet \\
\bullet & \bullet & \circ & \bullet & \circ & \bullet & \circ & \bullet
\end{bmatrix}, \quad
F_{3,4}(i, S^{\bullet}_2) = \begin{bmatrix}
i & i & i & i & i & i & \bullet & \bullet \\
\circ & \bullet & \circ & \bullet & \bullet & \bullet & i & i \\
\bullet & \circ & \bullet & \circ & \circ & \bullet & \circ & \bullet \\
\bullet & \bullet & \bullet & \circ & \bullet & \circ & \bullet & \circ
\end{bmatrix}.
$$

The vertical bars identify the 4 blocks. As can be seen each block is given by 1 black row, and the remaining rows filled, in this order, by one row of i's and the rows of S°_2 (or $S^{\bullet}_2$), from the first to the last. Using the above F matrices we can build the following 3-color $(3, 4)$-threshold scheme.

$$
B^1 = \begin{bmatrix}
1 & 1 & 1 & 1 & 1 & 1 & \bullet & \bullet & 2 & 2 & 2 & 2 & 2 & 2 & \bullet & \bullet & 3 & 3 & 3 & 3 & 3 & 3 & \bullet & \bullet \\
\circ & \bullet & \circ & \bullet & \bullet & \bullet & 1 & 1 & \circ & \bullet & \circ & \bullet & \bullet & \bullet & 2 & 2 & \circ & \bullet & \circ & \bullet & \bullet & \bullet & 3 & 3 \\
\circ & \bullet & \bullet & \bullet & \circ & \bullet & \circ & \bullet & \bullet & \circ & \bullet & \bullet & \circ & \bullet & \circ & \bullet & \circ & \bullet & \bullet & \bullet & \circ & \bullet & \circ & \bullet \\
\bullet & \bullet & \circ & \bullet & \circ & \bullet & \circ & \bullet & \bullet & \bullet & \bullet & \circ & \bullet & \circ & \bullet & \circ & \bullet & \bullet & \circ & \bullet & \circ & \bullet & \circ & \bullet
\end{bmatrix},
$$

$$
B^2 = \begin{bmatrix}
2 & 2 & 2 & 2 & 2 & 2 & \bullet & \bullet & 1 & 1 & 1 & 1 & 1 & 1 & \bullet & \bullet & 3 & 3 & 3 & 3 & 3 & 3 & \bullet & \bullet \\
\circ & \bullet & \circ & \bullet & \bullet & \bullet & 2 & 2 & \circ & \bullet & \circ & \bullet & \bullet & \bullet & 1 & 1 & \circ & \bullet & \circ & \bullet & \bullet & \bullet & 3 & 3 \\
\circ & \bullet & \bullet & \bullet & \circ & \bullet & \circ & \bullet & \bullet & \circ & \bullet & \bullet & \circ & \bullet & \circ & \bullet & \circ & \bullet & \bullet & \bullet & \circ & \bullet & \circ & \bullet \\
\bullet & \bullet & \circ & \bullet & \circ & \bullet & \circ & \bullet & \bullet & \bullet & \bullet & \circ & \bullet & \circ & \bullet & \circ & \bullet & \bullet & \circ & \bullet & \circ & \bullet & \circ & \bullet
\end{bmatrix},
$$

$$
B^3 = \begin{bmatrix}
3 & 3 & 3 & 3 & 3 & 3 & \bullet & \bullet & 1 & 1 & 1 & 1 & 1 & 1 & \bullet & \bullet & 2 & 2 & 2 & 2 & 2 & 2 & \bullet & \bullet \\
\circ & \bullet & \circ & \bullet & \bullet & \bullet & 3 & 3 & \circ & \bullet & \circ & \bullet & \bullet & \bullet & 1 & 1 & \circ & \bullet & \circ & \bullet & \bullet & \bullet & 2 & 2 \\
\circ & \bullet & \bullet & \bullet & \circ & \bullet & \circ & \bullet & \bullet & \circ & \bullet & \bullet & \circ & \bullet & \circ & \bullet & \circ & \bullet & \bullet & \bullet & \circ & \bullet & \circ & \bullet \\
\bullet & \bullet & \circ & \bullet & \circ & \bullet & \circ & \bullet & \bullet & \bullet & \bullet & \circ & \bullet & \circ & \bullet & \circ & \bullet & \bullet & \circ & \bullet & \circ & \bullet & \circ & \bullet
\end{bmatrix}.
$$

We give another example for $k = 3$, $n = 5$. Using again the S°_2 and $S^{\bullet}_2$ seen before, we have that

$$
F_{3,5}(i, S^{\circ}_2) = \begin{bmatrix}
i & i & i & i & i & i & \bullet & \bullet & i & i & i & i & \bullet & \bullet & i & i & \bullet & \bullet & \bullet & \bullet \\
\circ & \bullet & \circ & \bullet & \bullet & \bullet & i & i & \circ & \bullet & \bullet & \bullet & i & i & \bullet & \bullet & i & i & \bullet & \bullet \\
\circ & \bullet & \bullet & \bullet & \circ & \bullet & \circ & \bullet & \bullet & \bullet & \circ & \bullet & \circ & \bullet & \bullet & \bullet & \bullet & \bullet & i & i \\
\bullet & \bullet & \circ & \bullet & \circ & \bullet & \circ & \bullet & \bullet & \bullet & \bullet & \circ & \bullet & \circ & \bullet & \circ & \bullet & \bullet & \circ & \bullet \\
\bullet & \bullet & \bullet & \circ & \bullet & \circ & \bullet & \circ & \bullet & \circ & \bullet & \circ & \bullet & \circ & \bullet & \circ & \bullet & \circ & \bullet & \circ
\end{bmatrix}.
$$

Next we prove that the construction described above is correct.

Lemma 1. *Construction 1 builds a c-color (k, n)-threshold VCS, with pixel expansion $m = c\binom{n}{k}2^{k-2}$, where m' is the pixel expansion of the black and white scheme used as building block, and $\ell = 0$, $h \geq 1$.*

Proof. We start by proving the security property. We observe the following: Each base matrix consists of several blocks, and by construction there is one similar block per each color (either primary or secondary) with the only difference that for the primary color the block is made up from rows coming from S°_{k-1}, while for each secondary color the block is made up from rows coming from $S^\bullet_{k-1}$. Hence the security property of the new scheme follows directly from the security property of the $(k-1, k-1)$-threshold scheme given by the matrices S°_{k-1} and $S^\bullet_{k-1}$.

Now consider the contrast property. For a qualified set of participants each block for a secondary color contains either a row with all blacks, or it contains all the $k-1$ rows of $S^\bullet_{k-1}$. Recalling that the matrix $S^\bullet_{k-1}$ provides a perfect reconstruction of the black pixels, in both of the above cases we have that a secondary color is always superimposed to a black pixel. This implies that $\ell = 0$. For the primary color there will be at least one block that restricted to the qualified set of participants will consists of one row with the primary color and the remaining $k-1$ rows given by S°_{k-1}. Hence at least one pixel will be superimposed to all white pixels, and thus at least 1 pixel will be of the primary color (the exact number depends on the black and white scheme that one uses as a building block). Thus we have $h \geq 1$.

Finally the pixel expansion is easily computed observing that the number of blocks in each F matrix is $\binom{n}{k}$ and the width of each block is the same as the pixel expansion m' of the b&w scheme used as building block. Since there is one F matrix per each color, the pixel expansion is $m = c\binom{n}{k}m'$. $\quad\square$

The best, with respect to the pixel expansion, b&w (k,k)-threshold scheme with perfect reconstruction of black pixels is the scheme provided in [12]. Hence to build our c-color (k,n)-threshold schemes we use the b&w $(k-1, k-1)$-threshold scheme by Naor and Shamir whose pixel expansion is $m' = 2^{k-2}$. Hence Construction 1 gives a (k,n)-threshold scheme with pixel expansion $m = c\binom{n}{k}2^{k-2}$.

The pixel expansion of our schemes is in general worst than that of previous schemes. This is not surprising since our model requires an extra property. However in the case of $k = n$ we also achieve an improvement, with respect to the pixel expansion, over previous schemes. The pixel expansion of our c-color (n,n)-threshold schemes is $c2^{n-2}$. This is a factor of 2 better than the lower bound (1). Hence it is a factor of 2 better than the optimal c-color (n,n)-threshold schemes of [14, 7]. However, in our model, we use also white as a special color.

5   Optimal Pixel Expansion for $k = n$

In this section we give the sketch of a proof that in the model considered in this paper the c-color (n,n)-threshold scheme of Construction 1 is optimal with respect to the pixel expansion. The proof is similar to that used to prove that the Naor and Shamir b&w (n,n)-threshold scheme has optimal pixel expansion, because it basically argues that such a scheme must be used as a building block in our model.

Remember that each column of the base matrices is composed of 1 colored pixel and $n - 1$ black and white white pixels. Fix a color i and consider base matrix B^i. Since base matrix B^i reconstructs color i there must be at least one column consisting of 1 pixel of color i and $n - 1$ white pixels. Without loss of generality, assume that the color is placed on the first row.

In order to satisfy the security property for forbidden sets consisting of $n - 1$ participants, it is necessary that any other base matrix B^j, with $j \neq i$, has all the columns that have i on the first row and exactly $n - 2$ white pixels, while the remaining one have to be black (indeed if the exact same column appears in all base matrix then it is useless and can be deleted). This implies that base matrix B^i must contain all the $\binom{n}{1}$ columns which have a secondary color on the first row and in the remaining positions have $n - 2$ white and 1 black. But then reiterating this reasoning we have that base matrix B^i must contain all the $\binom{n}{2}$ columns that have i on the first row and in the remaining positions have $n - 3$ white and 2 black, and that it must contain all the $\binom{n}{3}$ columns with have j in the first row and in the remaining positions have $n - 4$ white and 3 blacks, and so on.

Hence it follows that base matrix B^i must have at least 2^{n-2} columns consisting of one row with the primary color i and the remaining columns which contains all the columns with an even number of black pixels and for each secondary j color at least 2^{n-2} columns consisting of one row with the secondary color j and the remaining columns which contains all the columns with an odd number of black pixels.

Hence base matrix B^i must have at least $c2^{n-2}$ columns and thus we have the following lemma.

Lemma 2. *The pixel expansion of a c-color (n, n)-threshold scheme is lower bounded by $c2^{n-2}$.*

6   Discussion and Conclusions

Observation 1. Although Construction 1 requires the b&w scheme used as a building block to have a perfect reconstruction of black pixels, the construction still works with other b&w schemes, but the resulting colored scheme will have $\ell > 0$. As remarked in [13], the recognition of the reconstructed color is easier for schemes with $\ell = 0$.

Observation 2. We can provide schemes for general access structures by using the same technique used for b&w schemes [2]. Such a technique builds schemes for general access structures starting from a (k, k)-threshold scheme. For each qualified set in the access structure we use a c-color (k, k)-threshold scheme, where k is the cardinality of the qualified set and we fill the remaining $n - k$ row with black. We then build the base matrices by simply concatenating the matrices described above for each qualified set.

Observation 3. We can transform a known scheme that uses the model of [13], such as the schemes of [13, 14, 5, 7] into a new scheme for the model introduced in this paper. Such a transformation has to eliminate the superposition of pixels with the same color. An easy way to this is to substitute each column of a base matrix that contains a certain number p of pixels of a given color i with p columns each of which substitutes the p pixels of color i with $p-1$ pixels of color $\circ$ and one pixel of color i, choosing the one pixel of color i in each of the p possible positions. Such a transformation, however, is in general not efficient in terms of pixel expansion, and yields schemes with pixel expansion worst than the one of the schemes provided in Section 4.

Conclusions. In this paper we have considered a new model for colored visual cryptography. Compared with previously used models our model requires an extra property, namely, that the reconstruction of the secret pixel must preserve the original color. We have provided a construction for c-color (k, n)-threshold scheme, for any number of color c, and for any value of k, n, with $2 \leq k \leq n$.

We prove that our c-color (n, n)-threshold schemes are optimal in our model. It remains open the problem of finding the optimal schemes for $k < n$.

The model considered in this paper stems from the observation that superimposing pixels of the same color one gets a darker version of that color, and thus, especially when superimposing many pixels, the reconstructed color can get very close, and thus indistinguishable, from the black color, which is usually used to make the scheme secure and is always present in the reconstruction. In a more general model one can consider the real properties of color superposition. As far as we know very few papers have tried this approach [11, 1, 10] and in all cases the schemes work for restricted sets of colors. An interesting direction of research would be to provide schemes that better exploit the real properties of color superposition.

Acknowledgments. The second author would like to thank Dr. Davide Stelitano for several discussions about the properties of light and colors which allowed us to understand the color superposition operation. We also thank Dr. Gianluca Caputo for several useful discussions.

References

1. A. Adhikari and S. Sikdar, A new $(2, n)$-Visual Threshold Scheme for Color Images. In Proceedings of INDOCRYPT 2003, Springer-Verlag LNCS 2904, pp. 148–161, 2003.
2. G. Ateniese, C. Blundo, A. De Santis, and D. R. Stinson, Visual Cryptography for General Access Structures. *Informatiosn and Computation*, No. 129 (2), pp. 86–106, 1996.
3. G. Ateniese, C. Blundo, A. De Santis, and D. R. Stinson, Extended Schemes for Visual Cryptography. *Theoretical Computer Science*, No. 250, pp. 143-161, 2001.
4. C. Blundo, P. D'Arco, A. De Santis, and D. R. Stinson, *Contrast Optimal Threshold Visual Cryptography Schemes*, SIAM J. on Discrete Math. 16, pp. 224-261, 2003.
5. C. Blundo, A. De Bonis and A. De Santis, Improved Schemes for Visual Cryptography. *Designs, Codes, and Cryptography*, No. 24, pp. 255–278, 2001.

6. C. Blundo, A. De Santis, and D. R. Stinson, On the Contrast in Visual Cryptography Schemes. *Journal of Cryptology*, No. 12(4), pp. 261-289, 1999.
7. S. Cimato, R. De Prisco and A. De Santis, Optimal Colored Threshold Visual Cryptography Schemes. To appear in *Designs, Codes, and Cryptography*.
8. P. A. Eisen and D. R. Stinson, Threshold Visual Cryptography Schemes With Specified Whiteness Levels of Reconstructed Pixels. *Designs, Codes and Cryptography*, No. 25, pp. 15-61, 2002.
9. T. Hofmeister, M. Krause, and H. U. Simon, Contrast-Optimal k out of n Secret Sharing Schemes in Visual Cryptography. *Theoretical Computer Science* n. 240, pp. 471-485, 2000.
10. Young-Chang Hou, Visual cryptography for color images. *Pattern Recognition*, Vol. 36, pp. 1619–1629, 2003.
11. H. Koga and H. Yamamoto, Proposal of a Lattice-Based Visual Secret Sharing Scheme for Color and Gray-Scale Images. *IEICE Trans. on Fundamentals of Electronics, Communication and Computer Sciences*, Vol. 81-A, no. 6, pp. 1262–1269, 1998.
12. M. Naor and A. Shamir, Visual Cryptography. In *Advances in Cryptology – EUROCRYPT '94*, Springer-Verlag LNCS 950, pp. 1–12, 1995.
13. E. R. Verheul and H. C. A. van Tilborg, Constructions and Properties of k out of n Visual Secret Sharing Schemes. *Designs, Codes, and Cryptography*, No. 11(2), pp. 179–196, 1997.
14. C-N. Yang and C.-S. Laih, New Colored Visual Secret Sharing Schemes. *Designs, Codes, and Cryptography*, No. 20, pp. 325–335, 2000.

On the Size of Monotone Span Programs

Ventzislav Nikov[1], Svetla Nikova[2,*], and Bart Preneel[2]

[1] Department of Mathematics and Computing Science,
Eindhoven University of Technology
P.O. Box 513, 5600 MB, Eindhoven, The Netherlands
v.nikov@tue.nl
[2] Department Electrical Engineering, ESAT/COSIC,
Katholieke Universiteit Leuven, Kasteelpark Arenberg 10,
B-3001 Heverlee-Leuven, Belgium
{svetla.nikova, bart.preneel}@esat.kuleuven.ac.be

Abstract. Span programs provide a linear algebraic model of computation. Monotone span programs (MSP) correspond to linear secret sharing schemes. This paper studies the properties of monotone span programs related to their size. Using the results of van Dijk (connecting codes and MSPs) and a construction for a dual monotone span program proposed by Cramer and Fehr we prove a non-trivial upper bound for the size of monotone span programs. By combining the concept of critical families with the dual monotone span program construction of Cramer and Fehr we improve the known lower bound with a constant factor, showing that the lower bound for the size of monotone span programs should be approximately twice as large. Finally, we extend the result of van Dijk showing that for any MSP there exists a dual MSP such that the corresponding codes are dual.

1 Introduction

Motivation and Related Work. Span programs have been introduced in 1993 by Karchmer and Wigderson in [14] as a linear algebraic model of computation. A span program for a Boolean function is presented as a matrix over a field with rows labelled by literals of the variables, and the size of the program is the number of the rows. The span program accepts an assignment if and only if the all-ones row is a linear combination of the rows whose labels are consistent with the assignment. A span program is *monotone* if only positive literals are used as labels of the rows.

One main motivation to study span programs is that lower bounds for their size imply lower bounds for formula size and other interesting complexity measures including branching program size. The class of functions computable by

* The work described in this paper has been supported in part by the European Commission through the IST Programme under Contract IST-2002-507932 ECRYPT, IWT STWW project on Anonymity and Privacy in Electronic Services and Concerted Research Action GOA-MEFISTO-666 of the Flemish Government.

C. Blundo and S. Cimato (Eds.): SCN 2004, LNCS 3352, pp. 249–262, 2005.

polynomial size span programs over $GF(2)$ is equivalent to the class of functions computable by polynomial size parity branching programs [7, 14]. Span programs over other fields are related to other logspace classes [1, 7, 14].

Monotone span programs (MSPs) are also closely related to the cryptographic primitive *secret sharing schemes*. The concept of *secret sharing* was introduced by Shamir [18] as a tool to protect a secret simultaneously from exposure and from being lost. It allows a so called *dealer* to share the secret among a set of entities, usually called *players*, in such a way that only certain specified subsets of the players are able to reconstruct the secret while smaller subsets have no information about it. Monotone span programs are equivalent to a subclass of secret sharing schemes called *linear secret sharing schemes* (LSSSs). The size of MSPs measures the amount of information that has to be given to the participants in LSSSs. Lower bounds on MSPs imply lower bounds on the length of the shares in LSSSs.

In cryptographic multi-party protocols a general question is to find a "good measure", so that "often" the protocols are polynomially efficient in the number of players. Let *complexity* mean the total number of rounds, bits exchanged, local computations performed, etc. The best measure known for the *efficiency* of an SSS protocol is the *Monotone Span Program Complexity* [8] (which is the size of the MSP) and it coincides with the complexity in terms of linear secret sharing schemes over finite fields. Thus the question of estimating the MSP complexity (i.e. the size of the MSP) is a central question in several areas.

In a series of works [3, 5, 11] a lower bound for the size of an MSP has been proven. Later, Gal [12] proved that the MSP size is in the worst case superpolynomially (in the number of players) lower bounded. In addition it was proven in [4] that the size of MSPs over two fields with different characteristics is incomparable.

Our Results. We focus on studying the properties of MSPs related to their size. Using the results of van Dijk [10] (connecting codes and MSPs) and a construction for dual MSPs proposed by Cramer and Fehr [9] we prove a nontrivial upper bound for the size of MSPs. This result was announced in part in [16]. On the other hand using the same approach as in [3, 11] (critical families) together with the dual MSP construction of Cramer and Fehr [9] we improve the known lower bound with a constant factor; we show that the lower bound for the size of an MSP should be approximately twice as large. The rank of the matrix has been used a number of times to prove lower bounds on various types of complexity. In particular it has been used for the size of monotone formulas and monotone span programs [13]. We show that the nullity (the dimension of the kernel) of the matrix also should be taken into account when estimating the size of MSPs, since the nullity is linked to the rank of the matrix used in the dual MSP. Next we extend the result of van Dijk [10] showing that for any MSP $\mathcal{M}$ there exists a dual MSP $\mathcal{M}^{\perp}$ such that the corresponding codes $\mathcal{C}$ and $\mathcal{C}^{\perp}$ are dual.

Organization. In the next section we recall some definitions and notations that will be used later in the paper. In the first part of Sect. 3 we give some known properties of MSPs, then we describe our results: we modify the dual MSP construction of Cramer and Fehr and present an upper bound for the size of MSP in terms of the number of minimal and maximal sets in the access structure computed by the MSP. In Sect. 4 we first present definitions and known results related to the approach developed in [3, 11, 12]; then we improve the known lower bound for the size of an MSP.

2 Preliminaries

Let us denote the players in a Secret Sharing Scheme by P_i, $1 \leq i \leq n$, the set of all players by $\mathcal{P} = \{P_1, \ldots, P_n\}$ and the set of all subsets of $\mathcal{P}$ (i.e., the power set of $\mathcal{P}$) by $P(\mathcal{P})$. We call the groups which are allowed to reconstruct the secret *qualified* and the groups which should not be able to obtain any information about the secret *forbidden*. The set of qualified groups is denoted by Γ ($\Gamma \subseteq P(\mathcal{P})$) and the set of forbidden groups by Δ ($\Delta \subseteq P(\mathcal{P})$). The set Γ is called *monotone increasing* if for any set A in Γ any set containing A is also in Γ. Similarly, Δ is called *monotone decreasing*, if for each set B in Δ each subset of B is also in Δ. A monotone increasing set Γ can be efficiently described by the set Γ^- consisting of the *minimal elements* in Γ, i.e., the elements in Γ for which no proper subset is also in Γ. Similarly, the set Δ^+ consists of the *maximal elements* (sets) in Δ, i.e., the elements in Δ for which no proper superset is also in Δ. The tuple (Γ, Δ) is called an *access structure* if $\Gamma \cap \Delta = \emptyset$. It is obvious that (Γ^-, Δ^+) generates (Γ, Δ). If the union of Γ and Δ is equal to $P(\mathcal{P})$ (so Γ is equal to Δ^c, the complement of Δ), then we say that the access structure (Γ, Δ) is *complete* and we denote it just by Γ. Throughout the paper we will consider *connected access structures*, i.e., the access structures in which every player is in at least one minimal set. For a complete access structure the dual access structure could be defined as follows. The *dual access structure* $\Gamma^\perp$ of an access structure Γ, defined on $\mathcal{P}$, is the collection of sets $A \subseteq \mathcal{P}$ such that $\mathcal{P} \setminus A = A^c \notin \Gamma$.

In most of the works (e.g. [3, 5, 11, 14]) the connection between MSPs and monotone Boolean functions has been exploit. Here we will show that there is one-to-one correspondence between complete access structures and monotone Boolean functions. Associate with every player P_i a Boolean variable x_i. Then with any set $A \subseteq \mathcal{P}$ we associate a variable $x_A = (x_1, \ldots, x_n)$ by fixing $x_i = 1$ if and only if $P_i \in A$; x_A is sometimes called the *characteristic vector* of A. Now a one-to-one mapping between f and Γ is defined in the following way: $f(x_A) = 1$ if and only if $A \in \Gamma$. A *minterm* of a monotone function is a minimal set of its variables with the property that the value of the function is 1 on any input that assigns 1 to each variable in the set, no matter what the values of the other variables are. Using the mapping between access structures and monotone functions, it is easy to see that minterms correspond to minimal sets. A *maxterm* of a monotone function is a minimal set of its variables with the property that the value of the function is 0 on any input that assigns 0 to each variable in the set, no matter what the values of the other variables are. Recall the one-to-one mapping between f and Γ. With this mapping in mind it is not difficult to verify that maxterms are equivalent to maximal sets. Let $f(x_1, \ldots, x_n)$ be a monotone Boolean function. Let $f^*(x_1, \ldots, x_n) = \overline{f(\overline{x_1}, \ldots, \overline{x_n})}$, sometimes f^* is called the dual function of f. In fact the minterms of f^* are exactly the maxterms of f. Using again the one-to-one mapping between f and Γ it follows that if access structure Γ corresponds to a monotone function f, then the function f^* corresponds to the dual access structure $\Gamma^\perp$.

An SSS is linear if the dealer uses only linear operations to share (reconstruct) the secret amongst the participants. Each *linear SSS* (LSSS) can be viewed as derived from a monotone span program computing its access structure [8]. On the other hand, each monotone span program gives rise to an LSSS. Hence, one can identify an LSSS with its underlying monotone span program. Such an MSP always exists, because MSPs can compute any monotone access structure (see [2, 11, 14]). An important parameter of the MSP is its size, which turns out to be also the size of the corresponding LSSS (the sum of all shares).

Let us describe some of the tools we will employ. An $m \times d$ matrix M over a field $\mathbb{F}$ defines a map from $\mathbb{F}^d$ to $\mathbb{F}^m$ by taking a vector $v \in \mathbb{F}^d$ to the vector $Mv \in \mathbb{F}^m$. Associated with an $m \times d$ matrix M (or a linear map) are two natural subspaces, one in $\mathbb{F}^m$ and the other in $\mathbb{F}^d$. They are defined as follows. The *kernel* of M (denoted by $\ker(M)$) is the set of vectors $u \in \mathbb{F}^d$, such that $Mu = \mathbf{0}$. The *image* of M (denoted by $\mathrm{im}(M)$) is the set of vectors $v \in \mathbb{F}^m$ such that $v = Mu$ for some $u \in \mathbb{F}^d$. The dimension of the image of M is called the *rank* of M, and the dimension of the kernel of M is called its *nullity*. A central result of linear algebra, called *the rank and nullity theorem* states that the dimensions of these two spaces add up to d, the number of columns in M. It is well known that the *column rank* of a matrix M (being the maximal size of a linearly independent set of columns of M) is equal to the *row rank* of M (which is the maximal size of an independent set of rows). The space generated by the rows of a matrix M will sometimes be denoted by $\mathrm{span}(M)$.

For an arbitrary matrix M over a field $\mathbb{F}$, with m rows labelled by $1, \ldots, m$ and for an arbitrary non-empty subset A of $\{1, \ldots, m\}$, let M_A denote the matrix obtained by keeping only those rows i with $i \in A$. In the sequel $\mathbf{v}^i$ will denote a vector but $\mathbf{v}_i$ stands for the i-th coordinate of the vector $\mathbf{v}$. With the standard inner product $\langle \mathbf{v}, \mathbf{w} \rangle$ we write $\mathbf{v} \perp \mathbf{w}$, when $\langle \mathbf{v}, \mathbf{w} \rangle = 0$. For an $\mathbb{F}$-linear subspace $\mathcal{V}$ of $\mathbb{F}^d$, $\mathcal{V}^\perp$ denotes the collection of elements of $\mathbb{F}^d$, that are orthogonal to all of $\mathcal{V}$ (the orthogonal complement). It is again an $\mathbb{F}$-linear subspace. For all subspaces $\mathcal{V}$ of $\mathbb{F}^d$ we have $\mathcal{V} = (\mathcal{V}^\perp)^\perp$. Other standard relations are $(\mathrm{im}(M^T))^\perp = \ker(M)$ or $\mathrm{im}(M^T) = (\ker(M))^\perp$, as well as $\langle \mathbf{v}, M^T \mathbf{w} \rangle = \langle M\mathbf{v}, \mathbf{w} \rangle$.

Let $\mathbb{F}$ be a finite field and let the set of secrets be $\mathcal{K} = \mathbb{F}^{p_0}$, with $p_0 = 1$. Associate with each player P_i ($1 \leq i \leq n$) a positive integer p_i such that the sets of possible shares for player P_i, is a linear subspace $\mathcal{S}_i = \mathbb{F}^{p_i}$. Denote by $p = \sum_{i=1}^{n} p_i$ and by $N = p_0 + p$, then the sharing space $\mathcal{S} = \mathcal{S}_1 \times \cdots \times \mathcal{S}_n = \mathbb{F}^p$ and $\mathcal{K} \times \mathcal{S} = \mathbb{F}^N$.

Definition 1. *[10] Consider the vector* $\mathbf{v} \in \mathbb{F}^N$. *The coordinates in* $\mathbf{v}$, *which belong to player* P_i *are collected in a sub-vector denoted by* $\mathbf{v^i}$ *and the coordinates that correspond to the secret, i.e., to the dealer* $\mathcal{D}$ *are collected in a sub-vector denoted by* $\mathbf{v^0}$ *or in other words* $\mathbf{v} = (\mathbf{v^0}, \mathbf{v^1}, \ldots, \mathbf{v^n})$ *where* $\mathbf{v^i} \in \mathbb{F}^{p_i}$. *The* p-*support of a vector* $\mathbf{v}$, *denoted by* $sup_p(\mathbf{v})$, *is defined as the set of coordinates* i, $0 \le i \le n$ *for which* $\mathbf{v^i} \ne \mathbf{0}$, *i.e.,* $sup_p(\mathbf{v}) = \{i \; : \; \mathbf{v^i} \ne \mathbf{0}\}$.

Now we give a formal definition of a Monotone Span Program.

Definition 2. *[14] A* Monotone Span Program *(MSP)* $\mathcal{M}$ *is a quadruple* $(\mathbb{F}, M, \varepsilon, \psi)$, *where* $\mathbb{F}$ *is a finite field,* M *is a matrix (with* m *rows and* $d \le m$ *columns) over* $\mathbb{F}$, $\psi : \{1, \ldots, m\} \to \{1, \ldots, n\}$ *is a surjective function and* ε *is a fixed non-zero vector, called* target vector, *e.g., the column vector* $(1, 0, \ldots, 0)^T \in \mathbb{F}^d$. *The size of* $\mathcal{M}$ *is the number* m *of rows and is denoted as* $\text{size}(\mathcal{M})$.

As ψ labels each row with an integer i from $\{1, \ldots, m\}$ that corresponds to player $P_{\psi(i)}$, we can think of each player as being the "owner" of one or more rows. Also consider a "function" φ from $[P_1, \ldots, P_n]$ to $\{1, \ldots, m\}$ which gives for every player P_i the set of rows owned by him (denoted by $\varphi(P_i)$). In some sense φ is the "inverse" of ψ. For any set of players $B \subseteq \mathcal{P}$ consider the matrix consisting of rows these players own in M, i.e. $M_{\varphi(B)}$. As it is common, we shall shorten the notation $M_{\varphi(B)}$ to just M_B. The reader should be aware of the difference between M_B for $B \subseteq \mathcal{P}$ and for $B \subseteq \{1, \ldots, m\}$.

An MSP is said *to compute* a (complete) access structure Γ when $\varepsilon \in \text{im}(M_A^T)$ if and only if A is a member of Γ. We say that A is *accepted* by $\mathcal{M}$ if and only if $A \in \Gamma$, otherwise we say that A is *rejected* by $\mathcal{M}$. In other words, the players in A can reconstruct the secret precisely if the rows they own contain in their linear span the target vector of $\mathcal{M}$, and otherwise they get no information about the secret. There exists a so-called *recombination vector* $\boldsymbol{\lambda}$ such that $M_A^T \boldsymbol{\lambda} = \varepsilon$ hence $\langle \boldsymbol{\lambda}, M_A(s, \boldsymbol{\rho})^T \rangle = \langle M_A^T \boldsymbol{\lambda}, (s, \boldsymbol{\rho})^T \rangle = \langle \varepsilon, (s, \boldsymbol{\rho})^T \rangle = s$ for any secret s and any random vector $\boldsymbol{\rho}$. It is easy to check that the vector $\varepsilon \notin \text{im}(M_B^T)$ if and only if there exists a vector $\boldsymbol{k} \in \mathbb{F}^d$ such that $M_B \boldsymbol{k} = \mathbf{0}$ and $k_1 = 1$. Technically these properties mean that when we consider the restricted matrix M_A for some subset A of $\mathcal{P}$, the first column is linearly dependent on the other columns if and only if $A \notin \Gamma$.

Note 1. [3, 11] It is well known that the number d of columns in an MSP $\mathcal{M}$ can be increased without changing the access structure computed by it. The space generated by the 2-nd up to the d-th column of M does not contain even a non-zero multiple of the first column. Without changing the access structure that is computed, we can always replace the 2-nd up to the d-th column of M by any set of vectors that generates the same space.

3   On Upper Bounds for the Size of MSPs

We will start with some known properties of MSPs. Cramer and Fehr [9] proposed a method to construct the dual MSP (i.e. the MSP computing the dual access structure $\Gamma^\perp$) starting from the MSP computing a given access structure Γ.

Lemma 1. *[9] Let an MSP $\mathcal{M} = (\mathbb{F}, M, \varepsilon, \psi)$ compute Γ. Denote by $\boldsymbol{\lambda}$ a solution of the equation $M^T \boldsymbol{\lambda} = \boldsymbol{\varepsilon}$ and let $\mathbf{b}^1, \mathbf{b}^2, \ldots, \mathbf{b}^\ell$ denote an arbitrary generating set of $\ker(M^T)$, $(l = nullity(M^T))$. Then $\mathcal{M}^\perp = (\mathbb{F}, M^\perp, \boldsymbol{\varepsilon}^*, \psi)$ is an MSP computing $\Gamma^\perp$, where $M^\perp = [\boldsymbol{\lambda}, \mathbf{b}^1, \mathbf{b}^2, \ldots, \mathbf{b}^\ell]$ and $\boldsymbol{\varepsilon}^*$ is the column vector $(1, 0, \ldots, 0)^T \in \mathbb{F}^{\ell+1}$.*

Note 2. Let us define the $d \times (\ell+1)$ matrix $\overline{E}$ to be a zero matrix except for the entry in the upper left corner which is 1, or in other words $\overline{E} = \varepsilon(\varepsilon^*)^T$. Then it follows from the construction proposed in Lemma 1 that the matrices M and $M^\perp$ satisfy the following equation $M^T M^\perp = \overline{E}$.

In his Ph.D. thesis van Dijk [10] investigates the more general setting when more than one secret (e.g. $s_1, \ldots, s_{p_0} \in \mathbb{F}$) should be shared with an access structure. Note that this approach allows consideration of incomplete access structures. Van Dijk proposed a method (using the generalized vector space construction) to build matrices which have the properties equivalent to the MSP. Recall that we consider only the case $p_0 = 1$, i.e. $s \in \mathbb{F}$. It is worth to note that because of [10–Lemma 3.4.14] when we share only one secret (i.e. $p_0 = 1$), the generalized vector space construction that computes (Γ, Δ) coincides with the generalized vector space construction that computes Note that this is exactly the case for an MSP, where we consider only one secret and a complete access structure.

Definition 3. *([10–Definition 3.2.2]) Let $\Gamma^- = \{X_1, \ldots, X_r\}$. Then the set of vectors $C = \{\mathbf{c}^i \in \mathbb{F}^m : 1 \leq i \leq r\}$ is said to be* suitable *for the access structure Γ if C satisfies the following properties called $g(\Gamma)$ respectively $d^-(\Delta)$.*

- $supp_P(\mathbf{c}^i) = X_i$ for $1 \leq i \leq r$;
- *For any vector $(\mu_1, \ldots, \mu_r)$ in $\mathbb{F}^r$, such that $\sum_{i=1}^r \mu_i \neq 0$, there exists a set $X \in \Gamma = \Delta^c$ satisfying $X \subseteq supp_P(\sum_{i=1}^r \mu_i \mathbf{c}^i)$.*

In the next theorem van Dijk provides an important link between a parity check matrix of a code generated as a span of suitable vectors and the MSP matrix.

Theorem 1. *([10–Theorem 3.2.5, Theorem 3.2.6]) Let $\Gamma^- = \{X_1, \ldots, X_r\}$. Consider a set of vectors $C = \{\mathbf{c}^i : 1 \leq i \leq r\}$. Let H be a parity check matrix of the code generated by the linear span of the vectors $(1, \mathbf{c}^i)$, $1 \leq i \leq r$ and let H be of the form $H = (\boldsymbol{\varepsilon} \mid H')$ (This can be assumed without loss of generality). Then the MSP with the matrix M defined by $M^T = H'$ computes the access structure Γ if and only if the set of vectors C is suitable for Γ.*

There is a tight connection between an access structure and its dual. It turns out that the codes generated by the corresponding sets of suitable vectors are orthogonal.

Theorem 2. *([10–Theorem 3.5.4]) Let $\Gamma^- = \{X_1, \ldots, X_r\}$ be an access structure and $(\Gamma^\perp)^- = \{Z_1, \ldots, Z_t\}$ be its dual. Then there exists a suitable set $C = \{\mathbf{c}^i : 1 \leq i \leq r\}$ for Γ if and only if there exists a suitable set $C^\perp = \{\mathbf{h}^j : 1 \leq j \leq t\}$ for $\Gamma^\perp$.*

Suppose there exists a suitable set C for Γ and a suitable set $C^\perp$ for $\Gamma^\perp$. Let C^* be the code defined by the linear span of vectors $\{(1, \mathbf{c^i}) : 1 \leq i \leq r\}$ and let $C^\perp$ be the code defined by the linear span of vectors of $\{(1, \mathbf{h^j}) : 1 \leq j \leq t\}$. Then the codes C^* and $C^\perp$ are orthogonal to each other.

Note that C^* and $C^\perp$ are not necessarily each other's dual. Now we point out that the suitable set of vectors are in fact the solutions $\boldsymbol{\lambda}$ of the equation $M^T \boldsymbol{\lambda} = \boldsymbol{\varepsilon}$ or in other words the suitable set of vectors consists of recombination vectors.

Lemma 2. *Let $\Gamma^- = \{X_1, \ldots, X_r\}$ be the access structure computed by MSP $\mathcal{M}$. Also let $\boldsymbol{\lambda^i} \in \mathbb{F}^m$ be the recombination vector that corresponds to X_i. Then the set of vectors $C = \{\boldsymbol{\lambda^i} : 1 \leq i \leq r\}$ defines a suitable set of vectors for the complete access structure Γ.*

Recall that Cramer and Fehr [9] proposed a method to construct the dual MSP (i.e., the MSP computing the dual access structure $\Gamma^\perp$) starting from the MSP computing the given access structure Γ (see Lemma 1). Now we will slightly modify their construction.

Lemma 3. *Let MSP $\mathcal{M} = (\mathbb{F}, M, \boldsymbol{\varepsilon}, \psi)$ compute access structure Γ. Let $\Gamma^- = \{X_1, \ldots, X_r\}$ be the set of minimal sets in Γ. For each X_i denote the corresponding recombination vector by $\boldsymbol{\lambda^i} \in \mathbb{F}^m$, so $M^T \boldsymbol{\lambda^i} = \boldsymbol{\varepsilon}$ and $sup_P(\boldsymbol{\lambda^i}) = X_i$. Then there exists an MSP $\mathcal{M}^\perp = (\mathbb{F}, M^\perp, \boldsymbol{\varepsilon^*}, \psi)$ computing $\Gamma^\perp$, where $M^\perp = [\boldsymbol{\lambda^1}, \boldsymbol{\lambda^1} - \boldsymbol{\lambda^2}, \ldots, \boldsymbol{\lambda^1} - \boldsymbol{\lambda^r}]$ and $\boldsymbol{\varepsilon^*}$ is a column vector $(1, 0, \ldots, 0)^T$ of suitable length.*

Proof. We will follow the proof of Cramer and Fehr with some minor changes. Note that for any X_i there may be several recombination vectors $\boldsymbol{\lambda^i}$; we pick one of them and denote it by $\boldsymbol{\lambda^i}$. Note also that the vectors $\boldsymbol{\lambda^1} - \boldsymbol{\lambda^2}, \ldots, \boldsymbol{\lambda^1} - \boldsymbol{\lambda^r}$ from $\ker(M^T)$ may not generate the full kernel space.

If $A^c \notin \Gamma$, then there exists a vector $\mathbf{k}$ such that $M_{A^c}\mathbf{k} = \mathbf{0}$ and $\mathbf{k}_1 = 1$. Define $\boldsymbol{\lambda^*} = M_A \mathbf{k}$, or equivalently define $\boldsymbol{\lambda^{**}} = M\mathbf{k}$. Note again that $\boldsymbol{\lambda_A^{**}} = \boldsymbol{\lambda^*}$ and $\boldsymbol{\lambda_{A^c}^{**}} = \mathbf{0}$. Then $(M_A^\perp)^T \boldsymbol{\lambda^*} = (M^\perp)^T \boldsymbol{\lambda^{**}} = (M^\perp)^T (M\mathbf{k}) = ((M^\perp)^T M)\mathbf{k} = (M^T M^\perp)^T \mathbf{k} = \boldsymbol{\varepsilon^*}$, thus $A \in \Gamma^\perp$.

On the other hand, if $A^c \in \Gamma$, then there exists a vector $\widetilde{\boldsymbol{\lambda}}$ such that $M^T \widetilde{\boldsymbol{\lambda}} = \boldsymbol{\varepsilon}$ and $sup_P(\widetilde{\boldsymbol{\lambda}}) \subseteq A^c$, i.e. $\widetilde{\boldsymbol{\lambda}}_A = \mathbf{0}$. Note that we can even choose $\widetilde{\boldsymbol{\lambda}}$ to be in the linear span of the vectors $\boldsymbol{\lambda^1}, \boldsymbol{\lambda^2}, \ldots, \boldsymbol{\lambda^r}$. Now by the definition of $M^\perp$, it follows that there exists a vector $\mathbf{k}$ such that $\mathbf{k}_1 = 1$ and $M^\perp \mathbf{k} = \widetilde{\boldsymbol{\lambda}}$, i.e. $M_A^\perp \mathbf{k} = \mathbf{0}$, thus $A \in \Delta^\perp$ which concludes the proof. $\square$

Thus Lemma 3 improves the construction of Cramer and Fehr (see Lemma 1) showing that a matrix with fewer columns suffices. Recall that $r = |\Gamma^-|$ and $t = |\Delta^+|$. Let

$$\bar{r} = \dim \ \text{span}\{\boldsymbol{\lambda^i}; 1 \leq i \leq r\}. \tag{1}$$

Analogously define $\bar{t}$ for the dual MSP $\mathcal{M}^\perp$. Note that $\bar{r} \leq r$ and $\bar{t} \leq t$. Combining Lemma 3 and Note 1 yields a construction of an MSP with particular properties.

Lemma 4. *Let Γ be a connected access structure and let $\Gamma^{\perp}$ be its dual. Then there exist MSPs such that $M^{\perp}$ has size $m \times \bar{r}$ and M has size $m \times \bar{t}$, where $\bar{r}$ is defined by (1).*

Lemma 5. *Let Γ be a connected access structure and let $\Gamma^{\perp}$ be its dual. Then there exists an MSP program computing Γ with size:*

$$m = \bar{r} + \bar{t} - 1.$$

and such that the matrix $M^{\perp}$ has size $m \times \bar{r}$ and matrix M has size $m \times \bar{t}$.

Proof. Let $H = (\varepsilon \mid M^T)$ and $H^{\perp} = (\varepsilon \mid -(M^{\perp})^T)$. We prove (see Lemma 2) that the vectors $(1, -\boldsymbol{\lambda}^i)$ generate the code $\mathcal{C}$ since they are a suitable set of vectors. From the construction of the dual MSP (see Lemma 3) it follows that the generator matrix M can be rewritten as $G = (\varepsilon \mid -(M^{\perp})^T)$. But the last observation implies that these matrices are the same, i.e. $G = H^{\perp}$ holds. It is now straightforward to obtain the equality $\bar{r} + \bar{t} = m + 1$. Finally, note that because of Lemma 4 we have for M and $M^{\perp}$ that $M^{\perp}$ has size $m \times \bar{r}$ and M has size $m \times \bar{t}$. $\qquad\square$

Now we are ready to state the main result in this section.

Theorem 3. *Let Γ be a connected access structure and let $\Gamma^{\perp}$ be its dual. Let $|\Gamma^{-}| = r$ and $|(\Gamma^{\perp})^{-}| = t$. Then for any field $\mathbb{F}$, there exists a monotone span program $\mathcal{M}$ computing Γ with size satisfying the following upper bound:*

$$size(\mathcal{M}) \leq r + t - 1.$$

Proof. From Lemma 5 and the obvious facts that $\bar{r} \leq r$ and $\bar{t} \leq t$ we obtain that $m \leq r + t - 1$. $\qquad\square$

Note 3. By Definition $(\Gamma^{\perp})^{-} = \{Z_1, \ldots, Z_t\}$ implies that $\Delta^{+} = \{Y_1, \ldots, Y_t\}$, with $Z_j = Y_j^c$. In other words the size of an MSP is limited from above by the sum of the number of minimal and the number of maximal sets minus one.

We will provide an alternative proof of Lemma 5 using van Dijk's approach. Recall that the matrix G is the generator matrix of the code $\mathcal{C}^*$, generated by the suitable set of vectors $(1, \mathbf{c}^i), 1 \leq i \leq r$. The matrix H is the parity check matrix of the code $\mathcal{C}^*$; it is of the form $H = (\varepsilon \mid M^T)$. Analogously we have the matrix $G^{\perp}$ as a generator matrix of the code $\mathcal{C}^{\perp}$, generated by a suitable set of vectors $(1, \mathbf{h}^j), 1 \leq j \leq t$. The matrix $H^{\perp}$ is a parity check matrix for the code $\mathcal{C}^{\perp}$, is of the form $H^{\perp} = (\varepsilon \mid (M^{\perp})^T)$. Here we will use MSP $\mathcal{M}^{\perp}$ with target vector $-\varepsilon$. If we summarize the results from Theorems 1 and 2 we have:

$$\begin{aligned} GH^T &= HG^T &= 0 \\ G^{\perp}(H^{\perp})^T &= H^{\perp}(G^{\perp})^T &= 0 \\ G(G^{\perp})^T &= G^{\perp}G^T &= 0 \end{aligned}$$

As we pointed out the codes $\mathcal{C}^*$ and $\mathcal{C}^{\perp}$ are not necessarily each other's dual, i.e. $H^{\perp}H^T = H(H^{\perp})^T \neq 0$. Thus our goal now is to prove that for any MSP $\mathcal{M}$ there exists an MSP $\mathcal{M}^{\perp}$ such that $\mathcal{C}^*$ and $\mathcal{C}^{\perp}$ are dual, i.e. $\mathcal{C}^* = \mathcal{C}$.

Lemma 6. *Denote the linear span of the rows of matrices G and $H^\perp$ by $span(G)$ respectively $span(H^\perp)$. There are matrices G and $H^\perp$ such that $span(G) = span(H^\perp)$.*

Proof. As van Dijk proved in Theorem 2, $span(G) \subseteq span(H^\perp)$ (since $G(G^\perp)^T = G^\perp G^T = 0$). Note that these equations also mean that vectors $(1, \mathbf{c^i}); 1 \le i \le r$ and $(1, \mathbf{h^j}); 1 \le j \le t$ are orthogonal. Thus the matrices have the following form:

$$
H = \begin{pmatrix} (1, \mathbf{h^1}) \\ (1, \mathbf{h^2}) \\ \vdots \\ (1, \widetilde{\mathbf{h}}^1) \\ (1, \widetilde{\mathbf{h}}^2) \\ \vdots \\ (0, \overline{\mathbf{h}}^1) \\ (0, \overline{\mathbf{h}}^2) \\ \vdots \end{pmatrix}
\quad
H^\perp = \begin{pmatrix} (1, \mathbf{c^1}) \\ (1, \mathbf{c^1}) \\ \vdots \\ (1, \widetilde{\mathbf{c}}^1) \\ (1, \widetilde{\mathbf{c}}^2) \\ \vdots \\ (0, \overline{\mathbf{c}}^1) \\ (0, \overline{\mathbf{c}}^2) \\ \vdots \end{pmatrix}
\quad
M^T = \begin{pmatrix} \mathbf{h^1} \\ \mathbf{h^2} - \mathbf{h^1} \\ \mathbf{h^3} - \mathbf{h^1} \\ \vdots \\ \widetilde{\mathbf{h}}^1 - \mathbf{h^1} \\ \widetilde{\mathbf{h}}^2 - \mathbf{h^1} \\ \vdots \\ \overline{\mathbf{h}}^1 \\ \overline{\mathbf{h}}^2 \\ \vdots \end{pmatrix}
\quad
(M^\perp)^T = \begin{pmatrix} \mathbf{c^1} \\ \mathbf{c^2} - \mathbf{c^1} \\ \mathbf{c^3} - \mathbf{c^1} \\ \vdots \\ \widetilde{\mathbf{c}}^1 - \mathbf{c^1} \\ \widetilde{\mathbf{c}}^2 - \mathbf{c^1} \\ \vdots \\ \overline{\mathbf{c}}^1 \\ \overline{\mathbf{c}}^2 \\ \vdots \end{pmatrix}
$$

The matrix H consists of the row vectors $(1, \mathbf{h^j})$ and probably other vectors of the form $(1, \widetilde{\mathbf{h}}^j)$ and/or $(0, \overline{\mathbf{h}}^j)$ and all of them are orthogonal to $(1, \mathbf{c^i})$. Analogously, the matrix $H^\perp$ consists of the row vectors $(1, \mathbf{c^i})$ and probably other vectors of the form $(1, \widetilde{\mathbf{c}}^i)$ and/or $(0, \overline{\mathbf{c}}^i)$ and all of them are orthogonal to $(1, \mathbf{h^j})$. First, note that in the matrix $\overline{E}$ defined in Note 2 the entry in the upper left corner could be any non-zero number. Now this entry is -1 since we choose the target vector in $\mathcal{M}^\perp$ to be $-\varepsilon$. Consider the equation $(M^\perp)^T M = M^T M^\perp = \overline{E}$ from Note 2. This equation implies that the vectors $\mathbf{h^1}$, $\mathbf{h^j} - \mathbf{h^1}$, $\widetilde{\mathbf{h}}^j - \mathbf{h^1}$ and $\overline{\mathbf{h}}^j$ are orthogonal to the vectors $\mathbf{c^1}$, $\mathbf{c^i} - \mathbf{c^1}$, $\widetilde{\mathbf{c}}^i - \mathbf{c^1}$ and $\overline{\mathbf{c}}^i$, except that $\langle \mathbf{h^1}, \mathbf{c^1} \rangle = -1$ should hold. Now using the orthogonality relations between the vectors $(1, \mathbf{c^i})$ and the vectors $(1, \mathbf{h^j})$, $(1, \widetilde{\mathbf{h}}^j)$, $(0, \overline{\mathbf{h}}^j)$ and also between $(1, \mathbf{h^j})$ and $(1, \mathbf{c^i})$, $(1, \widetilde{\mathbf{c}}^i)$, $(0, \overline{\mathbf{c}}^i)$ we obtain:

$$\langle \overline{\mathbf{h}}^j, \widetilde{\mathbf{c}}^i \rangle = 0, \quad \langle \overline{\mathbf{c}}^i, \widetilde{\mathbf{h}}^j \rangle = 0, \quad \langle \overline{\mathbf{h}}^j, \overline{\mathbf{c}}^i \rangle = 0, \quad \langle \widetilde{\mathbf{h}}^j, \widetilde{\mathbf{c}}^i \rangle = -1.$$

Thus, we have

$$\langle (0, \overline{\mathbf{h}}^j), (1, \widetilde{\mathbf{c}}^i) \rangle = 0, \quad \langle (0, \overline{\mathbf{h}}^j), (0, \overline{\mathbf{c}}^i) \rangle = 0,$$

$$\langle (1, \widetilde{\mathbf{h}}^j), (1, \widetilde{\mathbf{c}}^i) \rangle = 0, \quad \langle (1, \widetilde{\mathbf{h}}^j), (0, \overline{\mathbf{c}}^i) \rangle = 0.$$

Hence H is orthogonal to $H^\perp$, i.e. $H(H^\perp)^T = H^\perp H^T = 0$ holds. But, now it immediately follows that $span(G) \supseteq span(H^\perp)$. Hence $span(H^\perp) = span(G)$, which completes the proof. □

Define

$$\tilde{r} = \dim \ \mathrm{span}\{(1, \mathbf{c^i}); 1 \leq i \leq r\}, \qquad (2)$$
$$\tilde{t} = \dim \ \mathrm{span}\{(1, \mathbf{h^j}); 1 \leq j \leq t\}.$$

Now we are in position to prove the following result.

Lemma 7. *Let Γ be a connected access structure and let $\Gamma^{\perp}$ be its dual. Then there exists an MSP program computing Γ of size m satisfying:*

$$m = \tilde{r} + \tilde{t} - 1.$$

and such that the matrix $M^{\perp}$ has size $m \times \tilde{r}$ and the matrix M has size $m \times \tilde{t}$.

Proof. We have that G is an $\tilde{r} \times (m+1)$ matrix, since $\tilde{r}$ is the dimension of the code $\mathcal{C}$. It also follows that $\tilde{r} \leq r$. On the other hand H is a parity check matrix of code $\mathcal{C}$. Hence H is an $(m+1-\tilde{r}) \times (m+1)$ matrix, and thus M is an $m \times (m+1-\tilde{r})$ matrix, since $H = (\varepsilon \mid M^T)$.

Analogously we have that $G^{\perp}$ is a $\tilde{t} \times (m+1)$ matrix, since $\tilde{t}$ is the dimension of the code $\mathcal{C}^{\perp}$. Also it follows that $\tilde{t} \leq t$. On the other hand $H^{\perp}$ is a parity check matrix of the code $\mathcal{C}^{\perp}$. Hence $H^{\perp}$ is an $(m+1-\tilde{t}) \times (m+1)$ matrix, and thus $M^{\perp}$ is an $m \times (m+1-\tilde{t})$ matrix, since $H^{\perp} = (\varepsilon \mid (M^{\perp})^T)$. Note that M and $M^{\perp}$ have the same size m. As a consequence of Lemma 6, i.e. from $\mathrm{span}(G) = \mathrm{span}(H^{\perp})$ the following equality holds: $\tilde{r} + \tilde{t} = m + 1$. $\qquad \square$

Recall that the vectors $\boldsymbol{\lambda^i}$ form a suitable set of vectors. Note that Lemma 7 actually restates Lemma 5.

Corollary 1. *Let $\mathcal{M}$ be an MSP program computing Γ, and $\mathcal{M}^{\perp}$ be an MSP computing the dual access structure $\Gamma^{\perp}$. Let the code $\mathcal{C}^{\perp}$ have the parity check matrix $H^{\perp} = (\varepsilon \mid (M^{\perp})^T)$ and the code $\mathcal{C}$ have the parity check matrix $H = (\varepsilon \mid M^T)$. Then for any MSP $\mathcal{M}$ there is an MSP $\mathcal{M}^{\perp}$ such that $\mathcal{C}$ and $\mathcal{C}^{\perp}$ are dual.*

4   On Lower Bounds for the Size of MSPs

In earlier works [3, 5, 11, 12] a lower bound for the size of an MSP has been proven. As we pointed out the problem of estimating the size of an MSP is related to many problems in complexity theory such as (symmetric) branching programs, (undirected) contact schemes, formula size as well as with the complexity of some distributed protocols in cryptography.

That is why it should not surprise the reader that the notation in this section differs from the original author's notation. The idea used in [3, 11, 5, 12] is to show that if the size of a span program (i.e., the number of rows in the matrix) is too small, and the program accepts all the minimal sets of the access structure then it must also accept an input that does not contain a minimal set. The latter means that the program does not compute the access structure, since any input accepted by the MSP should contain at least one minimal set.

Beimel et al. [3] introduced a notion of a *critical family*, which we will redefine as the notion of *critical set of minimal sets*.

Definition 4. *Let $\Gamma^- = \{X_1, \ldots, X_r\}$ be the set of minimal sets in the access structure Γ. Let $\mathcal{H} \subseteq \Gamma^-$ be a subset of the set of minimal sets. We say that a subset $\mathcal{H} \subseteq \Gamma^-$ is a* critical set of minimal sets *for Γ^-, if every $X_i \in \mathcal{H}$ contains a set $B_i \subseteq X_i$, $|B_i| \geq 2$, such that the following two conditions are satisfied.*

B1. The set B_i uniquely determines X_i in the set $\mathcal{H}$. That is, no other set in $\mathcal{H}$ contains B_i.

B2. For any subset $Y \subseteq B_i$, the set $S_Y = \cup_{X_j \in \mathcal{H}, X_j \cap Y \neq \emptyset}(X_j \backslash Y)$ does not contain any member of Γ^-.

Note that Condition $B2$ requires that S_Y does not contain any minimal set of Γ, not just a minimal set from $\mathcal{H}$. We can rewrite the set S_Y also as

$$S_Y = \cup_{X_j \in \mathcal{H}, X_j \cap Y \neq \emptyset}(X_j \cap Y^c) = (\cup_{X_j \in \mathcal{H}, X_j \cap Y \neq \emptyset}X_j) \cap Y^c$$
$$= (\cup_{X_j \in \mathcal{H}, X_j \cap Y \neq \emptyset}X_j) \backslash Y.$$

Thus we can restate $B2$ as follows:
$B2'$: For any subset $Y \subseteq B_i$, there is no member of Γ^- which is contained in the set $S_Y' = \cup_{X_j \in \mathcal{H}, X_j \cap Y \neq \emptyset}X_j$ and is a subset of Y^c.

Theorem 4. *[3, 11, 5, 12] Let Γ be an access structure, and let $\mathcal{H}$ be a critical set of minimal sets for Γ. Then for every field $\mathbb{F}$, the size of any monotone span program $\mathcal{M}$ computing Γ*

$$size(\mathcal{M}) \geq |\mathcal{H}|.$$

Proof. [sketch]
Let M be the matrix of a monotone span program computing Γ, and let m be the number of rows of M. Any minimal set of $\mathcal{H}$ is accepted by the program. By definition, this means that, for every $X \in \mathcal{H}$, there is some recombination vector $\boldsymbol{\lambda}_X \in \mathbb{F}^m$ such that $M^T \boldsymbol{\lambda}_X = \boldsymbol{\varepsilon}$, where $\boldsymbol{\lambda}_X$ has nonzero coordinates only at rows labelled by variables from X. For any given X there may be several such vectors, we pick one of them and denote it by $\boldsymbol{\lambda}_X$.

Since $\boldsymbol{\lambda}_X$ is taken from $\mathbb{F}^m$, the number of linearly independent vectors among the vectors $\boldsymbol{\lambda}_X$ for $X \in \mathcal{H}$ is a lower bound for m, i.e., for the size of the span program computing Γ. Thus the following lemma concludes the proof.   □

Lemma 8. *[3] Let Γ be an access structure, and let $\mathcal{H}$ be a critical set of minimal sets for Γ. Then the recombination vectors $\boldsymbol{\lambda}_X$ for $X \in \mathcal{H}$ are linearly independent.*

Gal [12] derives a superpolynomial (in the number of players) worst case asymptotic lower bound for the size of MSPs, showing that there are access structures Γ, with suitable critical sets of minimal sets $\mathcal{H}$. In [17] the authors argued that there are cases in which asymptotically the number of columns and the number of rows (the size of MSP) are identical. Beimel *et al.* observe also that sizes of a MSP and its dual MSP are equal.

Theorem 5. *[3, 11] For every field $\mathbb{F}$, $size(\mathcal{M}) = size(\mathcal{M}^{\perp})$.*

Note that $size(\mathcal{M}) \geq \max(|\mathcal{H}|, |\mathcal{H}^{\perp}|) \geq \frac{|\mathcal{H}| + |\mathcal{H}^{\perp}|}{2}$. Now we are ready to prove the main theorem of this section, the improvement of the bound of Beimel *et al.* [3] (see Theorem 4).

Theorem 6. *Let Γ be an access structure and $\Gamma^{\perp}$ be its dual, let $\mathcal{H}$ be a critical set of minimal sets for Γ and let $\mathcal{H}^{\perp}$ be a critical set of minimal sets for $\Gamma^{\perp}$. Then for any field $\mathbb{F}$, the size of any monotone span program $\mathcal{M}$ computing Γ is bounded from below by the sum of the sizes of both critical minimal sets minus one, i.e.,*

$$size(\mathcal{M}) \geq |\mathcal{H}| + |\mathcal{H}^{\perp}| - 1.$$

Proof. Let M be the matrix of a monotone span program computing the access structure Γ, and let m be the number of rows of M. Let $\Gamma^- = \{X_1, \ldots, X_r\}$ be a set of minimal sets in the access structure Γ and let $\Delta^+ = \{Y_1, \ldots, Y_t\}$ be a set of maximal sets in $\Delta = \Gamma^c$.

For each minimal set X_i consider the corresponding recombination vector $\boldsymbol{\lambda}^i \in \mathbb{F}^m$, so $M^T \boldsymbol{\lambda}^i = \boldsymbol{\varepsilon}$ and $\sup_P(\boldsymbol{\lambda}^i) = X_i$. Recall that the recombination vector $\boldsymbol{\lambda}^i$ corresponds to the vectors $\boldsymbol{\lambda}_X$ in the original proof of Beimel *et al.* [3] (see Theorem 4). For any X_i there may be several such vectors; in that case we pick one of them and denote it by $\boldsymbol{\lambda}^i$. From the proof of Beimel *et al.* (see Lemma 8) it follows that for any critical set of minimal sets $\mathcal{H}$ of Γ^- the corresponding recombination vectors $\boldsymbol{\lambda}$ are linearly independent. Now consider the vectors $\boldsymbol{\lambda}^1 - \boldsymbol{\lambda}^i$ for $i = 2, \ldots, r$. It is easy to see that all these vectors are in the kernel of the transposed matrix M^T, i.e. in $\ker(M^T)$. Therefore for any $\mathcal{H}$ we have $\text{nullity}(M^T) \geq |\mathcal{H}| - 1$.

For each maximal set Y_i consider a vector $\mathbf{k} \in \mathbb{F}^d$ such that $M_{Y_i}\mathbf{k} = \mathbf{0}$ and $\mathbf{k}_1 = 1$. For any given Y_i there may be several such vectors, again we pick one of them. Define $\widetilde{\boldsymbol{\lambda}^i} = M\mathbf{k}$. Note that $\sup_P(\widetilde{\boldsymbol{\lambda}^i}) = Y_i^c \in (\Gamma^{\perp})^-$. From the proof of Lemma 1 as well as from the proof of Lemma 3 we have that $(M^{\perp})^T \widetilde{\boldsymbol{\lambda}^i} = \varepsilon^*$. Hence we have the same correspondence between recombination vectors $\widetilde{\boldsymbol{\lambda}^i}$ and sets $Y_i^c \in (\Gamma^{\perp})^-$ as we have for recombination vectors $\boldsymbol{\lambda}^i$ and sets $X_i \in \Gamma^-$. Applying again the result of Beimel *et al.* Lemma 8 but for the dual access structure $\Gamma^{\perp}$ we obtain that for any critical set of minimal sets $\mathcal{H}^{\perp}$ of $(\Gamma^{\perp})^-$ the corresponding recombination vectors $\widetilde{\boldsymbol{\lambda}^i}$ are linearly independent. Now note that by construction the vectors $\widetilde{\boldsymbol{\lambda}^i}$ are in the image of the matrix M, i.e. $\widetilde{\boldsymbol{\lambda}^i} \in \text{im}(M)$. Hence $\text{rank}(M) \geq |\mathcal{H}^{\perp}|$. On the other hand since the row rank is equal to column rank we have $\text{rank}(M^T) = \text{rank}(M) \geq |\mathcal{H}^{\perp}|$.

The last step is to apply the rank and nullity theorem for the transposed matrix M^T:

$$m = \text{rank}(M^T) + \text{nullity}(M^T) \geq |\mathcal{H}^{\perp}| + |\mathcal{H}| - 1,$$

which completes the proof. $\square$

Note that the worst case superpolynomial asymptotic estimation for the size of MSPs due to Gal [12] does not change because of this relation.

Revisiting the proof of Theorem 6 we notice that $\text{nullity}(M^T) = \bar{r} - 1$ and $\text{rank}(M^T) = \bar{t}$. Hence we have actually three different proofs of the fact that $m = \text{rank}(M^T) + \text{nullity}(M^T) = \bar{r} + \bar{t} - 1$ (see also Lemma 5 and Lemma 7). Now observe that $|\mathcal{H}| \leq \bar{r}$ and $|\mathcal{H}^{\perp}| \leq \bar{t}$ give the lower bound (Theorem 6) and that $\bar{r} \leq r$ and $\bar{t} \leq t$ give the upper bound (Theorem 3). Note that the lower bound is achieved if there exist critical minimal and maximal sets with exactly (the maximum possible number) $\bar{r}$ and $\bar{t}$ elements. However, how one can efficiently build an MSP computing Γ with the smallest size remains still an open question.

5   Conclusions

In this paper we have shown an upper and improve the lower bound for the size of monotone span programs. Next we extend the result of van Dijk showing that for any MSP there exists a dual MSP such that the corresponding codes are dual.

Acknowledgements

The authors would like to thank Anna Gal, Ronald Cramer, Berry Schoenmakers and the anonymous referees for the valuable comments and remarks.

References

1. E. Allender, R. Beals, M. Ogihara, The Complexity of Matrix Rank and Feasible Systems of Linear Equations, ACM STOC'96, 1996, pp. 161-167.
2. A. Beimel, Secure Schemes for Secret Sharing and Key Distribution, *Ph.D. Thesis*, Technion, 1996.
3. A. Beimel, A. Gal, M. Paterson, Lower Bounds for Monotone Span Programs, *Computational Complexity*, 6, 1996/1997, pp. 29-45.
4. A. Beimel, E. Weinreb, Separating the Power of Monotone Span Programs over Different Fields, *FOCS'03*, 2003, pp. 428-437.
5. L. Babai, A. Gal, A. Wigderson, Superpolynomial Lower Bounds for Monotone Span Programs, *Combinatorica* 19 (3), 1999, pp. 301-319.
6. E. Brickell, Some Ideal Secret Sharing Schemes, *J. of Comb. Math. and Comb. Computing* **9**, 1989, pp. 105-113.
7. G. Buntrock, C. Damm, H. Hertrampf, C. Meinel, Structure and Importance of the Logspace-mod Class, *Math. Systems Theory* 25, 1992, pp. 223-237.
8. R. Cramer, I. Damgard, U. Maurer, General Secure Multi-Party Computation from any Linear Secret Sharing Scheme, *EUROCRYPT'2000*, Springer-Verlag LNCS 1807, 2000, pp. 316-334.
9. R. Cramer, S. Fehr, Optimal Black-Box Secret Sharing over Arbitrary Abelian Groups, *CRYPTO 2002*, Springer-Verlag LNCS 2442, 2002, pp. 272-287.

10. M. van Dijk, Secret Key Sharing and Secret Key Generation, *Ph.D. Thesis*, 1997, TU Eindhoven.
11. A. Gal, Combinatorial Methods in Boolean Functions Complexity, *Ph.D. Thesis*, Chicago, Illinois, 1995.
12. A. Gal, A Characterization of Span Program Size and Improved Lower Bounds for Monotone Span Programs, *Computational Complexity*, Vol. 10, No. 4, 2001, pp. 277-296.
13. A. Gal, P. Pudlak, Monotone Complexity and the Rank of Matrices, *Inform. Proc. Lett.* 87, 2003, pp. 321-326.
14. M. Karchmer, A. Wigderson, On Span Programs, *Proc. of 8-th Annual Structure in Complexity Theory Conference*, 1993, IEEE Computer Society Press, pp. 102-111.
15. V. Nikov, S. Nikova, B. Preneel, J. Vandewalle, Applying General Access Structure to Metering Schemes, *WCC* 2003, *Cryptology ePrint Archive*: Report 2002/102.
16. V. Nikov, S. Nikova, B. Preneel, Upper Bound for the Size of Monotone Span Programs, *ISIT 2003*, 2003, pp. 284.
17. P. Pudlak, J. Sgall, Algebraic Models of Computations and Interpolation for Algebraic Proof Systems, *Proof Complexity and Feasible Arithmetic*, DIMACS Series in Discrete Mathematics and Theoretical Computer Science 39, 1998, pp. 279-295.
18. A. Shamir, How to Share a Secret, *Commun. ACM*, 22, 1979, pp. 612-613.

Universally Composable DKG with Linear Number of Exponentiations

Douglas Wikström

Royal Institute of Technology (KTH),
KTH, Nada, S-100 44 Stockholm, Sweden

Abstract. Until now no distributed discrete-logarithm key generation (DKG) protocol is known to be universally composable. We extend Feldman's verifiable secret sharing scheme to construct such a protocol. Our result holds for static adversaries corrupting a minority of the parties under the Decision Diffie-Hellman assumption in a weak common random string model in which the simulator *does not choose* the common random string.

Our protocol is optimistic. If all parties behave honestly, each party computes $O(3.5k)$ exponentiations, and otherwise each party computes $O(k^2)$ exponentiations, where k is the number of parties. In previous constructions each party always computes $\Omega(k^2)$ exponentiations.

1   Introduction

The ability of a group of parties to jointly generate a public key for which the secret key is shared is a cornerstone of threshold cryptography. Without a method to do this securely the parties must resort to a preliminary phase in which a trusted key generating party is present. In some applications no natural trusted party exists, e.g. electronic voting. When a discrete-logarithm based cryptographic primitive is used, distributed key generation often amounts to generating a public key $y = g^x$ for which the corresponding secret key x is secretly and verifiably shared among the parties. Following Gennaro et al. [14] we call a protocol that does this securely a DKG protocol.

1.1   Previous Work

The problem of constructing a DKG protocol was first investigated by Pedersen [25]. His basic building block was a new non-interactive verifiable secret sharing scheme [24] based on ideas of Feldman [8]. Pedersen DKG has been used as a subprotocol in numerous constructions in the literature, but it has never been verified that Pedersen DKG composes correctly in general. Indeed, Gennaro et al. [14] pointed out that the Pedersen DKG may generate a public key which is biased by the adversary. They also gave a new modified protocol and gave a more careful analysis. Adaptively secure protocols for DKG where given by Canetti et al. [6] and Jarecki and Lysyanskaya [21]. Independently, Frankel, MacKenzie and

C. Blundo and S. Cimato (Eds.): SCN 2004, LNCS 3352, pp. 263–277, 2005.

Yung gave key generation protocols secure against adaptive adversaries in several papers [9, 10, 11, 12]. They also considered threshold variants of RSA. Recently, Gennaro et al. [13] investigated the security of the original Pedersen DKG, i.e. how the adversary can benefit from biasing the public key. They show that under certain circumstances the adversary gains very little from this additional power.

Canetti [5] and independently Pfitzmann and Waidner [26], proposed security frameworks for reactive processes. We use the former framework, i.e. the Universally Composable security framework (UC-security). Both frameworks have composition theorems, and are based on older definitional work. The initial ideal-model based definitional approach for secure function evaluation is informally proposed by Goldreich, Micali, and Wigderson in [17]. The first formalizations appear in Goldwasser and Levin [18], Micali and Rogaway [23], and Beaver [3]. Canetti [4] presents the first definition of security that is preserved under composition. See [4, 5] for an excellent background on these definitions.

1.2   Contribution

We give a protocol that securely realizes the ideal DKG functionality in a universally composable way under the Decision Diffie-Hellman assumption. Thus, our protocol can be plugged as a subprotocol in any setting where a DKG protocol is needed. Our result holds in a very weak common random string model in that the simulator does not choose the common random string.

Let k be the number of parties. Our protocol is optimistic and each party computes only $O(3.5k)$ exponentiations if all parties behave honestly and $O(k^2)$ otherwise. In previous constructions each party computes $\Omega(k^2)$ exponentiations.

Pedersen commitments [25] are not used at any point in our protocol. We think it is particularly nice to see that Feldman's original ideas can be used directly.

We note that in work independent of ours, Abe and Fehr [1] have announced an adaptively UC-secure DKG protocol. Each party computes $\Omega(k^2)$ exponentiations in their protocol, and the security rests on the DDH-assumption.

1.3   Universally Composable Security

Throughout this paper we employ the universally composable security framework (UC-framework) of Canetti [5]. Our result does not depend on technicalities of any particular flavor, but to avoid any ambiguity we review in Appendix A the precise definitions we use. The idea of UC-security is to define security such that if a protocol π "securely realizes" a functionality $\mathcal{F}$, then π can be plugged in as a subprotocol in *any* setting where a functionality $\mathcal{F}$ is needed. Thus, the model allows modular analysis of the security of protocols, and guarantees that the security properties of a protocol is preserved regardless of where it is used.

The framework is formalized by defining a real model in which the protocol π executes, and an ideal model which essentially contains the functionality $\mathcal{F}$ the protocol should realize. The protocol π is said to *securely realize* $\mathcal{F}$ if for each adversary $\mathcal{A}$ in the real model there exists an ideal adversary $\mathcal{S}$ in the ideal model such that no environment $\mathcal{Z}$ can distinguish between executions in the real and ideal models. A hybrid model is a real model where the protocol π is given access to additional functionalities $\mathcal{F}'$. The protocol π'', where each call to $\mathcal{F}'$ is replaced by an invocation of a protocol π' is called the *composition of π and π'*. The UC-composition theorem says that π'' securely realizes $\mathcal{F}$ if π securely realizes $\mathcal{F}$ in the $\mathcal{F}'$-hybrid model and π' securely realizes $\mathcal{F}'$.

1.4   Notation

Throughout, $M_1, \ldots, M_k$ denote the participating parties, which are modeled as interactive Turing machines. We abuse notation and use M_j to denote both the machines themselves and their identity. We write $\mathcal{M}_{k/2}$ to denote the set of *static* polynomial time *non-uniform* Turing machines that can corrupt a minority of the parties.

We use the term "randomly" instead of "uniformly and independently at random". We assume that G_q is a group of prime order q with generator g for which the Decision Diffie-Hellman Assumption holds, e.g. a subgroup G_q of prime order q of $\mathbb{Z}_p^*$ for some $p = \kappa q + 1$. We take $\log p = n$ to be our security parameter, and assume that computing an exponentiation in G_q takes time corresponding to computing at least n multiplications in G_q. This allows us to express the complexity of our procotol in terms of the number of exponentiations computed.

Assumption 1 (Decision Diffie-Hellman). *Let $e_1, e_2, e_3 \in \mathbb{Z}_q$ be randomly chosen. The (non-uniform) Decision Diffie-Hellman assumption for G_q states that for all polynomial time non-uniform Turing machines A, $\forall c > 0$, $\exists n_0$, such that for $n > n_0$:*

$$|\Pr[A(g^{e_1}, g^{e_2}, g^{e_3}) = 1] - \Pr[A(g^{e_1}, g^{e_2}, g^{e_1 e_2}) = 1]| < \tfrac{1}{n^c}.$$

We use $\mathcal{C}_\mathcal{I}$ to denote the ideal communication model. It routes authenticated messages between the parties, the ideal adversary, and the functionalities. The first component of a list handed to $\mathcal{C}_\mathcal{I}$ is the identity of the receiver. The adversary decides when $\mathcal{C}_\mathcal{I}$ delivers messages. The notion of a bulletin board is intuitively clear.

Functionality 1 (Bulletin Board (cf. [28])). The ideal *bulletin board* functionality, $\mathcal{F}_{\mathrm{BB}}$, running with parties $M_1, \ldots, M_k$ and ideal adversary $\mathcal{S}$.

1. $\mathcal{F}_{\mathrm{BB}}$ holds a database indexed on integers. Initialize a counter $c = 0$.
2. On receiving $(M_i, \mathtt{Write}, m_i)$, $m_i \in \{0,1\}^*$, from $\mathcal{C}_\mathcal{I}$, store (M_i, m_i) under c in the database, hand $(\mathcal{S}, \mathtt{Write}, c, M_i, m_i)$ to $\mathcal{C}_\mathcal{I}$, and set $c \leftarrow c + 1$.
3. Upon receiving $(M_j, \mathtt{Read}, c)$ from $\mathcal{C}_\mathcal{I}$ check if a tuple (M_i, m_i) is stored in the database under c. If so hand $((\mathcal{S}, M_j, \mathtt{Read}, c, M_i, m), (M_j, \mathtt{Read}, c, M_i, m_i))$ to $\mathcal{C}_\mathcal{I}$. If not, hand $((\mathcal{S}, M_j, \mathtt{NoRead}, c), (M_j, \mathtt{NoRead}, c))$ to $\mathcal{C}_\mathcal{I}$.

Goldwasser and Lindell [19] show that authenticated broadcast can be securely realized with respect to *blocking* $\mathcal{M}_{k/2}$-adversaries. On the other hand Lindell, Lysyanskaya and Rabin [22] show that composable authenticated broadcast can not be realized for *non-blocking* $\mathcal{M}_B$-adversaries if $B > k/3$. A non-blocking adversary is an adversary that never delays the delivery of messages to honest parties indefinitely. The following lemma follows straightforwardly from [19].

Lemma 1. *There exists a protocol* π_{BB} *that securely realizes* $\mathcal{F}_{BB}$ *with respect to blocking* $\mathcal{M}_{k/2}$-*adversaries.*

In many constructions the parties are assumed to be able to communicate secretly with each other. In the UC-framework this was modeled by Canetti [5]. Below we give a slightly modified variant, better suited for our setting.

Functionality 2 (Multiple Message Transmission). The ideal multiple message transmission, $\mathcal{F}_{MMT}$, with parties $M_1, \ldots, M_k$ and ideal adversary $\mathcal{S}$.

1. In the first activation expect to receive a value $(\texttt{Receiver})$ from some party M_j. Then hand $((\mathcal{S}, \texttt{Receiver}, M_j), \{(M_i, \texttt{Receiver}, M_j)\}_{i=1}^{k})$ to $\mathcal{C}_{\mathcal{I}}$.
2. Upon receiving $(M_j, \texttt{Send}, M_i, m_j)$ from $\mathcal{C}_{\mathcal{I}}$, hand $((\mathcal{S}, M_j, \texttt{Send}, M_i, |m_j|), (M_i, M_j, m_j))$ to $\mathcal{C}_{\mathcal{I}}$.

From Claim 16 in Canetti [5] and the fact that the Cramer-Shoup cryptosystem [7] is chosen ciphertext secure in the sense of Rackoff and Simon [27] under the Decision Diffie-Hellman assumption in G_q, the lemma below follows.

Lemma 2. *There exists a protocol* π_{MMT} *that securely realizes* $\mathcal{F}_{MMT}$ *under the Decision Diffie-Hellman assumption in* G_q.

A common assumption used in the construction of protocols is the existence of a common random string (CRS). A common reference string is different from a CRS in that it may have additional structure, or be generated together with a trapdoor which allows easy simulation. Previous DKG-protocols require the existence of a common reference string $g, h \in G_q$ such that the simulator knows $\log_g h$. When this is not the case the protocols can not be simulated. We make no such assumptions. Our simulator is *not* allowed to choose the CRS. Thus, our CRS can truly be a random string defined by a physical experiment.

Functionality 3 (Common Random String (CRS)). The ideal common random string, $\mathcal{F}_{CRS}$, running with parties $M_1, \ldots, M_k$ and ideal adversary $\mathcal{S}$ simply chooses $h_1, h_2, h_3 \in G_q$ randomly and hands $((\mathcal{S}, \texttt{CRS}, h_1, h_2, h_3), \{(M_j, \texttt{CRS}, h_1, h_2, h_3)\}_{j=1}^{k})$ to $\mathcal{C}_{\mathcal{I}}$.

2   Distributed Key Generation

The functionality below captures the notion defined by Gennaro et al. [14], but in the language of the UC-framework. A public key $y = g^x$ is generated and given to all parties. Each party also receives a share s_j of the secret key x.

Functionality 4 (Distributed Key Generation (DKG)). The ideal *Distributed Key Generation over* G_q, $\mathcal{F}_{DKG}$, running with generators $M_1, \ldots, M_k$, and ideal adversary $\mathcal{S}$ proceeds as follows. Let $t = \lceil k/2 - 1 \rceil$.

1. Wait for $(\texttt{CorruptShares}, \{j, s_j\}_{j \in I_M})$ from $\mathcal{S}$, where I_M is the set of indices of corrupted parties.

2. Choose $a_\iota \in \mathbb{Z}_q$ randomly under the restriction $a(j) = s_j$ for $j \in I_M$, where $a(z) = \sum_{\iota=0}^{t} a_\iota z^\iota$. Then define $s_j = a(j)$ for $j \notin I_M$, and set $y = g^{a_0}$.
3. Hand $((S, \texttt{PublicKey}, y), \{(\texttt{PublicKey}, y, s_j)\}_{j=1}^{k})$ to $\mathcal{C}_\mathcal{I}$.

Note that the adversary chooses the shares handed to corrupted parties.

Recall the verifiable secret sharing scheme of Feldman [8]. A dealer shares a secret $a_0 \in \mathbb{Z}_q$ by choosing $a_\iota \in \mathbb{Z}_q$ randomly and forming a polynomial $a(z) = \sum_{\iota=0}^{t} a_\iota z^\iota$ of degree t. Then it publishes $\alpha_\iota = g^{a_\iota}$ and hands a share $s_j = a(j)$ to the j:th party. This allows the receiver of a share s_j to verify its correctness by checking that $g^{s_j} = \prod_{\iota=0}^{t} \alpha_\iota^{j^\iota}$. If a share is not correct the receiver complains and forces the dealer to publish a correct share. To recover the secret the receivers simply publish their shares. This allows anybody to find a set of correct shares and Lagrange interpolate the secret. The distribution step of Feldman's protocol gives a way to share the secret key x corresponding to a public key $\alpha_0 = g^x$.

Next we give an informal description of our protocol. The parties are partitioned into three sets and each set is assigned a random generator $h_f \in G_q$. Each party runs a copy of Feldman's protocol, but using its set's generator. Instead of verifying each individual dealer's shares and public information, they are combined within each set of parties. This allows efficient verification. The basic idea behind this trick was taken from Gennaro et al. [15]. If some party is malicious, the efficient way of verifying shares is abandoned and individual verifications are performed. From this each party M_j computes a combined share s_j, the sum of all correct shares it received. Then each party publishes $\beta_j = g^{s_j}$. Note that this time all parties use the common generator g. Then the parties verify the correctness of the β_j's and construct a joint key $y = g^x$, for which x is the secret to which the combined shares s_j correspond. If the verification fails each party is essentially required to prove that its β_j is correct. This allows all parties to agree on a set of correct β_j from which the joint key can be constructed.

Let $\{\Omega_1, \Omega_2, \Omega_3\}$ be a partition of $\{1, \ldots, k\}$ such that $||\Omega_f| - |\Omega_{f'}|| \leq 1$ for $f \neq f'$. Define $f(j)$ to be the value of f such that $j \in \Omega_f$. All parties always verify that their input is contained in G_q or $\mathbb{Z}_q$ as expected by the protocol.

Protocol 1 (Distributed Key Generation (DKG)). Let $t = \lceil k/2 - 1 \rceil$. The Distributed Key Generation protocol with generators $M_1, \ldots, M_k$.

Preliminary Phase
1. Hand (`Receiver`) to $\mathcal{F}_{\text{MMT}}$.
2. Wait for (`Receiver`, M_l) for $l = 1, \ldots, k$ from $\mathcal{F}_{\text{MMT}}$.
3. Wait for (`CRS`, h_1, h_2, h_3) from $\mathcal{F}_{\text{CRS}}$.

Key Generation Phase
4. Define f by $j \in \Omega_f$. Choose $a_{j,\iota} \in \mathbb{Z}_q$ randomly, and define $a_j(z) = \sum_{\iota=0}^{t} a_{j,\iota} z^\iota$, $\alpha_{j,\iota} = h_f^{a_{j,\iota}}$, and $s_{j,l} = a_j(l)$. Hand (`Send`, M_l, `Share`, $s_{j,l}$) to $\mathcal{F}_{\text{MMT}}$ for $l \neq j$ and (`Write`, `PublicElements`, $\{\alpha_{j,\iota}\}_{\iota=0}^{t}$) to $\mathcal{F}_{\text{BB}}$.
5. Wait until $(M_l, \texttt{PublicElements}, \{\alpha_{l,\iota}\}_{\iota=0}^{t})$ appears on $\mathcal{F}_{\text{BB}}$ and a message $(M_l, \texttt{Share}, s_{l,j})$ is received from $\mathcal{F}_{\text{MMT}}$ for $l \neq j$. Choose a random n-subset

$A_j \subset \{0, \ldots, t\}$ (if $t < n$ then $A_j = [k]$), compute $\theta_{j,f,\iota} = \prod_{l \in \Omega_f} \alpha_{l,\iota}$ for $f = 1, 2, 3$ and $\iota \in A_j$. Then hand (Write, Products, $\{\theta_{j,f,\iota}\}_{\iota \in A_j, f \in \{1,2,3\}}$) to $\mathcal{F}_{\mathrm{BB}}$.

6. Wait until $(M_l, \text{Products}, \{\theta_{l,f,\iota}\}_{\iota \in A_l, f \in \{1,2,3\}})$ appears on $\mathcal{F}_{\mathrm{BB}}$ for $l \neq j$. Then verify that $\theta_{l,f,\iota} = \theta_{l',f,\iota}$ for $\iota \in A_l \cap A_{l'}$. If not go to Step 12. If so define $\theta_{f,\iota} = \theta_{l,f,\iota}$ for any l such that $\iota \in A_l$.

7. Verify that $h_f^{\sum_{l \in \Omega_f} s_{l,j}} = \prod_{\iota=0}^{t} \theta_{f,\iota}^{j^\iota}$, for $f = 1, 2, 3$. If so, hand (Write, Complaints, $\emptyset$) to $\mathcal{F}_{\mathrm{BB}}$. Otherwise, go to Step 12.

8. Wait until $(M_l, \text{Complaints}, \Delta_l)$ appears on $\mathcal{F}_{\mathrm{BB}}$ for $l \neq j$. If all $\Delta_l = \emptyset$ set $I_1 = \{1, \ldots, k\}$. Otherwise, go to Step 13.

9. Define $s_j = \sum_{l \in I_1} s_{l,j}$ and set $\beta_j = g^{s_j}$. Then hand (Write, ConstructPublicKey, β_j) to $\mathcal{F}_{\mathrm{BB}}$.

10. Wait until $(M_l, \text{ConstructPublicKey}, \beta_l)$ appears on $\mathcal{F}_{\mathrm{BB}}$ for $l \in I_1$. Verify that $\beta_j = \prod_{i=1}^{t+1} \beta_i^{\prod_{l \neq i} \frac{l-j}{l-i}}$. If so set $I_2 = \{1, \ldots, t+1\}$. If not, go to Step 15.

11. Define $y = \prod_{i \in I_2} \beta_i^{\prod_{l \neq i} \frac{l}{l-i}}$ and output (PublicKey, y, s_j).

Handle Cheating with the $s_{l,i}$ and $\alpha_{l,\iota}$.

12. Verify for $l = 1, \ldots, k$ that $h_{f(l)}^{s_{l,j}} = \prod_{\iota=0}^{t} \alpha_{l,\iota}^{j^\iota}$. Let Δ_j be the set of indices l for which inequality holds. Then hand (Write, Complaints, Δ_j) to $\mathcal{F}_{\mathrm{BB}}$.

13. Wait until $(M_l, \text{Complaints}, \Delta_l)$ appears on $\mathcal{F}_{\mathrm{BB}}$ for $l \neq j$. Let $\Gamma_j = \{l \mid j \in \Delta_l\}$. Then hand (Write, Refutes, $\{s_{j,l}\}_{l \in \Gamma_j}$) to $\mathcal{F}_{\mathrm{BB}}$.

14. Wait until $(M_l, \text{Refutes}, \{s_{l,i}\}_{i \in \Gamma_l})$ appears on $\mathcal{F}_{\mathrm{BB}}$ for $l \neq j$ and replace old values of $s_{l,j}$ with the new. Let I_1 be the set of l such that $h_{f(l)}^{s_{l,i}} = \prod_{\iota=0}^{t} \alpha_{l,\iota}^{i^\iota}$ for all i such that $(l, i) \in [k] \times \{j\} \cup \bigcup_{i'=1}^{k} (\Delta_{i'} \times \{i'\})$. Then go to Step 9.

Handle Cheating with the β_l.

15. Set $c_{f,j,0} = \sum_{l \in \Omega_f \cap I_1} s_{l,j}$ and choose $c_{f,j,\iota} \in \mathbb{Z}_q$ for $\iota > 0$ randomly. Define $c_{f,j}(z) = \sum_{\iota=0}^{t} c_{f,j,\iota} z^\iota$, $\gamma_{j,\iota} = g^{c_{1,j,\iota} + c_{2,j,\iota} + c_{3,j,\iota}}$, $\delta_{f,j,\iota} = h_f^{c_{f,j,\iota}}$, and $\zeta_{f,j,l} = c_{f,j}(l)$. Then hand (Send, M_l, Share2, $(\zeta_{1,j,l}, \zeta_{2,j,l}, \zeta_{3,j,l})$) to $\mathcal{F}_{\mathrm{MMT}}$ for $l \in I_1$ and hand (Write, PublicElements2, $\{\gamma_{j,\iota}, \delta_{1,j,\iota}, \delta_{2,j,\iota}, \delta_{3,j,\iota}\}_{\iota=1}^{t}$) to $\mathcal{F}_{\mathrm{BB}}$.

16. Wait for $(M_l, \text{PublicElements2}, \{\gamma_{l,\iota}, \delta_{1,j,\iota}, \delta_{2,j,\iota}, \delta_{3,j,\iota}\}_{\iota=1}^{t})$ on $\mathcal{F}_{\mathrm{BB}}$ for $l \in I_1$. Set $\gamma_{l,0} = \beta_l$ and $\delta_{f,l,0} = \prod_{i \in \Omega_f \cap I_1} \alpha_{i,\iota}$. Verify $g^{\zeta_{1,l,j} + \zeta_{2,l,j} + \zeta_{3,l,j}} = \prod_{\iota=0}^{t} \gamma_{l,\iota}^{j^\iota}$ and $h_f^{\zeta_{f,l,j}} = \prod_{\iota=0}^{t} \delta_{f,l,\iota}^{j^\iota}$. Let Δ_j' be the set of indices for which the verification fails. Then hand (Write, Complaints2, Δ_j') to $\mathcal{F}_{\mathrm{BB}}$.

17. Wait until $(M_l, \text{Complaints2}, \Delta_l')$ appears on $\mathcal{F}_{\mathrm{BB}}$ for $l \in I_1$. Let $\Gamma_j' = \{l \mid j \in \Delta_l'\}$. Then hand (Write, Refutes2, $\{\zeta_{1,j,l}, \zeta_{2,j,l}, \zeta_{3,j,l}\}_{l \in \Gamma_j'}$) to $\mathcal{F}_{\mathrm{BB}}$.

18. Wait until $(M_l, \text{Refutes2}, \{\zeta_{1,j,l}, \zeta_{2,j,l}, \zeta_{3,j,l}\}_{i \in \Gamma_l})$ appears on $\mathcal{F}_{\mathrm{BB}}$ for $l \in I_1$ and replace the old values of $\zeta_{f,l,j}$ with the new. Let I_2 be the lexicographically first set of l such that $g^{\zeta_{1,l,i} + \zeta_{2,l,i} + \zeta_{3,l,i}} = \prod_{\iota=0}^{t} \gamma_{l,\iota}^{i^\iota}$ and $h^{\zeta_{f,l,i}} = \prod_{\iota=0}^{t} \delta_{f,l,\iota}^{i^\iota}$ for all i such that $(l, i) \in I_1 \times \{j\} \cup \bigcup_{i'=1}^{k} (\Delta_{i'}' \times \{i'\})$. Then go to Step 11.

All shares corresponding to a partition Ω_f are verified together. One can also consider verifying smaller sets together if some cheating is expected. Then if cheating is detected, fewer shares have to be verified individually. This changes the security analysis only slightly.

Remark 1. Theoretically, it suffices that each party chooses an $e(n)$-subset in Step 5, where $e(n)$ is a function such that $e(n)/\log n = \Omega(1)$.

Theorem 1. *The protocol π above securely realizes $\mathcal{F}_{\mathrm{DKG}}$ with respect to $\mathcal{M}_{k/2}$-adversaries in the $(\mathcal{F}_{\mathrm{BB}}, \mathcal{F}_{\mathrm{MMT}}, \mathcal{F}_{\mathrm{CRS}})$-hybrid model under the DDH-assumption.*

If all parties behave honestly, each party computes $O(3.5k)$ exponentiations in G_q. In the worst case each party computes $O(k^2)$ exponentiations.

Corollary 1. *If π is composed with π_{MMT}, the result holds in the $(\mathcal{F}_{\mathrm{BB}}, \mathcal{F}_{\mathrm{CRS}})$-hybrid model. If also composed with π_{BB} the result holds in the $\mathcal{F}_{\mathrm{CRS}}$-hybrid model for* blocking *adversaries.*

Some intuition behind the construction and for the proof of Theorem 1 follows. Since the adversary could potentially generate the shares it distributes *after* receiving shares from all honest parties, it can choose the shares it distributes such that the combined shares s_j of corrupted parties take on certain values. This is why we must allow the ideal adversary to do this in the DKG functionality as well (the distribution of y is unbiased).

Already after the public elements $\alpha_{j,\iota}$ are published the simulator can extract the secrets of corrupt parties, compute the resulting final combined shares, and feed them to the ideal functionality. To simulate honest dummy parties, the ideal adversary generates in the second step public elements β_j that appear correct to the corrupt parties, but they are carefully chosen such that the public key y output by a protocol execution is identical to the public key output by the ideal functionality. This implies that the $\alpha_{j,\iota}$ and β_j are inconsistent. This fact must be hidden from the adversary and environment such that the latter can not distinguish a simulation from a real execution. This must hold despite that the environment knows all shares s_j at the end of an execution.

The use of three independent generators h_1, h_2 and h_3 in the first phase ensures that no adversary or environment can check if the final shares s_j correspond to the public elements $\alpha_{l,\iota}$. The adversary is essentially given a tuple $(h_1, h_2, h_1^{e_1}, h_2^{e_2}, (1-b)e_3 + b(e_1 + e_2))$, where $h_1, h_2 \in G_q$ and $e_1, e_2, e_3 \in \mathbb{Z}_q$ are random, and must guess b. This problem is related to the DDH-problem as follows. Consider a tuple (h_1, u, v, w), where $(u, v, w) = (h_1^{e_1}, h_1^{e_2}, h_1^{be_1 e_2 + (1-b)e_3})$. This is a DDH-tuple if $b = 1$. Define $h_2 = u = h_1^{e_1}$, $U = h_1^\sigma / v = h_1^{\sigma - e_2}$, $V = w = h_2^{(1-b)e_3 + be_2}$, and $W = \sigma$ for a random σ. Then (h_1, h_2, U, V, W) is a tuple of the first type and $b = 1$ precisely when (u, v, w) is a DDH-triple. In fact we have translated an instance of the DDH-problem to an instance of a problem that the adversary and environment must solve to distinguish a simulation from a real execution of our protocol.

Although the UC-framework allows it, we have not used any trapdoor for the common random string in the simulation. In fact the common random string is not even chosen by the simulator. Thus, we feel that our use of the common random string is very mild.

Proof (Theorem 1 and Corollary 1). It is easy to verify the complexity claim in the non-optimistic case by counting.

The optimistic case is not as obvious. In Step 4 we invoke a corollary in Section 8.5 in Aho, Hopcroft, and Ullman [2] which says that kth degree polynomial over $\mathbb{Z}_q$ can be evaluated in k points using at most $k \log^2 k$ arithmetic operations (i.e. $+$, $-$, $\times$, $/$) in $\mathbb{Z}_q$. Thus, this step is performed in time corresponding to compute k exponentiations.

In Step 5 each party computes n products, each having k factors. This corresponds to computing k exponentiations.

In Step 7 the exponents j^ι are computed iteratively using the recursion $j^\iota = j \cdot j^{\iota-1}$. The cost is at most k multiplications, and ignored. Similarly the cost of the multiplication of the exponentiated elements is ignored. Thus, the cost of this step is $k/2$ exponentiations, since this is how many ordinary exponentiations are performed.

In Step 10 and Step 11 k ordinary exponentiations are computed, but we must also consider how to compute the exponents in these products. We note that the products are almost factorial (here it is in fact necessary to have $I_2 = \{1, \ldots, t+1\}$), i.e. $\prod_{l \neq i}(l-i) = (1-i)(2-i) \cdot \ldots \cdot ((i-1)-i)((i+1)-i) \cdot \ldots \cdot (t+1-i)$. We compute all factorials $1!, 2!, 3!, \ldots, (t+1)!$ in $\mathbb{Z}_q$ and their inverses. Then each of our exponents can be formed using only 4 multiplications. Thus, all exponents can be computed using at most $O(k)$ multiplications, and the total cost of the two steps corresponds to k exponentiations.

In total each party computes $O(3.5k)$ exponentiations.

We construct an ideal adversary S that runs any hybrid adversary A as a blackbox. Then we show that if S does not imply that the protocol is secure, the DDH-assumption is broken.

THE IDEAL ADVERSARY S. Let I_M be the set of indices of generators corrupted by A. The ideal adversary S corrupts the dummy generators $\overline{M}_j$ for $j \in I_M$. The ideal adversary is best described by starting with a copy of the original hybrid ITM-graph $(V, E) = \mathcal{Z}'(\mathcal{H}(A, \pi^{\overline{\pi}^{(\mathcal{F}_{BB}, \mathcal{F}_{MMT}, \mathcal{F}_{CRS})}}))$ where $\mathcal{Z}$ is replaced by a machine $\mathcal{Z}'$ that we define below. The adversary S simulates all machines in V except those in A', and the corrupted machines M_j for $j \in I_M$ under A':s control.

Simulation of Links $(\mathcal{Z}, A)$, $(\mathcal{Z}, M_j)$ *for* $j \in I_M$. S simulates $\mathcal{Z}'$ and $\overline{M}_j$ for $j \in I_M$, such that it appears as if $\mathcal{Z}$ and A, and $\mathcal{Z}$ and M_j for $j \in I_M$ are linked directly.

1. When $\mathcal{Z}'$ receives m from A, m is written to $\mathcal{Z}$, by S. When S receives m from $\mathcal{Z}$, m is written to A by $\mathcal{Z}'$. This is equivalent to that $\mathcal{Z}$ and A are linked directly.
2. When $\mathcal{Z}'$ receives m from M_j for $j \in I_M$, m is written to $\mathcal{Z}$ by $\overline{M}_j$. When $\overline{M}_j$, $j \in I_M$, receives m from $\mathcal{Z}$, m is written to M_j by $\mathcal{Z}'$. This is equivalent to that $\mathcal{Z}$ and M_j are linked directly for $j \in I_M$.

Extraction from a Corrupt Generator. Note that since the last t generators M_j which distributes their shares $s_{j,l}$ may be corrupted, the adversary can choose

$s_{j,l}$ for $j \in I_M$ such that $s_j = \sum_{l \in I_1} s_{l,j}$ takes on any values of its choice. The ideal adversary $\mathcal{S}$ must somehow extract the s_j for $j \in I_M$ and then hand them to $\mathcal{F}_{\mathrm{DKG}}$ to ensure that the shares s_j for $j = 1, \dots, k$ that eventually ends up at the environment are consistent with the output public key y.

When the last $(\texttt{Write}, \texttt{Complaints}, \Delta_j)$ message before executing Step 9 appears on $\mathcal{F}_{\mathrm{BB}}$ for $j = 1, \dots, k$, interrupt the simulation of $\mathcal{F}_{\mathrm{BB}}$.

There are two cases. If there were no complaints, we claim that $h_f^{\sum_{l \in \Omega_f} s_{l,j}} = \prod_{\iota=0}^{t}(\prod_{l \in \Omega_f} \alpha_{l,\iota})^{j^{\iota}}$ is satisfied for $j \notin I_M$ and $f = 1, 2, 3$. We argue that $\theta_{f,\iota} = \prod_{l \in \Omega_f} \alpha_{l,\iota}$. This is clearly the case if for each $\iota = 0, \dots, t$ there exists an honest party M_j such that $\iota \in A_j$. Thus, the probability of failure is bounded by $\Pr[\exists \iota \in [0, t], \forall j \notin I_M : \iota \notin A_j] \leq \sum_{\iota=0}^{t+1} \Pr[\forall j \notin I_M : \iota \notin A_j]$, where we used the union bound. From independence follows that the latter quantity equals $(t+1)\Pr[\iota \notin A_j]^{t+1}$ (for some arbitrary $\iota \in \{1, \dots, t+1\}$ and $j \notin I_M$). By construction $\Pr[\iota \notin A_j] = (1 - \frac{k}{k-n})$, which implies that the probability of failure is bounded by $(t+1)(1 - \frac{n}{k-n})^{k/2} \leq (t+1)e^{-n/2}$, which is negligible. Thus, with overwhelming probability, $\theta_{f,\iota} = \prod_{l \in \Omega_f} \alpha_{l,\iota}$. This implies that we can Lagrange interpolate $b_{f,i} = \sum_{l \in \Omega_f}(\sum_{j=1}^{t+1} s_{l,j} \prod_{l \neq j} \frac{i-l}{j-l}) = \sum_{l \in \Omega_f} s_{l,i}$ for $f = 1, 2, 3$ and compute $s_i = b_{1,i} + b_{2,i} + b_{3,i}$ for $i \in I_M$. If there were complaints, we have for $l \in I_1$ and $j \notin I_M$ that $h_{f(l)}^{s_{l,j}} = \prod_{\iota=0}^{t} \alpha_{l,\iota}^{j^{\iota}}$. This implies that the equation above holds for the new values of $s_{l,j}$ and we can Lagrange interpolate $s_i = \sum_{f=1}^{3} \sum_{l \in \Omega_f \cap I_1} s_{l,i}$ similarly to the above. To summarize, $\mathcal{S}$ can always extract s_j for $j \in I_M$ before deciding on β_j values.

The ideal adversary $\mathcal{S}$ hands $(\texttt{CorruptShares}, \{j, s_j\}_{j \in I_M})$ to $\mathcal{F}_{\mathrm{DKG}}$. $\mathcal{F}_{\mathrm{DKG}}$ then returns $(\texttt{PublicKey}, y)$. Below we describe the computations performed by $\mathcal{S}$ before the simulation of $\mathcal{F}_{\mathrm{BB}}$ continues.

Simulation of an Honest Generator. The next problem facing the ideal adversary $\mathcal{S}$ is how to simulate the honest generators M_j for $j \notin I_M$ such that the corrupt generators M_j for $j \in I_M$ output the same public key y as that output by the dummy generators $\overline{M}_j$ for $j \notin I_M$. The latter generators are beyond $\mathcal{S}$'s control and simply forwards the output from $\mathcal{F}_{\mathrm{DKG}}$. Intuitively, $\mathcal{S}$ must "lie" at some point, since it is already committed to a public key by the public $\alpha_{j,\iota}$ elements on $\mathcal{F}_{\mathrm{BB}}$. The "lie" must be carefully constructed such that the adversary can not identify it, and it must be constructed not knowing $\log_g y$.

First it computes $\beta'_j = g^{s_j}$ for $j \in I_M$ and sets $\beta'_0 = y$ and $I'_M = I_M \cup \{0\}$. These are the β'_j for $j \in I_M$ that *should* later be published by the corrupted generators if they behave honestly. Then $\mathcal{S}$ computes $\beta'_j = \prod_{i \in I'_M}(\beta'_i)^{\prod_{l \neq i} \frac{i-l}{i-l}}$, for $j \notin I_M$, and replace β_j with β'_j in the simulation of the honest generators M_j for $j \notin I_M$. The construction ensures that $\beta'_j = \prod_{i=1}^{t+1}(\beta'_i)^{\prod_{l \neq i} \frac{l-j}{l-i}}$. The simulated honest parties M_j for $j \notin I_M$ are instructed not to complain if $\beta_i = \beta'_i$ for $i \notin I_M$.

However, it may be the case that $\beta'_i \neq \beta_i$ for $i \in I_M$, in which case the honest generators must also simulate the handling cheating with the β_i. This is done using the same technique as above. $\mathcal{S}$ chooses $\zeta_{f,j,l}$ randomly for $l \in I_M$

and sets $\zeta_{f,j,l} = 1$ for $j \notin I_M$. Then it replaces the original values of $\gamma_{j,l}$ and $\delta_{f,j,l}$ for $j \notin I_M$ by $\gamma_{j,l} = \prod_{i \in I'_M} \gamma_{j,i}^{\prod_{i' \neq i} \frac{l-i'}{i-i'}}$ and $\delta_{f,j,l} = \prod_{i \in I'_M} \delta_{f,j,i}^{\prod_{i' \neq i} \frac{l-i'}{i-i'}}$. This ensures that $g^{\zeta_{1,l,j} + \zeta_{2,l,j} + \zeta_{3,l,j}} = \prod_{\iota=0}^{t} \gamma_{l,\iota}^{j^{\iota}}$ and $h_f^{\zeta_{f,l,j}} = \prod_{\iota=0}^{t} \delta_{f,l,\iota}^{j^{\iota}}$, for $j \in I_M$. The simulated honest generators are instructed to not complain despite that the above equations does not hold for their values of $\zeta_{j,l}$, when $j, l \notin I_M$. This implies that no $\zeta_{f,j,l}$ for any $j \notin I_M$ is ever published. Regardless if β_j for $j \in I_M$ are correct or not we have $y = \prod_{i \in I_2} \beta_i^{\prod_{l \neq i} \frac{l}{l-i}}$ where y is the value output by $\mathcal{F}_{\mathrm{DKG}}$. At this point the simulation of $\mathcal{F}_{\mathrm{BB}}$ is continued.

REACHING A CONTRADICTION. Suppose that $\mathcal{S}$ does not imply the security of the protocol. Then there exists a hybrid adversary $\mathcal{A}' = \mathcal{A}^{(\mathcal{S}_{\mathrm{BB}}, \mathcal{S}_{\mathrm{MMT}}, \mathcal{S}_{\mathrm{CRS}})}$, an environment $\mathcal{Z}$ with auxiliary input $z = \{z_n\}$, a constant $c > 0$ and an infinite index set $\mathcal{N} \subset \mathbb{N}$ such that for $n \in \mathcal{N}$: $| \Pr[\mathcal{Z}_z(\mathcal{I}(\mathcal{S}, \pi^{\mathcal{F}_{\mathrm{DKG}}})) = 1] - \Pr[\mathcal{Z}_z(\mathcal{H}(\mathcal{A}', \pi^{(\overline{\pi}_1^{\mathcal{F}_{\mathrm{BB}}}, \overline{\pi}_2^{\mathcal{F}_{\mathrm{MMT}}}, \overline{\pi}_3^{\mathcal{F}_{\mathrm{CRS}}})})) = 1]| \geq \frac{1}{n^c}$, where $\mathcal{S}$ runs $\mathcal{A}'$ as a black-box as described above, i.e. $\mathcal{S} = \mathcal{S}(\mathcal{A}')$.

Defining the Distinguisher. We are now ready to define a distinguisher D that contradicts the DDH assumption. D is confronted with the following test. An oracle first chooses $e_1, e_2, e_3 \in \mathbb{Z}_q$ and a bit $b \in \{0, 1\}$ randomly and defines $(u, v, w) = (h_1^{e_1}, h_1^{e_2}, h_1^{be_1 e_2 + (1-b)e_3})$. Then D is given (u, v, w) and must guess b.

There exists $j \neq i$ such that $i, j \notin I_M$ and $f(i) \neq f(j)$. Without loss we assume that $1, 2 \notin I_M$ and $f(1) = 1$ and $f(2) = 2$.

D does the following. It sets $h_2 = u$, and generates a random h_3. Then it simulates all machines and ideal functionalities as described above, except that

1. The simulation of M_1 and M_2 is special and depends on (u, v, w).

   $\mathcal{S}$ chooses $s_{j,l}$ randomly and defines $\omega_{j,l} = h_j^{s_{j,l}}$ for $j = 1, 2$ and $l \in I_M$. Then it chooses σ randomly in $\mathbb{Z}_q$ and sets $\omega_{1,0} = h_1^{\sigma}/v$ and $\omega_{2,0} = w$. Then it computes $s_{(1,2),l} = s_{1,l} + s_{2,l}$ for $l \in I_M$ and sets $s_{(1,2),0} = \sigma$. This allows the definition of $s_{(1,2),l} = \sum_{i \in I'_M} s_{(1,2),i} \prod_{j \neq i} \frac{l-i}{j-i}$, for $l \notin I_M$. Set $s_{1,l} = \log_{h_1} \omega_{1,l}$ and $s_{2,l} = \log_{h_2} \omega_{2,l}$ for $l \notin I_M$ (inclusive $l = 0$). These values are not known by $\mathcal{S}$, but we can still consider the equation system $(s_{j,l})_{l \in I'_M} = (l^{\iota})_{l \in I'_M, \iota \in [0,t]} (a_{j,\iota})_{\iota \in [0,t]}$. Denote by $(d_{l,\iota})_{l \in I'_M, \iota \in [0,t]}$ the inverse of $(l^{\iota})_{l \in I'_M, \iota \in [0,t]}$. Then $a_{j,\iota} = \sum_{l \in I'_M} d_{l,\iota} s_{j,l}$, for $j = 1, 2$.

   D sets $\alpha_{j,\iota} = \prod_{l \in I'_M} \omega_{j,l}^{d_{l,\iota}}$. Then the simulation is carried through as described above, except that M_j for $j \notin I_M$ replace $s_{1,j} + s_{2,j}$ in the sum $s_j = \sum_{l \in I_1} s_{l,j}$ by $s_{(1,2),j}$ (recall that $\mathcal{S}$ does not even know $s_{1,j}$ or $s_{2,j}$).
2. In the simulation of $\mathcal{F}_{\mathrm{DKG}}$, D instructs it to use the values s_j extracted from corrupt generators, and the values s_j generated by $\mathcal{S}$ in the simulation.

Concluding the Proof. If (u, v, w) is a DDH-triple, then $s_{1,l} = \log_{h_1} \omega_{1,0} = \sigma - e_2$ and $s_{2,l} = \log_{h_2} \omega_{2,0} = e_2$. Thus, $s_{1,l} + s_{2,l} = s_{(1,2),l}$, which gives $s_j = \sum_{l \in I_1} s_{l,j}$. This implies that the distribution of the output of D is identical to the distribution of $\mathcal{Z}_z(\mathcal{H}(\mathcal{A}', \pi^{(\overline{\pi}_1^{\mathcal{F}_{\mathrm{BB}}}, \overline{\pi}_2^{\mathcal{F}_{\mathrm{MMT}}}, \overline{\pi}_3^{\mathcal{F}_{\mathrm{CRS}}})}))$, since all inputs to $\mathcal{A}$ during the simulation are identically distributed to the corresponding inputs in a real execution.

If on the other hand (u, v, w) is not a DDH-triple, then $s_{1,l} = \log_{h_1} \omega_{1,0} = \sigma - e_2$ and $s_{2,l} = \log_{h_2} \omega_{2,0} = e_3$, which implies that $s_{1,l} + s_{2,l}$ is independently distributed from $s_{(1,2),l}$ for $l \notin I_M$. Since the former is used in the construction of $\alpha_{j,\iota}$ for $j = 1, 2$ and the latter is used to compute s_j, β_j and thereby y are independently distributed from $\alpha_{j,\iota}$. This is precisely the situation in the ideal model. Thus, the distribution of D in this case is identical to the distribution of $\mathcal{Z}_z(\mathcal{I}(\mathcal{S}, \bar{\pi}^{\mathcal{F}_{\mathrm{DKG}}}))$.

This implies that the DDH-assumption is broken (Definition 1), and the theorem is true. The corollary follows from Lemma 2 and Lemma 1 by use of the composition theorem of the UC-framework (Theorem 2 in Appendix A).

Acknowledgments

I thank Johan Håstad for helpful discussions in general and in particular for helping me to correct an error in a preliminary version.

References

1. M. Abe, S. Fehr, *Adaptively Secure Feldman VSS and Applications to Universally-Composable Threshold Cryptography*, to appear at Crypto 2004. (full version at Cryptology ePrint Archive, Report 2004/118, http://eprint.iacr.org/, May, 2004).
2. A. Aho, J. Hopcroft, J. Ullman, *The Design and Analysis of Computer Algorithms*, ISBN 0-201-00029-6, Addison Wesley, 1974.
3. D. Beaver, *Foundations of secure interactive computation*, Crypto '91, LNCS 576, pp. 377-391, 1991.
4. R. Canetti, *Security and composition of multi-party cryptographic protocols*, Journal of Cryptology, Vol. 13, No. 1, winter 2000.
5. R. Canetti, *Universally Composable Security: A New Paradigm for Cryptographic Protocols*, http://eprint.iacr.org/2000/067 and ECCC TR 01-24. Extended abstract appears in 42nd FOCS, IEEE Computer Society, 2001.
6. R. Canetti, R. Gennaro, S. Jarecki, H. Krawczyk, T. Rabin, *Adaptive security for threshold cryptosystems*, Crypto '99, LNCS 1666, pp. 98-115, 1999.
7. R. Cramer, V. Shoup, *A Practical Public Key Cryptosystem Provably Secure against Adaptive Chosen Ciphertext Attack*, Crypto '98, pp. 13-25, LNCS 1462, 1998.
8. P. Feldman, *A practical scheme for non-interactive verifiable secret sharing*, 28th FOCS, pp. 427-438, 1987.
9. Y. Frankel, P. MacKenzie, M. Yung, *Adaptively-secure distributed threshold public key systems*, In Proc. of 7th Annual European Symposium 1999, LNCS 1643, pp. 4-27, 1999.
10. Y. Frankel, P. MacKenzie, M. Yung, *Adaptively-secure optimal-resilience proactive RSA*, Asiacrypt '99, LNCS 1716, pp. 180-194, 1999.
11. Y. Frankel, P. MacKenzie, M. Yung, *Adaptive Security for the Additive-Sharing Based Proactive RSA*, Public Key Cryptography 2001, LNCS 1992, pp. 240-263, 2001.

12. Y. Frankel, P. MacKenzie, M. Yung, *Adaptively secure distributed public-key systems*, Theoretical Computer Science, Vol. 287, No. 2, September 2002.
13. R. Gennaro, S. Jarecki, H. Krawczyk, T. Rabin, *Secure Applications of Pedersen's Distributed Key Generation Protocol*, RSA Security '03, LNCS 2612, pp. 373-390, 2003.
14. R. Gennaro, S. Jarecki, H. Krawczyk, T. Rabin, *Secure Distributed Key Generation for Discrete-Log Based Cryptosystems*, Eurocrypt '99, LNCS 1592, pp. 295-310, 1999.
15. R. Gennaro, M. O. Rabin, T. Rabin, *Simplified VSS and Fast-track Multiparty Computations with Applications to Threshold Cryptography*, In Proc. of the 1998 ACM Symposium on Principles of Distributed Computing, 1998.
16. O. Goldreich, *Foundations of Cryptography*, Cambridge University Press, 2001.
17. O. Goldreich, S. Micali, and A. Wigderson, *How to Play Any Mental Game*, 19th STOC, pp. 218-229, 1987.
18. S. Goldwasser, L. Levin, *Fair computation of general functions in presence of immoral majority*, Crypto '90, LNCS 537, pp. 77-93, 1990.
19. S. Goldwasser, Y. Lindell, *Secure Multi-Party Computation Without Agreement*, In Proc. of the 16th DISC, LNCS 2508, pp. 17-32, 2002.
20. S. Goldwasser, S. Micali, C. Rackoff, *The Knowledge Complexity of Interactive Proof Systems*, SIAM Journal of Computing, Vol. 18, pp. 186-208, 1989.
21. S. Jarecki, A. Lysyanskaya, *Adaptively Secure Threshold Cryptography without the Assumption of Erasure*, Eurocrypt 2000, LNCS 1807, 221-242, 2000.
22. Y. Lindell, A. Lysyanskaya, T. Rabin, *On the Composition of Authenticated Byzantine Agreement*, 34th STOC, pp. 514-523, 2002.
23. S. Micali, P. Rogaway, *Secure Computation*, Crypto '91, LNCS 576, pp. 392-404, 1991.
24. T. Pedersen, *Non-interactive and information-theoretic secure verifiable secret sharing*, Crypto '91, pp. 129-140, 1991.
25. T. Pedersen, *A threshold cryptosystem without a trusted party*, Eurocrypt '91, pp. 129-140, 1991.
26. B. Pfitzmann, M. Waidner, *Composition and Integrity Preservation of Secure Reactive Systems*, 7th Conference on Computer and Communications Security of the ACM, pp. 245-254, 2000.
27. C. Rackoff, D. Simon, *Noninteractive zero-knowledge proofs of knowledge and chosen ciphertext attacks*, 22:nd STOC, pp. 433-444, 1991.
28. D. Wikström, *A Universally Composable Mix-Net*, Proceedings of First Theory of Cryptography Conference (TCC '04), LNCS 2951, pp. 315-335, 2004.

A   Review of the UC-Security Framework

In this section we give a short review of the universally composable security framework of Canetti [5]. This framework is very general, quite complex, and hard to describe both accurately and concisely. We have chosen to use a slightly simplified approach. For a general in depth discussion, intuition, and more details we refer the reader to Canetti [5]. Note that we consider only static adversaries.

Following Goldwasser, Micali and Rackoff [20] we define the parties to be interactive Turing machines, and denote the set of interactive Turing machines by ITM.

Canetti assumes the existence of an "operating system" that handles the creation of subprotocols. This is necessary to handle protocols with a large number of possible trees of calls to subprotocols, but for our purposes we may assume that all subprotocols are instantiated already at the start of the protocol.

Canetti models an asynchronous communication network, where the adversary has the power to delete, modify, and insert any messages of his choice. To do this he is forced to give details for exactly what the adversary is allowed to do. This becomes quite complex in the hybrid model. We instead factor out all aspects of the communication network into a separate concrete "communication model"-machine. The real, ideal, and hybrid models are then defined solely on how certain machines are linked. The adversary is defined as any ITM, and how the adversary can interact with other machines follows implicitly from the definitions of the real and ideal communication models.

Since each protocol or subprotocol communicate through its own copy of the "communication model", and all protocols are instantiated at the start of the protocol we need not bother with session ID:s. Such ID:s would clearly be needed if our protocols would be rewritten in the more general original security framework, but it is notationally convenient to avoid them.

We also assume that we may connect any pair of machines by a "link". Such a link is more or less equivalent to the notion of a link as defined by Goldreich [16]. Thus, the following is meaningful.

Definition 1. *An* ITM-*graph is a set* $V = \{P_1, \ldots, P_t\} \subset$ ITM *with a set of links* E *such that* (V, E) *is a connected graph, and no* P_i *is linked to any machine outside* V. *Let* ITMG *be the set of* ITM-*graphs.*

During the execution of an ITM-*graph, at most one party is active. An active party may deactivate itself and activate any of its neighbors, or it may halt, in which case the execution of the* ITM-*graph halts.*

The real communication model models an asynchronous communication network, in which the adversary can read, delete, modify, and insert any message of its choice.

Definition 2. *A* real communication model $\mathcal{C}$ *is a machine with a link* l_{P_i}, *to* P_i *for* $i = 1, \ldots, k$, *and a link* $l_{\mathcal{A}}$ *to a real adversary* $\mathcal{A}$, *defined as follows.*

1. *If* m *is read on* l_s, *where* $s \in \{P_1, \ldots, P_k\}$, *then* (s, m) *is written on* $l_{\mathcal{A}}$ *and* $\mathcal{A}$ *is activated.*
2. *If* (r, m) *is read on* $l_{\mathcal{A}}$, *where* $r \in \{P_1, \ldots, P_k\}$, *then* m *is written on* l_r, *and* r *is activated.*

The ideal communication model below captures that the adversary may decide if and when to deliver a message from an ideal functionality to a party, but it can not read the contents of the communication.

Definition 3. *An* ideal communication model $\mathcal{C}_{\mathcal{I}}$ *is a machine with a link* l_{P_i}, *to* P_i *for* $i = 1, \ldots, k$, *and links* $l_{\mathcal{F}}$, *and* $l_{\mathcal{S}}$ *to an ideal functionality* $\mathcal{F}$ *and an ideal adversary* $\mathcal{S}$ *respectively. Its program is defined as follows.*

1. *If a message m is read on l_s, where $s \in \{P_1, \ldots, P_k\}$, then (s, m) is written on $l_{\mathcal{F}}$ and $\mathcal{F}$ is activated.*
2. *If a message (s, m) written on $l_{\mathcal{F}}$ is returned unaltered[1], m is written on l_s. If not, any string read from $l_{\mathcal{F}}$ is interpreted as a list $((r_1, m_1), \ldots, (r_t, m_t))$, where $r_i \in \{\mathcal{S}, P_1, \ldots, P_k\}$. For each m_i a random string $\tau_i \in \{0, 1\}^n$ is chosen, and (r_i, m_i) is stored under τ_i. Then $((r_1, |m_1|, \tau_1), \ldots, (r_t, |m_t|, \tau_t))$, where $|m_i|$ is the bit-length of m_i, is written to $l_{\mathcal{S}}$ and $\mathcal{S}$ is activated.*
3. *Any string read from $l_{\mathcal{S}}$ is interpreted as a pair (b, τ), where $b \in \{0, 1\}$ and τ is an arbitrary string. If $b = 1$ and (r_i, m_i) is stored in the database under the index τ, m_i is written on l_{r_i} and r_i is activated. Otherwise $(\mathcal{S}, \tau)$ is written to $l_{\mathcal{F}}$ and $\mathcal{F}$ is activated.*

An *adversary* can normally corrupt some subset of the parties in a protocol. A *dummy party* is a machine that given two links writes any message from one of the links on the other. There may be many copies of the dummy party. We write $\overline{P}$ for dummy parties. The ideal model below captures the setup one wishes to realize, i.e. the environment may interact with the ideal functionality $\mathcal{F}$, except that the adversary $\mathcal{S}$ has controls the communication.

Definition 4. *The* ideal model *is defined to be a map* $\mathcal{I} : \mathrm{ITM}^2 \times \overline{\mathrm{ITM}}^* \to \mathrm{ITMG}$, *where* $\mathcal{I} : (\mathcal{F}, \mathcal{S}, \overline{P}_1, \ldots, \overline{P}_k) \mapsto (V, E)$ *is given by:*
$V = \{\mathcal{C}_{\mathcal{I}}, \mathcal{F}, \mathcal{S}, \overline{P}_1, \ldots, \overline{P}_k\}$ *and* $E = \{(\mathcal{S}, \mathcal{C}_{\mathcal{I}}), (\mathcal{C}_{\mathcal{I}}, \mathcal{F})\} \cup \bigcup_{i=1}^{k} \{(\overline{P}_i, \mathcal{C}_{\mathcal{I}})\}$.

If $\overline{\pi} = (\overline{P}_1, \ldots, \overline{P}_k)$, we write $\mathcal{I}(\mathcal{S}, \overline{\pi}^{\mathcal{F}})$ instead of $\mathcal{I}(\mathcal{F}, \mathcal{S}, \overline{P}_1, \ldots, \overline{P}_k)$ to ease notation. The real model is supposed to capture the properties of the real world. The parties may interact over the real communication model.

Definition 5. *The* real model *is defined to be a map* $\mathcal{R} : \mathrm{ITM}^* \to \mathrm{ITMG}$, *where* $\mathcal{R} : (\mathcal{A}, P_1, \ldots, P_k) \mapsto (V, E)$ *is given by:* $V = \{\mathcal{C}, \mathcal{A}, P_1, \ldots, P_k\}$ *and* $E = \{(\mathcal{A}, \mathcal{C})\} \cup \bigcup_{i=1}^{k} \{(P_i, \mathcal{C})\}$.

Let $(V, E) = \mathcal{I}(\mathcal{F}, \mathcal{S}, \overline{P}_1, \ldots, \overline{P}_k)$. Then we write $\mathcal{Z}(\mathcal{I}(\mathcal{F}, \mathcal{S}, \overline{P}_1, \ldots, \overline{P}_k))$ for the ITM-graph (V', E') defined by $V' = V \cup \{\mathcal{Z}\}$, and $E' = E \cup \{(\mathcal{Z}, \mathcal{S})\} \cup \bigcup_{i=1}^{k} \{(\mathcal{Z}, \overline{P}_i)\}$. We use the corresponding notation in the real model case.

A hybrid model is a mix between a number of ideal and real models, and captures the execution of a real world protocol with access to some ideal functionalities. It is also a tool to modularize security proofs. It may be viewed as if we "glue" a number of ideal and real models onto an original real model.

Definition 6. *Suppose that we are given* $(V, E) = \mathcal{R}(\mathcal{A}, \pi)$, $\pi = (P_1, \ldots, P_k)$. *Let* $(V_j, E_j) = \mathcal{I}(\mathcal{S}_j, \overline{\pi}_j^{\mathcal{F}_j})$, $\overline{\pi}_j = (\overline{P}_{j,1}, \ldots, \overline{P}_{j,k})$ *for* $j = 1, \ldots, t$, *and* $(V_j, E_j) = \mathcal{R}(\mathcal{S}_j, \pi_j)$, $\pi_j = (P_{j,1}, \ldots, P_{j,k})$ *for* $j = t + 1, \ldots, s$.
We denote by $\mathcal{H}(\mathcal{A}^{(\mathcal{S}_1, \ldots, \mathcal{S}_t)}, \pi^{(\overline{\pi}_1^{\mathcal{F}_1}, \ldots, \overline{\pi}_t^{\mathcal{F}_t}, \pi_{t+1}, \ldots, \pi_s)})$ *the* hybrid model *defined as the ITM-graph* (V', E'), *where* $V' = V \cup \bigcup_{j=1}^{t} V_j$ *and*
$$E' = E \cup \bigcup_{j=1}^{t} E_j \cup \bigcup_{i=1}^{k} \left(\{(\mathcal{S}_i, \mathcal{A})\} \cup \bigcup_{j=1}^{t} \{(P_i, \overline{P}_{j,i})\} \right)$$

---

[1] This special rule simplifies security proofs.

Similarly as above we write $\mathcal{Z}(\mathcal{H}(\mathcal{A}^{(\mathcal{S}_1,\dots,\mathcal{S}_t)},\pi^{(\overline{\pi}_1^{\mathcal{F}_1},\dots,\overline{\pi}_t^{\mathcal{F}_t},\pi_{t+1},\dots,\pi_s)}))$ to denote the ITM-graph (V'',E'') defined by $V'' = V' \cup \{\mathcal{Z}\}$, and $E'' = E' \cup \{(\mathcal{Z},\mathcal{A})\} \cup \bigcup_{i=1}^{k}\{(\mathcal{Z},P_i)\}$.

Note that all real subprotocols π_j, for $j = t+1,\dots,s$, above may be integrated into the original real protocol π. Thus a hybrid model with no ideal functionalities involved is equivalent to a real model, except that it may use several communication models.

The concept of hybrid models is generalized in the natural way, e.g. we write $\mathcal{H}(\mathcal{A}^{(A_1^{\mathcal{S}_{11}},A_2^{\mathcal{S}_{21}})},\pi^{(\pi_1^{\overline{\pi}_1^{\mathcal{F}}},\pi_2^{\overline{\pi}_2^{\mathcal{F}}})})$ for a hybrid model for a real protocol that executes two subprotocols, where each subprotocol has access to a separate copy of the ideal functionality $\mathcal{F}$. Some care needs to be taken when defining the adversary for such models. If an adversary corrupts a party, it automatically corrupts all its sub-parties that are involved in subprotocols[2].

We also write $\mathcal{Z}_z$ to denote that $\mathcal{Z}$ takes auxiliary input z, and always assume that in any execution of such an ITM-graph, $\mathcal{Z}$ is activated first.

The following definition is somewhat sloppy in that we have not defined the notion of $\mathcal{M}$-adversaries rigorously, but it is a class of adversaries.

Definition 7 (Secure Realization). *Let $\mathcal{F}$ be an ideal functionality. Let $\pi = (P_1,\dots,P_k)$, and let $\overline{\pi}_j = (\overline{P}_{j,i},\dots,\overline{P}_{j,i})$ be the corresponding dummy parties for $\mathcal{F}_j$, for $j = 1,\dots,t$.*

Then $\pi^{(\overline{\pi}_1^{\mathcal{F}_1},\dots,\overline{\pi}_t^{\mathcal{F}_t})}$ realizes $\overline{\pi}^{\mathcal{F}}$ securely with regards to $\mathcal{M}$-adversaries if for all $\mathcal{M}$-adversaries $\mathcal{A}^{(\mathcal{S}_1,\dots,\mathcal{S}_t)}$ with auxiliary input $z = \{z_n\}$, $\exists \mathcal{S} \in$ ITM such that $\forall c > 0$, $\exists n_0$, such that $\forall n > n_0$:

$$|\Pr[\mathcal{Z}_z(\mathcal{I}(\mathcal{S},\overline{\pi}^{\mathcal{F}})) = 1] - \Pr[\mathcal{Z}_z(\mathcal{H}(\mathcal{A}^{(\mathcal{S}_1,\dots,\mathcal{S}_t)},\pi^{(\overline{\pi}_1^{\mathcal{F}_1},\dots,\overline{\pi}_t^{\mathcal{F}_t})})) = 1]| < \frac{1}{n^c}.$$

Since the dummy parties are of no real importance we also say that π realizes $\mathcal{F}$ in the $(\mathcal{F}_1,\dots,\mathcal{F}_t)$-hybrid model.

Canetti [5] proves a powerful composition theorem that can handle polynomially many instances of a constant number of ideal functionalities, but we only need the following weaker special case.

Theorem 2 (Composition Theorem). *Suppose that $\pi^{(\tilde{\pi}_1^{\mathcal{F}_1},\dots,\tilde{\pi}_t^{\mathcal{F}_t})}$ securely realizes $\tilde{\pi}^{\mathcal{F}}$, and that $\pi_i^{(\tilde{\pi}_{i1}^{\mathcal{F}_{i1}},\dots,\tilde{\pi}_{it_i}^{\mathcal{F}_{it_i}})}$ securely realizes $\tilde{\pi}_i^{\mathcal{F}_i}$, for $i = 1,\dots,l$, with regards to $\mathcal{M}$-adversaries.*

Then $\pi^{(\pi_1^{(\tilde{\pi}_{11}^{\mathcal{F}_{11}},\dots,\tilde{\pi}_{1t_1}^{\mathcal{F}_{1t_1}})},\dots,\pi_l^{(\tilde{\pi}_{l1}^{\mathcal{F}_{l1}},\dots,\tilde{\pi}_{lt_l}^{\mathcal{F}_{lt_l}})},\tilde{\pi}_{l+1}^{\mathcal{F}_{l+1}},\dots,\tilde{\pi}_t^{\mathcal{F}_t})}$ securely realizes $\tilde{\pi}^{\mathcal{F}}$ with regards to $\mathcal{M}$-adversaries.

---

[2] The most general definition allows some violations of this rule.

An Algebraic Approach to NTRU $(q = 2^n)$ via Witt Vectors and Overdetermined Systems of Nonlinear Equations

J.H. Silverman[1], N.P. Smart[2], and F. Vercauteren[2]

[1] Mathematics Department, Box 1917,
Brown University, Providence, RI 02912, U.S.A.
joseph_silverman@brown.edu
[2] Dept. Computer Science, University of Bristol,
Merchant Venturers Building, Woodland Road,
Bristol, BS8 1UB, United Kingdom
{nigel,frederik}@cs.bris.ac.uk

Abstract. We use the theory of Witt vectors to develop an algebraic approach for studying the NTRU primitive with q parameter equal to a power of two. This results in a system of nonlinear algebraic equations over $\mathbb{F}_2$ having many symmetries, which is reminiscent of the approach of Courtois, Murphy, Pieprzyk, Robshaw and others for studying the structure of block ciphers such as the AES. We study whether this approach to NTRU provides any immediate security threat and conclude that under the most favourable assumptions, the method is of asymptotic interest but is completely impractical at current or likely future parameter sizes.

1 Introduction

NTRU [7] is a public key encryption scheme whose security is based on a polynomial factorisation problem in the ring $\mathbb{Z}_q[X](X^N - 1)$. It is an interesting system to study for a number of reasons. Firstly, it does not depend on the traditional hard problems, such as factoring or discrete logarithms, on which other practical public key schemes are based. Indeed the best known heuristic attack is that of finding a short vector in a lattice, which appears to be a very hard problem. Furthermore, schemes based on factoring or discrete logarithms can be broken in the quantum setting using Shor's algorithm [16]. Currently, there is no quantum algorithm which significantly improves the classical approach to breaking NTRU. Secondly, the basic arithmetic operations in NTRU are particularly simple making it suitable for use in constrained environments where traditional public key schemes have difficulty. Thirdly, it appears unique amongst the practical public key encryption schemes in that there is a possibility of mounting attacks based on the property of imperfect decryption [8], which has led to interesting developments in the area of provable security.

C. Blundo and S. Cimato (Eds.): SCN 2004, LNCS 3352, pp. 278–293, 2005.
© Springer-Verlag Berlin Heidelberg 2005

Algebraic attacks on block and stream ciphers have been of considerable interest in the research literature over the last few years. Starting with the XL and FXL algorithms of Courtois, Klimov, Patarin and Shamir [3], a number of papers has appeared studying applications of the XL algorithm to the security of block and stream ciphers, see for example [4, 5, 12]. These algebraic attacks work by reducing the determination of the secret key in a cryptographic system to the solution of an overdetermined system of quadratic equations over a small finite field. Then using the technique of linearisation, this nonlinear system is mapped into a large system of linear equations. The resulting linear system is then solved and the key is recovered. There is some controversy over the precise practicality of these algebraic attacks in various situations. For example, it is not known whether the XL algorithm runs in subexponential time for systems that are only slightly overdetermined.

In this paper we reduce the problem of recovering an NTRU private key to an overdetermined system of quadratic equations over $\mathbb{F}_2$. Experimentally we find that these systems of equations tend to have a single solution, which is encouraging since from the prior literature on the XL algorithm, it appears that XL has a better chance of success if there is a unique solution. This leads us to perform numerical experiments (in small dimension) testing the applicability of the XL algorithm to the system of nonlinear equations derived from NTRU problem instances. These experiments reveal that from a practical perspective, the method is unlikely to be successful at current or likely future parameter sizes.

The paper is organised as follows: In Section 2 we briefly describe the NTRU encryption algorithm so as to fix notation. Then in Section 3 we recall the basic theory of Witt vectors and use it to reduce the problem of determining the NTRU private key to that of solving an overdetermined system of quadratic equations. In Section 4 we report on our numerical experiments applying the XL algorithm to the resulting system of equations. Finally in Section 5 we give some conclusions of our work.

We end this introduction by noting that the technique based on Witt vectors introduced in this paper applies to many cryptosystems other than the NTRU cryptosystem. The isomorphism $\mathbb{Z}_{2^m} \cong W_m(\mathbb{F}_2)$ implies that virtually any cryptosystem based on arithmetic modulo 2^m (together with logical operations and rotations) can be analysed using Witt vectors. This remark applies to symmetric key cryptosystems that could not previously be algebraically analysed due to their use of arithmetic modulo 2^m, for example to RC5 [13], RC6 [14] and IDEA [10].

2   The NTRU Cryptosystem

2.1   Notation

We denote the ring of integers by $\mathbb{Z}$ and the integers modulo q by $\mathbb{Z}_q$, which we shall assume are represented by elements in the interval $(-\lceil q/2 \rceil, \lfloor q/2 \rfloor]$. For N

a positive integer, we identify the set $\mathbb{Z}^N$ (respectively $\mathbb{Z}_q^N$) with the ring of polynomials

$$P(N) = \frac{\mathbb{Z}[X]}{(X^N - 1)}, \quad \text{respectively} \quad P_q(N) = \frac{\mathbb{Z}_q[X]}{(X^N - 1)},$$

via the natural association $f = (f_0, f_1, \ldots, f_{N-1}) = \sum_{i=0}^{N-1} f_i X^i$. Note that the modulus q is not necessarily prime, hence $\mathbb{Z}_q$ is not in general a field.

Two polynomials $f, g \in P(N)$ are multiplied by the cyclic convolution product, since we are working modulo $X^N - 1$, an operation that we denote by $\star$ to distinguish it from ordinary multiplication $\cdot$ in $\mathbb{Z}$ or $\mathbb{Z}[X]$. Let $h = f \star g$. Then for each $0 \leq k < N$, the kth-coefficient h_k of h is given by

$$h_k = (f \star g)_k = \sum_{i=0}^{k} f_i g_{k-i} + \sum_{i=k+1}^{N-1} f_i g_{n+k-i} = \sum_{i+j \equiv k \bmod N} f_i \cdot g_j.$$

This is the ordinary polynomial product reduced modulo $X^N - 1$, so it is both commutative and associative. The symmetric representation of $\mathbb{Z}_q$, i.e. reducing in the interval $(-\lceil q/2 \rceil, \lfloor q/2 \rfloor]$, implies that the product of two polynomials with coefficients of small absolute value will again be a polynomial with small coefficients. We write $P_q^\star(N)$ for the multiplicative group of units in $P_q(N)$ and we denote the inverse polynomial of $f \in P_q^\star(N)$ by f_q^{-1}.

We also need a "small" element p of $P(N)$ that is relatively prime to q, by which we mean that p and q generate the unit ideal in $P(N)$. Typically one chooses p to be 2, 3 or $2 + X$. In this paper we concentrate on the case $p = 2 + X$, since that is the choice made in the NTRU challenges [2]. However, our methodology applies to other values of p. Reduction of a polynomial in $P(N)$ modulo $2+X$ proceeds by rewriting each integer coefficient $n = 2a+b$ as $(-X)a + b$ and then iterating. It is easily seen that reduction modulo $2 + X$ always leads to a polynomial with coefficients in $\{0, 1\}$.

We denote the quotient ring $P(N)/(p)$ by $P_p(N)$, we let $P_p^\star(N)$ be the multiplicative group of units in $P_p(N)$, and we write f_p^{-1} for the inverse polynomial of $f \in P_p^\star(N)$.

2.2   The NTRU Primitive

We sketch the NTRU cryptosystem as developed in [7]. The public parameters consist of values for (N, p, q) as above. The value of q is chosen to lie between $N/2$ and N and may be chosen to aid computation. For example for the "recommended" security parameter $N = 251$ for "standard security" one could choose $q = 128$ or $q = 127$ so as to aid in reduction modulo q.

Other required parameters are various integers d which are used to define several families of binary polynomials of $P_q(N)$ as follows: The notation $\mathcal{L}(d)$ is used to denote the set of polynomials in $P_q(N)$, with d coefficients equal to 1 and all other coefficients set to zero. These sets are used to define three sets of polynomials $\mathcal{L}_f$, $\mathcal{L}_g$ and $\mathcal{L}_r$. The standard [1] contains two common choices for these sets. In this paper we focus on the following choice; the other case can be dealt with in a similar (but slightly more complicated) manner.

We first define the sets $\mathcal{L}_f = \{1 + p \star F : F \in \mathcal{L}(d_f)\}$, $\mathcal{L}_g = \mathcal{L}(d_g)$ and $\mathcal{L}_r = \mathcal{L}(d_r)$, for certain integer parameters d_f, d_g and d_r. Notice that with the above choice of $f \in \mathcal{L}_f$, we have $f_p^{-1} = 1$.

A public key encryption algorithm consists of three subprocedures: A key generation algorithm, an encryption algorithm and a decryption algorithm. For the convenience of the reader, we describe these three procedures in Appendix A. We do not describe these procedures for NTRU here since, for the purposes of this article, it suffices to know that a private key is generated by choosing random $f \in \mathcal{L}_f$ and $g \in \mathcal{L}_g$ and computing $f_q^{-1} \in P_q^\star(N)$ and $f_p^{-1} \in P_p^\star(N)$, which for our choice of $\mathcal{L}_f$ equals 1. Then the private key consists of the pair (f, f_p^{-1}) and the public key is the polynomial h defined by the formula

$$h \equiv p \star f_q^{-1} \star g \pmod{q}.$$

Breaking an NTRU key is the problem of recovering f from a given h.

The traditional way to try to break an NTRU public key, in the sense of recovering the private key, is to embed the NTRU problem into a lattice as a shortest (or closest) vector problem and use lattice reduction techniques to try and recover the private key. Whilst lattice reduction algorithms themselves run in polynomial time, this method is unlikely to work for large key sizes since the resulting reduced lattice basis only approximates the shortest lattice vector to within an exponential factor.

Lattice based attacks are currently the best known heuristic attacks against NTRU. The best known deterministic attack is based on a meet-in-the-middle strategy, see [9, 17]. It has complexity roughly

$$\frac{1}{\sqrt{N}} \binom{N/2}{d_f/2}. \tag{1}$$

It is highly advisable to choose N to be a prime. Firstly, this tends to maximise the probability that the private key has an inverse modulo p and q. More importantly, the use of composite N leads to so called composite attacks on NTRU [6], which can significantly reduce the time needed to recover the private key. It is also important to choose N sufficiently large. Parameter sets with $N = 107$ have been broken via lattice techniques in a few hours of computer time [11]. Depending on the desired level of security, recommended choices for N (see [1]) include 167, 251, 347 or 503.

3   Reduction to Algebraic Equations over $\mathbb{F}_2$

In this section we show how the NTRU problem for $q = 2^n$ leads in a natural way to a system of nonlinear equations over $\mathbb{F}_2$. Since $q = 2^n$, we can apply a lifting strategy by considering the equality $f \star h \equiv p \star g \pmod{2^m}$ for intermediate values $0 < m \leq n$ and equate the bits of the coefficients of both sides. In particular, for $m = 2$ (i.e. working modulo 4) we obtain a highly structured system of N quadratic equations in N binary variables. The most elegant approach to this analysis is based on the theory of Witt vectors over $\mathbb{F}_2$.

3.1   Witt Vectors over $\mathbb{F}_2$

We briefly set the Witt vector notation needed to analyse NTRU. For the convenience of readers who are not familiar with the construction of the ring of Witt vectors, we have sketched the basic theory in Appendix B. For the general theory of Witt vectors, we refer the reader to [15–Section II.6].

The ring of Witt vectors of length m, denoted $W_m(\mathbb{F}_2)$, is the set $\mathbb{F}_2^m$ of m-tuples, but with special addition and multiplication laws so that the map

$$W_* : W_m(\mathbb{F}_2) \longrightarrow \mathbb{Z}_{2^m}$$

$$[a_0, \ldots, a_{m-1}] \longmapsto \sum_{i=0}^{m-1} a_i 2^i \pmod{2^m} \tag{2}$$

is an isomorphism of rings. The precise construction of the map W_* and the ring operations on $W_m(\mathbb{F}_2)$ are described in Appendix B, but as an example, we write them down for $m = 2$:

$$[a_0, a_1] + [b_0, b_1] = [a_0 + b_0, a_0 b_0 + a_1 + b_1]$$
$$[a_0, a_1] \cdot [b_0, b_1] = [a_0 b_0, a_0 b_1 + b_0 a_1]$$

3.2   Generating Algebraic Equations over $\mathbb{F}_2$ for NTRU

The isomorphism between the ring of Witt vectors $W_m(\mathbb{F}_2)$ of length m and the ring $\mathbb{Z}_{2^m}$ transforms NTRU private key recovery into the problem of solving a system of nonlinear equations over $\mathbb{F}_2$. To see why this is true, consider the fundamental relation

$$f \star h \equiv p \star g \pmod{2^m} \tag{3}$$

for some $m \leq n$. Applying the inverse of the map W_* to the coefficients of the polynomials, we obtain the same equation in the ring $W_m(\mathbb{F}_2)[X]/(X^N - 1)$, i.e. in the ring of polynomials modulo $X^N - 1$ whose coefficients are in the ring of Witt vectors of length m.

To ease notation, for any element $e \in W_m(\mathbb{F}_2)[X]/(X^N - 1)$, we will denote the coefficients of e in $W_m(\mathbb{F}_2)$ by $\mathbf{e}_0, \ldots, \mathbf{e}_{N-1}$, i.e. $e = \sum \mathbf{e}_i X^i$. Comparing the coefficients in equation (3) gives rise to mN equations over $\mathbb{F}_2$, since each coefficient of each X^k is a vector of length m over $\mathbb{F}_2$. Explicitly, equating the coefficients of X^k on the two sides of (3) leads to the formula

$$\sum_{i+j \equiv k \pmod{N}} \mathbf{f}_i \, \mathbf{h}_j = \sum_{i+j \equiv k \pmod{N}} \mathbf{p}_i \, \mathbf{g}_j \quad \text{in the ring } W_m(\mathbb{F}_2). \tag{4}$$

To illustrate this approach, we explicitly compute these equations for our choice of parameter sets $\mathcal{L}_f$ and $\mathcal{L}_g$ and modulus $p = 2 + X$. Recall that we have set $\mathcal{L}_f = \{1 + p \star F : F \in \mathcal{L}(d_f)\}$ and $\mathcal{L}_g = \mathcal{L}(d_g)$. Since $p = 2 + X$ and since $g = \sum g_i X^i$ has *binary* coefficients, we conclude that

$$p \star g \equiv \sum_{k=0}^{N-1} \mathbf{R}_k X^k \quad (\text{mod } 2^m) \quad \text{with} \quad \mathbf{R}_k = [g_{k-1}, g_k, 0, \ldots, 0] \in W_m(\mathbb{F}_2).$$
(5)

(As usual, indices are taken modulo N.) Similarly, writing $F = \sum F_i X^i \in \mathbb{F}_2[X]$, we have

$$f \equiv 1 + (2 + X) \star F \equiv \sum_{i=0}^{N-1} \mathbf{f}_i X^i \quad (\text{mod } 2^m)$$

with $\mathbf{f}_i \in W_m(\mathbb{F}_2)$ given by

$$\mathbf{f}_i = \begin{cases} [1 + F_{N-1}, F_0 + F_{N-1}, F_0 F_{N-1}, 0, \ldots, 0] & \text{if } i = 0, \\ [F_{i-1}, F_i, 0, \ldots, 0] & \text{if } 1 \le i < N. \end{cases}$$

Write $h \equiv \sum \mathbf{h}_i X^i$ with $\mathbf{h}_i = [h_{i,0}, h_{i,1}, \ldots, h_{i,m-1}]$. Then

$$f \star h \equiv \sum_{k=0}^{N-1} \mathbf{L}_k X^i \quad \text{with} \quad \mathbf{L}_k = \sum_{i+j \equiv k \ (\text{mod } N)} \mathbf{f}_i \mathbf{h}_j. \tag{6}$$

Note that with the notation in (5) and (6), the fundamental relation (4) says that $\mathbf{L} = \mathbf{R}$. We will exploit this fact by equating the first two coordinates of $\mathbf{L}$ and $\mathbf{R}$.

The initial Witt ring operation functions are $S_0(\mathbf{a}, \mathbf{b}) = a_0 + b_0$ and $P_0(\mathbf{a}, \mathbf{b}) = a_0 b_0$ (see Table 4 in Appendix B), so we find that

$$g_{k-1} = R_{k,0} = L_{k,0} = \sum_{i+j \equiv k \ (\text{mod } N)} f_{i,0} h_{j,0} = h_{k,0} + \sum_{i+j \equiv k \ (\text{mod } N)} F_{i-1} h_{j,0}.$$

Replacing k by $k + 1$, this gives a formula

$$g_k = h_{k+1,0} + \sum_{i+j \equiv k+1 \ (\text{mod } N)} F_{i-1} h_{j,0} \tag{7}$$

expressing g_k as an $\mathbb{F}_2$-linear combination of the F_i. Similarly, using the four Witt ring operation functions from Appendix B Table 4,

$$S_0 = a_0 + b_0, \qquad S_1 = a_0 b_0 + a_1 + b_1, \qquad P_0 = a_0 b_0, \qquad P_1 = a_0 b_1 + b_0 a_1,$$

we compute

$$g_k = R_{k,1} = L_{k,1}$$

$$= \sum_{\substack{i<s \\ i+j\equiv k \ (\mathrm{mod}\ N) \\ s+t\equiv k \ (\mathrm{mod}\ N)}} f_{i,0}h_{j,0}f_{s,0}h_{t,0} + \sum_{\substack{i+j\equiv k \ (\mathrm{mod}\ N)}} (f_{i,0}\,h_{j,1} + f_{i,1}\,h_{j,0})$$

$$= \sum_{\substack{i<s \\ i+j\equiv k \ (\mathrm{mod}\ N) \\ s+t\equiv k \ (\mathrm{mod}\ N)}} F_{i-1}F_{s-1}h_{j,0}h_{t,0} + h_{k,0} \sum_{\substack{s+t\equiv k \ (\mathrm{mod}\ N)}} F_{s-1}h_{t,0}$$

$$+ \sum_{\substack{i+j\equiv k \ (\mathrm{mod}\ N)}} (F_{i-1}\,h_{j,1} + F_i\,h_{j,0}) + h_{k,1}. \qquad (8)$$

Notice that (8) expresses g_k as an $\mathbb{F}_2$-quadratic combination of the F_i.

Equating the two formulae (7) and (8) for g_k, we arrive at a system of N quadratic equations over $\mathbb{F}_2$ in the N variables $F_0, F_1, \ldots, F_{N-1}$. We further observe that the resulting system of quadratic equations has a high degree of symmetry. Indeed, there are two sets of indices S and T such that each equation $L_{k,1} - g_k = 0$ can be written as

$$\sum_{\substack{i<j \\ i,j\in S_k}} F_iF_j + \sum_{i\in T_k} F_i + h_{k,0} \sum_{i\in S_k} F_i = h_{k+1,0} + h_{k,1}, \qquad (9)$$

with

$$S_k = \{i+k \pmod N \,|\, i\in S\} \qquad \text{and} \qquad T_k = \{i+k \pmod N \,|\, i\in T\}.$$

Example 1. We give an example with $m = 2$ illustrating the nice structure of the system of quadratic equations. We let $N = 17$, $q = 2^7$, $d_f = 6$ and $d_g = 5$, and for the private key we take

$$f = 1 + p \star F$$
$$= 1 + (2 + X) \star (X^{14} + X^{11} + X^6 + X^5 + X^4 + X)$$
$$= X^{15} + 2X^{14} + X^{12} + 2X^{11} + X^7 + 3X^6 + 3X^5 + 2X^4 + X^2 + 2X + 1,$$
$$g = X^{15} + X^{13} + X^{12} + X^7 + 1.$$

The corresponding public key is

$$h = 105X^{16} + 45X^{15} + 32X^{14} + 119X^{13} + 53X^{12} + 89X^{11} + 67X^{10} + 3X^9$$
$$+ 86X^8 + 52X^7 + 56X^6 + 69X^5 + 101X^4 + 81X^3 + 52X^2 + 6X + 29.$$

Given h, we can easily compute the index sets S and T and the constant terms of the quadratic equations (9); we obtain

$$S = \{0, 1, 3, 4, 5, 6, 7, 11, 12, 13, 16\},$$
$$T = \{3, 6, 7, 8, 15\},$$
$$[h_{k+1,0} + h_{k,1}]_{0\leq k<N} = [0, 1, 1, 1, 1, 0, 0, 0, 0, 0, 0, 1, 1, 1, 1, 1, 1].$$

In this case, the system of equations (9) has only one solution, namely that given by the coefficients of $F = X^{14} + X^{11} + X^6 + X^5 + X^4 + X$.

3.3   Additional Equations

As we have seen, the results of Section 3.2 with $m = 2$ can be used to derive N inhomogeneous quadratic equations over $\mathbb{F}_2$ in the N variables $F_0, \ldots, F_{N-1}$. However, due to our choice of parameters, we know that exactly d_f of the values of the F_i are equal to one and the rest are zero. This immediately gives us an extra linear equation

$$\sum_{i=0}^{N-1} F_i \equiv d_f \pmod 2.$$

We can similarly make use of the second least significant bit of d_f to obtain a quadratic relation on the F_i. Precisely, if we write $d_f \equiv d_{f,0} + 2d_{f,1} \pmod 4$ with $d_{f,0}, d_{f,1} \in \{0, 1\}$, then

$$\sum_{i<j} F_i F_j \equiv d_{f,1} \pmod 2.$$

Using other bits of d_f will result in similar equations, but unfortunately they are no longer quadratic, but instead will have higher degree.

Thus using the results of Section 3.2 with $m = 2$, we obtain $N + 2$ inhomogeneous quadratic equations over $\mathbb{F}_2$ in the N variables $F_0, \ldots, F_{N-1}$. The study of such systems of equations has already received much attention in cryptography, see for example [3, 4, 5, 12], via the XL algorithm. In the next section we consider how the XL algorithm may be applied to analyse our system of equations.

4   Experiments with the XL Algorithm

We have conducted extensive experiments with small values of N and found that the system of $N + 2$ quadratic equations corresponding to $m = 2$ almost always has a unique solution, namely the target private key F. Very rarely we found that the system of equations had more than one solution, but even then there was only one solution with the correct Hamming weight d_f.

Thus the formulae derived in Sections 3.2 and 3.3 generally give us a (slightly) overdetermined system of multivariate polynomial equations (of degree 2) whose solution is the desired private key. Such systems of equations might lend themselves to XL-type techniques as described in [3, 4, 5, 12]. We note that in general, solving such systems is NP-hard. However, this is a worst case analysis, and as a practical matter we are more interested in the average case difficulty of our more special problem.

In the paper [3], Courtois, Klimov, Patarin and Shamir propose an algorithm called XL to solve overdetermined systems of multivariate polynomial equations over a finite field. We restrict attention to equations of degree at most two. In this case, the equations defining the system are multiplied by monomials of degree less than $D - 2$ to produce equations of degree at most D. This results in a much larger number of equations, albeit of much higher degree. Note since we are working in characteristic 2, the degree of the monomial equals the number of variables occurring in the monomial. The monomials of degree greater than one in this enlarged system are then replaced by "dummy variables", a technique called linearisation. The resulting linear system is solved, and one hopes that the original system is solved at the same time. Note that the method only works if the resulting system of linear equations has rank approximately equal to the number of linearised variables.

The arguments of [4], where multivariate quadratic equations over $\mathbb{F}_2$ are studied, imply that if the number of equations n_e is roughly equal to the number of variables n_v, then the XL algorithm runs in exponential time. The authors of [4] conjecture that the XL method runs in polynomial time when $n_e = O(n_v^2)$, and that it does not run in polynomial time when $n_e/n_v^2 \to 0$. However, for systems where the number of equations is slightly larger than the number of variables, the authors in [3] leave as an open question whether the XL algorithm might in fact run in subexponential time.

In our situation with $m = 2$, we derived $N + 2$ quadratic equations in N variables. Since $N + 2$ is only slightly larger than N, it is not clear that we obtain any advantage. This led us to conduct the following experiments and to analyse the XL algorithm as applied to the specific set of $N + 2$ inhomogeneous equations in N unknowns described in Sections 3.2 and 3.3.

After linearisation, we obtain

$$\alpha = (N + 2) \sum_{j=0}^{D-2} \binom{N}{j}$$

linear equations in at most $\beta = \sum_{k=1}^{D} \binom{N}{k}$ variables. We let γ denote the number of linearly independent equations, i.e. γ is the rank of the matrix associated to the system of linear equations, and we set

$$\mu = \frac{\gamma}{\alpha} = \text{proportion of the linear equations that are independent.}$$

The XL algorithm will succeed if $\beta = \gamma$ (or at least if $\beta \approx \gamma$), i.e. if $\alpha \cdot \mu \approx \beta$. A straightforward analysis (cf. [4]) implies that we need to choose

$$D \gtrapprox \frac{N}{\sqrt{\mu(N + 1)}}.$$

In such a situation, the complexity of actually solving the resulting linear system is $O(\beta^{2.3})$ using sparse linear algebra techniques.

4.1   (# of Variables) ≈ (# of Independent Equations)

We are assuming that we have more linear equations than variables. In this section we assume that the number of *independent* equations γ is approximately equal to the number of variables β, since if this does not happen, then we are unlikely to be successful. In other words, we study the situation when

$$\lambda = \frac{\gamma}{\beta} \approx 1.$$

If $\lambda = 1$, then the system has a unique solution, but in general this will not be the case. If $\lambda < 1$, then the system of equations does not uniquely determine the value of the variables. Instead, it determines a vector subspace V_λ of solutions whose dimension is

$$\dim(V_\lambda) = (\# \text{ of variables}) - (\# \text{ of indep. equations}) = \beta - \gamma = \beta(1 - \lambda).$$

The XL algorithm thus reduces the original problem to that of performing an exhaustive search through the vectors in the space V_λ, where

$$\#V_\lambda = 2^{\dim(V_\lambda)} = 2^{\beta(1-\lambda)}. \tag{10}$$

Remark 1. If there is a meet-in-the-middle search, the exponent in (10) should be divided by 2. We also note that in small numerical examples, we often found that back substitution yielded parts of the desired solution even when the solution space was large. See Remark 2 below.

Table 4.1 gives, for various values of N and d_f, the smallest value of D such that $\alpha > \beta$. In other words, assuming that $\lambda \approx 1.0$, the table gives the smallest value of D such that the XL method has a chance of recovering the secret key. The table also gives the associated value of β, the resulting $O(\beta^{2.3})$ linear system complexity, the comparable complexity value (1) for the meet-in-the-middle attack of [9, 17], and the value of λ necessary to make the search space complexity $2^{\beta(1-\lambda)}$ from (10) equal to the linear system complexity $O(\beta^{2.3})$. In other words, the value of λ in the last column is the solution to $\beta^{2.3} = 2^{\beta(1-\lambda)}$ and represents the proportion of linear equations that need to be independent in order to make the complexity of finding the solution space V_λ approximately the same as the complexity of searching through the solution space. (But see Remark 2 which suggests that somewhat smaller values of λ may still be useful.)

Assuming $\lambda = 1$, then Table 4.1 shows that eventually the algebraic XL-based approach is more efficient than the previously best known deterministic attack. This is still true if we only have $\lambda \approx 1$, but the last column of the table suggests that the difference $1 - \lambda$ needs to be extremely small. In other words, we need an extremely high proportion of the equations to be independent in order to succeed. We further note that, even under the most favourable (and unlikely) assumption that $\lambda = 1$, the data in Table 4.1 shows that the advantage of the XL-based approach only occurs for $N > 1000$, which is considerably larger than any value used in practise [1, 2, 7].

4.2   Experimental Evaluation of λ

The validity of the runtime estimates derived in Section 4.1, especially as given in Table 4.1, depends on the assumption that λ is very close to 1 when we choose

Table 1. Complexity Comparison

N	d_f	D	β	$\beta^{2.3}$	$\frac{1}{\sqrt{N}}\binom{N/2}{d_f/2}$	$\beta^{2.3} = 2^{\beta(1-\lambda)}$
200	68	14	$\approx 10^{22}$	$\approx 10^{49}$	$\approx 10^{26}$	$\lambda \approx 1 - 10^{-20}$
400	134	20	$\approx 10^{34}$	$\approx 10^{77}$	$\approx 10^{53}$	$\lambda \approx 1 - 10^{-32}$
600	200	25	$\approx 10^{45}$	$\approx 10^{102}$	$\approx 10^{81}$	$\lambda \approx 1 - 10^{-42}$
800	268	28	$\approx 10^{52}$	$\approx 10^{119}$	$\approx 10^{108}$	$\lambda \approx 1 - 10^{-49}$
1000	334	32	$\approx 10^{61}$	$\approx 10^{139}$	$\approx 10^{136}$	$\lambda \approx 1 - 10^{-58}$
1200	400	35	$\approx 10^{68}$	$\approx 10^{156}$	$\approx 10^{163}$	$\lambda \approx 1 - 10^{-65}$
1400	468	37	$\approx 10^{74}$	$\approx 10^{169}$	$\approx 10^{191}$	$\lambda \approx 1 - 10^{-71}$

Table 2. Experimental values of λ

N	D	dim	λ_{min}	λ_{max}	$\overline{\lambda}$
11	3	561	0.96	1.00	0.99
13	3	1092	0.92	1.00	0.97
17	4	9401	0.91	1.00	0.99
19	4	16663	0.87	1.00	0.97
23	4	44551	0.95	0.96	0.95

a value for D for which $\alpha > \beta$. In order to investigate this assumption, we carried out the following experiments.

For various small values of N and various values of d_f and d_g, we generated NTRU keys and formed the set of $N+2$ inhomogeneous quadratic equations in N variables described in Section 3. We applied XL linearisation with increasing values of D until we obtained a value of D that made $\alpha > \beta$. We then computed the rank γ of the resulting matrix and the ratio $\lambda = \gamma/\beta$ of independent equations to variables. Unfortunately, the size of the matrices grew very rapidly, so were were only able to perform experiments with small values of N.

For each value of N, we generated 10 keys. Table 4.2 gives the results of our experiments. The table lists the minimum, maximum, and mean values of λ over the 10 experiments, as well as the value of D required and the column dimension of the eventual linear system, i.e. the number of columns in the matrix.

Remark 2. Although often we were unable to obtain a system of full rank, it is an interesting experimental observation that in most cases we were able to recover a significant proportion of the underlying NTRU private key using back substitution. In other words, although we expect to have to search the entire space of solutions to find the NTRU private key, it happened that many of the coefficients of the private key were already determined. We do not know to what extent this is an artifact of our use of small values of N and to what extent it might continue to hold for cryptographically interesting values of N. In any case, it is a topic that merits further study.

We also considered a variant of the XL algorithm called FXL. In FXL, one fixes the value of some of the the variables and then applies the XL algorithm to

Table 3. Experimental λ values using FXL

N	D	c	λ_{min}	λ_{max}	$\overline{\lambda}$	$\perp$
11	3	385	0.99	1.00	0.99	0.2
13	3	793	0.99	1.00	0.99	0.1
17	3	2516	0.80	0.95	0.93	0.9
19	4	12615	0.92	1.00	0.99	0.2
23	4	35442	1.00	1.00	1.00	0.1

the remaining variables. (This may be compared with the zero-forcing technique of May [11].) The effect of FXL is to reduce the number of variables whilst maintaining the number of equations. Thus not only does the resulting system of linear equations have smaller dimension, but one might also expect the value of λ to be larger. We experimented with this variant by fixing one or two variables. Note that there are two cases, since either the fixed variables have been guessed correctly, or they have been guessed incorrectly.

Table 4.2 gives the results of our experiments fixing one of the private key variables. We give the values of λ_{min}, λ_{max} and $\overline{\lambda}$ for the cases that the guessed fixed value was correct. For the final column of Table 4.2, labelled $\perp$, we performed experiments in which the guessed fixed value was incorrect. The listed value gives the proportion of such experiments for which the resulting matrix was consistent, i.e. gave a solution. Thus the value in column $\perp$ represents the probability that one would not be able to tell that an incorrect guess had been made for the fixed coordinate. In each row of Table 4.2, we performed 10 experiments with the correct guess and 10 experiments with the incorrect guess.

We conducted a similar set of experiments in which we fixed (guessed) the value of two of the variables. However, the results were worse than when fixing one variable. Hence it appears that fixing variables does not lead to an improvement for our problem, at least for the small size of N considered here.

5   Conclusion

We have shown how the NTRU primitive can be reformulated, using Witt vectors, into a system of overdetermined nonlinear (quadratic) equations over $\mathbb{F}_2$. We have thus introduced the tool of Witt vectors into the field of cryptographic analysis. We have studied how one can attempt to solve this nonlinear system by reducing it to a much larger system of linear equations using the XL algorithm. We note that the analysis of the XL algorithm is itself quite controversial and that its effectiveness is not well understood. We performed experiments using equations generated from the NTRU primitive with small parameters and found that the rank of the eventual XL linear system is a good, but not a perfect, indicator of success.

If the XL algorithm behaves as claimed by its inventors and if it turns out either that the resulting linear systems have very close to full rank or that almost full rank is not actually necessary for success, then the approach described in this paper provides the asymptotic best known deterministic attack against NTRU. However, even under the most favourable assumptions, our method is less efficient than known methods at the largest current recommended parameter values. We have found no evidence to support the assertion that XL performs as claimed by its inventors, nor evidence to refute their claims. Further research on the applicability and efficiency of the XL algorithm is thus warranted, as is further research on the other questions raised in this paper.

References

1. Consortium for Efficient Embedded Security. *Efficient embedded security standards #1: Implementation aspects of NTRU and NSS, Version 1*, 2002.
2. NTRU CryptoLab. *Challenge Problems* Available from http://www.ntru.com/cryptolab/challenges.htm.
3. N. Courtois, A. Klimov, J. Patarin and A. Shamir. Efficient algorithms for solving overdefined systems of multivariate polynomial equations. *Advances in Cryptology – EUROCRYPT 2000*, Springer-Verlag LNCS 1807, 392–407, 2000.
4. N. Courtois and J. Patarin. About the XL algorithm over $GF(2)$. *CT-RSA 2003*, Springer-Verlag LNCS 2612, 141–157, 2003.
5. N. Courtois and J. Pieprzyk. Cryptanalysis of block ciphers with overdefined systems of equations. *Advances in Cryptology – ASIACRYPT 2002*, Springer-Verlag LNCS 2501, 267–287, 2002.
6. C. Gentry. Key recovery and message attacks on NTRU-composite. *Advances in Cryptology – EUROCRYPT 2001*. Springer-Verlag LNCS 2045, 182–194, 2001.
7. J. Hoffstein, J. Pipher and J.H. Silverman. NTRU: a ring-based public key cryptosystem. *Algorithmic number theory – ANTS III*, Springer-Verlag LNCS 1423, 267–288, 1998.
8. N. Howgrave-Graham, P.Q. Nguyen, D. Pointcheval, J. Proos, J.H. Silverman, A. Singer and W. Whyte. The impact of decryption failures on the security of NTRU encryption. *Advances in Cryptology – CRYPTO 2003*, Springer-Verlag LNCS 2729, 226–246, 2003.
9. N. Howgrave-Graham, J.H. Silverman and W. Whyte. A meet-in-the-middle attack on an NTRU private key. NTRU Cryptosystems Technical Report #004, Version 2, June 2003.
10. X. Lai. On the design and security of block ciphers. ETH Series in Information Processing, 1992.
11. A. May and J.H. Silverman. Dimension reduction methods for convolution modular lattices. *Cryptography and Lattices*, Springer-Verlag LNCS 2146, 110–125, 2001.
12. S. Murphy and M. Robshaw. Comments on the security of the AES and the XL technique. Unpublished Manuscript, 2002.
13. R.L. Rivest. The RC5 encryption algorithm. *Fast Software Encryption, Second International Workshop*, Springer-Verlag LNCS 1008, 86–96, 1995.
14. R.L. Rivest, M. Robshaw, R. Sidney and L. Yin. The RC6 block cipher. Submission to AES process, 1998.
15. J.-P. Serre. *Local Fields*. Springer-Verlag GTM 67, 1979.
16. P.W. Shor. Polynomial-time algorithms for prime factorization and discrete logarithms on a quantum computer. *SIAM J. Comput.*, **26**, 1484–1509, 1997.
17. J.H. Silverman and A. Odlyzko. A Meet-In-The-Middle Attack on an NTRU Private Key. *Technical Report #004*, NTRU Cryptosystems, 1997.

A   NTRU Key Creation, Encryption and Decryption

In this appendix we briefly recall the key generation algorithm, encryption algorithm and decryption algorithm for the NTRU public key cryptosystem. We follow the notation of Section 2.1. For a more detailed description of NTRU, see [1, 7].

Key Creation.

The generation of public/private keys proceeds as follows:
1. Choose random $f \in \mathcal{L}_f$ and $g \in \mathcal{L}_g$.
2. Compute $f_q^{-1} \in P_q^\star(N)$ and $f_p^{-1} \in P_p^\star(N)$.
3. If one of these inverses does not exist, choose a new f. Otherwise f serves as the secret key.
4. Publish the polynomial $h \equiv p \star f_q^{-1} \star g \pmod{q}$ as the public key.

Note that for the above parameter choices we have $f_p^{-1} = 1$, so we do not have to compute this value. Other versions of the NTRU algorithm may have $f_p \neq 1$.

Encryption.

NTRU encryption is probabilistic, in the sense that encrypting the same message twice will result in different ciphertexts. To encrypt a plaintext $\mathcal{M}$, which we consider as given by a polynomial in $P_p(N)$, we perform the following two steps.
1. Choose random $r \in \mathcal{L}_r$.
2. Compute $e = \mathcal{E}_h(\mathcal{M}; r) = r \star h + \mathcal{M} \pmod{q}$.

Decryption.

Given a ciphertext e and a private key (f, f_p^{-1}), decryption proceeds as follows:

Step 1. First we compute $p \star r \star g + \mathcal{M} \star f$ as an element of $P_q(N)$ via,

$$a \equiv e \star f \equiv r \star p \star f_q^{-1} \star g \star f + \mathcal{M} \star f \equiv p \star r \star g + \mathcal{M} \star f \pmod{q}.$$

Step 2. Under suitable assumptions, it is (usually) the case that the value of a from Step 1 is exactly equal to $p \star r \star g + \mathcal{M} \star f$ in $P(N)$. We then switch to reduction modulo p and compute

$$a \star f_p^{-1} \equiv p \star r \star g \star f_p^{-1} + \mathcal{M} \star f \star f_p^{-1} \equiv \mathcal{M} \star f \star f_p^{-1} \equiv \mathcal{M} \pmod{p}.$$

and recover the plaintext $\mathcal{M} \in P_p(N)$. Note that for the above parameter choices this calculation simplifies to $a \equiv \mathcal{M} \pmod{p}$, since $f_p^{-1} = 1$.

In this paper we have simply considered the structure of the NTRU keys themselves.

B   The Ring of Witt Vectors over $\mathbb{F}_2$

In this appendix we briefly recall the construction of the ring of Witt vectors $W_m(\mathbb{F}_2)$ of length m. The ring $W_m(\mathbb{F}_2)$ is isomorphic to the ring of integers modulo 2^m, but it has the useful property that the ring operations are described purely in terms of polynomials. For the general theory of Witt vectors, we refer the reader to [15–Section II.6].

A Witt vector of length m is simply an element of $\mathbb{F}_2^m$, i.e. a vector consisting of m components in $\mathbb{F}_2$. To turn this set into a ring, we need to define an addition law and a multiplication law. These operations are defined by the requirement that the map

$$W_* : W_m(\mathbb{F}_2) \longrightarrow \mathbb{Z}_{2^m}$$
$$[a_0, \ldots, a_{m-1}] \longmapsto \sum_{i=0}^{m-1} a_i 2^i \quad (\mathrm{mod}\ 2^m) \tag{11}$$

is a ring isomorphism.

Clearly, the operations in $W_m(\mathbb{F}_2)$ will be more complicated than component-wise addition and multiplication, since we need to take carry bits into account. We thus have to find functions (multivariate polynomials)

$$S_0, \ldots, S_{m-1}, P_0, \ldots, P_{m-1} \in \mathbb{F}_2[X_0, \ldots, X_{m-1}]$$

such that for all Witt vectors $\mathbf{a} = [a_0, \ldots, a_{m-1}]$ and $\mathbf{b} = [b_0, \ldots, b_{m-1}]$, we have

$$W_*([S_0(\mathbf{a}, \mathbf{b}), \ldots, S_{m-1}(\mathbf{a}, \mathbf{b})]) \equiv W_*(\mathbf{a}) + W_*(\mathbf{b}) \quad (\mathrm{mod}\ 2^m),$$
$$W_*([P_0(\mathbf{a}, \mathbf{b}), \ldots, P_{m-1}(\mathbf{a}, \mathbf{b})]) \equiv W_*(\mathbf{a}) \cdot W_*(\mathbf{b}) \quad (\mathrm{mod}\ 2^m).$$

The easiest way to compute the functions $S_0, \ldots, S_{m-1}$ and $P_0, \ldots, P_{m-1}$ is to use Witt polynomials. The ith Witt polynomial $W_i \in \mathbb{Z}[X_0, \ldots, X_i]$ is defined by

$$W_i(X_0, \ldots, X_i) = X_0^{2^i} + 2X_1^{2^{i-1}} + \cdots + 2^i X_i. \tag{12}$$

One then proves [15] that there are unique polynomials

$$\varphi_0, \ldots, \varphi_{m-1}, \psi_0, \ldots, \psi_{m-1} \in \mathbb{Z}[X_0, \ldots, X_{m-1}, Y_0, \ldots, Y_{m-1}]$$

with the property that for all $0 \le i < m$,

$$W_i(\varphi_0, \ldots, \varphi_i) = W_i(X_0, \ldots, X_i) + W_i(Y_0, \ldots, Y_i),$$
$$W_i(\psi_0, \ldots, \psi_i) = W_i(X_0, \ldots, X_i) \cdot W_i(Y_0, \ldots, Y_i). \tag{13}$$

Table 4. The first few Witt addition and multiplication polynomials

$S_0(\mathbf{a}, \mathbf{b}) = a_0 + b_0$
$S_1(\mathbf{a}, \mathbf{b}) = a_0 b_0 + a_1 + b_1$
$S_2(\mathbf{a}, \mathbf{b}) = a_0 b_0 a_1 + a_0 b_0 b_1 + a_1 b_1 + a_2 + b_2$
$S_3(\mathbf{a}, \mathbf{b}) = a_0 b_0 a_1 a_2 + a_0 b_0 a_1 b_2 + a_0 b_0 b_1 a_2 + a_0 b_0 b_1 b_2$
$\quad + a_1 b_1 a_2 + a_1 b_1 b_2 + a_2 b_2 + a_3 + b_3$
$P_0(\mathbf{a}, \mathbf{b}) = a_0 b_0$
$P_1(\mathbf{a}, \mathbf{b}) = a_0 b_1 + b_0 a_1$
$P_2(\mathbf{a}, \mathbf{b}) = a_0 b_0 a_1 b_1 + a_0 b_2 + b_0 a_2 + a_1 b_1$
$P_3(\mathbf{a}, \mathbf{b}) = a_0 b_0 a_1 b_1 a_2 + a_0 b_0 a_1 b_1 b_2 + a_0 b_0 a_1 b_1 + a_0 b_0 a_2 b_2$
$\quad + a_0 a_1 b_1 b_2 + a_0 b_3 + b_0 a_1 b_1 a_2 + b_0 a_3 + a_1 b_2 + b_1 a_2$

The polynomials S_i for addition and P_i for multiplication may then be recovered as $S_i = \varphi_i \bmod 2$ and $P_i = \psi_i \bmod 2$. The first few addition and multiplication polynomials are listed in Table 4.

Example 2. Let $m = 4$ and consider the Witt vectors $\mathbf{a} = [1,0,1,1]$ and $\mathbf{b} = [1,1,1,0]$. Then we have $W_*(\mathbf{a}) \equiv 13 \pmod{16}$ and $W_*(\mathbf{b}) \equiv 7 \pmod{16}$, so $W_*(\mathbf{a}) + W_*(\mathbf{b}) \equiv 4 \pmod{16}$ and $W_*(\mathbf{a}) \cdot W_*(\mathbf{b}) \equiv 11 \pmod{16}$. Computing the functions $S_0, \ldots, S_3$ and $P_0, \ldots, P_3$, we indeed obtain

$$[S_0(\mathbf{a}, \mathbf{b}), \ldots, S_3(\mathbf{a}, \mathbf{b})] = [0,0,1,0] \quad \text{with} \quad W_*([0,0,1,0]) = 4, \quad \text{and}$$
$$[P_0(\mathbf{a}, \mathbf{b}), \ldots, P_3(\mathbf{a}, \mathbf{b})] = [1,1,0,1] \quad \text{with} \quad W_*([1,1,0,1]) = 11.$$

Efficient Cryptanalysis of
RSE(2)PKC and RSSE(2)PKC

Christopher Wolf, An Braeken, and Bart Preneel

Department Electrical Engineering, ESAT/COSIC,
Katholieke Universiteit Leuven, Kasteelpark Arenberg 10,
B-3001 Heverlee-Leuven, Belgium
{christopher.wolf, an.braeken, bart.preneel}@esat.kuleuven.ac.be

Abstract. In this paper, we study the new class step-wise Triangular Schemes (STS) of public key cryptosystems (PKC) based on multivariate quadratic polynomials. In these schemes, we have m the number of equations, n the number of variables, L the number of steps/layers, r the number of equations/variables per step, and q the size of the underlying field. We present two attacks on the STS class by exploiting the chain of the kernels of the private key polynomials. The first attack is an inversion attack which computes the message/signature for given ciphertext/message in $O(mn^3 Lq^r + n^2 Lrq^r)$, the second is a structural attack which recovers an equivalent version of the secret key in $O(mn^3 Lq^r + mn^4)$ operations. Since the legitimate user has workload q^r for decrypting/computing a signature, the attacks presented in this paper are very efficient. As an application, we show that two special instances of STS, namely RSE(2)PKC and RSSE(2)PKC, recently proposed by Kasahara and Sakai, are insecure.

1 Introduction

1.1 PKC Schemes Based on Multivariate Quadratic Equations

In the last two decades, several public key cryptoschemes (PKC) have been proposed which use $\mathcal{M}$ultivariate $\mathcal{Q}$uadratic equations ($\mathcal{M}\mathcal{Q}$) over a finite field $\mathbb{F}$. A typical multivariate PKC public key $\mathcal{P}$ has the structure $S \circ \mathcal{P}' \circ T$. Here, $S \in \mathrm{GL}_n(\mathbb{F})$ and $T \in \mathrm{GL}_m(\mathbb{F})$ represent two linear transformations over the finite field $\mathbb{F}$. The system $\mathcal{P}'$ of m central equations in n variables of degree 2 is constructed with a trapdoor in order to speed up the decryption process. The secret key of the system consists of the triple $(S, \mathcal{P}', T)$. Depending on the structure of $\mathcal{P}'$, these schemes can be divided into several classes: *e.g.*, the initial polynomial substitution scheme from Fell and Diffie [8], C* schemes [17], HFE-like schemes [19, 6] or unbalanced oil-vinegar schemes [14]. All of them rely on the fact that the $\mathcal{M}\mathcal{Q}$-problem, *i.e.*, finding a solution $x \in \mathbb{F}^n$ for a given system $\mathcal{P}$ is computationally difficult, namely $\mathcal{N}\mathcal{P}$-complete (cf [9–p. 251] and [20–App.] for a detailed proof). Also decomposing $\mathcal{P}$ into $T, \mathcal{P}', S$ — called the Isomorphism of Polynomials Problem — is considered to be a hard problem if $S, \mathcal{P}', T$ do not have a special structure [21].

C. Blundo and S. Cimato (Eds.): SCN 2004, LNCS 3352, pp. 294–309, 2005.

In this paper, we concentrate on a special sub-class of $\mathcal{MQ}$-schemes, namely schemes which have a triangular structure for their central equations $\mathcal{P}'$ — triangular schemes for short. This idea is due to Shamir [22] who developed such schemes (Birational Permutations) over large finite rings. To guard against special types of attacks, he removed some initial equations. Goubin et $al.$ specialised the approach from [22] to the case of small finite fields, denoted TPM schemes (Triangle Plus Minus, [10]). They add to Shamir's construction some equations in the last step ("Plus" modification) and fall in a similar class as the scheme described in this paper (cf Fig. 2).

We now consider a further generalisation of the Birational Permutation and TPM family. These schemes are called STS (step-wise triangular schemes), which differ from the TPM class by allowing a "step" of more than one variable/equation in the triangular structure (cf Fig. 1 for regular STS). The step-width (number

$$
\text{Step 1} \begin{cases} y'_1 &= p'_1\,(x'_1,\ldots,x'_r) \\ &\vdots \\ y'_r &= p'_r\,(x'_1,\ldots,x'_r) \end{cases} \qquad \text{with } x'_i \in \mathbb{F}
$$

$$
\vdots
$$

$$
\text{Step } l \begin{cases} y'_{(l-1)r+1} = p'_{(l-1)r+1}\,(x'_1,\ldots,x'_r,\ldots,x'_{(l-1)r+1},\ldots,x'_{lr}) \\ \qquad\vdots \\ y'_{lr} \quad= \quad p'_{lr}\,(x'_1,\ldots,x'_r,\ldots,x'_{(l-1)r+1},\ldots,x'_{lr}) \end{cases}
$$

$$
\vdots
$$

$$
\text{Step } L \begin{cases} y'_{(L-1)r+1} = p'_{(L-1)r+1}\,(x'_1,\ldots,x'_r,\ldots,x'_{(l-1)r+1},\ldots,x'_{lr},\ldots,x'_{n-r+1},\ldots,x_n) \\ \qquad\vdots \\ y'_{Lr} \quad= \quad p'_{Lr}\,(x'_1,\ldots,x'_r,\ldots,x'_{(l-1)r+1},\ldots,x'_{lr},\ldots,x'_{n-r+1},\ldots,x_n) \end{cases}
$$

Fig. 1. Central Equations p'_i in a Regular STS Scheme

of new variables) and the step-height (number of new equations) is controlled by the parameter r. For Birational Permutations and TPM, the parameter r is fixed to 1. Therefore, they are a special case of STS (cf Sect. 1.2). The main part of this paper consists of the description of two very efficient attacks on STS schemes. They break STS in $O(mn^3 Lq^r + mn^4)$ and $O(mn^3 Lq^r + n^2 Lrq^r)$ — for m the number of equations, n the number of variables, L the number of layers, q the size of the ground field $\mathbb{F}$, and r the step-width/step-hight. The attacks are mainly based on the fact that the kernels of the private central polynomials p'_i form a descending chain of subspaces (cf Sect. 2.1). As the recently proposed schemes RSE(2)PKC and RSSE(2)PKC by Kasahara and Sakai belong to the STS family (cf Sect. 3), both schemes are covered by these attacks and thus highly insecure. As an application of the attacks described in this paper, we broke the challenge for RSE(2)PKC (cf Sect. 3.2).

1.2   Step-Wise Triangular Systems

A step-wise triangular scheme is defined over a finite field $\mathbb{F}$ with $q := |\mathbb{F}|$ elements and prime characteristic $\mathrm{char}(\mathbb{F})$. Over this field, we define multivariate quadratic polynomials

$$p_i(x_1,\ldots,x_n) := \sum_{1 \le j \le k \le n} \gamma_{i,j,k} x_j x_k + \sum_{1 \le j \le n} \beta_{i,j} x_j + \alpha_i, \qquad (1)$$

for $1 \le i \le m$ and $\alpha_i, \beta_{i,j}, \gamma_{i,j,k} \in \mathbb{F}$ (constant, linear, and quadratic terms). These polynomials form the public key as a system of equations $\mathcal{P} := (p_1,\ldots,p_m)$. The plaintext $x \in \mathbb{F}^n$ is transformed to the ciphertext $y \in \mathbb{F}^m$ as

$$y_i := p_i(x_1,\ldots,x_n) \text{ with } 1 \le i \le m .$$

The decryption, *i.e.*, the inversion of this mapping, uses a trapdoor (cf Fig. 2). This trapdoor consists of two linear transformations $S \in \mathrm{GL}_n(\mathbb{F})$, $T \in \mathrm{GL}_m(\mathbb{F})$ and central equations as outlined in Fig. 1. The public equations $\mathcal{P}$ are constructed as a composition of $\mathcal{P} := T \circ \mathcal{P}' \circ S$ where $\mathcal{P}'$ has a special triangular structure (cf Fig. 1). The two linear transformations may be seen as invertible matrices, we hence have $S \in \mathbb{F}^{n \times n}$ and $T \in \mathbb{F}^{m \times m}$, respectively. In our description, we always use a prime (') for denoting the secret central part of the system.

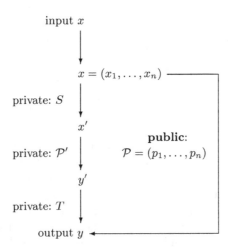

Fig. 2. $\mathcal{MQ}$-trapdoor $(S, \mathcal{P}', T)$ in STS

Let $r_1,\ldots,r_L$ be L integers such that $r_1 + \cdots + r_L = n$, the number of variables, and $m_1,\ldots,m_L \in \mathbb{N}$ such that $m_1 + \cdots + m_L = m$, the number of equations. Here $L \in \mathbb{N}$ denotes the number of layers or steps in the scheme, r_l represents the number of new variables (step-width) and m_l the number of equations (step-height), both in step l for $1 \le l \le L$. In a general step-wise Triangular Scheme (gSTS), the m_l private quadratic polynomials of each layer l, contain only the variables x'_k with $k \leq \sum_{j=1}^{l} r_j$, i.e., only the variables defined in all previous steps plus r_l new ones. The overall shape of the private polynomials leads to the name step-wise Triangular Scheme (STS).

When not mentioned otherwise, we concentrate on regular STS schemes (rSTS or STS for short) in this paper. For regular STS schemes we set $r_1 = \cdots = r_N = m_1 = \cdots = m_L$, which we denote by r. Moreover, $L = m/r$ and $m = n$. Note that the attacks we propose are also valid for the general STS schemes (cf Sect. 4.1). The structure of a regular STS has been outlined in fig. 1 and 2.

As we see in Fig. 1, there are exactly r new variables in an rSTS for each layer. This way one can compute an x for a given vector y with q^r attempts in each step. But as the legitimate user has a workload growing exponentially in r, this value has to be small in order to obtain a scheme of practical interest. The parameter r plays an important role for the complexity of our attack.

In order to decrypt a given ciphertext y, we need to invert the following steps: $x \xrightarrow{S} x' \xrightarrow{P'} y' \xrightarrow{T} y$. While S, T are bijections and also easy to invert, this is not so obvious for the central equations P'. In particular, these central equations may not form a bijection. Adding redundancy to the original message x or transmitting some additional redundancy, e.g., in form of its hash-value $h := H(x)$ where $H(\cdot)$ denotes a cryptographically secure hash function (e.g., see [18]), allows to pick the correct message x for a given input y. For a signature scheme, we do not need this redundancy as it is enough to obtain one $x \in \mathbb{F}^n$ such that $P(x) = y$ for a given y; in most cases, this will be the hash of a longer message. As this point is not important for our attack, we refer to [19, 12] for a broader discussion of this problem.

Remark: As already pointed out in the introduction, the Birational Permutation Schemes of Shamir are regular STS schemes with $r = 1$. However, they are not defined over a (small) finite field but over a (large) finite ring. The TPM class of Goubin and Courtois coincides with STS for the parameters $r_1 = u$, $m_L = v$, $m_1 = \cdots = m_{L-1} = r_2 = \cdots = r_L = 1$, i.e., we remove $u \in \mathbb{N}$ initial layers, add $v \in \mathbb{N}$ polynomials in the last step, and have exactly one new variable at all intermediate levels. As STS, this class is not defined over a ring but over a field.

Shamir's scheme was broken shortly after its publication in [2, 23, 3]. The TPM scheme of Goubin and Courtois has been broken in the paper that proposed it [10]. In fact, the aim of their construction was to show that Moh's TTM construction is weak. While we dwell on the basic ideas of the above attacks, it is necessary to extend them as they are not directly applicable to STS. In particular, Kasahara and Sakai conclude (cf [13–Sect. 4.3.III] and [12–Sect. 4.1.III]) that their constructions are secure against all known attacks — in particular, mentioning [10]. Although this observation is true, we will show in Sect. 2 that it is possible to generalise these attacks in a way that STS and consequently RSE(2)PKC and RSSE(2)PKC are covered by them, too.

1.3   Organisation

This paper is organised as follows: after this introduction, we move on to a cryptanalysis of regular STS schemes, showing both an inversion and a structural attack in Sect. 2. The following section deals with special instances like RSE(2)PKC and RSSE(2)PKC. In Sect. 4, we generalise STS. This paper concludes with Sect. 5.

2   Cryptanalysis

We now present two different types of attacks on STS. In the inversion attack (cf Sect. 2.3), we recover for given ciphertext y the corresponding message x. In the structural attack (cf Sect. 2.4), we build a linear equivalent version of the private key, denoted $(\tilde{S}, \tilde{\mathcal{P}}', \tilde{T})$. Using $(\tilde{S}, \tilde{\mathcal{P}}', \tilde{T})$, the attacker is in the same position as the legitimate user for deciphering a given message y or forging a signature on it. For both attacks, we first need some observations on kernels.

2.1   Chain of Kernels

Let p_i be a public key polynomial. For characteristic $\neq 2$, we can uniquely express its homogeneous quadratic parts in a symmetric matrix $P_i \in \mathbb{F}^{n \times n}$. We show this with a toy-example with three variables:

$$\begin{pmatrix} \gamma_{1,1} & \frac{\gamma_{1,2}}{2} & \frac{\gamma_{1,3}}{2} \\ \frac{\gamma_{1,2}}{2} & \gamma_{2,2} & \frac{\gamma_{2,3}}{2} \\ \frac{\gamma_{1,3}}{2} & \frac{\gamma_{2,3}}{2} & \gamma_{3,3} \end{pmatrix} ,$$

where the $\gamma_{i,j}$ represent the quadratic coefficients of $x_i x_j$ from the public polynomials as defined in (1). So, instead of evaluating the quadratic parts of p_i by the vector x, we may also perform $x P_i x^t$ as matrix-vector multiplications (here ^{t} denotes transposition). As division by 2 is not defined for characteristic 2, we use the form $P_i := L_i + L_i^t$ for lower triangular matrices L_i instead to obtain unique symmetric matrices. This way, we loose the quadratic coefficients $\gamma_{i,i}$ of the public polynomials. However, in characteristic 2, these quadratic terms are linear and we can therefore ignore them. To the knowledge of the authors, the above observation has been initially reported in [14] and is there credited to *Don Coppersmith*.

The private key polynomials p_i' may also be represented in the above matrix form. Following the notation outlined in the previous section, we denote the corresponding matrices P_i'. Obviously, the rank of each such matrix depends on its layer l. The matrices P_i' have a rank of rl in each layer l for $1 \leq l \leq L$ and we have

$$\ker_l' = \{a' \in \mathbb{F}^n | \ a_1' = \ldots = a_{rl}' = 0\}$$

as common kernels of the matrices P_i' for $(l-1)r < i \leq lr$. As these kernels are hidden by the linear transformation S, we also mark them with a prime $'$. Moreover, we denote by $a_i' \in \mathbb{F}$ for $1 \leq i \leq n$ the coefficients of the vectors $a' \in \mathbb{F}^n$.

We now study the effect of the linear transformation S, *i.e.*, the change of variables. As we have $\hat{p}_i := p'_i \circ S$ and $x' = S(x)$, we obtain $\hat{P}_i := SP'_i S^t$ in terms of the corresponding matrices. As S is invertible, we have $\text{Rank}(\hat{P}_i) = \text{Rank}(P'_i)$ and

$$\ker_l = \{a'S^{-1} \mid a' \in \mathbb{F}^n \wedge a'_1 = \ldots = a'_{rl} = 0\} \tag{2}$$

for the kernels of $\hat{P}_i$ for $(l-1)r < i \le lr$ and an unknown matrix S. Moreover,

$$\ker'_L \subset \ldots \subset \ker'_1 \text{ and consequently } \ker_L \subset \ldots \subset \ker_1 .$$

With the notation $T = (\tau_{i,j})_{1 \le i, j \le m}$, each individual public key matrix P_i can be expressed by

$$P_i = \sum_{j=1}^m \tau_{i,j}[SP'_i S^t] = \sum_{j=1}^m \tau_{i,j} \hat{P}_i .$$

The problem of finding the transformation T^{-1} and thus T has therefore been reduced to finding a linear combination of the public key (in matrix notation) which has a specific rank. In the following two subsections, we describe two algorithms which can be used for this purpose.

2.2 Recovering the Transformation T

Attacking the High-Rank Side. We start with an attack on the high-rank side (cf the algorithm in Fig. 3). The overall idea of this algorithm is to exploit the step-structure of STS. To do so, we observe that a correct random guess of a row-vector in T^{-1} will lead to a condition on the rank of the linear combination of the corresponding public key equations — expressed in matrix notation. More formally and also to verify the correctness of this algorithm, we consider the vector spaces

$$J_l := \{b'T^{-1} \mid b' \in \mathbb{F}^m \wedge b'_{lr+1} = \ldots = b'_m = 0\} \text{ for } 1 \le l \le L . \tag{3}$$

Obviously, they form a descending chain of subspaces and each of them has dimension $m - lr$. Therefore, when picking a random element $v \in_R J_{l+1}$, we have a probability of q^{-r} that the expression $v \in J_l$ holds. In addition, we have two efficient methods (matrixCheck or polynomialCheck, respectively) to check whether $v \in J_l$ or $v \notin J_l$. First, we concentrate on matrixCheck:

$$\text{matrixCheck}(P_1, \ldots, P_m, v, l) \text{ returns \textbf{true} iff } Rank(\sum_{i=1}^m v_i P_i) \le lr .$$

For the sake of the argument, we look at the problem in the T^{-1}-space, *i.e.*, after the linear transformation T^{-1} has been applied. Using the notation from (3), we consider vectors b' instead of v. Hence we have

$$M := \sum_{i=1}^m b'_i \hat{P}_i = \sum_{i=1}^{rl} b'_i \left(SP'_i S^t\right) = S \left(\sum_{i=1}^{rl} b'_i P'_i\right) S^t .$$

Observing the step-wise structure of the private key polynomials p_i' we conclude that the Rank$(M) \leq lr$. This yields the result.

The expected running time of the algorithm from Fig. 3 is therefore bounded by $O(mn^3 Lq^r)$: by picking at most cmq^r vectors for each layer (c being a small constant, e.g., 10), we can compute the vector spaces $J_1, \ldots, J_L$ with very high probability. Checking the matrix condition costs an additional factor of n^3 as we are processing matrices from $\mathbb{F}^{n \times n}$. In comparison, the running time of the other steps of the algorithm are negligible.

procedure highRankAttack($\mathcal{P}$)
    Input: $\mathcal{P}$: system of public equations
    Output: $\tilde{T}$: an equivalent copy of the transformation T
    $P_i \leftarrow$ computeMatrix(p_i); $J_L \leftarrow \mathbb{F}^m$
    for $l \leftarrow L - 1$ **downto** 1 **do**
       $J_l \leftarrow \{0\}$
       repeat
          $v \in_R J_{l+1}$
          if matrixCheck($P_1, \ldots, P_m$, v, l) $\vee$ polynomialCheck($p_1, \ldots, p_m$, v, l) **then**
             $J_l \cup \leftarrow \{v\}$
       until Dimension(J_l) $\overset{?}{=} lr$
       $\tilde{J} \leftarrow J_{l+1} \cap J_l$
       for $i \leftarrow 1$ **to** r **do**
          RowVector($\hat{T}, lr + i$) $\leftarrow$ BasisVector($\tilde{J}, i$)
    endfor
    return $\tilde{T} \leftarrow \hat{T}^{-1}$
endproc

Fig. 3. High-Rank Algorithm for Computing the Transformation $\tilde{T}$ for a Given System of Equations

In characteristic 2 we may apply Dickson's theorem instead to check directly for a given polynomial if it may be reduced to a form with less variables (procedure polynomialCheck). Unfortunately, the proof is a bit lengthy, we therefore refer to [16–Sec. 15.2, Thm. 4] for both the theorem and its proof. An algorithmic version of it can be found in [4–Sec. 3.2]. The time complexity of this algorithm is there estimated to be $O(n^3)$. Therefore, the overall complexity of the above algorithm remains the same: $O(mn^3 Lq^r)$.

Remark: In both cases, we will not be able to recover the original transformation T but the inverse of a linear equivalent copy of it, denoted $\hat{T}$ for the inverse and $\tilde{T}$ for the linear equivalent of T. In fact, we will recover versions of T in which the rows of $\tilde{T}$ are linear combinations of the rows of T within the same layer.

Attacking the Low-Rank Side. Instead of obtaining an equivalent copy of the transformation T directly, we can also exploit the fact that the kernels $K_i := \ker_i$ (cf (2)) form a descending chain — starting with the large kernel $\ker_1$. This algorithm (cf Fig. 4) is a little more subtle as it makes use of two different observations. The first one is that the kernels $\ker_i$ form a descending chain.

procedure lowRankAttack($\mathcal{P}$)
    Input: $\mathcal{P}$: system of public equations
    Output: $\tilde{T}$: an equivalent copy of the transformation T
    $P_i \leftarrow$ computeMatrix(p_i); $K_0 \leftarrow \mathbb{F}^n$; $J_0 \leftarrow \{0\}$
    for $l \leftarrow L$ **downto** 1 **do**
      repeat
        $w \in_R K_{l-1}$
        $J_l \leftarrow$ SolutionSpace($\sum_{i=1}^{m} v_i(wP_i) = 0$) for an unknown $v \in \mathbb{F}^m$
      until Dimension(J_l) $\overset{?}{=} lr$.
      $\tilde{J} \leftarrow J_l \cap \overline{J_{l-1}}$
      for $i \leftarrow 1$ **to** r **do**
        $\hat{t} \leftarrow$ BasisVector($\tilde{J}, i$); RowVector($\hat{T}, lr + i$) $\leftarrow \hat{t}$; $\hat{P}_{(l-1)r+i} \leftarrow \sum_{j=1}^{m} \hat{t}_j P_j$
      $K_l \leftarrow$ Kernel(P_{lr})
    endfor
    return $\tilde{T} \leftarrow \hat{T}^{-1}$
endproc

Fig. 4. Low-Rank Algorithm for Computing the Transformation $\tilde{T}$ for a Given System of Equations

Therefore, setting $\ker_0 := \mathbb{F}^n$, the statement $w \in \ker_l$ is true with probability q^{-r} for all $w \in_R \ker_{l-1}$ and $1 \leq l \leq L$. Second, the linear equation $\sum_{i=1}^{m} v_i(wP_i) = 0$ has q^{lr} solutions for unknown $v \in \mathbb{F}^m$ if and only if the vector w is in the kernel $\ker_l$. With $\tilde{J} := J_l \cap \overline{J_{l-1}}$ where $\overline{J_{l-1}}$ denotes the complement of the vector space J_{l-1}, we obtain dimension r for $\tilde{J}$ which yields r new linearly independent rows of the matrix T^{-1}. The algorithm will therefore terminate with a correct solution $\tilde{T}$ after $O(Ln^3q^r)$ steps on average. Thus it outperforms the algorithm from the previous section by a factor of m. As for the previous algorithm, we will not recover the original transformation T but an equally useful variant of it.
Remark: Specialised versions of the algorithms from fig. 3 and 4 can be found in [10] for the case of schemes with step-width 1 of the intermediate layers.

2.3   Inversion Attack

In the previous section, we discussed two different approaches to recover a linear transformation $\tilde{T}$ for given public key equations. In this section, we will use $\tilde{T}$ and the polynomials $\hat{p}_i := \tilde{T}^{-1} \circ p_i$ to solve the problem $y = \mathcal{P}(x)$ for a given vector $y \in \mathbb{F}^m$, i.e., for the $\mathcal{MQ}$-problem. We do so by computing a successive affine approximation of x, cf Fig. 5. This algorithm exploits the fact that the kernels $K_i := \ker_i$ for $1 \leq i \leq L$ have the form $\ker_l = \{a'S^{-1} \mid a' \in \mathbb{F}^n \wedge a'_1 = \ldots = a'_{rl} = 0\}$. Setting $K_0 := \mathbb{F}^n$ we have

$$\tilde{K}_l = K_{l-1} \cap \overline{K_l} = \{a'S^{-1} \mid a' \in \mathbb{F}^n \wedge a'_1 = \ldots = a'_{(l-1)r} = a'_{lr+1} = \ldots = a'_n = 0\}$$

for $1 \leq l \leq L$. Using this observation, we can "switch on" groups of r (hidden) variables x' and therefore manipulate the output of the polynomials $\hat{p}_i$ layer by layer. This is possible although we do not know the actual value of the secret matrix S. As the polynomial system $\hat{\mathcal{P}}$ inherits the layer structure of the original private polynomial system $\mathcal{P}'$, the solutions form a chain of affine subspaces $x+ < K_l >$ — where K_l has dimension $n - rl$ in step l. Therefore, we learn $r \log_2 q$ bits about the vector x for each level of recursion.

---

procedure inversionAttack($\mathcal{P}, \tilde{T}, K_1, \ldots, K_L, y$)
    Input: $\mathcal{P}$: system of public equations, $\tilde{T}$: linear transformation,
                $K_1, \ldots, K_L$: descending chain of kernels, y: target-value
    Output: X: a set of solutions for the problem $y = \mathcal{P}(x)$

    procedure recursivePart(x, l)
        if $l > L$ **then return** $\{x\}$
        $\tilde{K} \leftarrow K_{l-1} \cap \overline{K_l}; X \leftarrow \emptyset$
        for $w \in \tilde{K}$ **do**
            if $(\hat{p}_i(x + w) \stackrel{?}{=} \tilde{y}_i \; : \; (l-1)r < i \leq lr)$ **then** $X \cup \leftarrow$ recursivePart($x + w, l$)
        return X
    endproc

    $\hat{p}_i \leftarrow p_i \circ \tilde{T}^{-1} : 1 \leq i \leq m$
    $\tilde{y} \leftarrow y\tilde{T}^{-1}; K_0 \leftarrow \mathbb{F}^n$
    return recursivePart(0,1)
endproc

Fig. 5. Inversion Attack for $y = \mathcal{P}(x)$ and Given $\tilde{T}$

With this inversion attack, we are now in a similar position as the legitimate user: at each level, we have to try cq^r possible vectors and to evaluate r polynomials $\hat{p}_i$ — each step costing $O(rn^2)$. In case the STS is not a bijection, we may need to branch — but this is the same situation as for the legitimate user. The only additional overhead is the computation of the complement of vector spaces and to intersect them. Both can be done in $O(n^2)$. Assuming that $\mathcal{P}$ is a bijection, one application of this inversion attack has time-complexity $O(n^2 L r q^r)$.

2.4   Structural Attack

The starting point of the structural attack (cf Fig. 6) is the same as for the inversion attack, namely $ker_1 \supset \ldots \supset ker_L$. As we have computed the transformation $\tilde{T}$ in the previous step, we are able to compute the system of equations $\hat{\mathcal{P}}$, the corresponding matrices $\hat{P}_l$ and therefore their kernels for each layer $l : 1 \leq l \leq L$. Due to its internal structure, the vector space $\tilde{K} := K_{l-1} \cap \overline{K_l}$ consists of exactly r row-vectors of $\tilde{S}^{-1}$. We recover them in the for loop. As soon as we have recovered $\tilde{S}$, we apply it to the intermediate system of equations $\hat{\mathcal{P}}$, yielding $\tilde{\mathcal{P}}'$, an equivalent copy of the private key polynomials.

In terms of complexity, the second step of the structural attack is dominant: we need to evaluate m polynomials with $O(n^2)$ quadratic terms each. As each quadratic term has two variables, this costs $O(n^2)$ for each term. The overall time complexity is therefore $O(mn^4)$. So depending on the value q^r, either the structural or the inversion attack has a lower asymptotic running time as the constants are in the same range.

---

procedure structuralAttack($\hat{\mathcal{P}}$, K_1, ..., K_L)
    Input: $\hat{\mathcal{P}}$: system of equations; K_1, ..., K_L: descending chain of kernels
    Output: $\tilde{S}$: an equivalent copy of the secret transformation S
             $\tilde{\mathcal{P}}'$: an equivalent copy of the private key polynomials
    $K_0 \leftarrow \mathbb{F}^n$
    for $l \leftarrow 1$ **to** L **do**
        $\tilde{K} \leftarrow K_{l-1} \cap \overline{K_l}$
        RowVector($\hat{S}$, $(l-1)r + i$) $\leftarrow$ BasisVector($\tilde{K}, i$) : $1 \leq i \leq r$
    $\tilde{S} \leftarrow \hat{S}^{-1}$
    $\tilde{p}'_i \leftarrow \hat{p}_i \circ \tilde{S}^{-1}$: $1 \leq i \leq m$
    return $\tilde{S}, \tilde{\mathcal{P}}'$
endproc

Fig. 6. Structural Attack for a Given Sequence of Kernels $\ker_1, \ldots, \ker_L$

---

3   Special Instances of STS

In this section, we show that the two schemes RSE(2)PKC [13] and RSSE(2)PKC [12], recently proposed by Kasahara and Sakai, are special instances of STS — and will therefore fall for the attacks discussed in the previous section. In particular, we were able to break the challenge proposed in [13–Sect. 6] using an inversion attack (cf Sect. 2.3) in both cases.

3.1   RSSE(2)PKC

In RSSE(2)PKC, the private polynomials p'_i for $1 \leq i \leq r$ have a special form, namely

$$p'_{(l-1)r+i}(x') := \phi_{l,i}(x'_{(l-1)r+1}, \ldots, x'_{lr}) + \psi_{l,i}(x'_1, \ldots, x'_{(l-1)r}) \text{ for } 1 \leq l \leq L,$$

where $\phi_{l,i}$ and $\psi_{l,i}$ are random quadratic polynomials over $\mathbb{F}$ in r and $(l-1)r$ variables, respectively. In both cases, the constant part is omitted. To simplify programming, the linear terms βx_i are considered to be quadratic terms βx_i^2, for all $i \in \{1, \ldots, n\}$. This may be done as RSSE(2)PKC is defined over GF(2) and we hence have $x^2 = x$ for all $x \in \text{GF}(2)$.

We observe that this special construction of the private key polynomials does not affect our attack. In particular, the maximum rank for the corresponding matrices P'_i stays the same, namely lr for each layer. Unfortunately, for small values of r (in particular, $2 \leq r \leq 4$), there is a high probability that two polynomials $\phi_{l,i}, \phi_{l,j}$ for $i \neq j$ have the same coefficients: for $r = 2$, there is only one non-linear coefficient, for $r = 3$, there are only 3, and for $r = 4$, we obtain 6. The corresponding probabilities are therefore $2^{-1}, 2^{-3}$ and 2^{-6}, respectively, that the polynomials $\phi_{l,i}, \phi_{l,j}$ share the same quadratic coefficients. In a linear combination of these two polynomials, the rank of the corresponding matrix will therefore drop by r. This change defeats the lowRank algorithm from Fig. 4 as it only uses the matrix representation of the public key polynomials p_i. That way, it will not only find solutions of the layer l, but also for such linear combinations. To attack RSSE(2)PKC, it is therefore advisable to use the highRank algorithm from Fig. 3 in connection with Dickson's theorem (cf Sect. 2.2).

3.2   RSE(2)PKC

The system RSE(2)PKC is a special case of RSSE(2)PKC: the polynomials $\phi_{l,i}$ are required to be step-wise bijections, i.e., we have $(\phi_{l,1}, \ldots, \phi_{l,r}) : \mathbb{F}_2^r \to \mathbb{F}_2^r$ is a bijection for all $l \in \{1, \ldots, N\}$. This way, the whole system $\mathcal{P}$ becomes a bijection and it is possible to recover the solution x step by step without any ambiguity. As being a bijection is a rather strong requirement for a system of multivariate polynomials, the problem described in the previous section becomes more severe as we have far less choices for the coefficients in the quadratic terms. Still, using the high-rank rather than the low-rank attack should overcome this problem.

In [13–Sect. 3.2], the authors suggest $r \leq 10$ for their scheme which leads to $q^r = 2^{10}$. Therefore, we expect all attacks from the previous section to be efficient against these schemes.

Challenges. In [13–Sect. 6], Kasahara and Sakai propose two challenges with the following parameters: $\mathbb{F} = GF(2)$, $n = 100$ and $r = 4, 5$. Using a (highly unoptimised) Magma [1] programme, we were able to break this challenge in a few hours on an AMD Athlon XP 2000+. For our attack, we implemented the inversion attack against the low-rank side (cf sect. 2.2 and 2.3). As pointed out earlier, the attack should have been more efficient using an attack against the high-rank side in combination with Dickson's theorem (cf Sect. 2.2). In particular, we computed the solution x for the given value y. The two solutions are (in vector-notation, starting with x_1 at the left):

- $r = 4$: (0 0 1 1 0 1 0 0 1 0 0 0 0 1 1 0 0 0 1 1 1 0 0 1 1 0 0 1 0 0 0 1 1 1 0 0 0 1 1
  1 1 1 0 0 1 1 1 0 1 0 0 0 0 0 1 1 0 1 1 0 0 0 1 0 0 1 1 1 1 1 0 0 0 1 1 1 0 0 1 0 1 1 1
  1 1 1 0 0 1 0 0 1 1 0 1 0 1 0 0 1),

- $r = 5$: (1 1 1 0 0 1 1 0 1 0 1 1 1 0 0 0 1 0 0 0 0 1 0 0 1 0 0 0 1 1 0 1 0 1 0 0 1 1 0
  0 0 0 1 0 1 0 1 1 0 0 1 0 1 1 1 0 0 1 0 1 0 1 1 0 1 1 0 1 1 1 0 0 1 0 1 1 1 0 1 1 1 0 1
  0 1 0 1 1 0 0 1 1 0 0 1 1 0 0 1 1).

These results have been confirmed by Kasahara and Sakai [11].

Apart from the attacks presented in this paper, we also want to point out that the generic birthday attack for signature schemes applies against the parameter choice $q = 2$ and $n = 100$. In this case, the workload becomes only

$O(2^{50})$. As Kasahara and Sakai do not use special constructions as, *e.g.*, Feistel-Patarin-Networks [5], the generic birthday attack applies against RSE(2)PKC, RSSE(2)PKC, and also the hybrid type construction from the following section.

3.3 Hybrid Type Construction

In [12–Sect. 4.2], Kasahara and Sakai propose a so-called "hybrid type construction" to enhance the security of RSSE(2)PKC. To simplify explanation, we restrict to the case with two branches as this is sufficient to point out its vulnerability to the attacks described in this paper.

In this case, the private polynomials p'_i are partitioned into two sets: the polynomials $p'_1, \dots, p'_{m/2}$ are constructed as for RSSE(2)PKC (see above). However, the construction of the other polynomials now involves a third type of polynomial, denoted σ. For $L/2 < l \leq L$ and $1 \leq i \leq r$ we have:

$$p'_{lr+i}(x') := \phi_{l,i}(x'_{(l-1)r+1}, \dots, x'_{lr}) + \psi_{l,i}(x'_1, \dots, x'_{(l-1)r}) + \sigma_{lr+i}(x'_1, \dots, x'_{(L/2)}) .$$

As for $\phi_{l,i}$ and $\psi_{l,i}$, the polynomials σ_{lr+i} are quadratic polynomials with randomly chosen coefficients and no constant term α. All of them depend on the first $L/2$ variables only. Therefore, the overall structure of the private polynomials p'_i in terms of the rank of their matrix representation P'_i does not change and the attacks of this paper are still applicable.

4 Extensions of STS and Their Vulnerabilities

4.1 General Step-Wise Triangular Systems

As outlined in Sect. 1.2, regular STS may be generalised by different step-sizes and also different number of equations in each individual level, denoted $r_1, \dots, r_L \in \mathbb{N}$ and $m_1, \dots, m_L \in \mathbb{N}$, respectively. Moreover, we may consider these L-tuples as part of the private key; only their sums n and m are public. However, the internal structure of the private key keeps the same, in particular, we still obtain the chain of kernels of the private key polynomials. The only part of the attack we have to be careful about are the values r_1 and m_L, *i.e.*, the number of variables in the first layer and the number of equations in the last layer. If the first is too large, the attack at the low-rank side is no longer effective while a high value of the latter may preclude the attack from the high-rank side. Using gSTS for a signature scheme allows us $r_1 \gg m_1$. However, in this case we may not allow $r_L \ll m_L$ as this leads to a highly overdetermined system of equations — which has only very few solutions on average. The situation is reverse for encryption schemes. Here, we may have $r_L \ll m_L$ but not $r_1 \gg m_1$. As the system has a solution for $y = \mathcal{P}(x)$ by construction, a large value of m_L does not provide a problem here. Unfortunately, we are not able to find it back if the value for r_1 and consequently q^{r_1} is too large.

Therefore, gSTS will either fall to an attack from the high-rank or from the low-rank side. In both cases the construction is insecure. We want to point out that gSTS is a generalisation of the Triangular Plus-Minus (TPM) construction.

In particular, we relax the condition that there is only one new variable and one new equation at each intermediate level (cf Sect. 1.2).

4.2   Affine Transformations

In an attempt to strengthen gSTS, we investigate the replacement of the linear transformations S, T by affine ones, i.e., to include additional vectors $v_s \in \mathbb{F}^n$ and $v_t \in \mathbb{F}^m$.

Consider two affine transformations $S \in \mathrm{AGL}_n(\mathbb{F})$ and $T \in \mathrm{AGL}_m(\mathbb{F})$. Then there exists a unique, invertible matrix $M_S \in \mathbb{F}^{n \times n}$ (resp. $M_T \in \mathbb{F}^{m \times m}$) and an unique vector $v_s \in \mathbb{F}^n$ (resp. $v_t \in \mathbb{F}^m$) which describes the affine transformation S (resp. T) by $S(x) = M_S x + v_s$ where $x \in \mathbb{F}^n$ is an input vector (resp. $T(x) = M_T x + v_t$ for $x \in \mathbb{F}^m$). Moreover, we can rewrite the affine transformation S as $S(x) = (\overline{x} + v_s) \circ (M_S x)$ where $\overline{x}$ denotes the output of $M_S x$. In addition, we can rewrite the affine transformation T as $T(x) = (M_T \hat{x}) \circ (x + M_T^{-1} v_t)$, where $\hat{x}$ denotes the output of $x + M_T^{-1} v_t$. As M_T is an invertible matrix, the matrix $M_T^{-1} \in \mathbb{F}^{m \times m}$ exists and is unique. We now express the public key as a composition of the private key

$$\mathcal{P} = T \circ \mathcal{P}' \circ S$$
$$= [(M_T \hat{x}) \circ (\tilde{x} + M_T^{-1} v_t)] \circ \mathcal{P}' \circ [(\overline{x} + v_s) \circ (M_S x)]$$

where $\tilde{x}$ is the output of $\mathcal{P}' \circ [(x' + v_s) \circ (M_S x)]$ and $\hat{x}$ is the output of $(\tilde{x} + M_T^{-1} v_t) \circ \mathcal{P}' \circ [(x' + v_s) \circ (M_S x)]$. We have

$$\mathcal{P} = (M_T \hat{x}) \circ [(\tilde{x} + M_T^{-1} v_t) \circ \mathcal{P}' \circ (\overline{x} + v_s)] \circ (M_S x)$$
$$= (M_T \hat{x}) \circ \mathcal{P}'' \circ (M_S x)$$

for some system of equations $\mathcal{P}''$. As both $(\overline{x} + v_s)$ and $(\tilde{x} + M_T^{-1} v_t)$ are transformations of degree 1, they do not change the overall degree of $\mathcal{P}''$, i.e., as $\mathcal{P}'$ consists of equations of degree 2 at most, so will $\mathcal{P}''$. In addition, due to its construction, $(M_S, \mathcal{P}'', M_T)$ forms a private key for the public key $\mathcal{P}$ and the layer-structure of STS is not affected by these two operations.

Therefore, we can conclude that the use of affine instead of linear transformations does not enhance the overall security of STS. In fact, we are able to draw a similar conclusion for all such systems — as long as it is possible to replace the equation $\mathcal{P}'$ by an equation of similar shape. The corresponding observation for HFE has been made by Toli [24].

4.3   Degree Larger Than 2

In [13] and [12], Kasahara and Sakai generalise their construction to the schemes RSE(d)PKC and RSSE(d)PKC where $d \in \mathbb{N}$ denotes the degree of the public polynomials and $d \geq 2$. In their construction, terms of all degrees $1, \ldots, d$ appear in the public polynomials, e.g., linear and quadratic terms in RSSE(2)PKC and RSE(2)PKC (cf sect. 3.2 and 3.1). Therefore, we may apply the structural attack using the degree 2 terms in RSSE(d)PKC for $d > 2$, consequently retrieving the transformations $\tilde{S}$ and $\tilde{T}$, and then the corresponding private polynomials in the larger degree d. Similar, we may apply the inversion attack.

This construction is therefore not more secure. In addition, it leads to a much larger public key: the number of terms grows in $O(mn^d)$ for $d > 2$.

4.4 Highly Overdetermined Schemes

When the scheme has more equations than variables, *i.e.*, for $m > n$, we need to adapt the algorithm LowRankAttack (cf Section 2.2). Instead of picking one vector in each layer, we need to consider $\lambda := \lceil \frac{m}{n} \rceil$ vectors $v^1, \ldots, v^\lambda \in \mathbb{F}^n$ simultaneously. Now we have to solve the system of equations $\sum_{i=0}^{m} v_i^j (wP_i) = 0$ for $j \in \{1, \ldots, \lambda\}$ in order to have enough information for recovering the rows of $\tilde{T}$. As for the case $m \leq n$, this system of linear equations has q^{lr} solutions if and only if all vectors $v^1, \ldots, v^\lambda$ are in the kernel $\ker_l$. Consequently, the complexity for the LowRankAttack increases exponentially with λ and is equal to $O(mn^3 Lq^{\lambda r})$. In practice we will have small values for λ as highly overdetermined systems of quadratic equations are easy to solve [4].

5 Conclusion

In this paper, we have generalised the systems TPM, RSE(2)PKC, and RSSE(2) PKC to the step-wise triangular system (STS). In particular, we allow "steps" which contain more than one new variable (restriction in TPM) and give the private key polynomials p_i' more flexibility than in RSE(2)PKC or RSSE(2)PKC. We have presented two different types of attacks against the STS schemes: an inversion attack with complexity $O(mn^3 Lq^r + n^2 Lrq^r)$ and a structural attack with complexity $O(mn^3 Lq^r + mn^4)$. As the value of q^r has to be chosen rather small to derive a practical scheme, we conclude that STS is broken for all practical values (TPM uses 2 here while RSE(2)PKC and RSSE(2)PKC allow 1024 as maximal value). This is a new result for the special cases RSE(2)PKC and RSSE(2)PKC which have been considered to be secure against rank-attacks by their inventors. In particular, we were able to compute the solutions for the challenges proposed by Kasahara and Sakai (cf Sect. 3.2).

We have demonstrated that the existing generalisations of STS are either insecure or impractical. At present, it does not seem likely that there will ever be secure versions of STS schemes. In particular, we see no way of avoiding both the large kernel at one end and the small kernel at the other end — leave alone the chain of kernels — and still obtaining a scheme which may be used in practice for either encryption or signing.

Acknowledgements

We want to thank Taizo Shirai (Sony, Japan) for his help in connection with the challenge.

This work was supported in part by the Concerted Research Action (GOA) GOA Mefisto 2000/06, GOA Ambiorix 2005/11 of the Flemish Government and the European Commission through the IST Programme under Contract IST-2002-507932 ECRYPT. The second author was mainly supported by the FWO.

Disclaimer

The information in this document reflects only the author's views, is provided as is and no guarantee or warranty is given that the information is fit for any particular purpose. The user thereof uses the information at its sole risk and liability.

References

1. Computational Algebra Group, University of Sydney. *The MAGMA Computational Algebra System for Algebra, Number Theory and Geometry.* http://magma.maths.usyd.edu.au/magma/.
2. Don Coppersmith, Jacques Stern, and Serge Vaudenay. Attacks on the birational permutation signature schemes. In Cr [7], pages 435–443.
3. Don Coppersmith, Jacques Stern, and Serge Vaudenay. The security of the birational permutation signature schemes. *Jounal of Cryptology*, 10:207–221, 1997.
4. Nicolas Courtois, Louis Goubin, Willi Meier, and Jean-Daniel Tacier. Solving underdefined systems of multivariate quadratic equations. In *Public Key Cryptography — PKC 2002*, volume 2274 of *Lecture Notes in Computer Science*, pages 211–227. David Naccache and Pascal Paillier, editors, Springer, 2002.
5. Nicolas Courtois, Louis Goubin, and Jacques Patarin. *Quartz: Primitive specification (second revised version)*, October 2001. https://www.cosic.esat.kuleuven.ac.be/nessie/workshop/submissions/quartzv21-b.zip, 18 pages.
6. Nicolas T. Courtois. The security of Hidden Field Equations (HFE). In *The Cryptographer's Track at RSA Conference 2001*, volume 2020 of *Lecture Notes in Computer Science*, pages 266–281. D. Naccache, editor, Springer, 2001. http://www.minrank.org/hfesec.{ps|dvi|pdf}.
7. Douglas R. Stinson, editor. *Advances in Cryptology — CRYPTO 1993*, volume 773 of *Lecture Notes in Computer Science*. Springer, 1993. ISBN 3-540-57766-1.
8. Harriet Fell and Whitfield Diffie. Analysis of public key approach based on polynomial substitution. In *Advances in Cryptology — CRYPTO 1985*, volume 218 of *Lecture Notes in Computer Science*, pages 340–349. Hugh C. Williams, editor, Springer, 1985.
9. Michael R. Garay and David S. Johnson. *Computers and Intractability — A Guide to the Theory of NP-Completeness*. W.H. Freeman and Company, 1979. ISBN 0-7167-1044-7 or 0-7167-1045-5.
10. Louis Goubin and Nicolas T. Courtois. Cryptanalysis of the TTM cryptosystem. In *Advances in Cryptology — ASIACRYPT 2000*, volume 1976 of *Lecture Notes in Computer Science*, pages 44–57. Tatsuaki Okamoto, editor, Springer, 2000.
11. Masao Kasahara and Ryuichi Sakai. private communication, 3rd of April 2004.
12. Masao Kasahara and Ryuichi Sakai. A construction of public-key cryptosystem based on singular simultaneous equations. In *Symposium on Cryptography and Information Security — SCIS 2004*. The Institute of Electronics, Information and Communication Engineers, January 27–30 2004. 6 pages.

13. Masao Kasahara and Ryuichi Sakai. A construction of public key cryptosystem for realizing ciphertext of size 100 bit and digital signature scheme. *IEICE Trans. Fundamentals*, E87-A(1):102–109, January 2004. Electronic version: `http://search.ieice.org/2004/files/e000a01.htm\#e87-a,1,102`.

14. Aviad Kipnis, Jacques Patarin, and Louis Goubin. Unbalanced oil and vinegar signature schemes. In *Advances in Cryptology — EUROCRYPT 1999*, volume 1592 of *Lecture Notes in Computer Science*, pages 206–222. Jacques Stern, editor, Springer, 1999. Extended version: [15].

15. Aviad Kipnis, Jacques Patarin, and Louis Goubin. Unbalanced oil and vinegar signature schemes — extended version, 2003. 17 pages, `citeseer/231623.html`, 2003-06-11, based on [14].

16. F.J. MacWilliams and N.J.A. Sloane. *The Theory of Error-Correcting Codes*. Elsevier Science Publisher, 1991. ISBN 0-444-85193-3.

17. Tsutomu Matsumoto and Hideki Imai. Public quadratic polynomial-tuples for efficient signature verification and message-encryption. In *Advances in Cryptology — EUROCRYPT 1988*, volume 330 of *Lecture Notes in Computer Science*, pages 419–545. Christoph G. Günther, editor, Springer, 1988.

18. Alfred J. Menezes, Paul C. van Oorschot, and Scott A. Vanstone. *Handbook of Applied Cryptography*. CRC Press, 1996. ISBN 0-8493-8523-7, online-version: `http://www.cacr.math.uwaterloo.ca/hac/`.

19. Jacques Patarin. Hidden Field Equations (HFE) and Isomorphisms of Polynomials (IP): two new families of asymmetric algorithms. In *Advances in Cryptology — EUROCRYPT 1996*, volume 1070 of *Lecture Notes in Computer Science*, pages 33–48. Ueli Maurer, editor, Springer, 1996. Extended Version: `http://www.minrank.org/hfe.pdf`.

20. Jacques Patarin and Louis Goubin. Trapdoor one-way permutations and multivariate polynomials. In *International Conference on Information Security and Cryptology 1997*, volume 1334 of *Lecture Notes in Computer Science*, pages 356–368. International Communications and Information Security Association, Springer, 1997. Extended Version: `http://citeseer.nj.nec.com/patarin97trapdoor.html`.

21. Jacques Patarin, Louis Goubin, and Nicolas Courtois. Improved algorithms for Isomorphisms of Polynomials. In *Advances in Cryptology — EUROCRYPT 1998*, volume 1403 of *Lecture Notes in Computer Science*, pages 184–200. Kaisa Nyberg, editor, Springer, 1998. Extended Version: `http://www.minrank.org/ip6long.ps`.

22. Adi Shamir. Efficient signature schemes based on birational permutations. In Cr [7], pages 1–12.

23. Thorsten Theobald. How to break shamir's asymmetric basis. In *Advances in Cryptology — CRYPTO 1995*, volume 963 of *Lecture Notes in Computer Science*, pages 136–147. Don Coppersmith, editor, Springer, 1995.

24. Ilia Toli. Cryptanalysis of HFE, June 2003. arXiv preprint server, `http://arxiv.org/abs/cs.CR/0305034`, 7 pages.

The Decimated Sample Based Improved
Algebraic Attacks on the Nonlinear Filters

Miodrag J. Mihaljević[1] and Hideki Imai[2]

[1]Mathematical Institute, Serbian Academy of Sciences and Arts,
Kneza Mihaila 35, 11001 Belgrade, Serbia and Montenegro
miodragm@turing.mi.sanu.ac.yu
[2]University of Tokyo, Institute of Industrial Science,
4-6-1, Komaba, Meguro-ku, Tokyo, 153-8505 Japan
imai@iis.u-tokyo.ac.jp

Abstract. This paper proposes an improved approach for cryptanalysis of keystream generators based on a composition of a linear finite state machine (LFSM) and nonlinear mapping. The main feature of the proposed approach is that it is based on identification and selection for further processing certain suitable positions in the given sample so that only the decimated sample elements are relevant for the attacking. In a number of scenarios this yields a significant gain in the performance sometimes at the expense of a longer sample required or/and the pre-processing cost. The proposed approach employs novel methods for constructing the underlying overdefined system of equations relevant for the attacks and solving the system under a set of the hypothesis. Oppositely to the previously reported methods, the proposed ones also identify and use certain characteristics of the LFSM state-transition matrix in order to reduce the nonlinearity of the system. The novel construction of the equations yields a possibility for the trade-off between the required sample, pre-processing and processing complexity of the cryptanalysis. The pre-processing phase of the developed algorithm for cryptanalysis yields a collection of the output bit positions which are suitable for reducing the equations nonlinearity. The processing phase employs the output bits from the identified collection and it includes an exhaustive search over a subset of the secret key bits.

Keywords: stream ciphers, cryptanalysis, algebraic attacks, overdefined systems of equations, decimation, hypotheses testing.

1   Introduction

Recently, algebraic attacks have appeared as a powerful tool for cryptanalysis and security evaluation of certain encryption schemes and particularly stream ciphers including the nonlinear filter based keystream generators. Some early algebraic attacks on stream and related ciphers have been reported in [10], [11], [1] and [3]. Very recently, a number of general powerful algebraic attacks have been reported in [4], [5], [9] and [7].

C. Blundo and S. Cimato (Eds.): SCN 2004, LNCS 3352, pp. 310–323, 2005.
© Springer-Verlag Berlin Heidelberg 2005

A general paradigm of algebraic attacks is based on establishing and processing an overdefined system of the nonlinear equations. An algebraic attack can be roughly summarized as follows: (i) Describe the secret key as a largely overdefined system of (low-degree) nonlinear algebraic equations; (ii) If the number of equations exceeds the number of terms, linearise the system; i.e. treat each term as an independent variable and solve this (huge) system of linear equations. (iii) If the first step does not yield enough equations, try to solve the system employing other appropriate techniques (like Grobner basis, see [6], for example).

Motivation for the Work
General powerful algebraic attacks that have been recently reported are based on construction of the overdefined system employing (basically) only certain characteristics of the nonlinear function. Accordingly, the performance of these attacks strongly depend on the nonlinear part, and if this part does not have certain characteristics appropriate for cryptanalysis the attacks could become very complex or not feasible. So, an origin for this paper was addressing the following issue: Find a way to involve into the algebraic attack certain characteristics of the linear part of the generator in order to obtain more powerful attacks in the cases when the nonlinear part is heavily resistant against the reported algebraic attacks.

Contributions of this Paper
This paper yields a novel approach for developing algebraic attacks on the memoryless nonlinear filter based keystream generators. A novel method for constructing and solving the overdefined systems of the binary nonlinear equations relevant for the cryptanalysis is proposed. The proposed method assumes selection of a suitable subset of possible multivariate equations and the search over a set of hypothesis. Recall that the reported methods for construction of the overdefined systems are mainly based only on certain characteristics of the nonlinear function. Oppositely to the reported methods, the proposed one also identifies and employs certain characteristics of the state-transition matrix corresponding to the linear part in order to reduce the nonlinearity of the nonlinear equations related to algebraic attacks. The proposed construction of the system yields a possibility for the trade-off between the required sample, pre-processing and processing complexity of the cryptanalysis. The pre-processing phase of the developed method is independent of a particular sample and it consists of three consecutive stages: Particularly note that the first stage yields a collection of the output bit positions which are suitable for reducing the equations nonlinearity. The processing phase consists of two stages and it employs the output bits from the identified collection and includes an exhaustive search over a moderate subset of the secret key bits. Following the above framework an algorithm for algebraic attack is proposed, analyzed and its advantages in comparison with the reported ones are pointed out (see Table 1 and Table 2).

Organization of the Paper
The preliminaries including the specification of the nonlinear filter model under consideration in this paper are given in Section 2. Underlying ideas for the novel

approach and the framework for cryptanalysis of the nonlinear filter keystream generators are given in Section 3. The (basic) algorithms for cryptanalysis of the memoryless nonlinear filter generators employing algebraic attack is proposed in Section 4 and analyzed in Section 5. The proposed approach is compared with the relevant previously reported ones in Section 6. Finally, Section 7 yields a concluding discussion.

2   Preliminaries

2.1   Algebraic Normal Form of a Nonlinear Boolean Function

An m-variable Boolean function $f(x_1, x_2, ..., x_m)$ can be considered as a multivariate polynomial over $GF(2)$. This polynomial can be expressed as a sum of products representation of all distinct r-th order products ($0 \leq r \leq m$) of the variables as follows:

$$f(x_1, x_2, ..., x_m) = \bigoplus_{u \in GF(2^m)} \lambda_u \left(\prod_{i=1}^{m} x_i^{u_i} \right) , \quad \lambda \in GF(2) , \quad u = (u_1, u_2, ..., u_m) .$$

(1)

This representation of $f(\cdot)$ is called the algebraic normal form (ANF) of f. The algebraic degree of f, denoted by $deg(f)$ or simply d, is the maximal value of the Hamming weight of u such that $\lambda_u \neq 0$.

2.2   Matrix Representation of a Binary Linear Finite State Machine (LFSM)

A binary linear finite state machine (LFSM) can be described as $\mathbf{X}_t = \mathbf{A}\mathbf{X}_{t-1}$, where $\mathbf{A}$ is the **state transition matrix** (over $GF(2)$) of the considered LFSM. Let $\mathbf{X}_0$ be the column ($L \times 1$) matrix $[X_{L-1}, ..., X_0]^T$ representing the initial contents or initial state of the LFSM, and

$$\mathbf{X}_t = [X_{L-1}^{(t)}, ..., X_0^{(t)}]^T , \tag{2}$$

is the L-dimensional column vector over $GF(2)$ representing the LFSM state after t clocks, where $\mathbf{X}^T$ denotes the transpose of the L-dimensional vector $\mathbf{X}$. Accordingly,

$$\mathbf{X}_t = \mathbf{A}\mathbf{X}_{t-1} = \mathbf{A}^t \mathbf{X}_0, \quad \mathbf{A}^t = \begin{bmatrix} \mathbf{A}_1^{(t)} \\ \mathbf{A}_2^{(t)} \\ \mathbf{A}_3^{(t)} \\ \cdot \\ \mathbf{A}_L^{(t)} \end{bmatrix} , \quad t = 1, 2, ..., \tag{3}$$

where $\mathbf{A}^t$ is the t-th power over $GF(2)$ of the $L \times L$ state transition binary matrix $\mathbf{A}$, and each $\mathbf{A}_i^{(t)}$, $i = 1, 2, ..., L$, represents a $1 \times L$ matrix (a row-vector).

Linear feedback shift register (LFSR) and linear Cellular Automaton (CA) are particular LFSMs.

Example 1: LFSR.
An LFSR can be considered as a particular linear finite state machine described via certain linear operators as follows. The characteristic polynomial or feedback polynomial of the LFSR is

$$b(u) = 1 + b_1 u + \ldots + b_L u^L \tag{4}$$

and the recursion implemented by the LFSR is then

$$X_{L+t} = -b_1 X_{L+t-1} - \ldots - b_L X_t = b_1 X_{L+t-1} + \ldots + b_L X_t, \tag{5}$$

assuming operations over GF(2).

When the LFSR feedback polynomial being given by (4), then the state transition matrix $\mathbf{A}$ can be written as:

$$\mathbf{A} = \begin{bmatrix} b_1 & b_2 & b_3 & \ldots & & b_L \\ 1 & 0 & 0 & \ldots & & 0 \\ 0 & 1 & 0 & \ldots & & . \\ . & . & . & \ldots & & . \\ 0 & & & \ldots & 1 & 0 \end{bmatrix} = \begin{bmatrix} \mathbf{A}_1 \\ \mathbf{A}_2 \\ \mathbf{A}_3 \\ . \\ \mathbf{A}_L \end{bmatrix}. \tag{6}$$

2.3   Model of the Nonlinear Filter Keystream Generators

This paper considers a novel algebraic attack technique for cryptanalysis of a class of keystream generators for stream ciphers known as the nonlinear filter generators (see [8], for example). The model of the keystream generators under cryptanalytic consideration is displayed in Fig. 1 where LFSM denotes a known linear finite state machine with only the initial state $\mathbf{X}_0$ determined by the secret key, and $f(\cdot)$ denotes a known nonlinear memoryless function of K arguments.

Assumption 1. In the considered model, $f(\cdot)$ is nonlinear function such that it is computationally not possible to construct any multivariate relations between the function arguments and its output with the nonlinearity degree lower than d without employing linear combining of the basic multivariate equations.

Note that ANF of $f(\cdot)$ directly specifies one multivariate equation between the function arguments and its output which has the nonlinearity order equal to the algebraic degree of $f(\cdot)$, but in many cases additional multivariate equations with a lower nonlinearity order can be specified as well. When a linear combining of the equations is allowed, the linear combination can be with a lower degree than the component equations, assuming that enough many equations is available for the combining (see [5], for example).

In Fig. 1, $\mathbf{X}_0$ denotes the LFSM initial state, $\mathbf{X}_t$ and $\mathbf{A}^t$ denote the LFSM state and LFSM state transition matrix, respectively, at a time instance t, and let the generator output sequence be the sample available for the cryptanalysis.

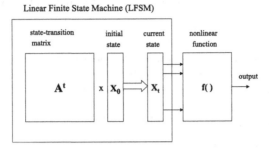

Fig. 1. Model of the keystream generators under consideration: The nonlinear filter

3   Origins, Underlying Ideas and Framework of Novel Approach for Algebraic Attacks

3.1   Origins and Underlying Ideas

The reported algebraic attacks on the nonlinear filters are based on identification of a nonlinear multivariate equation with the nonlinearity order d in the input arguments of $f(\cdot)$ and in general case can be of higher degree in the outputs. Note that this equation is established taking into account only the characteristics of the nonlinear functions $f(\cdot)$. According to [4], when we can evaluate around $\binom{L}{d}$ different instances of the identified equation, we can establish an overdefined system of nonlinear equations which can be solved by simple linearization and employment of the Gaussian elimination with the complexity proportional to $2^{\omega(log_2 L)d}$, where ω is a known constant ($\omega=2.7$, see [5] or [7], for example). Note that d contribute to the overall complexity in the exponential manner, and so it should be as small as possible. In [5], a method for reducing the nonlinearity order d of the involved equations is proposed: This method employs a pre-processing over the set of the equations via making appropriate linear combinations of the initial equations so that the resulting equations have reduced nonlinearity order. The underlying idea of the approach given in this paper has the same goal, i.e. reduction the nonlinearity order of the equations involved in the system to be solved via linearization and Gaussian elimination, but achievement of the goal is not based on the search for the appropriate linear combinations of the initial equations.

The underlying ideas of the novel approach can be summarized as follows: Reduce d of the initial multivariate equation via

- employment of a search over the set of hypotheses, and
- selection of a suitable subsequence of the nonlinear filter output sequence to be used for establishing the overdefined system of nonlinear equations with a reduced nonlinearity order.

The approach proposed in this paper takes into account not only the nonlinear part but certain (suitable) characteristics of the linear part originating from the following.

- At each time instance t the arguments of $f(\cdot)$ are certain elements of the state vector $\mathbf{X}_t = \mathbf{A}^t \mathbf{X}_0$ where $\mathbf{A}^t$ is the known matrix and $\mathbf{X}_0$ is the unknown initial state of LFSM.
- The LFSM initial state is considered as consisting of two suitably determined parts: one which should be determined by an exhaustive search, and the other which could be recovered via an appropriately designed algebraic attack, assuming that the first part is known due to the employed hypothesis.

3.2   Framework

This section proposes a framework for developing a novel family of algorithms for cryptanalysis of certain stream ciphers which fit to the model under consideration in this paper.

The proposed framework includes the preprocessing steps which are independent of particular sample elements (they should be performed only once) and the processing steps which should be performed for the given sample.

The main goals of the preprocessing are: (i) identification of the time instances t where certain arguments of $f(\cdot)$ depend only on a part of the LFSM initial state, and (ii) establishing the working system of equations with the reduced nonlinearity and deriving the general solutions for certain unknowns.

Taking into account only the time instances within $\mathcal{T}$, i.e. positions in the sample identified in the preprocessing, the central goals of the processing are: (i) For the given sample elements and a particular hypothesis evaluate the general solutions and obtain a candidate for the initial state; (ii) Recover the initial state via evaluation of the candidates over the set of hypothesis.

Three main components of the proposed framework are the following ones:

- *Sample Decimation.* Selection of suitable sample elements assuming that certain B bits of the LFSM initial state are known.
- *Conditional Algebraic Attack.* Mounting algebraic attack over the selected sample elements and obtaining the 2^B candidates for the initial state as a function of the B bits considered as known.
- *Hypotheses Testing.* Exhaustive search over 2^B hypothesis about the B bits and recovering the initial state.

Accordingly, assuming that certain necessary conditions are fulfilled, in a general case, the algorithm for cryptanalysis under development consists of the following three phases.

1. *Phase I.*
   - Suppose that certain B secret key bits (variables) will be recovered by the exhaustive search. (This assumption is recognized as a very useful one for developing efficient fast correlation attacks: see [11] and [2], for example.)
   - Determine a set $\mathcal{T}$ of time instances t where a subset of $f(\cdot)$ arguments depend only on the assumed B bits.

2. *Phase II.*
   Mount a general form of the algebraic attack taking into account only the time instances $t \in \mathcal{T}$ as follows:
   – specification of the initial system of equations;
   – construction of the working system of equations with the reduced non-linearity employing the assumption that certain B bits are known;
   – linearization of the constructed nonlinear equations;
   – solving the system of equations by Gaussian algorithm, and obtaining general solution for $L - B$ bits as a function of the B bits considered as known (this step is similar to the "slow pre-computation" approach [5], Section 4.1).
3. *Phase III.*
   – Substitution of the selected sample elements (corresponding to the time instances $t \in \mathcal{T}$) into general form of the solutions.
   – Testing the hypotheses on the assumed B bits, and recovering the initial state of LFSM.

4   Algorithm of New Algebraic Attack

Let at each time instance t, the following state elements are the arguments of $f(\cdot)$: $X_k^{(t)}$, $k \in \mathcal{K}$, and $\mathcal{K}$ is a subset of $\{0, 1, ..., L-1\}$ with the cardinality equal to K, and let $\mathcal{K}^*$ be a subset of $\mathcal{K}$. Note that:

$$X_k^{(t)} = \mathbf{A}_k^{(t)} \mathbf{X}_0 \ , \quad k \in \mathcal{K}, \quad t = 1, 2, \dots \ , \tag{7}$$

Assumption 2. At certain time instances $t \in \mathcal{T}$ the following is valid:

– For each $k \in \mathcal{K}^*$, $\mathcal{K}^* \subset \mathcal{K}$, the row vectors $\mathbf{A}_k^{(t)}$ have such forms that the state elements $X_k^{(t)}$, $k \in \mathcal{K}^*$, depend only on certain B elements of $\mathbf{X}_0$ with indices i, $i \in \mathcal{I}$, independent of the parameter t.

Let the cardinality of $\mathcal{K}^*$ is K^*. Let $|\mathcal{T}|$ denotes the cardinality of $\mathcal{T}$, i.e. total number of the time instances when Assumption 2 holds. The following statement can be directly proved: The contents of $\mathcal{T}$ depends on a particular LFSM, and can be obtained by a straightforward calculation.

A L G O R I T H M   I: The Decimation and Hypothesis Testing Based Algebraic Attack

– **Preprocessing**
   • *Preprocessing I - Sample Decimation.*
      ∗ *Input*: State transition matrix $\mathbf{A}$, positions $\mathcal{I}$ of B initial state bits known by the hypothesis, and the algorithm parameter N.

* *Search over the Powers of the State Transition Matrix*
  For each t, do the following
  1. Calculate $\mathbf{A}^t = \mathbf{A} \cdot \mathbf{A}^{t-1}$.
  2. Evaluate validity of Assumption 2 for current t.
  3. If Assumption 2 holds, include t into $\mathcal{T}$.
  4. Set $t \rightarrow t + 1$, and if $t \leq N$, go to the preprocessing Step 1; otherwise, go to the preprocessing output.
* *Output*: Set $\mathcal{T}$ of the selected time instances t.

- *Preprocessing II - Derivation of General Solutions.*
  * *Input*: Inputs of Preprocessing I and its output, set $\mathcal{T}$.
  * *The System of Equations Construction*:
    - Assume that B-bits pattern on the initial state index positions i, $i \in \mathcal{I}$ is known.
    - Taking into account only the positions $t \in \mathcal{T}$ and particular characteristics of LFSM states at these positions, specify the required initial system of $\binom{L}{K-K^*}$ nonlinear equations.
    - Perform the system linearization and derive expressions for $L-B$ initial state bits under assumption that the B-bits are known, obtaining the following relations:

$$x_j = \bigoplus_{t \in \mathcal{T}} c_j \phi_t(\{x_i\}_{i \in \mathcal{I}}) \,, \quad j \in \{1, 2, ..., L\} \bigcap \mathcal{I} \,, \qquad (8)$$

where $c_j \in \{0, 1\}$ are constants determined by the sample, and $\phi_t(\cdot)$ are known polynomial functions determined by Gaussian elimination procedure and the state transition matrix at time instances $t \in \mathcal{T}$.
  * *Output*: The general solutions (8) of $L - B$ bits under assumption that B bits are known.

- *Preprocessing III - Specification of a Dedicated Look-Up Table (LUT)*
  * *Input*: The functions $\phi_t(\{x_i\}_{i \in \mathcal{I}})$, $t \in \mathcal{T}$.
  * *Evaluation of LUT elements*: For each of 2^B different patterns of $[x_i]_{i \in \mathcal{I}}$ evaluate all the functions $\phi_t(\{x_i\}_{i \in \mathcal{I}})$, $t \in \mathcal{T}$.
  * *Output*: LUT of dimension $2^B \times O(2^{(K-K^*)log_2 L})$ where each the rows contains precomputed values of $O(2^{(K-K^*)log_2 L})$ "coefficients" $\phi_t(\{x_i\}_{i \in \mathcal{I}})$, $t \in \mathcal{T}$.

- **Processing Phase**
  - *Input*: Outputs of the preprocessing phase, and the keystream generator output sample.
  - *Processing Steps*:
    1. *Involving the Sample into General Solutions.*
       Substitute the sample elements corresponding to $\mathcal{T}$ into the general solutions (8).
    2. *Evaluation of the Solutions over the Set of Hypothesis*
       Evaluate the solutions (8) for all possible 2^B hypothesis on the B bits according to the following:

(a) Select previously not considered candidate for the B bits of initial state and employing (8) with involved sample bits, and LUT evaluate a candidate for the remained $L - B$ bits, obtaining a candidate for the entire initial state, as well.

(b) Generate the nonlinear filter output sequence of length at least equal to L.

(c) Compare the generated sequence and the corresponding segment of the given input sample.

If the sequences under comparison are identical accept the initial state determined by the considered hypothesis on B bits and the recovered $L - B$ bits as the correct one, recover the secret key and go to the processing phase Output.

Otherwise, continue examination of the candidates.

• *Output*: Recovered secret key.

5   Discussion on Required Sample and Algorithm Complexity

The complexity analysis in this section assumes that the output of function $f(\cdot)$ can be computed in time $O(1)$ (the same assumption is employed in [5]).

5.1   Arbitrary Positions of Nonlinear Filter Inputs

It is assumed that the employed LFSM is LFSR (or CA) with the primitive characteristic polynomial.

Proposition 1. The expected sample dimension N required for Algorithm I implementation should be greater than $2^{(L-B)} \binom{L}{K-K^*}$.

Sketch of the Proof. Algorithm I employs a system of $\binom{L}{K-K^*}$ equations corresponding to the positions of the generator output sequence where K^* arguments of the nonlinear function $f(\cdot)$ depend only on certain B bits. On the other hand in a statistical model corresponding to a sequence of the state-transition matrix powers, the probability that the pattern required by Assumption 2 appears is at most equal to $2^{-(L-B)}$. Accordingly, as an estimate we have the proposition statement.

Proposition 2. The time and space complexities of the pre-processing are $max\{O(2^{L-B+Q+(K-K^*)log_2 L});\ O(2^{\omega(K-K^*)log_2 L});\ O(2^{B+2(K-K^*)log_2 L})\}$ and $O(2^{B+(K-K^*)log_2 L})$, respectively.

Sketch of the Proof. Preprocessing consists of three consecutive phases, and the total time complexity is the sum of three corresponding complexities, but the maximum sum component is the dominant one. The sample decimation phase (Preprocessing I) has time complexity $O(2^{L-B+Q+(K-K^*)log_2 L})$ where $Q < B$ is a parameter which depends on the characteristics of employed LFSM and $f(\cdot)$. The Gaussian elimination phase (Preprocessing II) according to [4]-[5] has the time complexity $O(2^{\omega(K-K^*)log_2 L})$. The dedicated look-up table specification (Preprocessing III) has time complexity $O(2^{B+2(K-K^*)log_2 L})$. According to the structure of all preprocessing phases the dominant space complexity is determined by the required LUT dimension and so it is $O(2^{B+(K-K^*)log_2 L})$.

Proposition 3. The attack processing requires:
time complexity $O(2^{B+(K-K^*)log_2 L})$ and space complexity $O(2^{B+(K-K^*)log_2 L})$.

Sketch of the Proof. Algorithm I structure implies that the time complexity is sum of the time complexities of the main processing steps 1 and 2. According to the nature of these steps, the domminat complexity corresponds to the step 2. Time complexity of the step 2 is determined by the complexities of evaluation of the general solutions over 2^B hypotheses where $O(2^{(K-K^*)log_2 L})$ is time complexity of the evaluation employing LUT for a single hypothesis. The space complexity is determined by the space requirement for LUT.

5.2   Partially Concentrated Positions of Nonlinear Filter Inputs

Assumption 3. The considered LFSM is an LFSR with primitive characteristic polynomial and the state-transition matrix given by (6), such that $b_i = 0$ for $i_{min} \leq i \leq i_{max}$, $\mathcal{I} = \{1, 2, ..., B\}$, $i_{min} = B + 1$, $i_{max} = L - 1$, and $\Delta = m_{max} - m_{min} + 1$ where m_{max} and m_{min} corresponds to the largest and the smallest values in $\mathcal{K}^*$, respectively.

Proposition 4. When Assumption 3 holds, the expected cardinality of $\mathcal{T}$ is given by the following:

$$|\bar{\mathcal{T}}| = N \, 2^{-(L-B-1+2\Delta)} \quad,$$

where N is the available sample.

Sketch of the Proof. When $\mathbf{A}$ is the state transition matrix of an L-length binary LFSR with a primitive characteristic polynomial, than (3) implies that the sequence of the matrix powers $\mathbf{A}^t$ has period $2^L - 1$ because $\mathbf{X}_0$ is a constant vector and the sequence $\mathbf{X}_t$ has period $2^L - 1$.
On the other hand we have

$$\mathbf{A}^t = \mathbf{A}^{t-1}\mathbf{A}_0 \qquad (9)$$

where $\mathbf{A}_0 = \mathbf{A}$. Let

$$\mathbf{A}_0 = [\mathbf{AC}_1^{(0)}, \mathbf{AC}_2^{(0)}, ..., \mathbf{AC}_L^{(0)}]$$

and

$$\mathbf{A}^t = [\mathbf{AC}_1^{(t)}, \mathbf{AC}_2^{(t)}, ..., \mathbf{AC}_L^{(t)}] \,,$$

where each $\mathbf{AC}_i^{(0)}$ and $\mathbf{AC}_i^{(t)}$, $i = 1, 2, ..., L$, is an $L \times 1$ (column) matrix.
Let $\{x_n\}$ be the LFSR output sequence generated by the initial state $\mathbf{X}_0$ such that $X_{i_{max}}^{(0)} = 1$ and all other $X_i^{(0)}$, $1 \leq i \leq L$, $i \neq i_{max}$ are equal to zero.

Accordingly, and based on the proposition assumptions, the following can be directly shown: Each $\mathbf{AC}_i^{(t)}$, $i_{min} \leq i \leq i_{max}$ is equal to an L-length segment of $\{x_n\}$, and for any pair (i_1, i_2), $i_{min} \leq i_1 \leq i_2 \leq i_{max}$, we have that $\mathbf{AC}_{i_1}^{(t)}$ and $\mathbf{AC}_{i_2}^{(t)}$ correspond to the segments with the starting point difference equal to $i_2 - i_1$.

Finally, in the statistical model, the probability that an all-zeros pattern of length $L - B - 1 + \Delta$ will appear in the sequence $\{x_n\}$ is equal to $2^{-(L-B-1+\Delta)}$ and due to that always $b_L = 1$ (see (6)) the probability that Assumption 1 holds in a time instance t is equal to $2^{-(L-B-1+\Delta)} \cdot 2^{-\Delta}$. The above consideration implies the proposition statement.

The structure of Algorithm I directly implies the following statements.

Proposition 5. The sample dimension N required for Algorithm I implementation when Assumption 3 holds is proportional to $2^{(L-B+2\Delta)} \binom{L}{K-K^*}$.

Sketch of the Proof. Note that Algorithm I needs a sample in which the pattern required by Assumption 2 will appear around $\binom{L}{K-K^*}$ times, and the pattern required is a two dimensional $(L - B) \times \Delta$ one where $\Delta \geq K^*$. Accordingly, Proposition 4 imply the given estimation of the required sample.

So, when the inputs of $f(\cdot)$ are partially concentrated, a significantly smaller sample and pre-processing complexity are required in comparison with a general case.

Note. Assumption 3 has no impact to the time and space processing complexities, and they are given by Proposition 3.

6   Comparison with the Previously Reported Attacks

Taking into account Propositions 1 - 3, and the results reported in [5] and [7], the developed attack is compared with the best related ones previously published and the summary of comparison is given in Tables 1 and 2.

For the comparison purposes the following is assumed:
- the employed LFSM is LFSR of dimension L;
- the employed nonlinear Boolean function has the degree d and K arguments (K inputs from LFSR state assuming arbitrary positions) and $d = K$;
- e the parameter of the algorithms from [5] (see [5], Sect. 7.1 and 7.2) and in order to minimize the time complexity $e \approx K(1/\omega)$ where ω is the constant related to the algorithm for solving a system of linear equations ($\omega \approx 2.7$);
- B and K^* (see Assumption 2) are parameters of the proposed Algorithm I, $B < L$, $K^* < K < L$.

Also, it is assumed that the output of function $f(\cdot)$ can be computed in time $O(1)$ (the same assumption is employed in [5]).

Finally note that for simplicity, it is intentionally assumed that the both approaches [5] and [7] have the same preprocessing complexities although the more precise comparison is given in [7].

Table 1. Comparison of the time complexities of the proposed and previously reported attacks on the nonlinear filters (the processing complexity reported in [5] is corrected according to [7])

	Pre-Processing Complexity	Processing Complexity
CRYPTO'03, [5] $e < d < L$	$O(2^{(d+e)log_2 L})$	$max\{O(2^{(d+2e)log_2 L})$; $O(2^{welog_2 L})\}$
CRYPTO'04, [7]	$O(2^{(d+e)log_2 L})$	$max\{O(2^{(d+e)log_2 L+log_2 d+log_2 log_2 L})$; $O(2^{welog_2 L})\}$
proposed Algorithm I $e^* = K - K^* < e$; $Q < B < L$	$max\{O(2^{L-B+Q+e^* log_2 L})$; $O(2^{we^* log_2 L})$; $O(2^{B+2e^* log_2 L})\}$	$O(2^{B+e^* log_2 L})$

Table 2. Comparison of the required sample and the space complexities of the proposed and previously reported attacks on the nonlinear filters

	dimension of sample involved in processing	consecutive sample bit required	space complexity
CRYPTO'03, [5] CRYPTO'04, [7] $e < d < L$	$\sim \binom{L}{d}$	yes	$O(\binom{L}{d}\binom{L}{e})$
proposed Algorithm I $e^* = K - K^* < e$; $Q < B < L$	$\sim \binom{L}{e^*}$ decimated from $\sim 2^{L-B+Q}\binom{L}{e^*}$	no	$O(2^B \binom{L}{e^*})$

The following Table 3 yields a numerical illustration of the comparison given in Table 1. We assume attacking of the nonlinear filter which involve LFSR of length $L = 70$, and nonlinear function $f(\cdot)$ with $K = 6$ arguments and $deg(f) = 6$. The employed value of the parameter e in the reported algorithms [5] and [7] is $e = 2$, and the employed values of the parameters B and K^* in the proposed Algorithm I are $B = 35$ and $K^* = 4$, assuming partially concentrated inputs with $\Delta = 5$ (see Assumption 3 and Propositions 4 - 5, as well).

Table 3. An illustrative numerical comparison of the main characteristics of the proposed and previously reported attacks on the nonlinear filter, when the parameters in Table 1 take the following values: $L = 70$, $d = K = 6$, $e = 2$, $B = 35$ and $K^* = 4$

attack	CRYPTO'03 [5]	CRYPTO'04 [7]	proposed Algorithm I
length of required sample	$\sim 2^{48}$	$\sim 2^{48}$	$\sim 2^{57}$
consecutive sample bits required	yes	yes	no
space complexity (memory)	$O(2^{48})$	$O(2^{48})$	$O(2^{47})$
pre-processing complexity	$O(2^{48})$	$O(2^{48})$	$O(2^{58})$
attack complexity	$O(2^{60})$	$O(2^{54})$	$O(2^{47})$

7   Concluding Discussion

The paper proposes novel elements for security evaluation or cryptanalysis of certain stream ciphers which can be modeled via the nonlinear filter keystream generator, i.e. a linear finite state machine and a nonlinear Boolean function.

The main feature of the novel approach is that it employs certain characteristics of the generator linear part (the involved linear finite state machine) to identify positions of the generator output sequence where certain arguments of the nonlinear function depend only on a part of the generator initial state. Assuming that this part of the initial state can be considered as known one, a more suitable system of nonlinear multivariate equations can be established, and the assumed initial state part can be recovered via the exhaustive hypothesis testing later on.

The proposed approach consists of the following three main phases: (i) Selection of suitable sample elements assuming that certain B bits of the initial state are known; (ii) Mounting algebraic attack over the selected sample elements and obtaining the 2^B candidates for the initial state as a function of the B bits considered as known; (iii) Exhaustive search over 2^B hypothesis about the B bits and recovering the initial state.

The characteristics of the proposed approach are compared with the relevant previously reported techniques, and it is pointed out that in a number of scenarios the developed algorithm yields gains in comparison with the previously reported ones. (see Tables 1 and 2 for a general case, and Table 3 for a particular illustrative numerical case). Also note that the proposed approach does not require consecutive sample elements.

The proposed attack is limited to the simple nonlinear filters, and applicability of its underlying principles to the more general scenarios is an open issue. The proposed attack does not yield benefits in all the cases, but it could provide significant gains over the previously reported ones when: (i) a large sample is available, (ii) the employed memoryless nonlinear function has good algebraic immunity and when its parameter d is close to the parameter K and they have moderate values, (iii) the inputs from LFSR to the nonlinear filter are partially concentrated.

References

1. P. Camion, M.J. Mihaljević and H. Imai, "Two alerts for design of certain stream ciphers: Trapped LFSR and weak resilient function over GF(q)", SAC2002, *Lecture Notes in Computer Science*, vol. 2595, pp. 196-213, Feb. 2003.
2. P. Chose, A. Joux and M. Mitton, "Fast correlation attacks: An algorithmic point of view", EUROCRYPT 2002, *Lecture Notes in Computer Science*, vol. 2332, pp. 209-221, 2002.
3. N.T. Courtois, "Higher order correlation attacks, XL algorithm and cryptanalysis of Toyocrypt", ICISC2002, *Lecture Notes in Computer Science*, vol. 2587, pp. 182-199, 2003.
4. N.T. Courtois and W. Meier, "Algebraic attacks on stream ciphers with linear feedback", EUROCRYPT2003, *Lecture Notes in Computer Science*, vol. 2656, pp. 345-359, 2003.
5. N.T. Courtois, "Fast algebraic attacks on stream ciphers with linear feedback", CRYPTO2003, *Lecture Notes in Computer Science* vol. 2729, pp. 176-194, 2003.
6. J.-Ch. Faugere and G. Ars. "An algebraic cryptanalysis of nonlinear filter generators using Grobner bases". Available on the web, 2003. http://www.inria.fr/rrrt/rr-4739.html.
7. P. Hawkes and G. Rose, "Rewriting variables: the complexity of Fast algebraic attacks on stream ciphers", CRYPTO 2004, *Lecture Notes in Computer Science*, vol. 3152, pp. 390-406, 2004.
8. A.J. Menezes, P.C. van Oorschot, and S.A. Vanstone, *Handbook of Applied Cryptography*. CRC Press: Boca Raton, FL, 1997.
9. W. Meier, E. Pasalic and C. Carlet, "Algebraic attacks and decomposition of Boolean functions", EUROCRYPT 2004, *Lecture Notes in Computer Science*, vol. 3027, pp. 474-491, 2004.
10. M.J. Mihaljević and H. Imai, "Cryptanalysis of TOYOCRYPT-HS1 stream cipher", *IEICE Transactions on Fundamentals*, vol. E85-A, pp. 66-73, Jan. 2002.
11. M.J. Mihaljević and R. Kohno, "Cryptanalysis of fast encryption algorithm for multimedia FEA-M", *IEEE Communications Letters*, vol. 6, pp. 382-384, Sept. 2002.
12. M.J. Mihaljević, M.P.C. Fossorier and H. Imai, "Fast correlation attack algorithm with list decoding and an application", FSE2001, *Lecture Notes in Computer Science*, vol. 2355, pp. 196-210, 2002.

Non-randomness of the Full 4 and 5-Pass HAVAL*

Hirotaka Yoshida[1,2], Alex Biryukov[2], Christophe De Cannière[2,**],
Joseph Lano[2,***], and Bart Preneel[2]

[1] Systems Development Laboratory,
Hitachi, Ltd., 292 Yoshida-cho,
Totsuka-ku, Yokohama, 244-0817, Japan
[2] Katholieke Universiteit Leuven,
Dept. ESAT/SCD-COSIC Kasteelpark Arenberg 10,
B-3001 Leuven-Heverlee, Belgium
{hyoshida, abiryuko, cdecanni, jlano, preneel}@esat.kuleuven.ac.be

Abstract. HAVAL is a cryptographic hash function proposed in 1992 by Zheng, Pieprzyk and Seberry. Its structure is quite similar to other widely used hash functions such as MD5 and SHA-1. The specification of HAVAL includes a security parameter: the number of passes (that is, the number of times that a particular word of the message is used in the computation) which can be chosen equal to 3, 4 or 5. In this paper we cryptanalyze the compression functions of the 4-pass and the 5-pass HAVAL using differential cryptanalysis. We show that each of these two functions can be distinguished from a truly random function.

1   Introduction

A hash function is a cryptographic algorithm that takes input strings of arbitrary (or very large) length and maps these to short fixed length output strings. HAVAL is a cryptographic hash function proposed in 1992 by Zheng, Pieprzyk and Seberry [18]. Its structure is quite similar to other widely used hash functions such as MD5 [14] and SHA-1 [16]. It uses rotations, modular additions, and highly non-linear boolean functions. HAVAL operates in so called passes, where each pass consists of 32 steps. The recommended number of passes are 3, 4 and 5. Thus 3, 4 and 5 pass HAVAL would have 96, 128 and 160 steps (or rounds in block-cipher terminology) respectively. The hash value calculated by HAVAL is 256 bits long.

---

* This work was supported in part by the Concerted Research Action (GOA) Mefisto-2000/06 of the Flemish Government.
** F.W.O. Research Assistant, the Fund for Scientific Research – Flanders (Belgium).
*** Research financed by a Ph.D. grant of the Institute for the Promotion of Innovation through Science and Technology in Flanders (IWT-Vlaanderen).

C. Blundo and S. Cimato (Eds.): SCN 2004, LNCS 3352, pp. 324–336, 2005.
© Springer-Verlag Berlin Heidelberg 2005

In the case of HAVAL, several articles demonstrated collisions for the reduced 2-pass variants [10, 13, 8]. Recently, an efficient algorithm constructing collisions for the full 3-pass HAVAL has been described in [15]. The attack has a complexity of 2^{29} steps and requires a negligible amount of memory. However no weaknesses in the 4 and 5-pass HAVAL have been demonstrated so far.

In this paper we show a cryptanalysis of HAVAL in the cases where the number of passes equals the maximal security values: 4 and 5. Our analysis leads to an attack that detects the non-randomness of the 4-pass and the 5-pass HAVAL in encryption mode. We show how to distinguish the compression function of the 4 and 5-pass HAVAL from a random permutation. For convenience, we discuss the security of HAVAL focusing on the 4-pass version. Our discussion is easily extended to the 5-pass version. The security of the 4 and 5-pass HAVAL in hash mode remains an open problem.

The outline of this paper is as follows. In Section 2, we give a brief description of the HAVAL algorithm published in [18]. In Section 3, we present our differential attack on the HAVAL compression function used in encryption mode. We also discuss the practical implementation issues of our attack. In Section 4 we give experimental results. We conclude in Section 5.

2   Description of the HAVAL Hash Function

In this section, we give a brief description of the HAVAL hash function, which is sufficient to understand the concepts introduced in this paper. For a full description of HAVAL we refer to [18].

HAVAL is a hash function that is based on the well-known Davies-Meyer construction of hash functions ([12], p. 341). The variable-length message M is divided into 1024-bit blocks $M_0, M_1, \ldots, M_{n-1}$. The 256-bit hash value V_n is then computed as follows:

$$V_0 = IV; \ V_{j+1} = \texttt{compress}(V_j, M_j) = E(V_j, M_j) + V_j \ for \ 0 \le j < n,$$

where compress is the compression function, IV is a fixed initial value and E is a block cipher. As a block cipher E, one could choose either a known block cipher or a dedicated design. HAVAL chooses the latter option. The function E is an iterated design that only uses simple operations on 32-bit words. The 256-bit input V_j is loaded into 8 registers (A, B, C, D, E, F, G, H) and the 1024-bit message block is divided into 32 words of 32 bits $(X_0 \ldots X_{31})$.

The 8 registers are updated through a number of steps. One step of the compression function is depicted in Fig. 1. The HAVAL compression function consists of 96, 128 or 160 consecutive steps. Each sequence of 32 steps is grouped together into a pass, so that we say that HAVAL is 3,4 or 5-pass. In each pass, every word X_i is used exactly once. Every pass r has its own Boolean function f_r, 32 constants K_i, and a specified order in which the 32 words X_i are processed.

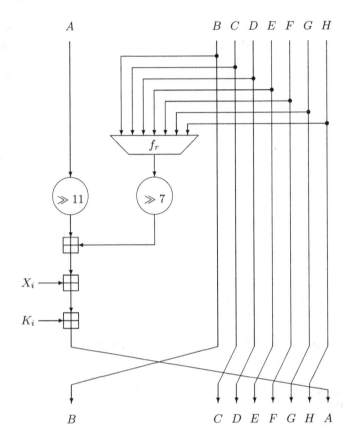

Fig. 1. One step of the compression function of HAVAL

3   Differential Cryptanalysis of the 4-Pass HAVAL in Encryption Mode

In this section, we will explain the HAVAL hash function in encryption mode in Section 3.1 and will study known attacks on the reduced 2-pass and the full 3-pass HAVAL in Section 3.2. We will present a differential cryptanalysis to find a weakness in the 4-pass HAVAL in Section 3.3 and provide solutions to the problems in its implementation in Section 3.4.

3.1   Cryptanalysis of Hash Functions in Encryption Mode

As mentioned above, one could construct a hash function from a block cipher using the Davies-Meyer construction. Inversely, one can construct a block cipher which is the HAVAL compression function with Davies-Meyer chaining peeled off. In the cipher, the message block M_j is viewed as the key, the chaining variable V_j acts as the plaintext block and $V_{j+1} = E(V_j, M_j)$ is the corresponding ciphertext block. In general, the block cipher constructed from a hash function in such a way is called a hash function in encryption mode.

We will analyze the 4-pass HAVAL in encryption mode. Such an analysis provides a better understanding of the strength of the HAVAL compression function. Our method can be easily extended to the 5-pass version.

Several cryptanalytic techniques ranging from differential cryptanalysis [1] to slide attacks [2] have been applied to study the security of well-known hash functions in encryption mode. For example, differential cryptanalysis of SHA-1 has been shown in [7]. A slide attack on SHA-1 and an attack on MD5 which finds one high-probability differential characteristic were given in [17].

Throughout this paper we will use the notion of a "step", as defined in the specification of HAVAL, instead of the block-cipher notion – "round". We will also use the notion of a "pass", which stands for 32 steps as explained above.

3.2   Known Attacks on the Reduced 2-Pass and the Full 3-Pass HAVAL

In this section we review the previously known attacks which find collisions for the reduced 2-pass and the full 3-pass HAVAL and explain why the techniques in these attacks are not applicable to the 4-pass HAVAL.

The main idea in all the attacks of finding a collision is that the attacker uses the simplicity of the message schedule that allows him to control over the differences in the 8 registers. What is used is a pair of message whose difference with Hamming weight one is in exactly one message word. The difference in the message word is injected into registers at exactly one step in each pass.

In the attacks on the reduced 2-pass HAVAL which have two passes out of three, the difference injections explained above happen at two steps [10, 13]. In between the two steps the difference in registers propagates. A differential propagation is found by applying the algebraic technique which is building a system of equations and solving it. The difference becomes zero at the last step in the propagation which means that a collision is found. When build the system, it is important to choose which message word have the difference. A good choice makes it possible for the difference in the registers to propagate for the small number of steps (e.g. 10), which allows the number of equations in the system to be small.

In the attack on the full 3-pass HAVAL, the algebraic technique as above is also applied [15]. The problem with this case is that the difference in the message word is injected into registers at three steps, such as 28, 38, and 69. The attack solves this problem by combining the algebraic technique and differential cryptanalysis. From step 28 to 38 the algebraic technique is applied to find an inner almost collision, which means a pair of values in registers which differs only in the small number of bit positions and then from step 39 to 69 a differential cryptanalysis is to find a differential propagation with a high probability, 2^{-29} such that the difference is zero at the last step of the propagation. The attack indicates a weakness in the compression function against differential cryptanalysis.

In case of the full 4-pass HAVAL, we tried to apply the same strategy as the case of the full 3-pass, however it was turned out to be difficult to find an inner almost collision by applying the algebraic technique. This is due to the fact that the different order of processing message words from the order in the case of 3-pass makes the system of equation more difficult to solve. Even if an inner almost collision is constructed, a differential cryptanalysis has to solve the problem of finding a differential propagation of many steps (typically, 65) with 3 time difference injection into the registers due to the message schedule, which is very difficult for the attacker to control over differences with a high probability. That is because the registers which the differences are injected from the message schedule into are not always as the attacker wants. We consider that it is easier to analyze the cipher in encryption mode where the differences in the register can be directly controlled than to do the cipher in hash mode where they can be controlled only through the message schedule. This observation above leads us to enhance differential cryptanalysis, instead of applying the algebraic technique, to find a weakness in the cipher in encryption mode.

3.3   Differential Cryptanalysis of the 4-Pass HAVAL

The technique of differential cryptanalysis has first been described in [1]. The aim of the approach is to find differential characteristics for the whole cipher. In [1], a differential characteristic is defined in the following:

Definition 1. *Associated with any pair of encryptions are the difference of its two plaintexts, the differences of its ciphertexts, the differences of the inputs of each round in the two executions and the differences of the outputs of each round in the two executions. These differences form an n-round characteristic. A characteristic has a probability, which is the probability that a random pair with the chosen plaintext difference has the round and ciphertext differences specified in the characteristic.*

In differential cryptanalysis, two difference operations are often used: $\Delta(X, X') = X \oplus X'$, $\Delta(X, X') = X - X'$. We will consider both cases in our cryptanalysis.

The strategy to perform the differential cryptanalysis can be mainly divided into two parts: In the first part we divide the function into several consecutive sub-functions and try to find differential characteristics with high probability for these sub-functions. In our analysis, each sub-function will consist of several steps in a certain pass. Hence all steps in such a sub-function will use the same non-linear Boolean function. In the second part the differential characteristics for each sub-function are concatenated so that they cover the whole cipher. However, it is difficult to do the second part of the analysis when the characteristics obtained in the first part have complicated forms. For instance, this is the case for SHA-1. In this paper, we present a method to solve this difficulty by combining these two parts into a single part.

The theoretical background of this method is the theory of Markov ciphers and their connection to differential cryptanalysis introduced by Lai *et al.* in [11]. For an iterated cipher E with the function $Y = T(X, Z)$ which takes the plaintext input as X, the subkey input as Z, we denote the conditional probability that β is the difference $\Delta Y(i)$ of the ciphertext pair after i steps of S, given that α is the difference of the plaintext pair, by $P(\Delta Y(i) = \beta | \Delta X = \alpha)$.

Recall that a sequence of discrete random variables $v_0, v_1, \ldots, v_r$ is a *Markov chain* if, for $0 \le i \le r$,

$$P(v_{i+1} = \beta_{i+1} | v_i = \beta_i, v_{i-1} = \beta_{i-1}, \ldots, v_0 = \beta_0) = P(v_{i+1} = \beta_{i+1} | v_i = \beta_i).$$

A Markov chain is called *homogenous* if $P(v_{i+1} = \beta | v_i = \alpha)$ is independent of i for all α and β. A Markov cipher is defined as follows:

Definition 2. *An iterated cipher with the function T is a Markov cipher if for all choices of α and β,*

$$P(\Delta Y = \beta | \Delta X = \alpha, X = \gamma)$$

is independent of γ when the subkey is uniformly random.

We now state the following theorem using our notation.

Theorem 1. *If an r-step iterated cipher is a Markov cipher and the r step keys are independent and uniformly random, then the sequence of differences $\Delta X = \Delta Y(0), \ldots, \Delta Y(r) = \Delta Y$, is a homogenous Markov chain.*

In the case of HAVAL, we denote 8 consecutive steps[1] of E by T. We assume that the cipher E, obtained by iterating T, is a Markov cipher. This allows us to search for differentials rather than characteristics. The goal of our attack is to find a high probability differential for the 4-pass and the 5-pass HAVAL.

Our goal is to study differential properties of the 4-pass HAVAL. We will consider low Hamming weight differentials and their propagation: we study the behavior of the 4-pass HAVAL compression function when we apply input differentials of weight 1 and 2. At the output, we only observe output differentials of weight 1 and 2. We will check whether these observations are in accordance with the randomness criteria we would expect from a cryptographic hash function.

Let $\mathcal{A}$ be the set of all the bit strings of length 256:

$$\mathcal{A} = \{0, 1\}^{256}.$$

Let $\mathcal{B}$ be the subset of $\mathcal{A}$ where each element has Hamming weight equal to 1:

$$\mathcal{B} = \{\Delta \in \mathcal{A} | Ham(\Delta) = 1\}.$$

Let $\mathcal{C}$ be the subset of $\mathcal{A}$ where each element has Hamming weight equal to 2:

$$\mathcal{C} = \{\Delta \in \mathcal{A} | Ham(\Delta) = 2\}.$$

---

[1] A single step of HAVAL is clearly a bad candidate for T since only one 32-bit word changes per step and only one 32-bit word of key-material is mixed in.

Let $\mathcal{D}$ be the union set of $\mathcal{B}$ and $\mathcal{C}$:

$$\mathcal{D} = \mathcal{B} \cup \mathcal{C}.$$

Let $\mathcal{E}$ be a set of integers where each element is greater than 0 and is less than or equal to the size of $\mathcal{D}$:

$$\mathcal{E} = \{1, 2, \ldots, 2^8 + \frac{2^8 \cdot (2^8 - 1)}{2}\}.$$

Using the first consecutive 8 steps in the s-th pass, we build a matrix M_s. To do so, we first define a function g mapping $\mathcal{D}$ to $\mathcal{E}$ in the following manner. If $\Delta \in \mathcal{B}$, let k be the position of 1 in Δ. Otherwise, let h be the high position of 1 in Δ and let l be the low position of 1 in Δ. The function g is defined as follows:

$$g(\Delta) = \begin{cases} k - 1 & \Delta \in \mathcal{B} \\ h - l - 1 + \sum_{i=0}^{l-1}(256 - i) & \Delta \in \mathcal{C}. \end{cases}$$

It is easy to see that g is bijective. The aim of the function g is to establish an ordering for the elements of $\mathcal{D}$.

Now, let's denote the function which consists of the first consecutive 8 steps in the s-th pass as T_s. To construct a matrix M_s, we randomly choose a (sufficiently large) subset R of $\mathcal{A}$. The cardinality of the subset R is denoted by $\#R = r$. For i and j in $\mathcal{E}$, we define each entry $a_{ij}^{(s)}$ in the matrix M_s as follows:

$$a_{ij}^{(s)} = \frac{\#\{p \in R | g^{-1}(j) = \Delta(T_s(p), T_s(\Delta(p, g^{-1}(i))))\}}{r}.$$

The entry $a_{ij}^{(s)}$ estimates the probability of the differential where the input difference is $g^{-1}(i)$ and the output difference is $g^{-1}(j)$. We assume that one pass of HAVAL behaves as a 4-round Markov cipher with T_s as the round transformation[2]. Thus the matrix M_s is a transition matrix of the corresponding Markov chain. Raising this matrix to the fourth power as M_s^4 allows us to see the probabilities of 32-step differentials for the s-th pass. Calculating the composition $\mu = \mu_4^4 \circ \mu_3^4 \circ \mu_2^4 \circ \mu_1^4$ allows us to see the differential structure of the 4-pass HAVAL, where the function μ_s is defined by a matrix multiplication as $\mu_s(X) = X \cdot M_s$. For example, we can see high probability differentials for the whole cipher. What is of most interest now is the highest value in the matrix $M = \mu(I)$. This highest value corresponds to a particular low-weight differential which has a high probability.

The approach described here has several complications with respect to a memory-efficient and fast implementation, which we will now explain into more detail.

---

[2] Our experiments indicate that this assumption is reasonable. The ten best differentials for 16 steps produced by experiment and the ten best differentials computed via M_s^2 were at most a factor 1.28 apart. Also some variation across the different keys has been observed.

3.4   Implementing the Matrices M_s and Their Multiplication

We had to resolve some implementation issues for the $N \times N$ matrix M_s. The value of N is quite large:

$$N = 2^8 + \frac{2^8 \cdot (2^8 - 1)}{2} \approx 2^{15},$$

If we implement the matrix M_s as such, the required memory size is $8 \cdot 2^{30} \approx 8GB$ when using 64-bit variables to represent each element of M_s. This is quite large and not efficient at all. Simulations show that the matrix M_s is very sparse: Because of the diffusion of T_s, the hamming weight of the output differences are very likely to be more than 2 and thus most output differences will be discarded in our approach. And those that do have a Hamming weight of at most 2 only occur in a limited number of places in the matrix. This helps us for the efficient implementation. The number of nonzero entries of a row in a matrix is typically 100 but we make the number a parameter, namely d, which is useful as will be shown. For each row, we will now only store the nonzero entries, together with the column in which this nonzero entry occurs. Furthermore, we also store the row itself for each row. This is useful to reduce the time complexity which will be explained later. Every non-zero $a_{ij}^{(s)}$ in the M_s is stored as a triplet $(i, j, a_{ij}^{(s)})$ in its implementation. In that case, the memory complexity is only $2^{15} \cdot d \cdot (2 + 2 + 8) \approx 5MB$ when using 16-bit variables to represent each row i and column j.

In order to implement the multiplication of the two matrices M_s, we have to implement one matrix M_s as a list of rows and the other matrix as a list of columns. The representation of M as a list of columns can be easily obtained from the representation as a list of rows by a straightforward and efficient transposition algorithm. In addition to the memory for the two lists, the memory for the product matrix is allocated. However, we have a problem with the memory for the product matrix after one multiplication. A theoretical estimation shows that about 26% of the entries in the product matrix will be non-zero, which was confirmed by our experiments. This means that the product matrix is not sparse any more. This motivates the following idea of pruning the matrix. After the generations or multiplications of the matrix M_s, we only keep high-value entries in M_s, cutting the entries below a fixed low value q. To obtain a high probability for the whole cipher, it is sufficient to obtain high probabilities after every 8 steps. This also motivates the idea of pruning. We now keep the matrix sparse all the steps. Taking into account that the multiplications can be done on the fly, the memory complexity of computing the matrix M for the whole cipher is $15MB$.

The time complexity of generating the matrix M_s can be shown to be $r \cdot 2^{16}$ computations of T_s. When we take r equal to 2^{20} (which seems to be enough to obtain a matrix with sufficient statistical significance), this results in a time complexity of 2^{36} computations of T_s. As for the multiplication of the matrices, we can find a fast implementation. As mentioned above, the matrix M_s is implemented as an array with dimension two where each element is a triplet

$(i, j, a_{ij}^{(s)})$. If the matrix is sorted by the first element and afterwards by the second element in the triplets, then it can be implemented as an array with dimension one. Now all we have to do is the multiplication of two sorted arrays with dimension one. In this case, the multiplication of the matrices has a time complexity of $N \cdot d = 2^{15} \cdot 100 \approx 2^{21.6}$ computations, each of which is a few of multiplications and additions of two 64-bit variables. Note that this significantly reduces the number of computations of entries during the multiplication of the matrices hence is much faster than straightforward implementation which has a time complexity $N^2 \cdot d^2 \approx 2^{43.3}$. To compute the matrix M for the whole cipher requires the generations of the matrix M_s 5 times and the multiplication of matrices 15 times. Taking into account their time complexities and what is done during one computation in each case, the time complexity in total is dominated by the former, which is 2^{38} computations of T.

4   Experimental Results

We report some experimental results which we obtained by using the techniques described above. In our experiments, we used the reference implementation of HAVAL available at [9] and the cut-away value q in Section 3.4 is set to be 2^{-12}. Since different passes use different non-linear functions, it is interesting to see the differential structure for each of the 4 different passes. Therefore we search for the best probability over 8 and 32 steps in the s-th pass.

Before doing that, we need some preparation. We focus on the observation of 8 steps to see whether the experimental results are stable. That is very important: if the results were not stable yet, the error will be amplified due to the multiplication of matrices. Our simulations convincingly showed that increasing the number of plaintexts r to 2^{20} is sufficient in order to obtain precise experimental results.

Table 1. The best probability for 8 steps in the case of $\Delta(X, X') = X \oplus X'$

	$r = 2^{16}$	$r = 2^{20}$	$r = 2^{24}$
$s = 1$	$2^{-5.916521}$	$2^{-5.992885}$	$2^{-5.996883}$
$s = 2$	$2^{-6.947432}$	$2^{-7.023257}$	$2^{-7.009951}$
$s = 3$	$2^{-6.969333}$	$2^{-6.996482}$	$2^{-6.992622}$
$s = 4$	$2^{-6.594859}$	$2^{-6.660011}$	$2^{-6.677051}$

Table 1 presents a typical experimental results that we observed for the 4-Pass HAVAL. It shows the measured probability for 8 steps for each of the 4 passes, and this for increasing samples r. As a difference function we used $\Delta(X, X') = X \oplus X'$. Note that in the above experiment, we consider the input difference $\Delta_{in} \in \mathcal{B}$ to make it feasible in terms of time complexity to obtain the result for r equal to 2^{24}. However, in all the following experiments we will use the entire set $\mathcal{D}$.

Table 2. The best probability for 8 and 32 steps in the case of $\Delta(X, X') = X \oplus X'$

	8 steps	32 steps
$s = 1$	$2^{-5.992885}$	$2^{-26.670829}$
$s = 2$	$2^{-7.023257}$	$2^{-30.992364}$
$s = 3$	$2^{-6.996482}$	$2^{-30.908851}$
$s = 4$	$2^{-6.660011}$	$2^{-29.360996}$

Table 2 shows the best probability of a differential characteristic for all 4 passes ($s = 1, 2, 3, 4$), and this both for 8 steps and 32 steps. In these experiments we used 2^{20} as a value for r, and again used the difference function $\Delta(X, X') = X \oplus X'$.

For both the 4-pass and the 5-pass HAVAL, we can now calculate the best probability with which all the differential characteristics we consider by computing the matrix M in Section 3 in which the highest entry is the best probability. We learn from Section 3 that it is practical to compute the matrix M because the time complexity is 2^{38} computations of 8 steps and the memory complexity is $15MB$.

The result is that the best probability is 2^{-125} for the 4-pass HAVAL and 2^{-168} for the 5-pass HAVAL. Each of these two probabilities is much greater than the probability 2^{-256} that we would expect from a truly random hash function. This means that both the 4-pass and the 5-pass HAVAL have a significant weakness of randomness.

Taking into account that each of these our results has been obtained with a fixed randomly chosen key, there could be an occupancy problem if our results are affected by the choice of the key. There are two points to be stressed:

For the full 4 and 5-Pass HAVAL we fix both the input and the output differences. Thus occupancy is not a problem there. On the other hand we gather probabilities for the matrix M by experiment, so we could potentially experience occupancy problem, which would result in slightly higher key-dependent probabilities.

We carried out some experiments for the 8 steps of each pass which show that probabilities collected for the matrix M are not key-dependent and hold on average. We encrypted 2^{20} plaintext pairs to check that results of Table 2 for 8 steps remain the same for 5 different keys $K_1, K_2, \cdots, K_5$. The following table 3 shows the best probabilities over different keys. The table 3 shows that results of Table 2 for 8 steps remain the same for these keys, which means the best probabilities are not affected by the choice of the key.

Next we consider not only the probabilities and but also their pairs of input difference and output difference to see if the differential structure of 8 steps is affected by the choice of the key. In fact, in the case of the 2nd pass, the best probabilities in the table 3 are achieved at exactly the same pair of input difference and output difference. In the cases of the other passes, the best probabilities in the table 3 are achieved at several different pairs of input and output differences. Therefore we present for each pass, the probabilities over different keys

Table 3. The best probabilities over different keys

Key	1st pass	2nd pass	3rd pass	4th pass
K_1	$2^{-5.992885}$	$2^{-7.012381}$	$2^{-6.972267}$	$2^{-6.647129}$
K_2	$2^{-5.979194}$	$2^{-6.977285}$	$2^{-6.997537}$	$2^{-6.651963}$
K_3	$2^{-5.974168}$	$2^{-6.980409}$	$2^{-7.007947}$	$2^{-6.668383}$
K_4	$2^{-5.984237}$	$2^{-6.979541}$	$2^{-7.005823}$	$2^{-6.676664}$
K_5	$2^{-5.990521}$	$2^{-6.983540}$	$2^{-6.972958}$	$2^{-6.682163}$

Table 4. The high probabilities at the same pair of input difference and output difference for each pass

Key	1st pass	2nd pass	3rd pass	4th pass
K_1	$2^{-5.992885}$	$2^{-7.012381}$	$2^{-6.972267}$	$2^{-6.647129}$
K_2	#$2^{-5.997537}$	$2^{-6.977285}$	#$2^{-7.010606}$	$2^{-6.651963}$
K_3	$2^{-5.974168}$	$2^{-6.980409}$	#$2^{-7.009896}$	#$2^{-6.687684}$
K_4	#$2^{-5.988511}$	$2^{-6.979541}$	$2^{-7.005823}$	#$2^{-6.686834}$
K_5	#$2^{-6.000352}$	$2^{-6.983540}$	#$2^{-7.015938}$	#$2^{-6.684284}$

at the same pair of input and output difference in the table 4 in which each triplet where the probability is not the best is indicated by #. Fortunately, the probabilities for each pass are very close which means the differential structure of 8 steps is not affected by the choice of the key.

These discussions show that our results hold on average for any key and are not affected by the occupancy problem.

Our method contains multi-paths. This means that various trails exist that go from one input difference to one output difference. Therefore an interesting question is how many multi-paths are included into the best probability. We carried out some experiments with 2^{20} plaintexts and found an answer to the question. The best probability $2^{-124.6}$ with which the input difference e_{160} goes to the output difference e_{176} includes 12 multi-paths. On the other hand, a probability $2^{-125.9}$ with which the input difference e_{139} goes to the output difference e_{155} includes the maximum number of multi-paths observed, 42. For both probabilities above, the input and output difference have Hamming weight 1.

Another point we need to check is which difference notion is most effective in our attack: $\Delta(X, X') = X - X'$ or $\Delta(X, X') = X \oplus X'$. In Table 5, we present the results for the case of the difference operation $\Delta(X, X') = X - X'$, where the number of samples r equals 2^{16}. The table shows the best probability over 8 and 32 steps in the s-th pass for the 4-Pass HAVAL. By comparing this table with Table 2, we can see that the difference operation $\Delta(X, X') = X \oplus X'$ is more effective. One of the possible reasons why this happens is that due to the non-linear function, each step of the 4-Pass HAVAL uses XOR operation 4 to 8 times while it uses arithmetic additions only 3 times. This makes the step function XOR-friendly which means that differences can go though paths with paying relatively small probabilities when using the operation. $\Delta(X, X') = X \oplus X'$.

Table 5. The best probability for 8 and 32 steps in the case of $\Delta(X, X') = X - X'$

	8 steps	32 steps
$s = 1$	$2^{-6.860449}$	$2^{-27.638838}$
$s = 2$	$2^{-7.426353}$	$2^{-34.011164}$
$s = 3$	$2^{-7.642448}$	$2^{-34.337646}$
$s = 4$	$2^{-7.536476}$	$2^{-30.437003}$

Note that these results can not be used immediately to distinguish outputs of the 4-Pass or the 5-Pass HAVAL in hash mode from truly random outputs, though they show a surprising property.

We explain what we have done in details and what we will be able to do for the future research. We limited ourselves to search for all the paths where the differences have a hamming weight less than 3 not only at input and output but also at every 8 steps, which is a strong condition on the paths. It is surprising to find a path with a very good probability under this limited circumstance. This means that we found a probability which is a lower bound for the differentials. It would be interesting to see how high the best probability be when the condition is relaxed. In order to do this, a more efficient algorithm has to be found.

We describe what would be necessary for a hash function which is secure against our attack. One of the necessary conditions to apply our attack is that the weight of a low-weight difference is likely to remain to be low after 8 steps. This is the case for the 4-Pass and the 5-Pass HAVAL. For a hash function with a good diffusion, this is not the case even after a small number of consecutive steps. Our attack is not applicable to such a function.

5   Conclusions

We have analyzed the compression functions of the 4-pass and the 5-pass HAVAL. Surprisingly, our result shows that the use of highly non-linear functions, which is the main focus of the design of HAVAL, does not result in a hash function which is significantly strong against differential cryptanalysis. With our approach, we identified differentials with probabilities $> 2^{-125}$ for the 4-pass HAVAL and $> 2^{-168}$ for the 5-pass HAVAL, which is much higher than the probability 2^{-256} we would expect from a random function.

It is difficult to see if and how the weakness of randomness in the compression function can be exploited to find collisions for the HAVAL hash function. This remains an open problem. The strategy for our attack is quite general so that we can analyze the compression functions of other hash functions with the approach described in this paper.

Acknowledgements

The authors would wish to thank Bart Van Rompay, Antoon Bosselaers, Soichi Furuya, Souradyuti Paul, and several anonymous reviewers for helpful comments and useful discussions.

References

1. E. Biham, A. Shamir, *Differential Cryptanalysis of the Data Encryption Standard*, Springer-Verlag, 1993.
2. A. Biryukov, D. Wagner, *Advanced slide attacks*, Eurocrypt 2000, LNCS 1807, B. Preneel, Ed., Springer-Verlag, pp. 589–606, 2000.
3. B. den Boer, A. Bosselaers, *Collisions for the compression function of MD5*, Eurocrypt 1993, LNCS 765, T. Helleseth, Ed., Springer-Verlag, pp. 293–304, 1993.
4. I. Damgård, *A design principle for hash functions*, Crypto 1989, LNCS 435, G. Brassard, Ed., Springer-Verlag, pp. 416–427, 1990.
5. H. Dobbertin, *The status of MD5 after a recent attack*, Cryptobytes, Vol. 2, No. 2, pp. 1–6, Summer 1996.
6. H. Gilbert, H. Handschuh, *Security Analysis of SHA-256 and Sisters*, SAC 2003, LNCS 3006, M. Matsui, R. Zuccherato, Eds., Springer-Verlag, pp. 175–193, 2004.
7. H. Handschuh, D. Naccache, *SHACAL*, Submission to the NESSIE project, 2000. Available from http://www.gemplus.com/ smart/r_d/publications/pdf/HN00shac.pdf.
8. Y.-S. Her, K. Sakurai, S.-H. Kim, *Attacks for finding collision in reduced versions of 3-pass and 4-pass HAVAL*, International Conference on Computers, Communications and Systems, CE-15, pp. 75–78, 2003.
9. Calyptix Security, *HAVAL source code (reference implementation)*, available at http://www.calyptix.com/downloads.html.
10. P. Kasselman, W. Penzhorn, *Cryptanalysis of reduced version of HAVAL*, Electronics letters, Vol. 36, No. 1, pp. 30–31, January 2000.
11. X. Lai, J. Massey, *Markov Ciphers and Differential Cryptanalysis*, Eurocrypt 1991, LNCS 547, D. Davies, Ed., Springer-Verlag, pp. 17–38, 1991.
12. A. Menezes, P. van Oorschot and S. Vanstone, *Handbook of Applied Cryptography*, CRC Press, 1997.
13. S. Park, S. H. Sung, S. Chee, J. Lim, *On the security of reduced versions of 3-pass HAVAL*, ACISP 2002, LNCS 2384, J. Seberry, L. Batten, Eds., pp. 406–419, 2002.
14. R. Rivest, *The MD5 message-digest algorithm*, Request for Comments (RFC) 1321, Internet Activities Board, Internet Privacy Task Force, April 1992.
15. B. van Rompay, A. Biryukov, B. Preneel, J. Vandewalle, *Cryptanalysis of 3-Pass HAVAL*, Asiacrypt 2003, LNCS 2894, C. Laih, Ed., Springer-Verlag, pp. 228–245, 2003.
16. National Institute of Standards and Technology, FIPS-180-2: *Secure Hash Standard (SHS)*, August 2002.
17. M. Saarinen, *Cryptanalysis of Block Ciphers Based on SHA-1 and MD5*, FSE 2003, LNCS 2887, T. Johansson, Ed., Springer-Verlag, pp. 36–44, 2003.
18. Y. Zheng, J. Pieprzyk, J. Seberry, *HAVAL – a one-way hashing algorithm with variable length of output*, Auscrypt 1992, LNCS 718, J. Seberry, Y. Zheng, Eds., Springer-Verlag, pp. 83–104, 1992.

Controlling Spam by Secure Internet Content Selection

Amir Herzberg

Computer Science Department, Bar Ilan University, Ramat Gan, Israel
herzbea@cs.biu.ac.il
http://AmirHerzberg.com

Abstract. Unsolicited and undesirable e-mail (spam) is a growing problem for Internet users and service providers. We present the Secure Internet Content Selection (SICS) protocol, an efficient cryptographic mechanism for spam-control, based on allocation of responsibility (liability). With SICS, e-mail is sent with a content label, and a cryptographic protocol ensures labels are authentic and penalizes falsely labeled e-mail (spam). The protocol supports trusted senders (penalized by loss of trust) and unknown senders (penalized financially). The recipient can determine the compensation amount for falsely labeled e-mail (spam). SICS is practical, with negligible overhead, gradual adoption path, and use of existing relationships; it is also flexible and appropriate for most scenarios, including deployment by end users and/or ISPs and support for privacy (including encrypted e-mail) and legitimate, properly labeled commercial e-mail. SICS improves on other crypto-based proposals for spam controls, and complements non-cryptographic spam controls.

1 Introduction

E-mail main (and initial) use is professional and personal communication. However, e-mail is very efficient and low-cost; therefore, a growing fraction of e-mail messages contains other types of content, mostly advertisements. Many users, and providers, find themselves wasting substantial resources dealing with such messages, which are often undesired. There are few conventions for identifying advertising or other potentially undesired messages, e.g. prepending the string 'ADV' to the subject line, allowing mail servers and user agents to quickly discard them. Unfortunately, most messages containing potentially-undesired content do not contain appropriate label for the type of content; indeed, the senders often use different evasive techniques to make it hard to distinguish between the messages and desirable professional/personal communication. We use the term spam for messages containing potentially undesirable content, with misleading (or no) label. Spam, and our solution (SICS), apply also to other forms of 'push' content such as pop-up web pages and instant messaging (where spam is sometimes called spim), although we mention mostly e-mail. Spamming wastes considerable machine and human resources - most notably, the recipient's time. Indeed, spamming is reducing the usefulness of e-mail as a communication mechanism these

C. Blundo and S. Cimato (Eds.): SCN 2004, LNCS 3352, pp. 337–350, 2005.

Table 1. Categorization of spam controls by use of cryptography and of trusted entity

	Non-cryptographic spam controls	Cryptographic spam controls
Trust-based spam controls	Unlisted recipient e-mail address	Sender / domain authentication
	Unique unlisted address per sender	Pay to send
	Senders whitelist	Signing e-mail and label
	Caller-ID (source identification)	*Secure Internet Content Selection*
	Senders / domain blacklist	*(SICS)*
Spam controls without any Trusted entity	Heuristic proof of (manual) work	Cryptographic proof of work
	Return address validation	
	Content-based filtering	

days. Many users reduce or avoid using e-mail, most limit the distribution of their e-mail address, and many desirable messages are lost by aggressive (human and automated) filtering. As a result, there are many proposals and mechanisms trying to control and prevent spam; see review in the full version [9].

We categorize spam-controls in Table 1, using two attributes: the use of cryptography, and the use of trust. In particular, spam can be almost completely prevented by accepting only cryptographically-authenticated e-mail from trusted senders. However, this creates three serious problems. The first problem is migration: it is difficult to force all senders to adopt this (or any particular) spam-control measure. The second problem is openness: an important feature of e-mail is that it allows mail from unknown senders, so spam-controls need to allow also mail from untrusted senders. The third problem is efficiency: SMTP and its server implementations are very efficient, allowing reasonably-priced servers to handle large amounts of e-mail; this should be preserved, and cryptographic mechanisms can pose significant processing overhead. As a result of these problems, this extereme form of spam control is impractical. In fact, most existing spam controls avoid relying on cryptography, and many of them avoid the dependency on trusted entities; see Table 1. Unfortunately, all of the previously proposed and existing spam controls are weak, penalize (or charge) senders, or result in loss of universality (openness). SICS uses both cryptography and trusted (third-party) entities, however, it allows universal e-mail and penalizes only spammers.

Our Contributions. The Secure Internet Content Selection (SICS) proposal refines previous spam-control proposals using cryptography and trust (source authentication, pay to send and signing labeled messages). We believe our improvements address the three main concerns regarding the use of trust and cryptography, namely migration, openness and efficiency. In particular, in Section 4 we present a migration plan, providing value to early adopters of SICS. In Section 5 we show how SICS can support unknown, untrusted senders, by forcing spammers to compensate recipients and service providers (and without requiring payments from non-spammers, as in previous proposals [10, 2, 18, 5, 6]).

Content Selection Labels. Like some other recent spam-control proposals [15, 2], SICS focuses on ensuring that messages contain truthful labels.

SICS extends the Platform for Internet Content Selection (PICS) W3C recommendations [12, 11], and could be used to provide improved security for PICS-compliant applications (e.g. browsers limited to 'non-offensive' content, used mostly for children).

1.1   E-Mail Security and Threats

In order to allow secure use of e-mail, several standards and systems offer encryption and source authentication mechanisms for e-mail messages, e.g. S/MIME [13] and PGP [19]. The S/MIME standard is implemented in many e-mail products, and PGP has enjoyed wide recognition and substantial number of installed clients. However, only few e-mail users use these or other cryptographic mechanisms to protect their e-mail messages.

We are especially concerned with the lack of source authentication, which means that spoofing of the identity of the e-mail source (the sender) is trivial. We observe that receivers do not always need to authenticate the identity of the source of e-mail. More frequently, receivers care mostly about the properties of the sender or of a particular message. We focus on identifying and filtering spam - unsolicited and undesirable e-mail, including offensive content, malicious content (e.g. virus) and/or advertising content, when not clearly labeled. We do not consider e-mail messages that contain properly labeled advertising content as spam.

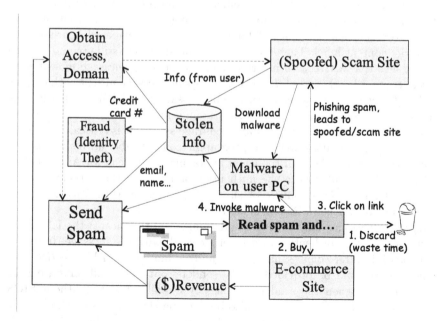

Fig. 1. The Vicious Cycle of Spam

Spam is closely related to other threats to computer security, and in particular to different forms of malicious software ('malware') such as viruses and Trojan horses, and also to spoofed web sites and other online scams. As shown in Figure 1, there is a 'vicious cycle' in which spam plays a central role. For details, see the full version.

2 Secure Internet Content Selection in a Nutshell

We begin by describing the basic operation of the SICS protocol, in typical scenarios after SICS is deployed by both sender and recipient; we later discuss advanced features, including the migration process. Internet content selection involves at least two entities: an originator, e.g. Alice, and a recipient, Bob. Alice sends some content or message m to Bob. To help Bob decide if and how to use m, Alice attach to m a content label l (or rating). Before m reaches Bob, it passes Bob's Content Filter (CF) agent. Bob defines to the Content Filter some policy, specifying acceptable vs. unacceptable content labels; the content filter should discard or retain messages with unacceptable content labels, and deliver to Bob only messages with 'desirable' content labels. The content filter CF may also add some additional label, e.g. classifying messages based on likelihood of being spam.

For simplicity, we assume that all parties agree on a universal mapping ('oracle') *Label* from messages to their 'correct' content labels (extensions to multiple mappings are trivial, e.g. see 'Rating Systems' in PICS). However, content-filtering agents cannot compute *Label* efficiently and precisely (if such an 'ideal' content filtering software is possible, SICS is not needed). The content filter may use some efficient estimate of *Label*, such as content-based heuristics, to confirm the content label. Therefore, the content filter may still err and pass to Bob messages that arrive with incorrect content labels. A message m sent with incorrect content label $l \neq Label(m)$ is called *spam*; message m sent with correct label $l = Label(m)$ is *non-spam*. An e-mail message is unlabeled when it does not contain any content label (i.e., 'legacy' e-mail message).

To encourage correct labeling (and discourage spam), it is critical to endorse the content label, by attaching a cryptographic content label authenticator (or simply authenticator). We call the agent endorsing labels (e.g. for Alice) a Rating Service (RS), and denote the authenticator by A_{RS}; the authenticator is the result of public key signature or shared-key Message Authentication Code (MAC), applied by Alice's Rating Service .

The Rating Service may generate and endorse (authenticate) the label l on its own, or endorse (authenticate) a label received, with the message, from the sender, possibly after some 'sanity check' and/or modification by the RS. The Rating Service could be provided by the sender's outgoing mail server, e.g. to support labeling when the sender runs legacy e-mail software (without SICS support). The Rating Service could also be done on the sender's machine .

Now that we have introduced the sender (Alice or A), recipient (Bob or B), Rating Service (RS) and Content Filter (CF), it may be helpful to refer to

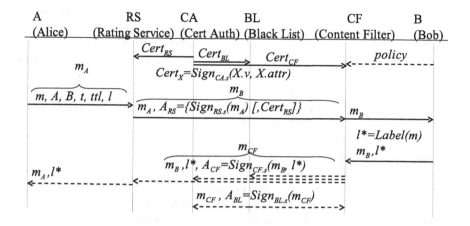

Fig. 2. Overview of the Secure Internet Content Selection (SICS) Protocol

Figure 2, which presents an overview of the Secure Internet Content Selection (SICS) protocol. The BL (black list) and CA (certification authority) parties are optional; and the dashed arrows are used only when a 'false negative' labeled message arrives. Further details follow.

Alice sends to the Rating Service RS the message m, the identities of Alice and Bob (A and B), the current time t, the maximal acceptable delivery time ttl and the content label l. Let m_A denote the set of all the fields sent by Alice, i.e. $m_A = \{m, A, B, t, ttl, l\}$. If the label l or time to live ttl are absent, then the RS adds them (e.g. using default value for l). If l is specified by Alice, then RS may validate it.

The Rating Service RS endorses the label l by attaching to m_A an authenticator A_{RS}. We use the following *notation*: fields (e.g. keys) belonging to a party are denoted by the name of the party followed by dot and the name of the field, e.g. the secret signature key s of RS is denoted by $RS.s$. The authenticator is normally a digital signature by the private signing key $RS.s$ of the RS, plus an (optional) certificate signed by an entity denoted CA (for *certificate authority*), namely: $A_{RS} = \{Sign_{RS.s}(m_A)[, Cert_{RS}]\}$. The certificate of entity X ($X \in \{RS, BL, CF\}$) is a signature by CA over the public signature-validation key $X.v$ of X, together with some attributes $attr$ which CA declares hold for X, such as the identity of X, e.g. $Cert_{RS} = Sign_{CA.s}(RS.v, attr)$.

The RS next sends the complete e-mail message, together with the attached authenticator, to the recipient, using the standard e-mail protocol (SMTP). The RS may also attach to the message its public-key and/or attribute certificates, $Cert_{RS} = Sign_{CA.s}(RS.v, attr)$. The certificate contains the public signature-validation key $RS.v$ of RS, and a list of attributes $attr$ assigned to RS by a Certification/Attribute Authority, which we denote CA. The attributes $attr$ describe properties that CA attributes to RS, and in particular its IP address and domain name, which CF can immediately validate. Other attributes provide information about the trustworthiness of RS, e.g. 'this ISP has been spam-free for the last year', or provide identification information allowing CF to sue RS.

The certificate is needed when the CF does not trust RS. The certificate should convince CF to accept the content labels endorsed by RS. Usually, this implies financial risk to RS if it endorses (authenticates) false labels (spam), and/or compensation to Bob and/or CF.

When Bob receives spam, he should complain and send the correct label $l^* = Label(m)$ to Alice, via CF and RS.

In theory, the rating service RS could eliminate all risk of paying penalties due to having authorized spam (false content labels), simply by (manually) inspecting each message for validating or for assigning it a correct content label. However, this is clearly too expensive (and very intrusive on sender's privacy). Therefore, the rating service RS must manage risk of inadvertently endorsing spam.

To allow the RS to manage this risk, we limit its liability and financial exposure to spam messages identified as such before their time-to-live (ttl) expired. Rating services could use different mechanisms to protect themselves from the risk due to messages whose time-to-live is still valid. This includes (manually) inspecting some messages, i.e. evaluating $Label(m)$, on a random basis (which may be expensive and intrusive), using heuristic approximation of $Label(m)$ and requiring sufficient deposit from the sender (Alice) for compensation in cases of spam.

From discussions with ISPs, it appears that many of them are already using financial penalties to extract damages from spammers, typically by shutting down accounts (and retaining fees). Therefore, such ISPs can easily run a rating service RS charging senders for spam.

Users can bound their liability to damages from spam originating from their accounts, sent by some unauthorized spamming software ('malware' - virus, etc.), e.g. by placing appropriate limits on the total amount of liability in outgoing messages, enforced by their rating service RS.

When detecting a false digitally-signed label, the content filter CF may also send this 'proof of spam' complaint to one or more Black List (BL) servers and/or Certificate Authorities (CA). The Black List servers uses this to create lists of spamming mail servers and rating services; these lists are used to avoid the spammers, by SICS content filters and by legacy mail servers. The Certificate Authorities uses the 'proof of spam' to revoke (or not extend/issue) certificates for non-trustworthy rating services. Both CF and BL also sign these lists; this allows recipients to discard false 'proofs of spam', which may be sent to cause confusion or waste of resources (as a 'Denial of Service (DoS)' attack). The CF and BL may also attach their certificates, and if a particular content filter CF or black list BL sends false reports, then this information could also be distributed by (other) black-list servers as a 'proof of fault', to further reduce the potential for DoS attacks (these mechanisms are not shown in the figure).

3   Secure Content Selection: Design Criteria

We now identify the design criteria and requirements from a secure (internet) content selection solution, roughly in order of (diminishing) importance. For lack of space, this version only lists the criteria:

- Legacy support: no interference with 'legacy' (unlabeled) mail.
- Smooth migration path.
- Minimize manual user work.
- Allow use of existing mail clients, with minimal new UI, and no usage change, including e-mail addresses, e-mail to multiple recipients, and mailing-lists.
- Allow any legitimate content (including explicit advertising and 'potentially offensive' content), on the basis of the recipient-defined policy.
- Easy interoperability across providers.
- Facilitate use of e-mail security and privacy mechanisms (encryption).
- Mail received should conform to the recipient's policy.
- Prevent 'Framing' of conforming participants.
- Allow filtering and rating by intermediate mail servers.
- Limit the damage due to breach of trust.
- Minimal, acceptable overhead in computation, communication, messaging or otherwise.
- Stateless, replicable services/servers.

4   Bootstrapping SICS: Providing Value to Early Adopters

We recommend that SICS server and client deployments would always contain both Rating Service and Content Filter services. This allows any two SICS-enabled parties along the path from sender to recipient, to use SICS rating and content-filter services. In the first and second subsections, we show that even when only a single party along the path from sender to recipient deploys SICS, then there are significant value to this party from SICS. In the third subsection, we explain how a SICS sender and recipient can establish trust, even in the absence of a trusted certification authority.

4.1   Sending SICS-Enabled E-Mail to New or Legacy Recipients

We first consider the scenario where the sender, or the sender's outgoing mail service (usually operated by the sender's ISP), is SICS-enabled, but the recipient may not support SICS. Currently, e-mail clients and ISPs often receive 'spam complaints' from different spam filters and e-mail recipients, containing spam messages sent using the client's e-mail address. However, e-mail source addresses are easy to spoof; it is therefore difficult for the sender, and/or her ISP, to determine whether the complaint is the result of an actual spam sent by the client (possibly by a virus on the client's machine), or the result of a spoofed source address (possibly generated by a virus on another machine). This distinction is important, to warn the client when her computer is infected, and to penalize clients who intentionally (or due to negligence, e.g. virus) send spam.

Similarly, SICS could be used by the recipient's mail server, or by intermediate mail servers, to confirm 'spam complaints' regarding mail sent via the mail server. This allows the mail server to confirm, easily, the mail server from which the spam came, more securely and conveniently than by consulting the content of the complaint and the log files kept by the mail server (which is the current practice). This will allow more accurate black list reporting and other penalty mechanisms, encouraging mail servers to be more careful in preventing spam through them.

Let us consider the case of a SICS-enabled mail server. When the SICS-enabled mail server receives an e-mail message without a SICS label, it attaches a SICS label as a MIME attachment ('part') to it before transferring it toward the recipient. If the original message contained a multipart MIME type, the SICS label is simply added as an additional part of the existing multipart MIME type. Otherwise, when the original message contains only a single (MIME or ASCII) part, then the server transforms the message into multipart MIME and includes the original message as one part, and the SICS label as another part. The SICS label itself consists of the following parts:

1. A simple textual message identifying this as a SICS label and recommending the use of SICS-enabled mail reader.
2. A SICS rating for the content, based on the agreement between the server and the server or client from whom it received the e-mail, and possibly on the result of a content-based filter run by the server. Typically, this will be a basic, broad indicator, e.g. 'no advertisement'.
3. A (possibly compressed) copy of the original message headers, allowing precise identification of the server or client responsible for it. If the server maintains the headers in log files, it may include an appropriate pointer instead of a copy of the headers.
4. Hash values for the two parts above of the SICS label, and for all the other parts in the (original) message.
5. A digital signature over the hash values, using the private signing key of the SICS-enabled server.
6. Optionally, one or more certificates of the server, and/or links to repository containing such certificates.

4.2   SICS Deployed by Recipient or Recipient's Mail Server

Upon initialization, a SICS recipient generates a secret key k for a pseudo-random function f, e.g. implemented by a block cipher such as AES. It then uses this key, to generate pairs $n, f_k(n)$ where n is a unique identifier (counter or random), and f is a pseudo-random function; we refer to such pairs $n, f_k(n)$ as a *SICS ticket*. Then, either Bob himself or Bob's SICS-enabled mail reader can provide a SICS ticket to each new correspondent, typically by encoding it as part of a special e-mail address for Bob, which this sender should use, as in [7]. SICS-enabled senders can use n as an identifier and $f_k(n)$ as a shared key with which they secure initial communication with Bob, as we discuss in the next subsection.

Legacy senders use the SICS ticket as an e-mail address for Bob. RFC822 [14] allows e-mail addresses in the form *phrase* < *addr − spec* >, where *phrase* is any sequence of words, which is forwarded but ignored by the mail servers, and *addr − spec* is the 'simple' e-mail address, e.g. `Bob@mail.org`. Therefore, SICS encodes $n, f_k(n)$ as one or two words in *phrase*. The length of n should suffice to ensure uniqueness, e.g. 32 bits, and the length of $f_k(n)$ should suffice to prevent guessing, e.g. 64 bits; with typical encoding, the length of the resulting SICS ticket phrase is in the order of 20 characters, which seems acceptable for efficiency and ease of use (even for manual typing).

Bob can specify how many messages, and possibly which kind of messages, are allowed from each SICS ticket address (or class of addresses he defined); once receiving spam from an address, it is invalidated and future messages from it are ignored. Or, if Bob still trusts that the sender is not a spammer, and the spam was by someone else (e.g. copied on a note from the sender to Bob), then Bob instructs the SICS-enabled mail reader to generate new ticket $n', f_k(n')$ and send it to the sender.

A SICS-enabled mail reader will normally not pass to Bob messages received without a ticket (or an appropriate SICS-label). Bob may allow some exceptions; in particular, Bob may want to permit incoming messages without a ticket, if the sender address appears in Bob's address book or if Bob earlier sent a message to this sender; usually such 'waiver' will be removed upon identification of spam from this sender. When an incoming message without a SICS label or ticket is blocked, the SICS-enabled mail reader may respond by sending back a SICS ticket' and a request to re-send the message together with the ticket (possibly by hitting 'reply'). This will confirm, at least, that the sender is able to receive e-mail as well as to send e-mail, getting rid of much of the spam (using spoofed source address). Of course, such an address may still belong to a spammer, and Bob's e-mail reader may be more suspicious regarding messages coming from it, e.g. running more critical content-based filter, or restricting the number of such messages delivered to Bob during the same day.

4.3   Establishing 'Web of Anti-spammers', or: Trust Without CA

In the previous two subsections, we argued that SICS may provide some (limited) benefits even if deployed only by a single participant (sender, recipient or mail server) along the e-mail path. In this subsection we consider the case where two (or more) of the participants along the path have installed SICS enabled mail agents. In Section 2, we explained the operation of SICS between a rating service and a content filter that trusts it. We also briefly explained how the content filter can establish trust in an unknown rating service, using a certificate stating that this is a trustworthy non-spammer, from a trusted certification authority. In this subsection we show two methods for the content filter to establish trust in a rating service (or sender), without requiring a trusted certification authority. The first method extends the technique in the previous subsection, namely the use of a per-sender e-mail address for the recipient, , e.g. $<n, f_k(n)>$ Bob@mail.org, where $n, f_k(n)$ is a ticket which the content filter generates using the secret, random key k (and the known pseudo-random function f). As before, the user may transfer the per-sender address (containing the ticket) manually to the sender, e.g. printed on 'customized' business cards. Alternatively, the content filter may send the per-sender e-mail address in e-mail to the sender, possibly with a request to re-send the original message with a SICS label or ticket.

When a SICS Rating Service, run by the sender or ISP, receives an e-mail address $<n, f_k(n)>$ Bob@mail.org containing a SICS ticket, it considers $k' = f_k(n)$ as a shared secret key with the recipient Bob@mail.org; it then uses k' to authenticate the messages (and SICS labels) it sends to Bob, as explained in Section 6.

This simple mechanism allows pairs of SICS-deploying users and ISPs to establish a 'secure pipe' between them, preventing spoofing of e-mail; it therefore allows the content filter to establish more and more trust in the rating service's SICS labels (as long as Bob does not authenticate spam!). In particular, the rating service RS uses k' to authenticate a special SICS message to Bob, containing the public signature-validation key of the rating service $RS.v$, authenticated by a message authentication code $MAC_{k''}(RS.v)$ using key k'' derived from k' as in Section 6. This allows Bob to gain trust in $RS.v$. This can be useful if the rating service RS, e.g. owned by Alice, starts using another client, to which she transfers her private key but not the shared secret key.

In the full version, we explain how to extend this mechanism, and create a 'PGP-like' web of trust [19] allowing automated, secure establishment of trust in SICS labels between individuals, building on the existing social networks connecting them.

5   No Free Spam

If SICS is used in countries with appropriate digital signature laws, then Bob or CF may be able, in principle, to sue RS for damages due to spam (falsely) endorsed with false label by RS. However, this process is usually impractical or impossible. In this subsection, we explain how to automate the compensation for spam to the content filter and recipient, by using guaranteed-payment authorities and certificates.

A *guaranteed-payment certificate authority (GPCA)* is a special kind of CA, which CF trusts, to make payments per an agreement between them. This implies that CF could trust ratings signed by $GPCA$. However, if the $GPCA$ has to handle and sign every message, this would cause substantial processing overhead and delay. We prefer a solution where $GPCA$ is involved only in exceptional situations, mainly when RS endorses falsely labeled e-mail (spam).

Therefore, we propose that $GPCA$ is contacted only once per period by RS, as a special kind of certificate/attribute authority. However, CF and $GPCA$ must first establish an agreement, allowing CF to 'honor' certificates signed by $GPCA$ (knowing that $GPCA$ will compensate it for spam). The agreement identifies the following fields:

1. An identifier ('account') for CF, denoted $CF.id$, which rating services must include explicitly in the (signed) label; this ensures that CF cannot ask for compensation for messages not endorsed specifically for it.
2. A public signature-validation key $GPCA.v$ of $GPCA$. This allows validation of signatures by the $GPCA$ (on certificates to rating services RS).
3. A non-negative 'compensation amount function' caf, whose input is the label l sent with the email m, and the correct label $Label(m)$; and where for every label l holds $caf(l, l) = 0$.
4. A period during which this agreement holds and a maximal amount of compensation by $GPCA$ to CF for false negative ratings, over the entire period. This allows $GPCA$ to control its risks due to an agreement, similarly to the use of the ttl field with messages (to control the risks of the rating service).
5. An agreement identifier $agreement.ID$, which RS includes in the (signed) labels for which this agreement applies. This allows $GPCA$ to use multiple agreements concurrently with CF, e.g. to handle the case where one agreement expires or when the maximal amount of compensation in it is reached.

The process of sending e-mail with guaranteed-payment certificates is quite similar to the process described in Section 2, when RS attaches a certificate from a 'regular' certificate authority CA. Namely, RS attaches to the message a certificate $Cert_{RS} = Sign_{GPCA.s}(RS.v, attr)$. However, we have some specific requirements from the attributes $attr$ in the certificate. In particular, $attr$ must indicate the identity and/or public key of CF, i.e. $CF.id$ and/or $CF.v$, a maximal liability amount per validity period and a validity period. The rating service RS should also include in the authenticator $A_{RS} = Sign_{RS.s}(m_A)$, or simply in the label l (which is part of m_A), the values of $CF.id$ and $CF.v$. We also assume that labels are unique (if necessary, add a serial number), to prevent 'double deposits'.

In this solution, $GPCA$ needs the ability to transfer money from RS to CF. This may be simple, e.g. by requiring RS to deposit an amount with $GPCA$. However, to support interoperability on a global scale, we need to consider the case where there is no long-term, direct trust relationship between $GPCA$ and RS. We can solve this if $GPCA$ has long-term trust relationship with some other guaranteed payment authority $GPCA'$, which has trust relationship with RS. Namely, $GPCA'$ makes an agreement a' with $GPCA$, who uses this to make appropriate agreement with CF. This extends efficiently, allowing an arbitrarily long 'chain of trust' between guaranteed-payment service providers, linking the rating service RS and the content filtering service CF. For details, see the 'payment routing protocol' of [8].

The guaranteed payment services allow SICS to provide another useful service, namely monetary compensation to recipients and processors of properly marked (commercial) e-mail messages. Some legitimate, respectable corporations may be interested in such a mechanism, whereby they pay a small, predefined amount to the recipients of their advertisements and/or to the mail servers involved in processing them. Moreover, guaranteed-payment services may be useful for other payment applications, unrelated to e-mail, e.g. person to person payments and micropayments; see [8].

6   Supporting Confidential (Encrypted) Messages

There are two ways to support encrypted messages. In the first option, we use the following property of all practical public key (and hybrid) cryptosystems: decryption recovers the randomness used during encryption, i.e. $D_{B.d}(E_{B.e}(p,r)) = (p,r)$. The message m includes the public encryption key, i.e. $m = E_{B.e}(p,r)||B.e$ (the RS authenticates also the public encryption key, preventing key spoofing attacks [1]). The recipient sends the pair (p,r) in the complaint, allowing everybody to validate the plaintext against the label. However, this option requires the third party validating the complaint to be able to encrypt using the same scheme, i.e. to have an implementation of the same cryptosystem. This may sometimes be a problem, e.g. if the parties want to use a proprietary cryptosystem. Also note that this method does not work well for shared key cryptosystems, where (as usually) the same key encrypts many messages, since it requires exposing the key.

The other option allows the use of arbitrary public key encryption and shared key encryption. The sender concatenates to the ciphertext a commitment to the plaintext using a secure commitment scheme, i.e. $m = E_{B.e}(p,r)||commit_{ck}(p)$, where ck is an optional public commitment key. However, this implies that confidentiality depends (also) on the confidentiality of this commitment scheme.

7   Conclusions and Discussion

The Secure Internet Content Selection (SICS) protocol, which we presented in this paper, is a relatively simple cryptographic protocol, which may aid in controlling spam, including different forms of messages sent with undesirable content and with misleading representation and labels. The protocol meets the many design goals presented, and in particular it 'punishes' spammers, or more precisely rating services that endorse messages sent with false, inaccurate or misleading labels. This is important, as usually spammers have a financial incentive, which they may share with seemingly-disinterested rating service, creating an incentive to endorse spam. Recipients, by defining appropriate policies to their content filter, can define an arbitrarily large compensation for spam. In reality, we expect that eventually most ISPs and e-mail client developers will agree on some reasonable default values, e.g. based on the pricing scheme of sending postal letters of different classes and priorities (corresponding to e-mail messages marked with different priorities).

The biggest obstacle to the acceptance of SICS, and many other of the more advanced spam controls, may be the fact that it requires cooperation between (honest) senders and recipients, and/or their mail servers. Indeed, there are many aspects in the design, described in Section 4, which are specifically targeted to support the gradual migration and adaptation, and provide value even to early adopters.

Another significant obstacle may be our requirement of 'punishing' spammers, mainly by financial penalties. This may require modification to the agreements between Internet and e-mail service providers and their customers, especially to ensure a deposit to cover fines for possible future spamming. We believe, however, that this process is inevitable, especially in light of the current insecurity of most computers connected to the Internet these days. Indeed, from discussions with some Internet connectivity providers, it turns out that many of them already apply financial penalties to spammers, typically by closing spamming accounts (with a financial implication).

We also believe that most users will agree to set a reasonable limit for messages sent daily, which translates into limited spamming value and limited damage to the consumers as well as to spam recipients and e-mail servers carrying the spam. In fact, we hope and believe that many users will appreciate the value of becoming aware of a penetration to their computer, by their ISP informing them of spam originating from their computer. Growing user awareness may also result in development and adoption of better computing security mechanisms. In this way, SICS may help reduce the number of insecure computers connected to the Internet, thereby 'breaking' the 'vicious cycle of spam' illustrated in Figure 1. Internet security may further benefit from the message authentication and confidentiality (encryption) facilities, based on SICS mechanisms for establishing shared secret keys between senders and recipients. In particular, this may make it more difficult for e-mail viruses to propagate and will help to prevent other e-mail spoofing, phishing and eavesdropping attacks.

Acknowledgment

The author developed some of the basic ideas in this work together with graduate student Jonathan Levi, at 2002-2003; Ron Rivest encouraged the author to complete the unfinished work following the discussion in [4]. Jonathan also provided helpful comments to this manuscript.

This work benefited from discussions on the cryptography@metzdowd.com mailing list, including different ideas and proposals related and similar to ours, in particular see [4]. Thanks to owner and moderator, Perry Metzger, and the other participants. Special thanks to John Gilmore, whose criticism in [4] was instrumental in improving the design, especially to prevent censorship. Free, uncensored and spam-free communication is important to all of us.

This work was supported in part by National Science Foundation grant NSF CCR 03-14161 and by Israeli Science Foundation grant ISF 298/03-10.5.

References

1. Ross Anderson and Roger Needham. Robustness principles for public key protocols. In Proc. Int'l. Conference on Advances in Cryptology (CRYPTO 95), volume 963 of Lecture Notes in Computer Science, pages 236–247. Springer-Verlag, 1995. http://citeseer.nj.nec.com/article/anderson95robustness.html
2. The Coordinated Spam Reduction Initiative, Microsoft corporation, February 2004.
3. Philip DesAutels (Ed.), Yang-hua Chu, Brian LaMacchia and Peter Lipp, PICS Signed Labels (DSig) 1.0 Specification, W3C Recommendation, http://www.w3.org/TR/REC-DSig-label, May 1998.
4. Victor Duchovni, John Gilmore, Amir Herzberg, Ben Laurie, Perry Metzger and others, messages to the cryptography@metzdowd.com list , January 2004.
5. Cynthia Dwork, Andrew Goldberg and Moni Naor, On Memory-Bound Functions for Fighting Spam, Advances in Cryptology - CRYPTO 2003, LNCS 2729, Springer, 2003, pp. 426-444.
6. Cynthia Dwork and Moni Naor, Pricing via Processing or Combating Junk Mail, Crypto '92, pp.139 - 147, 1992.
7. Eran Gabber, Markus Jakobsson, Yosi Matias, Alain Mayer, Curbing Junk E-Mail via Secure Classification, proceedings of Financial Cryptography, pp. 198-213, Feb. 1998.
8. Amir Herzberg, Micropayments, pp. 245-280, chapter 12 in Payment Technologies for E-Commerce, Editor Prof. Weidong Kou, Springer-Verlag, ISBN 3-540-44007-0, 2003.
9. Amir Herzberg, Controlling spam by secure internet content selection (full version), in preparation.
10. Kevin McCurley, Deterrence Measures for Spam, presented at the RSA Conference, January, 1998.
11. Jim Miller (Ed.), Tim Krauskopf, Paul Resnick and Win Treese, PICS Label Distribution Label Syntax and Communication Protocols Version 1.1, W3C Recommendation, http://www.w3.org/TR/REC-PICS-labels, October 1996.
12. Jim Miller (Ed.), Paul Resnick and David Singer, Rating Services and Rating Systems and Their Machine Readable Descriptions Version 1.1, W3C Recommendation, http://www.w3.org/TR/REC-PICS-services, October 1996.
13. Request for comments 2633, Ramsdell, B., Editor, S/MIME Version 3 Message Specification, June 1999.
14. David Crocker, Request For Comments 822, Standard for the Format of ARPA Internet Text Messages, http://www.ietf.org/rfc/rfc822.txt, August 1982.
15. Vincent Schiavone, David Brussin, James Koenig, Stephen Cobb, Ray Everett-Church, Trusted Email Open Standard - A Comprehensive Policy and Technology Proposal for Email Reform, An ePrivacy Group White Paper, available at http://www.eprivacygroup.net/teos/teos_release.pdf, May, 2003.
16. Alan Schwartz and Simson Garfinkel, Stopping Spam, O'Reilly & Associates 1998.
17. Technical responses to spam, Taughnnock Networks whitepaper, November 2003.
18. An overview of E-Postage, Taughnnock Networks whitepaper, June 2003, Updated February 2004.
19. Phil R. Zimmerman. The Official PGP User's Guide. MIT Press, Boston, 1995.

On Session Identifiers in Provably Secure Protocols

The Bellare-Rogaway Three-Party Key Distribution Protocol Revisited*

Kim-Kwang Raymond Choo, Colin Boyd, Yvonne Hitchcock,
and Greg Maitland

Information Security Research Centre,
Queensland University of Technology,
GPO Box 2434, Brisbane, QLD 4001, Australia
{k.choo, c.boyd,y.hitchcock, g.maitland}@qut.edu.au

Abstract. We examine the role of session identifiers (SIDs) in security proofs for key establishment protocols. After reviewing the practical importance of SIDs we use as a case study the three-party server-based key distribution (3PKD) protocol of Bellare and Rogaway, proven secure in 1995. We show incidentally that the partnership function used in the existing security proof is flawed. There seems to be no way to define a SID for the 3PKD protocol that will preserve the proof of security. A small change to the protocol allows a natural definition for a SID and we prove that the new protocol is secure using this SID to define partnering.

1 Introduction

An important direction in the computational complexity approach for protocol proofs was initiated by Bellare and Rogaway in 1993 with an analysis of a simple two party entity authentication and key exchange protocol [5]. They formally defined a model of adversary capabilities with an associated definition of security, which we refer to as the BR93 model in this paper. Since then, the BR93 model has been further revised several times. In 1995, Bellare and Rogaway analysed a three-party server-based key distribution (3PKD) protocol [6] using an extension to the BR93 model, which we refer to as the BR95 model. The most recent revision to the model was proposed in 2000 by Bellare, Pointcheval and Rogaway [4], hereafter referred to as the BPR2000 model. The proof approach by Bellare *et al.* has been applied to the analysis of public key transport based protocols [9], key agreement protocols [10, 20], password-based protocols [4, 7, 8], conference key protocols [11, 12, 13, 14], and smart card protocols [22].

An important difference between the various models is in the way partner oracles are defined (i.e. the definition of partnership). The BR93 model defines

---

* This work was partially funded by the Australian Research Council Discovery Project Grant DP0345775.

C. Blundo and S. Cimato (Eds.): SCN 2004, LNCS 3352, pp. 351–366, 2005.
© Springer-Verlag Berlin Heidelberg 2005

partnership using the notion of matching conversations, where a conversation is a sequence of messages exchanged between some instances of communicating oracles in a protocol run. Partnership in the BR95 model is defined using the notion of a partner function, which uses the transcript (the record of all SendClient and SendServer oracle queries) to determine the partner of an oracle. The BPR2000 model defines partnership using the notion of session identifiers (SIDs) and it is suggested that SIDs be the concatenation of messages exchanged during the protocol run. We examine partnering in the BR95 model and observe that the specific partner function defined in the proof of security for the 3PKD protocol is flawed. Consequently, the BR95 proof is invalidated, although not irreparably so. More interestingly, we also demonstrate that it does not seem possible to introduce a practical definition of partnership based on SIDs in the 3PKD protocol.

In a real world setting, it is normal to assume that a host can establish several concurrent sessions with many different parties. Sessions are specific to both the communicating parties. In the case of key distribution protocols, sessions are specific to both the initiator and the responder principals, where every session is associated with a unique session key. To model the real world implementation, the most recent definition of partnership based on SIDs in the BPR2000 model seems most natural. SIDs enable unique identification of the individual sessions. Without such means, communicating hosts will have difficulty determining the associated session key for a particular session.

We consider the use of SIDs to establish partnership analogous to the use of sockets in establishing connections between an initiating client process and a responding server process in network service protocol architecture [23]. A socket [18, 19] is bound to a port number so that the TCP layer can identify the application to which that data is destined to be sent, analogous to a SID being bound to a particular session enabling communicating principals to determine to which session messages belong. Since the initial development of sockets in the early 1980s, the use of sockets has been prevalent in protocols such as TCP/IP and UDP. In fact, Bellare et al. [4] recognised that SIDs are typically found in protocols such as SSL and IPSec.

The inability to define a unique SID in the 3PKD protocol so that the communicating principals can uniquely distinguish messages from different sessions leads one to question the practicality and usefulness of the protocol in a real world setting. In our view, the design of any entity authentication and/or key establishment protocol should incorporate a secure means of uniquely identifying a particular communication session among the many concurrent sessions that a communicating party may have with many different parties. One outcome of this work is such a means of session identification.

We consider the main contributions of this paper to be:

1. the observation that session identifiers are necessary for real world use of provably secure protocols,
2. demonstration of a flaw in the specific partner function used in the BR95 proof of security that invalidates the proof, and

3. proposal of an improved 3PKD protocol with a proof of security using a definition of partnership based on SIDs.

The remainder of this paper is structured as follows: Section 2 briefly explains the Bellare-Rogaway models. Section 3 describes the 3PKD protocol and the specific partner function used in the existing proof of security for the protocol. It also contains a description of a 3PKD protocol run that demonstrates a flaw in the proof due to its use of an inadequate partner function, followed by a description of how to fix it. Section 4 demonstrates that it does not seem possible to successfully introduce a definition of partnership based on SIDs to the 3PKD protocol. We then propose improvements to the 3PKD protocol. Section 5 describes the general notion of the proof of security for the improved protocol. Finally, Section 6 presents the conclusions.

2   Overview of the Bellare-Rogaway Model

Both the BR93 model [5] and the BPR2000 model [4] define provable security for entity authentication and key distribution goals. In the same flavour, the BR95 model [6] specifically defines provable security for the key distribution goal. In this section, we will focus on the BR95 and the BPR2000 definitions of security.

In all three models, the adversary $\mathcal{A}$ is a probabilistic machine that controls all the communications that take place between parties by interacting with a set of $\Pi^i_{U_1,U_2}$ oracles ($\Pi^i_{U_1,U_2}$ is defined to be the ith instantiation of a principal U_1 in a specific protocol run and U_2 is the principal with whom U_1 wishes to establish a secret key). $\mathcal{A}$ also interacts with a set of $\Psi^j_{U_1,U_2}$ oracles, where $\Psi^j_{U_1,U_2}$ is defined to be the jth instantiation of the server in a specific protocol run establishing a shared secret key between U_1 and U_2. The predefined oracle queries are described informally as follows.

- The SendClient(U_1, U_2, i, m) query allows $\mathcal{A}$ to send some message m of her choice to $\Pi^i_{U_1,U_2}$ at will. $\Pi^i_{U_1,U_2}$, upon receiving the query, will compute what the protocol specification demands and return to $\mathcal{A}$ the response message and/or decision. If $\Pi^i_{U_1,U_2}$ has either accepted with some session key or terminated, this will be made known to $\mathcal{A}$.
- The SendServer(U_1, U_2, i, m) query allows $\mathcal{A}$ to send some message m of her choice to some server oracle $\Psi^i_{U_1,U_2}$ at will. The server oracle, upon receiving the query, will compute what the protocol specification demands and return the response to $\mathcal{A}$.
- The Reveal(U_1, U_2, i) query allows $\mathcal{A}$ to expose an old session key that has been previously accepted. $\Pi^i_{U_1,U_2}$, upon receiving this query and if it has accepted and holds some session key, will send this session key back to $\mathcal{A}$.
- The Corrupt(U_1, K_E) query allows $\mathcal{A}$ to corrupt the principal U_1 at will, and thereby learn the complete internal state of the corrupted principal. The corrupt query also gives $\mathcal{A}$ the ability to overwrite the long-lived key of the corrupted principal with any value of her choice (i.e. K_E). This query can be used to model the real world scenarios of an insider cooperating with

the adversary or an insider who has been completely compromised by the adversary.

- The $\mathsf{Test}(U_1, U_2, i)$ query is the only oracle query that does not correspond to any of $\mathcal{A}$'s abilities. If $\Pi^i_{U_1,U_2}$ has accepted with some session key and is being asked a $\mathsf{Test}(U_1, U_2, i)$ query, then depending on a randomly chosen bit b, $\mathcal{A}$ is given either the actual session key or a session key drawn randomly from the session key distribution. The use of the $\mathsf{Test}(U_1, U_2, i)$ query is explained in Section 2.4. Note that $\Pi^i_{U_1,U_2}$ must be fresh, as defined in Section 2.3.

The definition of security depends on the notions of partnership of oracles and indistinguishability. In the BR95 model, partnership of oracles is defined using a partner function whose purpose is to enable a mapping between two oracles that should share a secret key on completion of the protocol execution. In the BPR2000 model, partnership of oracles is defined using SIDs. The definition of partnership is used in the definition of security to restrict the adversary's Reveal and Corrupt queries to oracles that are not partners of the oracle whose key the adversary is trying to guess. To avoid confusion, we will explicitly indicate which definition of partnership is used.

2.1   Notion of Partnership in the BR95 Model: A Partner Function

No explicit definition of partnership was given in the BR95 model since there is no single partner function fixed for any protocol. Instead, security is defined predicated on the existence of a suitable partner function. Before defining the partner function, we need the notion of a transcript. A transcript T is defined to be a sequence of communication records, where a communication record is a combination of SendClient and SendServer queries and responses to these queries. At the end of a protocol run, T will contain the record of the Send queries and the responses.

Definition 1 (BR95 Partner Function). *A partner function f in the BR95 model is syntactically defined to be a polynomial-time mapping between an initiator oracle and a partnering responder oracle (if such a partner exists), which uses the transcript T to determine the partner of an oracle.*

Let A and B be some initiator and responder principals, and also i and j be some instances of A and B respectively. The notation $f^i_{A,B}(T) = j$ denotes that the partner oracle of $\Pi^i_{A,B}$ is $\Pi^j_{B,A}$. The initial values $f^i_{A,B}(T) = *$ and $f^j_{B,A}(T) = *$ mean that neither $\Pi^i_{A,B}$ nor $\Pi^j_{B,A}$ has a BR95 partner. Two oracles are BR95 partners if, and only if, the specific BR95 partner function in use says they are. The specific BR95 partner function used in the proof of security for the 3PKD protocol will be discussed in Section 3.3.

2.2   Notion of Partnership in the BPR2000 Model: SIDs

Partnership in the BPR2000 model is given by Definition 2. It is defined using the notion of SIDs, whose construction is by the concatenation of message flows in the protocol. In the BPR2000 model, an oracle who has accepted will hold the associated session key, a SID and a partner identifier (PID). Note that any oracle that has accepted will have at most one BPR2000 partner, if any at all. In Section 4.1, we demonstrate that it does not seem possible to define partnership based on SIDs for the 3PKD protocol.

Definition 2 (BPR2000 Definition of Partnership). *Two oracles, $\Pi^i_{A,B}$ and $\Pi^j_{B,A}$, are BPR2000 partners if, and only if, both oracles have accepted the same session key with the same SID, have agreed on the same set of principals (i.e. the initiator and the responder of the protocol), and no other oracles besides $\Pi^i_{A,B}$ and $\Pi^j_{B,A}$ have accepted with the same SID[1].*

2.3   Notion of Freshness

Definitions of security in both BR95 and BPR2000 models depend on the notion of freshness of the oracle to whom the Test query is sent. Freshness is used to identify the session keys about which $\mathcal{A}$ ought not to know anything because $\mathcal{A}$ has not revealed any oracles that have accepted the key and has not corrupted any principals knowing the key. Definition 3 describes freshness in the BR95 model, which depends on the notion of partnership in Definition 1.

Definition 3 (BR95 Definition of Freshness). *Oracle $\Pi^i_{A,B}$ is fresh (or it holds a fresh session key) at the end of execution, if, and only if, oracle $\Pi^i_{A,B}$ has accepted with or without a partner oracle $\Pi^j_{B,A}$, both oracle $\Pi^i_{A,B}$ and its partner oracle $\Pi^j_{B,A}$ (if such a partner oracle exists) have not been sent a Reveal query, and the principals A and B of oracles $\Pi^i_{A,B}$ and $\Pi^j_{B,A}$ (if such a partner exists) have not been sent a Corrupt query.*

The definition of freshness in the BPR2000 model restricts the adversary $\mathcal{A}$ from sending a Corrupt query to any principal in the protocol. We adopt the BR95 version because it offers a tighter definition of freshness since for $\Pi^i_{A,B}$ to be fresh, the adversary is not restricted from sending Corrupt queries to principals apart from the principals of oracle $\Pi^i_{A,B}$ and its partner oracle $\Pi^j_{B,A}$ (if such a partner exists).

2.4   Definition of Security

Security in both the BR95 and BPR2000 models is defined using the game $\mathcal{G}$, played between a malicious adversary $\mathcal{A}$ and a collection of $\Pi^i_{U_x,U_y}$ oracles for players $U_x, U_y \in \{U_1, \ldots, U_{N_p}\}$ and instances $i \in \{1, \ldots, N_s\}$. The adversary $\mathcal{A}$ runs the game simulation $\mathcal{G}$, whose setting is as follows.

- **Stage 1:** $\mathcal{A}$ is able to send any SendClient, SendServer, Reveal, and Corrupt oracle queries at will in the game simulation $\mathcal{G}$.

---

[1] Although the original paper required both parties to accept with the same PID, we have corrected this typographical error.

- **Stage 2:** At some point during $\mathcal{G}$, $\mathcal{A}$ will choose a fresh session on which to be tested and send a Test query to the fresh oracle associated with the test session. Note that the test session chosen must be fresh (in the sense of Definition 3). Depending on a randomly chosen bit b, $\mathcal{A}$ is given either the actual session key or a session key drawn randomly from the session key distribution.
- **Stage 3:** $\mathcal{A}$ continues making any SendClient, SendServer, Reveal, and Corrupt oracle queries of its choice. (In the BR95 model, this stage is omitted and $\mathcal{A}$ was required to output the guess bit b' immediately after making a Test query. However, such a requirement is not strong enough, as discussed by Canetti and Krawczyk [15]. They mentioned including this stage to fix the problem, as proposed by Bellare, Petrank, Rackoff, and Rogaway in an unpublished paper.)
- **Stage 4:** Eventually, $\mathcal{A}$ terminates the game simulation and outputs a bit b', which is its guess of the value of b.

Success of $\mathcal{A}$ in $\mathcal{G}$ is measured in terms of $\mathcal{A}$'s advantage in distinguishing whether $\mathcal{A}$ receives the real key or a random value. $\mathcal{A}$ wins if, after asking a Test(U_1, U_2, i) query, where $\Pi^i_{U_1, U_2}$ is fresh and has accepted, $\mathcal{A}$'s guess bit b' equals the bit b selected during the Test(U_1, U_2, i) query. Let the advantage function of $\mathcal{A}$ be denoted by $\mathsf{Adv}^{\mathcal{A}}(k)$, where $\mathsf{Adv}^{\mathcal{A}}(k) = 2 \times \Pr[b = b'] - 1$.

The BPR2000 model defines security for both entity authentication and key establishment goals, whilst the BR95 model defines security only for key establishment. In this paper, we are interested only in the notion of key establishment in the BPR2000 model since the 3PKD protocol does not consider entity authentication as its security goal. We require the definition of a negligible function.

Definition 4 ([1]). *A function $\epsilon(k) : \mathbb{N} \to \mathbb{R}$ in the security parameter k, is called negligible if it approaches zero faster than the reciprocal of any polynomial. That is, for every $c \in \mathbb{N}$ there is an integer k_c such that $\epsilon(k) \leq k^{-c}$ for all $k \geq k_c$.*

The definition of security for the protocol is identical in both the BR95 model and the BPR2000 model, with the exception that different definitions of partnership and freshness are used in the respective models.

Definition 5 (Definition of Security [4, 6]). *A protocol is secure in the BR95 model and secure under the notion of key establishment in the BPR2000 model if both the validity and indistinguishability requirements are satisfied:*

1. *Validity: When the protocol is run between two oracles in the absence of a malicious adversary, the two oracles accept the same key.*
2. *Indistinguishability: For all probabilistic, polynomial-time (PPT) adversaries $\mathcal{A}$, $\mathsf{Adv}^{\mathcal{A}}(k)$ is negligible.*

3 A Flaw in the BR95 Proof of the 3PKD Protocol

In this section, we describe the 3PKD protocol and an execution of the protocol run in the presence of a malicious adversary, followed by an explanation of the specific partner function used in the BR95 proof. Using an execution of the protocol as a case study, we demonstrate that the specific partner function used in the BR95 proof enables a malicious adversary to reveal a session key at one oracle, where the same session key is considered fresh at a different, non BR95 partner oracle.

3.1   3PKD Protocol

The 3PKD protocol in Figure 1 involves three parties, a trusted server S and two principals A and B who wish to establish communication. The security goal of this protocol is to distribute a session key between two communication principals (i.e. the key establishment goal), which is suitable for establishing a secure session. Forward-secrecy and mutual authentication are not considered in the protocol. However, concurrent executions of the protocol are possible.

In the protocol, the notation $\{message\}_{K_{AS}^{enc}}$ denotes the encryption of some message under the encryption key K_{AS}^{enc} and the notation $[message]_{K_{AS}^{MAC}}$ denotes the computation of MAC digest of some message under the MAC key K_{AS}^{MAC}. K_{AS}^{enc} is the encryption key shared between A and S, and K_{AS}^{MAC} is the MAC key shared between A and S. Both keys, K_{AS}^{enc} and K_{AS}^{MAC}, are independent of each other.

$$
\begin{array}{ll}
1. & A \longrightarrow B : R_A \\
2. & B \longrightarrow S : R_A, R_B \\
3a. & S \longrightarrow A : \{SK_{AB}\}_{K_{AS}^{enc}}, [A, B, R_A, \{SK_{AB}\}_{K_{AS}^{enc}}]_{K_{AS}^{MAC}} \\
3b. & S \longrightarrow B : \{SK_{AB}\}_{K_{BS}^{enc}}, [A, B, R_B, \{SK_{AB}\}_{K_{BS}^{enc}}]_{K_{BS}^{MAC}}
\end{array}
$$

Fig. 1. 3PKD protocol

The protocol begins by having A randomly select a k-bit challenge R_A and send it to the B with whom she desires to communicate. Upon receiving the message R_A from A, B also randomly selects a k-bit challenge R_B and sends R_B together with R_A as a message (R_A, R_B) to the server S. S, upon receiving the message (R_A, R_B) from B, runs the session key generator to obtain a session key SK_{AB}, which has not been used before. S then encrypts SK_{AB} with K_{AS}^{enc} and K_{BS}^{enc} to obtain ciphertexts α_A and α_B, and computes the MAC digests β_A and β_B of the strings $(A, B, R_A, \{SK_{AB}\}_{K_{AS}^{enc}})$ and $(A, B, R_B, \{SK_{AB}\}_{K_{BS}^{enc}})$ under the keys K_{AS}^{MAC} and K_{BS}^{MAC} respectively. S then sends messages (α_A, β_A) and (α_B, β_B) to A and B respectively in Steps 3a and 3b of the protocol.

3.2   Execution of Protocol Run in the Presence of a Malicious Adversary

Figure 2 depicts an example execution of the 3PKD protocol run in the presence of a malicious adversary, which will be used to demonstrate that the specific partner function used in the BR95 proof enables a malicious adversary to reveal a session key at one oracle, where the same session key is considered fresh at a different, non partner oracle. Consequently, the BR95 proof will be shown to be invalid.

1.	$A \longrightarrow B$ (intercepted by $\mathcal{A}$) : R_A
1($\mathcal{A}$).	$\mathcal{A}$ (impersonating A) $\longrightarrow B$: R_E
2.	$B \longrightarrow S$ (intercepted by $\mathcal{A}$) : R_E, R_B
2($\mathcal{A}$).	$\mathcal{A}$ (impersonating B) $\longrightarrow S$: R_A, R_B
3a.	$S \longrightarrow A$: $\qquad\qquad\qquad \{SK_{A,B}\}_{K_{AS}^{enc}}, [A, B, R_A, \{SK_{A,B}\}_{K_{AS}^{enc}}]_{K_{AS}^{MAC}}$
3b.	$S \longrightarrow B$: $\qquad\qquad\qquad \{SK_{A,B}\}_{K_{BS}^{enc}}, [A, B, R_B, \{SK_{A,B}\}_{K_{BS}^{enc}}]_{K_{BS}^{MAC}}$

Fig. 2. Execution of protocol run in the presence of a malicious adversary

An active adversary $\mathcal{A}$ intercepts and deletes the message R_A sent by A to B. $\mathcal{A}$ then sends a fabricated message R_E to B impersonating A. B, upon receiving the message R_E, and believing that this message originated from A, also randomly selects a k-bit challenge R_B and sends R_B together with R_E as a message (R_E, R_B) to the server S. $\mathcal{A}$ then intercepts and deletes this message (R_E, R_B), and sends the fabricated message (R_A, R_B) to S impersonating B. S, upon receiving the message (R_A, R_B) from $\mathcal{A}$, and believing that this message originated from B, runs the session key generator to obtain a unique session key SK_{AB}, which has not been used before. S encrypts SK_{AB} with the respective principals' encryption keys (i.e., K_{AS}^{enc} and K_{BS}^{enc}) to obtain the ciphertexts α_A and α_B respectively. S also computes the MAC digests (i.e., β_A and β_B) of the strings $(A, B, R_A, \{SK_{AB}\}_{K_{AS}^{enc}})$ and $(A, B, R_B, \{SK_{AB}\}_{K_{BS}^{enc}})$ under the respective keys K_{AS}^{MAC} and K_{BS}^{MAC}. S then sends the messages (α_A, β_A) and (α_B, β_B) to A and B respectively in Steps 3a and 3b of the protocol.

Immediately after both A and B have verified and accepted with the session key SK_{AB}, $\mathcal{A}$ sends a Reveal query to A and obtains the session key SK_{AB} from A. This enables the adversary $\mathcal{A}$ to break the protocol as shown in the following section. Figure 3 shows the oracle queries associated with Figure 2.

3.3   The Partner Function Used in the BR95 Proof

The specific partner function used in the BR95 proof is defined in two parts, namely the partner of the responder oracle and the partner of the initiator oracle. Let f be the partner function defined in the BR95 proof, $\Pi_{A,B}^i$ be the initiator oracle, and $\Pi_{B,A}^j$ be the responder oracle. Both values $f_{A,B}^i(T)$ and $f_{B,A}^j(T)$ are initially set to $*$, which means that neither $\Pi_{A,B}^i$ nor $\Pi_{B,A}^j$ is BR95 partnered. The description of f is now given, where T is the transcript with which the adversary terminates the execution of the protocol run.

BR95 Partner of the Initiator Oracle: The first two records of T associated with queries of the oracle $\Pi_{A,B}^i$ are examined. If the first record indicates that $\Pi_{A,B}^i$ had the role of an initiator oracle, was sent a SendClient($A, B, i, *$)

On query of q:	Return:	Append to T:
SendClient$(A, B, i, *)$	R_A	$\langle q, R_A \rangle$
SendClient(B, A, j, R_E)	(R_E, R_B)	$\langle q, (R_E, R_B) \rangle$
SendServer$(A, B, s, (R_A, R_B))$	$((\alpha_{A,i}, \beta_{A,i}), (\alpha_{B,j}, \beta_{B,j}))$	$\langle q, ((\alpha_{A,i}, \beta_{A,i}), (\alpha_{B,j}, \beta_{B,j})) \rangle$
SendClient$(A, B, i, (\alpha_{A,i}, \beta_{A,i}))$	$Accept_{A,i}$	$\langle q, Accept_{A,i} \rangle$
SendClient$(B, A, j, (\alpha_{B,j}, \beta_{B,j}))$	$Accept_{B,j}$	$\langle q, Accept_{B,j} \rangle$
Reveal(A, B, i)	$SK_{A,B,i}$	

Fig. 3. Oracle queries associated with Figure 2

query and replied with R_A, and the second record indicates that $\Pi_{A,B}^i$'s reply to a SendClient$(A, B, i, (\alpha_A, \beta_A))$ was the decision $Accept$, then T is examined to determine if some server oracle, $\Psi_{A,B}^k$, sent a message of the form (α_A, β_A') for some β_A'. If so, determine if this message was in response to a SendServer$(A, B, k, (R_A, R_B))$ query for some R_B, and if this is also true, determine if there is a unique j such that an oracle $\Pi_{B,A}^j$ generated a message (R_A, R_B). If such an oracle $\Pi_{B,A}^j$ is found, then set $f_{A,B}^i(T) = j$, meaning that the BR95 partner of $\Pi_{A,B}^i$ is $\Pi_{B,A}^j$.

Suppose that the adversary terminates the execution of the protocol run in Figure 3 with some transcript T_1. According to the BR95 partner function f, $\Pi_{A,B}^i$ has no BR95 partner because although there is a SendServer$(A, B, k, (R_A, R_B))$ query for some R_B, there does not exist a unique j such that an oracle $\Pi_{B,A}^j$ generated a message (R_A, R_B). Hence, $f_{A,B}^i(T_1) = *$.

BR95 Partner of the Responder Oracle: The first two records of T associated with queries of the oracle $\Pi_{B,A}^j$ are examined. If the first record indicates that $\Pi_{B,A}^j$ had the role of a responder oracle, and was sent a SendClient(B, A, j, R_A) query, and the second record indicates that $\Pi_{B,A}^j$ accepted, then determine if there is a unique i such that an oracle $\Pi_{A,B}^i$ generated a message R_A. If such an oracle $\Pi_{A,B}^i$ is found, then set $f_{B,A}^j(T) = i$, meaning that the BR95 partner of $\Pi_{B,A}^j$ is $\Pi_{A,B}^i$.

For the execution of the protocol run in Figure 3, $\Pi_{B,A}^j$ has no BR95 partner because although $\Pi_{B,A}^j$ accepted, there does not exist a unique oracle $\Pi_{A,B}^i$ that it generated a message R_E (recall R_E is fabricated by $\mathcal{A}$). Hence, $f_{B,A}^j(T_1) = *$. Hence, we have shown that the protocol state is not secure since $\mathcal{A}$ can reveal a fresh non partner oracle, either $\Pi_{A,B}^i$ or $\Pi_{B,A}^j$, and find the session key accepted by $\Pi_{B,A}^j$ or $\Pi_{A,B}^i$ respectively. It is possible to fix the flawed partner function used in the BR95 model, as shown below.

The only differences between the fixed definition of an initiator's partner and the original definition are that the server may think that the initiator and responder roles are swapped, and that the nonce output by B on behalf of A, R_A', need not be identical to the nonce output by A itself, R_A. The definition of a responder's partner has been made analogous to that of an initiator's partner.

Using the fixed partner function in our example execution, $\Pi_{A,B}^i$'s partner is $\Pi_{B,A}^j$ and $\Pi_{B,A}^j$'s partner is $\Pi_{A,B}^i$.

Fixed BR95 Partner of the Initiator Oracle: The first two records of T associated with queries of the oracle $\Pi_{A,B}^i$ are examined. If the first record indicates that $\Pi_{A,B}^i$ had the role of an initiator oracle, was sent a SendClient$(A, B, i, *)$ query and replied with R_A, and the second record indicates that $\Pi_{A,B}^i$'s reply to a SendClient$(A, B, i, (\alpha_A, \beta_A))$ was the decision *Accept*, then T is examined to determine if some server oracle, $\Psi_{A,B}^k$ or $\Psi_{B,A}^k$, sent a message of the form (α_A, β_A') for some β_A'. If so, determine if this message was in response to a SendServer$(A, B, k, (R_A, R_B))$ or SendServer$(B, A, k, (R_B, R_A))$ query for some R_B, and if this is also true, determine if there is a unique j such that an oracle $\Pi_{B,A}^j$ generated a message (R_A', R_B) for any R_A'. If such an oracle $\Pi_{B,A}^j$ is found, then set $f_{A,B}^i(T) = j$, meaning that the BR95 partner of $\Pi_{A,B}^i$ is $\Pi_{B,A}^j$.

Fixed BR95 Partner of the Responder Oracle: The first two records of T associated with queries of the oracle $\Pi_{B,A}^j$ are examined. If the first record indicates that $\Pi_{B,A}^j$ had the role of a responder oracle, was sent a SendClient(B, A, j, R_A') query and replied with (R_A', R_B), and the second record indicates that $\Pi_{B,A}^j$'s reply to a SendClient$(B, A, j, (\alpha_B, \beta_B))$ was the decision *Accept*, then T is examined to determine if some server oracle, $\Psi_{A,B}^k$ or $\Psi_{B,A}^k$, sent a message of the form (α_B, β_B') for some β_B'. If so, determine if this message was in response to a SendServer$(A, B, k, (R_A, R_B))$ or SendServer$(B, A, k, (R_B, R_A))$ query for some R_A, and if this is also true, determine if there is a unique i such that an oracle $\Pi_{A,B}^i$ generated a message R_A. If such an oracle $\Pi_{A,B}^i$ is found, then set $f_{B,A}^j(T) = i$, meaning that the BR95 partner of $\Pi_{B,A}^j$ is $\Pi_{A,B}^i$.

4   A Revised Protocol

We now revisit the construction of SIDs in the BPR2000 model and demonstrate that it does not seem possible to define partnership based on SIDs in the 3PKD protocol. We then propose an improvement to the 3PKD protocol with a natural candidate for the SID. Consequently, the protocol is practical in a real world setting.

4.1   Defining SIDs in the 3PKD Protocol

Bellare, Pointcheval, and Rogaway [4] suggested that SIDs can be constructed on-the-fly using fresh unique contributions from the communicating participants. Uniqueness of SIDs is necessary since otherwise two parties may share a key but not be BPR2000 partners, and hence the protocol would not be considered secure. Within the 3PKD protocol, the only values that A and B can be sure are unique are R_A and R_B. However, the integrity of only one of R_A and R_B is preserved cryptographically for each party in the protocol. Since the integrity of a SID consisting of R_A and R_B is not preserved cryptographically, attacks such as the one proposed in Section 3 are possible. An alternative would be to use an externally generated SID, such as a counter, but the use of such a SID would be inconvenient. Hence, it does not seem possible to use SIDs to successfully define partnership in the 3PKD protocol.

4.2   An Improved Provably Secure 3PKD Protocol

In order for partnership to be defined using the notion of SIDs in the 3PKD protocol, we propose an improvement to the protocol as shown in Figure 4. In the improved 3PKD protocol, S binds both values composing the SID, R_A and R_B, to the session key for each party, using the MAC digests in message flows 3a and 3b.

$$
\begin{array}{l}
1. \quad A \longrightarrow B : R_A \\
2. \quad B \longrightarrow S : R_A, R_B \\
3a. \ S \longrightarrow A : \{SK_{AB}\}_{K^{enc}_{AS}}, [A, B, R_A, R_B, \{SK_{AB}\}_{K^{enc}_{AS}}]_{K^{MAC}_{AS}}, R_B \\
3b. \ S \longrightarrow B : \{SK_{AB}\}_{K^{enc}_{BS}}, [A, B, R_A, R_B, \{SK_{AB}\}_{K^{enc}_{BS}}]_{K^{MAC}_{BS}}
\end{array}
$$

Fig. 4. An improved provably secure 3PKD protocol

The primitives used in the protocol are the notions of a secure encryption scheme [16] and a secure message authentication scheme [17]. Both notions are now relatively standard. For the security of the underlying encryption scheme, we consider the standard definitions of *indistinguishability of encryptions* (IND) due to Goldwasser and Micali [16] and *chosen-plaintext attack* (CPA). For the security of the underlying message authentication scheme, we consider the standard definition of existential unforgeability under *adaptive chosen-message attack* (ACMA) due to Goldwasser, Micali, and Rivest [17].

Theorem 1 *The improved 3PKD protocol is a secure key establishment protocol in the sense of Definition 5 if the underlying message authentication scheme is secure in the sense of existential unforgeability under ACMA and the underlying encryption scheme is indistinguishable under CPA.*

5   Security Proof

The proof of Theorem 1 generally follows that of Bellare and Rogaway [6], but is adjusted to the different partnering function used. The validity of the protocol is straightforward to verify and we concentrate on the indistinguishability requirement. The security is proved by finding a reduction to the security of the underlying message authentication scheme and the underlying encryption scheme.

The general notion of the proof is to assume that there exists an adversary $\mathcal{A}$ who can gain a non-negligible advantage in distinguishing the test key in game $\mathcal{G}$ (i.e. $Adv^{\mathcal{A}}(k)$ is non-negligible), and use $\mathcal{A}$ to break the underlying encryption scheme or the message authentication scheme. In other words, we consider an adversary $\mathcal{A}$ that breaks the security of the protocol.

Using results of Bellare, Boldyreva and Micali [2], we may allow an adversary against an encryption scheme to obtain encryptions of the same plaintext under different independent encryption keys. Such an adversary is termed a multiple eavesdropper, $\mathcal{ME}$. In the 3PKD protocol, the server, upon receiving a message from the responder principal, sends out two ciphertexts derived from the encryption of the same plaintext under two independent encryption keys. Hence, we consider a multiple eavesdropper $\mathcal{ME}$ who is allowed to obtain encryptions of the same plaintext under two different independent encryption keys. The formal definition of $\mathcal{ME}$ is given by Definition 6.

Definition 6 ([2, 6]). *Let $\Omega = (\mathcal{K}, \mathcal{E}, \mathcal{D})$ be an encryption scheme with security parameter k, $\mathcal{SE}$ be the single eavesdropper and $\mathcal{ME}$ be the multiple eavesdropper, and $\mathcal{O}_{k_A}$ and $\mathcal{O}_{k_B}$ be two different independent encryption oracles associated with encryption keys k_A and k_B. We define the advantage functions of $\mathcal{SE}$ and $\mathcal{ME}$ to be:*

$$Adv^{\mathcal{SE}}(k) = 2 \times Pr[\mathcal{SE} \leftarrow \mathcal{O}_{k_A}; (m_0, m_1 \xleftarrow{R} \mathcal{SE}); \theta \xleftarrow{R} \{0,1\}; \gamma_A \xleftarrow{R} \mathcal{O}_{k_A}(m_\theta)$$
$$: \mathcal{SE}(\gamma_A) = \theta] - 1$$
$$Adv^{\mathcal{ME}}(k) = 2 \times Pr[\mathcal{ME} \leftarrow \mathcal{O}_{k_A}, \mathcal{O}_{k_B}; (m_0, m_1 \xleftarrow{R} \mathcal{ME}); \theta \xleftarrow{R} \{0,1\};$$
$$\gamma_A \xleftarrow{R} \mathcal{O}_{k_A}(m_\theta), \gamma_B \xleftarrow{R} \mathcal{O}_{k_B}(m_\theta) : \mathcal{ME}(\gamma_A, \gamma_B) = \theta] - 1$$

Lemma 1 ([2]). *Suppose the advantage function of $\mathcal{SE}$ against the encryption scheme is ϵ_k. Then the advantage function of $\mathcal{ME}$ is at most $2 \times \epsilon_k$.*

As a consequence of Lemma 1, an encryption scheme secure against IND-CPA in the single eavesdropper setting will also be secure against IND-CPA in the multiple eavesdropper setting [2].

An overview of the proof of Theorem 1 is now provided[2]. The proof is divided into two cases since the adversary $\mathcal{A}$ can either gain her advantage against the protocol by forging a MAC digest with respect to some user's MAC key or gain her advantage against the protocol without forging a MAC digest.

5.1   Adaptive MAC Forger $\mathcal{F}$

Following the approach of Bellare, Kilian and Rogaway [3], we quantify security of the MAC scheme in terms of the probability of a successful MAC forgery under adaptive chosen-message attack, which we denote by $Pr[Succ^{\mathcal{F}}(k)]$. For

---

[2] A complete proof appears in the extended version, which can be downloaded from http://sky.fit.qut.edu.au/~boydc/papers/

the MAC scheme to be secure under chosen-message attack, $\Pr[\text{Succ}^{\mathcal{F}}(k)]$ must be negligible. In other words, the MAC scheme is considered broken if a forger $\mathcal{F}$ is able to produce a valid MAC forgery for a MAC key unknown to it.

The first part of the proof of security for the improved 3PKD protocol assumes that the adversary $\mathcal{A}$ gains her advantage by forging a valid MAC digest for a MAC key that $\mathcal{A}$ does not know. More precisely, we define MACforgery to be the event that at some point in the game $\mathcal{A}$ asks a SendClient$(B, A, j, (\alpha_{B,j}, \beta_{B,j}))$ query to some fresh oracle $\Pi_{B,A}^{j}$, such that the oracle accepts, but the MAC value $\beta_{B,j}$ used in the query was not previously output by a fresh oracle. We then construct an adaptive MAC forger $\mathcal{F}$ against the security of the message authentication scheme using $\mathcal{A}$, as shown in the following attack game, $\mathcal{G}_{\mathcal{F}}$.

- **Stage 1:** $\mathcal{F}$ is provided permanent access to the MAC oracle $\mathcal{O}_{x'}$ associated with the MAC key x' throughout $\mathcal{G}_{\mathcal{F}}$.
- **Stage 2:** $\mathcal{F}$ runs $\mathcal{A}$ to produce a valid MAC forgery for the MAC key x' that is known to neither $\mathcal{F}$ nor $\mathcal{A}$. By examining all oracle queries made by $\mathcal{A}$, $\mathcal{F}$ outputs the MAC forgery.

The objective of $\mathcal{F}$ is to output a valid MAC forgery for a MAC message which was not previously asked of $\mathcal{O}_{x'}$. It is shown in the proof that $\Pr[\text{MACforgery}] \leq N_p \cdot \Pr[\text{Succ}^{\mathcal{F}}(k)]$, where N_p is polynomial in the security parameter, k. Hence, $\Pr[\text{MACforgery}]$ is negligible if the message authentication scheme in use is secure.

5.2   Multiple Eavesdropper Attacker $\mathcal{ME}$

The second part of the proof assumes that the adversary $\mathcal{A}$ gains her advantage without forging a MAC digest. We construct another algorithm $\mathcal{ME}$ that uses $\mathcal{A}$ against the security of the encryption scheme, whose behaviour is described by the attack game $\mathcal{G}_{\mathcal{ME}}$ shown below and in Figure 5. The objective of $\mathcal{ME}$ is to correctly predict the challenge bit θ in the game simulation $\mathcal{G}_{\mathcal{ME}}$ (i.e. have $\theta' = \theta$).

- **Stage 1:** $\mathcal{ME}$ is provided permanent access to two different encryption oracles $\mathcal{O}_{k_A}$ and $\mathcal{O}_{k_B}$ associated with encryption keys k_A and k_B respectively throughout the game $\mathcal{G}_{\mathcal{ME}}$.
- **Stage 2:** $\mathcal{ME}$ chooses a pair of messages (m_0, m_1) of equal length and hands them to the challenger. The challenger then chooses a random challenge bit, θ (i.e., $\theta \xleftarrow{R} \{0, 1\}$), and returns the ciphertexts γ_A and γ_B to $\mathcal{ME}$, where $\gamma_A = \mathcal{E}_{k_A}(m_\theta)$ and $\gamma_B = \mathcal{E}_{k_B}(m_\theta)$.
- **Stage 3:** $\mathcal{ME}$ runs $\mathcal{A}$ to determine whether m_0 or m_1 was encrypted as γ_A and γ_B. By examining all oracle queries made by $\mathcal{A}$, $\mathcal{ME}$ outputs her prediction, θ'.

We denote the probability that $\mathcal{ME}$ correctly guesses the challenge bit θ by $\Pr[\text{Succ}^{\mathcal{ME}}(k)]$, and observe that for the encryption scheme to be IND-CPA, $\text{Adv}^{\mathcal{ME}}(k) = 2 \times \Pr[\text{Succ}^{\mathcal{ME}}(k)] - 1$ must be negligible. It is shown in the proof

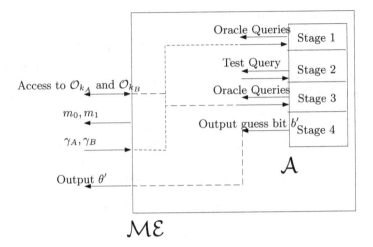

Fig. 5. Game $\mathcal{G}_{\mathcal{ME}}$

that $(\mathsf{Adv}^{\mathcal{A}}(k)|\overline{\mathsf{MACforgery}}) = N_p^2 N_s \cdot \mathsf{Adv}^{\mathcal{ME}}(k)$, where N_p and N_s are polynomial in the security parameter. Hence, $(\mathsf{Adv}^{\mathcal{A}}(k)|\overline{\mathsf{MACforgery}})$ is negligible if the encryption scheme in use is secure.

5.3 Conclusion of Proof

The proof concludes by observing that:

$$
\begin{aligned}
\mathsf{Adv}^{\mathcal{A}}(k) = {} & (\mathsf{Adv}^{\mathcal{A}}(k)|\mathsf{MACforgery}) \times \Pr[\mathsf{MACforgery}] \\
& + (\mathsf{Adv}^{\mathcal{A}}(k)|\overline{\mathsf{MACforgery}}) \times \Pr[\overline{\mathsf{MACforgery}}] \\
\leq {} & \Pr[\mathsf{MACforgery}] + (\mathsf{Adv}^{\mathcal{A}}(k)|\overline{\mathsf{MACforgery}})
\end{aligned}
$$

Hence, $\mathsf{Adv}^{\mathcal{A}}(k)$ is negligible when the encryption scheme and message authentication scheme in use are secure against IND-CPA and secure against existential forgery under ACMA respectively, and therefore the improved 3PKD protocol is also secure.

6   Conclusion and Future Work

By making a small change to the 3PKD protocol we have allowed SIDs to be defined in a natural way. This makes the improved protocol a more useful tool for practical applications since we have provided a simple way to identify which secure session key should be used on which communication channel. At the same time we would argue that the resulting definition of partnering is more intuitive, and consequently we believe that our proof of security is more straightforward than the one presented by Bellare and Rogaway in their original paper.

As a result of our findings we would recommend that all provably secure protocols should use partnering definitions based on SIDs. This situation is common for two-party protocols [4, 10, 15]; even if a SID is not explicitly used in the security definition, one can easily be defined from the fresh inputs of each principal. When it comes to multi-party protocols the situation is not so clear. While protocols which use only broadcast messages [21] have a natural SID, protocols which utilise point-to-point messages do not have this property [12, 13]. It would be interesting to know whether the protocols without broadcast messages can be provided with a secure means to obtain a shared SID.

References

1. M. Bellare. A Note on Negligible Functions. *Journal of Cryptology*, 15(4):271–284, 2002.
2. M. Bellare, A. Boldyreva, and S. Micali. Public-key Encryption in a Multi-User Setting: Security Proofs and Improvements. In *Advances in Cryptology – Eurocrypt*, pages 259 – 274. Springer-Verlag, 2000. LNCS Volume 1807.
3. M. Bellare, J. Kilian, and P. Rogaway. The Security of the Cipher Block Chaining Message Authentication Code. *Journal of Computer and System Sciences*, 61(3):362–399, Dec 2000.
4. M. Bellare, D. Pointcheval, and P. Rogaway. Authenticated Key Exchange Secure Against Dictionary Attacks. In *Advances in Cryptology – Eurocrypt*, pages 139 – 155. Springer-Verlag, 2000. LNCS Volume 1807.
5. M. Bellare and P. Rogaway. Entity Authentication and Key Distribution. In *Advances in Cryptology*, pages 110–125. Springer-Verlag, 1993.
6. M. Bellare and P. Rogaway. Provably Secure Session Key Distribution: The Three Party Case. In *27th ACM Symposium on the Theory of Computing*, pages 57–66. ACM Press, 1995.
7. S.M. Bellovin and M. Merritt. Encrypted Key Exchange: Password-Based Protocols Secure Against Dictionary Attacks. In *Symposium on Security and Privacy*, pages 72–84. IEEE, 1992.
8. S.M. Bellovin and M. Merritt. Augmented Encrypted Key Exchange: A Password-Based Protocol Secure Against Dictionary Attacks and Password File Compromise. In *1st Annual Conference on Computer and Communications Security*, pages 72–84. ACM, 1993.
9. S. Blake-Wilson and A. Menezes. Security Proofs for Entity Authentication and Authenticated Key Transport Protocols Employing Asymmetric Techniques. In *Security Protocols Workshop*. Springer-Verlag, 1997.
10. S. Blake-Wilson and A. Menezes. Authenticated Diffie-Hellman Key Agreement Protocols. In *Selected Areas in Cryptography*, pages 339–361. Springer-Verlag, 1998.
11. C. Boyd and J.M.G. Nieto. Round-optimal Contributory Conference Key Agreement. In *Public Key Cryptography PKC 2003*, pages 161–174. Springer-Verlag, 2003. LNCS Volume 2567.
12. E. Bresson, O. Chevassut, and D. Pointcheval. Provably Authenticated Group Diffie–Hellman Key Exchange — The Dynamic Case. In *Advances in Cryptology - Asiacrypt 2001*, pages 209–223. Springer-Verlag, Dec 2001.
13. E. Bresson, O. Chevassut, and D. Pointcheval. Dynamic Group Diffie–Hellman Key Exchange under Standard Assumptions. In *Advances in Cryptology - Eurocrypt 2002*, pages 321–336. Springer-Verlag, May 2002.

14. E. Bresson, O. Chevassut, D. Pointcheval, and Jean-Jacques Quisquater. Provably Authenticated Group Diffie–Hellman Key Exchange. In *8th ACM Conference on Computer and Communications Security*, pages 209–223. ACM Press, Nov 2001.

15. R. Canetti and H. Krawczyk. Analysis of Key-Exchange Protocols and Their Use for Building Secure Channels. In *Advances in Cryptology - International Conference on the Theory and Application of Cryptographic Techniques*, volume 2045, pages 453–474. Springer-Verlag, Berlin, Heidelberg, May 2001.

16. S. Goldwasser and S. Micali. Probabilisitic Encryption. *Journal of Computer and System Sciences*, 28:270–299, 1984.

17. S. Goldwasser, S. Micali, and R.L. Rivest. A Digital Signature Scheme Secure Against Adaptive Chosen-Message Attacks. *SIAM Journal on Computing*, 17(2):281 – 308, 1988.

18. The Internet Engineering Task Force. *RFC 0204 Sockets in Use*, Aug 1971. http://www.ietf.org/rfc.html/.

19. The Internet Engineering Task Force. *RFC 0147 Definition of a Socket*, May 1971. http://www.ietf.org/rfc/rfc0147.txt?number=0147.

20. M. Jakobsson and D. Pointcheval. Mutual Authentication and Key Exchange Protocol for Low Power Devices. In *Financial Cryptography*, pages 178–195. Springer-Verlag, Berlin, Heidelberg, 2001.

21. J. Katz and M. Yung. Scalable Protocols for Authenticated Group Key Exchange. In *Advances in Cryptology - Crypto 2003*, pages 110–125. Springer-Verlag, 2003.

22. V. Shoup and A. Rubin. Session Key Distribution Using Smart Cards. In *Eurocrypt*, pages 321–331. Springer-Verlag, 1996.

23. W. Stallings. *Data and Computer Communications – 7th Edition*. Prentice Hall, 2004.

How to Embed Short Cycles into Large Nonlinear Feedback-Shift Registers

Le Van Ly and Werner Schindler

Bundesamt für Sicherheit in der Informationstechnik (BSI),
Godesberger Allee 185–189,
53175 Bonn, Germany
{LeVan.Ly, Werner.Schindler}@bsi.bund.de

Abstract. We construct nonlinear feedback shift registers with short cycles. Our method is to embed nonlinear feedback shift registers with small state spaces into nonlinear feedback shift registers with large state spaces. Algebraic analysis of our embedding indicates that detecting the embedded 'small' feedback shift register in the large feedback register is infeasible without additional information. As an application we propose a low-cost group-identification scheme.

Keywords: Nonlinear feedback shift register, short cycles, systems of algebraic equations, invariant theory, low-cost group identification.

1 Introduction

Cryptographic applications often use feedback-shift registers as primitives. Then, in most cases their *cycle structure* is of crucial importance. The *cycle structure* of the feedback-shift register is given as follows: we call a state u *periodical* with respect to a feedback-shift register F if the sequence $u, F(u), F \circ F(u), \ldots$ is periodical. The set of periodical elements splits into disjoint subsets, the so-called *cycles*, by the iterative application of F.

For linear feedback-shift registers (LFSRs) the cycle structure is well understood. Using primitive feedback polynomials ensures that the state space falls into two cycles. The first cycle consists of the single element $\{(0, \ldots, 0)\}$ whereas the second cycle is the complement of the first, [6]. Furthermore, it is easy to check whether a polynomial is primitive, although it is not a trivial task to find one. Using LFSRs with non-primitive feedback polynomials is not very common in practice.

In the nonlinear case, some interesting results about nonlinear feedback shift registers (NLFSRs) with randomly chosen feedback functions exist as well: for instance, about distributions of cycle lengths, linear complexity profiles, etc. Moreover, Golomb showed in [2], Part III, the existence of NLFSRs with particular properties.

However, unlike in the linear case there are no simple, general criteria that characterize the cycle structure of a given NLFSR. Therefore, in general exhaustive search is the only method to compute the cycle structure. But this is not

C. Blundo and S. Cimato (Eds.): SCN 2004, LNCS 3352, pp. 367–379, 2005.

practically feasible, if the state space is large, which is a necessary condition for the majority of cryptographic applications. Without exhaustive search the determination of the cycle structure is only possible for very simple feedback functions. Hence for randomly chosen feedback functions, although in general there exist periodical states with short cycles, it is practically infeasible to find them.

In this paper we shall take advantage of this fact. We create NLFSRs in which we "embed" periodical states that have short cycle lengths. More precisely, we start with an arbitrary feedback shift register on a small state space K^m with feedback function f_0, so that we can do exhaustive search to investigate its cycle structure. With respect to f_0 we describe an embedding of K^m into K^n ($n > m$ large) and construct a family of feedback functions on K^n in such a way that these coincide with f_0 on the embedding. Although our construction is quite elementary, it seems to be practically infeasible to decide whether a given feedback function has such an embedded small feedback function f_0 or even to recover f_0 unless a sufficient number of elements in the embedding are available (Sect. 3).

The plan of the paper is as follows. In the second section we describe the embedding. Section 3 presents the cryptographic properties of our construction: In which cases is it possible to reconstruct f_0. In Section 4 we discuss a low-cost group-identification scheme that uses our construction as the cryptographic primitive. Finally, we give our conclusions.

2   Embedding Short Cycles into Large Nonlinear Feedback-Shift Registers

2.1   The Embedding

Let K be a finite field and m, n integers so that $m < n$. To a feedback function $f_0 : K^m \to K$ we associate the feedback-shift register given by $F_0 : K^m \to K^m$, $\boldsymbol{x} := (x_0, ..., x_{m-1}) \mapsto (x_1, ..., x_{m-1}, f_0(\boldsymbol{x}))$. Furthermore we denote its ℓ-fold by $F_0^{(\ell)}(\boldsymbol{x}) := F_0 \circ F_0 \circ ... \circ F_0(\boldsymbol{x})$ (ℓ-times). The paper hinges on the following embedding of K^m into K^n by f_0:

$$\iota_{f_0,n} : K^m \to K^n, \boldsymbol{x} \mapsto (\boldsymbol{x}, f_0(\boldsymbol{x}), f_0 \circ F_0(\boldsymbol{x}), ..., f_0 \circ F_0^{(n-m-1)}(\boldsymbol{x})).$$

Clearly, $K = \mathbb{F}_2$ is the case of most practical importance, but we do not need to restrict us to this case. The following lemma on the properties of $\iota_{f_0,n}$ is elementary but crucial for the rest of the paper.

Lemma 1. *(i) For $\boldsymbol{x} \in K^m$ let $\boldsymbol{u} := (u_0, ..., u_{n-1}) := \iota_{f_0,n}(\boldsymbol{x}) \in \iota_{f_0,n}(K^m) \subset K^n$. Then $F_0^{(j-m)}(\boldsymbol{x}) = (u_{j-m}, ..., u_{j-1})$ for $j = m, ..., n$.*
(ii) For $j = m, ..., n - 1$ consider functions $g_j : K^n \to K$ given by $\boldsymbol{y} \mapsto f_0(y_{j-m}, ..., y_{j-1}) - y_j$. Then these mappings are trivial on the embedding, that is, $g_j|_{\iota_{f_0,n}(K^m)} \equiv 0$.

Proof. Assertion (i) follows by induction on j. For $\boldsymbol{u} \in \iota_{f_0,n}(K^m)$ there is a unique $\boldsymbol{x} \in K^m$ with $\iota_{f_0,n}(\boldsymbol{x}) = \boldsymbol{u}$. From (i) we conclude $u_j = f_0(u_{j-m}, ..., u_{j-1})$ for $j > m - 1$, which proves (ii).

This leads us to the central result of this paper:

Theorem 1. *Let $g_m, ..., g_{n-1}$ be defined as in Lemma 1. Furthermore consider a mapping $f : K^n \to K$ that is constructed from f_0 as follows:*

$$f(\boldsymbol{y}) = f_0(y_{n-m}, ..., y_{n-1}) + \sum_{j=m}^{n-1} g_j(\boldsymbol{y})h_j(\boldsymbol{y}), \qquad (1)$$

where $h_m, ..., h_{n-1} : K^n \to K$ are arbitrary mappings. (We say: "f_0 is embedded into f".) Then the corresponding feedback-shift registers F and F_0, respectively, coincide on the embedding of K^m into K^n by $\iota_{f_0,n}$, more precisely, for all $\boldsymbol{x} \in K^m$ it holds

$$F(\iota_{f_0,n}(\boldsymbol{x})) = \iota_{f_0,n}(F_0(\boldsymbol{x})).$$

Proof. Let $\boldsymbol{u} = \iota_{f_0,n}(\boldsymbol{x})$. Applying Lemma 1 (i) and (ii) we obtain $f(\iota_{f_0,n}(\boldsymbol{x})) = f_0(u_{n-m}, ..., u_{n-1}) = f_0 \circ F_0^{(n-m)}(x_0, ..., x_{m-1}) = f_0 \circ F_0^{(n-m-1)}(F_0(\boldsymbol{x}))$. This equals the right-most component of $\iota_{f_0,n}(F_0(\boldsymbol{x}))$, which verifies Theorem 1.

If we identify K^m with its embedding $\iota_{f_0,n}(K^m)$ Theorem 1 delivers a family of feedback shift registers on K^n that coincide with F_0 on this embedding. Consequently, the embedding $\iota_{f_0,n}$ maps cycles of F_0 into cycles of F. More precisely,

Corollary 1. *Let $\boldsymbol{z}_0 \in K^m$ so that $F_0^{(\ell)}(\boldsymbol{z}_0) = \boldsymbol{z}_0$. Then the analogous property holds for $\boldsymbol{z} := \iota_{f_0,n}(\boldsymbol{z}_0) \in K^n$ with respect to F, i.e., $F^{(\ell)}(\boldsymbol{z}) = \boldsymbol{z}$.*

2.2   Bijective Feedback-Shift Registers

Suppose that G defines a feedback-shift register on the state space K^r with feedback function $g : K^r \to K$. Remind that a state $\boldsymbol{x}$ is called *periodical* with respect to G, if the sequence $\boldsymbol{x}, G(\boldsymbol{x}), G^{(2)}(\boldsymbol{x}), \ldots$ is periodic, and that the set of periodical elements splits into cycles.

Depending on the application it may be reasonable to choose feedback shift registers that have no non-periodical states. As any non-periodical state is attained at most once, all elements are periodical if and only if G is bijective. For example, the feedback-shift register with feedback function $g(\boldsymbol{x}) := x_{r-1}$ has only $\#K$ periodical elements, namely the states where all components are identical.

The next lemma gives criteria for feedback-shift registers to be bijective:

Lemma 2. *Let $G : K^r \to K^r$ be the corresponding feedback-shift register to $g : K^r \to K$. Then the following holds:*

(i) G is bijective if and only if the mapping $t \mapsto g(t, c_1, ..., c_{r-1})$ is a bijection of K for all $(c_1, ..., c_{r-1}) \in K^{r-1}$.

(ii) If g is of the form $g(\boldsymbol{x}) = x_0 + s(x_1, ..., x_{r-1})$ for a mapping $s : K^{r-1} \to K$, then G is bijective. For $K = \mathbb{F}_2$ the converse also holds.

Proof. Assertion (i) and the first claim of (ii) are obvious. The final statement is shown in [2], Theorem 1, 115f.

Therefore, if we want our polynomial constructed in Theorem 1 to be bijective, we may choose f_0 and the h_i's as follows:

Proposition 1. *Let $f_0 : K^m \to K$ be of the form $f_0(\boldsymbol{x}) = x_0 + s(x_1, \ldots, x_{m-1})$ for a function $s : K^{m-1} \to K$. Embed f_0 into $f : K^n \to K^n$ as follows:*

$$f(\boldsymbol{y}) = f_0(y_{n-m}, ..., y_{n-1}) - g_m(\boldsymbol{y}) + \sum_{j=m+1}^{n-1} g_j(\boldsymbol{y})h_j(y_1, ..., y_{n-1}).$$

Then the feedback-shift register F with feedback function f is bijective. Hence, all states are periodical with respect to F.

Example 1. Let $K = \mathbb{F}_2$ and $(m, n) = (10, 20)$. We constructed our large feedback function $f : K^{20} \to K$ accordingly to Proposition 1 from a small feedback function $f_0 : \mathbb{F}_2^m \to \mathbb{F}_2, \boldsymbol{x} \mapsto x_0 + x_2 x_9 + x_5$, and randomly chosen mappings $(h_{11}, ..., h_{19})(y_1, ..., y_{19}) = (y_1, y_{15}, y_4, 1, y_1, y_2, y_5, y_{12}, y_8)$ (see Appendix). This yields

$$
\begin{aligned}
f = {} & y_1 y_3 y_{10} + y_4 y_5 y_{12} + y_1 y_7 y_{14} + y_2 y_8 y_{15} + y_4 y_{11} y_{15} + y_5 y_9 y_{16} \\
& + y_{10} y_{12} y_{17} + y_8 y_{11} y_{18} + y_3 y_4 + y_1 y_5 + y_1 y_6 + y_2 y_6 + y_5 y_7 + y_4 y_8 \\
& + y_2 y_9 + y_8 y_9 + y_1 y_{10} + y_1 y_{11} + y_2 y_{11} + y_5 y_{12} + y_8 y_{12} + y_4 y_{13} + y_6 y_{13} \\
& + y_{12} y_{13} + y_8 y_{14} + y_1 y_{15} + y_2 y_{15} + y_7 y_{15} + y_{12} y_{15} + y_2 y_{16} + y_5 y_{17} \\
& + y_{12} y_{18} + y_8 y_{19} + y_{12} y_{19} + y_0 + y_1 + y_4 + y_5 + y_9 + y_{14} + y_{15}.
\end{aligned}
$$

The feedback function f decomposes the state space $\mathbb{F}_2^n$ into cycles as follows:

cycle length	1	2	15	22	69	152	301	661	875	1504	17543	72995	234189	720201
# cycles	2	1	4	1	1	1	1	1	1	1	1	1	1	1

The embedded cycles induced by f_0 have length $(1, 1, 15, 15, 15, 15, 301, 661)$.

3   Cryptographic Properties of the Embedding

In this section we assume $f_0 : K^m \to K$ to be a feedback function, which is embedded into $f : K^n \to K$ as described in Theorem 1. Furthermore, denote the corresponding bijective feedback-shift registers by F_0 and F, respectively.

The goal of this section is to investigate the question: Which data suffice to decide, whether a given feedback function has an embedded smaller feedback function, or even to reconstruct this embedded feedback function?

We investigate different (crytographically interesting) situations. More particularly, we shall show:

- Given only F, it seems to be hard to decide whether there is an embedded smaller feedback function and to reconstruct it.
- Given enough embedded states $z_0, ..., z_r$, where $z_i \in \iota_{f_0,n}(K^m)$, it is easy to compute f_0.
- Given F and one embedded state $z \in \iota_{f_0,n}(K^m)$ with large enough cycle length, it is easy to compute f_0.
- Given F and linearly transformed embedded states $Tz_0, ..., Tz_r$ with secret $z_i \in \iota_{f_0,n}(K^m)$ and secret $T \in \mathrm{GL}_n(K)$, it is hard to compute f_0.

These statements hold, if we make the following reasonable assumptions about f_0 and f. As F should be efficiently computable, the degrees of f_0 and f should be small, about 2 and 4, respectively. But f_0 should not be too sparse. Moreover, m has to be so small that an exhaustive search over the state space K^m is possible, for example $m \approx 30$.

Remark 1. Some simple general properties of our construction are:

a) To check whether a candidate for f_0 is correct can be easily done, if f is known. We only need to verify for some states in K^m whether the feedback functions coincide on the embedding $\iota_{f_0,n}(K^m)$. Hence, having only a moderate number of candidates for f_0 one can do exhaustive search. For instance, for $K = \mathbb{F}_2$ knowing m and the degree d_0 of f_0 one has to check $2^{\sum_{i=0}^{d_0} \binom{m}{i}}$ candidates for f_0. Therefore $d_0 \geq 2$ is a necessary condition.
b) For $K = \mathbb{F}_2$ given only F the probability of picking an embedded state $z \in \iota_{f_0,n}(K^m)$ at random is 2^{m-n}, which is very low in our setting since in general we choose n much larger then m. (See also Theorem 13 in [2], 128.)

3.1   Reconstruction of f_0 from f

In the next two subsections we shall tackle the problem of reconstructing f_0 from f with algebraic methods. The first method is straightforward, whereas the second approach is a more sophisticated one making use of invariant theory. Both methods use Gröbner bases and elimination techniques [5].

It turns out that the first approach is more efficient for very sparse polynomials, whereas the second approach is faster if all polynomials are dense. But both are practically infeasible for large enough m and, for instance, $n = 4m$ (see appendix).

A Straightforward Algebraic Approach. Consider the residue class rings $P := K[X_0, ..., X_{m-1}]/(X_0^q - X_0, ..., X_{m-1}^q - X_{m-1})$ and analogously $Q := K[Y_0, ..., Y_{n-1}]/(Y_0^q - Y_0, ..., Y_{n-1}^q - Y_{n-1})$, where $q := \#K$. Seen from the algebraic point of view, the challenge is to decide for a given polynomial $f \in Q$ whether there exists a polynomial $f_0 \in P$ such that

$$f = f_0(Y_{n-m}, ..., Y_{n-1}) + \sum_{i=m}^{n-1} g_i h_i$$

for some $h_i \in Q$, where the g_i's are determined by f_0 as follows:

$$g_m := f_0(Y_0, ..., Y_{m-1}) - Y_m$$
$$g_{m+1} := f_0(Y_1, ..., Y_m) - Y_{m+1}$$
...
$$g_{n-1} := f_0(Y_{n-m-1}, ..., Y_{n-2}) - Y_{n-1}$$

One straightforward strategy to solve this problem is to make a similar approach as Lenstra's Linear-Algebra Attack against polynomial-based cryptosystem described by Koblitz [3], Chap. 5, §6. For this to work the following conditions have to hold:

- One needs a good guess on the degrees of the g_i's and h_i's, for instance by $\max_{i=1,...,m-n}(\deg g_i h_i) \approx \deg f$. (Note that $\geq$ holds.)
- No monomials cancel out, i.e. for every monomial in the support of g_i or h_i there has to be a monomial in the support of f that is a multiple of the first.

These conditions are likely to hold, if we assume f to be sparse. Then one is able to guess the supports of f_0 and of the h_i's by looking at the support of f. An attacker puts up the coefficients as unknowns, computes the polynomial combination and extracts equations by comparing coefficients with f. Solving these equations yields f_0.

Example 2. As the systems of equations in our setting are very large, in this example we consider a simplified situation omitting f_0. For $K = \mathbb{F}_2$ we construct a polynomial
$$f = g_0 h_0 + g_1 h_1 = Y_0 Y_1 Y_2 + Y_1 Y_2 + Y_1 + Y_2$$
from $g_0 = Y_0 Y_1 + 1$, $g_1 = Y_1 Y_2 + 1$ and $h_0 = Y_2$, $h_1 = Y_1$. (Note that the notations are modified in this example.) The task is now to reconstruct g_0.

An attacker knows that the degree of g_0 has to be at least 2, therefore he guesses the degree of the h_i's to be 1. Hence, candidates for the support of $g_0 \in \mathbb{F}_2[Y_0, Y_1]$ are $Y_0 Y_1$, Y_1 and 1. This leads to the following guess on h_0's support: Y_2, Y_1 and 1. Similarly for g_1 and h_1, we yield $\{Y_1 Y_2, Y_1, Y_2, 1\}$ and $\{Y_0, Y_1, Y_2, 1\}$, respectively. Therefore, an attacker conjectures the support of g_0 to be $Y_0 Y_1, Y_0, Y_1, 1$, introduces unknowns γ_i, and puts $\tilde{g}_0 = \gamma_0 Y_0 Y_1 + \gamma_1 Y_0 + \gamma_2 Y_1 + \gamma_3$ and accordingly $\tilde{g}_0, \tilde{g}_1$. Additionally, he sets $\tilde{h}_0 = \gamma_4 Y_2 + \gamma_5 Y_1 + \gamma_6$ and $\tilde{h}_1 = \gamma_7 Y_0 + \gamma_8 Y_1 + \gamma_9 Y_2 + \gamma_{10}$. Comparing coefficients of the equation $\tilde{h}_0 \tilde{g}_0 + \tilde{h}_1 \tilde{g}_1 = f$ results in the following system of quadratic equations:

$$\gamma_1 \gamma_5 + \gamma_1 \gamma_8 = 0$$
$$\gamma_1 \gamma_6 + \gamma_2 \gamma_8 + \gamma_1 \gamma_9 + \gamma_2 \gamma_9 = 1$$
$$\gamma_2 \gamma_5 + \gamma_1 \gamma_7 + \gamma_2 \gamma_7 + \gamma_3 \gamma_8 + \gamma_1 \gamma_{10} + \gamma_3 \gamma_{10} = 1$$
$$\gamma_3 \gamma_5 + \gamma_1 \gamma_{11} = 0$$
$$\gamma_2 \gamma_6 + \gamma_4 \gamma_8 + \gamma_3 \gamma_9 + \gamma_4 \gamma_9 + \gamma_2 \gamma_{10} + \gamma_4 \gamma_{10} = 1$$
$$\gamma_3 \gamma_6 + \gamma_2 \gamma_{11} = 0$$
$$\gamma_4 \gamma_5 + \gamma_3 \gamma_7 + \gamma_4 \gamma_7 + \gamma_3 \gamma_{11} = 0$$
$$\gamma_4 \gamma_6 + \gamma_4 \gamma_{11} = 1$$

This system leads to three solutions: $Y_1 Y_2 + Y_1 + 1$, $Y_1 Y_2 + Y_2 + 1$, and $Y_1 Y_2 + 1$ for g_0.

To estimate success-probability of this approach we have to answer some questions: Firstly, as mentioned before this approach only works if the above conditions hold for the monomials. How likely are these conditions to hold in our situation? Secondly, in contrary to Lenstra's approach to polynomial-based schemes, we now have to guess more supports and have to consider a system of quadratic polynomial equations. How complex can this system be?

One crucial value is the number of unknowns one has to consider. This number is roughly bounded by

$$\sum_{i=0}^{d_1} \binom{m}{i} + (n-m) \sum_{i=0}^{d_2} \binom{n}{i},$$

where $d_1 = \deg f_0$ and $d_2 = \max \deg h_i$. For instance for $d_1 = 2$ and $d_2 = 1$ (the minimal possible degrees) we obtain $1 + m + \frac{m(m-1)}{2} + (n-m)(n+1)$, which is a huge number, if someone wants to solve a system of nonlinear equations. Nevertheless, this bound is not very precise, for instance in the case that all polynomials are sparse. Moreover, the system of equations we have to consider is in general overdetermined.

Therefore, in order to get a deeper insight in that algorithm, we made some experiments with MAGMA. (Exact computation times are displayed in the Appendix. These computations exhibit the following:

- The number of variables grows very fast.
- The fact that the systems of equations are overdetermined helps to compute Gröbner bases, such that we were able to compute Gröbner bases of systems with a large number of variables.
- Also due to the overdetermination we often got only one solution for f_0.
- Allowing the polynomials g_i and h_i to be quadratic, for $K = \mathbb{F}_2$ we weren't able to compute Gröbner bases for m greater than 5 and $n = 4m$.

These observations indicate that such a linear algebra approach is hopeless for these kind of problems.

A Sophisticated Algebraic Approach by Invariant Theory. The previous algebraic approach does not make use two facts: We do not need the exact h_i's in order to test whether a candidate for f_0 is embedded into f. We only need to reduce the number of candidates for f_0 to a manageable number. Moreover the g_i's are constructed by shifts of the indices. Hence, the goal is to represent f in terms of invariant theory.

Firstly, we introduce the following notations: Let us consider the mappings as polynomials of the residue-class ring $Q := K[Y_0, ..., Y_{n-1}]/I$ with $I = (Y_0^q - Y_0, Y_1^q - Y_1, ..., Y_{n-1}^q - Y_{n-1})$ and $q = \#K$. The group action of an element σ of the symmetric group $\mathrm{Sym}(n)$ is defined by the algebra homomorphism $\cdot^{\sigma} : Q \rightarrow Q$

given by $Y_i \mapsto Y_{\sigma(i)}$. For $t \in 0, ..., n-1$ we denote the *shifts* by t by σ_t, that is $\sigma_t \in \mathrm{Sym}(n)$ with $\sigma_t(i) \mapsto i + t \pmod{n}$.

To every polynomial $f \in Q$ we associate its *shift-invariant* polynomial

$$f^\alpha := \sum_{t=0}^{n-1} f^{\sigma_t},$$

that is invariant under the action of $\{\sigma_t : t = 0, ..., n-1\}$. Some obvious properties of these operations are

Lemma 3. *(i)* *For $r, s \in \{0, ..., n-1\}$ it holds $(f^{\sigma_r})^{\sigma_s} = f^{\sigma_{r+s(\bmod n)}}$.*
(ii) *The mapping $.^\alpha : Q \to Q, f \mapsto f^\alpha$ is a vector-space homomorphism, in particular: $(f + g)^\alpha = f^\alpha + g^\alpha$.*
(iii) *The mapping $.^\alpha : Q \to Q, f \mapsto f^\alpha$ does not respect the algebra structure of Q: in general $(fg)^\alpha \neq f^\alpha \cdot g^\alpha$.*

Let us now complete the sequence $g_m, ..., g_{n-1}$ defined in Lemma 1 as follows:

$$g_0 := f_0(Y_{n-m}, ..., Y_{n-1}) - Y_0,$$
$$g_1 := f_0(Y_{n-m+1}, ..., Y_{n-1}, Y_0) - Y_1,$$

$$...,$$

$$g_{m-1} := f_0(Y_{n-1}, Y_0, ..., Y_{m-2}) - Y_{m-1}.$$

Then obviously σ_t transfers the g_i's into each other: $g_i^{\sigma_t} = g_{i+t(\bmod n)}$. Moreover the construction of Theorem 1 can then described by $f - Y_0 = \sum_{i=0}^{n-1} g_i h_i$, if we choose $h_0 = 1$, $h_1 = ... = h_{m-1} = 0$, and $h_m, ..., h_{n-1}$ as before. This gets us in the position to formulate our next result.

Proposition 2. *Let f_0 be embedded into f as described in Theorem 1. Then there exists a polynomial $h \in Q$ such that*

$$(f - Y_0)^\alpha = (g_0 h)^\alpha.$$

For example, this holds for $h = \sum_{i=0}^{n-1} h_i^{\sigma_{n-i}}$.

Proof. Simple substitutions and reformulation yield

$$(f - Y_0)^\alpha = \left(\sum_{i=0}^{n-1} g_i h_i\right)^\alpha = \sum_{r=0}^{n-1}\sum_{i=0}^{n-1} (g_i h_i)^{\sigma_r} = \sum_{r=0}^{n-1}\sum_{i=0}^{n-1} (g_i)^{\sigma_r}(h_i)^{\sigma_r}$$

$$= \sum_{r=0}^{n-1}\sum_{i=0}^{n-1} g_{i+r(\bmod n)}(h_i)^{\sigma_r} = \sum_{k=0}^{n-1} g_k \sum_{i+r=k(\bmod n)} (h_i)^{\sigma_r}$$

$$= \sum_{k=0}^{n-1} g_k \left(\sum_{i=0}^{n-1}(h_i)^{\sigma_{n-i}}\right)^{\sigma_k} = \sum_{k=0}^{n-1} (g_0 h)^{\sigma_k} = (g_0 h)^\alpha.$$

The previous proposition leads to the following algebraic approach to reconstruct f_0 from f:

1. Compute $(f - Y_0)^\alpha$.
2. Guess the degrees of g_0 and h and put up the polynomials with the coefficients as unknowns.
3. Solve the quadratic system of equations induced by $(f - Y_0)^\alpha = (g_0 h)^\alpha$.
4. From every candidate for g_0 derive a candidate f_0' for f_0, test whether f_0' coincides with f by applying both functions iteratively to several embedded states $\iota_{f_0',n}(x)$ with $x \in K^m$.

Like for the first algebraic approach described in Subsection 3.1, we implemented this second approach in MAGMA and made experiments on a PC. These computations exhibit the following:

- For sparse polynomials the second approach puts up systems of equations with much more unknowns than in the first approach. The reason is that the shift-invariants polynomials are in general dense, and therefore the second approach does not exploit sparsity.
- For dense polynomials the second approach puts up systems of equations with less unknowns than in the first approach. The reason is that in the second approach only two polynomials have to be considered.
- No experiments determined if the degree of f_0 was at least two.

Hence, although for dense polynomials the second approach is theoretically more efficient than the first one, practically already in the smallest relevant case the algorithm is infeasible.

3.2   Reconstruction of f_0 from Embedded States

Given an embedded state $z = \iota_{f_0,n}(x) \in \iota_{f_0,n}(K^m)$ we get $n - m$ linear equations in the coefficients of f_0 by considering

$$f_0(z_0, ..., z_{m-1}) = z_m$$
$$f_0(z_1, ..., z_m) = z_{m+1}$$
$$...$$
$$f_0(z_{n-m-1}, ..., z_{n-2}) = z_{n-1}.$$

Clearly, if the attacker is able to extract at least $\sum_{i=0}^{d_0} \binom{m}{i}$ linear independent equations in this way he can determine f_0. Hence, he requires at least $\frac{\sum_{i=0}^{d_0} \binom{m}{i}}{n-m}$ embedded states.

Since consecutive states do only yield one additional equation, the knowledge of F and of exactly one embedded state z only suffices for the determination of f_0, if the cycle length of z is large enough. More precisely, if ℓ is the length of the cycle containing z then ℓ has to be larger than $\sum_{i=0}^{d_0} \binom{m}{i}$.

3.3   Reconstruction from Linear-Transformed Embedded States

In this subsection we shall consider linear-transformed embedded states $u_0 := T z_0, ..., u_r := T z_r$ with $z_i \in \iota_{f_0,n}(K^m)$, $T \in \mathrm{GL}_n(K)$. We distinguish two cases:

Case 1. The task is to compute the linear transformation T from the knowledge of f_0 and $u_0, ..., u_r$. Like in the previous subsection, one is able to derive equations from a linear-transformed embedded states $z = T^{-1}u$ as follows:

$$f_0(z_0, ..., z_{m-1}) = z_m$$
$$f_0(z_1, ..., z_m) = z_{m+1}$$
$$...$$
$$f_0(z_{n-m-1}, ..., z_{n-2}) = z_{n-1}.$$

But this time we get nonlinear equations of degree $\deg f_0$ in n^2 unknowns (the entries of T^{-1}). If n and the degree of f_0 are large enough, it is very likely that this system of equations is practically unsolvable.

The complexity can be estimated as follows: Given sufficient linear-transformed embedded states the system of equations becomes so overdetermined that it can be linearized [5]. Then Gaussian elimination solves the associated matrix in

$$O\left(\left(\sum_{i=0}^{d_0} \binom{n^2}{i}\right)^3\right)$$

time. For instance, for $\deg f_0 = 2$ and $n = 2^7$ we yield $\approx ((2^6 \cdot 2^7)^2)^3 = 2^{78}$.

Case 2. In the case that one only knows F and linear-transformed embedded states $u_0, ..., u_r$ the above approach yields a system of algebraic equations of degree $d_0 + 1$ in $n^2 + \sum_{i=0}^{d_0} \binom{m}{i}$ unknowns, where d_0 is the degree of f_0. Therefore, in this case it is even more likely that this system of equations is practically unsolvable.

4   Applications

In this section we point out some general consequences of our results. After that, we discuss a low-cost identification scheme that uses our construction as the cryptographic primitive. We expect further cryptographic applications.

4.1   General Consequences

The main consequence resulting from this paper is:

When using NLFSR with "random-looking" feedback function received from a non-trusted party, one cannot be sure that nobody knows states lying in short cycles.

Therefore in a setting where one party gets a feedback function and "random" states from another party, the receiver has to be aware of the threat that the other party might have constructed a feedback function with embedded short cycles.

For instance, in the case that the central component of a key generation mechanism is an NLFSR, the knowledge of states with short cycle length might be helpful for deceptions. A potential victim, however, is able to exclude extremely short cycle lengths by checking the cycle length of a received state to a particular bound. If he wants to be absolutely sure that he did not receive an embedded state, he can even do the approach described in Section 3.2 to check whether for this state an embedded feedback function f_0 exists. But that might be too costly if the "bad" state is hidden in a lot of "good" states.

4.2   Low-Cost Group Identification

In order to show that our construction is also a useful cryptographic primitive, we present a *low-cost non-interactive group-identification scheme* for the following situation:

We consider a large group $\{\mathcal{U}_0, ..., \mathcal{U}_r\}$ of users who need access to some device or room. There is a key-distribution center $\mathcal{A}$ that equips group members with keys. If a group member wants to have access to a device, his key is verified by a verifier $\mathcal{V}$. Furthermore, we assume the verifier to have only small memory, small computing power, and no possibility to interact with a prover $\mathcal{U}_i$ or to set up an online connection to $\mathcal{A}$.

A simple example for our setting is the key management at a faculty in the university. Some faculty members have access to the library, the photocopy machine, the computer room or the server room. They apply for some key at the administration, and after that their key is checked by some low-cost device at the door or at the machine.

There are three simple solutions for this setting:

(i) One possibility is to give the verifier $\mathcal{V}$ a list of valid keys. Then $\mathcal{V}$ only checks whether the user has one of these keys. But this requires large memory capacities if the number of users is large.

(ii) More common in practice is to give every member the same key in order to save memory space. But then misdeeds cannot be traced back to single members.

(iii) A third solution is to provide the users with different "valid" keys and to give the verifier the ability to check the validity.

The third case is typically realized by symmetric block ciphers, for instance AES. The key distribution center provides a user $\mathcal{U}_i$ with the pair $(x_i, \text{AES}_k(x_i))$ using a secret key k, which is also known by the verifier $\mathcal{V}$ so that $\mathcal{V}$ is able to check the correctness of the pair. (The value x_i is typically some hash value of the identity of the user.)

However, this solution requires the verifier $\mathcal{V}$ to be able to compute a block cipher. For instance, for the execution of AES the verifying device has to store large tables overtaxing low-cost devices. Therefore we propose the following scheme that realizes case (iii) with the construction introduced in this papers. The verifier only has to do a simple linear transformation and to execute an NLFSR. The scheme works as follows:

Set Up. The key-distribution center $\mathcal{A}$ generates a feedback function F with an embedded feedback function f_0 (as described in Theorem 1 or more specific in Proposition 1) and an embedded state $z \in \iota_{f_0,n}(K^m)$ with cycle length

$\ell \geq r$. Moreover, $\mathcal{A}$ chooses a linear transformation $T \in \mathrm{GL}_n(K)$ and a randomly chosen permutation $\sigma \in \mathrm{Sym}(\ell)$.

Key Distribution. A group member $\mathcal{U}_i$ gets secretly his key $\boldsymbol{k}_i := TF^{(\sigma(i))}(\boldsymbol{z})$ and the verifier $\mathcal{V}$ the secret T^{-1}. The verifier $\mathcal{V}$ also gets the feedback function f and the cycle length ℓ, but both data need not to be kept secret.

Verification. The verifier $\mathcal{V}$ verifies a key $\boldsymbol{k}_i$ by checking whether $F^{(\ell)}(T^{-1}\boldsymbol{k}_i)$ equals $T^{-1}\boldsymbol{k}_i$.

Clearly, this scheme is secure against *dishonest users*, as follows from the argumentation in Subsection 3.3. Even in the case that all users cooperate they cannot reveal the secrets T or f_0 and therefore are not able to construct another state $\boldsymbol{k} \in K^n$ that is a valid key. The scheme, however, is not secure against eavesdropping and cheating-verifier attacks, because the provers always use the same keys. But this holds for almost every non-interactive scheme.

Furthermore, in contrast to block-cipher-based schemes a pure *verifier-intrusion attack* on our scheme does not suffice to reveal the secret f_0, as discussed in Subsection 3.1. An attacker also needs some valid keys, according to Subsection 3.2. Note that, because of the same reason a real verifier is in the position to reveal the secret f_0 after getting several valid keys.

Remark 2. We point out that our scheme provides a hierarchy among keys as follows: Let $\boldsymbol{z}, \boldsymbol{z}' \in K^n$ with cycle length ℓ, ℓ', respectively, so that ℓ is a proper divisor of ℓ'. Then certainly $F^{(\ell)}(\boldsymbol{z}) = F^{(\ell')}(\boldsymbol{z})$. That means $T\boldsymbol{z}$ is a valid key for all verifiers accepting $T\boldsymbol{z}'$, but not conversely. Therefore, depending on the prime factorization of all embedded cycle lengths we are able construct keys with different "power".

Related Work. Summing up, our scheme provides group-identification for a large group in a setting where only low-cost devices are available. For this setting we did not find any solution in the vast literature on entity authentication (see, for instance, [1], [4]). All other schemes needed at least a large memory, a hashfunction, or a symmetric-key cipher.

Our scheme also differs from low-cost *radio-frequency identification (RFID) based systems* because these schemes only allow low-cost sender tags, but need powerful tag readers (see, for instance, [7]). Theoretically our scheme would work with low-cost RFID chips only, but in practice we then need some mechanism against eavesdropping.

5   Final Remarks

In contrast to the linear case only little is known about the cycle structure of nonlinear feedback-shift registers (NLFSRs). In this paper we gave new results on this topic: We constructed NLFSRs with short cycles. The technique is to embed small NLFSRs into large NLFSRs. We showed that our embedding yield an NLFSR that algebraic analysis cannot distinguish from a random NLFSR.

Furthermore, we discussed the question which additional data suffice to detect the embedded NLSFR. For instance this is possible with the knowledge of embedded states. We showed that all properties of our embedding fit together in such a way that it works as the cryptographic primitive of a low-cost group-identification scheme.

References

1. D.W. Davies, W.L. Price, *Security for Computer Networks*, Wiley & Sons (1998).
2. S.W. Golomb, *Shift Register Sequences*, revised Edition, Angean Park Press, Laguna Hills (Cal.) (1982).
3. N. Koblitz, *Algebraic Aspects of Cryptography*, Springer, Berlin (1998).
4. A.J. Menezes, P.C. van Oorschot, S.A. Vanstone, *Handbook of Applied Cryptography*, CRC Press (1997).
5. D. Lazard, *Gröbner bases, Gaussian elimination, and resolution of systems of algebraic equations*, EuroCAL 1983, pages 146-156.
6. R.A. Rueppel, *Analysis and Design of Stream Ciphers*, Springer, Berlin (1986).
7. S.E. Sarma, S.A. Weis, D.W. Engels, *RFID Systems and Security and Privacy Implications*, Cryptographic Hardware in Embedded Systems — CHES 2002, Lecture Notes in Computer Sciences Volume 2523, pages 454-470, Springer (2002).

Appendix: Experimental Results

We made experiments to estimate the number of unknowns and the complexity of the system of quadratic equations obtained by the algebraic approach in Section 3.1. For $\deg f_0 = 2$, $\deg h_i = 2$ and different integers m we proceed as follows:

1. Put $n = 4m$.
2. Choose randomly polynomials $f_0 \in \mathbb{F}_2[X_0, ..., X_{m-1}]$ and $h_m, ..., h_{n-1} \in \mathbb{F}_2[Y_0, ..., Y_{n-1}]$ so that $\# \operatorname{Supp} f_0 = 2$ and $\# \operatorname{Supp} h_i = 1$.
3. Retrieve g_j from f_0 and compute $f = f_0(Y_{n-m}, ..., Y_{n-1}) + \sum_{i=m}^{n-1} g_i h_i$.
4. Execute the algebraic approach assuming that $\deg f_0$ and $\deg h_i$ are known.

Results. In all experiments the number of solutions for f_0 has been one or zero. If we have received a solution, it was correct and we got back f_0. Our average values and computation times with MAGMA on a PC (1,4 GHz Pentium, 512 MB RAM) were:

m	$\# \operatorname{Supp} f$	Number of unknowns	Number of equations	Time in seconds
2	11	60	78	270
3	17	124	261	640
4	24	222	681	33,290
5	31	338	1402	> 1 day

Remark 3. We chose the polynomials f_0 and h_i's artificially sparse, as for more dense polynomials the algorithm did not terminate at all.

Author Index

Lecture Notes in Computer Science

For information about Vols. 1–3266

please contact your bookseller or Springer